Portia Robinson is Associate Professor of History at Macquarie University. She is the editor of *Macquarie Colonial Papers*, a series publishing the work of postgraduate students. Her own publications include *The Hatch and Brood of Time: A Study of the First Generation of Native-born White Australians, c. 1788–1828* (1985). Professor Robinson's current research in the period 1770–1830 includes gender and criminality in Western Europe and Australia; migrant women to New South Wales; and a documentary history of the Irish in Australia.

THE WOMEN of BOTANY BAY

---

*A reinterpretation of the role of women
in the origins of Australian society*

PORTIA ROBINSON

PENGUIN BOOKS

Penguin Books Australia Ltd
487 Maroondah Highway, PO Box 257
Ringwood, Victoria 3134, Australia
Penguin Books Ltd
Harmondsworth, Middlesex, England
Viking Penguin, A Division of Penguin Books USA Inc.
375 Hudson Street, New York, New York, 10014, USA
Penguin Books Canada Limited
10 Alcorn Avenue, Toronto, Ontario, Canada M4V 1E4
Penguin Books (N.Z.) Ltd
182-190 Wairau Road, Auckland 10, New Zealand

First published by the Macquarie Library Pty Ltd, 1988
Revised edn, published in Penguin, 1993
10 9 8 7 6 5 4 3
Copyright © The Premier of the State of New South Wales, 1988, 1993

All rights reserved. Without limiting the rights under copyright reserved above, no part of this publication may be reproduced, stored in or introduced into a retrieval system, or transmitted, in any form or by any means (electronic, mechanical, photocopying, recording or otherwise), without the prior written permission of both the copyright owner and the above publisher of this book.

Typeset in 9/10 pt Aster by Photoset Computer Service Pty Ltd, Sydney
Made and printed in Malaysia through SRM Production Services Sdn. Bhd.

National Library of Australia
Cataloguing-in-Publication data:
Robinson, Portia.
The women of Botany Bay.
Includes index.
ISBN 0 14 014698 9.
1. Women – Australia – History. 2. Women – Australia – Social conditions. 3. Women prisoners – Australia – History. 4. Australia – History. I. Title.
994.0082

*For MARY
and all the women of Botany Bay,
past and present*

and Joyce and Betty Shaw

Foreword

Every generation writes its own history in its own image. Historians of preceding generations have written eloquently on the role of British men in planting their way of life, their institutions and their values in the ancient continent of Australia. The historians of this generation are beginning to write about women and the Aborigines. Works dealing with such subjects are probably best written by women and Aborigines. They require something more than industry, zeal and scholarship. They can be written well only by writers with a great moral passion and what Henry James called a 'quantity of felt life'.

Portia Robinson has both these qualities in abundance. She is already known to the academic world and the reading public for her book, *The Hatch and Brood of Time*. Now she comes before us again with this passionate and lively history of *The Women of Botany Bay*. It is not necessary for me to sum up the contents of the book. Portia Robinson is angry, and rightly angry with the picture men painted of the pioneer white women in Australia. She has written a hymn of praise to those women. This is not the work of a contrite man. It is the work of a woman who has both the eye of pity and the passionate heart. She has a message for this generation. I believe her work will in time give us a new picture of the past. Academics will doubtless comb over the work. The reading public will know that their eyes have been opened to a new picture of our past.

Manning Clark
1988

Contents

Foreword		vii
Preface		xi
Author's Preface		xiii
Preface to the Revised Edition		xiv
Contemporary Terms and Expressions		xv
Acknowledgements		xvii
Convict Ships Carrying Women Transported to New South Wales		xx
Conversion Table		xxiv

Introduction
'SHE WAS COME OF DECENT PEOPLE...' — 1

1 'GUESTS OF HIS MAJESTY' — 11
   The convict women of Great Britain

2 'THE INCREASING DEPRAVITY OF THE AGE' — 37
   Female criminality and transportation

3 'THE REFUSE OF LONDON' — 63
   Crime and punishment in English society

4 'THE GODS GO A-BEGGING' — 81
   From Newgate to Botany Bay

5 'POOR PETITIONERS' OR 'NOTORIOUS OFFENDERS'? — 103
   Crime and punishment in Irish society

6 'STATIONED IN PARADISE'? — 127
   Irish women transported to New South Wales

7	**'A GREAT AND BITTER GRIEF'** *The convict wives*	155
8	**'WOMEN OF PROVEN GOOD CHARACTER'** *Women and crime at Botany Bay*	187
9	**'A WOMAN IS A WORTHY THING'** *Women and labour at Botany Bay*	217
10	**'THE SWORD OF GOD AND GIDEON'** *Marriage and morals at Botany Bay*	247
11	**'SHE SANG HER TOIL AND TROUBLE'** *Family women of Botany Bay*	271

Conclusion
'THE WOMEN OF BOTANY BAY' — 293

Abbreviations — 301

Notes — 304

WOMEN TRANSPORTED TO NEW SOUTH WALES — 368

List A.	Women transported from England, 1788–1827	370
	A–1: Women transported	370
	A–2: Aliases or variant names	424
	A–3: Women listed on the indents of more than one ship	436
List B.	Women transported from Ireland, 1791–January 1828	437
	B–1: Women transported	437
	B–2: Aliases or variant names	469

Indexes — 476

Women Mentioned in the Text — 476
General Index — 486

Preface

This is a pioneering book and a revelation. It tells the story of Australia's pioneer convict women and is the result of ten years' intensive research by historian Dr Portia Robinson of Macquarie University.

Through this seminal work we now have access for the first time to the lives and histories of the women who were transported to the colony of New South Wales in the first forty years of white settlement.

Very little has been published about these women, convicts themselves or 'convict' wives, as the free women who came to join their convict husbands were labelled. *The Women of Botany Bay* redresses this neglect and confronts our misunderstandings and ignorance of who these women were, where they came from and above all, what they contributed to the society that grew from those harsh beginnings. Myth, assumption and legend which has hidden the truth about the convict women for so long gives way in this fascinating work to a thorough documentation and perceptive interpretation of their role in the development of the Australian economy and society. They were working women, family women, bush and town women. They went into business, sometimes alone, sometimes as partners. They farmed the land. They prospered and established themselves in the community. They created lives for themselves and their children. In this book they speak for themselves, and to us, their heirs, and take their proper place in the mainstream of our history for the first time.

The exceptional quantity and quality of information on the individual women of the period 1788–1828 is one of the hallmarks of this book. As Portia Robinson states in the Acknowledgements, thousands of women and men in Australia, England, Scotland, Wales and Ireland have supported this project by contributing information and family records and history. Together with the author's inspiration and dedication they have made this work possible.

No project of this scope can be completed without generous financial backing. This was forthcoming in the first few years from academic research grants and over the past three years in the form of a major Bicentennial grant from the NSW Government. As well, the generous contribution by British Airways to travel costs made it possible for Portia Robinson to uncover vital records overseas. I join her in offering my personal thanks to all these and other donors and of course to the men and women who gave their time and knowledge to enrich all our lives through this work.

All sorts of readers will find much to relish and discover in *The Women of Botany Bay*. Portia Robinson's immense achievement as a historian and writer is entirely deserved and I am sure will be widely acknowledged in the public response to this book.

Professor Di Yerbury, AM
Vice-Chancellor, Macquarie University
September 1988

AUTHOR'S PREFACE

The Women of Botany Bay is a history of the European women who came to New South Wales as convicted felons or as the free wives of convicts. Its aim is to allow these women to speak for themselves after some 200 years of silence, neglect and misinterpretation. My interpretation is based on the re-creation of the individual and collective British and Australian lives of every woman convicted in England, Ireland, Scotland and Wales and transported to New South Wales between 1787 and 1828 and as many of the forgotten 'convict wives' as could be traced.

The contribution of these women in the formation of a distinctive, unique 'Australian' society and their determinative influence on the nature, structure and characteristics of an 'Australian' female society, has been ignored, glossed over and distorted. By re-creating their own lives, before and after transportation, a new source of evidence is presented on which their roles within colonial society and their influence on both social and economic colonial development may be reassessed.

The Women of Botany Bay intends no disrespect to either the white native-born women or the black native-born women to whose land they came, nor to those 'genteel ladies' who accompanied husbands and fathers as free settlers or the free wives of civilian and military officials. These three groups are outside the scope of this present work.

The Women of Botany Bay is my own interpretation of the evidence collected from Great Britain, Ireland and Australia.

Preface to the Revised Edition

I am grateful to Penguin Books for the opportunity to revise the original text and notes for *The Women of Botany Bay*. The editorial advice and expertise of my editor, Beryl Hill, has been invaluable.

I thank those readers who sent further information – and the odd correction – which is now incorporated in this edition.

To Joyce and Betty Shaw, who have not only checked, rechecked and checked again but painstakingly indexed this volume, thanks are inadequate.

Portia Robinson
1992

Contemporary Terms and Expressions

absolute pardon — A man or woman who received an absolute pardon was restored to the position of a free person. They could leave New South Wales, if they wished.

assigned servant — A man or woman convict whose services were assigned for a certain period, under certain conditions to a private master or mistress.

Botany Bay — This description of New South Wales did not infer a geographical location. It was linked with the infamous and degraded connotations of a convict colony.

came free — Men, women and children who arrived in the colony unconvicted were said to have 'come free'. The contemporary term 'came free' is used throughout the text.

concubine — The description used by Samuel Marsden to describe the women not legally married in 1806.

conditional pardon — A man or woman conditionally pardoned became technically free,

xvi Contemporary Terms and Expressions

	but could not leave the colony until the expiry of the original sentence imposed in Britain.
convict	A man or woman under sentence of the law. Contemporaries seldom distinguished between a convict and an ex-convict, frequently referring to both as 'convict'.
emancipist	Technically, an emancipist was an emancipated convict, that is, one who had been freed by pardon, either absolute pardon or conditional pardon. It was used loosely to refer to all ex-convicts and has continued to be used in this sense.
'exclusives', *'of the first water',* *'pure merinoes'*	Terms describing the respectable men and women who were unconvicted, free of all criminal taint.
fatal tree, *gallows tree,* *three-legged mare*	The scaffold.
government servant	A man or woman convict whose services were retained by the government.
'launched into eternity', *'turned off'*	Executed.
ticket-of-leave	A convict permitted to work for himself/herself under certain conditions and to support himself/herself while still under sentence of the law. This 'indulgence' could be revoked.
unblessed unions	De facto relationships. Again, the description is Samuel Marsden's.

ACKNOWLEDGEMENTS

The Women of Botany Bay began as a study of colonial women in 1977. It was financed first by Macquarie University, then by the Australian Research Grants Scheme. In 1985 the Premier's Department of the New South Wales Government funded the research so that it could be completed as a Bicentennial Project. British Airways contributed the frequent travel which made research in Great Britain and Ireland possible. Men and women throughout Australia, Great Britain, Ireland and Europe all contributed voluntarily their personal records and data relating to individual women transported to New South Wales. Volunteers on both sides of the world gave generously of their time to collect, collate and file a massive amount of data. I hope that everyone who became involved with 'Our Women' will take this as a personal statement of my gratitude and appreciation.

A Steering Committee was appointed at my request to administer the Government Grant of $258 000. The encouragement, advice, cooperation and patience of the members of the Committee is more than appreciated: The Chairman, Mr J. E. Moore (Premier's Department), Professor Barry Leal, Deputy Vice-Chancellor (Academic), Professor Edith-Mary Johnston and Mr Brian Lidbury of Macquarie University.

Ken Morton of British Airways made it possible to unearth, copy and bring to Australia a wealth of contemporary documentary material without which this volume would have had far less data on the British and Irish lives of our first women pioneers. Thanks, too, for the unfailing kindness and helpfulness of the staff of many British Airways flights towards a lone traveller weighed down with documents which she would not let out of her sight.

Thanks to those employed on the project – their dedication and deep involvement is well-remembered. Gloria Webb, as Project Secretary, cheerfully took on the role of Australian coordinator and 'did all things' – and more – that were required. Isobel Low, as British coordinator, not only found contacts and sources, but unearthed valuable data in Sussex, Hampshire and Cambridge. Dr Christine Kinealy, Irish coordinator, established contact with local authorities throughout Ireland and painstakingly searched all contemporary newspapers and journals finding sources hitherto unknown. At Macquarie University, Monica Perrot, Annette Salt, Ann Duffy, Jennifer Allison, Jenny Pearce, Ann Major and Betty Robinson were invaluable. It was Siva, our computer consultant, who overcame so many of the difficulties caused by the nature of contemporary data and who devised solutions to the problems of thousands of 'our women' who would not conform to expected patterns. Linda Paolini not only typed an unwieldy manuscript but did so almost overnight and acted as proofreader. To all who were employed on the project, thank you.

Thanks to the voluntary workers who gave so unstintingly of time and expertise – Joyce and Betty Shaw whose patience, precision, expertise and unfailing encouragement became legendary; to Lois Carrington who, despite all obstacles, combed Britain for crime; Aileen L'Amie of the University of Ulster; Andy Anderson of Lincoln; to Pam Quick, Jill Warren, Dot Pederson – and to all those who came so willingly to Macquarie University and worked, checked and copied endlessly; to all the members of the 'Women of Botany Bay – Colleen to Matilda' Association for their loyalty, support, encouragement, friendship and the data and documents they have so willingly contributed.

Thanks to colleagues who listened with patience, discussed, commented, even disputed – and continued to encourage. Dymphna and Manning Clark, as always, my 'heart-warmers'; Professor Gareth Roberts who eased so many problems; Dr Frank Clarke upon whose friendship, advice and judgment I have come to rely so heavily; Professor Don Aitkin (ANU); Associate Professor Bruce Harris; Associate Professor Raoul Mortley; Dr John Walmsley; Dr George Raudzens; Dr Trevor McClaughlin; Dr George Liik; Dr John Eddy, SJ; Professor F. X. Martin OSA (Dublin); Professor Antony Low (Cambridge); Professor Guy Cabourdin (France); Dr Ian Duffield (Edinburgh);

Russell and Rebecca Dobash (Stirling); Antoinette Fauve-Chamoux (Paris); Lilly Askne (Sweden); Dr Clare O'Reilly (Dublin); Anne Neary (Dublin); Dr Kevin Whelan (Dublin); Dr William Nolan (Dublin); Patrick Nolan (Kilkenny); Dr Deidre Beddoe (Wales); Joan Ward and Zena Hodgkinson of Sydney.

Thanks to Susan O'Reilly, AM, who was the first to take an active and continuing interest in our Irish Colleens of Botany Bay; to Professor Dianne Yerbury, AM, who continued to encourage and give practical support; to His Excellency Ambassador Joseph Small, former Irish Ambassador to Australia and to Sir Peter Lawler, former Australian Ambassador to Ireland, with gratitude for assistance, advice and friendship. I am also grateful to the Duke of Edinburgh for his encouragement.

Thanks to institutions which made research not only more comfortable but more efficient: History Department, RSSS and University House (ANU, Canberra); the Naval and Military Club (London) which provided not only a warm welcome but made writing, research and meeting facilities available; Elaine McLean and BBC Glasgow; the many libraries, public record offices and archives, the local and family history societies on both sides of the world, especially the Public Library of Cambridge and the Record Offices of York, Edinburgh, Winchester and London. To the Mitchell Library Sydney, the Archives Authority of New South Wales, the Macquarie Library, the National Library Canberra, the National Library Dublin, the British Museum – thanks for the way in which staff smoothed and helped with problems and responded cheerfully to almost impossible requests.

Thanks to my editor, Susan Butler, for her expertise, good sense and friendliness, and to Beryl Hill, the editor of the Penguin edition.

Thanks to family and friends who have shared so many years of research with such forbearance and tolerance: Edith and Harry Ferguson; my sons, Tim and Leigh Robinson; Clyde Robinson for providing a quiet refuge in which to write; Lee Robinson OAM, for the professionalism of his advice; most of all to the one who has had the most to bear, my husband, Ron Robinson.

Convict Ships Carrying Women Transported to New South Wales

In the following lists Roman numerals appearing after the name of a ship indicate which ship it is out of a number of ships allotted a particular name. Numbers in brackets refer to the specific voyage of the ship to New South Wales. For example, *Friendship II* (2) is the second ship of that name making its second voyage to New South Wales. *Surprize* (1) does not appear in the list, although *Surprize* (2) does, because on its first voyage *Surprize* did not carry convict women.

1 SHIPS DEPARTING FROM ENGLAND

Ship	Date of arrival Sydney Cove, New South Wales	Source
Charlotte	26 January 1788	4/3998 Bound Indents, AONSW
Friendship I	26 January 1788	4/3998 Bound Indents, AONSW
Lady Penrhyn	26 January 1788	4/3998 Bound Indents, AONSW
Prince of Wales	26 January 1788	4/3998 Bound Indents, AONSW

Convict Ships **xxi**

Ship	Date of arrival Sydney Cove, New South Wales	Source
Lady Juliana	3 June 1790	Lists vary: HO 11/1, reel 87, p 15; CO 201/4, p 105, reel 1, no 2
Neptune	28 June 1790	4/3998
Mary Ann	9 July 1791	COD 9
Albemarle	13 October 1791	COD 9, COD 131
Pitt	14 February 1792	COD 9
Royal Admiral	7 October 1792	COD 9
Kitty (1)	18 November 1792	COD 9
Bellona	16 January 1793	COD 9
William	10 March 1794	Reel 392, p 99
Surprize (2)	25 October 1794	COD 9
Indispensable (1)	30 April 1796	COD 9
Britannia III (1)	18 July 1798	COD 9
Speedy	15 April 1800	4/3999
Earl Cornwallis	12 June 1801	COD 138, p 13ff
Nile	14 December 1801	COD 138
Glatton	11 March 1803	2/8261, p 123ff
Experiment I	24 June 1804	COD 138
William Pitt	11 April 1806	COD 139
Alexander I	20 August 1806	COD 139, p 219ff
Sydney Cove	18 June 1807	COD 139
Speke (1)	16 November 1808	COD 139
Aeolus	26 January 1809	COD 139
Indispensable (2)	18 August 1809	COD 139
Canada (2)	8 September 1810	COD 131
Friends	10 October 1811	COD 139
Minstrel (1)	25 October 1812	4/4004
Wanstead	9 January 1814	COD 140
Broxbornebury	28 July 1814	COD 141
Northampton	18 June 1815	COD 141, p 59
Mary Anne I (1)	19 January 1816	COD 147, p 127 ff
Lord Melville I (1)	24 February 1817	COD 142

Convict Ships

Ship	Date of arrival Sydney Cove, New South Wales	Source
Friendship II (2)	14 January 1818	COD 143
Maria I (1)	17 September 1818	2/8268, p 325ff, 4/3499, p 89
Morley (3)	30 September 1820	COD 148
Providence II (1)	7 January 1822	COD 150
Mary Anne I (2)	20 May 1822	COD 150, p 109
Lord Sidmouth (3)	27 February 1823	COD 151
Mary III (1)	18 October 1823	4/4009A
Brothers (1)	7 May 1824	4/4009A
Grenada (3)	23 January 1825	2/8261, p 361ff
Henry (2)	27 February 1825	2/8262, p 167
Midas (1)	17 December 1825	4/4009A
Grenada (4)	23 January 1827	4/4012
Princess Charlotte (2)	6 August, 1827	4/4012, p 131ff
Harmony (1)	27 September 1827	4/4012, p 180ff
Louisa	3 December 1827	4/4013, p 1ff

Notes

1 Fourteen women who had been convicted in Dublin were sent from Ireland to join the 'English' convict women on the *Kitty*. Two of the 'English' were Welsh women tried in Carmarthen.

2 Women tried in England sailed on the *Janus*, 3 May 1820 and the *Lord Wellington*, 20 January 1820, which departed from Cork after embarking women tried in Ireland.

3 The *Minstrel* which arrived on 22 August 1825 brought 121 male convicts to the Colony, *not* 121 female convicts as listed in Bateson, *The Convict Ships*..., p 385. See 4/4009A and 2/8270, Musters and Papers: *Minstrel*, AONSW.

4 Bound Manuscript Indents 1788–1835 were 'made up in the colony in the office of the Colonial Secretary ... mostly copies or originals of the indentures with the owners of the ships contracting to transport the convicts, not always with list of prisoners attached.' 4/3998–4/4002. *Guide to the Convict Records in the Archives Office of New South Wales*, p 52.

2 SHIPS DEPARTING FROM IRELAND

Ship	Date of arrival Sydney Cove, New South Wales	Source
Queen	26 September 1791	COD 9
Boddingtons	7 August 1793	COD 9
Sugar Cane	17 September 1793	COD 9
Marquis Cornwallis	11 February 1796	COD 9
Britannia I (2)	27 May 1797	COD 9 (or SZ115)
Minerva	11 January 1800	4/3999, p 1ff
Anna/Luz St Anna/Anne	21 February 1801	COD 138
Hercules I	26 June 1802	COD 138
Atlas I	7 July 1802	COD 138
Rolla	12 May 1803	COD 138
Tellicherry	15 February 1806	COD 139
Experiment II	25 June 1809	COD 139
Providence I	2 July 1811	COD 139
Archduke Charles	16 February 1813	COD 140
Catherine	4 May 1814	COD 140
Francis & Eliza	8 August 1815	COD 141
Alexander II	4 April 1816	COD 142
Canada (4)	6 August 1817	COD 143, p 329
Elizabeth I (2)	19 November 1818	COD 145
* *Lord Wellington*	20 January 1820	COD 147
* *Janus*	3 May 1820	COD 147; 4/3502, pp 37-8
John Bull	18 December 1821	COD 149
Woodman (1)	25 June 1823	X41; COD 151
Almorah (3)	20 August 1824	4/4010; 4/4009A
Mariner (2)	10 July 1825	4/4009A
Lady Rowena	17 May 1826	4/4011, p 46
Brothers (2)	2 February 1827	4/4012
Elizabeth II	12 January 1828	4/4013, pp 1-59

* The *Janus* and the *Lord Wellington* carried convict women who had been tried in England in addition to those tried in Ireland.

Conversion Table

Imperial measurements have been retained in the text as used by contemporaries in the interests of historical accuracy and commonsense. The following are approximate conversions:

1 inch	2.5 centimetres	1 ton	1 tonne
1 foot	0.3 metre		
1 yard	0.9 metre	1 gallon	4.5 litres
1 mile	1.6 kilometres		
1 acre	0.4 hectares		
		£1 (one pound)	$2.00
		1s (one shilling)	10 cents
1 ounce	28 grams	1d (one penny)	0.8 cents
1 pound	450 grams		

Introduction
'She was come of decent people...'

... she said she had not broken her fast, and wished him to give her something – he had known her ten years before, and she was come of decent people...

—Trial of Sarah Cramsie, County Antrim Assizes,
26 March 1825

Botany Bay, although no jewel in the Crown, was a British colony, a colony where, almost without exception, the settlers were from British stock. But it was not a replica of British society for most of the colonists during the foundation years were from the one level of society, defined by their contemporaries as belonging to 'the criminal class ... those who normally commit crimes ... the poor and the indigent'. They did not, therefore, bring with them to New South Wales a familiarity with, or expectation of, those standards, values, customs, obligations and privileges which were an intrinsic part of the British hierarchical social system. Instead, they brought with them the memories of experiences which had resulted directly from their economic and social background as members of the lowest order of British society.

To contemporaries, New South Wales was inhabited almost exclusively by 'the scum, the sweepings of the gaols, hulks, and prisons', men and women who became 'infinitely more depraved' in that penal colony than at the time of their arrival. It was accepted that Botany Bay had been founded as a convict colony, a place to which felons would be transported as the most severe form of punishment short of death itself. Their transportation was not expected to lead to any significant reformation of morals or manners, for even the increasing harshness, severity and deprivations of imprisonment in Britain had failed to reduce the numbers of second and third offenders. It was certainly not considered that banishment among their own kind might lead to any level of economic independence, prosperity or social respectability. What class distinctions could there be among those who had arrived as convicts? Without question, they would remain as vile, as infamous, as criminal and immoral as they were known to be in Britain.

Assumptions such as these were not confined to the foundation years of New South Wales. They continued to be expressed and accepted well into the nineteenth century in Britain and the shame attaching to this 'convict taint' was still evident among mid-twentieth century Australians. The English description 'Botany Bay' continued to infer all the infamy of criminality and immorality, of crime and punishment, long after it had ceased to refer to a specific geographic location. Any changes in the nature and structure of the population, any development of a new and distinct system of class hierarchy based on the economic achievements of those 'depraved' convicts was unremarked in Britain. Neither was there recognition of the tremendous physical changes in New South Wales during the administration of Governor Lachlan Macquarie. By 1820 settlement had spread far beyond the struggling penal camp that had been Botany Bay. The townships and settlements scattered throughout and beyond the Cumberland Plain were as indicative of the increasingly ex-convict 'free' communities as was the bustling seaport of Sydney itself. Respectable Britishers, however, continued to believe in the infamy and degradation of the inhabitants of Botany Bay.

This was not the opinion of the men and women who had adopted New South Wales as their homeland, nor was it the opinion of their native-born children. The most distinguished of those children, William Charles Wentworth, himself the illegitimate son of a convict woman, unhesitatingly named the first privately-owned colonial newspaper the *Australian*. There was no colonial shame, no stigma attached to his public identification with a convict Botany Bay for, in the colony itself, 'Australia' was replacing 'Botany Bay'. Visitors, free settlers, officials, soldiers, the convicts themselves who arrived in New South Wales in the latter years of the Macquarie decade, expecting to find the debauchery, inebriety and licentiousness believed in Britain to be characteristic of the colony, were astounded at its 'civilisation'. Instead of huts and hovels they saw mansions 'which would grace Hanover Square . . . streets as long as Oxford Street', 'magnificent churches and public buildings, roads and bridges, shops and businesses of all descriptions, neat cottages for labourers, fine carriages for the wealthy . . . everything belied it was a convict colony'.

This commendable development 'in the short space of thirty years' was, of course, judged and praised by English standards.

What was found to be 'un-English' was peculiar to the colony itself. This was the tangible and visible evidence of the punishment of British criminals. The chain gangs which slowly worked their miserable way along George Street, 'half-starved and near-naked', the reports of the living dead at Norfolk Island and Port Arthur, the flagrant immorality of the abandoned convict women at Parramatta Female Factory, all these were the 'un-English' 'cruel' aspects of the colony, characteristics condemned as indigenous to Botany Bay.

The transportation system, designed to settle and maintain the convict colony, had been born from the English criminal law and nurtured by continuing British attitudes towards crime, criminals and punishment. It was, therefore, these 'un-English' aspects of New South Wales which continued to be emphasised, to dominate opinions and to shape attitudes in Britain. British visitors might praise the unexpected 'civilisation' of Botany Bay but they remained unaware that colonial development owed much to an intrinsic and unrecognised feature of that transportation system: the unexpected opportunities it had given to the transported convicts. There was little, if any, recognition that it was mainly the labour, industry and enterprise of the men and women who had arrived as convicts which had built and developed a penal camp into a free settlement.

It had been the peculiar and unique nature of the convict colony which had allowed and encouraged individual response to the opportunities for material advancement at all levels of society, convicted and free. For a price in human endeavour, the lands of Australia offered far greater rewards for labour than any which could have been imagined by a British labourer, tradesman or military officer, or dreamed of by any country servant girl or working woman in any of the towns and cities of Great Britain.

It was the level of economic success which resulted from individual response to those opportunities which created the first 'Australian' class system among those who had arrived as convicts. Colonial society remained divided by the stigma of criminal conviction, but those who arrived as convicts did not necessarily or inevitably remain the uniform 'criminal class' they had been in Britain. Within convicted society there developed the normal hierarchical levels and gradings of contemporary society, but all based on economic achievement or failure in the colony.

That convicted women as well as men were part of this social and economic development of a penal colony into a free society was unnoticed by contemporaries, ignored or misrepresented by later generations of historians and commentators. The colonial women of New South Wales remained tainted with the description 'the convict women of Botany Bay'. The conviction of most of them for major felonies in Britain had made them even more infamous than the male convicts in the opinions of their respectable British contemporaries, their prosecutors, their gaolers. That they *were* criminal women meant, to contemporaries, that they were also degraded, vicious, depraved and dissolute whores, characteristics supported not only by the 'evidence' of their lifestyles prior to their conviction, but by the reports of their obscene and abandoned behaviour in the prisons and gaols of Britain which was clear proof that they were depraved women, incapable of reformation. That such women were transported to Botany Bay was the basis of the assumption that there could only be one class of women in that penal colony – convict women, women so devoid of any sense of decency or shame, so lacking in any of the expected womanly virtues that 'their very children imbibed vice with their mothers' milk'.

Their reputation was a British, not a colonial one. It was firmly based on their status as convicted felons, British criminals from the lowest orders of society. Contemporaries had little doubt as to their viciousness for British newspapers reported almost daily on the alarming and increasing depredations of highwaywomen, of female footpads, cutpurses, pickpockets, shoplifters, housebreakers – and worse. Did not women and girls, singly, in pairs or in gangs, attack, assault and rob indiscriminately throughout Britain? Were not the good people from almost every marketplace, village, town and city aware of the increasing number of crimes by women in their own localities? And were not those women who were apprehended, tried and convicted for these offences against their neighbours and their betters, 'lost as they were to every species of depravity', far worse than the men? Officials, and would-be reformers who visited the prisons holding the convicted women awaiting death or transportation, certainly thought so. They reported again and again that these wretched females were 'of the lowest and worst description, the very scum both of the city and country'.

With such a reputation in their home country, what standards of decency, honesty and morality could be expected in a convict colony? What hope of reformation could there be for second and third offenders, women whom no punishment could reclaim from their evil ways? Women who had previously been whipped, or burnt in the hand, imprisoned, sent to the Houses of Correction – and again come before the Courts and found guilty of the same offences. Was not the learned judge correct in his summing up that these 'night-walking strumpets who infest our streets' belonged at Botany Bay?

Their British reputation continued to dominate attitudes towards the women of Botany Bay. There was little comment on the differing patterns of behaviour which emerged in their colonial lives, little recognition of their roles within colonial society, especially as ex-convict, technically free women. The emergence and growth of a new social structure of class among women who had shared the same class origins in their native country passed unobserved. Many of these convict women endured with their free sisters the fears and privations of a pioneering life in the isolation of the outlying settlements, in the strange and alien loneliness of the Australian bush. They too knew the fear and danger of floods, of bushfires, of droughts. They too experienced the anguish of childbirth and child-death far from the assistance and comfort of other women. They endured equal privations, faced the same dangers and fears as the few free migrant women in the early years of the penal settlement. Despite their very real involvement as the first European women to settle the Australian bush, these convict and ex-convict women did not become a part of the legends and mythology of the bush. Nor did those women who remained in the towns and townships as working women, as family women, or as both, find any place in the history of early Australia, although they were as enterprising in their economic activities as were the transported men. Either by themselves or with husbands or male partners, these women 'of no trade' set up small businesses, opened shops, became market women, dealers and street-sellers, worked as dressmakers, seamstresses, milliners, laundresses, washerwomen, pastrycooks and confectioners, sometimes employing other women in these trades. The ex-convict women who married convict or ticket-of-leave men found themselves in a new role as 'wives', for they became the technical head of the family, a convict being ineligible to own land or to apply for licences. The ex-convict wife, therefore, was the one who petitioned for land grant, lease or licence. She was the one who, with testimonials to her 'proven good character' applied for government licences to brew, to distil, to bake, to own or lease an inn or public house, to engage in trade, to sell to the Commissariat. It was the convict wife who applied for any indulgence, such as additional convict servants, assigned men or women with specific skills or trades, or for the loan of government cattle.

This direct involvement of many ex-convict women, single, married or widowed, in the economic life of the colony was not only ignored by contemporaries but overlooked by most historians. The economic role of colonial women and the very nature of the colonial economy became so distorted that a mid-twentieth century historian could claim that 'the social and economic conditions of the first fifty years ... fostered whores not wives'.

All of the convicted women needed to establish new lives in the colony almost in defiance of their unsavoury British reputation. The determining influence on their individual responses to the new conditions, opportunities and difficulties they found at Botany Bay was not their British criminality with its associated expectations of depravity, immorality and vice, but the experiences which had been commonplace before their conviction. It was the contrast between those experiences as women of the lowest order of British society and as colonial women, with opportunities both as family women and working women, that was determinative for the nature of the emerging 'Australian' female society. Despite this, despite success or failure in New South Wales, these women remained the victims, not of the male-dominated penal society, but of the vast misunderstanding which existed between British assumptions and the reality that was New South Wales.

It has taken almost two hundred years for the British and colonial lives of Australia's first women pioneers to be reconstructed. It has taken almost as long for a reinterpretation of their role in and contribution to Australian society on the basis of their own lives within their own times. To their own children, there was little shame or disgrace in their 'convict' parentage. These native-born children knew their parents through their colonial achievements and failures, possibly unaware of their British reputations. The real taint and stigma of convictism became entrenched in colonial attitudes following the drastic changes within the transportation system from the 1820s, increasing with the Victorian emphasis on respectability, morality and class consciousness which came to New South Wales with each new shipload of British migrants throughout the nineteenth century. This 'shame' of convict origins gradually entered the Australian consciousness, fostered by the 'pure merinos' of colonial society, bolstered by the increasing migration of free and respectable families at all levels of the social scale. The labour, the enterprise, the contribution of the first 'convict' settlers was ignored. There remained only horror, revulsion and rejection of the 'convict' origins of Australian society.

It was not until 1922 that there was any significant swing of the pendulum against this shame of Australia's tainted origins. In that year Professor G. A. Wood gave a paper to the Royal Australian Historical Society entitled 'The Convicts'. Wood's new interpretation was revolutionary in the sense that it rejected entirely the traditional 'depravity and infamy' of Australia's first convict settlers. According to Professor Wood our founding fathers were not the despicable and degraded criminals guilty of the vilest of crimes. They were, he argued, the real victims of a harsh British social and criminal code. Innocent and manly, these 'village Hampdens' suffered the effects of a relentless and uncaring policy instigated by the British aristocracy to protect their property, wealth and privileges. At the most, these despairing and starving men stole a loaf of bread, or poached a rabbit, or thieved a handkerchief as an alternative to death from starvation for themselves and for their families. For these trivial offences they suffered the agonies of transportation and, at Botany Bay, were flogged and ironed and starved and worked until death was a merciful release from unendurable hardships.

Wood's view emphasised the compassion, pity and pride with which, he argued, Australia's origins should be viewed. Shame, if shame there were, should be transferred from the miserable victims to their oppressors, the British upper classes safe and secure in the mother country. Pity for the miserable wretches who suffered helplessly under the tyranny and inhumanity believed to typify the transportation system replaced the shame of the convict taint. This nobility of suffering became evident in the horror of banishment, of ceaseless toil without reward, of the spiritual deprivation and desolation, of lives dragged out in misery and pain, without hope, without purpose.

It was from this view of Australia's origins that the myth or legend of the 'noble convict' grew. Gradually, very gradually, gaining popular acceptance, replacing the stigma of convict ancestry with pride in those innocent 'victims'. The legend of the noble convict, however, was a male legend. The nobility of suffering, the injustice, the miseries, the fearsome cruelties, did not include the convicted women. They were damned to remain without place or acknowledgement in the history of their adopted country, their colonial lives overshadowed and submerged by their British reputation.

The noble convict legend is an undeserved apology for the men (and women and children) who *were* Australian society in its foundation years. It had given a new perspective to the Australian legend, had brought into open discussion aspects of early Australia which had remained obscured and neglected. But the 'innocent and manly victims' theory was as biased and distorted as the belief that the convicts were degraded, vile criminal outcasts. The first settlers needed no apology, nor did they need their crimes whitewashed. It would be as erroneous to claim that all the convicted men were honest, sober and industrious, and all the women dutiful and virtuous – even sober – as it would to assert that they were the victims of a harsh and oppressive system.

Suffering, inhumanity, cruelty, spiritual deprivation – all were part of the convict system, and their influence cannot be underestimated. The despair and failure, the desolation of mind and body were characteristics which must take their place beside the successes and triumphs, great and small, the hopes, the dreams, the achievements of Britain's exiles. It was this multiplicity of experiences which shaped the new and distinct society which grew from Botany Bay to become 'Australia', experiences which were not necessarily based on the attitudes, values and expectations of the Old Country, nor rooted in the great heritage of Europe's civilisation. Britain's outcasts came to a land new to Europeans but where an ancient and unrecognised civilisation had stood still for time beyond the compass of the mind.

The suffering and misery which came with the Europeans to the old land of Terra Australis was integral to the origins of the society created at Botany Bay. It cannot be ignored or glossed over; neither should it be stressed and emphasised for it was not the determining characteristic of the new society. It was the dark side of the European heritage, the physical embodiment of the criminal law of England. As such it entered the Australian consciousness and remained embedded in the mythology as a dominant feature of Australia's founding years.

The first faint attempts to reinterpret the role of convict women damned them still further, for the feminist writers of the second half of the twentieth century described their colonial contribution on the evidence of the opinions and reports of a handful of 'respectable' contemporaries interpreted in accordance with prevailing mid-twentieth century feminist theories. This resulted in an excuse-explanation of the place of convicted women in colonial society. It accepted the contemporary assumption, based mainly on the British reputations of these women, that they continued their immoral behaviour in the male-dominated penal colony, but excused it. The reason? These women had no economic or social value to New South Wales except as sexual objects. This being so, argued the mid-twentieth century feminists, they became the 'victims of victims', the convict men. They were the lowest level of colonial society, forced to prostitute themselves to survive. This argument is almost a 'noble female convict' legend, owing much to Wood's theories of the 1920s. Wood claimed that the convict men had been forced by circumstances beyond their control to become petty thieves in order to survive and to feed their starving families in Britain. The feminist writers argued that the convict women were also forced by the economic and social circumstances of the colony to become the unhappy victims who had no alternative to prostitution and 'enforced whoredom'. Whatever may have been the motivation, the first Australian women were labelled the 'damned whores' of Botany Bay, with no awareness of the distinction between convict women and ex-convict women, no awareness of the complexity and diversity of the emerging structure of colonial female society in New South Wales.

These women need no excuse, nor do they need apologists. Nor can the assumption that they were the oppressed victims of convict society remain unchallenged. They may have arrived in New South Wales as a uniform class of despised felons, tainted with all the vile and infamous connotations of that word 'convict', but their responses to colonial opportunities and disadvantages were as stridently varied and determinative as were those of the women who came free and unconvicted. English, Irish, Scottish, Welsh or Cornish, country women or town women, married, widowed or single, thieves, robbers, pickpockets, skilled or illiterate, young or old, diseased or healthy, all of those women who came to Botany Bay reacted according to their own individual responses to a life of exile in a convict colony. It is only on this evidence, the evidence of their individual lives, that their contribution to colonial society may be assessed.

1
'GUESTS OF HIS MAJESTY'

The convict women of Great Britain

> *... vagrants and disorderly women of the very lowest and most wretched class of human beings, almost naked, with only a few filthy rags almost alive with vermin, their bodies rotting with distemper, and covered with itch, scorbic and venereal ulcers.*
>
> – William Smith, Middlesex Gaols, 1776

The women of Botany Bay were the criminal women of Great Britain, women exiled from their homeland to serve sentences of penal servitude in England's convict colony of New South Wales. These were the women believed to typify the debauchery, depravity and criminality which was Botany Bay. To all civilised nations England's penal settlement was what it purported to be, a colony of thieves, murderers and pickpockets, of felons so debased that the only fit punishment for their crimes was banishment from respectable society to a distant and uninhabited part of the globe where they would spend their lives with their own kind.[1]

Assumptions regarding convicts, convictism and a convict settlement were all intertwined in attitudes towards the women of Botany Bay. On their British reputations alone they were damned by contemporaries as dissolute and immoral, lacking any of the expected virtues of decent women. As felons in a convict colony what could be expected of them but a continuation and extension of those characteristics which had led to their convictions in their native land? There were sufficient pious contemporaries to observe and report on the behaviour of the women at Botany Bay to give substance in Britain to the accuracy of these assumptions. Chaplain Richard Johnson saw these convicts as 'preferring lust to their very souls' and Chaplain Samuel Marsden reported that their children, spawned in drink, 'imbibed vice with their mother's milk', while reports of the licentiousness, the brawling, the profanity and the obscenity of the women at the Parramatta Female Factory would make accounts of the notorious behaviour of the women confined in Newgate Gaol pale into insignificance.[2]

The opinion of the visiting Spanish expedition in 1793, that the women of Botany Bay excelled even the notorious women of Rio in the arts of enticement and prostitution, remained unchallenged.[3]

The term 'convict women' continued to be used indiscriminately to describe the women of England's penal colony. Most but not all of the women who came to New South Wales during the first forty years of white settlement arrived as convicted felons. It was not until 1828 that the combined total of adult came-free women and adult native-born women almost equalled the total number of women who had arrived convict. The structure of colonial female society, however, was as diverse and complex as that of male society. The diversity was accentuated by the distinction – often overlooked by both colonial and British commentators – between those who were serving their sentences and were, in actual fact, 'convicts', and those who had either served their full sentences or had been pardoned and were thus technically free, restored to that society from which they had been barred by their criminal offences.[4]

It was not only the ex-convict women who retained the stigma of convictism. The free wives of convicts, the women who had come to New South Wales voluntarily to rejoin their convicted husbands, were so closely associated with convictism through their marriages that they, too, became women of Botany Bay. In most cases this extension of the husband's convictism to the free wife was reinforced by the class origins of those wives, most of whom came from the same background in Britain as the convict women.

The minority of colonial women who had come free were outside convict society, divorced, as it were, from the evils inherent in convictism. Yet they, too, were not a uniform class of women and differed in their social and economic status even more than the women who had been transported. These were the free women settlers of New South Wales, the nucleus of that respectable society of gentlewomen in which Elizabeth Macarthur could find only three or four members by the end of 1791.[5] In the foundation years, most of these women were the wives of civilian and military officials and many were temporary residents, spending only that time in New South Wales during which their husbands were appointed to official positions. Most of the thirty-one wives who accompanied the soldiers and non-commissioned officers of the Royal Marines in 1788 returned with their husbands when the Royal Marines were replaced by the New South Wales Corps.[6] Most of the wives of the higher-ranking officials were in the colony only for that period of their husbands' tour of duty. Mrs Johnson, Mrs King, Mrs Paterson, Mrs Putland and Mrs Macquarie left their individual marks on the emerging female society, but were temporary 'Ladies of Botany Bay'.

The free women who came as the wives and daughters of settlers, tradesmen, traders, publicans and shopkeepers, and the free girls and women who accompanied the gentlewomen as their servants, emphasised the social and economic distinctions which existed among the came-free inhabitants of Botany Bay. The yardstick by which status and position was allocated or achieved in the colony was civil condition. Every man, woman and child was entitled to privileges or subject to disabilities in accordance with their status as bond or free. Within these two wide categories all colonists found their place defined by their economic level of success. What was unexpected in the structure of 'convict' society was that there would be men and women whose enterprise would place them among the wealthiest in the colony, rivalling even the purest of the 'pure merinos' in their achievements. That women who had arrived as convicts would also be sufficiently enterprising and industrious as to play significant economic roles in the colony as well as become the honest and respectable wives of successful emancipists, was even more unexpected and so out of keeping with the widely-accepted assumptions as to their depravity and uselessness as to be unbelievable to contemporaries. The successes of the ex-convict women, the positions they obtained within convict society, by their own efforts or as wives or partners of their men, remained unrecognised by British officials and commentators and did nothing at all to lessen the belief that their colonial role remained in keeping with their British criminality, that they were the drunken whores and debased prostitutes of colonial society, women who deserved the infamous description 'women of Botany Bay'.

It was, without doubt, the British criminality of the women of Botany Bay which determined attitudes and assumptions towards their roles within colonial society. That criminality, however, implied an erroneous assumption as to the uniformity of their backgrounds, lifestyles, characteristics, attitudes and values. This assumption was in direct contrast to the diversity of their lives prior to conviction in England, Ireland, Scotland or Wales, to the variety and range of experiences, causes and consequences which had led to those convictions, and even to the variety of ages, native places, occupations, and family situations of the women themselves. Admittedly there were shared characteristics, even among the English and the Irish women, characteristics such as familiarity with poverty and destitution, shared class origins of membership of the lower orders of British society, occupational skills limited to those traditionally associated with the domestic labour of women, close experience of the conditions and rewards for unskilled or semi-skilled labour and a certainty of the lack of opportunity for economic advancement for even the most industrious of women seeking 'a place' or means of livelihood either in their native parishes or in the cities and towns of Britain. Individual experiences before conviction for a major statutory offence, however, were almost as diverse as the individual responses of the transported women to life in England's penal colony.

The emphasis on their criminality was determinative not only of contemporary assessments of the contribution of the convict women to Australian society but also influenced historical interpretations of the nature of Australian society in its origins. It was not their criminality, however, which was to be the major influence on their responses to colonial life. Far more determinative were the social and economic circumstances of their lives before conviction. This was overlooked by contemporary commentators who were almost obsessed with the significance of their being convicts, women found guilty of crimes 'of the darkest description'. The neglect of this vital factor in almost all historical interpretations and explanations of the role and contribution of women to the origins of an Australian society has caused distortion and misrepresentation of the real role and contribution of the 'convict' women. It is only in recent years that historians and sociologists have begun to see women not primarily as women in society, not exclusively as 'women in history', but as a whole and vital part of a society. Convict society, interpreted solely within the limits of convictism, leads to an interpretation as inaccurate and distorted as previous accounts which entirely overlook that women were an actual and living part of that society. In this way, Russel Ward's scholarly account of *The Australian Legend* is marred by the lack of any acknowledgement that women, too, were part of that past from which Australian mythology developed.[7] At the other end of the scale, the rehash of the old nineteenth-century 'convict novels' found in Robert Hughes's *Fatal Shore* perpetuates this traditional interpretation of the nature of the women convicts of Australia. Comments such as, 'It was the sense of helplessness, above all, that ground the women prisoners down', and the harping emphasis on the Female Factory at Parramatta, 'the colony's main marriage market', belittle and minimise the wide and varied contribution of the women of Botany Bay to the society which was to become their own.[8]

What manner of women were they, these convict women of Botany Bay, these European women and girls transported from all parts of the British Isles? Most of them would spend the remainder of their lives in New South Wales, but they were not aware of the vastness of their adopted country although they were vividly conscious of the great distance which separated them from their homeland. They knew nothing of the extent of pasture and arable lands and of wastelands which lay behind the barrier of the mountain ridges. To them, New South Wales was a limited settlement, limited to the boundaries of the Cumberland Plain which stretched some forty miles by twenty (sixty-five kilometres by thirty-two) along the coastline of the Pacific Ocean. For these women, and for their men, 'outlying settlement' meant the districts outside the townships of Sydney and Parramatta, spreading gradually to include Hunter's River, Newcastle and Moreton Bay to the North, Liverpool, Jervis Bay and Illawarra to the south, and west beyond the Bathurst Plains. To the east was that impenetrable barrier, the sea, a barrier which prevented them, as surely as the iron bars of a cage, from returning to the land they had known since childhood. For almost all of the convicted women, New South Wales was to be their adopted homeland for the remainder of their lives and they, their men and their colonial-born children, its pioneers.[9]

These first white Australian women were the products of their European heritage. Almost without exception they shared a common European ancestry, their British heritage differing according to their place of birth, their parentage, their skills or lack of skills, their occupation and their place of residence. They were women familiar with the civilisation of their own times only so far as it touched their class or place in society. They were women to whom public physical punishment was neither extraordinary nor barbarous. They were women who, almost without exception, had no expectations of 'rising above their station in life'; women familiar with the exploitation of child labour, with poor working conditions, with overcrowded and unsanitary housing in cottage, room or lodging; women who had known and lived through the dangers of infant, child and juvenile disease and who, in many cases, had survived childbirth and the complications of lying-in. They were women representative of the lower classes and unemployed of England, Ireland, Scotland and Wales during the late eighteenth and early nineteenth centuries and it was these characteristics and these social origins which were transferred with the convict women to Botany Bay.[10]

Any understanding of the responses of these women to life at Botany Bay, individually and collectively, must rest on a recognition and appreciation of the social and economic conditions from which they came. Their living conditions prior to conviction, their customary and accepted standards of housing, diet, hygiene, their expectations from labour and its rewards, are in almost all cases overlooked by historians intent on portraying the horrors and sufferings of the convicts of New South Wales under the transportation system. For the women, the conditions of the Female Factory itself were but the shadow of the reality that they had known during their confinement in the prisons and bridewells of Britain.

Before conviction the everyday living conditions of almost all the transported women were characterised by squalor, poverty, dirt and disease in either urban or rural localities. With the increasing movement of people to London and other urban centres, overcrowding in the metropolis became notorious. Many of the newcomers were unable to find employment or any means of subsistence, apart from begging or crime. Whole districts became vast 'lodging houses' where even among the employed it was commonplace for a family to live in one small unventilated room. A contemporary description of late-eighteenth-century London shows conditions which would have been familiar to the many women convicted in the metropolis:

it will scarcely appear credible ... that persons of the lowest class do not put clean sheets on their beds three times a year ... that from three to eight individuals of different ages often sleep in the same bed ... The room occupied is either a deep cellar, almost inaccessible to the light, and admitting of no change of air; or a garret with a low roof and small windows the passage to which is close, kept dark, and filled not only with bad air, but with putrid excremental effluvia from a vault at the bottom of the staircase ... [all] favour the accumulation of heterogeneous filth ...[11]

It was the very poor, especially the single women, the washerwomen, the charwomen, the street-sellers, the silk-winders, streetwalkers and those of 'no trade' who lived in these cellars and garrets, not only in London, but in Dublin, Glasgow,

Edinburgh and all the major cities and towns of Britain. The few respectable contemporaries who were sufficiently charitable as to express horror at this abject poverty, described the plight of those women forced to give birth alone in such surroundings:

poor women, in a state of child-bearing ... are of all objects the most miserable. They are quite unfit for labour ... and consequently deprived of the means of supporting themselves in their great day of affliction. Their lodgings are generally in extreme cold garrets open to every wind that blows, or in damp uncomfortable cellars underground, subject to floods from excessive rain.[12]

Many of these urban women who were unemployed in Britain had a child to maintain, while the women in similar situations in Dublin had three or four, or even more children entirely dependent on their mothers' exertions for their support and subsistence. In Britain and in Ireland, the girls and women of the cities and towns who 'were in an unfortunate line of life' and worked as street women, lived in a shared room, garret or cellar, or even, as Mary Partridge (*Pitt*) who was transported in 1792, 'in the coal shed'. Ann Wakelin, servant to Mr Myers of Air Street, Piccadilly, 'resided in a stall in the same street'. When Elizabeth Burkitt (*Indispensable*) was tried at Middlesex Sessions in 1795, her prosecutor described how he 'was loathe to make a fuss when he missed his watch and saw her with it in her hand' (after he had spent the night with her) because 'there were others in the room'. Margaret Kennedy, tried Middlesex Sessions 1796, lived in the notorious criminal district of St Giles, in Dyot Street, but 'worked' Bloomsbury, making use of the lanes and courtyards for her 'line of work'. The numbers of transported women found guilty of theft while 'attending to their trade' in courtyards, lanes, passageways and alleys might suggest a lack of any privacy in their shared room, although, from the evidence at numerous trials, there appeared no reluctance on the part of two or three women to take home a man or men at the same time.[13]

These living conditions were not confined to the poor of London. The squalor and the filth which characterised the 'homes' of the poor grew with the spread of the industrial towns and cities. Manchester, for example, was completely unable to deal with the problem of housing a growing labour force. In 1795 the appalling conditions, the open sewers, the primitive privies, the enormity of the squalid overcrowding was described by a contemporary:

... Manchester may bear comparison with the metropolis itself in the rapidity with which whole new streets have been raised, and its extension on every side towards the surrounding country; so it unfortunately vies with, or exceeds, the metropolis, in the closeness with which the poor are crowded in offensive, dark, damp, and incommodious habitations, a too fertile source of disease.[14]

This was the background familiar to Manchester women such as Ellen Fraser, Sarah McCormick, Isabella Oldfield and Jane Parkinson, all of whom were transported on the First Fleet. Not one of these women gave any evidence of possessing a trade, skill or calling at their trials in Manchester, although Jane Parkinson described herself to the Surgeon of the *Lady Penrhyn* as 'a milliner'. All four were 'singlewomen' according to their indictments, although Ellen Fraser was charged with William Fraser and resumed living with him after transportation to Botany Bay – one of their colonial sons was christened by Chaplain Johnson in June 1789 and another in July 1791.[15] What comparisons Ellen Fraser and her companions from Manchester may have made with colonial living conditions and those they had experienced in the slums of Manchester is unknown.

As historian James Walvin points out, it was not only in the major cities of Britain that the living conditions of the poor were so deplorable:

Wherever urban industries existed in the eighteenth century there were to be found abject domestic circumstances; dirty, damp, overcrowded and unhygienic homes. This was particularly true of mining villages. But even those abject conditions were seen to be overwhelmed – in scale, intensity and consequence – by the dramatic growth of the English towns with their core of terrible housing. The age-old urban problems of London were rapidly replicated across the country.[16]

Overcrowded, unsanitary, unhealthy, with no facilities for hygiene or for washing of body or clothes, with primitive cooking arrangements, with no privacy and providing only the most basic of shelter, overrun with vermin, with rats, lice and bedbugs an accepted part of these ill-ventilated, damp and noisome living quarters, these were the everyday standards of 'homes' for the lower orders of British society. These conditions were reflected in the appearance and habits of many of the women sentenced to transportation, especially those who had spent months or years in the even more appalling conditions of Britain's gaols.[17] When first met by the surgeons of the transport ships, their physical appearance revolted these gentlemen and added to their conviction that the women were as morally destitute as they were physically unclean. Frances Wilson (*Friendship II*), a twenty-three-year-old stay-and-mantuamaker tried at York Quarter Sessions in 1816, was described by the transport surgeon as 'a filthy woman, delicate constitution, given to theft'. Isabella Thirkill (*Friendship II*), a forty-nine-year-old washerwoman from York was 'an insolent, offensive woman'. Elizabeth Voller (*Earl Cornwallis*) from Hampshire, Ann Evans (*Friends*) from Montgomeryshire, Janet Angus (*Midas*) from Perth, Hannah Edwards (*Experiment*) from Portsmouth – the convicted women from all parts of the British Isles had known no other standards of living except those familiar to all the women of their background and class in their native land.[18]

It was not only the locally-born women in need of assistance who created problems for local authorities in towns, cities and villages of Britain. The lack of any provision to relieve the distresses of men, women and children from other parishes became a problem of vast proportions. Despite some improvement with hospitals, dispensaries, and the rights of children 'without settlement' to be received into workhouses, the problems of the condition of the poor, employed, unemployed or 'out of a place' continued to plague local authorities. One of the greatest concerns was the problem of the vagrants, the beggars, the destitute who were far from their own parish and so not entitled to any charity or assistance from parish officers. The Mendicity Report of 1814-15 for London (see Table 1.1) is indicative of the enormity of this problem.

Table 1.1 Persons without settlement, London 1814–15[19]

Home parishes (within ten miles of the metropolis)	about 2231 persons	including 1384 children
Distant parishes	868	489
Ireland	1770	1091
Scotland	168	103 children
Foreign countries	59	29

Some of those 'without settlement' were part of the wandering population of 'comers and goers', well aware of the enormity of the problems of destitution which faced men and women with no claim on the charity of the parish in which they lived, problems which could and did lead to starvation and death from malnutrition. The extent of this internal migration, within England, Scotland and Wales and across the water from Ireland to English cities, towns and counties, is evidenced in the trials of those women and girls who were apprehended and convicted of crimes in towns and counties far from their native place. Women such as Elizabeth Evans, a married woman from Liverpool, who was sentenced to death at Salop in 1798, reprieved and transported on the *Earl Cornwallis*. Mary Rogers, another married woman from Liverpool, was sentenced to seven years' transportation at Shropshire Gaol Delivery in 1804 and arrived in New South Wales on the *William Pitt*. Catherine Clements, 'native-place Ireland', was sentenced at Chester Sessions of the Peace in 1809 and transported on the *Canada*. Not all indictments showed 'native place', but those sentenced for 'vagrancy' or as 'rogues and vagabonds' or, in Scotland, 'having the habit and repute of a thief' were usually women and girls 'without settlement'. That is, they were far from their own parish and not entitled to the charity of the local governors of the poor. Elizabeth Hurley (who could sign her name) was sentenced in Devon to seven years' transportation in 1798: 'She was a vagrant found at large, feloniously wandering abroad and begging after having been imprisoned as an incorrigible rogue.' She sailed for New South Wales on the *Earl Cornwallis* with another Devon vagrant, Mary Edwards, who had been sentenced at the Quarter Sessions of July 1800. 'She had been a vagrant before and had been confined for six months. She was now convicted of being an incorrigible rogue.'[21]

The number of rogues and vagabonds sentenced to transportation was not indicative of the numbers of vagrant women wandering the roads and lanes of Great Britain, for all rogues and vagabonds were not sentenced to transportation for their first offence. They were usually committed if 'found wandering abroad and lodging in Barns and outhouses and not giving a good account of themselves'. The Lee family were brought to Winchester Bridewell in January 1797 as rogues and vagabonds. Ann Lee, aged fifty-three and Martha Lee, twenty-four, were further charged with 'attempting to poison hogs belonging to Edward Whistler'. They were not transported but all received sentences of six months' confinement with hard labour for vagrancy, in accordance with the statutory punishment for 'Rogues and Vagabonds'. Were they to commit a second offence, all would certainly be sentenced to transportation as 'incorrigible rogues'.[20]

Lucy Vaughan was not so fortunate. Her case illustrates the 'progress' of a vagrant girl from 'rogue and vagabond' to 'incorrigible rogue' which could be punished with 'Two Years' Imprisonment and Whipping' or 'Transportation for Seven Years'. Lucy Vaughan was sentenced at the Quarter Sessions of her native Shrewsbury in July 1797. At the age of nineteen she was declared a 'rogue and vagabond' and given one month's hard labour. Two years later she appeared before the same court and received six months' hard labour with solitary confinement. In April the following year, still in Shrewsbury, she was sentenced again to 'one month with hard labour' for 'being a rogue and vagabond and wandering and lying in the open air'. Finally, early in 1804, she was sentenced in Shropshire to transportation for stealing muslin to the value of forty shillings. What contrasts did Lucy Vaughan find in her life in New South Wales after she arrived on the *William Pitt* in 1806? Did she leave anyone at all to lament her going? None of her trial papers mention parents, husband, children, friend or neighbour willing to supply any testimonial for Lucy Vaughan. To the respectable people of Shrewsbury and Shropshire, Lucy was undoubtedly a rogue and a vagabond who deserved to be at Botany Bay. There is no evidence that she continued her vagrant ways in the colony. She settled with James Squires, with whom she was still living in 1814, her days of 'lying in the open air' apparently over.[21]

During the early years of the nineteenth century the numbers of rogues and vagabonds committed at the county courts increased, as did the numbers of Irish women tried in England and sentenced to transportation. Some of these Irish migrants to England were single women, but most were married. These Irish family working women had come to Britain with their husbands, forced from their native land by poverty, famine, lack of employment, or as a result of the upheavals following rebellions. Most tried to find work in London or near the metropolis. One of the first Irish women to be sentenced and transported from London was Margaret Darnell who sailed with the First Fleet. She had been born in Dublin and had travelled to London in search of work and, after conviction for stealing one dozen knives and forks from an ironmonger in Chancery Lane, she was sentenced at the Old Bailey in 1787 to seven years' transportation. After a brief liaison with marine Charles Green – who gave his name to the son she bore him – she married former seaman Owen Cavanagh who had also come to the colony with the First Fleet. Cavanagh adopted her son, writing to Governor Macquarie in 1810 on his behalf as 'a sober and industrious' lad wishing to settle on his own land. Margaret Cavanagh's life in the colony was entirely different from the life she had known either in her home country or in London. She and her colonial husband were among the earliest settlers in the Hawkesbury District, where they had received an initial grant of one hundred acres. The value of the goods Margaret Darnell had stolen was estimated at six shillings. In 1808 Mrs Margaret Cavanagh sold land and garden in Pitts Row, Sydney, for £20. She had found her future – and her fortune – in New South Wales where, until her death in 1834, she remained a respectable family woman of Botany Bay.

Irish women sentenced in England were to follow Margaret Darnell on almost every female transport sailing from England to New South Wales. Most were married but few were granted the 'indulgence' of passage for husband or children. Mary Flynn, twenty-nine, convicted of stealing linen in 1791, was transported on the *Kitty*, her husband and children remaining in London. Susan Roberts from Mullingar, eighteen, convicted in 1801, arrived in New South Wales on the *Glatton* in 1803, her husband left behind in London. Most of these women had been confined in Newgate Gaol while waiting for their transport, and so were tarnished with that evil reputation of Newgate felons which had remained unchanged since William Smith's description of the women in Middlesex gaols in 1776:

vagrants and disorderly women of the very lowest and most wretched class of human beings, almost naked, with only a few filthy rags almost alive with vermin, their bodies rotting with distemper, and covered with itch, scorbic and venereal ulcers.

English, Irish, Scots or Welsh, these women left their prison where 'extortion, prostitution, and drunkenness were routine', where, it was claimed, 'gaol fever took more victims than did justice', and boarded the convict ships.[22] Were their expectations of life at the gaol of Botany Bay based on the experiences of life as they had known it in the gaols of England?

Few of the transported women, whether Irish, Scots or English, were the wives of men sentenced to transportation. An occasional petition requested that man and wife be transported to the same place 'or as near each other as we can with propriety be sent', or 'in the same ship', as in the petition of Elizabeth Maclean and Robert Harris, sentenced in 1819 at Dumfries, Scotland. Wives were often tried under their maiden name – as was Elizabeth Maclean – and this could delay official recognition of the married status of the woman, and so no attempts were made to transport man and wife together.[23]

In June 1815 Surgeon Arnold of the transport *Northampton* was sent a list of the convict women whose husbands had already been transported. This Report is one of the few pieces of official evidence relating to women who were convicted after the transportation of their husbands. It contained nine names of women aged between twenty and fifty years, who had been married in Scotland, Ireland, London and the major areas of Birmingham, Bristol and Manchester.

All of the transported husbands were tradesmen: buttonmaker, baker, cutler, weaver, dyer and scowerer, gardener, butcher, printer and husbandman. Does this suggest an economic rather than a criminal motivation for their offences? Criminals or victims of circumstances, few of these husbands and wives were reunited in New South Wales, for most husbands had been transported for several years and their whereabouts, or whether they were alive or dead, was unknown to their wives. Jane Ainsley, reported that her husband was 'Unknown, transported four or five years ago, was seven years in the *Captivity Hulk*'. Jane Ainsley, at thirty-six, had been apart from her husband for some twelve years at the time of her own conviction. Was it enforced widowhood as the result of transportation of the husband which had contributed to the criminal activities of the wife? This cannot be determined but it may be assumed that at least some of these nine women, especially with young families to support, may have stolen not from inclination but from desperation. The very small number of convict women who did claim to have a husband already transported contrasts with the greater number of free and unconvicted women who pleaded to be reunited with their transported husbands. It cannot therefore be assumed that the transportation of the husband automatically or invariably led to criminality on the part of the wife left in Britain.[24]

Only three of the *Northampton* women are known to have rejoined their convict husbands in New South Wales – Catherine Smith, Susannah Brazeley and Ann Noble. Catherine Smith was listed in the muster of 1822 as free by servitude, the wife of John Smith, householder of Sydney. Ann Noble, the woman from Armagh, rejoined her husband Robert, a former butcher. They settled in Liverpool, where they were still living in 1828. Susannah Brazeley and her husband Edward had a son, William, born in Sydney on 4 August 1817 and baptised at St Philip's on 8 February 1820.

There was little official concern for reuniting 'free' husbands with transported wives and no evidence of any belief or hope that the immorality and licentiousness of Botany Bay could be lessened by the encouragement of the 'free' husbands rejoining their wives. Very few 'free' husbands were permitted to rejoin their convict wives at government expense. Proportionately, they were a very minor percentage compared with the number of 'free' wives given assisted passages to rejoin their convicted husbands. The husband had to provide testimonials of good character and petition for permission from the British Secretary of State in the same manner as a 'free' wife seeking to join a transported husband. Should permission be granted, the British government would then inform the colonial governor, but such permission was rarely granted, and only to men with skills capable of supporting themselves and their families in New South Wales.

One of the women on the *Northampton*, Susannah Blake, was permitted to take her husband on the same transport, probably because he was 'a hard-working blacksmith' and there was always an unfilled demand for skilled blacksmiths in the penal colony. In 1813 the husband of convict Catherine Harvey was given government permission to 'work his passage out' on the transport *Fortune*. Under-Secretary Goulburn informed Governor Macquarie:

The Wife of this Person is a Convict, and sailed in the *Minstrel*, and he having been bred a Carpenter, and served in the Royal Navy, there is a reasonable Expectation that he will be able to support himself in the Colony without becoming a Burthen upon the Public.[25]

Was it the fear of added expense to the colonial expenditure which made the Home Office so reluctant to encourage husbands to rejoin convict wives in New South Wales? Was it that few of the husbands of convict women had trades which would ensure their capability to support themselves and their wives and children in New South Wales without any assistance from government? Or was it that few husbands applied for passages to follow their wives? Such requests were exceptional among the petitions and letters received by either the Colonial Secretary or the colonial governors. It was also exceptional for a petition to be received from the British husband requesting information as to whether a convict wife was alive or dead in distant New South Wales.[26]

For whatever official or private reason, whether the cause

was government policy or simply the reluctance of free men to venture to that distant penal colony with a convicted wife, almost all of the married women who were transported arrived at Botany Bay as technically single women. Legal or common-law wives or widows, they were as divorced from family ties as were the daughters, the unmarried spinsters, the single women of Britain and Ireland transported to New South Wales. Family women they may have been before their conviction but after arrival at Port Jackson they were women without the protection of husband, father or family and, to all intents and purposes, single women, women without kith or kin and believed unlikely to resume their former family status. This severance of all the personal relationships they had known was as traumatic for many of the women of Botany Bay as was their conviction for major statutory offences. It was an added social effect of the transportation system directly affecting the position of and attitudes towards the transported women in New South Wales.

It was not only the enforced separation from husbands which added to the punishment of family women. The official reluctance to allow transported women to be accompanied by their infants and young children placed further anguish on the women convicts who sailed from England and Ireland leaving behind children they knew they would never see again. The concern of the British government was not with humanitarian policies which would favour women criminals with young children, but to ensure that colonial expenditure was kept to a minimum. Expense took precedence over compassion. In the first few years there was little evidence that most family women would be separated from their children but, as the numbers transported continued to grow, especially from Ireland where large families were the norm, official reluctance to provide passages hardened into a policy with no room for pity for the women or concern for the fate of children left behind.

There were some twenty children of convict women on the First Fleet, some born in Britain, some on the voyage. It was not until the middle years of Macquarie's administration that such numbers were again permitted. Exactly what happened to the children left behind is not known; children of women who stood in the dock with infants in their arms; women who said at their trial 'Distress drove me to it'; women who petitioned for clemency for the sake of their 'fatherless babes'. Was the punishment of all the convict women who sailed for New South Wales without their children greater than that of their childless companions? How did they fit the stereotype of the damned whores of Botany Bay?[27]

Was it characteristic of morally destitute, debased and vile women to try, as so many of the convict women did, to have their children come with them, or follow them, in their banishment? In many cases in England and in Ireland, children described as 'fatherless' who had been with the mother since she was apprehended, sharing the gaol rations and conditions, were left behind when the mother was transported. Early in 1821 the Assistant-Overseer of the parish of Aston near Birmingham, petitioned Lord Sidmouth on behalf of Elizabeth Williams, sentenced to seven years' transportation, 'that the children of the above woman be allowed to accompany their mother to Botany Bay when she is transported. The boys are Edwin and John ... She has lately been removed to Stafford Gaol.' The reply was that, as 'the ship is on the point of sailing' the request could not be granted.[28] Children such as the Williams boys would have no other resource but to accept the charity of the parish workhouse, and even this 'benevolence' was only available to those who were in the parish of their birth.

Convict women in New South Wales continued attempts to obtain passages for the children they had left behind. Mary Jones (*Midas*), transported from Worcester for shoplifting, left a husband and four children in England. The visiting magistrate and the clergyman of St Nicholas' Rectory, Worcester, petitioned that husband and children be allowed to join her in New South Wales:

she has obtained a very comfortable situation in the family of Mr (I think Judge) Stephens and she tells him that as Tailors [her husband's trade] are much wanted there he might – on application to the proper authorities – be allowed to go out with his children to New South Wales.

The husband, Thomas, was thirty-eight, the children aged three, seven, nine and eleven-and-a-half. The reply? 'It is not in in Mr Peel's power to comply with the request'. Did her 'comfortable situation' ease Mary Jones's separation from her family?[29]

Family women and single women were transported from all parts of the British Isles. About 44 per cent were tried and convicted in Ireland and came to New South Wales from both county and town gaols and places of confinement. On the British mainland, women were convicted from the far north of Scotland to the southern parts of Cornwall, from Wales to Devon, from the Islands of Skye and of Man, to the Isle of Wight and the

Scilly Isles, from all of the large industrial centres. Table 1.2 gives an analysis of the trial places (where known) of women and girls transported from England, Scotland and Wales between 1788 and 1826.

Table 1.2   Trial places of 3390 women transported from England, Scotland and Wales, 1788–1826

		%
	England	96.4
	Scotland	1.9
	Wales	1.2
England:	Cornwall	0.3
	English Counties*	52.6
	London/Middlesex	43.8

*The largest proportion of county women came from Lancaster (9.4%).

These percentages suggest that at least half of the women transported from England were familiar with urban life rather than rural, and that almost half came from London and surrounding districts. To assume from these figures that most of the women of Botany Bay were women from urban areas of Britain would be as erroneous as to assume that those women tried in county districts were invariably county women with the skills and backgrounds traditionally associated with country women. These figures are for trial place only and do not represent the native place of the women tried. To assume that trial place equates with native place distorts both the influence and the proportion of women from Scotland, Wales and Ireland among the women transported from England, and gives a false impression of the balance between urban and rural women among the women of Botany Bay.

It was not until 1815 that native place was regularly recorded for women sentenced to transportation. From that date, almost all of the women convicts who came to New South Wales were identified by their native place. An analysis of native place compared with trial place shows clearly that there was far more 'coming and going' among the unemployed, working and family women of the lower orders of British society than has previously been appreciated. It has always been recognised that London was the centre for increasing internal migration of men and women seeking employment or opportunities. It is known that migration across the Irish Sea to England brought numerous Irish men and women to Liverpool, Manchester and London. The comparison of native place with trial place supports these assumptions. Additionally, it shows, first, that Irish women were found in almost every county and major town of England and, second, the extent of internal British migration within the English counties and towns and from Wales, Scotland and Cornwall to English counties. It cannot therefore be deduced from the location of trial place that women were either urban or rural, that their skills or lack of skills were those of country women or town women.

Among the 106 women landed from the *Northampton* in 1815, at least 42 per cent had not been tried in their native place. Not only did this indicate the extent to which women travelled in search of employment, it also indicated the large proportion of women from the lower orders who were without any resource to poor law or parish relief in times of distress or unemployment. The alternatives after loss of employment caused by dismissal, accident, sickness, misfortune, pregnancy or simply termination of seasonal work, were begging, crime or destitution. Destitution away from the parish of one's birth could itself lead to conviction as a rogue and vagabond, or for vagrancy. Elizabeth Asker (*Mary Ann*), discharged from her place as a servant, was guilty of theft committed immediately following her dismissal. She returned to the house of her former employer and stole clothing, which she then pawned. Other women, such as Martha Anderson (*Earl Cornwallis*), who was sentenced at Northumberland Quarter Sessions in 1796 as 'an idle and disorderly person', after apprehension by the constable of Alnwick and conveyed to Morphet Gaol, for which he received ten shillings. Martha Anderson, guilty of larceny, had no witnesses on her behalf and the people who gave evidence against her – the innkeeper of Morphet, the baker and his wife of the same parish, two constables, and a wagoner from Berwick-on-Tweed – received a total of £4 13s 0d for their expenses.

The pattern of 'comers and goers' among the *Northampton* women was typical for the women on the transports which followed. The *Mary Anne* arrived at Sydney Cove on 19 January 1816 and landed 101 convict women. At least 31 per cent had not been tried in their native place, and others had been tried in different parts of their own counties. Occupation did not appear to influence whether a women travelled to a different part of Britain, although the majority of women transported from England were domestic servants. Mary Mazagora, a seamstress from Liverpool, was tried in Warwick; another seamstress, Isabella Hewett from London, was tried in Surrey; Mary Supple, Irish washerwoman from Cork, was tried in Kent. A servant from Derry was tried in Northumberland, another from Staffordshire was tried in Chester, and servants from Cork, Down, Dublin, Hull, Limerick, Sligo, Staffordshire, Southampton and Wicklow were all tried at Middlesex, as was a needlewoman from Sussex, a shoebinder from Dorset, a straw-hatmaker from Hertfordshire and a dressmaker from Wiltshire. Another dressmaker from Armagh was tried in Nottingham, and a confectioner from the same Irish county also tried in Nottingham. Women with a skill or trade, women who were, or hoped to be, domestic servants, were among the married women, the widows, the single women, who made up the 'comers and goers' who travelled the highways, roads and lanes of Britain, alone or with husband and children, searching for work. That they formed so high a proportion of the women transported from England to Botany Bay indicates the lack of success so many had in their search for a livelihood far from their native place.

There was little change from this pattern until the mid- to late-1820s when an increasing number of women from Northern Ireland, especially from Belfast, were convicted in the courts of Scotland and transported on ships sailing from English ports. In addition an increasing number of women from Scotland were sentenced to transportation in the courts of England, in particular in London or Middlesex, while women from Wales were tried in county courts throughout England.

The *Grenada* arrived at Sydney Cove in 1827 with 88 convict women who had been tried in England. Of these, 13.6 per cent were Irish-born, seven of whom were convicted in London, three in Liverpool, one in Manchester and one in Hull. Two Edinburgh-born women were tried in London (both servants) and another, a straw-bonnet-maker, in Nottingham. There were women from Warwick sentenced in Staffordshire and Birmingham, servants from Canterbury, Denbeighshire and Essex sentenced in Manchester, housemaids from Kent and Devon sentenced at Exeter, servants from Nottingham tried in Suffolk and Leicester, from Gloucestershire tried in Wiltshire. Londoners were tried in Kent (for stealing a watch) and in Nottingham (for picking pockets).

Three convict women on the *Grenada* indicated the growing numbers of women from places outside the British mainland who were becoming a part of the English criminal population. Hannah Pritchard 'of no education' was a washerwoman from

Bengal sentenced to transportation for stealing money in Manchester. Mary Ann Thompson, who could read and had two children, was a house servant, 'a native of America', when she, too, was convicted of stealing-money in Manchester. Mary Ann Webber was a twenty-nine-year housemaid from Guernsey – 'she reads and has three children' – when she was found guilty of stealing in Exeter.

At the end of 1827 this pattern of conviction away from native place was becoming more accentuated and numbers of women transported from towns and counties distant from their birthplaces continued to increase in the 1830s with the increasing numbers of women convicts sent to New South Wales and Van Diemen's Land. The *Louisa*, which arrived in the same year as the *Grenada*, was one of the first transports to include any significant numbers of women tried in the courts of Scotland and to include women from Belfast tried in both Scotland and England. Among the ninety women who landed at Sydney Cove, nineteen (21.1 per cent) had been sentenced in Scotland. They came from Glasgow, Edinburgh, Perth, Aberdeen, Argyllshire, Paisley, Shetland, Dumfries, County Down, Belfast and the East Indies. Ann Durrant, the native of the East Indies, was tried in Aberdeen where she had come with her seaman-husband. She was thirty-six when convicted of receiving stolen goods and allowed to take her youngest child to New South Wales, while her two elder children remained with her husband in Scotland. She had her own initials, those of her husband and one of her children, tattooed on her left arm. She went to the Female Factory on arrival to await assignment and was employed at the Factory at the time of the 1828 Census. There is no record of her child surviving in New South Wales, or of the fate of the husband and the children left in Aberdeen.

That many of the women who were transported to Botany Bay were women who had already travelled far from their birthplaces eased the transition from local society in Britain to the society of Botany Bay where women from all parts of Britain were thrown together in the confined settlement of the penal colony. Mary Thomas (*Mary Anne*), for example, transported in 1816, had come from Wales to York City in search of employment as a servant. Mary Thomas, and the many women like her from all the parts of Great Britain and Ireland, were clearly distinguishable by their speech as 'strangers' in the place where they were tried and convicted.[30] For the women from Ireland, there was the added 'strangeness' of a 'foreign' religion and the overtones of rebellion, violence and lawlessness. When all of the 'travelled' women found themselves sharing their daily life on the transports and at Botany Bay with women of different dialects and backgrounds, problems of speech and different customs were not so great as for those girls and women who had not left their native place until on their way from prison to transport ship. For these women, the strangeness of speech itself could add to the despair of their 'unhappy situation'.

The extent to which women left the places of their birth and travelled throughout Britain in search of employment in the latter half of the eighteenth century was not typical of the traditions of their class. Mendicants, tinkers, gypsies, vagrants and some seasonal workers had wandered throughout Britain since time immemorial but the honest working-girl or woman would not have expected to travel far from the place of her birth. The decreasing opportunities for employment and the increasing demands of the industrial districts in Britain encouraged this internal migration, as did the poverty and lack of employment in Ireland. Many of the travelling women saw London as their goal and many of these hopeful seekers after security found instead that their journey from home led not to constant employment but to the prison of Newgate, and from there to the transports which would take them to Botany Bay.

The convict women were mature by contemporary standards when they arrived in New South Wales. Statistical data for the death rate in England and Wales is almost non-existent for the eighteenth century, and there are numerous variables in determining the age and place of death. Constant migration, for example, of women from their native places affected the relationship between rural and urban death, for there were no statistics to show the duration of the life of the woman after she had left a rural district to settle in an urban centre. The low life-expectancy of women was further affected by the high incidence of deaths in children five years and under, especially in urban districts. Infant mortality was excessively high during the childhood years of the transported women, and over half of the infants born in London between 1739 and 1789 died before they reached five years of age. In cities such as Manchester and Liverpool the mortality rate of young children was even higher. In 1835 the *Lancet* published a table (see Table 1.3) estimating the incidence of death for the hundred-year span 1730–1830.

Table 1.3 Incidence of death, children below the age of five years, London, 1730-1830

	%
1730-49	74.5
1750-69	63.0
1770-89	51.5
1790-1809	41.3
1810-29	31.8

Allowance must be made for underestimation in these percentages. Not only were contemporary statistics frequently unreliable and often contradictory, but they were often 'grossly underestimated' as a result of the many defects in the system of registering the deaths of infants and young children.[31]

The decrease from 74.5 to 31.8 per cent was affected by the advances in medical hygiene, improvement in midwifery and by the increasing availability of medical help and advice for the poor during this period. Not only were there improvements in the lying-in hospitals, and assistance more generally available – but still limited – to women and single girls, but general dispensaries were established so that the poor could seek both treatment and advice. The first of these dispensaries was established in London in 1798. The number of 'poor persons' seeking advice or treatment is a clear indication of the deplorable state of health of many Londoners. In 1802 according to a contemporary involved in the Dispensary Movement, 'Dispensaries in the metropolis extended a system of medical relief ... to the poor unknown to any other part of the globe. About 50,000 poor persons are thus annually supplied with medicine and advice gratis.' How many of the 'poor women' of London sought help at the Dispensaries is not known, but the number treated annually indicates the need of the poor for treatment for the many diseases and sicknesses prevalent in the city. It also confirms the deplorable state of health of so many of the women when they boarded the transport ships.[32]

Exact age for the transported women was difficult to determine, some of the women themselves being unsure as to the exact year of their birth, others adding a year or two while in prison in the hope of gaining a stay of transportation as 'aged convicts', while others reduced their trial age by several years before arrival in New South Wales, apparently in the belief that this would enhance their future prospects.

The ages of individual women varied from eight years to

eighty, but the average age at the time of trial was in the mid-twenties, those sentenced in Ireland being slightly older than those from England.[33] The great variation on this average age was significant for the roles of the transported women in the convict colony. Young girls, for example, knew that they faced the rest of their lives in New South Wales, with little opportunity of returning to Britain after their sentences were served – girls as young as Sarah Sullivan, who was barely eleven years old when sentenced to transportation at the Middlesex Sessions of 1805 for stealing six yards of cotton from a draper's shop with the help of two accomplices aged fourteen and fifteen. Sarah Sullivan was transported on the *Alexander*, arriving at Botany Bay at the age of twelve years. Many of the girls from London were under sixteen when convicted. Rebecca Reeson was fifteen when sentenced for stealing ten handkerchiefs from a draper in London. She was transported on the *Alexander*. Mary Ruby shoplifted six yards of ribbon worth three shillings and sixpence, and was transported at the age of fifteen on the *Broxbornebury* in 1814. Other young shoplifters included Juliet Shaw, sixteen when she sailed on the *Sydney Cove*, and Ann Rochfort, also sixteen, transported on the *Britannia*. Some of these very young girls had been sentenced to death, as had Mary Gray or Carney to whom 'Mercy was extended because of her youth'. She came to Botany Bay on the *Northampton* in 1815 instead of hanging from the gallows of Newgate. At the other end of the scale were women as old as Dorothy Handland, convicted of perjury on behalf of her 'friend' William Till in 1787. Handland, alias Gray, was eighty-two when tried, and eighty-three on arrival at Botany Bay.[34]

Among the transported women were older family women, young mothers of infant children, women widowed and without means of earning their livelihood, and the incorrigible rogues and vagabonds, the girls and women to whom thieving and crime were the only way of life that they knew, girls who would say indignantly at their trial 'He wanted me to go with him for threepence ... I would not go with any gentleman for threepence'. That argument over her price led to yet another felon being transported to Botany Bay. The threepenny girls, the pickpockets, the shoplifters, the highwaywomen, the burglars, all the thieves and women criminals of Britain and Ireland unlucky enough to be apprehended, tried, convicted and sentenced to transportation and finally shipped to their place of banishment, these were the women of Botany Bay.

These women had survived the child-killing diseases, had

lived despite the sordid filth of their homes and the gaols in which they had been confined in Britain. They had experienced poverty, destitution and the deprivations consequent on unemployment or irregular work. They had subsisted on an inadequate and uncertain diet, and many had known the necessity of begging to keep themselves and their children alive. To them, sickness, disease, death and near-starvation were the commonplace and the expected. This was the British background of so many of the convict women sentenced to transportation, and these were the familiarities of life and the memories they brought with them to Botany Bay.

2
'THE INCREASING DEPRAVITY OF THE AGE'

Female criminality and transportation

The vast increase of petty robberies is a proof too flagrant not to be lamented of the increasing depravity of the age. All crimes begin by slow degrees, and creep upwards till they brave even justice in the face...

—*Public Advertiser*, 17 November 1788

That criminal women as well as men were sentenced to transportation to Botany Bay was not unusual or extraordinary, causing neither adverse nor favourable comment among contemporaries. England had banished her troublesome women for centuries, from headstrong queens and ladies of the royal blood to the not-so-virgin 'virgin maids' of Henry VIII. Many a Moll Flanders had found her fortune in the colonies of North America, and many more were to sail as white bond slaves throughout the eighteenth century. Banishment was a traditional and legal method of ridding the kingdom of the malcontents, the dissenters, the troublemakers, the worthless vagabonds, the incorrigible rogues, the idle and the dissolute. As a statutory punishment for major felonies, transportation was an integral part of the English criminal code. Transportation of male and female felons in the eighteenth century had benefited the North American colonies by providing a steady source of cheap white labour and, on the other hand, had economically benefited the Mother Country by reducing the expenses of enlarging or maintaining gaols in England.[1]

To sentence women, as well as men, to transportation to 'Botany Bay on the East Coast of New South Wales' was in complete agreement with contemporary theories and practices towards the punishment of criminal women. To the women who were sentenced to transportation this banishment did not appear an extraordinary or unexpected punishment. It simply took its place beside the gallows, the whips, the pillories, the instruments for burning, branding or mutilating, and the most feared punishment of all, the faggots of the execution fires. In most cases transportation was thought of as the humane alternative to death.

That New South Wales was established as a convict colony, inhabited principally by convicted felons who 'must work or starve', was central to the opportunities which developed in the colony for those outcast prisoners. The colony was founded in a manner unique in the history of English colonisation, but the official reasoning of His Majesty King George III was simple for contemporaries to accept. There were the usual criticisms of any government decision: 'any old woman in the three kingdoms could devise a better plan' grumbled one newspaper correspondent, while another queried the expense of providing felons with such luxuries as nightcaps to warm their shaved and deloused heads. A third questioned the virtues of sending such atrocious offenders to a life of ease in the earthly paradise of Botany Bay.[2] To most thinking contemporaries, however, there was nothing unusual in this method of ridding Great Britain of the felons crammed into every gaol and place of confinement. A colony of thieves had not been the first solution offered to the increasing and embarrassing domestic problem of too many prisoners with no place to be confined in Britain and no place willing to receive them outside the British Isles. While waiting to subdue the rebellious Americans, England had simply moored rotting hulks on the Thames as holding gaols for men sentenced to transportation. The conditions on these hulks caused more prisoner deaths than all of Britain's common hangmen. More prisoners suffered from infirmities, chronic diseases and disabilities, infections and debilities than in any Regiment of the Line in the midst of the most adverse battle conditions.[3]

The 'temporary' hulks were to remain, a source of constant embarrassment to the government, an ever-present danger to the neighbouring populace. Not only had England failed to subdue those rebellious colonists, she had been unable to persuade the victorious Americans, triumphant in the full flush of victory and misted with the dreams of a brave new world severed from mother's apron strings, that they should continue to accept the white slave labour of the criminals of the Old World into their promised Utopia. Within this context, the reasoning of King George was self-evident:

The several gaols and places of confinement of felons in this Kingdom being in so crowded a state that the greatest danger is to be apprehended, not only from their escape, but from the infectious distempers, which may hourly be expected to break out.[4]

That the gaols were overcrowded, inadequate, crumbling, unhygienic, and disease-ridden were not reasons for contemporaries to consider building new and bigger gaols. Systematic confinement of felons within Britain for any lengthy period was not part of the contemporary theory or practice of penology. The only inquiry into the feasibility of building penitentiaries at home as an alternative to transportation was in Ireland in the early 1790s. The Lord Lieutenant of Ireland had requested individual reports and opinions from County Grand Juries. Opinions varied, but there was an unmistakable consensus of opinion from all counties that transportation was far preferable to the building and maintaining of prisons in the home country. It was all a matter of expense. The Grand Jury of Donegal summed up the general opinion: 'They appear to think some scheme of the kind might be necessary, but said that the idea was quite a new one, new to them and that they were at a loss what opinion to form about it and seemed much afraid of the expense.'[5]

The suggestions were not implemented, and men, women and children were transported from Ireland in increasing numbers from 1791, hopefully saving their counties the expense of their punishment.

That British and Irish gaols were crammed with felons awaiting transportation was incontestable evidence to contemporaries of the spiralling crime rate and the depravity of the lower orders. There was little speculation or investigation into the actual causes of crime, apart from a smug agreement that poverty was the principal cause. What caused poverty was less significant and normally attributed to the 'feckless and indolent nature' of the lower orders and their reluctance to labour or to work at an honest trade. This was little consolation to the numerous victims of thefts, robberies, street assaults, or to the shopkeepers and tradesmen, to the masters of light-fingered domestic servants, to the publicans whose pewter pots had an almost fatal attraction for those who would melt them down to counterfeit the coin of the realm, to the lodging-house keepers who would lose bed, bedding, and the entire contents of rented rooms.

Reports of crimes published in the newspapers gave substance to the assumption that the criminals were without any of the attributes of 'respectable' men and women, that they would have neither pity nor compassion for little children, for the aged, the lame, the poor. Typical were reports published regularly in the London *Public Advertiser* at the end of the eighteenth century. A man, who had come to London to take up a position as 'Assistant in a Pastry cook's Shop',

> was robbed in the Bishop's Walk, Lambeth, of a new Hat, a new Coat and Waistcoat, a Silver Watch, two Guineas and some Silver, a Pair of plated Shoe-Buckles, and even his very Shoes, by two Footpads. He begged hard for his Shoes, but to no Purpose.

In March the same year the callousness and indifference of criminals was shown clearly when 'a labouring Man was stopped in the Middle of Upper Moorfields by two Footpads, who took from him Twopence Halfpenny, which was all that he had, and damn'd him for having no more Money.'[6]

Reports of the crimes of women and girls showed the same alarming lack of compassion. Sixteen-year-old Sarah Saunders (*Glatton*) 'stole the apparel from a child's person' and had two previous convictions for the same offence, involving assault of the children. Sarah Slater (*Alexander*) assaulted nine-year-old Elizabeth Cummings and 'stole her goods and clothes'. Mary Marshall 'knocked a man down and robbed him violently of a pound note'. Ann Daly 'seized Mrs Ormsby [a neighbour] by the throat and put her hand in her pocket and took out her money ... and Rose Molloy saw her being seized by the throat and with force held against the door ...'[7] It was not surprising that a correspondent in the *Public Advertiser* lamented that 'The vast increase in petty robberies is a proof too flagrant not to be lamented of the increasing depravity of the age. All crimes begin by slow degrees and creep upwards until they brave even the face of justice.'[8]

With men and women so audacious in their own country, with criminals so violent and so vicious, could it not be expected that they would 'brave the face of justice' when confined together on the shores of Botany Bay? Contemporaries certainly thought so, and branded the convicts sent to New South Wales as the most infamous and depraved of Britain's criminal class.

The traditional and accepted remedy for crime was increasing severity of punishment. To ensure fear of punishment, would-be criminals must be deterred by dread of physical suffering so great that 'the malefactor would draw back his hand in horror at the aweful [sic] consequences of his act'.[9] This dread was the fear of pain, physical pain, legally inflicted to punish the body of the criminal. This had been the basis of legal punishment from time immemorial, for punishment of the body was the traditional and accepted form of deterrence. Such punishments had included mutilation until well into the eighteenth century, with the slitting of nostrils, slicing of ears, and branding on the hand or face. The body of the criminal was itself a symbol of the retribution which a wronged society would exact from offenders, and was left to rot in chains throughout the English countryside or given to the surgeons for public dissection.[10]

It could not be expected that contemporary legislators, penal theorists, humanitarians, even well-intentioned commentators, would consider deeply alternative forms of punishment or ponder on the underlying causes of crime in Britain in the late eighteenth to early nineteenth centuries. That would have been outside the contemporary framework of ideas and practice. One of the very few to inquire into and report on causes of increasing crime in the late eighteenth century was a London magistrate, Patrick Colquhoun. Colquhoun saw the problem primarily as an administrative one: too many offenders escaped detection, committal, prosecution and conviction because of bureaucratic inefficiency. His remedy lay in suggesting the organisation of a proper system of police in the metropolis, establishing the office of Prosecutor for the Crown, and revising the 'known abuses in the system of granting pardons'. Furthermore, he saw features of the criminal code as contributing significantly to the steady increase in crime, features such as the imperfections in the penal code itself, which imposed sentences of unnecessary severity on a multiplicity of crimes of varying degrees. A man or woman, he might have argued, could be hanged for stealing a handkerchief, a hat, an umbrella, a shawl. Where was the deterrent to the theft with violence, assault, even murder, in the course of a robbery, if the punishment were the same for all offences?[11]

There was little distinction between criminal men and criminal women in Britain either in the crimes they committed, the degree of viciousness and callousness they showed their victims, or in their punishments. Apart from prison reformer Elizabeth Fry, few commentators saw women-prisoners in any special category based on their sex. Women were equally subject to imprisonment and to the punishment of physical pain as were the men, facing branding, whipping, hanging, and burning at the stake. As with male criminals, the official and traditional attitude prevailed, that fear and terror of physical suffering would be the solution to increasing female criminality.

In 1821 the Third Report of the Committee of the Society for the Improvement of Prison Discipline (London) made specific reference to the punishment of women. The Society recommended strongly that prisons must become an object of terror, or their function as deterrents to crime would cease. This terror was to include continuous toil, but not of a productive kind as had been proudly introduced by the Preston House of Correction where 'an idle hand is rarely found. There are one hundred and fifty looms in full employ from each of which the average weekly earnings are five shillings'. The Society advocated:

We would banish all the looms of Preston jail, and substitute nothing but the tread-wheel, or the capstan, or some species of labour where the labourer could not see the results of his toil, – where it was monotonous, irksome, and dull as possible ... pulling and pushing, instead of reading and writing, – no share in the profits – not a single shilling.

For the female felons there were to be special restrictions, their femininity itself was to be suppressed and they were to be forbidden any normal 'womanly' activities:

There would be no tea and sugar – no assemblage of female felons round the washing-tub, nothing but beating hemp, and pulling oakum, and pounding bricks – no work but what was tedious, unusual, and unfeminine.[12]

The object of imprisonment was neither the reformation nor the education of the felon nor the training in any skill, nor labour which might ensure an opportunity to secure an honest livelihood after sentence was served. It was simply to deter further criminal offences by the dread of returning to the harshness, discipline and deprivations of prison life. The Society for the Improvement of Prison Discipline had none of the pious compassion of the 'amiable and excellent Mrs Fry', and argued most forcibly that 'her's is not the method to stop crime'. The overriding aim was 'to keep the multitude in order, and to be a terror to evildoers ... by the planned and regulated and unrelenting exclusion of happiness and comfort'.[13]

How did this strict regime of ceaseless and unproductive toil, this deprivation for the women prisoners of any vestige of womanly comforts or activities, this constant emphasis on discipline of the body and subjection of the spirit, compare with the punishment of transportation to Botany Bay? Theoretically, transportation was the most severe punishment short of death. It implied constant and irksome toil for many long years, with no hope of return to family, home or friends, a life without hope, dragged out in misery and suffering on a distant shore.[14] In practice, however, transportation could replace hopelessness and despair with opportunity and incentive, 'irksome toil' with labour for self-advancement and, far from denying women any womanly role within society, place the female felon squarely within the accepted role of 'virtuous' women, that of wife or mother. No comparison between conditions in the women's prisons of Great Britain and the conditions for the female convicts in New South Wales could favour the systematic confinement of women in their own country as either preferable or more advantageous to the women themselves.

Punishment of the body remained the touchstone of penal legislation well into the nineteenth century. That punishment should be commensurate with the specific crime was a secondary consideration. Until 1826 all felonies were punishable by death. The increasing number of misdemeanours which were declared capital felonies during the reign of the first three Georges led to more and more sentences of transportation for men and women who, prior to the promulgation of the specific statute declaring their offence capital, would have been punished by whipping, branding, standing in pillory, or confinement in a house of correction. It was this multiplicity of capital offences which filled Britain's gaols with convicts awaiting death or transportation to New South Wales. The enormous increase in the number of these offences is shown vividly in a House of Commons Debate in which F. Bruxton told his fellow parliamentarians that 'in the past 150 years, from the accession of Charles 2nd to the present time, 187 offences have been declared capital'. Of these, 36 were introduced during the reign of the Stuarts, 156 under the reigning House of Brunswick: 'More crimes have been denounced capital in the reign of His Present Majesty, than in the reigns of the Plantagenets, the Tudors and the Stuarts combined.'[15]

That all the convict women were guilty of major felonies directly influenced contemporary assumptions as to their characteristics. There could be no expectations that individual felons were identified by their individual crime, thus lessening or increasing, the degree of guilt. No other attitude could be expected. Catherine Rourke was transported on the *Sugar Cane* for 'stealing a butter-boat'; Mary Rooney (*Sugar Cane*) stole a hat; another Mary Rooney, some twenty years later, was transported on the *Archduke Charles* for 'stealing two quarts of whiskey'; Margaret Quinn (*Rolla*) was guilty of highway robbery and assault; Bridget Geoghegan (*John Bull*) and Elizabeth Graham

(*Elizabeth*) were murderesses, while Jane Burne (*John Bull*) had attempted to poison her husband. All were equally 'felons of the darkest complexion', all sentenced to transportation for seven years.[16]

It was not until the early 1820s that parliamentarians gave serious consideration to the problems arising from the continuing expansion of the number of offences decreed capital. Their attitudes, comments and opinions reflected contemporary assumptions regarding crime, punishment and criminals. In 1819 Sir James Mackintosh introduced a motion into the House of Commons to appoint a Select Committee 'to consider of so much of the Criminal Laws as relates to Capital Punishment in Felonies'. Mackintosh spoke at length on the extent of capital punishment, dividing crimes which carried the death penalty into three categories: 'murder and associated acts; arson, highway robberies and piracies and similar; frauds of various kinds ... [including] others of the most frivolous and fantastic nature ... about 150 in number'.

It was only the last group, Mackintosh argued, who should be excluded from the punishment of death. His opinions reflected clearly the unchanging attitude of his class towards any offences, major or minor, which affected private property: 'whatever attacks the life or dwelling of a man ought to be punished by death'.[17] When it is considered that New South Wales was populated by such criminals, almost all having 'attacked the property' of others, the distrust and disgust shown by British officials towards the population of that colony may be more easily understood. But there was still no qualification of guilt by consideration of 'degrees of criminality', either among first or frequent offenders, among the young or the old, among the professional thieves and cutpurses and the petty thief.

In London seventeen-year-old Frances Cranmer (*Indispensable*) heard the judge pronounce her sentence of death for 'burglariously breaking and entering the dwelling house of David Levy'. That she had stolen almost every movable article in the house could not make her punishment any greater than that of Ann Wicks (*Mary Ann*), who had 'burglariously and feloniously broken into and entered the dwelling house of John Jordan' and had taken away his goods worth three shillings and eightpence. Both girls were to be hanged. Both sentences were commuted to transportation at the end of the Sessions, and both came to Botany Bay believed to be equally 'steeped in the infamy' of their convictions for major felonies.

In 1826 Robert Peel attempted to consolidate the criminal

code by amalgamating the numerous individual statutes which had created individual capital offences, such as the single statute which made 'receiving stolen pewter' a hanging offence and which must have been greatly welcomed by the publicans and innkeepers of England. It was not Peel's intention to lessen the punishment for any individual crime but to improve the effectiveness of the administration of the criminal code. Peel's continued emphasis on the enormity of the crime of theft, despite the nature of the item stolen, is in itself evidence of the reasoning behind contemporary assumptions as to the depravity, the criminality and the viciousness of the convicts transported to Botany Bay. Peel told the House of Commons:

I select the laws relating to theft in the first instance because I consider the crime of theft to constitute the most important class of crime. There are acts no doubt of greater malignity, of a much more atrocious character than the simple act of robbery; but looking to the committals and convictions for crime, it will at once be seen, that those for theft so far exceed the committals and convictions for any other species of offence, that there can be no question of its paramount importance in the catalogue of offences against society.

In 1826 there were no less than ninety-two statutes relating to the punishment of theft.[18] As L. L. Robson has shown, almost all the convicts, men and women transported to Botany Bay were guilty of some form of larceny. This is clearly supported by an analysis of the individual crimes of both the Irish and the English women.[19] It was not until 1832 that any serious moves were made in the House of Commons to abolish capital punishment for certain offences, and this was stridently opposed by Peel. Leave was sought to introduce a Bill to abolish the death penalty for 'horse-stealing, sheep-stealing, cattle-stealing, also in cases of stealing from a dwelling house, no person being put in fear therein . . . ' In his opposition, Peel stressed that 'the greatest caution was necessary at every step, in order not to excite the prejudices of society against the alteration [i.e. removal of the death penalty], by too rapidly weakening the present protection of property.'[20]

It was not the increasing number of committals and convictions which plagued the legislators so much as the apparent lack of any effective deterrence in the punishments of death or transportation. Jeremy Bentham, who, more than any of his contemporaries, had the ability to see into the problem of Britain's spiralling crime rate, argued to no effect that the fear of death was no deterrent to 'a degraded and wretched class of men, who do not set the same value upon life [as those who make the laws]'. To the 'highest classes . . . death is considered a great evil, and an ignominious death as the greatest of evils'. To those most likely to commit crimes, however, 'the habitual infamy of [their] lives renders them inaccessible to the infamy of punishment'. To these men and, presumably, women, 'indigence and hard labour is more formidable than death'.[21]

British attitudes towards Botany Bay were strongly influenced by this certainty of the 'respectable classes' that there was a direct link between crime and the indolence of the criminal class which made them adverse to any form of honest labour. This belief was reinforced by the acceptance that the 'criminal class' were, almost without exception, the lower orders of British society and that 'convict' equated with poverty, unemployment and lack of skills or enterprise. If punishment were to be effective, either in Britain's gaols or in far distant New South Wales, it must be inextricably linked with labour, for the antidote to crime was the fear of confinement with unremitting, ceaseless toil. In the convict colony the yardstick for respectability, for evidence of reformation of manners, was tangible proof of industrious labour which had led to material improvement in the life of the ex-convict. Testimonials to support an 'honest, sober and industrious' character were the prerequisites for the granting of indulgences, these characteristics being accepted as undeniable proof of moral reformation. The Protestant work ethic, which was the antithesis of all the presumed characteristics of the British criminal class, became the standard by which colonial achievement was established.

It was this apparent dichotomy between the feckless nature of the convicts in Britain, transported because they thieved and stole rather than worked, and the respectability they gained in the penal colony as a direct result of their own labour and economic achievements, which was at the base of the development of an Australian society. This economic-based respectability was not limited to male convicts. For the women prisoners, too, their own labour in the colony could and did provide the path to respectability within their colonial society.

From the viewpoint of the criminal women, transportation had been dreaded almost as much as death itself. In one or two cases women had actually refused mitigation, preferring the known certainty of the hangman's noose to the dread of the unknown prison of Botany Bay. The punishment of banishment, even with penal servitude, was a departure from the tradition of 'pain for the body' of the offender, as it encompassed wide emotional and spiritual distress and desolation. In practice, transportation lacked that essential ingredient of punishment – the infliction of pain and physical suffering. It provided instead clothing, food, care, and even a modicum of liberty, on the long voyage to Botany Bay and, once in the colony, it provided a prison where the bars were of the criminals' own making, for the deprivation of liberty, the confinement or physical punishment followed conviction for colonial offences.

Among the transported women were those who were no stranger to the pain the law could and did inflict. Sophia Brannigan had been 'burned in the hand for theft' as had Ann Reed. Mary Bowman had been whipped for a previous offence.[22] Most of the transported women had shared their prisons with other women whom they had seen ride on the cart from gaol to the gallows for their public executions. Many had heard the judge read the sentence of death and had waited until the end of the Sessions to learn if they, too, were to die on the gallows or be granted the indulgence of transportation; women such as Penelope Mackenzie in Aberdeen who listened to the judge decree that she

be carried from the Bar back to the Tolbooth of Aberdeen therein to be detained till Friday the eighth day of June next and upon that day betwixt the hours of two and four in the afternoon to be taken from the said Tolbooth to the common place of Execution of the said Burgh and then and there to be hanged by the Neck upon a Gibbett until she is dead by the Hands of a Common Executioner.

Until the time of her execution she was to receive only the barest subsistence rations of bread and water.[23]

Fear of death on the public gallows was graphically described by Margaret Dunn, awaiting execution in Dublin's Newgate gaol in 1812:

I have endeavoured to reconcile my mind and submit to it with fortitude and resignation... One thousand times since that awful day I have thoughts on addressing Your Lordship, not for the purpose of saving my life, but for a mitigation of the manner of my death... [will say] with my last breath of my innocence of the crime... I now supplicate Your Lordship – allot to me any other death but that of being hanged, for I do not dread death in any other way... ware my head to be severed from may body, ware my brains to be blown out, ware I to be burned at a stake, I should meet my fate and be resigned but O my Lord, the idea of being hanged fills my soul with horror, distracts and interrupts me in the time of my prayer, my nature and the delicacy of my sex forbids it.

Was it the eloquence of Margaret Dunn that gained her respite from death?[24] The horror and dread of death on the public gallows was more poignantly, if less eloquently, expressed by two young girls in Marlbro' Gaol who wrote to the Lord Lieutenant of Ireland 'In Great Haste' that they were to be hanged on the next Thursday morning. Their fear of death might have been in contradiction to Bentham's argument that death was no deterrent to the men and women of their class, but the desperation of their plea is unmistakable: '[we beg] Your Excellency to get us poor innocent females at least a respite as Judge Dawnes promised us ... if it does not leave Dublin on receipt of this we will be strangled early next Thursday morning'. Their plea was unanswered and these two young girls were hanged outside their local gaol on that Thursday morning, the ritual required by the law witnessed by all those confined within the prison and most of the inhabitants of their native town.[25]

All of these experiences were accepted as commonplace for the men and women awaiting trial or punishment. Girls and women awaiting transportation or death shared their misfortunes with other women uncertain if they were to live or die. They had intimate knowledge of the many individual tragedies and misfortunes of their fellow prisoners, they knew the variety of circumstances which had led to punishment, and they knew how slight was the possibility of obtaining any mitigation of that punishment on the grounds of pity, compassion, or understanding. They, and women of their class, were beyond pity to their respectable contemporaries for their felonies had placed them outside respectable society, suitable only for the gallows or the convict ships.

The women in the gaol of Castlebar knew of the miserable state of Bridget Hennegan and of the rejection of the petition that was sent to the Lord Lieutenant of Ireland on her behalf. This plea was typical of the numerous petitions from or about Irish family women awaiting death or banishment. Bridget Hennegan, suffering 'from the general calamity of these perilous times – and having Six helpless Starving Children, without any Guide or Support', begged that the remainder of her sentence be remitted for 'if she is kept in prison ... her destitute family will die of want'. She had been guilty of a petty larceny and sentenced to six months' confinement in Castlebar Gaol. She claimed that she had been accused and convicted because the pernicious system of Ribbonism was beginning to spread thro the Town and Country about Ballina – Memorialists said husband [he had served sixteen years in the North Mayo Militia] had Informations lodged against her Prosecutors for a charge of Ribbonism who – to avoid the ends of Justice – brought the charge against her ...[26]

There were girls and women who had been tried and convicted with other family members and had seen young sons or daughters, brothers or sisters, husbands, fathers or mothers, 'cast for death' or ordered to be whipped or branded for their part in a joint crime. Elizabeth Smith, transported for fourteen years on the *Speke* 'had a child in her arms' when she was sentenced. Her companion, ten-year-old Mary Crawley, was sentenced to death. Elizabeth Waring, sentenced to fourteen years' transportation for robbery, heard her sixteen-year-old son sentenced to death as her accomplice. Ann Bedford, a married woman, was indicted with twelve-year-old James Kitchener for receiving stolen goods. She was sentenced to transportation for fourteen years, the boy sentenced to be publicly whipped.[27]

First-hand knowledge of these personal tragedies reinforced the hopelessness of appealing for pity to a blind official justice. This was not, however, evidence of an exceptionally callous and merciless society in which the legislators, the administrators, the men of property and privilege, were intent solely on retribution and deterrence by the infliction of physical sufferings on the individual who transgressed their laws, abused their rights. As the crime was the evidence of the depravity of the age, so the punishment of the offender was the public expression of justice. The common people themselves showed no hesitation or reluctance to take part in the rituals of public executions, burnings, brandings or mutilations. There was little visible sign of compassion in the way they and their children fought to obtain better seats to view the hangings, to watch the knives of the surgeons publicly dissect the bodies of executed criminals, and they joined wholeheartedly in the 'sport' of baiting the unfortunates confined in pillory or stocks.

Compassion, if compassion there were, was evidenced through the actions of individuals rather than from the behaviour of crowds. A prison inspector, a prison surgeon, a few turnkeys, a local clergyman or magistrate, would on occasion try to intervene on behalf of a specific prisoner by petitioning for mitigation of sentence or release. Catherine Kit was seen as 'a fit object for mercy' by her gaolers, who wrote to the Lord Lieutenant of Ireland on her behalf:

A Poor Unfortunate Woman the Mother of Three Children who had during her Imprisonment Suffered Uncommon distress haveing been Delivered of A Child Since her transmittal to this preason [sic] from which and other Causes she is reduced to a most Deplorable Condition.

For Catherine Kit, convicted felon, there was neither pity nor pardon. She sailed alone to Botany Bay on the *Minerva*.[28]

It was not only the petitioners who were so acutely aware of the lack of compassion in the execution of the laws of England. Those who shared the confinement in the gaols, friends, neighbours, the 'respectable' gentlemen who provided testimonials in support of mitigation of sentence, all knew the circumstances of the petitioner and the result of the petition. On every transport ship there were women who had unsuccessfully tried to obtain pardons so that they could remain with husbands and children. Was it that, as convicts, they were 'undeserving' of any indulgences? Or was it that expense, or fear of expense, continued to influence all discussions, arguments and plans for the transportation of convicts to Botany Bay?

Could compassion be expected? Why should leniency and mercy be granted to a convicted criminal when there was little concern over the plight of the 'deserving poor', the sufferings of the orphans, the deprivations and miseries which came with old age, or sickness, disease, lack of employment, or followed the many misadventures and mishaps which brought calamity to men and women without economic or social reserves for times of distress.

There was little official or public concern for the conditions in the places of confinement of Britain and Ireland. The women waiting to be transported lived in unbelievable filth, squalor and deprivation. Few had the benefits of the 'enlightened charity' of Elizabeth Fry and her ladies, and had no experience at all of a prison as a place other than where malnutrition and even death followed the inadequate diet, where disease and filth were encouraged by the lack of any facilities for washing of person or clothes, where primitive open sewers served men, women and children alike, and where the sick, the diseased, the dying, the newborn, the lame, the insane, the murderers and petty thieves, the young and the old, were herded together in conditions similar to those described by a visitor to Colbath Fields prison at the end of the eighteenth century:

Men and women, boys and girls, were indiscriminately herded together, in this chief county prison, without employment or wholesome control;

while smoking, gaming, singing and every species of brutalizing conversation and demeanour tended to the unlimited advancement of crime and pollution.[29]

Gloucestershire County Gaol was described by John Howard in his report on *The State of the Prisons*:

there is only one court for all the prisoners and one day room for men and women felons ... Many prisoners died here ... eight died before Christmas 1778 of the small-pox; and in 1783 several died of that disorder and the gaol-fever ... Only one sewer. No bath ... There is no separation of the women ... The licentious intercourse of the sexes is shocking to decency and humanity. Many children have been born in this gaol ... [30]

In 1815 Inspector General of Prisons, Forster Archer, claimed that 'greater attention cannot be paid to their [i.e. the women convicts] Health nor can more humanity be exemplified than is by those employed in their care'. The consequences of prison conditions, however, remained clearly visible in the physical condition of many of the prisoners delivered to the convict ships. Archer commented that

The cases of Persons afflicted with Contagious diseases arriving in the Dublin ships at Cork where hithertofore very numerous – Within the last six years they have not been nearly frequent ... We have not Hulks for their confinement, nor a General Depot at Cork Harbour where the Sick or Convalescent might with safety be committed ... Persons afflicted with fever or Dysentery are taken to the City Gaol of Cork which has neither Court Yard or Airing Ground attached, here they remain till death or recovery ensue ... [31]

Individual petitions stressed the 'debility', 'disease and evil putrifications of the body' which so often followed long imprisonment. Elizabeth Boyle pleaded from the City Gaol of Londonderry in October 1804 that

Petitioner hath been Confined in said Gaol, Since the month of March last ... That Petitioner is now of the age of eighteen years and was at the time of her imprisonment in good health but from Long Confinement the same has been greatly injured ... [32]

The journals of the prison surgeons who accompanied the deportees from Dublin to the prison ships at Cork detail the appalling physical condition of so many of the women sent to New South Wales. On 15 June 1805, when the prisoners bound for the transport, the *Tellicherry*, had reached Kilkenny on their way to Cork, the surgeon recorded that 'Catherine Kiernan has been sick on the road with a violent vomiting and is now in High Fever'. She was reported 'in much the same way' when the group reached Waterford. On the 19 June the surgeon noted the following: 'Ellen Fergusson is free from fever but is very weak ... two women are mending – Nancy Farrel has a scrofulous sore and is becoming very offensive from her dirt – the straw should be thrown out'.

The women waited at Cork 'until the *Tellicherry* was ready to receive them' but the straw which was their bedding was 'so bad ... that there is danger of sickness from it'. The Captain of the *Tellicherry* sent a sail to the prison for the women to spread over the rotting, body-filthy, vermin and lice-infested straw. The surgeon added 'Ann Farrell [sic] is very bad with the sore and she is a filthy object'. On 30 July twelve of the women were considered 'fit' to board the *Tellicherry*, but

The convicts are very badly off – They have no straw, save a little scraped together for the sick, the other Convicts are laying on the ballast. The air is very bad in the Prison and they allow but 12 on the deck at the time [in Cork Harbour] ... The consequence is that the fever has broke out and is spreading ... Catherine Cox and Catherine Masterton ... ill with the Dysentery ... Half of them are full of the itch ... [33]

Contemporaries did not question the inadequacies of the gaols. With the exception of the 'misguided' Mrs Fry, all emphasis was on the increasing severity of prison life, and the deprivation from all that was not essential to maintain life. The chastisement of the body of the prisoner through continuous, monotonous toil, by sparse and basic diet, by the removal of all hope that prison life would be anything other than ceaseless labour under the most stringent discipline, these were the features to be developed to their utmost.[34] The individual prisoners remained as the examples to society of the horrifying consequences of crime for both men and women.

Was it as a result of the unendurable hardships of prison life that some women felons petitioned for 'immediate transportation'? Eliza Brown in Phillipstown Gaol in 1820 had been apprehended in a house which she had entered for 'refreshment' and was taken up with the owner, 'a suspicious character who Petitioner never saw in her life before'. She was unable to raise bail in consequence of 'her friends living in a remote part of the Kingdom', and so was sentenced to seven years' transportation. She petitioned that she be sent immediately to Botany Bay 'and relieve her out of her present distressed situation'. Her plea was granted, and she arrived in New South Wales on the *John Bull* in 1821.[35]

Official concern for the well-being of those men and women who were released from British gaols was limited to the hope that they would dread any return to prison and so curb their criminal instincts. It was not until 1793 that there was any firm evidence of concern by the public for the ex-prisoners in Britain. In that year the following suggestion was made by a newspaper columnist:

one more public institution is much wanted in this Country. It is a place where criminals, released from hard labour or imprisonment may have the opportunity of earning bread by some coarse employment and perhaps of acquiring characters which may restore them effectually to society.

When it is considered that from want of such an opportunity these persons are released, and are under the necessity of committing depredations, it is wonderful that, though humanity does not interfere to save them from further guilt and from death, the good policy of protecting public property and quiet should not have produced such an institution.[36]

The object of the suggestion was to prevent further crime. No official comment followed this article, and little if anything was done to assist the ex-prisoner in Britain.

It was apparently not recognised in Britain that transportation as a punishment was more than a means of removing criminals from 'the scene of the crime', more than an ultimate solution to England's crime problem by ridding the mother country of her most vile and unwanted subjects, most of whom would be unable to return. This punishment of transportation, by its very nature, aided 'reformation' by offering opportunities for work and for self-advancement. Was this not generally discussed because most of those who were transported, especially among the women, were believed to be beyond redemption? If this were so, it would reinforce the belief that contemporaries saw only the crime, the criminal and his or her criminal 'propensities', not the economic and social distresses which may have contributed to at least a proportion of the offences. Botany Bay, therefore, could not be considered as a place of reformation of character, morals or habits. To British contemporaries, it remained a 'vast brothel', a place 'of the utmost degradation of body and soul', where the men and women sent as criminals remained to pollute the colony with their infamy and viciousness.[37]

When it was planned to resume transportation from Britain after the end of the American War of Independence, and Botany Bay was settled upon as the site for the proposed colony of thieves, the question most important to the colony's development and future welfare was who was to be transported. The vital question for the British government, however, was how much expense could be saved in Britain and in New South Wales in the establishment of this colony. The two requisites were not mutually exclusive in theory, but in practice the result weighed heavily in favour of the minimum of expenditure by the mother country. During the nine months between the announcement of the decision to settle Botany Bay as a penal colony and the sailing of the First Fleet on 13 May 1787, the man appointed to head the expedition and to become its first governor, Captain Arthur Phillip, faced almost insuperable difficulties in ensuring adequate ships, supplies, food and clothing, medicines, stores – all that would be needed for the voyage and for the maintenance of the colony in its first two years. At one period Phillip became so exasperated that he wrote to Lord Sydney to ensure that he would not be blamed if he lost half the garrison and convicts – which was highly probable – 'crowded and victualled in such a manner for such a long voyage'. Was it that the lack of official concern for the physical well-being of convicted felons in Britain's gaols was simply extended to those felons unfortunate enough to have been chosen for transportation?[38]

By 1787 the hulks and prisons of Great Britain were crammed to overflowing with men, women and children sentenced to transportation. This situation was not alleviated by the comparatively few felons transported prior to the arrival of Governor Macquarie. Despite increasing numbers transported after the Napoleonic Wars, only a small proportion of the felons confined in Britain were actually sent to New South Wales. Who was to be selected – and why? Philip had expected 'healthy young men and breeding women'. Perhaps there seemed little need to insist that those chosen had at least the rudimentary skills needed to establish a colony, to build the huts, to bake the bread, to brew, to sew, to clear and farm the land. The 191 convict women who sailed from England on that First Fleet were to be the pioneer women of the new settlement, yet few of their backgrounds would suggest that they were fitted for this role. Most had been 'in service'. Skills? Most of the First Fleet women were 'singlewomen of no trade'. One was an artificial-flowermaker, another a charwoman, another a bookbinder. Rebecca Davison (*Lady Penrhyn*) was a needlewoman, Elizabeth Hayward (*Lady Penrhyn*) an apprentice clog-maker. Nor were they particularly healthy, although only three died on the voyage: one as the result of an accident aboard ship, another of 'old age and dropsy' and a third of 'consumption, already in an advanced state when she embarked'. Phillip complained that many 'had diseases of long standing' and that 'many [of the men and women] had been discharged from the Venereal Disease Hospitals as incurable'; some had lost the use of their limbs, and one, Rebecca Boulton, was an idiot.[39]

A minority of the women selected for transportation in 1787 were such vicious characters as to support the belief in Britain that the convict women were irreclaimable. Despite their disorderly, vicious, immoral, degraded and drunken behaviour on the voyage and in the first two or three years of settlement, despite 'breaking through the bulwarks to get at the sailors', some of these 'notorious whores' settled in the colony in common law or legal relationships, bore children, lived self-supporting and at least outwardly 'honest and industrious' lives. One of these women, Jasmin Allen, transported from Middlesex for assault and housebreaking, was described at her trial as a 'lustyish woman with black hair ... she seems to be a drunkard and unreliable'. After six months in Newgate gaol, she was selected for transportation on the *Lady Penrhyn*. She was flogged at least twice in the first years of settlement, receiving fifty lashes for buying a stolen shirt on 12 January 1789. 'Tam' remained in the colony until her death in the Benevolent Asylum in 1825. She was then about seventy-six years old, had had no further colonial convictions, and was described as 'Free at Death'.

Their colonial reputation, however, was not enhanced by the behaviour of women such as Ann Fowles, whose early colonial life justified the reputation of a 'wild, wanton whore of Botany Bay'. Ann Fowles was frequently before the colonial courts in 1788, and, in June 1789, she was convicted of stealing clothes and provisions and sentenced to be publicly flogged with fifty lashes for three successive Thursdays, to have her head shaved, and to wear a canvas cap with the word 'thief' on it. Her four-year-old daughter who had come with her on the *Lady Penrhyn*, was taken from her as 'she was a woman of abandoned character', and sent to Norfolk Island as 'a public child', to be taught 'reading, writing and husbandry' far from the evil influence of her mother. Ann Fowles later married John Holt at Parramatta in 1801, and lived with him until she died at the age of about fifty-nine, apparently physically unharmed by 'vicious youth'.

Another of the First Fleet women who enjoyed an unenviable reputation in the early years of the colony was Rebecca Davison (*Lady Penrhyn*), whose London life strongly suggested that she earned her living as a prostitute as well as a thief. She married William Holmes on Norfolk Island. For a colonial offence she was sentenced 'to be stripped and tied to the cart... and to receive twenty-five lashes on the West Side [of Norfolk Island] twenty-five on the East Side and ten at Buckingham Township' where the farm she shared with her husband was located. After her husband died in 1797, Rebecca married, or formed alliances with Thomas Prior, James Horral, and possibly a William Smith. She was buried as 'Rebecca Horral' in 1809.

The profligate, irreclaimable reputation of Botany Bay's women was further added to by the youngest woman transported on the First Fleet, thirteen-year-old Elizabeth Hayward (*Lady Penrhyn*). Mary Johnson, the chaplain's wife, took the girl into her household as a servant, but early in 1789 the chaplain charged her with insolence, and she was punished with thirty lashes. She was then aged fourteen or fifteen. She was sent to Norfolk Island in 1790, where she had at least two living children, George and Mary Haywood. By 1820 she was living at Port Dalrymple, married to Joseph Lowe.[40]

The First Fleet women were atypical in that they were sent to found a colony, not to live in an established settlement. There was also no certainty that the colony would be a success. Those women who committed offences, who were drunken, disorderly, quarrelsome and abusive, were simply continuing their previous lives in a new type of gaol, a penal camp where they were almost unrestricted as to how and where they would live. It was the notorious behaviour which was recorded in the trials of the courts and in the despatches of the governors and which added colour to accounts of life at Botany Bay.

Were these assumptions justified? Were the women – and the men – selected from among those sentenced to transportation as 'fit objects' for Botany Bay the most depraved and vicious of the felons crowded into Britain's gaols? Or were they selected for their usefulness in the colony? An analysis of the crimes, skills, age and health of the women sent to New South

Wales during the first forty years shows how unaltered the haphazard process of selection of convicts for transportation continued to be throughout the convict period. Phillip complained that the sending of the diseased, the sick, the crippled and the old, cleared the gaols of Britain – 'but what of the colony?'[41]

Macquarie sent a strongly critical request to Bathurst on the 'system' of selecting men and women for transportation, to which Forster Archer wrote a detailed counterchatge and reply vindicating the administration in Ireland. Archer gave as example the *Three Bees* and the *Catherine* which left the Cove of Cork for Falmouth on 28 October 1813 with 219 men and 98 women. Seventy of the women had embarked at the dock of Dublin and had remained on board at the Cove of Cork, and all prisoners were confined on the ships for over two months while the transports were at Falmouth. Archer described in detail the care taken to maintain the health of the women:

Women are continually both in Harbour and at Sea, admitted to the Decks – Two were delivered on board the Dublin ship, it was considered dangerous to move them from the very Hot atmosphere of the Hold to an Hospital, they however soon recovered and were embarked perfectly well in the *Three Bees* at Cork ... greater attention cannot be paid to their health nor can more humanity be exemplified than is by those employed in their case.

It was because of this care, because of the continual access to the decks, Archer claimed, that the Irish women arrived in New South Wales in such excellent health.

As to Macquarie's complaint that a large proportion of 'aged convicts' were transported who became a burden on the settlement, Archer argued that the complaints of the colonial governor were simply based on his wish to have only 'young, Healthful men and Breeding women' sent to the colony. If this were to be the case, the effects on the prisoners in the gaols of Britain would be severe, morally and physically, for the older hardened villains would corrupt the young and incite disobedience and disorder. Archer claimed that

In respect of age very old persons of either sex unless they are Habitual Offenders or persons guilty of atrocious Crimes are seldom Transported – these are either detailed in their respective prisons or at the Gaol of Cork after embarkation and with the Lord Lieutenant's approbation are in some time liberated on bail.[42]

Every transport to arrive in New South Wales, however, did include women 'advanced in years'. Dorothy Handland of the *Lady Penrhyn* was eighty-two when she disembarked at Sydney Cove.[43] Elizabeth Beckford, from the same ship, was aged seventy. In the following transports aged convicts, feeble, infirm, diseased, crippled and those, like Mercy Parker of 'tender constitution' were transported with the young and healthy.

'Mrs Bartlett' was sixty-six when sentenced to transportation at Maidstone in Kent in 1819. Her son petitioned that her sentence be mitigated: 'she is so very ill. She spits blood and is so weak that she can scarcely stand and some days keeps to her bed ... I hope you can have the heavy fine she must pay mitigated as she is ruined with law and illness of five years.'

Hannah Bowsted was sent from Yarmsworth for transportation in December 1821. The mayor sent a letter to Lord Sidmouth: 'she is above the age mentioned in the letter [containing transportation requirements]. She is forty-six years but in good health and fit to undergo the voyage.'[44]

This suggests that some standardisation of requirements was made in the early 1820s. Whether or not it was effective cannot be estimated. It is probable that the practice described by Forster Archer continued, that is, 'convicts advanced in Life universally in the prisons extend their ages for the purpose of exciting compassion in hope of being for that cause detailed'. The final selection remained with the gaolers and the 'problems', those requiring extra care and expense, those creating disturbances, were the most favoured for transportation by their gaolers.

The case of Elizabeth Birkett illustrates the extraordinary lengths to which certificates of illness could be ignored by British officials. The Chief Officer of the *Wellington* had sent Elizabeth Birkett ashore after he had examined her hands, saying, 'if she was on the water for one month he should be obliged to throw her overboard'. The Captain became 'very angry' when she was brought back again, and said, 'Take her away for I will have nothing to do with her'. The woman had come from Nottingham Gaol with a letter to the mayor:

Thomas Basnett the Gaol Surgeon is now in attendance ... the complaint under which Elizabeth Birkett labours was a high degree of Scorbic Disease but in no degree of a contagious nature or make her unfit to be transported.

After the refusal of the Captain to have her back on board the *Wellington*, she was sent to the *Janus* where it was found that

> she had symptoms of slight inflammation of the bowels with dysentery of ten days previous duration. Although the symptoms have subsided and she is in better health she is not strong enough to encounter seasickness so requests she be sent ashore.
>
> ... when received on the *Wellington* (eight months ago) she was much affected by a cutaneous disease and had to be sent ashore. She has since had an attack of pleurisy.

The 'policy', if policy there were towards transporting the old and the sick, was explained very clearly in the letter of the chief surgeon who examined 'the female convict from Nottingham' in May 1819 at the request of Lord Sidmouth. He found that she had

> an herpetic Disease which is certainly likely to be increased by salt provisions and a sea-voyage. At the same time I must observe that if surgeons of transports were allowed to pick the prisoners and take none but those who are young and in perfect health the persons of this country must ere long be ... besides offering an opportunity to convicts of rendering themselves in general appearance unfit for removal.[45]

More humanity – or expediency – was shown in one isolated case in April 1819 in which the two surgeons at Preston County Gaol requested Lord Sidmouth to remit the sentences of thirteen old, 'wealthy' [*sic*], infirm prisoners of the gaol:

> They would be much more comfortable in the respective workhouses of the Townships to which they belong. The Female part of the prison is crowded to excess as so many are being sent from Lancaster during the repairs at Lancaster Castle. Something must be done to keep the prison in a healthy state during the approaching warm season of the year.

The list of these women, aged between fifty-six and seventy-six, all sentenced to transportation, shows that most were old offenders with two, three, four and even five convictions. One, Mary Stambles, had been previously transported. Was it humane consideration for their age that they were respited from transportation, or was it that they were an encumbrance on an exceptionally crowded gaol? The four discharged, the youngest of the 'old women', sent their thanks to Lord Bathurst, hoping 'that the remaining eight may also be liberated'.[46]

'The increasing depravity of the age' 61

Overcrowding of gaols was an increasing and continuing problem for local authorities. Gaolers in most of the English counties wrote to the Secretary of State urging that those sentenced to transportation be removed as soon as practicable because of the overcrowded state of the gaols. William Jamison, Under-Sheriff of Nottingham, wrote in 1821: 'I am desired to state to your Lordship that the Prison is now too crowded'. That same year, P. Harward, Justice of the Peace for the County of Gloucester, referred to the overcrowding in the Gloucester County Gaol 'as both the visiting magistrates are indisposed' and requested the immediate removal of the nine male and three female prisoners sentenced to transportation. These were Ann Lloyd, Agnes Ball and Ann Malcolm. The latter had had 'no return of fits for the last twelve months and is exceeding anxious to be removed'.[47]

The men and women sentenced to transportation to Botany Bay were intended in theory to 'suffer' their punishment as soon as they were convicted. Almost all of the transported women, however, had spent up to twelve months in Newgate or a county gaol, some waiting three and four years to be transported.[48] Their county gaolers were anxious to be rid of them; the Navy Office wrote to Sidmouth of 'the great necessity' to embark convict and free women with all possible speed as 'the lengthened time of confinement of some on board is likely to produce sickness during the voyage besides the great expense of daily demurrage'.[49] Expense, to the counties, to the contractors, to the Navy, to anyone at all, appeared to be a strong motivation to transport convicted felons with all possible dispatch. Their offences had made them unworthy to live among decent people, unwanted and feared by many of their contemporaries, despised and rejected by the respectable section of society. The only fit place for them was at England's penal colony of Botany Bay where they would live among their own kind, convicts in a convict colony suffering the consequences of their infamy, depravity and criminality.

3
'THE REFUSE OF LONDON'

Crime and punishment in English society

... filthy in their persons, disgusting in their habits, obscene in their conversations.

—Joseph John Gurney, London, 1819

It was London, and the everyday life of London which was familiar to such a large proportion of the women transported from England. London itself, its society, its peoples, its workforce, its poor, its shops, public houses, workplaces and lodging houses, these were the familiarities which the convict women from Newgate brought with them to the penal colony, and these were the standards by which they measured colonial life.

A greater contrast between London and the settlement at Port Jackson would be difficult to imagine. London was one of the most cosmopolitan cities of the civilised world. It not only had its own population of London-bred at all levels of society, but was temporary or permanent home for the 'comers and goers', the wandering seasonal workers, the itinerant tramps, beggars and vagabonds, the migrating and travelling men, women and children from all parts of the British Isles – and beyond. Dorothy George, and more recently James Walvin, have shown that there were 'sizeable communities of Europeans ... French Huguenots, European Jews ... and pockets of black slaves'; that 'the strong, the willing, the able, the enterprising along with the wretched and the maimed found their various ways to London to seek a livelihood'.[1] There were women in all of these categories who would be sent from London to Botany Bay.

London acted as a beacon to young country girls in search of domestic work – and older women and widows seeking an alternative to the workhouse of their parish. Many of these found no employment, no honest way of earning a living. Almost all the women transported from Newgate claimed to be servants, or 'in domestic service', some pleading at their trials that they had been unable to find a place in London. When Ellis Wallis (*Broxbornebury*) was sentenced for shoplifting fifty yards of ribbon, she told the judge: 'My Lord, I humbly implore you to extend mercy to an unfortunate female. I came to London to get a place of servitude; not succeeding in my endeavours has been the cause of my being brought here . . .'

Three years earlier Elizabeth Smith (*Friends*), accused of feloniously stealing clothes worth five shillings from the child who was carrying them, said: 'I came from Somersetshire . . . I had been in London five weeks'. Aged thirty-three, she was sentenced to seven years' transportation. Others who were 'from the country' included women such as Ann Taylor, thirty and married, who was a lace-maker 'out of the West Country', sentenced to seven years' transportation for stealing from a dwelling house. Married woman Catherine Turner (*Surprize*), twenty-three, from Worcester, was sentenced to seven years for stealing monies from a dwelling house. Elizabeth Gulliver (*Kitty*), eighteen, from Somersetshire, seven years for stealing wearing apparel. Sarah Baker (*Broxbornebury*), a sixteen-year-old servant from the country who had received her notice, stole an umbrella, a pair of shoes, £13 in notes, a ring and two brooches from her master in Great Portland Street. She was apprehended on the coach at Aldgate on her way home to the country. She returned some of the items she had stolen, but said 'I would wish to have the property I am going to suffer for'. Christina Morris (*Janus*) said quite bluntly at her trial: 'I took the things to carry me to Scotland to my friends.'

It was not only women from the counties of England who were drawn to London by the hope of a better livelihood. Single women and women with their families came from all over Ireland. Most tried to find some form of domestic work and those who were unhappy with their positions, or 'in distress' or simply light-fingered with their employer's possessions, found instead that they were confined in Newgate and bound for Botany Bay.[2]

One feature of Botany Bay which would not have been unfamiliar to the women transported from London was the presence of the Aboriginal inhabitants in the penal colony. Women from London were accustomed to the numbers of black men and women in the metropolis. Some were seamen, others were slaves or ex-slaves who had made their way to London and had been discharged by their masters – or abandoned – or had 'run' or deserted their owners. They did not form 'communities' in London, but lived where and how they could, still greatly disadvantaged by the uncertainty of their legal position as free men and women or as slaves, and many lived in distressing circumstances in the poorest parts of the city. Those among the 'vagrant blacks' forced to beg for survival, were nicknamed 'St Giles black birds',[3] many becoming a part of the London criminal world, either as victims or as offenders. On 1 November 1788 the *Public Advertiser* reported the 'shocking assault' and murder of a 'mulatto woman ... found in a ditch in Robinson's lane, Chelsea':

Her skull is laid bare in many places, and one of her ears was found by her on the ground in a vast quantity of blood, and a piece of large stick with many marks of blood on it, supposed to have been broke by some inhuman wretch beating her ... She had been near thirty years a valuable servant to a respectable family who brought her from the East Indies. Her name is Sylvia and about eight years ago she married ...

Another black man, John P. Halliday, was violently assaulted in an open field by nineteen-year-old Mary Oakes, who robbed him of his possessions and left him lying in the field. She was sentenced to death, respited, and sailed for Botany Bay on the *Nile* in 1802.

In August 1788 Donald (alias Daniel) Love was convicted of a misdemeanour, and sentenced to be put in the pillory for an hour and then to be flogged 'at the court's time on the 25th September in four different parts of the town, nine lashes at each place'. His offence? 'Stealing and selling Negroes, the property of others'. In the same edition of the *Public Advertiser* which reported this misdemeanour, 'a free Negro man ... was committed to gaol ... charged with murdering a Negro slave the property of Mr E. Burton. He was found guilty of manslaughter'. Just outside of London in Surrey, Rackly Mason 'a free black man convicted of manslaughter was sentenced to be burnt in the hand; which was immediately put into execution in the face of the Court'.

Black women were also transported to New South Wales. 'Susannah' was a 'Negro, bought as a girl in the East Indies by Mrs Bridges'. In 1795 Susannah was convicted of stealing large quantities of wearing apparel from her master, Mr Bridges. She was sixteen years old.[4]

As historian Ian Duffield argues, black men and women were commonplace in the cities, major towns and seaports of Britain. That they were accepted by the lower classes without question could explain why there is so little recorded comment on the lives of the non-Aboriginal black women of early New South Wales. When Clara Ward, convicted in Bengal, arrived in New South Wales on the *Campbell Macquarie* as a transported felon, there was no comment on her colour.[5] Contemporary records in the colony only refer to the black women convicts or ex-convicts when they came to official notice, as in the case of the inquest into the death of Elizabeth Mandeville who was described as 'a woman of colour, a native of London' by Surgeon William Bland. At her trial in Middlesex Elizabeth Mandeville, 'a black girl', had been accused and convicted with her white accomplice in circumstances which strongly indicated that prostitution and thieving from their 'victims' was their normal means of subsistence.

The mixture of accents and dialects concentrated in the settlement of New South Wales would have caused little comment from the women of London, for one of the notable characteristics of London was the variety of its accents. The convict women shared their gaol quarters and their transport berths with women and girls from all over Britain and, from time to time, from as far distant as 'the Americas', Quebec, Lisbon, Germany and France. Absconded London servants were identified by accent as well as physical characteristics; one woman, for example, being described in the *The Hue and Cry* as 'speaks with a strong Lancashire accent'.[6]

It was not only the variety of the origins of its inhabitants which made London a city of such vast contrasts. Houses, shops, streets, parks, gardens were all stark evidence of the gulf between the rich and the poor. A German visitor to the city in 1780, von Archenholtz, described this 'astonishing contrast':

The east end, especially along the shores of the Thames, consists of old houses, the streets there were narrow, dark and ill-paved, inhabited by sailors and other workmen who are employed in the construction of ships and by a great part of the Jews. The contrast between this and the West End is astonishing; the houses here are mostly new and elegant; the squares are superb, the streets straight and open – If all London were well-built there would be nothing in the world to compare with it.[7]

On this occasion von Archenholtz was concerned with the physical description of London more than with the poverty of so many of its inhabitants or with the London criminals, equally 'at home' plying their trade in both the West and East Ends.

Women who lived, worked and thieved in the East End, even

in that dockyard district described by von Archenholtz, were among the women transported to Botany Bay. Hannah Swinney (*Speke*) was one example of a 'Dockland girl'. A servant in one of the boarding houses for seamen, she was convicted of stealing four curtains from the house. Mary French (*Friends*) was another. Her husband was a nightwatchman on the docks, and the man with whom he lodged, Andrew Foster, was 'unhappy' when he wanted to bring his wife to lodge with him, for he knew she 'had been in trouble'. Foster's reluctance was well-founded. Mary stole goods worth fourteen shillings and sixpence from Foster while her husband was at work.

London was a city of great poverty, squalor, distress, and even starvation, for its 'have-nots'. Some of these were the individuals whom Patrick Colquhoun called the 'casual poor' when he wrote in 1800:

The number of persons who, with their families find their way to the metropolis, from the most remote quarters of Great Britain and Ireland is inconceivable ... those virtuously brought up in the country ... unable to find employment ... left finally with nothing else to pawn ... live in such miseries which often exceeds anything the human mind can conceive ... for they will not steal and are ashamed to beg.[8]

Women fitting this description are not easy to find among those sentenced to transportation or death. A major problem in determining motivation for crime, however, is the nature of available evidence. There are few remaining contemporary sources sufficiently detailed or reliable on which to base any satisfactory analysis. Newspaper reports are partial, and may not necessarily be typical, average or even generally applicable. Reporters tended to concentrate on the sensational 'newsworthiness' of crime and to stress the sordid, the horrifying or the humorous. Journal articles were more inclined to theorise than to detail accounts of actual crimes and criminals. Any investigation into the criminality, the character and possible motivation of the women transported to Botany Bay, must rest primarily on judicial records – indictments, trial papers, gaol reports – supported, where they exist, by petitions, pleas in mitigation of sentence, and surgeons' reports. Obviously, there are problems inherent in this heavy reliance on 'judicial' evidence. J. M. Beattie argued convincingly in tracing 'The Pattern of Crime in England, 1600–1800' that 'it is the extent to which indictments provide a guide to criminality rather than to the level of reporting or the efficiency of the administrative system, or to some other variable', that their significance rests.[9] Admittedly, this is the problem when attempting to compile statistics, for example, the incidence, growth or pattern of crime in a definite place for a defined period. It is the unreported, undetected crime, 'the dark figure', the unknown and the unmeasurable, which reduces the reliability of the investigation.

In the case of the women transported from London, this restraint does not apply. The analysis based on their offence, indictment, trial and sentence, is for *all* women in their category. There is no sampling or selective process. Mayhew's estimate that only 10 per cent of all criminals were actually apprehended in this period would affect any investigation into crime based on the judicial records, but it would not affect this analysis of the women transported. It must, however, be considered that within the wider community of London these women were the convicted criminals, less skilled at evasion, less fortunate at avoiding detection. The most obvious danger from reliance on the judicial accounts of their trials is that of bias arising from pity for the accused, especially in the minority of cases where the plea was distress or destitution: 'I am a stranger unable to find work'; 'I have seven fatherless children'; 'I was in dire need'; 'Distress drove me to it'. Ann Rogers and Jane Jones, sentenced to death at the age of fifteen, but respited and transported to Australia for life on the *Broxbornebury* in 1814, had pleaded: 'We were in great distress'. 'They had broken into a public house and stolen food and clothes. Mercy was recommended by the jury 'because of their youth and good characters'.[10] Judicial records must be analysed with a critical eye, not 'the eye of pity'.

Which of the women from London could be classified as Colquhoun's 'casual poor'? Perhaps Mary Williams and her daughter Eliza, aged thirteen, both sentenced to death for coining and uttering in 1814? The plea? 'Distress caused me to infringe on the laws of my country'. Was it that same distress which had led to the mother's prior one-year term of imprisonment for the same offence? Or the daughter's one year in the House of Correction in 1810 at the age of nine, again for the same offence? Or was Mary McCarty (*Broxbornebury*) a more deserving case? 'I am a poor woman with three children, without a father'. Aged forty-four, she had shoplifted twenty-four yards of calico. Or Elizabeth Wilmot who arrived in New South Wales on the *Canada* in 1810, convicted of stealing a guinea 'because I was going into hospital'. Or Elizabeth Payne (*Friends*), thirty-two, who was transported for stealing ten pairs of stockings and pleaded 'I have a dying husband at home'. Or twenty-nine-year-old Mary Randall, convicted on twenty counts of disposing of forged banknotes. Her plea? 'I was in distress, I had no residence'. Or Elizabeth Norman,

a decayed belle of sixty [with] her country-looking middle aged woman servant [who] took lodgings in Edgeware Road and stripped them of plate and other articles ... [she] was formerly an authoress, and had written 'The Child of Woe' an exquisite romance, which had a great run, but her faculties and sight had failed her ... [11]

There were cases where the 'inconceivable misery' of her life would qualify the woman prisoner for membership of the 'casual poor'. Was it desperation which led Ann Owen (*Wanstead*) to steal seven shillings' worth of goods from a pawnbroker? Judge and jury indicated that they believed this to be the case when they extended 'mercy to her on account of her being distressed' and her death sentence was commuted to transportation for life and her child permitted to accompany her. Her plea? 'I was very much in distress. I applied to the Parish to take my child; they refused. I have a bad state of health and am very poor. I am not able to go into service.'

Such cases as that of Ann Owen were not typical. A soldier's widow, Margaret Cox, was transported for seven years on the *Indispensable* for breaking and entering. Was she 'forced into crime'? Very few of the London women – perhaps not more than four or five – pleaded that they were in distressed circumstances because of the execution, imprisonment or transportation of the husband. Mary Mercer, transported on the *William Pitt* for theft, pleaded: 'I was distressed because my husband was on the *Glatton*.' Had she hoped to rejoin him in New South Wales? Sarah Best (*Britannia*), transported for stealing a cotton counterpane worth five shillings: 'the prisoner was the wife of Colin Reculist who was executed'.

An analysis of the women tried in London or Middlesex indicates that very few of those transported to Botany Bay would qualify for membership of London's 'casual poor', the women who would not 'steal or beg'. These were more likely to be found among the 'free passengers', the wives of men transported to New South Wales who had received permission to rejoin their husbands in the convict colony at government expense. Many of these free women lived in 'inconceivable misery', but 'neither begged nor stole'. Their petitions supported by testimonials from officials concerned in their plight show the distress, destitution, even starvation, that faced these women and their children after the husband was transported.[12] Few took the criminal solution of Eleanor Rice (*Northampton*), convicted of breaking, entering and stealing. Rice pleaded: 'I was in distress ... my husband had left me.'

Women such as Elizabeth Surman could more aptly be called 'the casual poor'. Her body was found by an agent with those of two other women in an empty house in Stonecutter Street. She was the daughter of a respectable jeweller, and only six years old when both her parents died. She then lived with a succession of friends and relatives, working as silk-winder or servant. She was discharged from her last employment (by a washerwoman with six children) because of her ill-health. Having no 'domicile rights', although her father had been a respected churchwarden, she ended up sleeping in the streets of London. She came to an empty house, starving, and lay down beside the corpses of two women who had died of starvation, not realising they were dead. She was found dead a few days later, literally starved to death.[13] There were no avenues of poor relief or help open to her, but she had neither begged, stolen nor prostituted herself. Death by starvation was the 'final solution' for those of the poor who would not beg or steal.

Colquhoun's description of that class whom he saw as the alternative to the casual poor was more appropriate for most of the girls and women sentenced to transportation from London:

those who came to the city and formed connections with others who live by petty or more audacious offences ... the young female part of such families too often become prostitutes while the males pursue acts of depredation upon the Public.[14]

The offences of the young London girls transported to Botany Bay show that the females, as well as the males, were as likely 'to commit acts of depredation'. Into which category would fourteen-year-old Sarah Johnson (*Britannia*) fall? Convicted in 1797 for the theft of a shift, an apron, a black silk bonnet and a scarlet cloak – all valued at three shillings and sixpence – she pleaded: 'I did it from necessity and want'. Was it that the child needed clothes to obtain a 'respectable' position? Or thirteen-year-old Esther Gamble (*Friends*), who lived with her sister in Homer Street, Marylebone, and was sentenced to death for stealing goods worth £54 15s 0d. Her sentence was commuted to transportation for life 'because of her confession and her youth'. Elizabeth Stacey (*Speke*), sixteen, had been 'turned out' from her place as a servant, and returned to rob her former mistress. She said, 'I went to this woman's house. I took a chisel and opened the door. I went and took those things out of the drawer'. Because of her youth Elizabeth Stacey's death sentence was commuted to life transportation. Elizabeth Allen, known as 'Bett', certainly did not fit any picture of the 'casual poor' of London. Tried with two accomplices for highway robbery, she had 'dragged him [the victim], while he was very drunk, out of a public house and robbed him'. After a stay in Newgate, Elizabeth Allen sailed for New South Wales on the *Britannia* in 1798. How could motivation for these crimes be attributed? The pleas of the women had little effect on the severity of their sentences, and most judges remained unmoved by the personal distresses of the defendants.

What of families tried and convicted together? Was this evidence of criminal lifestyles? Ann Baker was transported for seven years for theft, and her father, Thomas Baker, received fourteen years for receiving his daughter's stolen goods. Ironically, Ann was servant to James Hardy Vaux, and had stolen from a man who was himself to be transported to Botany Bay for life – on two occasions.[15] Sarah Swatman (*Morley*) and her entire family were committed for theft of linen. Sarah, aged fifty-seven, was employed as a laundress for Hatchett's Hotel in Piccadilly and took the linen home, where her husband and family helped her wash it. Only Sarah and her daughter Esther were convicted of the theft of fifty-seven tablecloths and sixty-two napkins and seventeen pillowcases, and they sailed to Botany Bay. A 'couple' convicted together, Mary Brown and Benjamin Noble – he was forty-six, she twenty-five – and sentenced to death for stealing forty yards of woollen cloth, made what might have been an attempt to impress the judge with their moral standards 'Yes ... they lived together ... but not as man and wife', as his wife was still living. Whether or not their plea fell on disinterested judicial ears, the death sentence was respited for both. Mary Brown was transported for life on the *Morley*, her 'live-in friend' Benjamin Noble followed – without his wife. Mary Shadwell who was transported on the *Friends*, was tried with her mother-in-law for stealing promissory notes. Susan Skelton (*Wanstead*) was transported for shoplifting, her ten-year-old son William was sentenced to death. Eleanor Flynn (*Friends*) and her mother were charged with stealing from Eleanor's employer.

Where there is poverty, there is crime. Throughout the period of transportation to New South Wales, contemporaries were convinced that crime was increasing in Britain, especially in the cities and large manufacturing towns. Punishment of death and of transportation were not having the desired deterrent effect on the criminal poor, and London, that centre of the British universe, was believed to have the highest incidence of crime. There was a continual flow of letters published in the daily and weekly newspapers from concerned citizens. One 'respectable citizen of London' wrote an open letter to the Lord Mayor of the city in 1793, in which he complained of

those numerous and audacious equalizers of property who daily annoy the citizens of London whilst they are industriously providing the support of themselves and their families . . .

It needs no comment, My Lord, when hourly experience tells us that a number of daring pickpockets continually infest the public streets of the City; it must strike the most superficial observer that something must be wrong when impunity is the concomitant of guilt.
— *Public Advertiser*, 6 August 1793[16]

This 'respectable citizen' did not specify the abandoned girls and women of London who, in gangs, with accomplices or alone, 'infested the streets and byways of London, preying on the unwary'. Could his description of 'that class of thieves by which the city is infested' be applied to the women transported from London? What of Mary Carty, Mary Sowden, Jane Curtis (all transported on the *Alexander*), and Alice Swinns and Ann Leisted, a 'teenage gang' who broke into Hannah Welch's house and stole her goods and money? Were they 'poor, hungry paupers who peculate to support an almost expiring existence'?

Poverty was an integral part of the life of cities in the late eighteenth and early nineteenth centuries. Nowhere was it more obvious to the 'respectable' resident, the casual visitor, to all inhabitants, than in London. The London poor, men, women, children, orphans, widows, the lame and the sick, appeared as countless as the sands of the shore. Families huddled together in the streets, ragged children and sickly infants begged from passers-by. The deformed, the mutilated, the gross and the obscene exploited their misfortunes, displayed their deformities and supplicated with the beggars and the destitute.[17] Few contemporaries drew the dividing line between the 'deserving poor' and the 'criminal poor'. Poverty itself was frequently regarded as sufficient evidence of criminality. Their outward appearance, unwashed, unkempt, 'half-naked and starved', rather than inspiring pity from the good citizens of London, added to the expectations of criminality. Those who tried to help the needy, who took pity on the destitute, often found that this was misplaced sympathy, and the good samaritans were robbed for their kindness.

Elizabeth Bason, transported on the *Lord Wellington* in 1820 (respited from death), had been taken into the house of her 'acquaintance', Mrs Longstaff, when she was out of work and homeless. In return, she stole Mr Longstaff's pocket book and £38. Twenty-eight-year-old Mary Newbury (*Speke*) was 'a young woman lately come out of the Workhouse'. She had 'nowhere to go', so Susannah Powell, aged ninety-five, took her in and gave her a place in her home. She responded by stealing six guineas from her aged benefactor. Judith Lightly 'had been in prison', but had been helped by the family of James Guy who 'had known her for seven or eight years'. Twenty-six-year-old Judith stole goods worth fifteen shillings from that family and was transported to Botany Bay on the *Speke* in 1808. Mary Johnston (*Maria*), twenty-five, had asked for charity from Eliza Bond. Mary had nowhere to go because her mother was in the alms house. She repaid Eliza's charity by returning to her benefactor's house, breaking in, and stealing clothes. She was sentenced to death, her sentence commuted to transportation for life. Elizabeth Gibbs (*Northampton*) broke into Thomas Yarrow's house and stole goods from him – 'she had been given permission to use his facilities to boil potatoes'. These, and similar cases where advantage was taken of kindness and assistance, may have been 'the tip of the iceberg' and 'the dark figure' of unreported gratitude far higher than indicated in the trials at London or Middlesex. Where the prosecutor was aware that conviction would mean death or transportation for the accused, there could have been a reluctance among the humanitarian-minded to prosecute. One fact is indisputable: the women who were transported for thefts from their benefactors could not, by any stretch of the imagination, be called 'the deserving poor'.

To the Londoner, to the resident, new arrival or casual visitor from the counties or abroad, the poor, deserving or not, were obvious in all parts of the city. Most 'respectable' Londoners continued to believe that poverty itself was a contributing cause to the ever-increasing crime rate, as was 'the feckless nature ... and indolence' of many of the lower orders who preferred crime to honest labour.

Whatever the causes, London enjoyed the unenviable reputation of being the major centre of crime, a place where even the Watch was not safe, where a lady could not walk unaccompanied in the Strand without fear of being physically attacked and robbed, as poor Mary Price discovered when she was assaulted and robbed by 'fresh-complexioned' Sarah Townsend (*Surprize*). Sarah had come from the Isle of Wight to find her fortune in the city of London. Her manner of 'finding' that fortune led her to be transported to Botany Bay. Mrs Ward, another resident of London, was stopped 'behind Whitechapel as she made her way from Stephney to Leadenhall ... by two footpads who robbed her of four guineas, nine shillings and sixpence, took her ring from her finger and beat her severely'.

Even servants could not escape the footpads: 'a gentleman's servant with a quantity of fish was stopped near Holborn by a couple of footpads who robbed him of fifteen shillings and his wallet'.[18]

The good citizens of London were not safe in their own homes from the 'depredations' of the city's criminals. Throughout the period of transportation, the two most common offences for which women were transported from London were stealing from employers and stealing from dwelling houses. Thefts from dwellings were usually after 'breaking and entering' but this part of the charge was frequently dismissed, in all probability not because it had not taken place, but because it reduced the penalty from death to transportation. Thefts from dwellings were often accompanied by assault or 'putting the [victim] in fear and danger'. This was the case for two sisters, Rebecca and Elizabeth Armstrong, who were at home when their sixteen-year-old servant, Agnes Vallance, broke into their house and stole household goods, linen and clothing from her employers. For this offence, Agnes Vallance was transported on the *Indispensable*. A different case was that of Alice Burroughs and Amelia Evans, aged nineteen and twenty-one, and transported on the *Indispensable* for stealing – but not in the dwelling house. Their case was an exception to the old adage 'honour among thieves', or at least among friends; they were convicted of stealing quantities of clothing from Lucy Stodford who lived with them in their house.[19]

Londoners were not safe in public houses, or even when in the houses of acquaintances. Ann Tracey, thirty-three, and her young son Peter, aged nine, were both sentenced to death for assaulting William Whitnell in their house, with the complicity of Mary Brown. Whitnell had been 'put in fear' as the three 'took from his person and against his will a man's hat value 6sh, a linen apron value 4d, six cups and saucers value 1sh and 6d, an iron shovel value 1sh and a tinder box value 6d . . . his property.' Both women were transported on the *Britannia* and Peter recommended for 'mercy'.

Travellers were certainly not safe on the King's Highway, where the 'highwayman' was frequently a young woman either alone or with a gang of women. Elizabeth Ford aged twenty-three and barely 4 feet 6 inches tall, and Ann Taylor, twenty-eight, were transported on the *Surprize* for 'assaulting Samuel Evan on the Highway and taking his watch'. Both returned to Newgate after their trial to await the sailing of the transport for Botany Bay. Ann Lamb, aged twenty-seven, and her husband John, with Ann Clarke, received death sentences for assaulting Richard Hill on the King's Highway and taking his watch, seal, key and silk string. Both Ann Lamb and Ann Clarke were transported on the *Indispensable*. Both were typical of the London 'highwaywomen' who assaulted and robbed unwary travellers to and from the City of London. Letters, diaries and journals of the time mention travelling to and arriving at London 'without incident', their writers obviously relieved to have escaped the welcoming attentions of the fraternity of the road.[20]

Crime, violence and poverty were 'normal' characteristics of everyday London life. They were not regarded as exceptional, unexpected or remarkable; unfortunate, creating a problem of vast proportions, even distressing, but not abnormal. Respectable citizens took what precautions they could to protect their lives and their property and looked to the law with its increasing severity of statutory punishment for an increasing number of crimes denoted felonies to deter the malefactors, the flash coves, the cutpurses and pickpockets, 'the light-fingered gentry' of the brotherhood and sisterhood of the streets. The reading public continued to find daily evidence in their newspapers of the increasing prevalence of crime, with reports of 'brutal murders', highway robberies, assaults, thefts and burglaries, of accounts of men 'lured' into alleyways by molls and strumpets, stripped of their watches, pocketbooks, seals and fobs – even their breeches; of unwary men taken to a room and waking up the next morning to find the girl and their belongings gone.[21]

Familiarity with crime and the extent of violence, criminality, poverty and immorality did not breed contempt among the good people of London. It had, in one sense, a hardening effect. That is, it encouraged the severe punishments which were believed to deter crime. On the other hand, it became the basis for a strong and growing belief in the vicious nature, the depraved and degenerate characteristics of the felons convicted of major statutory offences. What reformation, what forgiveness, could be found for a fourteen-year-old servant who calmly fed her mistress and her baby arsenic over a period to ensure their deaths? Her reason? She would inherit her mistress's clothes. Where else did she belong but at Botany Bay? And what effect could the publication of her crime, her sentence and her destination have but to stress and give substance to the belief that 'Botany Bay was a land of thieves, murderers and prostitutes'?[22]

London crime was not covert nor necessarily cloaked by darkness. Any large gathering of its inhabitants became a field day for pickpockets, cutpurses, footpads and prostitutes and gave full employment to the London magistrates in the following week. Hanging days, traditionally public holidays, were notorious. Hogarth portrayed the thief picking a pocket as a guilty malefactor was about to be launched into eternity. Was this indicative of the 'aweful' effect of death as a deterrent to crime? There was no wish among the populace for hanging days to be abolished. When this was suggested, Dr Johnson's comment was 'innovation has run riot!' The public were not to be defrauded of their holiday, nor of the spectacle of criminals 'suffering' the extreme punishment of the law. The salutory effects of public hangings upon the inhabitants of London continued to be a major argument for their retention. In 1828 the *Morning Herald* reported the execution of Catherine Welch:

In the course of the morning a number of Charity children arrived in front of Newgate for the purpose of witnessing the execution; on their being seen by Mr. Cotton, the Ordinary, he went to them and admonished them as to the impropriety of their being present at such a scene; they immediately withdrew.[23]

It could reasonably be assumed that those Charity children had been sent to witness the execution of 'That unhappy woman' in the pious belief that such a sight would instil in them a horror and lasting dread of the consequences of crime.

In June 1788 *The Times* reported, with little commentary, the execution of Margaret Sullivan, burnt at the stake for colouring copper coins as silver.[24] It was fortunate for Bridget Joyce, who would have been forty-one at the time of Margaret Sullivan's burning, that this punishment fell into disuse. She was convicted in 1801 of passing 'counterfeit money at rate higher than it looked', and convicted a second time of the same offence in

78 *The Women of Botany Bay*

1813 and sentenced to death. She was respited, and, at the age of fifty-four, transported to New South Wales on the *Wanstead* in 1814. Was she aware of the women who had 'suffered' death by burning for similar offences?

Two years before the public burning of Margaret Sullivan, the *Daily Register* reported the burning of Phoebe Harrison. The 'mob' present showed little pity for the unhappy victim. After the flames had consumed her 'they amused themselves with kicking about her ashes, and similar to the practice of the savage Indians in America, expressed themselves in shouts of barbarous triumph.'[25]

The women transported to Botany Bay were familiar with the crowds who watched the public executions and, in all probability, numbers of them had been in such crowds. In February 1818, for example, the crowd which gathered to watch the executions of Mary Ann Jeines, Charlotte Newman, William Hutchman and John Attel was so numerous that the *Morning Advertiser* commented: 'scarcely ever [do we] recollect to have seen a larger assemblage on any occasion':

Most of the ropes were badly adjusted by the executioner. It was the subject of complaint; and it was evident to the populace, who twice rewarded his inattention by loud screams and hisses ... Hutchman expired in great agony and the women were deeply affected.[26]

Mary Ann Jeines and Charlotte Newman had come from Newgate for their execution. They had been sentenced at the same Sessions as most of the London women transported on the *Maria* and had shared the poor conditions of Newgate with women still waiting for their transport – or death. Hannah Bryant, twenty-eight, a servant sentenced to death and then reprieved for transportation for life, was in Newgate when the women were taken for execution, as were Mary Chambers, aged thirty-two and sentenced to seven years' transportation, and Mary Gilles, twenty-one, a servant sentenced to fourteen years. All three were transported on the *Maria*. Did any of these women think of their gaol-mates who had not had the luck to be respited and the chance of life at Botany Bay? From the numbers of women convicted in 1818 after this public execution, it would appear that the fear of death was little deterrent to the women criminals of London. Three months after the executions, Elizabeth Wingfield (*Lord Wellington*) and Hannah Polley were sentenced to be hanged for 'disposing of forged banknotes'. It was not until the end of the Sessions that both women knew they would escape death by transportation to Botany Bay.

Those women transported from London were well aware of the alternatives which would have been their punishment if they had not been sentenced to transportation: death on the gallows – in the early years, even death by burning – or long years of confinement in the harsh and indescribably severe gaols of London. There seemed, however, no deterrent strong enough to stop the women of London from thieving and stealing.

Theorists such as Sydney Smith believed that the greatest deterrent to crime was the fear of punishment, both corporal and spiritual punishment. Smith advocated gaols of the greatest severity: 'a gaol should be a place of suffering, from which men [and presumably women] recoil with horror – a place of real suffering, painful to the memory, terrible to the imagination'. Hard labour, seclusion from their fellows and a bare subsistence diet were Smith's remedy for both reform and punishment. 'Water, gruel and flour puddings' would be sufficient diet for men, women and children. The female felons must be kept in silence as much as possible and wear 'a dress of shame', eat only 'coarse food', and always be subjected to constant 'hard, incessant and irksome eternal labour'.[27] By contrast with this proposed regime for prisoners, life at Botany Bay could assume some equality with Paradise.

During the period of transportation, women in Britain received the same punishment as men for their crimes. They were not, however, subject to gibbeting – that is, leaving the hanged body to rot in chains as a warning and example to other would-be malefactors. Neither are there records of disembowelling or quartering of women. The single punishment reserved for women – especially husband-killers – was burning, and this was seldom invoked in the first quarter of the nineteenth century. Added to the sentence of death was the additional punishment dreaded even more than death itself: 'and the body be delivered to the surgeons for public dissection and anatomising'. This punishment had been legally added to the death sentence in cases of murder since the Act of 1752 and was enforced until its abolition in 1832. The same added punishment was also part of the New South Wales criminal code. On 18 July 1816, the death warrant for Elizabeth Anderson, signed by Lachlan Macquarie, read: 'Elizabeth Anderson tried and convicted of murder and sentenced to death to be carried out on 19th July and her body to be delivered to the surgeons.'[28]

Elizabeth Anderson, husband-killer, was atypical of the

women of Botany Bay, her crime exceptional. She was, however, the expected stereotype for the 'refuse of London', and, as a murderess, conformed to the expectations of the vicious callousness of women transported from the most notorious of Britain's gaols, Newgate. She represented all the assumptions as to the immorality, criminality and depravity of women who had brought with them to New South Wales their familiarity with the criminal life of London. Few of the surgeons on the transport ships would have questioned that the Newgate women who had been in their charge were capable of such crimes, few of the respectable citizens of London City would have commented that such a crime was committed in New South Wales, and few of the commentators on Botany Bay society would have seen a husband-murderer as exceptional or atypical in that convict colony.

The nature of their crimes, with the background of immorality, the apparent lack of any standards of decency or honesty, their very poverty and destitution, all supported the assumption that the women transported to the penal colony were the worst of London's criminals. It was only in New South Wales itself that it was apparent that few of these women continued their former lifestyles, fewer fulfilled the expectations of British or colonial officials, and only a minority would justify the opinions of their gaolers in London that they were totally irreclaimable. Their British reputation was undeniable as 'criminals of the darkest complexion' and, solely on an analysis of their offences and trials, the opinions of respectable commentators would be justified. What was lacking was any appreciation or recognition that, whatever may have been the reason, most of these London women merged into colonial society as the working and family women of Botany Bay.

4
'THE GODS GO A-BEGGING'

From Newgate to Botany Bay

'All I tell thee is a faint picture of reality; the filth, the closeness of the rooms, the furious manner and expressions of the women towards each other, and the abandoned wickedness, with which everything bespoke, are quite indescribable.'

—Elizabeth Fry, Newgate Prison, London, December 1813

The men, women and children who were convicted at the Old Bailey, London Gaol Delivery or the Middlesex Sessions were believed to be 'of the lowest and worst description' of the criminals of Great Britain. That almost 44 per cent of the women transported from England, Scotland and Wales had been tried in the metropolis confirmed the opinion that the women of Botany Bay were vicious, depraved, irreclaimable scum, 'the refuse of London'. Whatever may have been the motivation for their crimes, whether they had become part of London's criminal poor by necessity, by distress or by inclination, they were, to their respectable contemporaries, Newgate women who belonged on the gallows or at Botany Bay. As felons from Britain's most notorious women's prison, they were tainted with the unsavoury and inescapable stigma of women who were not only criminals but 'filthy in their persons, disgusting in their habits, obscene in their conversations'.[1] Some were London-born, others had come to London in search of employment, but all were considered London women, and all were familiar to a greater or lesser degree with the destitution London offered those without employment. All, without exception, knew the impossibility of regaining their 'characters' or securing honest employment after conviction for a major felony and confinement in Newgate Gaol.

The women and girls who came to Botany Bay direct from Newgate Prison were, with very few exceptions, the refuse of the city's criminal population. Ranging in age from eleven to seventy, single, married or widowed, they thieved and stole with impunity from masters, employers, benefactors, fellow-lodgers, relatives, the young, the old, the sick, the lame, the dying, the dead, and each other. Shoplifters, pickpockets, burglars, highway robbers, footpads, prostitutes, receivers, coiners, forgers and cheats, they were found guilty of every conceivable form of theft and assault. They attacked men, women and children violently, on the streets and highways, in the lanes, alleys and courtyards, in lodgings, in public houses and in their dwellings. They abducted infants and young children to strip them of their clothes and abandon them. Seldom was there an acceptable plea of distress to mitigate the offence. The most usual plea for leniency? 'I was intoxicated at the time'; 'I was in liquor'; 'I was very drunk'.[2]

Women tried and convicted in London at the Gaol Delivery, at the Old Bailey, or at Middlesex Quarter Sessions, were returned to Newgate Gaol to await their sentences – death, transportation, confinement in Newgate or the New Prison, or a term at a House of Correction. Most of the women sentenced to death or transportation had been employed at the time of their apprehension. It was probable that some of the accused women claimed an occupation to evade any possible stigma attached to a woman of no trade, the inference being that an unemployed woman lived by thieving or by prostitution. In many cases however, especially those involving theft by servants or former employees, the master or mistress was frequently the prosecutor leaving no doubt as to employment. Thomas Fowler gave evidence against his servant, Ann Barrett (*Sydney Cove*), who had stolen two sheets worth three shillings; Mary Jane Notra prosecuted her servant, Ann Blake (*Experiment*), for stealing clothing worth £2 11s 0d; Eleanor Blake (*Broxbornebury*), charged by her master, Phineas Tayasac, with stealing his watch, watch keys and seal, worth £10 10s 6d, pleaded it had been a gift in return for 'favours'; Jane Clements (*Mary Anne*), stole £62 in banknotes from the Hon. Alexander Murray when he visited her master's house, while Mary Johnson (*Aeolus*), a kitchenmaid, stole six silver teaspoons from her mistress, Mary Ward. All were transported from Newgate Gaol to Botany Bay.

Most of the transported women who gave an occupation at their trial in London or Middlesex were 'in service' as cook, housemaid, chambermaid, washerwoman, charwoman, nurse, nursemaid, or simply 'servant'. Other occupations were varied. They included an orange-seller, twenty-one-year-old Ann Berry (*Speke*) who stole an umbrella, and thirty-four-year-old Harriet Garvey (*Friendship*), a fortune-teller who made bonnets and added to her income by receiving stolen goods at her 'premises' in Frying Pan Alley, Petticoat Lane. Shoplifter Elizabeth Burke (*Speke*), twenty-one, 'washed for a young man, a sailor'. Mary

Clarke, eighteen, shoplifter, said 'I get my living from shoe-binding'. Mary Newman (*Canada*), thirty-four, 'stealing monies from a man': 'I make scissors, razors and spectacle cases'. Jane Nunn (*Sydney Cove*), thirty-four, who 'stole a petticoat from a line', described her trade enigmatically as 'I serve with asparagus'. Ann Rhodes, nurse, stole her employer's jewellery and was sentenced to death. Ann Tyler (*Sydney Cove*), forty-eight, 'worked making soldiers' coats and waistcoats'. Ann Taylor, forty-seven, a rent collector with a young son, received sentence of death for breaking and entering a dwelling house. Ann Horsley (*Canada*), thirty-eight, a chambermaid, stole her master's linen. Sarah Lester (*Glatton*), twenty-two, 'lived servant'. 'Bet' Ozely (*Albemarle*), forty-two, 'was a week woman to my [the prosecutor's] wife; a weekly servant'. Bet described her work as 'I worked journeywork with Mrs Thurston. My husband was abroad'. She received the death sentence for breaking, entering and stealing from her employer, a sentence commuted to transportation. All of these women were transported from Newgate Gaol to Botany Bay.

Most of the crimes of the women of London were offences against the 'working' people of the city, the tradesmen, shopkeepers, publicans and those members of the upper working classes and lower middle classes sufficiently affluent or conscious of their position to employ domestic help. Few women employed in occupations other than that of servant were convicted of stealing from their masters. An outspoken exception was Mary Owen (*Pitt*), who told the judge: 'I was forewoman and I looked on all those bits [the remnants she had stolen] as my perquisites. I had but eight shillings a week. I did a man's work. I have not witnesses, I am a stranger in the place.'

Where the prosecutor had been attacked by a highwaywoman, or was the victim of theft or assault by a prostitute, there was usually insufficient evidence to establish the social or economic status of the victim, apart from the value of the monies or goods stolen.[3] Among the numerous thefts from masters by domestic servants – notorious for their dishonesty – there were only half a dozen cases in which the employer was either upper middle class or a member of the aristocracy. Louisa Smith (*Canada*), nineteen, stole clothing worth £2 17s 6d from Lady Elizabeth Bingham in the house of Lord Lucan in Piccadilly. Margaret Graham (*Wanstead*), twenty-eight, stole goods valued at £3 5s from Stephen Moore, Earl of Mountershell. Twenty-six-year-old Sarah Newton (*Surprize*) from Staffordshire, stole a chair cover from Lady Lindsay. Mary Collins 'had waited on a young lady at Lord Dover's house' and was still 'a room maid, which was a place of trust, and had lived there for more than a year' when she was convicted of shoplifting and sentenced to transportation for seven years.

The servants of the London gentry were either skilled at evading detection or reluctant to jeopardise their living standards by theft. A servant to a gentleman or to a lady could confidently expect to be supplied with clothing of good standard, to have lodgings and food, to receive medical treatment as necessary. The hours were long, wages poor, privacy almost nonexistent, but the benefits of service in a 'good household' outweighed the disadvantages. For many girls and women, service with the gentry or professional classes was one way of escape from the poverty and restrictions of their origins. For family servants in the eighteenth and early nineteenth centuries there was the expected 'indispensable comfort of a servant, ... no gentleman [or lady] wanted to be surrounded by lousy, stinking ragamuffins'.[4] Roy Porter has described in vivid detail the privileged position of family servants of the gentry. Not only were many of the 'old' retainers treated frequently as members of the family, they were also entitled to 'perks' which greatly added to their incomes. Cooks, for example, expected concessions, usually money, from tradesmen for the patronage of the house, and were entitled to sell 'drippings and cinders' from the kitchen for their own benefit. Maids expected and received tips from visitors and frequently inherited their mistresses' cast-off clothing. These benefits were too highly prized to be lost by theft from the household.

Testimonials to 'undeniable character' and recommendations from former employers were obligatory for women seeking positions in 'genteel' establishments. Advertisements requested character testimonials and frequently stipulated 'No Followers allowed', possibly to maintain the reputation of the house and its servants. Women advertising for such positions included information that 'An exceptional recommendation will be given from the family with whom she lives', or, as in the case of 'a middle-aged woman seeking a position as Housekeeper in a small family, or to a single gentleman', specifying that she 'has no objection to confinement, having no encumbrance or followers; can have an undeniable character'. A woman seeking a position as 'Cook in a genteel family or a second cook where a man-cook is kept [is] a person who can have a good recommendation from her last place'.[5]

Loss of character, of course, led to instant dismissal, with the almost certain likelihood of no alternative employment available except 'the streets'. How many of London's prostitutes, those 'unfortunate women of the town' prepared to 'offer themselves for sixpence', were former servants who had lost their places through unwanted pregnancies, cannot be estimated. Not all the serving girls who caught the eye of the master or his sons were as fortunate as Richardson's *Pamela* to become the legal 'mistress' of the household.

Martha Jones (*Mary Ann*) certainly was not. Tried at the Old Bailey in 1790 for stealing from her former masters, Thomas Smith and John Knowles, brandy and wine merchants of Bishopsgate Street, she pleaded that she had been forced to leave her employment because 'there were no women in the house but her, and the men were always taking liberties with her'. Her plea was not accepted as mitigation of her offence. She was convicted and sent to Botany Bay.

Whatever may have been the cause, most of the women transported from London who described themselves as 'servants' had little first-hand knowledge of life in the households of the gentry or aristocracy of England. They were more likely to be familiar with the standards of the boarding and lodging houses, the taverns and public houses, sharing experiences similar to those of Catherine Kelly, thirty-nine-year-old cook to James Robinson, who claimed that the £5 17s she stole from him was wages owed her for the past six months. Her plea was unsuccessful, and she sailed for Botany Bay on the *Alexander*, sentenced to seven years' transportation.

The Newgate women brought with them to New South Wales more than a familiarity with the criminal life of London. They brought the experiences and the stigma attached to women of Newgate. They had shared confinement in England's most notorious women's prison with accused and convicted women from all parts of the United Kingdom. Whatever their circumstances had been before committal, they gained first-hand knowledge in Newgate of the squalor, the filth, the deprivation, the degradation and the hopelessness of life in His Majesty's gaols. It was a life where 'half-naked women, struggling together ... with the most boisterous violence, and begging with utmost vociferation' attempted to get money for food from visitors to the gaol. Elizabeth Fry was shocked at the condition of Newgate's women, and of the children and babies who accompanied their mothers: 'the filth, the closeness of the rooms, the furious manner and expressions of the women towards each other, and the abandoned wickedness, with which everything bespoke, are quite indescribable.'[6]

At the time of Elizabeth Fry's first visit to Newgate in 1815, numbers of the women she described were 'bound for Botany Bay' including most of the women who were to sail on the *Catherine* and the *Wanstead*. One who would have seen Elizabeth Fry was Frances Sage (*Wanstead*), seventeen, under sentence of death for stealing two seals and a ring from John Baykett Jarman. Her excuse? 'I was so much in liquor I did not know what I was doing'. She had little opportunity to be 'in liquor' in the twelve months she spent in Newgate before sailing for Botany Bay. Another was Jane Smith (*Wanstead*), twenty, shoplifter – thirty yards of muslin worth £5 – sentenced in February 1813 to seven years' transportation. Sarah Steward (*Wanstead*), twenty-seven, had stolen a shirt worth eighteen pence from James Lewis. Was she 'known to the court'? Her sentence: seven years' transportation. Justified or not, officials and the 'respectability' of British society considered these women beyond redemption, incapable of reformation, 'of the lowest and worst description, the very scum of the city and the country'.[7]

Newgate's women prisoners came from all parts of the United Kingdom. Their place of trial was not indicative of their native place. The women crowded into Newgate differed from those of their county sisters who had not ventured far from their place of birth, whether it had been Ayr, Penzance, Glamorgan, Kilkenny, Londonderry or Hull. For many of these county women who were sentenced to transportation after trial in their native place, it was probable that the journey by cart or coach to the ship waiting to take them to Botany Bay was as traumatic as the long sea voyage itself.[8]

One characteristic shared by all the Newgate women, whether London-born or not, was their notorious reputation for filth, obscenity and indecency. Elizabeth Fry and her friends were far more concerned with the reformation of the characters of these women than with their criminality. They saw their outward appearances as indicative of their moral degeneration. To these benevolent ladies, the ragged, unwashed, unkempt state of the Newgate women was evidence of their degradation, their complete lack of any moral standards. Their first aim, therefore, was to introduce standards of cleanliness and decent dress, believing that the reformation of the soul would follow the care of the body, and that this reformation of character would be hastened by 'useful toil and constant employment'. It seemed perfectly reasonable and logical to Elizabeth Fry that, by these methods, the women of Newgate could be raised from their brutish state to a decency approaching that which should be expected from their sex. There could be no more dreadful 'proceedings in the women's prison, no more begging, swearing, gaming, fighting, singing, dancing, dressing in men's clothing'.

Did Elizabeth Fry achieve her aims? Were the women transported Newgate after 1815 or 1816 more 'reformed' than their sisters who had been imprisoned awaiting transportation during the past thirty years or so? Elizabeth Fry certainly thought so, especially after she had formed the Association for the Improvement of Females at Newgate. Her emphasis remained on cleanliness, constant work, proper supervision and discipline, regular food, provision of decent clothing and bedding. Elizabeth Fry, as a Quaker, was a modest woman and avoided, as much as she could, publicity for her reformation – or attempted reformation – of the Newgate women. Visitors, however, expressed astonishment at changes brought about by her Association. The Lord Mayor of London expressed his amazement in no uncertain terms: 'instead of a scowl, a leer, or ill-suppressed laugh, I observed upon their countenances an air of self-respect and gravity, a sort of consciousness of their improved character and the altered position in which they were placed'.[9] Unhappily, when these same women were taken from Newgate to the convict transports, the descriptions of their character and appearance did not match these newly-acquired and praiseworthy characteristics.

It was one of the duties of the surgeon to report on the women in his charge during the voyage to New South Wales. Surgeon, Peter Cosgreave, of the *Friendship*, 1818, was highly critical of the lack of personal cleanliness, the immorality and the 'depraved' characteristics of most of the women on their way to Botany Bay. Few were rewarded with the comment 'quiet and industrious' as was Barbara Oliver, or 'quiet' Sarah Chandler. The nearest most of the other Newgate women came to 'acceptable' standards of conduct was 'quiet and filthy', the description of Mary Smith. The following were typical of the entries for Newgate women:

Mary Sheen:
    and female child: abusive and meddling, child dead.

Mary Ann Caffry:
    a thief, prostitute and blasphemous wretch.

Jane Barnes:
a character unworthy of any trust, except what concerns her profession (a thief).

Mary Williams:
a prostitute and insolent.

Emma Groom:
a designing blasphemous wretch and prostitute.

Helen Stewart:
filthy and lazy.

Margaret Duffy:
and four children: insolent and indolently inclined.[10]

The crimes of most of the Newgate women added to their unsavoury reputation. Among those women confined in Newgate gaol when it was first visited by Elizabeth Fry were Elizabeth Cook and Lucy Cooper, both transported on the *Broxbornebury*. Elizabeth Cook, a twenty-year-old servant, showed little evidence of 'the delicacy becoming a female' and certainly none of the milk of human kindness. Housekeeper for a family in New Road, St Georges, her master obtained a search warrant the day his wife died. She had been attended by Elizabeth Cook who had removed the ring from her dying mistress's finger and had stolen many of her belongings. The daughter of the dead woman identified her mother's possessions and Elizabeth Cook joined the women destined for Botany Bay. Lucy Cooper, with her long history of theft, appeared typical of the Newgate women. The day before Christmas 1812 she stole a shift and bedgown from the wife of the publican of the Cow Heel public house, for which offence she was fined one shilling and discharged. Two months later she was convicted for stealing from her lodging-house keeper. Did she have some intention of setting up house for herself? She stole – and managed to carry away – a bed, a bolster, a pair of sheets, a blanket, a tea kettle, a looking glass and a flat iron, all of which she passed out of her window, unobserved by the lodging-house keeper or his wife. At her trial she said she was a shoe-binder who had rented 'one pair of stairs back room furnished at five shillings a week' [*sic*]. Two months after this second offence she was charged with yet another theft from a lodging house and part of the first landlord's possessions were found when her room was searched. A pawn ticket, hidden in her room, led to the recovery of the bed at the nearby pawnbroker's. There were no mitigating circumstances and she joined the *Broxbornebury* on her way to Botany Bay.

Possibly the most reprehensible of 'female' crimes was stealing children. On almost every female transport which sailed from an English port there was at least one London woman who had stolen or assaulted a child for the purpose of stealing its clothes. On the *Alexander* in 1806 there were at least four women convicted of this offence. One, Martha Luke (*Alexander*), aged thirty, had been indicted on three previous occasions. Another, Ann Kelly (*Canada*), had kept the child for two days and stolen its clothes, worth one shilling and sixpence. The value of the clothes would not suggest that the child was from a wealthy or even well-to-do family; nor would the fact that the child was alone or unattended at the time of the abduction. Eighteen-year-old Mary Ann Jones (*Alexander*) stole the pinafore of the child she had abducted – it was worth one shilling and sixpence; Isabella Barnes (*Alexander*), stole the child's frock, worth one shilling and sixpence; Ann Roy (*Indispensable*), a linen frock, value one shilling and sixpence and a fluff skirt, value sixpence; Sarah Jones, who stole a frock worth two shillings from a five-year-old child, pleaded: 'Great distress drove me to do what I have done. If Your Lordship will be merciful to me I will leave London and never leave my native parish any more'. At forty-five Sarah Jones was not given the opportunity to return to her parish. She sailed to Botany Bay on the *Friends*. On that same transport was Mary Longfield who had stripped a child of all its clothes before abandoning it.

What manner of women were these assaulters of children? Mary Dean (*Glatton*) was sixteen and had five detainers against her for similar offences to the one for which she was transported: 'stealing a pair of gold earrings from a child'. Could Sarah Church (*Nile*) be believed when she pleaded 'I was very much in liquor; it is the very first time I ever committed an offence of this sort.' Mary Wilson, sixty-three, a London widow, stole a six-month-old infant, its clothing and a woman's cloak. She was transported to New South Wales on the *Surprize*.[11]

For judges and juries there were no extenuating circumstances for this crime. When Sarah Sims (*Indispensable*) stole a child, two years and nine months old, stripped her of her clothes and abandoned the little girl, sentence was passed with the following judgement (the child had been found abandoned, taken to the workhouse and eventually returned to her parents):

Prisoner, the wickedness and profligacy of your crime is so much superior to anything that we have heard of in this Court, at this session, that it makes it necessary that your judgment should be separated from the common felons and that you should immediately receive the sentence of the Court. The stealing of a few articles of wearing apparel would not itself receive a very severe sentence but when theft is attended with a very aggravated circumstance of depriving parents of a child it becomes in my mind a most gross and most heinous offence. It is in my mind very little short of the crime of murder. I have not words nor will I attempt to describe the feelings of the unfortunate parents who may be thus deprived of their children. I have to lament that the law in this land does not provide a distinct punishment equal and adequate to this act of profligacy of yours. But collaterally the court has power and so far as they have a power considering the offence of which you are convicted so far they will consider that you, not having any feeling for the happiness of others are in a situation to receive the just resentment of the law. I shall proceed to pass on you the severest sentence that the law of the land will permit me to pass, lamenting that I have not the power to pass one more severe than I am now about to do. The sentence of the Court is that you be transported for 7 years to parts beyond the seas to such place as His Majesty by the advice of his privy council shall be pleased to declare and appoint.

That such depraved women, guilty of such offences against children, which should have been abhorrent to all members of their sex, were transported to Botany Bay, did little to enhance the reputation of the women of that colony. Rather did it confirm the assumptions that these Newgate women were completely devoid of the most basic and fundamental characteristics of women. These opinions were strengthened by the evidence of court cases which showed clearly that these abandoned girls and women would steal with impunity from those in similar or even worse circumstances than themselves.

Lodgers in the same house, or sharing the same room, garret or cellar, stole from one another without compassion, without pity. Betsey Clarke and Mary Weston were transported on the *Sydney Cove* for stealing from Johanna Witts who shared their room. Alice Bunting, transported on the *Canada*, stole all the goods of Thomas Gibbs by breaking into his room which was next to hers. Mary Sheen, transported on the *Friendship*, stole the cap, gown and hat belonging to Mary Cummings who shared her lodging-house room.[12]

Nor was there any hesitation in robbing the lodging-house keeper. Eliza Pleasant (*Maria*) stole her landlord's watch and key; Elizabeth Jones and William Dean, who 'passed as man and wife', stole the household goods from their rented room; Mary

Buckley (*Britannia*) stole a pair of sheets and a counterpane belonging to her landlord, John Full, while Sarah Brooks, known as 'Sally', stole the bed, the bedding and the bedclothes in her furnished room, for which she was transported on the *Indispensable*. Mary Hardy (*Indispensable*), the wife of Robert Hardy, was transported for stealing money from her lodging-house keeper, while Charlotte Jennings, who rented a furnished room from Mary Simpson, stole the window curtains, a feather bolster, two pillow cases, a pair of linen sheets and a cotton counterpane, a looking glass, a pillow case and a bed tick. She was transported on the *Earl Cornwallis*. Margaret Watson (*Indispensable*) denied that she had stolen 'two half guineas, one hundred & twenty copper halfpence, a silver teaspoon, value 2/-, a garnet ring set in gold, value 2/- and a muslin apron value 4/-' from her lodging-house keeper, Andrew Quinlon of George's Alley, Field Lane in the Parish of St Andrew, Holborn. Ann Williams, transported on the *Speke*, shared a garret with William Perkins, from whom she stole £2 12s 0d.

The girls and women who stole indiscriminately from fellow-lodgers or from their landlords were not necessarily single women, or women living alone. Ann Johnson, seventeen and unable to read, lived in lodgings in Holywell Lane with her mother, sister and husband. She was transported on the *William Pitt* for stealing goods worth £1 10s 3d from their landlord. Margaret Hughes and Thomas Banks lived and stole together until she was transported on the *Friends* in 1811.

That these women thieved from fellow lodgers, often in the same or worse circumstances than themselves, that they stole almost as an occupation from their lodging-house keepers, added to the vicious, untrustworthy and criminal reputation of the women from London's lower classes.

It was not only the lodging-house keepers who were the victims of London's women thieves. Publicans were almost as popular a target. Forty-five-year-old Elizabeth Jenkins was convicted for stealing twenty-five pewter pots and eight quart pots. This was not her first offence and she was transported on the *Broxbornebury*. Her prosecutor, James Smith, proprietor of 'The Feathers' public house in Edgeware Road, said in evidence that he had lost £19 worth of pewter pots in the preceding five months. He knew the accused who frequently came to his public house and fetched beer for a Mrs Large who had rooms on the first floor of the house in which she lived. Elizabeth Jenkins pleaded that it was Mrs Large's children who used the fry-pan in her garret to melt down the pewter pots.

Publicans were robbed by their customers, their female lodgers, their servants and by women who broke into their premises and stole monies, goods, and, of course, pewter pots. What was the value of these pots? They could be sold to a fence but, more importantly, they could be melted down and used as the basis for counterfeiting coin. Sarah Barnes, transported on the *Mary Ann* was another 'pewter pot thief'. She was apprehended in her house in Cross Lane as she was melting down a pewter pot. She was found to have eight quart pots and five pint pots in her room, all the property of publican Thomas Elliott. Was this also the purpose behind Eleanor Packer's theft of four pewter quart pots and seven pint pots? She, too, was transported on the *Mary Ann*. It is probable that those convicted of the theft of a single pot simply intended to 'fence it'. Ann Lock, tried in December 1796 for the theft of one pewter pot valued at thirteen pence, pleaded: 'Poverty and the distress of my child drove me to it'. There was no mitigating plea by thirty-year-old Elizabeth Moore, transported on the *Britannia* for the theft of one quart pot valued at sixpence, or twenty-nine-year-old Sarah Clifford from Staffordshire, transported on the *Surprize* for the theft of one pewter pot, or forty-year-old Mary Squires, transported on the *Broxbornebury* for stealing one pewter pot worth fourteen pence. The publicans of London would be justified in their belief that the women of London were incorrigible thieves.

The high proportion of women who were second and even third offenders among the women waiting in Newgate to be transported to Botany Bay was further 'evidence' of the flagrant criminality of the convict women. Some of these were the receivers of stolen goods and their case histories suggest that this was their normal 'occupation'. Mary Rogers, transported on the *Broxbornebury* after her death sentence of 1812 was commuted, had been convicted of the same crime and sentenced to a year in the House of Correction in 1809 with 'prior convictions recorded'. Maria Tate, sentenced to death in 1803, despite her plea for mercy: 'I was very much intoxicated at the time', was transported on the *Experiment* in 1804 for uttering counterfeit money. She had already spent a year in the New Prison for a similar offence. Mary Russell, sentenced to death in 1814, was transported on the *Mary Anne* in 1816 for 'uttering [and] had a previous conviction for the same crime.' This was the case with two other women on the same transport – Charlotte Stanley and Mary Luscombe. Both had been convicted of a similar offence in 1810. Margaret Harrington, known as 'Peggy', convicted of 'uttering in 1803', imprisoned for one year, was convicted again in 1809 and sentenced to death. She was forty-five when she arrived in New South Wales on the *Canada*. Were those her only two offences? Without further evidence one can only surmise how she obtained her livelihood – it was said at her trial 'she was supposed to have a child' – between the time she was released from prison and the time she was next apprehended. It is more than probable that the professional women receivers of stolen goods gambled with the possibility of detection and apprehension. Their conviction, or second conviction, could not indicate the actual number of female receivers within the City of London. Their trials, however, do show how seldom they could support their plea for mercy with any mitigating circumstances of distress. Rather than being the 'support' of their children, they were more likely to employ those children and young adults as their thieves. The children – as young as nine years – were sometimes accused and tried with the parent and frequently received the same penalty of death. Ann Tracey, transported on the *Britannia*, was convicted with her nine-year-old son, Peter, who was sentenced to death. He was recommended for mercy on account of his youth. Husbands, too, were tried with their wives for the same offence. Richard White was hanged, his eighteen-year-old wife Mary Ann transported for seven years for receiving the goods he had stolen.[13]

The 'traditional' picture of the convicts as innocent victims sentenced to death or transportation for the theft of a loaf of bread or a pocket handkerchief is difficult to justify on the evidence of an analysis of the offences of the pickpockets, shoplifters, the 'breakers and enterers' of London. Death or transportation were more frequently imposed where there was violence associated with the offence, or the goods stolen exceeded the statutory figure. Highwaywomen were rarely sent to the Houses of Correction, and usually sentenced to death. If any pattern could be established, it was probable that the women transported were usually guilty of the more serious offences, were known to the Court, or were second or third offenders. Pickpockets were outnumbered by shoplifters, shoplifters by 'breakers and enterers'. The pickpockets usually worked alone, the shoplifters in pairs, or accompanied by small children, while burglaries of dwelling houses were frequently committed by gangs. All of these offences added to the belief that London women would steal and thieve wherever and whenever they could and that respectable citizens must be at all times on their guard.[14]

Pickpocketing, or theft from the person, was also linked with prostitution. Prostitution itself was not an indictable offence and the known prostitutes transported to New South Wales were convicted of thefts from the men they propositioned. It was with this group, the 'poor unfortunate women of the town', that the link between criminality and immorality was most evident. It was, however, unusual for the offence to be committed with violence. Pleas varied: 'he dropped his watch and I picked it up'; 'he offered me sixpence to go with him ... I would not go with any gentleman for sixpence' so, believing her reward was insufficient, she stole his watch. Or the theft took place 'after he had slept with her', 'had spent the night with her' or 'had gone to her room'. At least twelve of the women on the *Broxbornebury* had been transported for stealing watches or monies from men they had taken to their rooms. Of all the women transported from London who could accurately be described as prostitutes, the usual age was early to mid-twenties, although Sarah Mills (*Mary Ann*) at thirty-two was 'a widow obliged to go on the streets' and Elizabeth Booth (*Aeolus*) was forty. Not all were London-born – Elizabeth Mandeville, transported on the *Aeolus*, was a black woman. Some were married, as was Charlotte Roberts (*Canada*), who had two children and whose husband worked at Woolwich Docks. She had stolen the watch of the man she took to her room in Drury Lane. Some assaulted their victims. Mary Durant, transported on the appropriately named *Friends*, had 'lured William Gardener to her lodgings and, with two friends, Mary Kite and Elizabeth Ellis, threatened to murder him'. Sarah Bowyer (*Wanstead*), a married woman with 'a husband at sea', and Sarah Grimes, both of whom were sentenced to death for taking John Lewon home – he was lame – and attacking him violently and stealing his money and other goods.

Few of these women pleaded distress – they were more likely to plead 'intoxication' as evidence that they were not entirely responsible for their offences. Martha Doyle (*Speke*), at seventeen one of the youngest, pleaded she had 'no mother and her father cruelly told her to go on the town to earn a living'. Mary Macarthy (*Broxbornebury*) pleaded: 'I am a stranger in the country'. Mary Webb was more direct: 'I am as innocent as a child unborn', while Sarah Smith, transported on the *Experiment* was 'a poor unfortunate girl of the town who should have been in hospital'.

These, however, were the exceptions. There were sufficient numbers of women transported for theft who were identified, by themselves, the Court or the prosecutor, or by the circumstances of the theft, as women of the town, to give credence to the contemporary assumption that the London women transported to Botany Bay were as immoral as they were criminal. In addition, there was the unknown quantity, 'the dark figure', that is, women who were not identified at their trials as casual or professional prostitutes. When Colquhoun's estimate of some fifty thousand harlots and whores on the streets of London itself in 1800 is considered in relation to the number of women actually transported who were street-women, it may be suggested that most of those who lived by prostitution were either 'honest' when it came to the possessions of their client, or undetected, or unprosecuted by the victims.[15] The 'damned whores' of Botany Bay were among the unfortunates who were apprehended, tried and convicted. That there were women sent to Botany Bay who were whores, harlots and prostitutes is beyond doubt. Any key to motivation of distress, economic necessity, destitution or inclination, lies in their subsequent lives in New South Wales.

An analysis of the trials of the women convicted for theft in association with prostitution makes it clear why so many respectable Londoners were convinced that the women of Botany Bay were neither more nor less than habitual prostitutes, who added to the infamy of their 'profession' by robbing their clients. The difficulty is to explain why so few continued their 'occupation' in New South Wales. Catherine Lines, sentenced to transportation in September 1809 for 'feloniously stealing a watch worth £3 from Lemuel Lewellin after taking him to her room', was transported on the *Canada*. She was then aged forty-seven. By 1811 she had married William Noah, a convict clerk in the Lumber Yard who had been transported on the *Hillsborough*. She lived with him until his death at the age of seventy-nine in May 1827, at which time he was a self-employed carpenter. In the Census of the following year Catherine Lines was still living in their house in Phillip Street, Sydney, and described herself as 'housekeeper'. Her husband had kept a journal of events on the *Hillsborough* which was subsequently published. Was he aware of the crime for which his colonial wife was transported?[16]

Two *Canada* women tried together in 1809 were Margaret or Mary Wilby and Martha Hewison. They were transported for 'Feloniously stealing a watch worth £5 from Richard Thomas after taking him to their room'. Margaret Wilby was twenty-two when she was convicted. After arrival in New South Wales she was assigned as servant to Mr Cox and his family at Windsor where she met convict George Morley, transported for seven years on the *Royal Admiral*. They were married at St Matthew's, Windsor in June 1812. Martha Hewison was assigned to W. Hibbard of Parramatta. In October 1819 she married ticket-of-leave man William West and settled at Prospect, where she remained after his death. In 1828 she was listed as a householder with thirty acres, of which twenty were cleared and ten cultivated. Sarah Ann Drayton was transported on the *Wanstead* at the age of thirty-one, for stealing goods from Richard Baines after taking him home with her. She lived as a washerwoman in the colony until her death in 1817 at Windsor. No further convictions were recorded against her.[17]

Accounts of the trials of the women sent to Newgate to await transportation to Botany Bay continued to add to their infamous reputation. What could be expected from girls such as Charlotte Hopkins, convicted of stealing watch and money from the person of John Harwood of Piccadilly? Certainly she deserved to be a woman of Botany Bay. She was a servant 'out of a situation' when she and two other young women met the prosecutor at about half past eleven in the evening. 'She spent a few minutes with him in the passage of Dover Yard and then ran off, taking his watch and purse.' Harwood met her again in a public house three days later and had her searched, but found nothing. She was convicted on the evidence of other witnesses, including a publican who knew her and saw her changing money and a Sarah Thorn who swore she saw her pass Duck Lane with her arm around Harwood. Aged twenty-seven, Charlotte Hopkins/ Pearce was transported on the *Broxbornebury*.

Sarah Adams, also transported on the *Broxbornebury*, had met John Fitheridge and Thomas Jarvis in a public house and had accepted their invitation 'to take a walk with them'. After she had 'been private' with Fitheridge, Jarvis missed his leather bag and £5. Elizabeth Baker took home with her the sailor she met in Westminster. He had his wages of £80 with him in his pocket. It was gone when Elizabeth Baker left him at two o'clock the next morning. These and similar crimes were, to their contemporaries, certain evidence of the immoral characters of the women of London. The more notorious the crime, the stronger the evidence to contemporaries that the women transported to Botany Bay were, without doubt, the dregs and scum of the London underworld of crime, prostitution and vice.

Was this reputation of the women transported from Newgate justified? Were they the 'refuse of London'? From the individual histories of their offences, trials and convictions, there would seem little doubt. In the collective picture – in which there are, of course, many exceptions – the women appear as they are described by their contemporaries. Most could not be classified as the 'casual poor'. A more apt description was morally destitute, for they were women who, without scruple, could and did steal even from those who tried to help them. Elizabeth Heatherall was typical. She stole clothes, food and household goods from the charitable family who 'received her out of the Refuge for Unfortunate Females where she had been ever since she had returned from transportation'. Samuel Ireton and his wife employed her as a servant, giving her food and clothing, possibly from misplaced sympathy for the twenty-six-year-old who had been on her way to New South Wales three years previously when the ship was

taken by the French... she was landed on the Island of St. Antonia... brought back to Portsmouth... with the recommendation from the captain that she be given a free pardon for her good behaviour.

Her theft from her benefactors sent her back on her way to New South Wales where she arrived, this time without incident, on the *Mary Anne* in 1816.

Twenty-year-old Eleanor Connor (*Morley*) had been taken from the Refuge for the Destitute and given a place as a servant. She repaid this by stealing clothes from her benefactor, for which offence she was sentenced to transportation. Pity for these women from Newgate would be as much misplaced as for Ann Butler (*Lord Melville*), who stole household goods from Mrs Sarah Lee 'who had brought her home through charity', or Eleanor Emmett (*Sydney Cove*), who stole from Mrs Mary Pugmire who had 'taken her in because she had left her aunt and was in great distress'.

Were there no 'good women' transported from Newgate Gaol? Contemporaries doubted the extent of Mrs Fry's reformation of the convicted women. The Third Report of the Committee of the Society for the Improvement of Prison Discipline, noted that 'nobody respects Mrs Fry more than we do' but questioned the accuracy and reliability of reports which had claimed that:

The beneficial effects of their [The Ladies' Committees] exertions have been evinced by a progressive decrease in the number of female prisoners recommitted, which has diminished, since the visits of the Ladies to Newgate, no less than 40 per cent.

This 'extraordinary success' was questioned by this Committee on the grounds of lack of documentation: 'names, dates, certainties'.[18] The numbers transported from London did not decrease with the visits of Mrs Fry and her Ladies, even if allowance is made for the overall increase in population, committals and convictions from 1815. Second offenders continued to be sent back to Newgate – this time to await transportation to the only society for which they were considered fit members – the convict colony of Botany Bay.[19]

Mercy was rarely recommended by the jury because of 'good character'. One of the very few in this category was Eleanor Munroe, sentenced to death at the age of twenty-eight for stealing twenty-four yards of linen cloth worth thirty shillings. Of known good character before this offence, her death sentence was commuted to transportation and she sailed for New South Wales in 1815 on the *Northampton*.

Another exception was Catherine Fitzjohn, transported on the *Speedy*. Convicted of stealing clothing from the woman with whom she lodged, she pleaded:

My husband brought those things to me . . . I have been here [Newgate] ever since the Sessions before last and had nothing but what the gentlemen of the jail pleased to give me and my babe. I have no friend in the world.

Had women such as Margaret Bryan and Sarah Ward resorted to crime because of their need to support their children? Transported on the *Speke* in 1808 for shoplifting a shawl worth five shillings, Margaret Bryan had a child in her arms at the time of her trial. Sarah Ward, sentenced to death and sentence commuted to transportation for life in 1818, had 'disposed of forged notes'. She pleaded that she had to support her four small children. What became of those children when she sailed alone for New South Wales on the transport *Janus*?[20]

Very few of the Newgate women petitioned for pardon or for mitigation of sentence, or for permission to remain a prisoner in England rather than be transported to New South Wales. Those who did could either provide supporting evidence of good character, or of 'unsound mind'. Ann Levitt petitioned Lord Sidmouth after her conviction and her request was supported by character testimonials from former employers. She had been a widow for four years and had worked as a cook since her husband's Petition:

her conduct has been satisfactory ... she had been acquainted for some time with Mr. Goodwin ... who was unemployed and seeing his family in such distress ... was inclined to send them some articles to pledge ... and his wife begged ... to send her a gown which she did and was also pledged. By this time she had obtained a situation and asked Mr. Goodwin for her gown as she wanted to take her clothes with her. Mr. Goodwin said he had a note but it was not a good one. If she would go with him he would then show her where to pass it and she could have the money to get her gown out of pledge ...

She was detected and committed, tried and convicted. Her respectable relations and her employers supported her petition and she was one 'good woman' who did not sail for Botany Bay.[21]

Among the women of Botany Bay who had been 'detained' at Newgate were many who had lived in the prison under sentence of death. Although the death sentence was frequently pronounced, it was rarely carried out. Commutation to transportation was usually announced at the end of the Sessions and, until that time, the condemned girl or woman lived under the shadow of impending death by public hanging, with the added terror that her body would be delivered to the surgeons for public dissection. Some of these women under capital sentence saw others who had, like themselves, been 'cast for death', taken to their execution, and they knew that they, too, faced that same fate unless the mercy of commutation of sentence was granted.

One of the few sentenced to death for returning from transportation before the expiry of her sentence and who was extended mercy, was Sarah Cowden. Sarah had been 'delivered to the *Lady Juliana* to be transported to New South Wales', but she had escaped. Convicted in 1789, she was apprehended some three years later and pleaded that she 'has since been well-behaved ... she was at work at the silk way ... she has had an opportunity or two since she got away'. Sentenced to death, the jury and the Court both recommended mercy. The Judge, Lord Keynon, told her: 'If you are let loose I hope you will pursue the same line of industry which you have done according to the character you have been given this day'.

The inference here was that respectability and honest labour were the antidote to criminal propensity. Sarah Cowden, however, was not placing all her trust in her 'industrious character'. She pleaded that she was 'quick with child ... A jury of matrons was empanelled on [this application] ... and they returned

'The gods go a-begging' 101

a verdict that she was with quick-child upon which execution was stayed'. At the end of the Sessions capitally-convicted Sarah Cowden received a free pardon.[22]

There appears little pattern in the verdicts of the Court as to why one woman received a death sentence, another was sentenced to transportation, another fined a shilling, another given a month's imprisonment, all for similar offences. Was it perhaps that 'known' or second offenders were more likely to receive the more severe sentence?

Like the phantoms from a Newgate Calendar of Female Felons, the women sentenced to transportation in the courts of London and Middlesex were returned to Newgate Gaol to await their sentences. Willingly or not, they became a part of that criminal sisterhood of infamous repute. They shared their daily experiences with women waiting to be hanged, to be whipped, to be burnt in the hand, and those as yet unconvicted awaiting trial. They were all part of that prison, part of the infamous and degraded reputation it enjoyed: 'peopled with beings scarcely human, blaspheming, tearing each other's hair, or gambling with a filthy pack of cards for the very clothes they wore which often did not suffice even for decency'.[25]

These were the 'scum, the refuse' of London.

It was from Newgate that those women destined to be women of Botany Bay were taken to their convict transport. They were to begin a new life, a 'life' which was in many cases an alternative to death on the gallows. In all cases it was an alternative to long years of confinement in an English prison.

To the Newgate women, Botany Bay was an unknown prison, but whatever harshness and severities they may have imagined, these could not exceed the realities of the squalor, the degradation, the deprivation of the life they left behind them in London and in Newgate. As women of Botany Bay they would find opportunities beyond any dreams, exceeding even those hopes and ambitions which had led so many county girls and women to seek their fortunes in the great metropolis. So many of these had found instead the horrors of Newgate Gaol.

These Newgate women brought with them to Botany Bay both the familiarity and the despair they had known as part of London's criminal society. They left behind them family, husbands, children and friends. They brought to their new life that taint of criminality and immorality associated with their conviction of major statutory offences. Above all, the reputation of Newgate sailed with them to Botany Bay. Whatever changes there might be in their lifestyles in the penal colony, they would be unable to escape the condemnation and suspicion of the 'respectable' colonists. In the eyes of their contemporaries, these Newgate women would remain 'the scum, the refuse of London ... the disgrace of their sex'.

5
'POOR PETITIONERS' OR 'NOTORIOUS OFENDERS'?

Crime and punishment in Irish society

The Petitioner did not hesitate to acknowledge her Guilt She being extremely in want and distress... Her Husband having previous thereunto inlisted, which caused her to come from Kerry to Dublin in quest of him... whereby Distracted by Disappointment... in conjunction with the intolerable pressure of the foregoing Calamities... Petr has committed the Crime and cause of her present ignominous State...

—The Humble Petition of Judeth Murphy, a Convict
confined in the gaol of Kilmainham under rule of transportation,
Kilmainham Gaol, 5 February 1809

The Irish women transported to Botany Bay formed a distinct and distinctive group within colonial society. As convicts they shared with their English sisters all the infamy associated with proven criminality. As Irish they shared with their men the added stigma of rebellion and treason against King George combined with loyalty to the 'foreign' Church of Rome. In addition to their 'Irishness', many of these convict women came from backgrounds which differed from those of most of the women convicted in England, for more were married women, more were the mothers of young families, more were country women and, apart from the Dubliners, fewer were described as known streetwalkers. Fewer, too, were found guilty of crimes of violence such as assault or highway robbery. On the average, the Irish women who arrived at Botany Bay were an older group than the English women and almost all were aware of the impossibility of returning to their homeland when their sentences were served. Whether that sentence was for seven or fourteen years, the Irish women were technically banished for life from their native land.

At least half of the transported women of Botany Bay had been born in Ireland. The percentage may have been even higher for native-place was not invariably recorded on the trials in Great Britain. About 40 per cent of all the transported women sailed directly from Irish ports during the first forty years of white settlement of New South Wales. In addition, at least 10 per cent of those who were convicted in England had been born in Ireland. These were girls and women who had travelled to England or Scotland alone or with their families in search of work and had committed their offences near their places of employment.[1] One of the first to be transported in this way was Margaret Darnall (*Prince of Wales*), a Dubliner tried at the Old Bailey in April 1787 and transported with the First Fleet.

The first 'English' transport to carry both English-tried and Irish-tried women convicts was the *Kitty* on which fourteen women tried in English courts were joined by two tried in Wales and fourteen from Dublin.[2] The *Kitty* was one of the few exceptions to the general pattern which was to follow, for there appeared to be no clear-cut decision as to whether convicts should be transported directly from Ireland, brought to England to join 'English' ships, or whether convict transports should sail to New South Wales from England via Ireland to pick up Irish deportees.

The main concern of the English government was that transportation expenditure be kept to a minimum. William Richards, who had been the contractor for the First Fleet convicts, wrote to Nepean on 16 October 1792, enclosing terms for carrying Irish convicts to New South Wales. Richards proposed sailing to both Dublin and Cork. The Navy Office, anxious regarding cost, asked Dublin Castle to send all details of numbers to be transported and where the prisoners were confined. The reply received in London in October 1792 showed not only the numbers in Ireland awaiting transportation – as distinct from those sentenced to transportation – but also indicated the official attitude as to how the Irish were to be shipped to New South Wales. Cost was the major determinant. About 230 men and forty women (a ratio of slightly less than six to one) were waiting to embark for New South Wales:

The most convenient place for shipping them would be this Port [Dublin], as much the greater proportion of the convicts are now in the gaols of this City and County and the situation being central, the prisoners could be collected here from other ports with more facility and with less expense.

Such a vast number would need a ship 'of considerable dimensions' if all the men and women were to be transported at once. This added a navigational problem, for a large ship 'might not easily get over the Bar into the harbour [Dublin] and the Bay is too open and exposed to admit of a vessel lying there with safety in the winter'.

The solution proposed from Dublin was that two ships be employed, one to sail from Dublin the other from Cork Cove 'to which place the convicts might be ordered from the other counties of the kingdom'. Downing Street rejected this proposal, whether because of the probable difficulties of Dublin Harbour or because of the added cost of fitting out and contracting for two ships instead of one is not known.[3] What is known is that, except on rare occasions, convicts sentenced in Ireland embarked at Cork Cove on vessels which carried only Irish men and women. This was significant for Irish prisoners because it meant that the colonial officials in New South Wales were well aware that every transport which came to the colony directly from Ireland carried men and women identifiable as 'Irish', and who could therefore be expected to cause civil disobedience and dissension in the colony. This fear of the lawlessness of the Irish was not lessened by any specific knowledge of the crimes for which most of the Irish were transported, for few of the early 'Irish' convict ships carried detailed criminal records for either men or women. The *Minerva* was an exception, and the nature of the crimes listed under the heading 'characters explained' added to the belief that most were transported for political offences, seventy-four of the convicts on board the *Minerva* being identified as 'political' criminals and a further seven 'self-transportees'.[4]

Was it that the fear of rebellion had lessened by the 1820s? In September 1819 British officials were again considering the feasibility – and the cost – of bringing Irish convicts to England to embark for New South Wales, or of sending ships with English convicts to Ireland before departure for New South Wales. On 17 September Downing Street was advised by Dublin Castle that 'there are between fifty and sixty female convicts awaiting transportation. They will be furnished with clothing here and it will not be necessary to furnish any stores of that description in England'.[5]

It was at this time that both the *Janus* and the *Lord Wellington* embarked female convicts from both England and Ireland.

For colonial officials, 'Irish' was synonymous with Irish-tried. There was little, if any, recognition of the significance for colonial society, or of any possible dangers to the settlement, from the numbers of transported Irish-born men and women who were tried in English courts and transported from England. That Irish convicts and 'English' convicts sailed to New South Wales on different transports stressed the national differences. That Irish-born were tried and convicted in England, imprisoned in English gaols and transported on 'English' ships lessened to some extent the antagonism which existed in England and in the colony between the two national groups.

Perhaps more importantly, it meant that an unspecified number of Irish-born men and women arrived at Port Jackson as technically 'English' convicts and were treated as such by the colonial authorities.

In the counties of England the Irish women sentenced to transportation were almost invariably family women who were working as servants at the time of their offence, that offence being in most cases theft from their employers. Most had children but few were given permission to have their families follow them to New South Wales. Many of the husbands were former Irish farmers or country labourers who were welcomed in the English farming counties for they would 'reap the wheat' for lower wages than those demanded by the local labourers. This could and did lead to resentment against the Irish intruders, which was often expressed in riots, disturbances and physical assaults. In Bassingbourne in Cambridgeshire, a local disturbance was reported in the *Chronicle*:

Large portions of labourers of the Parish assembled together in a riotous and tumultuous manner, with a view to driving the Irishmen, who the farmers employes to reap their wheat, out of the Parish, many of them were beaten and others ran off thro' fear of further ill-usage ... the ring'leaders [were] arrested and placed in the County Gaol ... We insert this Caution to others against insulting or otherwise treating poor men, who take so much pains and suffer so many hardships to procure support for themselves and their families in a country where they have no Poor Rates to supply their wants.[6]

Not only were there frequent reports of these riots and disturbances among the English farming labourers and the immigrant Irish harvesters, there were also numerous accounts in London newspapers of 'affrays' and 'civil disturbances' in the city which were attributed directly to 'the barbarous and foreign practices of the Irish' and their 'turbulent and quarrelsome natures'. Irish weddings, funerals and christenings were notoriously responsible for many riotous clashes between English and Irish inhabitants of London's poorer districts. On 24 June 1793 the London *Morning Herald* reported a typical 'dreadful affray ... Early on Sunday morning ... in Oxford Buildings near Oxford Road'. The tone of this report is typical of the 'affrays' caused 'by chiefly Irish persons':

A large party of labouring persons of both sexes, chiefly Irish, had been collected at the house of one of them upon the occasion of a child's death. A dispute between an English and an Irishwoman interested the men, on both sides; and the latter, being by far the most numerous, not only conquered the English, of their own party, but began to commit violences in the neighbourhood. The watchmen were beaten, and the Capt. of the Paroles was so severely wounded that he is since dead. A party of the Foot-Guards who arrived about three in the morning, were assailed by brick-bats, one of which struck Lord Stoppard, the Commanding Officer, but the Military were immediately able to seize fifty-four of the rioters, of whom fourteen were lodged in Mount-Street Watch House, and forty in that of Marybone.

—*Morning Herald* (London), 24 June 1793

Incidents such as these not only added to ill-feeling against the Irish in England by officials, the military and the Watch but added fuel to the belief that they would be troublemakers and malcontents, the cause of disturbances in the penal colony of New South Wales.

Although these 'English' disturbances were seen as caused by the Irish-born living in England, there is no corresponding evidence to show any awareness by officials that Irish-born convicts on English ships were inherently a greater threat and danger to the safety and security of the voyage than their English-born messmates. Nor were the Irish-born women convicts tried in England seen as deeply 'steeped in infamy' as those on Irish transports. Riotous and rebellious behaviour was certainly expected from the Irish women transported on 'Irish' ships as much as from their men. Governor Hunter summed this up when he reported on the infamous behaviour of the Irish women who assisted their countrymen to mutiny on the way to New South Wales by grinding up glass and concealing it in the seamen's rations. 'What an importation!'[7] Such behaviour was to be expected from the refuse of Ireland.

There was little, if any, report of dissension based on nationality between English and Irish women transported on the same ship. Disputes and differences were almost invariably of a personal nature. Women from Dublin and women from London, women from Wicklow and women from Aberdeen, women from Donegal and women from Lincoln, women from most of the counties of England and Ireland sailed together as convicts, shared the same confined quarters, the same experiences, the same fears and hopes on the many months of the long voyage to the prison colony of Botany Bay. These experiences lessened the loneliness which faced so many women who suffered the added punishment of banishment from those who spoke their own dialect, who knew their own villages, towns or districts, who were familiar with all that was left behind. These women were to share the same conditions, the same opportunities, the same hardships in the colony, and the links and friendships formed on their transport ship, despite differences in dialect or native place, are evidenced in their everyday colonial lives, especially in the numbers who witnessed each other's marriage or the baptism of their children.

In Botany Bay there was widespread fear of the Irish convicts. This fear and the disruption, disobedience, turbulence and even rebellion they were assumed to be bringing to Botany Bay was particularly marked during the years immediately following the Rebellion of 1798. Almost every man, woman and child arriving convict from Ireland was regarded as being capable of treachery, treason and murder. Elizabeth Paterson, the lady wife of Colonel Paterson, expressed this dread in a private letter to her uncle in London, written shortly before the arrival of the *Minerva* with its cargo of 'political prisoners'. 'We shall all be murdered in our beds ... my fear is private assassination', for that was the 'habit' of the lawless Irish in their own country.[8] Few of the convicts on the *Minerva* could be described with accuracy as 'treasonable miscreants', dangerous cut-throats, but this was unrecognised in the colony. Their 'Irishness' was sufficient to damn them, one and all, as a threat and a danger to the colony. As for the women, they were believed to be 'far worse than the men', typified by that prototype of a rebellious, murderous Irish convict woman, transported convict Elizabeth Mulhall.

Elizabeth Mulhall was twenty-five when sentenced to die on the gallows of Kilkenny in the summer of 1800. She had been actively involved in the Rebellion of 1798 and was 'known to the English authorities'. So well-known that, when the despatch containing a report on her arrest and forthcoming trial was received by the English Cabinet, an instruction was despatched from Downing Street to the Lord Lieutenant of Ireland at Dublin Castle, urging that no mercy be shown Elizabeth Mulhall, no mitigation of sentence considered, and that she be punished relentlessly to the full extent of the law: 'Elizabeth Mulhall is an infamous character ... A plotter of most of the murders of the informers who were sacrificed in the County of Kilkenny'.

Was it that the judge in Ireland did not take kindly to instructions from Downing Street as to the verdict and sentence in a trial in his court? For whatever reason, mercy was shown Elizabeth Mulhall and instead of death on the gallows she was transported for life to Botany Bay. There she became the wife of a wealthy ex-convict trader and dealer who, shortly after their marriage, became insane, leaving his wealth in the hands of his wife. She later married another ex-convict, a landowner who was found drowned in his well within a few years of the marriage. That 'infamous plotter', Elizabeth Mulhall, again inherited a husband's wealth and lived comfortably in the colony until her death from natural causes in her late seventies. What had remained unnoticed when she was transported was that her crime was almost unique among the approximately 3000 Irishwomen who came as convicts to Botany Bay during the first forty years of white settlement.[9]

It was not only English officials who perpetuated the belief in the disruptive tendencies of the Irish convicts in New South Wales. The *Freeman's Journal* (Dublin) published reports, comments and news items from the convict colony, many of which emphasised the lawlessness, plots and schemes of the Irish in Australia. In January 1802 the *Freeman's Journal* published the full text of a Government Proclamation in New South Wales:

Notice: Notwithstanding the leniency shown to those concerned in a former attempt to create confusion in this Colony, yet it appears that several restless and turbulent characters are still forming designs to promote their diabolical schemes, for the destruction of all industry, public and private property, order and regularity; and to introduce murder, plunder and every kind of horror and confusion ... Disposed as the Governor has been not to credit any information he has received, yet the many corroborating evidences that have been given, compels him to take the necessary measures for securing the peace of the colony. Anxious to believe that these evil designs are only the frenzy of a few turbulent wretches whose aim is confusion he is willing to hope that when the different descriptions of persons in this colony reflect on the comforts and blessings they enjoy and may acquire in this colony by a very moderate industry, and the expectations that every prisoner may entertain that if his behaviour is honest, industrious and irreproachable, that he will in measure benefit by it ...

The *Freeman's Journal* added the comment that this Proclamation seemed to insinuate:

that there have been not only some insurrectional movements in the colony, but that subordination was not completely restored at the time of the Proclamation's publication ... it appears ... Botany Bay has become somewhat disturbed by traitors and incendiaries and it is not unlikely that some of them are miscreants of that description whom the laws have driven from this country, and what strengthens this opinion is that the mode said to be pursued there is similar to what miscreants practiced here, viz Secret and Anonymous inflammatory writings.

The Irish advice to the colonial Governor was 'to adopt all circumspection and vigilance he is master of, to prevent agitations and conspiracies against him, and the utmost he can do will not be more than sufficient'.[10]

Imagined or real insurrections in New South Wales added strength to the conviction that the transportation of Irish convicts would lead to risings and rebellions. Both Hunter and King were convinced that the conspiracy of 1800 was a planned insurrection, the work of that arch-plotter the convict priest Father Harrold and the transported United Irishmen. The would-be rebels had intended to imprison the departing Governor, Hunter, and to hang the new Governor, King. That so little official reprisal followed the abortive 'rising' may have indicated that the Governor believed it was only the minority of recently arrived Irish rebels who had been responsible. Father Harrold was simply publicly disgraced and sent to Norfolk Island.[11] After the Castle Hill Rebellion in 1804 there were ample grounds for the colonial officials to enforce stricter regulations to control possible rebels amongst the Irish convicts. That these rebels, and those of 1800, were almost exclusively convicted felons from Ireland, a country where so many of the inhabitants were not loyal to King George, was more significant than the fact that most were Catholic. As Marsden had so correctly observed 'when men become convicts, a difference of religious opinions is hardly discoverable amongst them'.[12] The combination of the known 'turbulence' of the Irish and their proven criminality by conviction for major statutory offences was sufficient to alarm the good citizens of Botany Bay. There were those among the colonial civil and military officials who could recall the terror that the 'viciousness' of Irish mobs had created in both Ireland and England. The *Morning Star*, for example, had reported on 10 March 1794:

By a letter from a respectable gentleman in Cork we learn the report of the mob having a guillotine was utterly unfounded, as was also that of their having planted the tree of liberty. They confined themselves entirely to taking and administering certain oaths to oppose certain laws.[13]

That credence had been given to the rumours of the bloodthirsty activities of the rebels was ample evidence of the fear and

112 The Women of Botany Bay

terror uprisings or threat of uprisings caused in Ireland. How much greater was that terror in a colony where almost every 'Irish' man and woman was also a convicted felon and where the convicts so greatly outnumbered the guards and the military?

The percentage of Irish women who came directly to the colony on the Irish convict ships was large enough to warrant that 'dread and fear' of the influence of Irish convicts on colonial society. In the first years of settlement, however, their numbers were small, the specific crimes, class origins and backgrounds unknown. The first transport to bring convicts directly from Ireland was the *Queen*, a former merchantman which sailed from Cork Cove in April 1791, arriving in Port Jackson the following September. On board were twenty-three Irish convict women (one died on the voyage) and four of their children. A free woman sailed with them, Mrs Ann Jamieson, the wife of Sergeant Jamieson of the New South Wales Corps; one hundred and twenty-six Irish convict men were also embarked at Cork. This was, in a sense, an experimental voyage for it was not yet assured that the convict colony would be a success. Nor were there definite regulations formulated as to which of the many men and women under sentence of transportation should be chosen to sail to Botany Bay.

The convict women on the *Queen* were not representative of the whole of Ireland. Fifteen were from Dublin, three from Armagh and one each from Kilkenny, Waterford, Limerick and Queen's County. Why these particular women were chosen is not known. The youngest was Mary Whelan, eighteen, a convicted Dublin rogue and vagabond, the oldest Margaret Stephenson, fifty, from Armagh. Most were in their early twenties and all except two sentenced to seven years' transportation. Four were accompanied by young children: Sarah Brennan from Dublin who embarked with her two-week-old daughter Margaret, Mary Connor with nine-month-old Judy Connor, Catherine Edwards with two-year-old son John, and Bridget McDonnell with one-year-old daughter Betty. Was there any official concern that these young children were going to a convict colony barely established as a struggling penal camp? Why were these particular women chosen from the crowded gaols and places of confinement throughout Ireland? Only two had been confined for more than a year; Bridget Nowlas [*sic*] was convicted in 1789 and Ann Slater had been confined 'under rule of transportation' since 1788 which did not suggest that the gaolers were ridding the gaols of those who had been confined for many years. What was to happen to the majority of these women whose sentences would expire

Poor petitioners' or 'notorious offenders'? **113**

some five or six years after arrival in New South Wales? These were questions and problems which do not appear to have been given serious consideration by either English or Irish authorities.

None of the women of the *Queen* are known to have returned to Ireland. Catherine Edwards from Dublin is believed to have been 'the pregnant woman' who attempted to escape from the colony with a party of twenty 'recently arrived' convict men (presumably from the *Queen*) in November 1791. The party had taken a week's provisions, tools and implements and had 'absconded . . . with the chimerical idea of walking to China or finding a settlement in this country where they would be received and entertained without labour'. They met with mishap, misfortune, accident, spearings by natives, and starvation, most returning to the settlement in 'a wretched and pitiable condition'. The pregnant woman from the *Queen* fared worst of all. This 'wretched female'

> had been separated from them [the men] for three days and wandered by herself, entirely ignorant of her situation, until she came to the water-side, where, fortunately, she soon after met the boat. Boats were sent down the next day and the woman's husband brought up from the settlement . . .

If this woman were Catherine Edwards, and she is the most likely among those who had arrived on the *Queen*, she was 'very near her time', for Thomas Driscal Edwards was born in January 1792. Her experiences 'lost in the Bush' did not appear to cause her permanent harm. Her 'husband', Dennis Driscoll, died at Parramatta in March 1792 and in 1796 she married Wickham Yearly at St John's, Parramatta. He received a conditional pardon the following year and they settled without further incident on land at Windsor.[14]

The women of the *Queen* were the first pioneer Irish-Australians. The way in which several faced the difficulties of a new settlement and showed the enterprise necessary to take advantage of the opportunities offered rather than succumb to the disadvantages, the difficulties, the privations and the dangers, exemplifies the responses of so many of the Irish women who were to arrive on the following transports. Some, such as Elinor McDonald, could be described as the prototype of the convict women who succeeded with their partner/husband. Others, like Ann Slater, managed mainly through their own efforts to become successful and independent landowners and farmers. Still

114 *The Women of Botany Bay*

others, such as Mary Davidson from Armagh who married Simon Burn, or Catherine Devereux who cohabited with Thomas Hill, were examples of the moderate success which made these former convict women self-supporting and independent in their adopted country, successes which, in exchange for enterprise, industry and perseverance, ensured the well-being of any colonial-born children.

Elinor McDonald had stolen 'a metal watch, chain and locket, value six guineas', a crime typical of the women convicted in Dublin. After six months in Sydney, she was sent to the settlement at Norfolk Island. Here she met Jonathon Griffiths, one of the four convicts chosen by Governor Phillip to accompany the settlers and the members of the New South Wales Corps who sailed to Norfolk Island on the *Supply*. McDonald and Griffiths remained on Norfolk Island until 1796, when they returned to the mainland and settled on one hundred acres granted Griffiths at Richmond, on the right bank of the river, just above the present bridge. This former Dublin thief lived on her property, until her death in 1831, by which time she was the earliest female settler still living in the Hawkesbury District. Many of her nine children had remained as settlers in the area. As Griffiths was a boatbuilder, he was frequently away from their property, and it was Elinor McDonald who was largely responsible for the management of the farm and the care of the two additional rented farms which Griffiths had settled on her in 1812. She was buried in the Richmond Church of England cemetery, and it was noted in the church records that 'a Roman Catholic priest officiated at the graveside'. Elinor McDonald/Griffiths, convicted thief, wife, mother, property-owner, had come a long way from the streets and lanes of Dublin.[15]

Bridget Nowlas or Nowland of the *Queen* had arrived in the colony at the age of thirty-seven, and showed the forthright and assertive manner by which so many of her convict countrywomen demanded the protection of their achievements in the penal colony. In 1810 she wrote to the newly-arrived Governor Macquarie requesting that he forthwith renew her lease on her house and property at The Rocks, Sydney. Lieutenant-Governor Paterson had granted her the lease some fifteen years previously. She informed Governor Macquarie that she had been in the colony nineteen years and during all that time 'had conducted herself well ... and by persevering application and honest industry had supported two children whose father had been drowned on a voyage to Lord Howes [*sic*] Island'. She had lived with John Evatt who had been transported from Ireland on the

Minorca. Together they had farmed fifteen acres at Richmond. Bridget Nowland, convicted Dublin thief, was granted the renewal of her leasehold. In the Muster of 1814 she was described as 'widow, free, off stores, Sydney'. Her sentence to penal servitude in 1789 had led to respectability, independence and material success.[16] Neither Bridget Nowlas nor Elinor McDonald conformed to expectations of the role of Irish convicts in New South Wales.

The backgrounds of the women tried in Ireland changed very little during the years which followed the departure of the *Queen*, nor did their overall responses to colonial life. It was the poverty of the people, the deprivation, hardship and starvation combined with revolt, rebellion, insurrection and civil disturbances which characterised Irish society of this period rather than the increasing industrialisation which characterised contemporary English society. The poverty of the working men and women and of many of the 'middling order' of Ireland is graphically evident in the description of diet in the various counties of Ireland which was included in 'Notes on the Corn Bill' published in the *Limerick Evening Post* on Saturday, 7 January 1815. The extract was taken from *A Statistical Survey of Ireland*, which reported that in Kilkenny 'the labourers live entirely on potatoes and milk'. In Adamstown, County Waterford, 'the food of the lower classes is chiefly oatmeal and a little milk'. In other parts of Waterford 'their food is generally potatoes and milk with a little change on festive days'. In County Clare

> the food of the middling order is potatoes milk and butter. The food of the very lower is extremely poor, being potatoes and sour milk for nine months of the year and potatoes and salt for about three months ... This poverty of diet creates poverty of [constitution?] and their confining themselves entirely to potatoes, generates scurvy and scrophulous disorders among them.

The poor and the 'middling order' of Irish counties seldom 'partake of animal food'. In County Meath they very occasionally had butter and eggs. In County Antrim potatoes and milk were the basic diet, and 'some have a little bacon or herrings, a little beef; others nothing during the winter but the poor man's diet of potatoes and salt'. In County Cork, 'a few of them' had meat on some Sundays as a supplement to their staple potatoes and milk. In Maghera, in the County of Londonderry, the chief food of the poor was the salted herrings brought in abundance from Scotland. This, 'together with the scarcity of milk ... renders them subject to many diseases'.

This was the diet familiar to most of the women transported from Ireland. In 1814, the year of the survey, there were fifty-four women in Irish gaols waiting for the transport to take them to New South Wales.[17] Two were in Antrim, Sarah McGrady and Catherine Neal, and four in Cork, Honora Barrett, Mary Bryan, Mary Casey and Mary Farrel. In all probability, none had known any diet other than that of potatoes and a little milk, and this, meagre as it was, was of a higher standard than the gaol rations. That these women had survived on such a basic and inadequate diet and had also lived through the many diseases so widespread among all the inhabitants of Great Britain, from measles and other child-killers to smallpox and venereal diseases, was strong evidence of the basic sturdiness of their constitutions. The change to rations issued on the convict transports and the still greater variety of diet in New South Wales, especially when the women were assigned as domestic servants, housekeepers and cooks, was in complete contrast to that staple diet of potatoes and a little milk most had known since their childhood.[18]

This familiarity with poverty, insufficient and inadequate diet, is also evident in the petitions from convicted Irish women to the Lord Lieutenant of Ireland, beseeching him to 'look with your usual humanity' at the plight of the poor petitioner and grant pardon or commutation of sentence.[19] These petitions also evidence a characteristic of so many of the transported Irish women which was to be determinative in their responses to colonial life. This was that most were family women with dependent children. Allowing for the natural bias in the pleas of the woman herself, or of those who wrote on her behalf, the petitions give vivid insight into the poverty, the hopelessness and the despair of so many women separated from their children, facing exile from their native land with the knowledge that those children must remain in Ireland, in many cases 'unprotected' and without any means of sustenance.

These petitions from female felons confined in Irish gaols show graphically the desperation of women awaiting transportation and still endeavouring to support infants and young children 'on the Gaol Allowance' or on 'the Charity of a Benevolent Publick'; women fearful for the future of children 'all dependent [on the imprisoned mother] for support and who must inevitably go to ruin'; women such as Charlotte Kavanagh who petitioned in 1807 that she had been convicted in Wicklow, taken to Dublin, then to Cork two years before and now 'that the Bottany [sic] ship has sailed three months ago petitioner was dayly expecting her pardon', an expectation which was not realised for this 'poor woman ... with five helpless Children whose Father was killed in the late Rebellion'.[20]

Margaret Delaney (*Almorah*) was a first offender, a married woman, the mother of two children, who had stolen a child's wearing apparel worth one shilling and eight pence. Employed as a housemaid at Cork, she begged not to be transported for the sake of her young children 'who if thrown upon the mercy of the world ... must certainly perish, the eldest being only Three Years of Age'. She also claimed she was innocent: she had simply pawned the child's clothing on behalf of another woman living in Cork. Her petitions were to no avail. What became of her infant children is not known, for there is no record of their arrival in New South Wales. Neither can the emotions of Margaret Delaney be reconstructed as she worked as a servant in the Parramatta Female Factory, knowing that she would never again see her homeland, her husband or her children. Did she continue to maintain her innocence of the crime which had cost her so dearly? Did she silently or vocally rebel against the cruelty of a blind justice impervious to all pleas for mercy? If so, she was not alone among the Irish female convicts transported to Botany Bay.[21]

The increasing number of convicts transported after the Napoleonic Wars, meant that more and more family women boarded the convict transports at Cork Cove, leaving infants and young children in Ireland. The proportion of married Irish women with children was far higher than the proportion of married women transported from English ports. The *Almorah* was a typical example of an Irish transport on which most of the women were married but few were accompanied by their infants or children.

Catherine Blake of Kildare, who could 'wash and make butter' was living in County Dublin when apprehended for the theft of 'some geese and hens'. She did not question the verdict but pleaded for mitigation of the sentence of transportation, for 'she had five small children who have no other support ... and are now left in a most destitute and forlorn state ... ' Her distress had aggravated health problems and she had been subject to 'frequent attacks of the falling sickness' since her confinement. Whether or not this 'falling sickness' was a ploy to gain respite from transportation, it did not affect the decision of the Lord-Lieutenant any more than the plight of the 'orphaned' children. Catherine Blake was taken from Kilmainham Gaol to Cork Cove and put on board the *Almorah* for that long voyage of exile from family and homeland.[22]

The *Almorah* was not unique. By the 1820s there were more

and more women on every transport which sailed from Cork who had petitioned for mitigation of sentence on account of their 'helpless children' whose fathers were either dead, or serving 'abroad' in His Majesty's navy or army. Few claimed to have husbands already serving sentences at Botany Bay. Most claimed, as did Catherine Stafford, that they were 'the sole support for their children'. Catherine Stafford, of 'sandy complexion, a little freckled, with dark brown hair and blue eyes', was a needlewoman and washerwoman from Cork who had been convicted of forgery in April 1820. She petitioned for clemency, saying she was 'the Mother of Eight children without a Father living, Solely depending upon Petitioner to Support them, without means but her daily Labour and Industry'. She also pleaded her innocence of the offence, claiming her former known good character. She had been prosecuted as an accomplice because 'she had lodged in a house where coining implements had been found'. The 'dead' husband was reunited with her in New South Wales, where he had been transported about five years previously and was still in government service. The indents of the *John Bull* did not name the twelve children who sailed with free or convict parents, but Catherine Stafford was noted as arriving with two children, Mary, twelve, and James, nine. By 1828 she had another daughter, Margaret, born in the colony in 1823. She continued to live with her Irish husband and, at the time of his death in March 1830, she was a shopkeeper in Pitt Street, Sydney. In that same year Catherine Stafford petitioned the governor to have her son Thomas assigned to her. Was this one of the six children she had left behind in 1819?[23]

That so many older Irish women, married or widowed, with children to support, were transported to New South Wales, raises questions and problems which must remain unanswered. Unanswered, that is, on the basis of quantitative evidence. What were the emotional effects of sentence of banishment from infants, young children and husbands, the knowledge that those children faced destitution, poverty, starvation, when the mother was exiled at distant Botany Bay, never to return to her homeland. How can these fears be measured as the lawful punishment for crime?

Was it fear for the infant she had had to leave behind in County Monaghan that caused Jane Shaw (*Almorah*) to suffer hysteria on the voyage to New South Wales?[24] And what of the attitude of Irish officials, from the Lord-Lieutenant who turned a deaf ear to all petitions from Irish mothers begging they be not separated from their 'defenceless babes' to the more humane gaolers, chaplains, surgeons and gaol inspectors who added testimonials to appeals for mitigation? Who can know what lay behind the actions of Catherine Marum (*Almorah*), born in County Kilkenny, working in Waterford ('she sews, spins and makes butter') and convicted at the age of twenty-five of theft from a dwelling? Catherine Marum, tall among her contemporaries, being five feet four inches, with pale freckled face, brown hair and grey eyes, had twins on board the *Almorah*, and both died. She named them Mary and Kitty McCarty, the father being McCarty the under-gaoler at Cork. Did Catherine Marum have hopes that she would evade exile from her native land through the influence of her gaoler?

There is no evidence of any official concern at local or central level for the well-being or care, or even subsistence, of children left alone in Ireland. In some cases the children were with the fathers; in others, it would appear probable that they had been left with grandparents when the mother, sometimes the father, went in search of employment in neighbouring towns or in Dublin City. What became of the children when their older guardians died, or when grandparents were unable to support their grandchildren, is unknown. Some may have become the 'desolate Boys', the juveniles received into penitentiaries and houses of industry after the commission of crimes or after being charged as vagrants. Others may have volunteered for naval or military service. Still others, both girls and boys, were themselves to be transported to New South Wales.[25]

The greatest effect for New South Wales was the influx of older family women, women who had been convicted mainly for thefts of clothing, food, animals or monies, women who had lived as married family women in Ireland and were transported as technically single women, bringing only the memory of their families to New South Wales and the despair for the motherless children whom they could not expect to see again.

Was it because they knew of no other lifestyle than that of family women that so many remarried in the colony, with or without 'benefit of clergy'? A cautious estimate would indicate that at least two-thirds of the women who had left children in Ireland married within a few years of arriving in New South Wales. In rare cases, the colonial husband was the Irish husband who had preceded his wife to the colony. One of these rare exceptions of resumed marriage was Mary Ann Bryan.

Mary Ann Bryan was listed in 1826 as 'ux Michael Bryan (Prisoner)'. This was the husband who had preceded her to the colony as a convict. The couple applied for and received permission to marry in the colony. Why they considered this necessary is unknown. There is no record that they were joined by their two children left in County Kildare.[26]

Many of the younger women transported on the *Almorah* who had been married in Ireland were listed as 'married in the colony' by 1826. Ellen Campbell, her husband in County Antrim, was twenty-three when listed as 'ux Thomas Brown (Prisoner)'; Bridget Carroll, with a husband and child in Limerick, married Michael Purtell, convict, in 1825, as did Ann Jennings with a husband and child in Cork and Mary Harvey with husband and two children in Queen's County. Two women listed as 'widows', Mary Hartigan, with an orphan child in Limerick, and Mary Ryan, with two children in Mullingar, were married in Sydney in 1825. Mary Ryan had obviously improved her 'violent and intemperate disposition' for which she had been handcuffed during the voyage to Botany Bay. Was it that all these 'family' women knew only a lifestyle as 'married' women? Was it that they had realised the impossibility of returning to their Irish families? It was not only the younger women convicts, but the women of forty, fifty, and over, who began new lives as colonial married women. Mary Coglan was forty-eight when she petitioned the governor for permission to accompany her husband John Creighton to Port Macquarie. Anne Connell was forty-six when Michael Hines applied for permission to marry her. After his death, she worked as a servant to William Todhunter and his wife Elizabeth in Cumberland Street, Sydney. Did she remember her seven children and her first husband who had remained in Cork?[27]

Among the women transported on the *Almorah* who had petitioned in vain for clemency for the sake of their children was Mary Coghlan, a 'very freckled, pale complexioned woman of forty-seven, with brown hair and blue eyes', who was convicted in Limerick City in July 1823. She petitioned the Lord-Lieutenant for mitigation of her sentence: she was

a Poor Widow with a Family of Three Children who are in a deplorable and wretched condition in Limerick City ... their Father had volunteered for the 68th Regiment of Foot [in Limerick City Militia] in which Corps he Died some years ago.

Her children did not come with her and Mary Coghlan, washerwoman from Limerick, became an assigned domestic servant until she 'married' Patrick Quin, convict from Ireland.[28]

There were Irish women who, years after they had been exiled to Botany Bay, tried to find the infants and children left behind in Ireland and petitioned the Colonial Secretary for permission to have the children given free passage to rejoin their mothers. In 1824 Mary McCarroll of Brickfield Hill, free by servitude, wrote that she 'has two daughters Ann and Elizabeth McCarroll, living at McPhefoe's Chandlery, Townsend Street Dublin'. Her husband, George Marshall, 'has valuable property, land and houses in the colony and they will be able to maintain the daughters'. Johanna McCarty petitioned in November 1825 while still a prisoner 'living in the District of Appin'. She was married and had two sons by a former marriage in Ireland, Bartholomew McCarty aged twelve and Timothy McCarty aged ten. The boys lived in Tralee in the County of Kerry and 'Mr Humphrey Denman, a respectable merchant of Tralee... may be contacted about the children'.[29] There is no record that the McCarroll daughters or the McCarty sons were permitted to come to New South Wales. It is unlikely that free passages were often granted in these circumstances. Distress, lack of means of support, death of other family members, none of these everyday occurrences were considered sufficiently exceptional to involve the British government in the additional expense of passage to New South Wales. Humanity and compassion were ruled by the probability of increased colonial expenditure.

Few of the women with children had husbands in Ireland who petitioned on their behalf. An exception was William Folks whose wife was confined in the gaol of County Kerry. He petitioned that her sentence had left him 'Burthened with three young helpless Children':

I am an old Infirm Man and having an unfortunate wife Mary Folks who was Tryed at the last Spring Assizes held in the City of Cork... being concerned in the felony of a few yards of Common Cotton... she... escaped in the Month of April last, Come to Tralee in the County of Kerry and has been apprehended... Your Petitioner humbly begs leave to State it was against his will she fell into bad Company...

The husband remained 'burthened' to bring up two of his children alone, for Mary Folks was transported on the *Almorah* with her youngest child, James.[30]

Another exception was Anne Donnelly who was granted mitigation of her sentence of transportation mainly by the efforts of her husband, Patrick, 'an honest, industrious poor man, nearly quite deaf'. She petitioned that she was 'of Weak and Credulous mind – easily made the dupe of designing persons' who had taken advantage of her. She claimed that: 'She had three small children to support with a Husband rendered Incapable of giving her any assistance from being deaf and without any trade. One of the said Children an Infant at the Breast'.[31]

In 1801 Bridget Boddican's husband had not been so fortunate. She was already on board the convict ship at Kingstown (Dun Laoghaire) sentenced to seven years' transportation when her husband, Daniel, a tailor, petitioned the Lord-Lieutenant to have pity on his young wife, who was with child, for she had only been in the company of a woman who had committed the theft with which she had been charged. The Lord-Lieutenant had no pity for pregnant Bridget Boddican and she sailed for Botany Bay, her young husband remaining alone at Kingstown.[32]

Among the Irish husbands and wives charged and convicted together, the case of Mary Murphy of Carlow illustrates the hardships of a woman confined with her children in the county gaol, as well as showing the attitudes of officials towards 'the low Irish'. Mary Murphy and her husband had been convicted in 1809 and both sentenced to seven years' transportation. The husband was sent to Botany Bay shortly after their trial, and the wife remained in Carlow Gaol:

a wretched prisoner ... dragging out a miserable existence striving to rear five children on the gaol allowance and the Benevolence and Charity of the Publick [her] wretched children must die of hunger if Your Grace will not be pleased to extend Mercy ...

The Inspector of Gaols, Forster Archer, supported the woman's petition but added: 'she having assumed her maiden name (a common practice among the low Irish) at her trial it was not known that she was the wife of Murphy sent to New South Wales in September 1810'.[33]

Differences between the Irish women transported from Ireland and the women transported from the mainland of Britain continued to be apparent throughout the first forty years of transportation. The differences were not only discernible between the Irish-born tried in Ireland and the English, Scottish and Welsh women tried in Britain, but between the Irish in Ireland and the Irish-born tried in England. A comparison of the backgrounds of women transported from Ireland with those of women transported from England shows that more single women were transported on 'English' ships but proportionately more of the married 'English' women were accompanied by their children. The 'English' women were markedly younger and more frequently guilty of more 'violent' crimes, that is, highway robbery and housebreaking.

The differing characteristics of 'English' and Irish women are evident from an analysis of the indents of the 'English' convict transport, the *Brothers*, which arrived in New South Wales in 1824. There were Irish-born women among the thirty-nine who were disembarked at Sydney. Bridget Hanning, convicted as a pickpocket at the Old Bailey, was a native of Limerick where she had six living children and a husband who was a sergeant in the 37th Regiment. None of the children accompanied her and she gave birth to her eleventh child on the voyage: 'the mother was infirm, the child puny ... another prisoner wet-nursed the infant; however it died, apparently from the mother accidentally lying on it'.[34]

Unlike most of the women on the Irish transport ships, few of the 'English' prisoners bound for Sydney on the *Brothers* were described as married with children. Among the 'English' 'family' women were: Sarah Bailey, a native of Wigan and convicted in London, a dressmaker who had robbed her lodging-house keeper. Her husband was a cabinetmaker in London and their twelve-year-old son Horatio was with his uncle; Margaret Boyle, a Catholic lady's maid from Dublin, was the wife of a pedlar in England and was permitted to take her two children, Sarah, aged four, and Henry eighteen months, with her. After her arrival at Sydney she married or cohabited with William Thurgate, a sailmaker of Argyle Street. (Her native-born children, Henry and Sarah, are listed as his children in the 1828 Census). Esther Bryant (CF) brought her fifteen-year-old son with her and rejoined her husband, Stephen, who had been transported in 1818. All three were living in Cambridge Street, Sydney in 1828. Eleanor Leech, a Dubliner convicted in London, was a housemaid who had stolen a shawl. She had a husband who was a soldier in the guards and a fifteen-year-old son, John, who lived with her father in Wales. Catherine Riley, born in Connaught, Ireland, and sentenced in London for receiving stolen goods, was a housemaid with a husband in London. She was 'suffered' to take her seven-year-old daughter Mary with her. Sarah Robinson, 'a native of Knutsboro' [*sic*], convicted at Chester for stealing money, brought her eight-month-old son John with her but left five children in Cheshire. Her husband had been sentenced to New South Wales eight years previously. There is no record that she – and her infant – rejoined the husband convicted in 1814. Elizabeth Wray, a native of Northumberland, convicted at Penrith ('a bad character ... mutinous'), was permitted to bring her one-year-old daughter with her. Thirty-two-year-old Jane Wheatley was an atypical convict. Born in Boston, she was convicted of stealing plants and pots in London. By trade a governess, her husband was a music master in Nottinghamshire and her son, Thomas Alfred, lived in Leicestershire. She was somewhat laconically described as having a 'purple complexion, dark brown hair and grey eyes'. Sarah Williams, a Londoner convicted in Shrewsbury, had a three-year-old child living with her husband in Manchester; Amelia Wilson, born in the Scilly Islands, a dressmaker and embroiderer convicted in London, was a widow, her only child Amelia, fifteen, a nurserymaid in London. The remaining women were not recorded as women with children in England.

The comparison of individual family situations between the convicts shipped from Ireland with those shipped from England is most marked in the different response of the authorities to the problem of women with young children. It may have been that comparatively few women transported from England had dependent children and that leniency was possible. The conditions of Ireland, both economic and social, combined with traditionally large families and aggravated by the lack of opportunity for employment, the loss of husbands by death, imprisonment, transportation or voluntary or forced enlistment in the army or the navy, left many Irish married women as technical widows. With almost non-existent help from local parishes in Ireland, the problem for women attempting to support large families was acute. Was it that their children were so numerous that British officials feared the Irish families, if permitted to accompany their convicted mothers, would simply add considerably to the colonial expenditure?

The greatest contribution of the Irish convict women to colonial society was their role and influence, collectively and individually, as family women. That so many were family women in their home country and, despite leaving children in their native land, despite the privations and despair they had known in Ireland's gaols, they resumed a family lifestyle in the penal colony. Was this the only known way of life for the women from the Irish countryside? For whatever reason, it was the family women of Ireland who contributed stability to the convict colony, helping to create a normality within a society which had been artificially created by the transportation system. It was a society in which adult men and a small proportion of adult women, almost all technically created single by banishment, were thrown together in the confined settlement of New South Wales, with the certain knowledge that there was little possibility of their ever returning to the lives and families they had left in the Old Country. The numbers of Irish women who did take up the only lifestyle familiar to them as wife and mother far outweighed those whose conduct and standards in the colony continued to mirror the immorality and criminality believed typical of the women of Botany Bay.

6
'STATIONED IN PARADISE'?

Irish women transported to New South Wales, c. 1790–1827

It appears... that Botany Bay has become somewhat disturbed by traitors and incendiaries and it is not unlikely that some of them are miscreants of that discription whom the laws have driven from this country... As shortly a new cargo of such 'worthies' are to be sent to that part of the world, it will behove the Governor to adopt all circumspection and vigilance he is master of, to prevent agitations and conspiracies, and the utmost he can do in that way will not be more than sufficient...

—Freeman's Journal (Dublin), 7 January 1802

There is little doubt that the women who were transported from Ireland were, in the opinion of the British and the colonial officials, the most depraved, dangerous and rebellious of all the women and girls transported to the English penal colony of Botany Bay. This opinion was not based on the collective or individual criminal records of these women, for very little was known of the specific crimes of the transported Irish. It was an opinion which rested primarily on the undisputed fact of their Irish nationality. That these women were both Irish and criminal was sufficient 'proof' that they were, and would continue to be, treacherous, untrustworthy, troublesome and disobedient. They, and their countrymen, could be expected 'to plot mischief were they stationed in Paradise'. Within the context of such assumptions, it is not surprising that no assessment was made by colonial authorities of the specific criminality of the Irish women. There was no official concern regarding the degree or nature of the criminality of the women transported from England, Scotland or Wales, so why should it occur to British or colonial officials to investigate the backgrounds of women from 'that Unhappy Country', Ireland? Why enquire into the nature and circumstances of the criminality of the Irish women? There was certainly no need to substantiate the belief that these women were more 'vicious' than their English sisters and a far greater threat to the security and well-being of New South Wales. This was accepted as self-evident from the known rebellious and turbulent nature of the Irish in their native land.

The roles of the Irish women in the development of an 'Australian' female society, as well as their contribution to and influence on the social and economic development of New South

Wales, cannot be assessed with any degree of accuracy if based solely on the assumptions of contemporaries as to their criminality before transportation. Furthermore, any explanation of their colonial lives can only be understood within the context of their previous 'Irish' lives. Central to all discussion and understanding is the reality of their criminal backgrounds in Ireland. It is only within this framework that assumptions as to their colonial roles may be tested and evaluated.

Despite the loss of many contemporary records, especially in the disastrous fire during the Easter Rising, there is remaining evidence on which an assessment may be made as to the criminality of the Irish women within the context of their own times, attitudes and values. This evidence includes both the personal data found in the Prisoners' Petitions and Cases and the reports of trial judges and gaol officials concerned in these petitions. Official data relating to individual prisoners, to crime and criminals, to punishment, to the state of gaols and prisons, is found in the Gaol Papers and Reports from both town and county gaols throughout Ireland. General Inquiries and Reports by Parliamentary Committees, Circuit Judges, Special Commissioners concerned with crime, punishment, poverty and civil disturbances, provide evidence of both the criminal and social background of the Irish men and women transported to New South Wales. Individual crimes were frequently reported in newspapers and journals throughout Ireland and, allowing for the journalistic bias of presenting the interesting, the unusual, the horrific, the violent and the frightening, these reports help to fill in the gaps left by the loss or destruction of contemporary court records. A combination of all these sources, critically evaluated, provides a framework within which the criminality of the Irish women transported to New South Wales may be assessed.[1]

Almost every woman transported from Ireland was Irish-born, for there was no internal migration of 'national' groups in Ireland as there was on the British mainland where women from Wales, Scotland, Cornwall – and Ireland – joined women from the various counties and towns travelling from place to place in search of employment. Undoubtedly, there was internal migration in Ireland, chiefly from the counties to Dublin, but remaining records are insufficient to indicate the native place of the transported women. Unlike Britain, few court records remain for the Irish women and men of this period. Trial place may be ascertained from the transport ships' lists and other official documents, but native place was rarely included. It was not until the early 1820s that native place, as given by the woman, was included with physical descriptions by the surgeons on the Irish transport ships.[2]

There is insufficient evidence to determine whether the pattern of travelling criminal women in Ireland was similar to that evident in the early 1820s, but it is a reasonable assumption that, for a proportion of the transported women convicted after 1790, their trial place was not their native place. This could distort assumptions on which colonial attitudes towards the Irish were based. The men and women from Galway and the western counties, for example, were more likely to speak Gaelic, thus further accentuating their 'Irishness' in the penal colony. This 'strangeness of dialect' was commented on by colonists who feared the disturbances the Irish were expected to bring to New South Wales. That they spoke together 'in their own tongue' was interpreted as plotting mischief and rebellion. According to the evidence of trial place, however, only 0.6 per cent of all Irish transported women in this period had been tried in Galway town or county. The numbers of Galway-born women tried in other counties before the 1820s, remains unknown.[3]

That women from Galway were tried in other counties is evidenced in the indents of the *Woodman*, which arrived in New South Wales in 1823, with native place recorded for all its ninety-four convict women. At least four native Galway women arrived on that transport after trial in Leitrim, Longford, Limerick and Waterford. Were these women unusual in age, occupation or crime from other Galway women who may have travelled from their birthplace and were sentenced to transportation in other counties of Ireland? Catherine Kirwan was twenty-five and married when sentenced to transportation in the summer of 1822, after conviction for picking pockets in Leitrim. She could milk and make butter, was five foot four inches, fresh-complexioned, with brown hair and grey eyes. She was reported to have been 'safely delivered of a healthy male child' during the voyage; she married again in the colony, three years after her arrival. Catherine Browne, sentenced for larceny in Limerick City, was skilled at milking and making butter. She was thirty-four when sentenced, 'of muscular habit, suffers from dysentery, 5′2½″ tall, sallow-faced, black-haired with light hazel eyes'. She, too, married within three years of her arrival in New South Wales, with no evidence of further criminal – or health – problems. Bridget Burke was employed as a servant in County Longford when convicted in the summer of 1821. Her age at her trial was thirty years, but on her arrival in the colony she gave her age as 'twenty-four'. This may have improved her marriage prospects, for later that year she married Martin Smith, a convict from the *Earl St Vincent*. She was described by the ship's surgeon as '5'0" lean and freckled complexion, red hair and grey eyes'. She had many health problems on the voyage to Botany Bay, reporting 'headache, pains, nausea, difficulty in breathing, pain in her side and thoracic pain'. None of these complaints appeared to persist, for in December 1825 she again applied for permission to marry. Mary Burke, whose age was also variable, was sentenced in County Waterford for stealing a lamb. She, too could milk and make butter. Like the other Galway women she was tall for her times, 5'3¼", fresh-complexioned, black-haired, and with light grey eyes. Aged twenty-two when convicted, she gave her age as nineteen to the transport surgeon, who found that she was 'scrophulous . . . has several glandular swellings in neck, and ulcers, and vomiting, nausea and dysentery' [*sic*]. There is no record of her marriage in the colony.

The women from Galway tried in counties far from their birthplace did not differ from other Irish transported women in respect of their age, their crime, their skills or their descriptions, with the exception that none of the Galway women were noted as 'pockpitted'.[4] They had, however, dialects and traditional and historical regional differences which would have been more apparent in New South Wales. It is reasonable to suppose that other Galway women who had left their native county, as well as women from all the counties of Ireland, were among women sentenced in all the town and county courts of the country. Place of trial, therefore, indicates only that most, but not all, of the women were native to the town or county in which they were convicted.

The crimes of the transported women differed little throughout Ireland. The chief difference was between Dublin and the counties, for there was a higher proportion of crimes in Dublin linked with prostitution, soliciting, or keeping a disorderly house. Crimes of violence – proportionately fewer than among the English-tried women – were not unique to Dublin, but scattered throughout the counties.

From about 1814 brief descriptions of individual crimes were noted on the ships' indents. This became more regular until, by the mid-1820s, almost every transported woman was identified by her crime. Table 6.1 indicates the specific offences of women convicted in Dublin during this period.

Table 6.1 Crimes of women transported from Dublin, 1814–27 (where known)

Crime	Total for Dublin
Felony of stealing	
monies/purse/pocketbook	93
clothing/wearing apparel	80
watch	46
cloth, ribbons, etc. [calico/linen/cotton/muslin/lace]	42
handkerchiefs	20
banknotes, etc.	16
spoons/plate	7
animals [geese/hens/fowl/sheep]	3
foodstuffs [ham/sugar/tea]	3
jewellery [brooch/ring/ear-ring]	3
child/children	2
Miscellaneous individual articles not specified	
burglary & robbery, etc.	25
robbing a person [includes 2 children]	19
shoplifting	11
felony/larceny/stealing	10
[2 indecipherable: jersey? rosewater?]	2
picking pockets	4
street robbery	2

Note: Individual offences classified under general heading are indicated by 'etc.'; miscellaneous includes 'individual' crimes, such as stealing prayer book, paper, ostrich feathers, looking glass; where two articles are described in the indent papers, the first is normally included under the appropriate heading.

Most of the offences were identified by the article stolen. Where the crime was recorded as 'picking pockets' or 'shoplifting' this did not indicate the total number of pickpockets or shoplifters and this may only be assumed on the basis of the article stolen. Pickpockets, for example, usually stole handkerchiefs, watches, monies, banknotes, purses or pocketbooks. Shoplifters stole ribbons, stockings, materials such as cotton, calico or lace, and articles of clothing such as caps, shawls, shoes or boots. 'House-robbers' stole almost every portable article in the house, from foodstuffs, jewellery and plate to sheets and chests. Violence, in the form of highway robbery and assault against the person, was seldom indicated on the ships' indents. With the exception of Elizabeth Gahan (transported for life on the *Elizabeth* in 1818 for the murder of her husband), very few of the Dublin women could be specifically identified as 'violent' from the nature of their offences as recorded on the ships' indents. It is the more detailed reports of selected trials published in contemporary newspapers and journals which indicate the degree of violence among Dublin's women criminals. The *Freeman's Journal* reported several cases in detail. Mary Brown was transported on the *Alexander* in 1816 for stealing 'a gold watch, seals and keys, the property of John Moore'. She and accomplice Judith Leeke were tried at the Sessions Court, Dublin:

This gentleman [John Moore, prosecutor] swore that he came out of a tavern about 1 o'clock in the morning when he had occasion to turn to a well immediately on coming out, when the two women at the Bar ran up to him, seized him with violence and pulled off the watch, seal and fob.
—*Freeman's Journal*, 23 May 1815

When sentenced, one of the prisoners 'a most hardened wretch' (Mary Brown) called out 'the d- - - - may care, sure we won't go alone!' Mary Brown was twenty years old at the time, a servant by trade.

Mary Marshall 'knocked down a man and robbed him of a pound note' in 1802, a similar crime to that of Mary Carroll, Hessy Burke and Elizabeth Murphy who were indicted in 1823 for 'knocking down John Hughes ... at St George's Quay and taking from his person by force while down, a pocketbook containing two bank notes and some silver and also a silver watch'. Some of the property was found on the persons of Murphy and Burke. Hessy Burke and Mary Elizabeth Murphy were sentenced to seven years' transportation, and arrived on the *Woodman* in 1823.[5]

Also on the *Woodman* was Margaret Byrne, a twenty-six-year-old Dubliner, by trade a scullery maid. She was tall among her contemporaries, being 'five feet five inches, of ruddy complexion, red hair, light blue eyes and pockmarked'. She was found guilty of stealing a pocket book containing three Bank of Ireland notes and other papers, the property of Thomas Boyd. Boyd described the circumstances of the theft:

[he] had the misfortune to go into a jig house in Barrack Street ... he was laid hold of by the woman and dragged into an open hall. She was

immediately joined by [her accomplice, also tried] who laid hold of him by the collar and robbed him of all he had ... they then thrust him out'.
—*Freeman's Journal*, 1 December 1821

Margaret Byrne served her sentence at the Female Factory, Parramatta, there being little opportunity for assignment for this 'violent' Dublin scullery maid.

Although there was some degree of violence associated with street robbery and robbing from the person and pickpocketing, fewer of the transported women of Dublin could be identified as guilty of violence than was the case with the women from Newgate Prison, London. Reports of Dublin crime involving girls and women give some indication of the background of the women sentenced to transportation. There is insufficient evidence to deduce with accuracy the numbers of Dublin women who lived wholly or in part by prostitution. References in trial papers and newspaper reports do, however, suggest a smaller percentage than that found among the women transported from London. Rose Walsh was transported on the *Catherine* in 1814 for stealing a watch. The *Freeman's Journal* report of her trial at the Recorder's Court in Dublin indicates clearly that her profession was that of prostitute:

Rose Walsh, one of the Cyprian tribe [a prostitute] who infest Dame Street was indicted for stealing a watch. The evidence was of such a curious nature as to fill the Court with laughter, but it proved fairly that the witness had been robbed by one of these 'guardians of the night'.
—*Freeman's Journal*, 23 August 1812

There was little laughter for Rose Walsh, who died on the voyage to New South Wales.

Neither was there any doubt as to the occupation of Dubliner Mary Shannon, transported on the *Tellicherry* in 1806. She had been convicted of stealing the watch of Richard Barret:

This was an amorous experiment and the prisoner influenced by the example of that godess who presides over her profession, wanted to pick fruit as the reward for her humility. The next essay will, however, most probably be at Botany Bay where she is condemned to a seven year noviceship to restore a vitiated constitution.

Mary Shannon was sufficiently 'restored' at Botany Bay to marry William Clarke at St John's, Parramatta.[6]

Elizabeth Coak, transported on the *Atlas* in 1802, was another of the Dublin 'guardians of the night'. Having had a drink of punch with a male friend in an ale house in Liffey Street 'his companion parted with him rather suddenly':

> he went in search of him and was accosted by a woman at the door of . . . a house in Liffey Street who told him walk in and that he could find the person he wanted then he went in and was ushered to a room with no fitting there except an old bed, that, having seated himself . . . Coak forcibly threw herself on him and rifled his pocket . . . having descended the stairs and laid hold [of Coak] he was seized by two other females at the bar who charged him on the watch for assault . . .

It was declared at the trial that the house in Liffey Street was 'a disorderly house'. In New South Wales Elizabeth Coak was employed by and lived with an ex-convict, Patrick Lennard, transported from Ireland on the *Queen*, who worked for himself as a fisherman. After his death, Elizabeth Coak, whose sentence had expired in July 1808, remained living in Parramatta 'free and off stores' until her death on 12 December 1817. At no time was she charged with any colonial misdemeanours or crimes. She was buried at St John's, and entered in the Church Register as 'Free, aged 43'.

Only a minority of the reported crimes of the Dublin women indicated any significant proportion of either violence or habitual prostitution associated with the offences of the women transported to New South Wales. The general picture was of women and girls who thieved and stole money, clothing or small items. There was a notable lack of women sentenced for receiving stolen goods, as well as of women who stole animals or foodstuffs. The criminal women of Dublin were more likely to 'earn their livelihood' by repeatedly stealing small articles. The women from the Irish counties, on the other hand, were more frequently first offenders, and more likely to come from a background of distress, poverty and destitution resulting from loss of husband or loss of employment.[7]

The shoplifters from town or county fitted the pattern of English offenders. Two or more would enter a shop, the accomplices distracting the shopkeeper's attention while the articles to be stolen were secreted about the person of one of the group. Margaret Doyle (*Rolla*) and Mary Tyrell (*Rolla*), also known as Higgins, stole five pieces of stamped muslin from shopkeeper John McDermott of Great Britain Street, Dublin, in 1802. He described the circumstances of the crime:

both prisoners came into the shop ... the one affected to bargain with his wife about the price of the muslin while the other, he presumed, took the five pieces away which he found on her person after she left the shop. He also found on the person of her who feigned to bargain with his wife, a piece of white muslin and a pair stockings of which he could not prove to be his own property ...

In New South Wales Mary Tyrell was employed by an ex-convict, William Whiteman, an Irishman who had arrived on the *Hercules*. Whiteman received a conditional pardon for good conduct and established himself as a farmer on a land grant at Evan. By 1828 Mary Tyrell was recorded as Mary Whiteman, forty-seven, living with her husband, William Whiteman, fifty, and their two colonial-born children, Sarah, born 1815, and Mary, born 1816. There is no evidence that in New South Wales this colonial farmer's wife reverted at any time to the light-fingered habits of her life in Dublin City.[8]

Mary Dunbar was another Dubliner who became a respectable farmer's wife in New South Wales. Guilty of stealing a coat, a waistcoat and other articles in 1792, she was transported on the *Sugar Cane*. By 1806 she was living with ex-convict Hugh Dogherty, a self-employed boatman who had been transported on the *Queen*; by 1814 she was 'wife to J [*sic*] Dogherty, landholder, Windsor'; by 1822 both were still listed together, and in 1828 Mary, aged fifty-three, and Hugh Dogherty, aged fifty-seven, were farming fifty acres at Surer Swamp, Portland Head. What became of the daughter who had accompanied her to Norfolk Island in 1794 is unknown. What is known is that, in almost forty years of colonial life, she was neither suspected nor accused of any crime or offence against the laws of her adopted country.[9]

Catherine Donnelly, a married woman, left one child in Northern Ireland when she was transported on the *Almorah* in 1824. She and her husband Hugh Brannigan were convicted of 'stealing from the person of Dr Isaac Burke in Ballinasloe Fair, £70 in Bank of Ireland notes and post bills'. The pickpockets were apprehended when Catherine Donnelly changed one of the notes on a Grand Canal Passage Boat, and both were transported for seven years. Described as 'very quiet, 4'11" black hair, hazel blue eyes', Catherine Donnelly was assigned to the family of William Waterhouse in Goulburn Street, Sydney, in 1823. She later rejoined her husband, who had arrived on the *Prince Regent* but remained employed by Waterhouse. Neither husband nor wife were known to have resumed their Irish pickpocketing habits in New South Wales.[10]

The trial descriptions provide an insight into the living conditions familiar to the women transported from Dublin. Elizabeth Jackson, tried in 1794 and transported on the *Marquis Cornwallis* in 1796, had been found guilty of stealing clothes. According to the *Freeman's Journal*, Elizabeth Jackson had visited a friend in the lodging house from which the clothes were taken. The prosecutor described the loss of his belongings:

James Gallagher swore that he lodged at 46 Mary's Lane and that the articles ... were taken in May last; that he missed them about 5.30 in the morning; that on going to bed, he left them on a chair at the bedside; that the prisoner was taken about nine in the morning with the clothes in her custody; that the door of the room was locked when he went to bed but that his landlord lay in the same room and got up before him, and on going out left the door open; that he fell asleep and that the prisoner, having access to a lodger in the house must have taken them.
— *Freeman's Journal*, 26 June 1794

Another lodger, Mary Carroll, confirmed this account, adding that, after he missed his clothes, she went downstairs into the street and alarmed the neighbours and told them of the robbery; she found the prisoner with the clothes – the clothes were worth more than three shillings. For three shillings' worth of old clothes Elizabeth Jackson was transported to Botany Bay, where she formed an alliance with ex-convict George Evans which lasted until his death. They had four colonial-born children, and in 1828 Elizabeth Jackson was described as 'widow' living with her son, George Evans, a farmer at Portland Head. She was then fifty-seven years old. Did she recall her youth in Dublin or was that theft of old clothes long forgotten, a part of that memory, veiled by time, of the poverty she had known as a criminal girl of Dublin's streets?[11]

It was believed by respectable contemporaries that only the most vicious, the most criminal of Ireland's refuse suffered transportation to Botany Bay – with the exception, of course, of those girls and women found guilty of crimes of such immensity that death on the gallows was the only fit punishment for their offences. Although the exact percentage cannot be determined from existing records, only a small proportion of all Irish women sentenced to transportation in Irish courts throughout Ireland were actually transported.[12] Were these 'deportees', as contemporaries believed, 'the worst characters', 'totally irreclaimable', 'vicious and depraved'? Were they even more dissolute and beyond redemption than the obscene, notorious and criminal women transported from London's Newgate Gaol? Remaining evidence would not suggest that it was only the worst of Ireland's criminal women who were sent to Botany Bay. Neither would such evidence suggest that those transported were always typical of Irish women convicted of major crimes. Evidence such as the Report Recommending Pardon from the Sentence of Transportation, compiled by the Superintendent of the Adult Female Penitentiary (Dublin) in 1812 indicates the grounds considered suitable for remitting sentence of exile.

The reasons for the recommendation for pardon ranged from 'very sickly and unable to bear confinement' (Elinor Delaney, receiver of stolen goods) to 'very industrious and well-behaved' (Mary Barrett, stealing stockings). The actual crime appeared secondary to the officials of the Penitentiary, the whole emphasis being on the 'reformation' shown by application to industry and proven good conduct. Mary Smyth had 'stolen a child', stripped it of its clothes, abandoned the child far from its home, and pawned the stolen clothes. To respectable contemporaries this was an abominable crime, one which an English judge had ruled deserved the fullest punishment the law allowed. Mary Smyth, however, received a pardon for 'she continues to conduct herself extremely well'. Sarah Patten had been found guilty of stealing one £100 note and had served three of her seven years' sentence at the Penitentiary when described as 'very quiet and being sickly and old recommended for Pardon'. Only one of the women recommended did not receive mitigation of her sentence of transportation: Jane Williams also known as Williamson, who had been convicted in September 1808 for stealing a banknote. Despite being recommended as 'extremely industrious and well-conducted', she was transported on the *Experiment*, arriving in New South Wales in 1809. Another, Catherine Brady (stealing a shirt), was recommended 'to be pardoned and sent to the House of Industry, being unfit for this place'. The remaining women were pardoned the remainder of their sentences, thus escaping transportation to New South Wales. There was no pattern in the degree or extent of the offences, which ranged from 'felony of a sock' (Mary McLoghlin 'has uniformly conducted herself well'), to stealing a watch, a shirt, sheets, banknotes, monies. This Report, and other recommendations for pardon or mitigation from the Gaol and Penitentiary authorities, all indicated that the prisoner was declared 'a fit object for mercy' if there were ample evidence of reformation, good conduct, visible improvement in morals and personal behaviour.[13]

A more detailed picture of crime, character and punishment of female felons in Ireland is in the list of convicts under sentence of death or transportation in Ireland in 1815 which had been requested from every Irish county by Forster Archer, the Inspector of Gaols. This Report gives some indication of which women were chosen as deportees, which received mitigation of sentences, and which were pardoned. In 1813 sixty-three of the women under sentence were transported, in 1814 fifty-four, and in 1815 ninety-one. The 1815 Report shows clearly that there is no consistency evident in decisions to transport or not to transport, with regard to crime, age, health or locality. The dominant characteristic of the transported women was their 'bad' or 'unreformed' characters. In County Antrim no women were listed among the eleven prisoners under sentence of death or transportation, although almost sixty of the transported Irish women came from that county. In Armagh (total women transported twenty-three) four of the eleven prisoners were women. The youngest, Elizabeth Brown, twenty, was transported on the *Alexander* (arrived New South Wales 1816). Elizabeth Brown was a servant who had stolen corduroy, and was sentenced to seven years' transportation. Both her health and character were described as 'Good'. Was it her age which made her a suitable 'object' for transportation? Her companion in Armagh Gaol, Mary Fitzpatrick, forty-six, guilty of receiving stolen goods, was in good health but of a 'Very Bad' character. Sarah Mooney, forty-seven, and Jane Reed, thirty-five, both of good health and character although guilty of stealing a piece of lace, remained in Ireland, serving their seven years in the county gaol.

In Cavan, from which seventeen Irish women were transported to New South Wales, none of the four women awaiting transportation were sent to Botany Bay. Susan Johnston, a nineteen-year-old shoplifter – 'good health and indifferent character' – served her sentence in Dublin's Kilmainham Gaol, as did her sister Margaret Johnston, twenty-five, another healthy but 'of indifferent character' shoplifter. Ann Donohoo, alias Reilly, a forty-nine-year-old shoplifter – 'good health, indifferent character' – joined the Johnston sisters in Kilmainham, while forty-year-old Alice Price, guilty of 'picking pockets', 'in good health and of good character', stayed in Cavan Gaol.

There were no women in Donegal Gaol in 1815, and only eight came directly from that county during the first forty years of transportation. In County Down (total of thirty-eight women to New South Wales) there were two women awaiting their transports, both young, both in good health and 'good in gaol'.

The two women held in 1815 in Drogheda Gaol were both sent to New South Wales on the *Alexander*. Catherine Goff, 21 and Ann Maginness, twenty-seven, both employed as servants, both guilty of picking pockets, were in good health and 'good in gaol'. A total of ten women were transported from Drogheda.

In Fermanagh (eight women transported) there were only two prisoners awaiting transportation: John Brown, a fifty-seven-year-old horse-thief sentenced to death but respited for transportation, and vagrant Ann Moore, thirty-two, who remained in Fermanagh, possibly because she was unable to provide 'security for her future good behaviour'. Such vagabonds and vagrants were usually transported. In Leitrim (six women transported) there were no female prisoners under sentence of death or transportation. In Longford (ten women transported) the only woman awaiting a transport was twenty-one-year-old vagrant Elizabeth Daugherty, who arrived in New South Wales the following year on the *Alexander*. There were no women in Louth County Gaol awaiting capital punishment or transportation (eleven came from this county). In Meath (seventeen women transported) all three women under sentence of transportation were sent on the *Alexander*: Margaret Perry, twenty-three, uttering forged notes, Catherine Wills, fifty, house robbery and Ann McKeon, twenty-four, picking pockets. No description of health or character was recorded. In Monaghan (twenty-four women transported) none were awaiting transportation, and in Tyrone (nine transported) Jane Wright, sentenced for 'forcible possession', remained in her county gaol.

In Tipperary at Clonmell (forty transported) three of the five women were transported on the *Alexander*: Mary Fennessy, twenty-six, convicted with her husband John of felony of banknotes, and both noted as in good health but 'very bad' characters; Bridget Kennedy, nineteen, guilty of perjury in court, no character comment; and Ann Ellis, thirty, 'felony of Cloaths', good health, character 'unknown'. The remaining two women were special cases: 'Baron George before whom these two women were tried directed the Sheriff to inform them he would have them removed to prisons in their home counties.'[14]

The pattern of circumstances which led to pardon continued vague and undefined throughout the whole period of transportation. There was only one certain plea which could mitigate a sentence of death and, in a few cases, delay transportation: this was 'I am with child'. Pregnancy did not mitigate an offence, although it saved many a woman from the gallows, for a woman 'with child' could not be hanged. One who took advantage of this loophole and 'pleaded her belly' was Sarah Geentry, who had been ordered for execution at the Assizes of Longford in 1808. Sentence was to be carried out on 20 July. Some ten months later a perplexed gaoler of Longford wrote to Dublin Castle for instructions:

this unfortunate woman having been found pregnant by a Jury of Matrons the Sentence was respited till further order ... She has not Shown any Appearance of Pregnancy and a Sufficient Time, in my Opinion, having elapsed, I directed that Sentence should be carried into Execution on Saturday 26th March ...

The humanity of this gaoler, or his desire not to overstep his powers, is shown in the final paragraph of his letter:

I know nothing further of the Merits of this Case and I write merely to afford His grace an opportunity of enquiry into it and of extending to this Woman any benefit which in Point of Law in Fact she may be thought entitled to.

Sarah Geentry was not 'an object for mercy'. She was hanged as scheduled on 26 March 1809.[15]

Death by hanging was feared by the women of Ireland. As Frances Bell exclaimed when sentenced to seven years' transportation for stealing a pair of buskins, 'Thank God, it can be no worse'. Frances Bell, from County Monaghan, was transported two years later on the *Mariner*, arriving in New South Wales in 1825. In October 1830 she married Joseph Alders at St Matthew's Church, Windsor. She died at Parramatta Hospital on 8 July 1833, 'Free at Death'.

A plea of innocence at the trial seldom changed the verdict, seldom influenced trial judges to make favourable response to subsequent petitions. Mary Doolan was a fifteen-year-old orphan of Dublin City when convicted of shoplifting in 1790. She petitioned for clemency, still protesting her innocence. Mary Doolan did not hang but arrived in New South Wales on the *Sugar Cane* in 1793. In the colony she became the wife, or common-law wife, of convict Joseph Chitham, a self-employed carpenter, and remained with him and their native-born children at Windsor until her death. No further charges were laid against her.

It was not only the 'good women', the despairing mothers of young children who petitioned against sentences of death, transportation or even imprisonment. Among the Irish women of

Botany Bay were women such as Mary Sullivan, a widow from County Kerry, transported on the *Almorah* in 1824 for killing sheep. At her trial she was described as 'a common streetwoman'. The surgeon of the *Almorah* found her 'very quiet, sews, spins and washes', adding 'she is pale complexioned, five feet three inches, lean and freckled with dark brown hair and blue eyes'. Common streetwoman of Ireland or not, quiet and freckled Mary Sullivan married within three years of arrival in New South Wales, and throughout her colonial life lived as a respectable family woman of Botany Bay.

Harriet Gordon, who described herself as a needlewoman, was transported on the *Woodman* in 1823 for felony of bank notes, her appeal dismissed by the judge for she, too, was 'nothing but a common streetwoman'. The ship's surgeon appeared to hold the same opinion of Harriet Gordon: 'aged 25, spare habit, appearance – scrophulous – has always led a vicious life' [*sic*]. Pale-complexioned, with brown hair and grey eyes, she married a ticket-of-leave Irishman, James Power, shortly after arrival at Sydney, and settled with him at Windsor. No records suggest she continued her 'vicious life' at Botany Bay.

Surgeons' Reports were not necessarily reliable or accurate, as the surgeon on the *Woodman* discovered when he described eighteen-year-old, flaxen-haired and blue-eyed Eliza Wheelan as 'has led an irregular life' with additional derogatory observations on her lack of morality. On a second and more detailed investigation, the same surgeon recorded that Eliza Wheelan, to his profound astonishment, was a virgin. Such a description appeared incongruous for a female felon.

The Irish women who were transported were not necessarily those who had been confined for long periods in their town or county gaol. Most were sent to the transport ships and deported within a year or less of sentencing.[16] In February 1818, out of a total of 548 'convicts under Rule of Transportation in the Gaols of Ireland', eighty-two were women. Sixty-five of these women had been sentenced to transportation in 1817 and were deported in 1818 on the *Elizabeth* which arrived in New South Wales in November 1818. Two more had been sentenced in 1816: Elizabeth Driscoll, a sixty-year-old shoplifter, and Mary Fitzgibbon, a thirty-two-year-old guilty of larceny from a shop. Both were from Cork, and both sailed on the *Elizabeth*. Sarah Jane Gibson, forty-five, from Queen's County was transported on the *Lord Wellington*, and Sarah Wilson, from Antrim, on the *Janus*, both arriving in New South Wales in 1820.

According to the number of women awaiting transportation

in Forster Archer's report of 1818, only thirteen of these women were not transported to New South Wales. This would include those severely ill, those who had died during confinement, and those who had received pardons or mitigation of the sentence of transportation. Table 6.2 compares the numbers confined in the various gaols with those actually transported:

Table 6.2 Women sentenced to transportation, Ireland, 1815-18

Gaol	Females under Rule of Transportation Feb. 1818	Females Transported after Feb. 1818	Females Transported Late 1817 per Canada
Dublin	24	22	
(Newgate 21; Kilmainham 3)			
Antrim	7	6	
Armagh	7	0	
Carlow	7	0	2
Cavan	2	2	
Clare	2	0	
Cork City	11	10	1
Cork Co.	6	3	
Donegal	1	0	
Downe	5	3	
Drogheda	5	1	1
Fermanagh	5	0	
Galway Co.	2	1	1
Galway Town	2	0	
Kerry	2	0	1
Kildare	2	2	
Kilkenny City	1	0	1
Kilkenny Co.	1	1	1
Kings County	2	2	
Leitrim	2	0	1
Limerick City	2	1	
Limerick Co.	2	0	
Londonderry	2	2	1
Longford	2	0	
Louth	2	0	
Mayo	2	0	4
Meath	3	3	1
Monaghan	2	2	

Gaol	Females under Rule of Transportation Feb. 1818	Females Transported after Feb. 1818	Females Transported Late 1817 per Canada
Queens County	4	3	
Roscommon	4	0	1
Sligo	1	1	
Tipperary	2	1	1
Tyrone	2	0	
Waterford City	2	0	
Waterford Co.	2	0	
Westmeath	1	1	
Wexford	2	0	
Wicklow	1	1	

* The *Canada* is included where appropriate, as the probability exists that some County Returns included women transported in the latter months of 1817.

Sources: Report of Forster Archer, Inspector of Prisons, 'Number of Convicts under Rule of Transportation in Gaols of Ireland', February 1818; Ships' Indents: *Elizabeth, Lord Wellington, Janus*; Gaol and Trial Reports; *Freeman's Journal*.

Note: Number transported based on 1815/1816/1817 trial date with transportation after February 1818.

Was it the expense of conveying prisoners from distant parts of Ireland to Dublin or to Cork to embark on the transports which reduced the numbers sent from county gaols? This would appear to have had little overall influence on decisions of gaolers and prison inspectors. In Cork itself, for example, only three of the six under sentence were transported. From nearby counties there was no consistent pattern which could be related to distance or expense of conveying prisoners to Cork. In Roscommon none of the four were transported, with the exception of one woman sent on the *Canada* in 1817. None were sent from Wexford, but both from Kildare and the only one under sentence in Kilkenny. On the other hand, six out of the seven were transported from distant Antrim, but only one from the four awaiting transportation in Galway. Twenty-two of the twenty-four from Dublin journeyed to Cork and embarked in 1818.[17] Distance from trial place to transport ship appeared to play as haphazard a part in the selection of women to be deported as any of the other considerations.

What type of women were they, these Irish criminals chosen for transportation to Botany Bay? Were they as described by their gaolers, by the surgeons on their transport ships, by their judges and prosecutors at their trial? Or were they the forlorn, the destitute, the hopeless, as so many of their own petitions, and those of their supporters, would suggest? There is bias inherent in any unqualified acceptance of either source of evidence, and almost all 'Irish' evidence conflicts with the pattern of colonial life adopted by most of these women.

The opinions of the Irish gaolers were almost unanimous in that the women to be transported were 'Bad Characters'. In Gaol Papers listing 'Convicts Under Sentence of Death or Transportation' many of the women who were to be transported on the *Almorah* or the *Elizabeth* were described in this way by their town or county gaoler. The character description was no indication of the future lifestyle of the woman in the penal colony. Jane Quigley, a twenty-five-year-old vagrant in Londonderry Gaol unable to raise the security required as guarantee for future good behaviour, was 'under rule of transportation ... a Bad Character'. On arrival in New South Wales she was sent to the Female Factory at Parramatta to await assignment, as was customary with newly-arrived female prisoners. She was assigned as a government servant is 1822, but had married by 1828. Her colonial husband, Fred Whitely (*Morley*), was a self-employed fisherman who had served his seven-year sentence. The pair lived in Kent Street, Sydney, with no evidence of the wife's former 'bad character'. Ellen Flaherty, eighteen and Rose Murtagh, thirty, both 'Bad Characters', were transported on the *Almorah* as punishment for house robbery. 'Bad' Ellen Flaherty was an assigned servant in Sydney, working as a housekeeper until she married John Rochester, a publican in Sussex Lane who had arrived as a free man in 1825. Rose Murtagh, calling herself Rosetta, married within a year of arrival in New South Wales, settling at Windsor, assigned to her husband. There is no evidence at all to show that either of these women continued their criminal lifestyle in the colony, or that they were 'women of bad character' in Botany Bay. To their Irish gaolers, however, they were infamous women convicted of major statutory offences and so unquestioningly 'Bad Characters'.

Age appeared to have had little influence on character descriptions of women confined in the gaols of Ireland. Elinor Keating, aged ten years and sentenced to death for burglary and robbery, was 'an Infamous Character', while Sarah Wilson, twenty, was described as 'An Infamous Sister to Elinor Keating'.

There is no colonial record of either of these 'notorious' sisters, apart from their listing on the indents of the *Elizabeth*.[18]

The colonial lifestyles of few of the transported Irish women were in accordance with the expectation that they were morally destitute, drunken, vicious and depraved whores and prostitutes. Most of the women on all of the convict ships which followed the *Queen* were more likely to merge easily into the role of 'family/working woman' rather than that of depraved whore or even 'vicious criminal'. Was this a direct result of their lives, attitudes and expectations before transportation? Most of these Irish women had been family women in their native land and had known no other lifestyle than that of wife, or widow, and mother before their convictions for major felonies.

Two characteristics emerge from an analysis of the colonial lives of these Irish women: first, the large proportion of women who remained with the man to whom they were originally assigned, and second, the proportion who married and became family women in the colony. Both of these characteristics are clearly evident among Irish women who arrived on the *Rolla* in 1803. Women such as Mary Barry, Bridget Byrne, Catherine Carter, Margaret Doyle, Catherine Hurley, Catherine Murphy, Mary Power and Judith Roe, all became the legal or common-law wives of the men to whom they were assigned.

Among the family women on the *Rolla* were Mary Cusadine from Clare who married J. Masterton (arrived convict per *Minerva*), a landholder at Liverpool and Catherine Laughlin from Kilkenny who, by 1814, had married the Gaoler at Windsor, where they lived with their five children. Other women who settled with new families in the colony included a former highwaywoman, Mary Quin from County Down (*Rolla*). She had been sentenced to be hanged at Newry, respited and transported on the *Rolla*. Shortly after arrival in New South Wales she married an ex-convict from the *Hercules*, Thomas Lynch. They and their two children remained living in Sydney. Not all married immediately or shortly after arrival. Mary Ryan from Clare (*Rolla*), 'exempt from working' in 1806 muster, married P. Hogan, by whom she was to have four native-born children. Jane Walsh of Westmeath (*Rolla*) also worked at the hospital before marrying G. Bidon and settling in Sydney. Mary McEntee from Meath (*Rolla*) was employed at the Female Factory as a seamstress until her marriage to Jonathan Hannah. The colonial lives of these family women bore no resemblance at all to the expected standards and characteristics of the Irish convict women.[19]

One of the women transported on the *Rolla* was typical of the expected stereotype of 'vicious, low Irish'. Ann Byrne had been tried in Dublin City in October 1800, and was frequently before the colonial courts after her arrival in New South Wales, charged with stealing or robbery. In 1806 she was a prisoner of the Crown serving a colonial sentence at the Female Factory. In 1815 Mary Anderson or Kelly, transported on the *Archduke Charles*, was charged with the possession of spirits, and she was gaoled when she refused to say how the spirits came into her possession. In 1826 she was again charged and again convicted, this time for 'a vicious assault' upon her husband.

Two other Irish women whose colonial lives conformed to the expected stereotype were Sarah Eyres and Rose Kenny, both from Dublin, both atypical of Dublin women. They petitioned for maintenance for their bastard children, fathered by seamen on their transport ship, the *Archduke Charles*. Both stressed to the magistrate that the fathers of their children had 'not the slightest objection' to 'leaving a sum of money for the support of the child'. It was the captain of the ship who refused to advance money for this purpose. The petition of Rose Kenny to the Sydney Bench of Magistrates is typical of many of the petitions for Maintenance in Bastardy and shows the background and circumstances which led to the appeal for support:

With submission I make bold to lay before you the unhappy situation I now labour under. Gentlemen – permit me to inform you I but lately arrived in the colony . . . a few days after I embarked on board necessity compelled me to cohabit with the carpenter of the ship during the whole of the Passage – and on my landing in Sydney I was induced to go into the General Hospital in order that I might receive medical aid, having been delivered of a son on board a few days previous to my coming on shore – Gentlemen – I now make bold to appear before you to make an affidavit to the Father of the child – as in a few days he will leave the Colony and I left destitute of maintenance/support of the infant – the man has not the smallest objection to leave me a sum of money for the support of the child provided Captain Jeffries will pay it down. [He] has perspectively asked Captain Jeffries to advance him money to the effect I am obliged to come to you upon, but all in vain, I therefore Gentlemen hope and trust you take my situation into consideration and order the man to remain with me in the Colony or Captain Jeffries to advance me some money on the wages due to him.[20]

This is a remarkable plea when it is considered that it is from a convict woman under sentence of the law in New South Wales. What 'necessity' caused her to cohabit with the carpenter is unknown, but that this cohabitation was for the entire duration of the voyage would support the opinion of Surgeon Peter Cunningham, who commented on the women convicts in his care in the early 1820s. It was Cunningham's belief that these 'long associations' were to the benefit of both woman and sailor, for they were not evidence of indiscriminate loose living but more akin to 'taking a mate', a settled relationship in which the woman benefited not only from the material comforts of extra tea and small luxuries, but from the far more important experience of living as a 'wife'. The sailor, in return, had the 'comforts' of care from the woman – washing, sewing, cleaning – so that the voyage was beneficial to both.[21] That Rose Kenny's carpenter had no objection to supporting their child – and may have been a party to her suggestion that he be allowed to remain in the colony – was not evidence of her 'flagrant immorality' but more indicative of the nature of their liaison. Furthermore, as a convict, Rose Kenny would not have been 'destitute' in New South Wales. She, and her child, would have been taken to the Female Factory where she would have been employed until her sentence had expired if she were not assigned as a servant to a colonist. Ships' carpenters, being absolutely essential to all ships and their skills allowing special privileges, it is unlikely that the captain would have agreed to release the father of Rose Kenny's son. There is no record to indicate that he did not sail with his ship. What became of the child is unknown, for the next reference to Rose Kenny is in the Muster of 1814, in which she was recorded as a single woman, convict, off stores, living in Sydney.

Most of the convict women transported on the *Archduke Charles* conformed to the pattern of the women on the *Queen*, the *Rolla* and the *Atlas*. They were women such as Mary Charlton, tried at Monaghan Assizes in August 1811 with Catherine McDonald and Susan Fitzgerald, and sentenced as vagrants to seven years' transportation. Mary Charlton was unable to give the required security for good behaviour, so was transported to New South Wales. On arrival she was assigned to Mr G. T. Palmer, landholder at Windsor. By 1822, by which time she was free by servitude, she had married Patrick McHale, an Irish ex-convict, who had received a conditional pardon and settled as a landholder at Parramatta. Susan Fitzgerald, convicted with Mary Charlton, was about fifty years old when she arrived in the colony. Shortly after arrival she married John Callaghan at St Matthew's, Windsor, a convict labourer from the *Atlas*.

By 1815 most of the 'new arrivals' from Ireland and from England were sent to the Female Factory at Parramatta to await private assignment. For most of the sixty-five women who arrived on the *Francis and Eliza* in August 1815, the first experience of life in the penal colony was the boat trip from Sydney up the Parramatta River to the Female Factory. They and their belongings were rowed by convict boatmen, some of whom were subsequently punished by flogging 'for taking three days to row the female convicts from Sydney to Parramatta when one day would suffice'. The women came from all parts of Ireland, were mainly servants, and mostly guilty of stealing, theft, uttering, passing or receiving stolen goods, highway robbery or pickpocketing. Thefts varied from that of Margaret Burns, a bootcloser of Dublin, born in Carlow, who was found guilty of stealing butter, to Elizabeth Healy, a Dublin servant who stole a watch, to Bridget Walsh of Sligo, who stole clothing. Bridget Burn had been tried at Wexford in March 1814. A native of Kilkenny, a servant by trade, she was described as 'pale complexion, brown hair, blue eyes'. Her crime:

Guilty of having in her custody without lawful excuse forged banknotes of the Bank of Ireland. It was also found upon her 71 forgeries of the Wexford Bank and several of Shaw's Bank. Crime committed in company with Margaret Mitchell.

Both were sentenced to fourteen years' transportation.

Most of the Irish convict women shared a background of poverty and deprivation, whether they were county women or city women. It cannot be determined with accuracy whether that poverty was the result of criminal inclination, that is, whether the transported Irish women were members of a 'criminal class', or whether crime had followed distress, unemployment, loss of husband or parent.

The entries on the indents of the transport ships evidence the 'everyday' nature of the crimes of most of the transported Irish – stealing wearing apparel, stealing clothing, stealing a watch, picking pockets, shoplifting muslin, calico, a bonnet, ribbons or stockings or lace, stealing foodstuffs, cash, banknotes, house robbery or theft from the dwelling, theft of a fowl, a duck, a pig, a cow or sheep-stealing. This in itself would appear to support an assumption that the offences were the result of 'hand to mouth' lifestyles. The case of Catherine Molloy illustrates the background familiar to those women who lived hand to mouth on the streets of the towns and cities of Ireland. Molloy, alias 'Pretty Kitty from her remarkable ugliness', was convicted at Cork City Assizes for stealing £10 from Humphrey Twomey. The offence was reported in detail in the *Freeman's Journal*, reinforcing the assumption that this crime was 'typical' of the women criminals of Ireland's cities: 'Pretty Kitty' had met the prosecutor 'a stout, well-looking young country fellow passing through North main street Cork on St Stephen's night'. A prosperous young pig-dealer, he had sold some pigs for £10. 'Pretty Kitty' put her arms around his neck and then put her hand into his pocket and took the money out and ran away:

In cross examination, he said that he was not drunk when the money was taken from him, he had not drunk much during the day for he was under a bond of conscience not to take more than a noggin of whiskey and four pints of porter every day; he had gone to the extent of his conscience but that was all.

He had found the prisoner the same night of the theft in Mr Barry's house in the same street, had sent for the constable who had searched her, but 'she had only 2 penny bits, and he never got any money since'. 'Pretty Kitty' was convicted,

and being an old inhabitant of the gaol from which she had been lately liberated, having escaped transportation to which she had been sentenced at a former Assizes by successfully affecting bad health ... His Lordship renewed the sentence that she is to be transported for seven years.[22]

There are petitions from transported women which balance the contemporary picture of assumed immorality and depravity, assumptions reinforced in many cases by the recorded opinions of the surgeons on the convict transports. At least eight of the 108 women who landed from the *Almorah* in August 1824 had petitioned for mitigation of sentence. Only one, Mary Ryan, was listed by the surgeon as 'handcuffed on voyage for insolent and intemperate disposition'. Mary Ryan, widow from Westmeath, was convicted in Dublin of passing a £1 forged note. She was then forty years old, employed as a baker in Dublin with two children in Mullingar. She petitioned the Lord Lieutenant while a prisoner confined in the Penitentiary Prison at Grange Gorman Lane in Dublin:

That Petitioner without asserting her Innocence, or acknowledging her Guilt presumes not to arraign the Justice of her Sentence, She being unable to disprove the Evidence on which she was convicted from the Circumstance of the person from whom She received said Note having fled on Petitioner's apprehension.

That Petitioner who was previous to the death of her Husband in Opulent and respectable Circumstances is now reduced to the utmost Misery, aggravated by having two helpless Fatherless female Children solely dependent on her, in this most pitiable Situation She has no refuge but your Excellency's Mercy, and Petitioner humbly anticipates, her former Unimpeachable Character (proven on her Trial by highly respectable Testimony) never to have been on any occasion heretofore Impeached will forcibly plead in her behalf.

Was it anguish at leaving two 'unprotected' young daughters behind which led to her 'intemperate disposition' on the convict ship? Or was it simply uncontrollable resentment at an uncaring authority which had ignored her pleas and overlooked her 'respectable' character testimonials? For whatever reason, Mary Ryan, convicted felon, widow, mother, arrived in the penal colony with the reputation of an insolent and intractable convict felon. Mary Ryan was finally granted a ticket-of-leave in August 1829 and settled at Parramatta. There is no record that her young children joined her in the colony. She and they had paid dearly for the passing of a single forged £1 note.[23]

All the other petitioners on the *Almorah* were mothers of young children, for whose sakes they begged for mitigation of sentence or permission to take their infants and children with them into exile. Mary Griffin, a widow from County Kerry who could 'sew, spin and wash', was sentenced to transportation for 'killing sheep' at the age of about forty-one. The ship's surgeon described her as 'very quiet' on the voyage to New South Wales. Her petition claimed that she had been prosecuted by her neighbour, Mary Sullivan, 'a noted thief and a woman who had been repeatedly in Gaol for various felonies'. Her crime?

having the flesh and pelts of two Sheep found in her house at Tralee which Memorialist got from the prosecutrix who brought them to her from the lands of Clounalassa being a distance of several miles near which place the prosecutrix lived and which sheep your Memorialist afterwards discovered the prosecutrix had stolen from Mr Williams...

Mary Griffin claimed she was

a poor Woman upwards of fifty years of age who has seven helpless Orphans and a mother Crippled from age whom she was endeavouring to support and that severe distress only induced her to accept of this flesh and pelts the Prosecutrix...

152 *The Women of Botany Bay*

Her appeal 'on her prostrate Kneews [*sic*]' was supported by the Gaoler of Tralee Gaol. He added to her petition:

I know the prosecutrix Mary Sullivan ... who has been repeatedly Committed to this prison for several larcencies to be a common Thief nor do I think she is entitled to creditt, She in this Case turned King's Evidence to Save herself. I also know the petitioner and believe her statement to be true. I do not think her a subject fit for transportation as from her age ... She could be of little advantage (if any) in any distant colony.

A second petition, sent after her arrival at the Convict Depot at the City of Cork, begged for mercy for 'the long confinement' prior to her trial was 'sufficient punishment on her to Remunerate her offence'. Mary Griffin had added ten years to her age in an effort to gain clemency:

Memorialist is a poor old infirm woman of the age of Sixty years and upwards, burthened with the charge of five fatherless children [seven Orphans in the previous Petition] and an old feeble woman, her Mother a Cripple were depending on the honest acquisition of Memorialist.

All appeals were to no avail. Mary Griffin sailed on the *Almorah*, leaving behind for ever her five or seven fatherless children and her old, crippled mother. Despite her infirmity and her age, Mary Griffin married again within two years of arrival in New South Wales.[24]

Ann Connell of Cork was 'very well behaved', according to the surgeon of the *Almorah*. A small woman, barely four feet ten inches, she had been employed as a spinner in Cork when she was convicted of stealing cloth. She appealed for mercy first on the grounds that she was innocent of the crime: 'She being standing in the street when [the two accusers] came up ... and gave her a piece of Cloth and Requested her to keep the same for a few Minutes until they would come back'. Both her accusers had been previously convicted, and both, when arrested for the theft of this piece of cloth, informed against her and said she stole it. Ann Connell claimed that 'She is upwards of Fifty four years of age ... very infirm ... the Mother of Eleven Children, Seven of whom are alive and all females ... under the age of twenty-one and unmarried.' In addition to this, when she was taken from the Depot at Cork to Cork Cove and put on board a convict ship, the Inspecting Doctor pronounced her to be too feeble and infirm to undergo a voyage to New South Wales and she was sent back to the Depot.

Ann Connell was not considered 'a fit Object for Mercy', and sailed to New South Wales, leaving her husband and seven unmarried daughters in Cork. There is no evidence that the family was ever reunited. In 1828 'old infirm Ann Connell' was employed as an assigned servant by William Todhunter of Sydney, a clerk in the Commissariat.[25]

Margaret Fowkes, 'very quiet' on the voyage, had a husband who was a soldier and three children when she was transported on the *Almorah*. A house servant from County Kerry found guilty of shoplifting, she was permitted to bring her son James with her to New South Wales. Two other children remained with their father in Ireland.[26]

Elizabeth French, who had a husband and child in Mullingar, begged for mercy on the grounds that the prosecutor had taken 'some remarkable freedoms' with her while she worked as his house servant:

during her time in his Service he [the Prosecutor] laid all schemes, and watched all Opportunities of seducing your Memorialist, and did fully accomplish the same ... and Memorialist being then dismissed from his service ... by reason of Prosecutor's Wife taken Notice of some remarkable freedoms which Created a great disunion between the Prosecutor and Wife, and caused your Memorialist to withdraw from that Neighbourhood ...

Unhappily for Elizabeth French, this

wicked and designing man ... did still continue his freedom with Memorialist ... and unfortunately did bring her to his house, and did give [her] a full opportunity of taking away the Cloaths that Memorialist were convicted for ...

The Lord Lieutenant did not look on Elizabeth French with that 'Eye of Tenderness', despite the confirmation of her good intentions by the Inspector and Chaplain of the Mullingar Gaol:

during her confinement, both previous to her Tryal and Since her Conviction, conducted herself with great propriety. She is a protestant and attends Divine Service very regularly – and Received the Sacrament on Easter Sunday given under my own hand ...

Poor Elizabeth French was not pursued to the colony, nor did she find 'designing men' intent on her moral destruction after her arrival in 1824. Possibly for her own protection, she remained working at the Female Factory at Parramatta.[27]

The petitions give vivid insight into the backgrounds of so

many of the transported Irish women from town and county. They suggest a background of poverty which, in most cases, leads to the assumption that for at least some of these women there was no alternative to crime. Many of the offences, 'stealing butter', 'stealing a watch', 'picking pockets', 'stealing in a shop', 'stealing a sheet', would support the assumption of 'crime for need'. On the other hand, there are the street robbers, the housebreakers, the few highwaywomen, the gangs, who could be classed as 'professional criminals'. Motivation in either case is impossible to attribute. Women from all categories – the butter-stealer, the husband-poisoner, the women who knocked down their victim and threw him unconscious into the Liffey – all were punished with the same sentence: 'transportation for seven years'.

For the 'Pretty Kittys' of Ireland, crime was an established way of life, the aim was simply to avoid long imprisonment or transportation. What of the older women like Mary Griffin and Ann Connell, the widows with large families? Had their lives been based on crime or petty thefts? What of widows like Mary Ryan 'reduced from opulent circumstances after the death of her husband'? Could all of these women be classed together as 'the refuse of Ireland', suitable only for transportation to the penal colony of Botany Bay?

What was unexpected and unrecognised by contemporary observers, critics and officials, was the disparity between the assumed 'Irish' lives of these women and their colonial lives. This was more significant than the lack of contemporary recognition that, although all were convicted for major statutory offences, all were not convicted for the same offences. Criminals in Ireland, most of the transported Irish women settled in New South Wales as 'respectable' family and working women and were never again before a court for a major or minor offence, or for a misdemeanour. There were exceptions, and these were to be found on every transport, English or Irish, and it was these exceptions whose criminality, drunkenness, filth and obscenities agreed with British expectations as to the characteristics of women convicts living in a penal colony.

7
'A GREAT AND BITTER GRIEF'

The convict wives

... being truly thankful for that Royal Mercy which hath spared the life of her dear unfortunate husband but being in great and bitter grief at the prospect of being separated for life from him with whom she hath always lived in cordial affection and agreement ...

—The Humble Petition of Tamar Worsfold, Surrey,
to the Rt Hon. the Lord Sidmouth, 10 May 1820

Much has been written of the anguish of the men and women exiled from their families by the punishment of transportation. There has been little corresponding concern with 'that great and bitter grief' of the wives, husbands and children left behind. Many of the 'convict wives' found themselves 'wholly unprovided for', 'in a most pitiable condition'. Some were newly married, some 'pregnant and very near the time', some with 'infants imbibing from the Breast... the mother's Wretchedness', others with numerous 'helpless children without means of support... relying on a benevolent Publick'. They included older women like Catherine Slater who pleaded 'so much proper feeling is shown on both sides', and Jane Booth 'married twenty-one years and cannot forget her former love... this long and tried affection on both sides'.[1]

The despair of these British women 'left wretched in their native land with no prospects but increasing misery' did not become part of that mythology of suffering and inhumanity which was to cloak the origins of Australian society. Nor was their plight of any concern to His Majesty's government. They were the 'Innocent victims of [the] husband's bad conduct', overlooked both by contemporary officials and by historians examining the social and economic effects of the transportation system in Britain and in New South Wales. The convict wives became the forgotten women of Botany Bay.

Many of the women left behind in Britain and in Ireland tried repeatedly to obtain free passages to New South Wales to rejoin their convict husbands. Many of those husbands did their utmost to bring their families to the penal colony. Those 'free convict wives' who were successful in obtaining passage to New

South Wales became a unique group within Botany Bay society, but there was no recognition, by contemporaries or later historians, of the distinct and significant contributions they made to that society. Free and unconvicted themselves they became part of 'convict' society for they were inextricably linked with criminality through the offences of the husbands. Not only did they form family groups among those still under the sentence of the law, but they found themselves in unexpectedly new domestic situations. It was the convict wife who frequently became the head of the household, with her husband assigned to her as government servant or as ticket-of-leave man, serving the remainder of that sentence imposed in Britain as servant to his wife. Many of these wives found that they must apply for land grants, leases or allotments, for licences to brew, to bake, to distil, to run inns or public houses, to tender for wheat or produce, to apply for any indulgence at all, including the assignment of convict labour, for the husband as convict was legally ineligible to own land or engage openly in many economic activities. It was the convict wife, therefore, who had duties, responsibilities and opportunities which were in complete contrast to those normally associated with the family woman in her native land.

What kind of women were they, these convict wives, prepared to leave all that was familiar and sail with their children to that distant and unknown penal colony, to undergo a voyage which, even to seasoned Royal Marines on a regular tour of duty was so dreaded that 'the mind hardly dared contemplate the outcome'?[2] Was it only as an escape from the horrors of their destitution, or was it 'that great and natural affection' for husbands lost to them, perhaps for ever, which prompted those petitions to the 'Noble Secretary of State'? Surely he was 'too just and generous a gentleman to visit the iniquity of the Husband upon the unoffending wife and innocent babes'? Whatever may have been the reasons for those pleas, it was the anxieties, the privations and the destitution as wives of convicted felons in Britain which directly influenced their responses to their new lives as free women of Botany Bay.

As with their 'fallen sisters', the influence of the convict wives on Botany Bay society reflected past experiences in their homelands. The most important similarity they shared with the convict women was their class origins. Most of the convict wives were from the lower orders of British and Irish society, sharing a lack of skills apart from those traditionally associated with the domestic work of women. The determinative difference was that the convict wives arrived in New South Wales as wives, as family women, free women joining husbands and resuming family life. The convict women, on the other hand, whether married, widowed or spinsters, arrived in New South Wales as technically 'single women'. Their reputation was not protected by accompanying husbands, nor, after arrival, were they expecting to take their place as wife within a family. They were female felons, to be assigned as the governor saw fit or as need arose, to work as directed as punishment for their crimes. Convict woman and convict wife, therefore, arrived at Port Jackson with differing expectations and faced entirely different assumptions from officials and inhabitants of Botany Bay as to their expected roles in the colony.

The anxieties in the petitions from the convict wives for permission to rejoin their husbands are the key both to the expectations they brought to the colony and the realities they found. Petitions from both wives and husbands need critical assessment, avoiding any undue influence from 'that Eye of Pity' so frequently invoked by the petitioner and so often ignored by the petitioned. They are, however, the first-hand accounts of the main participants in that great tragedy which was the English criminal code. A first reading shows the overwhelming desolation, destitution, deprivation and despair which faced so many British women after the conviction of their husbands. A second reading indicates the complete disregard of the British government for the secondary economic and social effects of transportation, results evident in almost all the cities, towns and villages of Great Britain. Concern at government level for the widespread results of human suffering resulting from national criminal policies was non-existent. Convict wives and children faced almost unimaginable poverty, many with no resource except to rely on the 'charity' of their parish. Both free wife and convicted husband knew the reality of starvation which faced the family far from their own parish, ineligible for poor support. Neither the practical problems of family survival after the conviction of the father nor the emotional upheaval of separation of husband and wife were influential in softening the heart of British officialdom and granting free passages to all wives who applied. Neither did the sheer volume of appeals lead to any official governmental enquiry into the distressed state of families of transported men. Such concerns were not the responsibility of His Majesty's government.

Typical of the petitions were those of Mary Harris and Mary Ashton. Mary Harris of Wiltshire wrote that the transportation of her husband Silas had 'left her with six children in the greatest distress to lament his loss'. Mary Ashton had been married more than ten years when her twenty-eight-year-old husband was transported for life. She pleaded that 'he has been kind and affectionate' and she was 'desirous of residing with him wherever he may be ... she was in poor and distressful circumstances, unable to pay the passage of their nine-year-old son'. Her plea was supported by 'two respectable neighbours ... one a shopkeeper at Woolwich'.[3]

The petitions from husbands showed as much concern for their deserted families as for their own position in gaol, on the hulks, or transported to Botany Bay. Francis Smith, 'under rule of transportation' in Downpatrick Gaol in Ireland, was so anxious for the fate of his family that he sent his sick wife to London with a petition for the Prince Regent that the family be allowed to accompany him in his banishment. He pleaded – unsuccessfully – that he 'feared for the consequences' if his wife were left in Ireland without his support, for 'my wife and child ... are ill with severe fever'.[4] Zachariah Phillips, at the age of fifty-nine, was 'getting very infirm from wounds received in service'. Not so infirm, however, that the size of his family was limited. As Zachariah waited on the hulk *Justina* to be transferred to the convict ship which was to take him to Botany Bay 'for seven long years', he petitioned that he be permitted to serve his sentence at home or that his family be allowed to accompany him. He was 'full of anxiety ... for the distress of his wife and five children and she is six months pregnant with the sixth child and deprived of the happiness, comfort and mainspring of their support'. Despite his record of almost twenty-two years' service in the Royal Navy – he had been invalided out after his return from India in 1814 – and despite strong recommendation for mercy from 'several very respectable gentlemen', his plea was unsuccessful. His long service in His Majesty's Navy was of no interest to the Secretary of State. The infirm Phillips sailed for Botany Bay, his family remained in Ireland, utterly dependent on the grudging support of the parish.[5] This 'punishment' for the family was equal to, if not greater, than the punishment of the guilty husband.

The unconcern of the British government for the economic distresses of the families of transported men was not remarkable, nor did it cause comment. Why should His Majesty's ministers interest themselves in what was very definitely a local matter? Poverty, poor relief, vagrancy, all were the responsibilities of the local authorities not the British government. There was no official 'Eye of Pity' evident in Downing Street when

Terence O'Brien, transported for seven years, petitioned that his destitute family be given free passage to rejoin him in New South Wales. His first petition was neither acknowledged nor answered. In despair, O'Brien tried again: 'Since then [the first petition] his wife and child have died of starvation ... he applies for leave to take his other young children with him to New South Wales'.

The death of a convict's wife and child from starvation warranted neither comment nor sympathy from Downing Street. Nor was officialdom concerned with the remaining children left orphaned with no means of support. Permission for them to go with their father was refused. There was, however, bureaucratic concern that this second plea might also go unanswered, reflecting unfavourably on the administration. A private letter from Downing Street suggested:

I suppose nothing could be done for him were he a worthier subject than by his own account he seems to be but as this is the second Petition he has sent us, it would be very desirable that he should receive an answer which I take it for granted that you will give him.

O'Brien's 'unworthiness', after all 'it appears he is now transported for the second time', outweighed any consideration for the fate of his children. He sailed on the *Mariner* at the age of forty-five to repay his debt to British society by labouring in the Iron Gang at Prospect.[6] Was the almost certain death of his children by starvation an accepted and unremarkable part of the punishment for his crime?

The same lack of official interest was evident in the cases brought to the attention of the Secretary of State where the wife and children were left far from their native parish with no rights of settlement and no call on the 'charity' of the local authorities. John Ryan was a Dubliner. He and his Irish family were living in Chelmsford when he was sentenced to transportation for life. Ryan was well aware of the consequences for his family and advised his wife to petition the Duke of York:

Petitioner [Jane Ryan] is a native of Dublin, Ireland and has no claim on any Parish to protect her and her infant child. She is at present in a state of starvation and begs the first possible passage to go to New South Wales.

This petition was refused. The death by starvation of a felon's wife and baby was not the responsibility of government. John

Ryan laboured alone 'for the term of his natural life' in New South Wales while his family starved to death in Chelmsford.[7]

At local level, the Governors of the Poor or officials from the parish and from the workhouse occasionally wrote to the Secretary of State on behalf of the more distressing cases which became their financial responsibility. It is a reasonable assumption that most of these semi-official pleas for convict wives were prompted by parish self-interest. The parish petition always stressed the 'great and continuing burthen' these families were to the local poor rates. They did not, however, overstress the privations suffered by these women and their children. The 'official' tone of these petitions highlighted the poverty and destitution, the hopelessness and despair of the women forced to apply for poor relief. Many of these parish petitions included pleas from the wives themselves, explaining 'the great desire to follow my husband and take my children with me', the 'great and pressing need ... to regain the support and protection of my dear husband' or 'to perish in misery and starvation as does the Babe at my Breast'. What other option was there for women such as Hannah Yardley 'so anxious to follow my husband' when she had six children living with her 'in very distressed circumstances and under the necessity of becoming chargeable to the parish for support'?[8] Many of these wives were reduced to begging or to 'reliance on the Publick Charity' as the only way in which they and their children could survive. Employment was difficult to obtain, especially with the 'encumbrances' of young children. In local communities, the stigma of the husband's conviction was an added preventive to the wife securing honest employment. Margaret Street wrote not only of the privations, the great distress, which had resulted from her husband's 'unfortunate ... inadvertence':

the scoffs and taunts her husband's [conviction] has brought upon them ... and the stigma which attaches on herself and her young children generally, when any one of which has had the temerity to infringe upon his country's laws ... and the only hopes of bringing them up in the paths of virtue, and of regaining that character in society, which we have at present unhappily lost ...[9]

Mrs Garland had received permission to join her convict husband in New South Wales and to take their six youngest children with her. The eldest son, aged sixteen, was refused passage. A second application on his behalf was unsuccessful:

She has been most laudably and successfully diligent in training her family in virtuous habits and the boy has been a special comfort under the disgrace brought upon them which she bitterly feels. The idea of parting with him for ever occasions the deepest distress. [She begs] ... That she may have her boy with her ... [he] is nearly 16 years of age but only looks 13.

The official decision was that no male children above the age of fourteen years could 'proceed to their fathers being convicts in New South Wales'.[10]

The daughter of Edward Scofield was also refused permission to accompany or join her father: 'Petitioner is twelve years of age, destitute of friend or parent to help her find employment or a situation to earn her Bread. [She] requests her father be liberated or at least remain in England.' Fifteen householders of her parish supported her plea and her claim that her father was innocent 'he could not have committed the crime as he was in bed at the time'. This former militia man – he had served twenty-two years and was retired on a pension of sixpence a day – was transported to Botany Bay on the *Shipley*. His young daughter remained in England.[11] Botany Bay became, more and more, the only hope and salvation for the British families of men transported to New South Wales. As more and more convicts were transported, so did the number of petitions from destitute wives and families increase.

These petitions, from wives, friends, parish officials, gaolers, surgeons, priests and chaplains, are far more than contemporary accounts of personal tragedies. They reflect clearly official and popular attitudes towards crime, criminals, punishment, poverty, charity and contemporary society. They unintentionally document that great and growing gulf between British perceptions of the nature of her penal colony and the colonial characteristics which were emerging at Botany Bay. Further, they evidence the changing assumptions of the lower orders of Britain towards life in the convict colony and the opportunities it offered. The great disparity between the realities of colonial life and the unchanging attitudes and assumptions of the 'respectable' classes of Britain as to the nature and characteristic of the convict colony is clearly evident in the petitions and letters from convicted family men.

At local level of parish or village those who considered themselves respectable, persisted in holding the belief that Botany Bay was neither more nor less than 'the receptacle for the scum, the sweepings of the gaols, hulks and prisons'. This assumption was nourished by the literate, and those with literary pretensions, in articles such as those by that self-proclaimed expert on New South Wales, Sydney Smith. It was Smith, perhaps more than any other non-official contemporary, who perpetuated the belief that England's penal colony was 'a sink of infamy in which the convicts of both sexes become infinitely more depraved than at the time of their arrival'.[12] One example of this acceptance of the continuing and growing 'infamy and viciousness' of Botany Bay was an atypical letter sent to Robert Peel by the magistrates of Norfolk in 1822:

Elisha Baker committed last Norfolk Sessions . . . is of so bad a character it is highly desirable that he should be sent to Botany Bay instead of being confined in the hulks . . . Although this man has a wife and six children and is settled in a Parish more burthened with poor than any other in this neighbourhood, the inhabitants would prefer the expense of their maintenance to having him amongst them.[13]

Such generosity on the part of the parish was almost unheard of. There was no consideration given to the wishes of the wife and six children who, quite conceivably, saw Baker in a different light and may have preferred to accompany him to New South Wales. The central point of the petition was directed at the removal of that 'vicious character' to the place where he belonged, Botany Bay. So great was this wish that the parish was prepared to support his family.

Wives left behind in Britain and husbands transported to New South Wales petitioned colonial officials, the British government officials and any respectable person they thought influential enough to intercede with the Secretary of State and obtain permission for wife and children to be granted free passages to New South Wales. Even the prosecutor was asked to petition the Secretary of State on behalf of the man who had wronged him. William Tidman, from whose barn Thomas Tatt had stolen quantities of wheat, wrote to Lord Sidmouth after Tatt had been sentenced to seven years' transportation:

My Lord,
The wife of Thomas Tatt which is now lying at Wollege under sentence of transportation for seven years for taking some wheat from me, requested me to lay before your Lordship her Petition not to send him from England having four male children which your Worship will have the goodness to remit that part of his sentence his wife and children will ever be in duty bound to pray, as I freely forgive him myself.[14]

164 *The Women of Botany Bay*

Many husbands wrote – or had written for them – letters to their wives, urging, even beseeching them to bring the children and come to a new life at Botany Bay. John Willmott, while aboard the *Canada*, requested that 'the wife whom he highly esteems' be allowed to sail with him to New South Wales. What influence he had is unknown, but Sarah joined him the following year, bringing with her the daughter born shortly after the father left England. Charles Ellis, transported in 1818 for seven years, wrote to his wife Rebecca in Sheffield three years later that he had become a clerk of the lumber yard in Sydney 'under the direction of Major Druitt':

he has more than 300 men under his control and a salary which will enable him to maintain his wife and children in a decent and comfortable manner. Major Druitt, Chief Engineer of the Colony, will attest to his good conduct, sobriety and integrity . . . [15]

John Gamble, transported from Durham for fourteen years in 1819, wrote to his wife Ann that he had received permission for his family to join him. He was in the service of Colonel Johnson as a coachman and had petitioned that he be emancipated and allowed to be fully self-supporting without further assistance from the government by being granted a suitable piece of land to farm. No less than 'thirty-one signatures [supported him] as a respectable and credible person'. Two years later, his wife and two children sailed to Botany Bay on the *Jupiter*.[16]

These and similar letters sent from convict husbands at Botany Bay stress the need to re-evaluate the emphasis which has been given to certain characteristics of convict society by 'respectable' contemporaries and perpetuated by later historians.

One of the most significant of those characteristics was the disproportionate ratio of women to men in New South Wales. There is no question at all that Botany Bay was a male-dominated society, numerically speaking. What is doubtful is the accuracy of the effects this was supposed to have had on the moral standards of society. That the ratio was never more than one woman to four men and, in the outlying settlements often as low as one to seven or eight, was the basis for the modern interpretation that the role of women in the origins of Australian society was that of 'degraded and prostituted victims of victims'. As women were in short supply it has been assumed that they were forced into prostituting themselves, forced into the lifestyles of harlots and whores. Historical 'evidence' as justification for this assumption was not difficult to find. Samuel Marsden himself publicly lamented the fate of the 'Unhappy Objects' with no economic or social alternative to a life of prostitution on the streets of Parramatta and Sydney Town.[17] What has been overlooked was not only the complexity of 'convict' society at Botany Bay, and the role of family women, but the role of the convict family men who did their utmost to recreate the normality of life as they had known it by bringing their wives and children to the colony. Convict men, acutely aware of the hardship which characterised the lives of their families in Britain and who worked, saved, petitioned and pleaded to bring those families to the security the convict colony could offer. Family life was unexpected in the convict colony and its existence among the convicted remained unremarked, unreported.

These transported men who had left wives and children in Britain, brought the conflicting influences of despair and normality to Botany Bay. The first cannot be measured, quantified or analysed, but had, nevertheless, lasting effects on that indefinable mystique of a people. Men without wives was as determinative as men without women for colonial society. The sum total of despair, of the misery of separation, of the certain knowledge of the poverty and sufferings of the family left in Britain, the anxiety and the helplessness, all this was a great but unrecognised part of that vast shadow of human desolation which clouded the European settlement of Australia.

The second influence, more measurable in terms of human conduct of men and women as family units within a society, was the existence of these families in a convict society, brought together by the actions of the convicted father. These were abnormal families in the sense that the fathers were convicted felons still under sentence of the law, who had nevertheless voluntarily assumed the responsibilities of family men within free society. Many were assigned to their free wives, but the family unit of free mother, convict father, came-free or native-born children, was evidence of the normality of life in a penal colony; a normality where the convict male did not necessarily lust after the degraded female convict, where the free mother found her own economic value to the family and to society was far greater than that in her homeland, and where the children grew and worked within the protection of a family. The disparity between the life of a convicted family man in New South Wales and that of a convicted family man in the hulks or gaols of Britain was almost unimaginable.[18]

Of course, Botany Bay was no Arcady. All transported husbands were not good men and true, nor were all convict wives faithful, industrious and deserving, nor were all colonial reunions successful. Mary Kette wrote to the governor that 'her coming had not brought her husband the happiness they thought'. Mary McPherson found that her husband had developed 'habits of intoxication' and, to her distress, 'when he was given the indulgence of being assigned to his wife, this encouraged him in habits of drinking and intoxication'.[19]

James Wiggins was transported to Botany Bay from Newbury in Berkshire in 1813, apparently unlamented by his wife. In 1821 the scandalised rector of Newbury wrote to Lord Sidmouth:

James Wiggins left a wife who now resides in my Parish and has applied to have read Banns to marry a man she has for a long time scandalously cohabited with.

James Wiggins was tried at Newbury and she has not heard from him since he left her and she believes or wishes him dead ... May I request whether James Wiggins is now living and in what part of the Colony?[20]

Mrs Wiggins's immoral behaviour was not typical of the wives left behind in Britain. It would have been considered far more appropriate for a woman in Botany Bay than for a wife in a Berkshire village.

Among the mass of petitions asking for information on the whereabouts of a transported husband, usually sent by wives who had been unsuccessful in their attempts to gain free passages, there are few which show any lack of concern as to whether the man is alive or dead. Most evidence deep concern for the fate of the prisoners in distant New South Wales. The family of William Holland, receiving no answer to their first inquiry, petitioned Lord Sidmouth a second time: 'The family is still distressed not to have heard the fate of their husband and brother and plead for an answer'. Did they ever hear that he remained as a labourer in the district of Airds where he had spent most of his seven years' servitude? Or was the reply similar to that received by the 'distressed wife' of James Knowles, sentenced in 1812: 'This Office cannot furnish this information'. The husband of Elizabeth Brown was also transported in 1812. Six years later she wrote: 'I am his wife and have two children and I never heard from him since he been gon'. Samuel Owen, a silk dyer was transported for theft from Manchester in 1816. In 1819 his wife tried to find out if he were dead or alive: 'he left a wife and children unprovided. There is a small sum of money that she will get on his death but she needs the particulars of the same, where and when he died.' What official reply his wife received is unknown, but reports of his death in 1819 were premature. Samuel was still living in Sydney in 1828. He was then sixty years of age and working as a servant in Goulburn Street, Sydney.[21]

One wife who did receive a reply to her query that she 'wishes to know if her husband is alive or dead' was Mary Parish of Staffordshire. Her petition showed that it was not unusual for contact to continue between a transported husband and his wife. Parish had been sentenced to transportation for fourteen years in 1817. Two years later his wife wrote:

she has not heard from him and fears her dear husband is dead. The other men who went abroad with him have written to their families but he has not and she wants to find out if he is dead or alive ... She has been told that she can write to the Transport Board and they can tell her if he arrived in New South Wales.

Eventually Mary Parish was told that her husband had arrived in New South Wales. Whether she then wrote to her 'dear husband' and tried to rejoin him is unknown. Ten years later he was a ticket-of-leave man, working as a nailor in Parramatta Road, Petersham.[22]

Complaints regarding 'coolness' between husbands and wives reunited in the colony were rare, considering the numbers of convict wives who did manage to obtain passage to New South Wales. If disagreements led to physical assault between the parties, this seldom came to the notice of the authorities. There were, for example, no 'disagreements' reported such as that which ended in the murder of convict Katherine Evans by her de facto husband after 'they had both been intoxicated, and had quarrelled on the night preceding and in the morning of the murder'.[23] Convict Edward Collman showed extraordinary restraint at the conduct of his wife after her arrival. Collman had been transported in 1819 and had repeatedly sought permission for his wife and children to join him. They arrived on the *Providence* – his wife Ann, their three children and 'a little girl, the daughter of the man she had been cohabitating with' since his transportation. Collman's brother had written to him of her 'atrocious behaviour' in England but the wife simply tore up the letter when shown it by her husband. She then 'formed an improper connection with William Cooper, clerk to Mr Meehan' who lived next door to them. Her husband applied to the governor for assistance when his wife took their seven-year-old son and openly lived with Cooper. Ann Collman was incapable of fidelity, for the second appeal from her husband reported that

'James Saunders brags in the Barracks about his cohabiting with her'. Collman, showing remarkable self-control, told the governor that he did not 'wish to injure his wife's character but is explaining his coolness to her'. He petitioned that, in these distressful circumstances, the government

> make him a clerk or in such other capacity as you may deem proper ... and be sent to a place remote from Sydney ... I would not wish even if possible never to breathe the same atmosphere with a woman so entirely lost to all sense of shame.

Edward Collman was granted his wish. He took what must have been his 'great and bitter grief' up country with him to Inverany [*sic*] where he was appointed constable to the Bench of Magistrates by a sympathetic officialdom. And his shameless wife? No more is heard of her, but doubtless this free woman continued to add to the vile reputation of the women of Botany Bay.[24]

Fortunately for the success of applications from convict wives, Ann Collman was a rare exception. She was also fortunate in her husband's forbearance. Barnabas Traynor was far more demanding of his wife. Traynor had been transported for life from County Wicklow and had received Macquarie's permission for his wife to come to him in New South Wales, for he was a man of proven good character and industrious habits. It would seem he was also determined to be master in his own household. His letter to his wife informing her that he had arranged her free passage was couched in such terms that 'the poor woman' applied to the gaoler at Wicklow to help her. Traynor had written 'he would wait two years for her arrival and after that period he would get another wife'. Although Mrs Traynor expressed her anxiety to rejoin her husband – and her distress at his letter – there is no record of her arrival in the colony nor of Traynor's 'remarriage' to a woman in Botany Bay.[25]

It is not possible to establish any pattern or to trace any definite policy in the responses to the applications for free passage and the success or failure of those applications. Neither the office of the Secretary of State nor the local parish authorities appeared certain of procedures to be followed or regulations which should be complied with. Practices varied from county to county, even from parish to parish. Decisions to assist or to recommend individual cases were based on either local knowledge of the petitioner or the wish to remove a financial burden from the parish rates, or a combination of both. One feature which does emerge clearly is that few of the applicants were from

London, most being county women. The convict wives who did arrive in New South Wales, therefore, did not have any of the stigma attached to the Newgate women and to the poor of the metropolis. The explanations for the comparatively few 'London' wives are, first, that most of the men transported from London were younger than those from the counties; second, more of those capitally convicted or sentenced to transportation in London were unmarried and, third, that it is probable that wives left unprovided for in London may have returned to their native parishes where this was possible so that they could apply for the relief of the poor.

Two exceptions were the families of James Hinnegan and Richard Hicks. Both petitions were atypical and both were successful. Cecilia Hinnegan wrote that she would sell everything she possessed to pay the passage for herself and her child if she were given permission to sail in the same ship as her unfortunate husband.

The petition regarding Hicks indicates the reaction of local officials and neighbours to his sentence of death for stealing. Was this plea for mercy linked with a hope that, if transported, the family of this 'poor man' could be assisted to join him in New South Wales thus relieving the parish of the added expense of their support?

I have been requested to write to Your Lordship respecting Richard Hicks a man who was resident ... in the County of Middlesex and was convicted at the Old Bailey Sessions ... for stealing ... and sentenced to be hanged. The Prosecutor and other respectable neighbours are most anxious to save the man from being executed and wish that this punishment might be commuted to Transportation. He has a wife and three children and if Hicks is sent to New South Wales a subscription would be entered into for the purpose of sending out his wife and children and by this means this Country would relieve themselves from the whole of the family which must otherwise be a Heavy Charge on the Parish ... A Petition most respectably signed has been in circulation in Hick's favour ...[26]

This concern for a condemned man was not only atypical of parish authorities but unexpected. The dominant feature in petitions involving local authorities was the heavy expense which devolved on the parish when a family was left destitute. The family of Hicks sailed to Botany Bay with the help of their respectable neighbours. The family of Hinnegan, paying their own passage, had no difficulty in obtaining government permission.

The British government had been unconcerned with the disruption of family life caused by the transportation of English criminals to the North American colonies in the eighteenth century. It remained unconcerned with personal tragedies when transportation was resumed after the American War of Independence and Botany Bay became the new receptacle for her outcasts. There was no discussion in the House of Commons, no committees set up to report on the social or economic consequences of transportation on the lower orders of British society. From time to time the moral implications of a colony of thieves where women were in short supply caused some slight discussion. The emphasis was on the problem of maintaining discipline, order and morality in a place with a shortage of women as sexual partners. The problems of wives without husbands, of marriages technically dissolved by the banishment of husband or wife, was not given precedence over the basic question of the sexual needs of convicts in a convict colony where this might affect penal discipline and colonial security.

At local level throughout Britain and Ireland, the concern for separation of husband and wife was fundamentally an economic one, for the family left behind became chargeable to the parish. Where were the humanitarians, so concerned with the welfare of the enslaved coloured peoples of the world, so unconcerned with the enormity of distress of the women and children of Britain? What of the charitable endeavours of the ladies of the local communities? Were they so anxious to 'reform' the fallen and convicted women that they had no time for the miseries of women left destitute through no crime of their own? The only individual concern was evidenced in semi-official or private letters from local clergymen, doctors, an occasional master of the workhouse or gaol superintendent, and, very occasionally, from a group of 'respectable neighbours', as in the case of Hicks.

No wives had been permitted to accompany the convicts on the First Fleet. And why should they? Felons in the hulks and gaols of Britain were not given the comfort of their wives and children. As one coffee-house wag expressed it, 'Why should Pitt grant this indulgence to convicts when he denied it to himself?' When the Second Fleet was preparing to sail there was a suggestion from Cabinet that the wives of convicts should be allowed to accompany their husbands. In 1789 Grenville wrote to Phillip:

nine hundred and thirty males and seventy-eight females have been embarked . . . the number of female convicts bearing a great disproportion to that of the males, it was thought advisable that such of the latter as were married should be allowed to take their wives with them on board the ships ... or even women that cohabited with them ... few of the latter descriptions of women have been prevailed upon to accede to the proposal ... [they] are to be furnished with the same articles [clothing and provisions] as the female convicts.[27]

There is no evidence which suggests the reason for this generosity on the part of the government nor why so few wives wished to avail themselves of the offer. Nor was this generosity repeated. It is probable that this initial 'indulgence' was linked with the problems Phillip had outlined to the British Cabinet in maintaining morality, discipline and order in a penal colony with such a marked imbalance of the sexes. Phillip had advised at least four possible solutions, all as strongly linked with maintaining civil order as much as with moral considerations.

The first solution was that native women from the aptly-named Friendly Islands be brought to the colony as 'companions for the men'. Phillip eventually decided that this was not practical, not from any considerations for the morality of such an action, nor with any concern for the future of a settlement where the parentage of its future generations would be a blend of British felons and imported native women. The obstacle was shortage of supplies which would cause these women to face possible starvation and death. Such a fate could not be tolerated by the humane governor.[28]

The second suggestion was a very clear indication of the attitudes of respectable, even 'enlightened', gentlemen of the time towards the standards of morality and decency expected from convicted felons. A certain place, Phillip wrote, could be set aside where those women who were willing could receive the visits of the men. Was this the germ of that assumption which was to gain such wide credence, that New South Wales was little more than an extensive brothel? Phillip was an understanding man. He foresaw no difficulties in accommodating the men of the colony. Neither did he foresee difficulties in selecting sufficient convict women prepared to take part in this scheme. He did admit that there might be some women of 'such tender years' that they were not yet steeped in infamy and vice, and these must be protected. On the whole, however, he was assured that his female charges lacked both 'virtue and honesty'.[29] This scheme suffered the same fate as that for the importation from the Friendly Islands. It remained a plan which was not put into effect – officially.

The third suggestion, legal marriage, appeared a part answer to the problem and Phillip attempted to promote this to the fullest possible extent. Marriage in the colony was, however, a very limited solution to the problem of men without women as sexual partners. It was no answer at all to the continuing problem of maintaining both morality and discipline in a prison camp without gaolers, without places of confinement where conduct could be both supervised and regulated. It was not only theoretical but practical considerations which plagued Phillip almost as much as did the maggots in his meat, the weevils in his flour. Not all the women convicts were desirable as marriage prospects – some were 'the perfect antidote to desire' – and not all were prepared to become 'partners' for the men. What of individual women such as eighty-two-year-old Dorothy Handland? Or that poor idiot girl Rebecca Bolton? What of the sick, the lame, the diseased and, more importantly, those who remembered the families they had left behind in the Old Country as a bar to marriage in the colony? It was certainly desirable to encourage colonial marriage but practical considerations appeared unsolvable.[30]

The married convicts who had been separated from their families were the group least considered by Governors Phillip, Hunter and King. Before leaving New South Wales, Phillip made his final suggestion to the British government by which the immorality in the colony might be lessened, if not overcome. This was that an incentive be offered to the convicted men to reform their vicious ways and become honest, industrious and deserving settlers in the colony. Proof of such reformation could lead to the indulgence of their wives and children being granted free passages to New South Wales.[31] There is no evidence of any enthusiastic response from the British government to this suggestion. With Phillip's departure the two Lieutenant-Governors who successively administered the colony until Hunter's arrival were more preoccupied with the well-being of the officers of the New South Wales Corps than with the sexual deprivations of the male convicts in their care. Without specific recommendations from the colonial government, British officialdom showed no interest in the private lives of the transported men and women, and few convict families sailed for Botany Bay. On the *Albemarle*, for example, there were 250 male convicts, six female convicts and two convict wives. Four wives sailed with the 262 convict men on the *Admiral Barrington*, one on the *Active* which brought 154 convicted men to the colony, and none on the *Matilda* which arrived with 205 male convicts, or on the *Britannia* which 'discharged 129 men at Port Jackson.' These ships all arrived in 1791, bringing a total of one thousand convicted men to the colony and six convict wives, one of the women on the *Albemarle* having died on the voyage. Was this indicative of British planning and concern for the well-being of the convict settlers in her convict colony?

Lack of policy, rather than any direct recommendations or instructions to colonial governors continued to characterise decisions regarding passages for convict wives. Passages were considered 'an indulgence' and were granted on the known character and worthiness of the convicted husband rather than on the circumstances in which his family found themselves after his deportation. Such indulgence might be granted to state prisoners, such as Byrne and Dwyer, whose wives and families were given passage on the *Tellicherry*, or in exceptional cases such as that of clergyman Henry Fulton, whose lady wife was permitted to accompany that reverend gentleman into exile.[32] The circumstances of the wife were rarely considered, except occasionally in cases where she had acted as informer or turned King's Evidence, thus placing her own life in danger. Celia Cosgrove was a convict wife who sailed on the *Woodman* to join her husband David. 'She had given information about a murder in Galway and she was sent with her child for safety.' Unhappily for this convict wife, her reputation was known on the *Woodman*, and she had to apply to the governor for 'protection from the noxious insinuations of some of the people who came with [her] on the *Woodman*'. Her husband David, who had arrived the previous year to serve a fourteen-year sentence, had already received the 'indulgence' of bringing his elder son, ten-year-old Patrick, with him. The husband now became the wife's government servant and she the titular tenant farmer at Cabramatta, where they lived far from the recriminations of their neighbours in Galway.[33] A just reward from the British government for 'honest and deserving informers'?

Comparatively small numbers of convict wives arrived in New South Wales during the first twenty or so years of settlement. Sometimes the wife accompanied the husband, but more often the family sailed on different transports. Daniel O'Neel and his free wife Sarah both arrived in 1815, he on the *Indefatigable*, she on the *Northampton*. This was unusual, for it was normally a year or even longer before passage could be arranged for the wife. Thomas Downes, who arrived on the *Minerva* in 1800 waited eight years for his wife Rosetta to join him.

In 1802 the British government made an atypical gesture by allowing thirty free wives to accompany their husbands on the

HMS *Calcutta*. Hobart explained the reason to the colonial administration:

> in consideration of some favourable circumstances which have appeared in the character of the husbands, it has been judged proper to allow the permission of accompanying them into exile and taking with them their children to the number of ten.[34]

Such indulgence did not become a regular practice. It was not until 1812 that convict wives became an official concern of the British government; concern in the sense that some 'policy' needed to be formulated, some action taken to show that Downing Street responded suitably to recommendations made by Select Committees of the House of Commons. This particular Select Committee had been set up to report on transportation to New South Wales. Doubtless many of its members were influenced by the widely accepted reports of the debauchery, drunkenness and depravity of that convict colony. Among the recommendations to improve the morality of Botany Bay was the recommendation that 'greater facility' be given by the government to granting passages for wives and children anxious to join their husbands in exile.[35] Bathurst had the task of explaining this recommendation to Macquarie. It was also necessary for him tactfully to alert the governor to the need to show compliance with Select Committee recommendations, while at the same time ensuring that any one of those recommendations did not add to the expense of colonial administration.

Passages for ten wives may not seem an adequate response to that 'further facility' recommended by the Select Committee. Rather would it appear a 'token' acquiescence by Bathurst to a government recommendation. Bathurst, cautious as ever, was acutely conscious of the need to restrain rather than increase colonial expenditure, a restriction not suffered by any Select Committee. The passage of free wives was inextricably linked with one unspoken question: who would be responsible for their maintenance and support after their arrival? Bathurst made this quite clear in his instructions to Macquarie: the wives permitted to sail on the *Kangaroo*

> had been recommended as of good character and industrious and it is hoped that few or none of them will become a Burthen to the Public Stores but on the contrary that their own Labour, added to that of their husbands' extra hours will be sufficient to procure them the means of

Subsistence; and they have all been informed that they are not to be victualled at the public expense after their arrival in the Colony.[36]

It would appear almost certain that these women owed their free passages not so much to their 'good characters' as to the need of the government to show a positive response to the Select Committee recommendations. What other reason could there be for overcoming, even in this small degree, that 'growing apprehension [in the British government] of the increasing number of rations issued in the Colony at Public Expense'? That permission for these wives to travel to New South Wales was regarded by Bathurst in the light of an experiment is shown clearly in the wording of his instructions to Macquarie:

You are not to consider yourself precluded from continuing to issue rations to these Women if it should be absolutely necessary, but I am to desire you will take early opportunity of acquainting me how far the expectation entertained here, as to the possibility of their being able to subsist themselves without assistance is well founded, as the further extension of this measure will depend on the result of the present experiment.[37]

This first 'convoy' of wives had seven long months in which to consider their future lives in the colony. The brig *Kangaroo* had been made 'of green timber', and prolonged stops were necessary in Rio to recaulk the entire 'upperworks, they having proved leakey', and at the Cape to refit the rigging which had been washed away in the heavy gales.[38] The sixteen free wives and 'a considerable number of children' who landed at Port Jackson would doubtless have shown great hesitation had there been any need whatsoever for them to return to Britain.

The expectation that all convict wives would prove no expense to the colonial public purse was not realised. In 1814 Macquarie wrote to Bathurst that he had been obliged to issue rations to free persons, including 'Wives of Convicts who arrived Free themselves, a Mr. Mathew [relative of Lord Gambier] with his family, a Mrs. Sims and her family and some others':

all these Persons arrived totally destitute of the means of Support, and are Unable either from their rank, Age, Sex or infirmities to support themselves. No alternative was left Me, but either see these Friendless Creatures Starve, or place them on the Bounty of His Majesty's Stores.

Macquarie added advice which effectively removed any blame from the governor himself for the need to place these free passengers on rations:

> The Inquiries now Instituted at Home in regard to the means of Subsistence possessed by Persons Soliciting permission to Come hither will, I trust effectively prevent Such Occurrences for the future and be attended with the happiest Consequences to the Persons themselves.[39]

It is probable that this suggestion by Macquarie prompted the adoption of the regulation – informal as it was – that any convict requesting the indulgence of a passage for his wife must first receive the recommendation of the colonial governor. Bathurst had replied to Macquarie's despatch by informing the governor that he had made the Home Department aware of the additional expenses which could be involved in granting free passages to convict wives. He added: 'Measures will be taken to prevent as far as possible the Embarkation of Wives of such Convicts who are either unwilling or unable to support them on Arrival.'

Bathurst added instructions that 'returns should be occasionally sent home of such Convicts who may have applied for permission for their Wives to join them'. It was to be the responsibility of the colonial governor to comment to the Home Department on whether or not 'such Persons have the means of maintaining wives and families'.[40] This despatch was sent from England in May 1816. Until it reached the colony, Macquarie continued to face those problems of additional expense. The moral issue of reuniting families, of alleviating the great distress and want of wives left in Britain, was not a consideration. Local poverty in the home country remained very definitely a local responsibility. Neither the British government nor the colonial administration considered that these problems were in any way their responsibility.

With the arrival of the *Broxbornebury* in 1814, Macquarie again explained to Bathurst that many of the free wives had to be rationed from the Public Store:

> Many of these Women [the convict wives] having large Families of Children, and None of them having the means of subsistence, I have been under the Necessity of putting them All on Store from time to time; had not this Act of Humanity been extended to them, they must have Perished from Want of Food.[41]

'A great and bitter grief' 177

With the arrival of the *Surrey* yet another problem of expense became apparent. What was to happen to the wife and family if the convicted husband had the misfortune to die before the arrival of his wife and children? What was to happen to the woman if the husband she accompanied died on the voyage? These possibilities had not been considered by Bathurst and his colleagues. It was Macquarie again who reported the unexpected but necessary expense this caused the colonial administration:

The Fever on Board the *Surrey* has deprived several of them [the wives] of their Husbands, by Which Means these poor Women are bereft of every Means Support for themselves and their Children and they are of Course supported ... at the Expense of Government.[42]

Problems such as this, to which no solution was offered by Bathurst, indicate the ad hoc fashion in which decisions were made in Britain about passages for convict wives. The success of applications from husbands in the colony and from wives in Britain was as unpredictable and erratic as the results of a lottery. That some 'system' did eventually develop may be attributed to the continual reports, suggestions and recommendations of Lachlan Macquarie.

Expense was unavoidable. Unavoidable until the British government realised that their only guarantee that a wife would not involve additional expense was a written certificate of recommendation from the governor in the colony, based on an investigation not only into the character of the husband but also his ability to support his wife. As Macquarie recommended to Bathurst:

I Conceive the Wives of Convicts should not be allowed Passages, or permitted to proceed hither unless they give Satisfactory Proof of their possessing the means of Supporting their families Without Becoming a Burthen on this Government, the Expense arising from the Victualling of those in Distress under the Present Circumstances is very Considerable.[43]

Two months after writing this despatch, the *Northampton* docked at Port Jackson with 110 women convicts and forty wives of convicts accompanied by their children. Macquarie was again faced with a 'weighty expense'. His recommendations, however, had their effect, and the numbers of wives permitted free passages were reduced considerably. The *Mary Anne* brought 101 convicted women and only fifteen convict wives. Fewer 'wives of Convicts and their Children' were given permission to sail in the

Friendship in 1817. It was not until the early 1820s that numbers of convict wives increased with every transport arriving in the colony. Local authorities, wives in Britain and husbands in New South Wales, were as unsure of the regulations and procedures for obtaining free passages as most of the colonial and British officials. One qualification was obvious to all: the good character of the convicted husband was an essential prerequisite for any indulgence. Mary Mulligan gave what she considered proof of the worthiness of her husband when she applied for passage for herself and their three children: 'His employer in New South Wales has given this Petitioner [the wife] a cheque for £10 which is clear proof of her husband's good character'. Not clear enough, it would seem, for William Horton. Mary and her children remained in Bailie'boro and her husband Peter continued as shepherd to that good employer, Alexander McLeod of Luskintyre.[44]

Ann Humphreys of the parish of Highworth in Wiltshire was more successful. She enclosed a letter she had received from her husband expressing 'a strong desire that she and her children should join him in his present situation where he has the ability to maintain them all, and she is very anxious to comply with her husband's wishes.'

Doubtless this natural anxiety was heightened by her position in Highworth. 'She and her three children had been Totally destitute of the means of support, being altogether dependent on the Parish.' It was the vicar of that parish who forwarded her petition to Lord Sidmouth with the strongest recommendations, not only to reunite the family, but to relieve his parish of the expense of maintaining the wife and children who had been 'born in lawful wedlock'.[45] The success of the application was in all probability due to the assurance that the husband could support his family.

It is quite improbable that Bathurst or any member of the British cabinet would have considered relieving the parish of Highworth of the financial burden incurred by poor rates for a convict's family and transferring that expense to colonial expenditure by the Crown. There was, however, less objection to providing a free passage if there were guarantee that no further expenses would be involved. Guarantee of this was very definitely the responsibility of the colonial governor, a duty to which Macquarie gave strict attention.

It was in December 1817 that Macquarie sent Bathurst the names of twenty-two convicts he had chosen from those who had applied to him for assistance in bringing their families to

New South Wales. Macquarie certified that these men 'are Considered capable of Supporting them on their Arrival here, free of Expense to the Crown'. His description of Simon McGuigan 'whose name stands at the Head of this List' indicates those qualities which Macquarie considered ample proof of 'worthiness':

Simon McGuigan ... has been Many years in this Colony, and by application and Industry has realised Sufficient property to Support his Family decently, were they here Altho' he could not Bear the Expense of their Passage; and his good Conduct gives him the fairest Claim to the Liberal Indulgence held out in Your Lordship's Dispatch to people of that Description.[46]

This 'Liberal Indulgence' did not become definite policy but continued to influence applications for free passages. An application, from a 'very distressed family with no means to support Life' after the transportation of the husband, was rejected by the Secretary of State on the grounds that

A regulation has been in force for some time not to send out wives of convicts until a certificate has been received from the Governor of the ability of the convict to maintain his wife and family on their arrival.[47]

Those most vitally concerned with securing free passages for destitute families were still the officials of the parishes to which the wives belonged. The concern remained entirely economic: the removal of 'burthens' on the parish. In whatever humanitarian terms their applications were couched, their success benefited the parish financially by transferring responsibility for maintenance of destitute wife and children to their proper guardian, the husband. Neither the government nor the parish questioned the assumption that a man convicted of a major felony and transported as a criminal to serve his sentence in a prison colony, would have the opportunity to support his family by his honest industry and diligence while still a prisoner of the Crown. The probability that the same man had been convicted of an offence closely linked with his inability to support that same family while a free man in his home country, remained unquestioned. This seeming paradox, that a guilty man of Botany Bay could support a family, an honest Britisher could not, was yet another example of the ambivalent attitude of the British respectability towards Botany Bay. Or was it simply further evidence of that complete lack of interest which characterised so many of the British government decisions regarding their expensive penal colony?

The common problem facing both parish and individual applying for assistance with passage to New South Wales was the complete ignorance of how and under what conditions passages would be granted and exactly who was responsible for incidental expenses. Mrs Stanfield of Lancashire was granted free passage for herself and her children after her husband had been transported 'for attending a radical meeting on George Moor at Yorkshire'. The township to which she belonged, however, 'would not grant her money to travel to the point of embarkation'. Fearful of forfeiting this 'liberal indulgence' she begged the Secretary of State for permission to travel on another vessel sailing soon so that she would have a little time to find money to travel from Lancashire to Portsmouth.[48]

Sarah Bell and her three children were on their way to the Irish transport which was to take them to New South Wales when one of her children developed smallpox. The surgeon who had to refuse to allow her to sail with the sick and contagious child took it upon himself to seek help for her from London:

I suggest she be sent to England to accompany a convict ship from there, but she needs money to support herself. She is at the Richmond Penitentiary House ... and what shall be done if she is not sent to England?

What indeed? Was it the surgeon himself or some unrecorded 'Publick Benevolence' which took pity on this convict wife's misfortune? Sarah Bell was one of the convict wives who sailed on the *Woodman*.[49]

Parish relief was barely enough to keep the wife alive. The weekly sum, even for a long period, would not equal the expense of a family's passage to New South Wales. Was it this which determined so many parish officials from offering either passage money or incidental expenses to the wives of transported men? The impossibility of a mother and five small children existing on three shillings and sixpence a week – the normal charity allowance in the early 1800s – did not influence the good parishioners and churchwardens of Bethnal Green to provide passage money for the wife of Thomas Newman, transported from that parish for life in 1818. They did, however, report her 'distressing circumstances' to the Secretary of State.[50]

The number of petitions from parishes asking for advice, seeking details of regulations regarding free passages for wives, even requesting 'forms' to submit, evidences the lack of knowledge both of government policy and an ignorance of colonial conditions. The parish was not concerned with what would happen to the family after arrival in Botany Bay. Their only consideration was how to get that family from their parish to New South Wales. As late as 1826 the Assistant Overseer of Chaverling parish wrote to 'the Home Department' asking if the wives and families of two men convicted at the last Assizes at Hartford and Essex 'could accompany them and at whose expense'. Two years earlier the churchwarden of the parish of Fressingfield in Norfolk had enquired 'if there were any allowances or encouragements for wives and families to join their husbands in New South Wales'.[51]

The Corporation of the Guardians of the Poor at Plymouth Workhouse were more direct in their approach for passage for 'Jane Davis and her two children under four years': 'she is unable to maintain [herself and the infants] and is reduced to great want and is obliged to apply to the Parish for relief. Her husband is awaiting transportation and she wishes to go abroad with . . . him.'

The Governor of the Workhouse, who was also Mayor of Plymouth, added a personal recommendation:

The bearer of this, whose Petition is enclosed is very desperate to go abroad with her husband . . . and has been advised to petition Lord Sidmouth as the woman is very solicitous to go as [in the event of] her remaining in this Country she is likely to be a great burthen on the Poor Rates of this Town, if you will be pleased to forward her petition to His Lordship you will much oblige the Corporation of the Guardians of the Poor.

Jane, with her children, took her petition from Portsmouth to London shortly before Christmas in 1819. How she managed in the bitter winter of that year and what was the outcome of her petition is unknown. Her husband, James, arrived alone in New South Wales on the *Shipley* in 1818. Transported for life he became a shepherd for the Macarthurs at Sutton Forest. Did that boy from Portsmouth speak of his young wife and children 'sentenced' to life on parish charity?[52]

There were parishes more charitable than that of His Worship the Mayor of Plymouth. When William Waters was convicted at Norfolk Assizes for sheep-stealing, his departure to Botany Bay left 'his wife in great distress with three children under six years of age [and] she is anxious to follow her husband to

Botany Bay and he is anxious she should'. The 'poor wife' pleaded: 'They will show their grateful sense of this Indulgence by his future reformed conduct and their joint endeavours to support their children in a course of honest and persevering industry.' Mrs Waters's petition was supported by the rector of their parish Fulmodesyome: 'the parishioners will be willing to assist this poor woman for her passage as His Lordship sees necessary'. His Lordship, however, apparently remained unimpressed by either the good intentions of the husband and wife, the distress facing the children, or the charity of the parish. There is no record of arrival in New South Wales.[53]

In the seemingly endless bundles of petitions from convict wives pleading for free passage to their husbands, there is no evidence at all of any doubt that their 'distressful circumstances' will end with their arrival at Botany Bay. Neither is there any anxiety for the future prospects of the children they are so desperate to take to that convict colony. It becomes increasingly apparent that, whatever may have been the assumptions of the respectability about that colony, the lower orders of British and Irish society saw Botany Bay not as a place of punishment but as a place where they could find opportunities unheard of in their homeland. Were these expectations based simply on desperation, on the hopelessness of their poverty in Britain? Were they influenced by the stories which filtered back from the colony, especially during the administration of Governor Macquarie, of unskilled convict men becoming landowners, publicans, independent working men able to support wives and families, even employ servants and labourers; of men with few or no skills who became well-established in the colonial economy? To the growing concern of His Majesty's government, it was the successes of the transported convicts rather than the 'horrors of the punishments of transportation' which appeared to have most influence on the lower orders of Britain. Irish convict John Lynch wrote at great length to his wife Mary, encouraging her to join him. The letter, a clear statement of the conditions in the colony as experienced by a convicted man, is the direct antithesis of that 'Sodom and Gomorrah' so often described in parliamentary debates, in contemporary British newspaper and journal articles:

My Dear Wife I take this favourable opportunity of writing these few lines to you of finding you in good health as I am at Present thanks be to God for it and not forgetting my children and your father and brothers and all well wishers.

And now I am to let you know that I am to send for you if you are willing to come and I will get you brought to me without any expence and if you are willing to come as soon as you Do Arive you are to get me a free man and you are to get 50 ackeres of Land as an Encouragement from Government and six months provision and that is to support us untill we have Got our own and that is another thing I have to mention to you that if I was a free man I would get £25 A year at the least and you that could milk and make butter would do better than I could for there is no women to do but men to make butter. And this I have to remark to you that no seven years man can obtain any Liberty untill he has served four years to one master. And this I have to remark to you not to be in the least Daunted at the coming of you to me for I never had such health as I had on sea and never got any sea sickness and sea sickness is nothing but a few days and if you do come bring a pount of tea or two with you and as much sugars as would do you three months once a day for if you get any Favourable wind you will come in that space of time and Cummiens wife that was sent from busheypark is come to her husband –

And now this Ierland that i am in is as holsome as Ierland and its now we have winter and our winter is finer than any summer in Ierland –

And if you come to go to Lynch the Shue maker that lives in Ennis and get a letter to his Daughter peggy. For she is married to one of the best Gentlemen in this Coloney and her self is a good Woman to any country men.[54]

Such letters were not uncommon. In 1815 Josiah Godber a machine-breaker, transported for life, wrote repeatedly to his wife of thirty years, his 'Dere Rebecca', describing the town of Sydney, his good 'master' and employment and the relative freedom he enjoyed. It was not, however, to improve her circumstances that he begged her to come to him: 'Oh my dere', he wrote, 'had I but known what it was to be torn asynder ... after all these years ... oh my dere all the powerrs ... would not have brought me hither'.[55]

Wives in Britain, however, continued to emphasise their distressing conditions, their abject poverty and destitution with no realisation at all that the humanity of the Secretary of State was directed by that single consideration of expense. Hannah Yardley wrote from Staffordshire two years after her husband William was transported for life that she had received a letter from her husband in New South Wales expressing a wish that his family join him. She had seven children, six living with her in very distressed circumstances. She added 'I am under the necessity of becoming chargeable to the Parish for support. I am very anxious to follow my husband and take my children with me'. She asked how she and her children could be 'conveyed to New South Wales and how they could be 'granted other allowances that are made in such case'.[56]

The success or failure of petitions from wives and convicted husbands formed no predictable pattern during the first forty years of transportation to New South Wales. The single factor which appeared to determine official response, both in Britain and in the colony, was an economic one. Would this 'indulgence' involve increase in colonial expenditure? Personal distresses, complete destitution of wife and family, proven industrious behaviour of the husband in the colony, the supporting testimonials from colonial employers or British parish officials, all were secondary to the question of whether or not it would be necessary to maintain the family in the colony at government expense. Added to this was the cost of passage to New South Wales and the cost of 'transporting' the free wife and family from whatever part of England, Ireland or Scotland where they had remained after the husband was convicted, to the port of embarkation and, in many cases, outfitting them for the journey.

The wife of John Proctor 'who very much encourages her to go to him' petitioned that she had no family and 'very small means of support, her husband being her only support'. She requested free passage to New South Wales and 'as she has no means of laying in a Sea Store that your Lordship would be pleased to allow her provisions for the voyage'. Matthew Kirkby was transported from Lancashire for fourteen years for having forged Bank of England notes in his possession. His wife, a weaver by trade, applied unsuccessfully for permission to take their two daughters, aged thirteen and seven, 'beyond the seas' with her husband. The family remained in Lancashire, the father working as a labourer at Cabramatta in New South Wales. Sarah Lawton sent her marriage certificate with her petition to Lord Sidmouth. She and her husband, a shoemaker, both of the parish of Wellingborough in Northampton, had been married little more than a year when William Lawton was sentenced to life transportation for burglary, leaving Sarah and her child with 'no means of obtaining a livelihood except by placing herself and the child on the Parish'. The young wife wrote that she was 'greatly attached to her husband' and begged to be allowed to sail with him. Was it fear of the expense of supporting wife and child which caused the application to be rejected?[57]

The degree of natural affection between husband and wife,

had the applicants only been aware, was of no concern to the British officials. Martin Donovan wrote:

[He] came by the *Mangles* and is from the Parish of Hook in Wexford County...he has left a wife, a child and orphan sister-in-law...he wants them all sent out. His sentence is for life and he cannot sleep the night thinking of their poor distress.

Could he support this family working as an assigned servant at West Bargo? Would not that family be far better off in the colony than starving in Clonmel in Ireland? These were not the pertinent questions. Phillip Butler was another transported man who obviously thought he could support his wife and three young children. He wrote to Governor Darling that he could keep all his family as he was qualified as a schoolmaster. In both cases, the plight of the families in Ireland was incidental.

For family men and women the added punishment, not only of separation from wives and children, but the certain knowledge of their distresses, their poverty, their destitution, added an immeasurable burden of suffering, a suffering which increased in accordance with the level of prosperity of the transported husband. This has been an unrecognised side of the 'horrors of transportation', equal in human misery to the overstressed physical punishments and inhumanity inherent in the workings of the transportation system.

That such family men existed among the transported convicts and that, where passages were given, these 'free-convict' families formed a nucleus of normality within a convict society, counteracts the distortion implicit in the acceptance of those contemporary opinions which painted New South Wales as 'a sink of iniquity', a recreated Sodom and Gomorrah. The expected 'depravity, vice and immorality' was not evident in the countless petitions from convicted men to have their families rejoin them in the colony.

This adds a new dimension to any understanding of convict society, as the plight of the wives in Britain shows that suffering, inhumanity, deprivation and even death from starvation were not the sole prerogative of convicted felons. In contemporary Britain, free and unconvicted women and children were left to starve, to live in greater desolation of mind and body than many of the inhabitants of Botany Bay. It is these women and children who were the innocent victims of the British criminal law. For those who did come to Botany Bay to take up or start anew their lives as 'wives', there would always be the undercurrent of familiarity with destitution and despair, the remembrance of their 'great and bitter grief'. In New South Wales, however, they were no longer the deserted wives of convicted felons, but free wives in a society which offered them and their families respectability and opportunities for economic independence.

8
'WOMEN OF PROVEN GOOD CHARACTER'

Women and crime at Botany Bay

The tendency of the women towards the men penned up in a ship, passing thro' hot weather, and on a salt diet, their sense of decency and shame broken down, restless, turbulant and impetuous in their disposition... women of the lowest and most depraved...

—Surgeon Superintendent James Hughes, Convict Transport

The great gulf between Britain's rich and her poor was one of the most rigid of social and economic distinctions. Custom, tradition, entrenched privilege had woven this as an iron thread throughout the entire fabric of social attitudes, assumptions and relationships. It was a distinction bred basically from class attitudes, from the assumption that heredity and inheritance created their own position and privileges so that it was the station in life of the parents which normally determined the lifestyle, opportunities or disabilities of every child born in Great Britain. For the children of the poor, escape from their preordained place in the social hierarchy was remote. These boys and girls were expected to work, to labour, almost as soon as they could walk. Daniel Defoe, an acute observer and a kindly man, found it most praiseworthy that in his whole tour of the Islands of Great Britain he found that 'the hands of children from the age of five were sufficient unto themselves' – children, that is, from the lower orders.[1]

There were, in effect, two distinct societies within the normal social hierarchical structure of Britain: a society of the rich and a society of the poor – the one respectable, the other needing guidance, inducement, even threats of punishment to maintain respectability. To describe this division as one between the haves and the have-nots oversimplifies the complexity and rigidity of the division. The poor, including the labouring poor, 'were not like us', either in their dress, their personal habits, their speech, customs, manners or appearance, their housing, their diet, their attitudes to life, to labour and its rewards. The gulf was as great and as insurmountable as the recognised social barrier which existed between the working classes and their employers. It had the added stigma of lack of respectability associated with poverty and this led to the expectation of criminal and licentious behaviour. It was far more difficult for a member of Britain's lower orders to gain any acceptance by the middle or upper classes – or even the upper working classes – than it was for the proverbial rich man to pass through the eye of the needle. Once convicted of an offence, whether misdemeanour or felony, once punished by the law, the criminal man or woman was forever a 'proven bad character', and conviction and punishment simply added confirmation to the assumptions and expectations of respectable society as to the criminality and depravity of the poor of Britain.

That the convict colony of New South Wales was populated almost entirely by men and women from Britain's lower orders, who had been transported as punishment for major felonies, led quite naturally to the assumption that Botany Bay was a criminal society in which all those undesirable traits associated with criminality and lack of respectability would be dominant. Most of the men and women transported were believed to be habitual offenders, unrepentant, incapable of reformation. It was known in Britain that imprisonment or physical punishment or both did not lead necessarily to reformation of the criminally inclined. The reverse was too often the case, young offenders learning from old lags, new associations formed in prisons to continue criminal activities after release, young women adversely influenced by the abandoned behaviour of women of notorious character and degraded immorality. These opinions were firmly supported by the published evidence of Select Committees, Reports on Prisons, and statistics relating to the high incidence of second and third offenders. Imprisonment in British gaols had failed to lead to the reformation of either manners or morals of habitual criminals or of first offenders. By 1820 there was official criticism of the ineffectiveness of 'enlightened' innovations which aimed at reformation by 'kindly' treatment, indulgences, training and even labour for payment while imprisoned. Even the reports and claims of Mrs Fry were questioned, and the effectiveness of her 'misguided methods' criticised. To most critics of Britain's penal system, the criminal was an object neither of pity nor of compassion. Redemption could be attained only by the severity of prison discipline, severity in every aspect of prison life, severity so intolerable that any man or woman committed to His Majesty's gaols would dread any return to such a life of deprivation, harshness and punishment. This theory was supported by a Report on the State of Prisons and Prison Discipline in 1820 which provided evidence to most respectable contemporaries that British prisons were filled with second and third offenders and were corrupt and vicious 'breeding grounds for crime'.[2]

If punishment or imprisonment in Britain were incapable of reforming criminals, how could contemporaries accept that transportation to a convict 'prison' colony might transform the scum of the criminal class into honest and industrious settlers? How could criminal women of infamous reputation in British gaols be expected to abandon their evil ways and become 'normal' family and working women in the prison colony of New South Wales? Such a belief was quite outside the contemporary framework of opinion and contrary to the evidence of characteristics of women imprisoned in the home country. Botany Bay was accepted as a convict settlement, so what inducements could contemporaries imagine existed in that vast gaol which would succeed in reforming the most hardened of habitual criminals? Surely that reformation was even more unlikely in a penal colony where the convicts lived among their own kind, part of a society of thieves, robbers, pickpockets, forgers, counterfeiters, shoplifters, highway robbers and worse. The women of the colony shared their immoral and depraved standards of life and were 'known' to be common prostitutes, women who would sell themselves for threepence and steal from the 'client', rob and thieve, drink themselves into insensibility, swear and curse with obscenities 'fit only for hell', bedraggled, dirty and unkempt, women who lacked any of the expected attributes of respectable females. It was significant that they arrived at a prison settlement as single women, not as part of a 'protected' family group for, by the very nature of the convict settlement, they had no choice but to associate with men and women convicted, like themselves, of crimes 'of the darkest complexion'. What hope could there be when even the example of 'good women' was so limited at Botany Bay as to be insignificant?

All matters considered, there was no room for respectable British contemporaries to question the assumption that the women of Botany Bay continued their criminal and immoral ways in the colony to which they were transported. Without doubt, those degraded wretches contributed equally with the men to the crimes against persons and property, to the vice, immorality, depravity and drunkenness which made that colony little more than an extension of hell itself.

Botany Bay, however, was as far from being a den of iniquity, an extensive brothel, as it was from being a paradise. Undoubtedly, it was a convict settlement and the need to maintain, supervise, discipline and punish the transported convicts was a major determinant in its administration and development. More importantly to the inhabitants, convict, ex-convict or free, it was a pioneer society, not in the sense of the American frontier pioneer settlements, but in the need and opportunities to develop the land and its resources, to 'create' a way of life which differed entirely from the known life of the home country. It was a government-controlled settlement, but one within which men and women, whatever their background, had the possibility of investing their initiative, industry and enterprise and, whether they drew the prizes or the blanks for their endeavours, were still able to secure a standard of living beyond comparison with that of their contemporaries who had served their sentences in British hulks and prisons. Few of the women under sentence were 'confined' as were the convicted women of Britain. Most were their own mistresses during the early years of assignment and, as the population grew, they served their sentences not as prisoners in deplorable overcrowded British gaols, but as servants in respectable households. Infringements of the rules brought punishment, but the opportunity for a 'respectable' life was there for the taking. The woman who committed colonial crimes lost more than her liberty, for she became a part of the criminal class of New South Wales, a group which differed in composition and nature from the criminal class of Britain, but was, nevertheless, the criminal underworld of Botany Bay.

Criminality was expected among the women of Botany Bay. It was not expected that the nature of this criminality would differ so markedly from that of women in any other European or American society. Criminality, crime, criminal class, were still defined according to British standards, attitudes and expectations and these definitions were increasingly inappropriate for colonial conditions. To take one example: Britain's 'criminal class' were her lower orders. Almost the entire population of New South Wales had originated from that same class level – the lower orders of Britain – but New South Wales was not inhabited exclusively by a 'criminal class'. The development of a small 'free society', the 'unconvicted' was accepted within the traditional British social structure brought to the colony by the higher civil and military officials and by the wealthier free settlers and their families. The development of a vast 'free society' among the ex-convict settlers was given as scant recognition as were the material achievements of members of the ex-convict inhabitants of the colony. To the exclusives, the 'pure merinos' who cherished their British-based claims to respectability and social superiority, the 'convict class' remained the criminal class, unfit to associate with the ladies and gentlemen 'of the first water' despite any proven reformation as shown in economic achievement, wealth or position. The complexity and diversity of the structure of 'convict society' was ignored, and although even the purest of the pure merinos would, if it were to his advantage, deal with former convicts in matters of trade, shipping and commerce, social contact was completely barred.

The criminal class of New South Wales was not the 'convict class' if convict were defined as transported felon sentenced in Britain or in British possessions to transportation to Botany Bay. These were the prisoners of the Crown, the government servants, the assigned servants, men and women under legal punishment of penal servitude for offences committed in their home countries. The criminals of New South Wales were those who committed colonial offences against the persons or property of other colonial residents. They came from all civil conditions in the colony – the convict under sentence, the serving marine, sailor or soldier, the ticket-of-leave men and women, the ex-convicts, the came-free settlers, wives or husbands of convicts, the 'foreign' sailors who skipped ship at Port Jackson, the native-born or came-free children of parents of all civil conditions, even members of the native Aboriginal tribes. The distortion created by contemporaries was to accept the British definition of 'criminal class' and apply it almost exclusively to the convict inhabitants of Botany Bay.

Crime itself differed in nature, degree, frequency and circumstance from crime in Britain especially crimes committed by women. Colonial crime is difficult to define for it was neither static nor measurable by the same standards throughout the period of transportation. It was influenced in the early years by the undeveloped nature of the colony itself and by the backgrounds of the women transported. It continued to be influenced indirectly by the changing economic and social conditions of Britain for these affected the number and 'type' of men and women chosen for transportation. The most determinative factor, however, was the nature of the colony itself, its stage of economic development, the extent of settlement, the number and dispersal of inhabitants, even the physical growth of towns and townships. Year by year the women prisoners arrived at a settlement which differed in appearance, characteristics and opportunities from the previous year. The more the colony grew to resemble a permanent settlement rather than a transient penal camp, the greater the number of inhabitants, the more extensive the development of small businesses, shops, taverns, inns and trade, the more opportunities there were for criminal offences similar to those in the towns of Britain. The most surprising characteristic – and the most unremarked – was how few of the women of Botany Bay became involved in crime as an occasional or permanent way of life.[3]

It would be completely inaccurate to suggest that there were not women at Botany Bay who were 'criminal' in the fullest sense of that word. There were colonial women as there were British women whose 'inclination' to a criminal way of life was unrestrained by any fear of punishment, any offer of inducements. There were women in Botany Bay who were as abusive, disorderly, drunken, vicious and criminal as any confined in London's Newgate Gaol or Dublin's Kilmainham Prison. There were colonial women who stole and thieved, who acted as receivers of stolen goods, who assaulted and robbed and maimed and murdered. There were the doxies and molls, the harlots and strumpets, the whores and common prostitutes, and there were women who became a part of the criminal class of Botany Bay, not because of their own immorality or criminality, but through their own close association with criminals. 'Honest' women, too, became involved in Botany Bay's criminal society through their husbands or male partners. Other women – usually those who had committed no colonial crime – became the victims of robbery, theft, lawlessness, violence, assault, rape or murder. In cases of assault, rape or 'depredations against their property', the colonial women were not reluctant to prosecute their assailants in the colonial courts and to demand punishment for the offender, retribution for themselves.

In the foundation years of the colony it was not only 'criminal' acts which were punishable by law. Breaches of discipline, from disorderly and riotous behaviour to disobedience or insolence, brought punishment from the magistrates, and punishment for breaches of the peace could be as severe as for thefts or robberies. In March 1803 Elizabeth Wilson and Mary Carrol were sentenced to public labour at Castle Hill for 'riotous and disorderly behaviour'. The following year Mary Tyrrell was sent to Newcastle for the same offence, and, at the same Sessions, Bridget Connelly received the same punishment for the theft of a bridle and saddle, as did Elizabeth McDuel, convicted of stealing 'a note of twenty shillings value'. Theft and disorderly conduct both received equal punishment. In 1820 Jane Marcus 'another most profligate character', was charged with cruel treatment of her husband 'a palsied and infirm old man' and with being 'a common nuisance in the streets of Sydney'. Her sentence was more lenient than those of the 'disorderly women' a decade or so previously: 'six months hard labour in the Factory at Parramatta'.[4]

Legal punishment in New South Wales was linked not only with criminal acts but with the need to maintain discipline among the inhabitants of the colony and to enforce standards of acceptable social behaviour in the settlement. To ensure the effectiveness of punishment for criminal offences, for insubordination or breaches of discipline, for drunkenness or unseemly behaviour, sentencing and the infliction of corporal punishment needed to be as public as possible, for the underlying aim of deterrence remained as strong in New South Wales as in Britain. The ultimate punishment, believed to be the ultimate deterrent, was death, and in all reports of colonial executions the emphasis was on the beneficial effects of witnessing the shameful death of a wrongdoer. Reporting the execution of a thief, the *Sydney Gazette* solemnly observed that 'this species of depradation [theft] had become frequent and required that its progress should be arrested by public example'. This execution was well-attended and the sufferer himself followed convention by warning the assembled populace not to follow his evil ways and piously hoping that his own shameful death would serve as a dread example.[5] Gallows speeches by men about to be 'launched into eternity' almost invariably followed this pattern which was in agreement with tradition, custom and popular expectations.

The cases of Ann Tibbutt, Mary Farrell, Marianne Wilkinson, Mary Hartley, Elizabeth Jones and Ann Tuckey, all evidence attitudes by colonial officials to women as offenders or as victims in major criminal cases. These cases also show the presumption that colonial women needed to establish their 'good character' in the colony and their own belief that it was to their advantage that they were presented to the Court as respectable married or family women.

Ann Tibbutt had come to New South Wales on the *Nile* in 1801 with her soldier husband John. Several years later she was violently assaulted by Michael Bryant who, according to Mrs Tibbutt's evidence, 'threw her down three times and threatened to give her a dig in the eye' if she screamed. She began her evidence at Bryant's trial for rape by saying: 'I live at the Hawkesbury and am a married woman'. She had visited the house of a friend and Bryant, who was there at the time, had followed her out as she left to go home. He 'followed her along the footpath' and said 'he wanted a bit of sport. I asked him if he thought I was a common prostitute'. Every time he threw her down, they got up – eventually – and walked together along the footpath. She asked him to go home with her and tell her husband. Bryant was quoted by a friend, Thomas Phillips, as saying: 'I had connection with the old Bitch' and her husband, John, gave evidence that when she arrived home, 'much frightened... her clothes were much tumbled and full of cow itch. She had violent retchings and was ill for several days'. Bryant was found guilty and sentenced to twelve months' hard labour in Sydney. As for that married woman, Ann Tibbutt, her reputation was vindicated, despite the leniency of the sentence, and she and husband John were still living together at Windsor in 1828.[6]

Mary Farrell, an ex-convict woman, threatened and raped by John Green in 1804, gave the following evidence at his trial:

At 6 o'clock in the morning Green jumped over a half door, holding a knife and said he would kill her if she would not lie with him... She replied that she was a married woman with children and not 'a person of the description you want'. He threw her to the ground, held a knife to her throat and raped her...

John Green was 'a black man... a Negro born in Philadelphia', transported on the *Coromandel*. He had gained a colonial reputation for criminal offences. The previous September he had been charged with 'feloniously stealing out of the dwelling house of William Mitchell sundry articles of wearing apparel' for which he was committed to the County Gaol of Sydney. After further examination 'as he was already a prisoner' he was taken to Parramatta where he 'suffered' a flogging. Two months later he escaped, and assaulted and raped Mrs Farrell. A week after his apprehension he was tried, convicted and sentenced to death for this unprovoked act of rape upon the body of this respectable married woman:

this brutal and inhuman assault aggravated, if it be possible by an infamous attempt to deprive her of existence by drawing a knife across her throat, which in an act of resistance she received on her right hand, and cutting a handkerchief she held there in it through many of its folds...

The report of the execution of Mrs Farrell's attacker showed the strength of the theory of deterrence as strongly in the colony as it did in Britain. At the moment of his death, Green publicly lamented his misspent life of vice and 'shed copious tears' that never again would he see his aged parents in America:

The malefactor was delivered over to the Provost Marshall, and in a cart conveyed to the spot at which he was to atone for his offences by an ignominious end, and by his aweful example to inspire a just abhorrence to crime ... Yielding to his fate, while the work of death was under preparation, he took leave of the populace in a short harangue, which he concluded with a fervent hope that his untimely end would operate to others as a wholesome warning against a life of vice and dissipation – and then departed for an unknown region.

Green had expressed no word of remorse for the woman who had been his victim and whose 'tears and entreaties' had produced not pity but threats of murder and further violence. This was unremarked by officials or onlookers. His admonition to avoid 'his melancholy fate' was applauded, for the law was not seen primarily as the legal avenger of the individual victim but as the instrument of enforcing standards of acceptable conduct.[7]

A comparison of the cases of Mrs Farrell and Mrs Tibbutt shows clearly that there was no doubt as to the lack of provocation or complicity by Mary Farrell in an attack which almost cost her life. There was also no question of her 'good character'. In the case of Ann Tibbutt there was little evidence of a determined struggle to protect her virtue, and the admission that she 'walked home' with her attacker in all probability added to the leniency of his sentence.

In the case of Marianne Wilkinson, two settlers and six convicts were accused and were sentenced to receive between eight hundred and one thousand lashes each for sexual assault 'attended by circumstances of infamy'. Nothing was known prejudicial to the woman's character, nor was evidence presented to suggest any promiscuity or irregularity in her colonial life. In sentencing the men, David Collins stressed the need for severity of punishment as

these unmanly attacks of several men on a single woman had frequently happened and had happened to some females who, through shame, concealed the circumstances. To such a height indeed was this dissolute and abandoned practice carried out that it had obtained a cant name and the poor unfortunate objects of this brutality were destroyed by a title expressive of the insults they had received.[8]

The case of Mary Hartley shows clearly the prejudicial influence on the Court of a woman's known 'bad character'. In May 1795 four men were charged with 'committing rape upon the body of Mary Hartley of Parramatta'. 'The Court was obliged to acquit the prisoners because of glaring contradictions in the witnesses'. At a second trial, two settlers and a convict were found guilty, the settlers sentenced to receive 500 lashes, the convict 300 as punishment for this offence. They eventually received half the number ordered, and were released. The summing up by the judge not only stressed the infamy of such an offence against a defenceless woman but also that Mary Hartley was of 'known bad character':

This was a most infamous transaction and, although the sufferer was of bad character, would have well warranted the execution of capital punishment on the three offenders, if the witnesses had not prevaricated in their testimony. They appeared to have cast off all feelings of civilised humanity, adopting as closely as they could follow the manners of the savage inhabitants of this country ... [9]

Where a woman of dubious reputation brought a charge of rape or indecent assault, she was aware that her own previous character would be investigated. It was also possible that she herself might be held up to public ridicule at the expense of her 'virtuous reputation' by reports of the case in the *Sydney Gazette*. These possibilities did not deter Ann Tuckey from bringing a charge of rape against Joseph Holt in 1808. The case was reported in the *Sydney Gazette* in such a facetious way as to stress the absurdity of the charge by this woman of questionable character:

Two witnesses who were both of the *fair* sex appeared to substantiate the testimony of the prosecutorix, upon her own declaration, in their presence, that the prisoner had ill-treated her ... he assaulted her chastity ... he had made use of language which the deponent's delicacy would scarce permit her to recapitulate. [She] was carrying a basket (which contained among other trifling articles of comfort a bottle of animating cordial) ... [she resisted her attacker] at the hazard of that reputation which was dearer to her than anything in life – except the basket itself.

Witnesses called by the defendant included Thomas Dunn who 'had had the misfortune to fall under a similar accusation from the same prosecutorix after a charge against him which must have endangered his life'. The woman, however, 'rather than face exposure', had withdrawn the charge. She accepted as recompense for 'the most atrocious injury which could be offered her... a bottle of spirits and four silver dollars'. After hearing this first witness for the defendant, the Court acquitted Holt 'without a moment's hesitation' and without a blemish on his character.[10]

The case of Elizabeth Jones showed contemporary attitudes towards a convicted murderess. Convicted in Essex, she had arrived on the *Neptune* sentenced to transportation for life. Shortly after her arrival, she married Thomas Jones at the Church of St Philip. In 1794 Jones received a grant of land, and the couple settled at the Eastern Farms with their two colonial-born daughters. Samuel Clode, a missionary, visited them shortly before his planned return to Tahiti, and when his body was found, butchered by an axe still stained with his blood and brains, Thomas and Elizabeth Jones were arrested with an accomplice, William Eldberry, and charged with this shocking murder. Jones was strong in his protestations that 'Samuel Clode was a man he so much loved and to whom he was indebted for his attention to him and to his family in times of sickness'. All three were taken to the pit where the body lay and Jones was ordered to look at the body and touch it. This was in accordance with the traditional belief that the wounds of the murder victim would bleed afresh at the touch of the murderer's hand. Jones showed no hesitation but said boldly: 'Yes, I will, and kiss him to [*sic*], if you please, for I loved him as my brother'.

His wife was implicated in 'this horrid deed' as much as her husband, although it was Jones and Eldberry who were believed to have actually killed the missionary. A trail of blood led from their house (freshly swept by the wife) to a pit where the body had been hidden with green boughs. All three were sentenced to death, the men to hang in chains after the execution, the woman's body to be cut down and delivered to the surgeons for dissection. The court ordered that the three were to be hanged upon the exact spot where the murder had taken place and that their house was to be pulled down and burnt. That these punishments were carried out in the criminal's own district, that all three suffered the ultimate degradation of their bodies after death, and that their property was publicly destroyed, reinforced the effect of deterrence by fear among the near neighbours. Until their arrest for murder, neither man nor wife had been regarded by officials or others as anything except deserving and industrious settlers, concerned only with the development of their farm and the well-being of their family.[11]

Was death by hanging as feared by the women of the colony as it was in Britain? Cases where a woman criminal was actually executed were comparatively rare in colonial New South Wales for reprieve usually followed capital conviction more often than in Britain. The reaction of Elizabeth Roanes (*Experiment*) to her death sentence in early November 1808 shows the horror of public execution:

The prisoner fell upon her knees and appeared most sensibly affected. In this supplicating posture, the power of speech forsook her, but yet her sad and pitiable countenance seemed to implore the intercession of her judges. She was returned to the place of her previous confinement there to await the awful period of atonement ...

Her crime had been 'breaking in and entering the dwelling of a non-commissioned officer of the New South Wales Corps' and his de facto wife 'and stealing therefrom a quantity of wearing apparel', their joint property. For Elizabeth Roanes there was clemency and the governor graciously reprieved her from her sentence of death. Was it that breaking and entering was not then so prevalent a crime that it needed the ultimate public retribution of execution to deter other would-be robbers?[12] There was no mitigation of sentence for Mary Grady (*Tellicherry*) sentenced to death for a similar offence the following year. On Saturday, 18 June 1809, twenty-year-old Mary Grady was publicly executed at Sydney. She had been sentenced to death the previous week for 'burglariously breaking and entering the house of Charles Stuart, at Parramatta between the hours of three and four in the morning of the 22nd of May and stealing therefrom cash and notes to a considerable sum.'

Her apprehension had resulted from her inability to read. The girl had taken several of the papers she had stolen to Mr Hassall and asked him to read them to her. Among them were Charles Stuart's certificate that his term of transportation had expired 'and several very remarkable notes of hand'. When sentence of death was pronounced she 'did not seem at all sensible of the awful predicament into which her crime had unhappily plunged her' and the evidence at her trial suggested that she may have been simple-minded. The terror of her punishment was evident at her execution the following week. At half past eleven she left the gaol with two male prisoners sentenced to execution:

They walked behind the cart on which the female delinquent was conveyed to her place of execution; – on approaching which she fainted several times, and as nearer she approached, appeared more and more affected by the horrors of her condition, of which she did not appear thoroughly sensible until her death warrant was read to her the day previous to her execution.[13]

Poor Mary Grady from County Kerry. Her sentence to life transportation led her to the gallows of Botany Bay.

Unlike the men who were executed, women were not expected to make a dying speech as they stood beneath the Gallows Tree. Was this attitude linked with their femininity, even as criminals? Reports of executions in the *Sydney Gazette* would suggest that the terror of their impending and shameful death robbed 'these frail objects' of the power to do other than attempt to pray to their Maker for forgiveness. These reports, however, in no way mitigated the infamy of the offences which had led to execution.

There was one certain way by which a capitally convicted woman could gain at least a temporary reprieve from 'hanging high on the Gallows Tree'. This was to plead 'I am with child', for a pregnant woman could not be executed until after the birth of the child. The plea, of course, would be rejected if proof were not forthcoming that the prisoner was pregnant. In 1789 Judith Jones (*Lady Penrhyn*) 'pleaded her belly' when she was sentenced to death by the Judge-Advocate. A jury of matrons was empanelled to determine the truth of the matter. In that small community of women it might have been expected that some leniency or pity could have been shown a fellow convict. That jury of women, however, reported to the Judge-Advocate that 'She is no more with child than he was himself'. Judith Jones was hanged forthwith, her execution witnessed by that jury of matrons. She gained the dubious honour of being the first white woman executed in New South Wales.[14]

Frances Moreton was more fortunate. Sentenced to death in 1798 for the theft of money from Charles Peat, there was no question of the truth of her plea that 'I am with child' for she was very near her time of delivery. Governor Hunter granted her a stay of execution and she was removed from Sydney Gaol but ordered to remain in the custody of a constable during her lying-in. There is no explanation as to why she was not returned to gaol, nor why her death sentence was commuted or revoked, but there is ample evidence that she lived to give birth to at least four more colonial children and that she died, not as an executed criminal 'reviled by her kind', but as a family woman of Botany Bay.[15]

Women who were murdered by their legal, common-law or de

facto husbands were often accidental victims of violence resulting from intoxication of one or both parties. Ann Smith and her husband Simon Taylor were believed by Surgeon Harris 'to always live in amicable terms of love and harmony together', and he gave evidence to the effect at Taylor's trial for the murder of his wife. In further evidence, a friend of the couple, Thomas Goldfinch, said Ann Taylor 'was dressed only in her shift and stays' on the day of the murder. It was further shown that the couple were from 'Fitzgerald's farm at Parramatta' and were 'in the habit of coming out of camp to get drunk and fighting'. On this occasion both were very intoxicated, and Taylor had called his wife 'a drunken bitch' and 'a nasty dirty bitch'. He 'beat her for a few hours and when confronted with the deed said she was only sleeping and cradled her head in his lap'. With awareness of his loss, Taylor's remorse was intolerable. In life he had affectionately called his Dublin-born wife 'My Old Tin Pot'. After his execution for her murder, this epitaph was carved on his tombstone:

> Beneath this stone lies Simon Taylor,
> Who was hung by Rice the gaoler,
> To hang on a Tree, it was his Lot,
> For knocking the bottom out of 'his old Tin Pot'.
> Now let no one be [indecipherable]
> For an innocent man was Simon Taylor.

The grave of his murdered wife was at St John's cemetery, Parramatta, but that of her 'affectionate' husband has vanished with time.[16]

All murdered wives, however, were not so affectionately remembered by their husbands, nor were their deaths directly attributable to the evil effects of intoxication. Mrs Julia Bates, the wife of an ex-convict sawyer at Kissing Point, was brutally and deliberately murdered by her husband: 'Julia Bates had been severely beaten and hit by an axe, nearly all the ribs on the right side fractured and the body burnt'. The husband was found guilty and hanged, showing appropriate remorse for his crime but not affection for his unfortunate wife. At an inquest into the unexplained death of Mrs Bennett of Parramatta, the mother of five children, evidence was given that her husband 'had been tried for the murder of two former wives', and acquitted on both charges. The coroner returned a verdict of death by 'Cause Unknown' with no suspicion attached to Bennett, except perhaps his unhappy choice of wives with a predisposition to die inexplicably.[17]

Women were seldom the victims of murders unassociated with domestic disagreements or overindulgence in liquor during the early years of the colony. The only important case linked with criminal assault in 1807 was that of 'Mary Smith, a decent, inoffensive woman employed as an instructress at Brickfield Hill' who had gone to Parramatta in search of property recently stolen from her:

The body of this unfortunate woman ... barbarously murdered was found in a ditch with a sheet nearly covering her. From the appearance of the body it was evident that the perpetrators had endeavoured to conceal their guilt by attempting to consume the unhappy object of their depravity ...

That same day John Kenny was apprehended on suspicion, tried and convicted. The murdered woman had chosen to stay the night in his house rather than with her friend Margaret Rees, for she had said to Mrs Rees that she knew Kenny was responsible for the robbery of her property and had seen her own handkerchief around his neck. Kenny had received her with every sign of friendliness, 'taking her cordially by the hand'. In his summing up the Judge-Advocate stressed the enormity of so vile a crime against a woman, one who 'could not defend herself against the violence ... of superior strength', a crime which was 'equally abhorred in every country', a 'violation of the laws of God, the voice of Nature, Reason and Mankind', which all demanded 'that whoever sheddeth Man's blood, by Man shall his blood be shed'. Kenny was publicly executed on 25 January 1807. After his execution the body 'remained the usual time suspended and was then sent to Parramatta to be hung in chains as an example and a warning of the consequences of such an abhorrent crime'.[18] Such murders were not characteristic of colonial society and were proportionately far less frequent than in contemporary Britain during this period.

Murder and attempted murder were not the prerogatives of a 'criminal class' and could result from neighbourhood quarrels, as well as from assaults linked with crimes against property. In 1802 Henry Hacking, the former quartermaster of the *Sirius* and a 'notorious drinker', was sentenced to death for the attempted murder of Mrs Ann Bowen, the wife of William Bowen. In the evidence against him, neighbour Elizabeth Ward said that she saw him with a musket pointing at Ann Bowen's fence and 'asked him if he intended to shoot anyone'. He replied 'No', then fired his musket into the garden where Ann Bowen was hanging out her clothes. She cried out, 'Oh, Hacking, I am dead!' Another witness, Thomas Willoughby gave evidence that he saw Hacking pass his house carrying a musket, and said, 'Sure if he is not come up to shoot Nancy'. Hacking escaped the gallows as there was evidence that the wounded woman did not immediately seek medical aid nor did she go to her bed. He died in Hobart in 1827, as unrepentant and drunken as he had lived.[19]

It was not until the 1820s that murder and manslaughter of women became more frequent in the convict colony, although still proportionately less than in contemporary Britain. The increase, slight as it was, could be directly linked with the increase in both the 'convict' and the free population, and with the changing conditions in the colony for convicts and ex-convicts following the adoption of the recommendations of Commissioner Bigge that New South Wales must become a place of both punishment for Britain's criminals and profit for the mother country.[20] Not only were increasing numbers of felons transported as a response to the deteriorating economic conditions and spiralling crime rate in Britain, but the pattern of crime indicated a far larger proportion of more violent and serious offences among the men and women transported than had been typical of the period preceding the departure of Governor Macquarie.

Murder was, of course, a 'normal' part of any society, convict or free. Was there a greater awareness of the possibility of violence among those colonial women who were employed by, or who employed, men and women who had been convicted of major felonies in Britain? The surgeons could certify that the women were 'free from any putrid infections or distemper', but character descriptions did little to encourage trust in many assigned servants. This description by the Keeper of York Castle which accompanied five women transported on the *Lord Melville*, who were later assigned as domestic servants in New South Wales, would do little to remove any misgivings or apprehensions of colonial employers:

Phillis Gordon, aged 30 ... 7 years ... feloniously stealing from furnished lodgings – 'Has been a very profligate character'.

Jane Graham/Wood, aged 33 ... Grand Larceny ... 14 years ... Bad ... Had been convicted of felony in the County of Gloucester and imprisoned for such offence within the Common penitentiary house in and for such county.

Ann Chapman aged 25 ... felony ... seven years 'a notorious thief'.

Elizabeth Wales aged 24 years ... vagrancy ... a very bad character.

Hannah Whiteby aged 52 ... wife of John Whiteby 'one of the worst of women'.[21]

Assigned female servants were returned by masters and mistresses who found them 'unfit for decent habitations' or disorderly, disobedient, drunken, slatternly or insolent – or pregnant – but few women servants were guilty of actual violence or assault upon their masters or mistresses. Those who were accused of such offences were usually charged in complicity with others, as in the case of Eliza Campbell (*Providence*), charged with six male assigned servants with 'wilfully and feloniously murdering their master, Mr J. Brackfield'. All were found guilty and executed.[22]

Female settlers in the outer districts were more 'in danger' from their servants than those in the towns and townships. Mrs Janet Mackellar, the wife of a settler at the Cowpastures in the District of Upper Minto and the mother of a young family, was murdered by one of her assigned male servants during the absence of her husband. The murderer, Lot McNamara, was hanged. Catherine Douglas, assigned servant to John Bennet of the Field of Mars, was murdered by fellow-convict John Clives. He was executed.[23] Both murderers and their victims had recently arrived in New South Wales and were in domestic situations which differed entirely from those with which they had been familiar in Britain.

Cases of assaults against women in the colony added to the 'evidence' accepted in England that Botany Bay was a lawless and vicious place. Cases of rape and assault upon children reinforced this belief in the depravity of colonial society. The question as to whether, in a penal colony, the violation of women and children by assault, violence, carnal knowledge or rape was considered less of an offence than in Britain is difficult to assess, either from the summing-up and verdicts of criminal trials or in reports in the colonial press. Punishment in cases involving children, however, was not so severe that it could be considered imposed as deterrence. Eliza McCabe was four years old when she 'suffered an assault' by James Deegan, 'rather an elderly man', who was sentenced to two years in the Iron Gang for the offence. Ann MacAdams was six when J. Hennessy attempted to rape the child (her mother prosecuted), as was Harriet Smith when assaulted by William Cunninghame, who was found guilty of 'violation of chastity'.[24] None of these attackers received the death penalty, and all their terms of imprisonment appeared inexplicably lenient when considered within the context of the crime.

In 1810 Ann Kennedy and her husband John made deposition that John Ingram had raped their young daughter. The mother sent a deposition, signed by her mark, that

Ingram was at her house on 9th July in the absence of her husband . . . she sent her daughter Jane, aged between eight and nine years 'to put up the goats' . . . she noticed that Ingram left too. Shortly after . . . she heard the child cry out faintly and knowing Ingram's general character ran out instantly fearing her child was in danger, [she caught him with the child, choking her, the clothing of both disarranged] . . . She 'washed the little child' . . .

Ingram was found not guilty because the Kennedys did not appear to prosecute on the day ordained, but they later gave evidence that the mother's 'agitation and grief made her so ill that she was unable to attend until this day to give evidence against her child's attacker'.[25] Ingram, however, escaped the punishment of the law for ravishing this young child.

The criminal women of Botany Bay were not a homogeneous class. They included married women, single girls, 'demoiselles of the ton [*sic*]', women who cohabited or formed de facto relationships, women who were young or old, women who were employed or were mistresses of their own businesses or partners with their husbands, women such as shoplifters Mrs Ralph, whose husband was a licensed baker, and Mrs New, wife of the publican of The Rocks. They were women from the towns of Sydney and Parramatta and from the townships and the outer settlements. If any, pattern of female criminality could be traced it was that crimes by women recently arrived in the colony exceeded those of the older inhabitants, that crimes by family women were far less than those by childless single women, that significantly fewer crimes could be linked with destitution and abject poverty than was the case in Britain. Few, if any, appeals were made for clemency because of distress, starvation or inability to support infants or young children, and female criminality increased proportionately with the growth of population and with the physical spread and development of the colony. The most significant feature of any pattern, however, was that the crime rate among colonial women was proportionately far lower than in the contemporary towns and villages of Britain.[26]

The offences of colonial women varied from drunkenness and disorderly behaviour to stealing from employers, receiving stolen goods, retailing illicit spirits, defrauding the government when employed in positions of trust, to assault, manslaughter and murder. Until the 1820s – and beyond – the punishment of colonial women continued to be influenced by the belief in fear as a deterrence, and that fear was the terror of physical suffering and deprivation. Colonial punishment was demonstrably more lenient than the statutory punishment for similar offences in Britain, and when a woman was executed her body was neither hung in chains nor exposed to the public for any lengthy period. There were no recorded cases in New South Wales of burning in the hand or mutilation of women criminals, and no colonial woman suffered execution by fire. After about 1800 flogging and whipping decreased as a punishment for women, as it did in Britain, but criminal women continued to suffer the public punishment and humiliation of being sentenced to wear an iron collar, to have their heads shaved, to be compelled to wear distinctive and drab clothing identifying them as criminals. The pillory and the stocks were used increasingly as punishments for misdemeanours and less serious offences and also those which were linked with unacceptable social behaviour. By 1826 drunkenness was still punishable by an hour or so in the stocks at the public market-place. Mrs Goodwin, a widow who had been sentenced to the stocks for drunkenness in 1816, was sentenced again for the same offence in 1826. In the same year Mary Grady, known as 'Timber Carriage' and 'a free demoiselle of the town', was sentenced to two hours in the stocks for drunken and disorderly behaviour, as was Jane Quigley (*Elizabeth*), the wife of a fisherman of Sydney, and Margaret Tully, a sixty-seven-year-old ex-convict farmer's wife.[27]

The confinement of women within a prison for long periods was, as in England, not a traditional colonial punishment. Women reconvicted in New South Wales of serious offences were increasingly punished by secondary transportation to penal settlements rather than confinement at Sydney or Parramatta. One of the continuing functions of the Female Factory at Parramatta was to serve as a place of comparatively brief confinement for those colonial women convicted of offences not considered sufficiently grave as to warrant transportation to Van Diemen's Land, to Newcastle, Moreton Bay or, in the early years, to Norfolk Island. Women such as Mrs Betty Dixon, who had been '37 years resident in the Colony', and was charged by Mrs Ogleby 'with very impolite behaviour', were sentenced to the Factory. Mary Davis, 'aged and blind', was sentenced to one month in the Factory for stealing a man's handkerchief valued at twopence. Miss Mary Scott 'of the Creole cast', was sent to the Factory for being 'drunk and disorderly', and Kitty Connor sentenced 'to the Parramatta Institution' for harassing her neighbours. Two atypical cases punished by confinement at the Female Factory were those of Mary Hartigan, a servant 'charged with wearing men's clothing and drunkenness', and Sarah Webb who, 'dressed in male attire', stole from a house in Argyle.[28] This 'unwomanly conduct' added to the gravity of the criminal offence of theft. These women were not only regarded as criminals by the Court but as women whose immodest and undesirable behaviour must be punished by confinement in the Female Factory. By the 1820s one of the functions of this colonial institution, the reformation of the prisoner, was developing more and more in accordance with the ideals of the Houses of Industry and Houses of Correction in Britain, especially under the benign guidance of Eliza Darling and her Ladies' Committees, who attempted to introduce the system of reformation by inducement and education in the mid 1820s. That is, not only was virtuous and good behaviour in the Factory rewarded both by money payments and by the quality and quantity of clothing issued, but the women were instructed in the arts of domestic service so that after release they would be capable of maintaining themselves by their own industry.[29]

Some of the changes in judicial attitudes to female criminality at Botany Bay are evidenced in the punishments of male and female receivers of stolen goods. One of the earliest cases in New South Wales involving women receivers was in December 1788. Convict James Daly, who had been sentenced to death for theft, was making his traditional gallows speech of repentance and warning before being 'turned off' when he identified two women convicts in the crowd, and lamented that they had induced him to commit the crimes for which he was about to suffer. They were his 'bad connections', the women who had received the profits of his thefts. Daly's accusation was not questioned as it was his dying deposition, and to lie as he was launched into eternity would bring him eternal damnation. Both women were taken into custody immediately, and one of them chosen as a public example of the punishment and degradation which would follow similar criminal offences. The woman – who has not been identified – had her head shaved and was forced to parade before the assembly 'clothed in a canvas frock, on which was painted in large letters, R.S.G. (receiver of stolen goods), and threatened with punishment if she were ever seen without it.' The shaving of the head was a humiliation feared even more by the women than a summary whipping. The reputation of the convict women, however, was so debased that few of the officials who witnessed this punishment believed that it would be of any preventative value for 'a great number of the prisoners of both sexes had too long been acquainted with each other in scenes of disgrace, for this kind of punishment to work much reformation among them.'[30] Nevertheless, the governor hoped that shame, and perhaps female vanity, might be some deterrent to a criminal act which, if committed in Great Britain, would have led to sentence of fourteen years' transportation or death.

Colonial women who acted as receivers of stolen property followed the tradition of 'professional' women criminals in Britain. These offences were premeditated, were usually conducted as an ongoing 'business' venture and acted as inducement to both petty and professional thieves. Most articles were stolen for the purpose of resale, the thief receiving payment from the fence. Without receivers, motivation for stealing would necessarily decrease. Punishment, therefore, was more severe for the colonial receiver which was in accordance with the underlying purpose of deterrence, but not invariably if the thief were a man and the receiver a woman. In New South Wales there was an even greater need to make public example of the punishment for this crime. Hand in hand with the presumption that the colony was inhabited by Britain's criminal classes went the belief that the natural indolence and criminality of the convicts would encourage them to live by 'depredations upon the property of others' rather than by honest industry. With the exception of the foundation years and the difficulties of initial establishment of the colony and of ensuring adequate rations and sufficient supplies of clothing, tools and household goods, few colonial crimes were committed for the sake of the articles stolen – with the exception of alcohol. Women receivers, however, continued to be punished differently from their male accomplices.

Rosamond Sparrow had been convicted in York in 1790. Had it been loneliness for her native country that led to her colonial marriage to a much older man, Joseph Hatton (*Scarborough*), who had been tried at the Castle of York in July 1794? The couple settled on a land grant at Eastern Farms, and nothing derogatory was heard about them until 'the young wife attacked her elderly husband':

a settler [who] was dangerously stabbed in the belly by his wife, a young woman . . . in a fit of jealousy and passion. On his recovery he earnestly requested that no punishment might be inflicted on her, but she might be put away from him.

After she was parted from her elderly but forgiving husband, Rosamond Sparrow lived with John Massie, and in 1799 both were charged with receiving stolen goods. Massie was sentenced to a public flogging of 500 lashes, and Rosamond Sparrow was ordered to have her head shaved, to wear an iron collar for six months, and to be confined at Parramatta Gaol for twelve months. Rosamond's elderly husband had consoled himself with another convict woman, Ann Smith, who bore the son who was to have his father's name. Joseph Hatton junior was baptised in 1800, and lived with his father on a land grant at Kissing Point. In 1828 the son still farmed the father's grant, in all probability completely unaware of the 'passionate jealousy' his 'elderly' father had inspired in his ill-fated colonial wife.[31]

Whether the crowd watching the shame, indignities and sufferings of the condemned man or woman were convicts themselves, or free men and women, appeared to have little influence on their responses. Public humiliation or public infliction of physical suffering on a colonial criminal appeared to have had as little deterrent effect in New South Wales as it had on the crowds who watched executions, mutilations, whippings, brandings and burnings in contemporary Britain. Jane McFae was well aware of the consequences if she were convicted of receiving stolen goods. In all probability she had witnessed the punishment and humiliation of Rosamond Sparrow. On 16 May 1800, six months after Sparrow's conviction, Jane McFae was tried with Thomas Day for receiving stolen goods, 'cloth and clothing, knowing them to have been stolen'. Both were found guilty and Day sentenced to fifty lashes and transportation to Norfolk Island for life. The Court, however, saw mitigating circumstances for Day: 'taking into Consideration the age, infirmity and other favourable circumstances'; it was recommended that the corporal punishment be forgiven. There was no mitigation for Jane McFae. She had her head shaved publicly and was sentenced to wear an iron collar for three months. The couple had been married in the colony in 1798 and Day, who had arrived convict, had received a conditional pardon in December 1794 and a land grant of thirty acres on 'the Flats at Upper Port Jackson' in the same month. The last colonial record to Jane McFae is in the Muster of 1806, in which she was listed as living with a soldier, Jo. Pilmore, and freed by servitude.[32]

It was only with the development of a 'free society' that the public shaming and punishment of women decreased in New South Wales, to be replaced by the imposition of statutory punishment of confinement in Factory, gaol or penal settlement in the same manner and for the same periods as for male offenders. Crime and punishment in New South Wales, so markedly linked with the convict nature of society and the convict origins of most of the inhabitants, altered in both nature and purpose as the free society became dominant over the convict, and as more and more of the convicted criminals of England became the ex-convict settlers of New South Wales.

By the late 1820s there was little significant difference in the attitudes to or the punishment of colonial criminals on the basis of their sex, although certain forms of physical punishment were still reserved almost exclusively for men. Male criminals continued to receive sentences for flogging, to be 'ironed', to work in road gangs, and, on occasion, to have their ears nailed to the pillory. None of these punishments were inflicted on women, even if guilty of the same offences.

The differing attitudes towards women criminals in the first thirty years or so of white settlement were clearly linked with what, to British and colonial officials, was their major characteristic, 'their vice'. Colonial 'vice' differed in both definition and connotation from 'vice' in Britain for it had little if any irreligious implications and was linked almost exclusively with immoral rather than criminal behaviour. Historian Michael Roberts has pointed out that the vices which the Society for the Suppression of Vice (London) hoped to eliminate included the following:

profanation of the Lord's Day and profane swearing; publication of blasphemous, licentious and obscene books and prints; selling of false weights and measures; keeping of disorderly public houses, brothels and gaming houses; procuring; illegal lotteries; cruelty to animals.[33]

Although Macquarie issued General Orders to prevent the Lord's Day becoming a working day, and offences such as 'driving a cart on Sundays' were punishable in the magistrates' courts, as indeed was 'shooting a neighbour's dog on Sunday', there was little if any link between the religious significance of certain crimes and the lack of religious observance among many of the colonial women.[34] Disorderly behaviour was an expected characteristic of convicted women and was seen primarily, if not exclusively, as the result of inherent immorality and promiscuity.

An overindulgence in liquor was believed to be the cause of almost every civil disturbance and 'habits of inebriation' a major cause of the unruly, disorderly behaviour of the convict women.

This continued to be seen as a constant problem by colonial officials, many of whom openly blamed the women of the colony not only for their own inebriety but for enticing the men into drunken stupor. When a sailor was convicted of supplying convict women with drink in 1788, he was forgiven and the women flogged because they had 'enticed him' to commit the offence.[35] Women had been charged with 'disturbing the peace', quarrelling and fighting, abusive and disorderly behaviour from the beginning of settlement. Most of the cases were closely linked with drunkenness. The case of Ann Farmer (*Prince of Wales*) was typical of the problems intoxication added to Phillip's attempts to maintain order and regularity in the infant settlement. Ann Farmer, a 'Newgate woman', created such disturbance in the women's camp early in August 1788 that the guard were sent to investigate. She was found 'very much in liquor... lying in a heap in the corner of her tent'. She refused to go with the guard, and the officer who was then called found her 'far too intoxicated to move'. The following day she was charged with 'making a riot at 12 o'clock at night'. She was discharged on her own evidence that the trouble had been caused by the loss of her own hut – a tree had fallen on it – and other convicts had stolen her possessions. The officer, Captain Baker had, she claimed, 'offered to take some very indecent liberties with her which she had refused'.[36]

Phillip's leniency to Ann Farmer was not in accordance with his public warnings on the severity of punishment which would follow any offences or disturbances in the colony. Shortly after the arrival of the First Fleet at Port Jackson, Phillip's Commission was publicly read on a 'Spot of Ground that had been cleared for a Parade' and at which were assembled 'all the Officers of the Several departments, the Convicts, Men and Women' the Battalions and 'every Body from on board the Ships that could be spared'. Phillip addressed the assembly and spoke of the opportunities which were open to the convict settlers, adding that if there were transgressions, he would allow the law to take its course. He may have been lenient on the voyage to the colony, but now punishment could be expected for all wrongdoers. One of those present, Surgeon George Worgan of the *Sirius*, reported that Governor Phillip

> was convinced, he told them, that there were a Number of good Men among them, who, unfortunately, from falling into bad Company, from the influence of bad Women, and in a rash moment of Intoxication, had been led to violate the Laws of their Country, by committing Crimes

which in a serious Moment of Reflection, they thought of with Horror and Shame, and of which now, they sincerely repented ...

Phillip appeared to have a far lower opinion of the women in his charge and less hope that they might be redeemed from their vicious and evil ways than the men, lacking, as they did 'either virtue or honesty'. The governor told the convicts that 'sorry he was ... that there were some Men and Women amongst them, so thoroughly abandoned in the Wickedness, as to have lost every good Principle'.[37] For the women, intoxication was not simply the 'result of a rash moment' but an ingrained characteristic.

This belief in the inherent 'wickedness' of the convicts was evident in all official comment throughout the period of transportation. Their 'wickedness' was evidenced in their drunkenness and consequent dissipation and debauchery which, combined with indolence and aversion to labour, led to the committal of colonial crimes. Was intoxication responsible for crime at Botany Bay to any more marked degree than it was in Britain? The women of London and Middlesex had pleaded for mercy on the grounds that, 'I was very drunk' or 'I was intoxicated' or 'I was much in liquor', but these same pleas were seldom recorded as a defence in any of the colonial trials in which a woman was the defendant.

Was it overindulgence in liquor which led to the problems of self-confessed 'tipsy' Mary Joyce? If so, she was fortunate in the understanding of her judge. Mary Joyce had built up a sizeable business, ironing and washing at her premises in The Rocks, when she was accused in May 1811 by Mrs Stacey, one of her customers, of stealing some 'twenty-five articles she had left with her overnight to be ironed'. When Mrs Stacey called to collect them, Mary Joyce told her that they had been stolen from her house while she was out. The Chief Constable, John Redmond, gave evidence that the prisoner had come to him on the Sunday morning and said she had been 'tipsy' and lost the articles. Jane Lloyd (*Lady Juliana*), the owner of the house in which they were found, swore that the prisoner had given them to her as payment of a debt. Mary Joyce swore that this was not true – she had been drinking in the house with Jane Lloyd and had left the bundle of clothes there, and when she came back for them Jane Lloyd said she would not give them to her until she had paid her liquor debt. The Court found in favour of the prisoner, Mary Joyce, overlooking her fondness for liquor. She was discharged, and the clothes returned to their rightful owner.[38]

Whether or not the crimes by colonial women were the result of drunkenness, this plea was rarely recorded in the colonial courts. It was, however, often mentioned in the evidence of a number of colonial trials for criminal offences. In June 1814 Dennis McCarty was tried for 'assaulting and beating John Williams, a constable'. Jane Bayly, 'called Jenny' (*Indispensable*), gave evidence that: 'I go by the name of Jane McKay. I have lived eleven years last harvest with the prisoner at the Bar ...' That evening she 'had a few words with McCarty and he struck her and set her nose a bleeding'. She shrieked out 'Murder', and called Williams the constable to take her to gaol for protection because McCarty would surely kill her. Williams told him to stop ill-treating her, and he replied, 'I can do what I like with my own woman'. Williams got hold of her by the hand and was going to take her out when she said to McCarty, 'How can you let me go, he only wants to take me in the Bush'. At this outburst, McCarty sprang up, hit Williams with a hoe, knocked him down, and jumped on him until 'he bled a good deal ... Jane McKay then went to Williams and wrapped the smock around his head and then put it into her mouth and said she would eat his hearty blood'. She excused her behaviour by telling the judge: 'I won't swear that I was not so drunk that I did not know what I was about. I was sitting on Mary Long's bedside [she was her lodger] when I was in my shift'. The upshot of this fracas, all the result of the fickle and changing affections of Jane McKay, was that her de facto husband was sentenced to solitary confinement on bread and water for three months. Whether or not the two resumed living together is unknown, but by 1814 McCarty was again confined in gaol and of Jane Bayly/McKay there was no trace.[39]

Most of the cases in which women were the defendants in the colonial courts involved some form of theft. A typical case was that of Jane Jones (*Glatton*), assigned servant, who in 1805 was accused of stealing articles belonging to her master, Mr Atkins; his wife identified his property. Although she strongly denied the charge when the articles were found at her house, she was found guilty and sentenced to 'transportation for seven years to commence from the expiration of the time of her previous sentence'.[40] Another case involved convicts Bridget Conoboy (*Atlas*) and Catherine Murphy (*Hercules*), who were convicted of shoplifting nine pairs of cotton stockings from Robert Jenkins, shop owner of Pitt Street, Sydney. The prosecutor claimed that 'the prisoners came to his shop and stole the stockings while he was at the back of the shop'. This was corroborated by his assistant Charles Vining. Both were found guilty and sentenced to be hanged.[41] Some fifteen years later greater leniency was shown Catherine Elliott, who was found guilty of shoplifting from the Sydney shop of Charles Pickering. She was not hanged but sentenced to the Factory for three months, her four small children allowed to accompany her.[42] In the same year Anne Campbell (*Louisa*), from Stirling, Scotland, was found guilty of stealing from Mrs Dillon's shop, and sentenced to twelve months' confinement at the Factory. Apparently this Scottish lass found life at the Factory not to her liking and 'bolted'. Recaptured, she was 'ordered to be returned to the Factory and to have her flowing ringlets shaved off'.[43] All of these women were still convicts under sentence at the time of their colonial offences.

By the mid-1820s the increasing frequency of thefts by colonial servants was shown in cases reported regularly in the *Australian*. These thefts were not confined to those committed by convict women or assigned servants, as had previously been the case. Ann Gatty was 'a native ... a young girl ... only five weeks in service' who robbed her mistress, Mrs Reynolds. She was sentenced to six months in the Factory. Maria Hunt and her husband were 'free emigrants from England', employed as servants to Barnet and Mrs Levy when charged with stealing from their master. Mrs Mary Cole, servant to Mrs Anne Whiting, stole three ducks and was sent to the Factory for three months. She had arrived as the daughter of free immigrants. A convict woman, Elizabeth Piggett (*Mariner*), was accused of theft by her mistress in 1825. She strongly denied the charge but was convicted and sentenced to three years' transportation.[44] Was her sentence greater because she was a convict? There is insufficient evidence to establish any pattern which could suggest a definite prejudice by the courts against a convict charged while still under sentence or any corresponding leniency to a native-born or free immigrant woman. On the other hand, there were numerous cases which did not conform to any pattern or any expected verdict. An atypical case was that of convict Mary Dunlevey (*Mariner*), charged by her mistress with absconding unlawfully. The woman pleaded she had intended only 'a short absence'. Described in court as 'fair, fat and over forty ... and yet could run like a greyhound, and so she did ... ', Mary Dunlevey was sentenced to a term in the Factory, which effectively put a temporary stop to her 'running'.[45]

There is no explanation of the consideration shown in an occasional case, such as that of Sophia Davis, acquitted of a charge of drunkenness when she pleaded that she was 'a stranger in the colony'. Stranger she may have been, but she had arrived as a convict a few months earlier on the *Midas*, and it is unlikely that her 'strangeness' was the only mitigating circumstance for her disorderly behaviour. Colonial officials guarded against a repetition of the results of her loneliness in Sydney Town by assigning her to James Bowman at distant Patrick's Plains, where she remained far from the temptations of the town. Conversely, Mary Ward (*Indispensable*), 'free', found that 'her fifteen years' residence in the Colony' was of no avail when she was 'again charged with drunkenness' in 1826. She was sentenced to six weeks in the Factory.[46]

The ways in which colonial women reacted to both civil and criminal situations they regarded as unjust is an indication of their recognition of their own rights in their adopted country. Convict, ex-convict or free, most showed little hesitation in charging offenders whatever their position within colonial society. The first instance of this was the first action brought before the New South Wales Court of Civil Jurisdiction. In July 1788 Susannah Holmes and Henry Kable, both transported felons, charged Duncan Sinclair, the master of the *Alexander*, with illegal retention of their possessions. Although technically ineligible to sue in a British court, the pair won their action and the master was ordered to make restitution.[47] In 1809 Catherine Cotton had no hesitation in demanding redress from the action of Captain Cummings who had 'selected that part of the North Shore known as Cotton's Point' as his land grant. Mrs Cotton affirmed that she had purchased that portion of land from a soldier, Lewis Williams, but Captain Cummings did not recognise her title to the land as 'she had lost the chit' given her as proof of ownership by Williams. The land had been expensive to clear and cultivate, and she had been unable to continue to improve it 'because a man [presumably her assigned servant] had been killed on it'. She requested the governor to give her a formal grant to confirm her ownership of the property. Handwritten on the side of her petition was the comment that 'if what she says is correct, Captain Cummings cannot have "Cotton's Point" '.[48]

In June 1826 Mrs Jenkins, who had subscribed one pound to the School for Female Servants, charged Sir John Jamieson with breach of the peace. She claimed that his carriage had run into hers at the races held in Hyde Park, causing her damage and inconvenience. The verdict of guilty would have had little effect on Sir John, apart from the temporary loss of his coachman who was sentenced to three days on the treadmill.[49]

In 1826 Susan Cooper was ordered to be sent from gaol to the Parramatta Factory, but petitioned that the case was unjust because all the documents relating to the conviction had been lost. The result? A reply from the colonial secretary that 'Susan Cooper's case has met with the gracious consideration of His Excellency ... She should not suffer because the documents to this effect have been lost'.[50]

Cases reported in the *Australian* between 1825 and 1828 evidence the ways in which colonial women unhesitatingly charged offenders against their property, their person, their family or their reputation. On 15 December 1825 Mrs Susanna Raymond, who kept the Market House in Sydney, brought charges against 'a black, a native of New York' for stealing from her. On 26 January Clara Parsons of Phillip Street charged 'Shiek Brown ... a man of colour' with leaving stolen property at her house. He was convicted of stealing, partly on her evidence. In that same month Mrs Dillon, a shopkeeper of Pitt Street, charged her employee, Martha Morris, with embezzlement. Neither was it unusual for female assigned servants to stand up for their rights in the colonial courts. A female prisoner (name unknown) charged Constable Thomas Kinton with cruelty to her in July 1826, and won her case. On that same day Catherine Brown brought charges of assault against an assigned servant in the same household as herself. The man, Thomas Kelly, was convicted.[51]

Women at Botany Bay who became involved in colonial crime as victims, as accessories, as prosecutors or as criminals, were not only convict women. As in all societies, crime was not limited by social or economic class. The patterns of female criminality which emerge among the colonial women reinforce the need to reappraise the role of women within colonial society. Contrary to contemporary expectations and beliefs, the convict women did not become the criminal women of Botany Bay, nor did they form a homogenous criminal class. The emphasis on the criminality of the convict women, and all the infamous connotations this implies, distorts not only the roles of these women within colonial society but misinterprets the nature, incidence and pattern of colonial crime. Furthermore, such an emphasis overlooks the social and economic changes in the colony, changes which affected crime as greatly as all other facets of colonial life. With the gradual development of a new structure of class based upon material success, it became completely erroneous to describe the criminal class of New South Wales according to British definitions. The convict women of Britain were not the criminal women of New South Wales.

9
'A WOMAN IS A WORTHY THING'

Women and labour at Botany Bay

A woman is a worthy thing:
They do the wash and do the wring;
'Lullay, lullay' she doth thee sing;
And yet she hath but care and wo.
—Anonymous, *Oxford Book of Medieval Verse*

The first female labour force in New South Wales was convict, and women's work in the colony continued to be inextricably linked with convictism and with the social origins of the convict women. Both men and women were sentenced to transportation for terms of penal servitude, but the major difference in practice was that the very existence and survival of the settlement depended on the labour of men while the labour of the women convicts was often unnecessary, unsuitable and even unwanted by colonial officials. Women were needed only for domestic work, work that was in accordance with the basic and traditional domestic skills of women, and the minority of women with trade skills – with the exception of the few weavers and spinners – had little opportunity while convicts to use those skills in government or private employ. As the 'home' occupation of most of the women convicts was servant, or some branch of domestic or country service, it was not remarkable that almost all of the women convicts who worked at 'Public Labour', or were assigned to masters and mistresses in New South Wales, were employed in some form of domestic service. It was after sentence was served or after pardon or, in some cases, after marriage, that the women who had arrived as convicts became a more diverse and enterprising part of the economic life of the penal colony.

Where female convict labour was required by government or private master it was for traditional women's work – to cook, to clean, to wash, to mend, to sew and knit, to bake and perhaps to brew, to make butter and cheese, to tend children and to nurse the sick. It was not envisaged by either the British or the colonial authorities that the convict women would play any other than a domestic role within the labour force of New South Wales, with the exception of those who could be employed at the Parramatta Factory in 'the linen and woollen manufactories'. There was no expectation that some of the women might be as enterprising, ambitious and successful as the industrious ex-convict men, that they might set themselves up as dealers, shopkeepers, marketwomen, hatmakers, dressmakers, shirtmakers, seamstresses, mantua-makers, pastrycooks, confectioners, bakers, laundresses 'of fine linen', washerwomen 'for the quality'; that they would apply for and obtain government licences to bake, to brew, to distil and to run public houses, inns and taverns and places of refreshment as 'women of proven good character', that they would engage in trade, in importing and exporting, that they would tender for government contracts as suppliers of necessities to the Orphan School, to the Female Factory, to the Commissariat, to Government House itself; that they would obtain official positions and responsibilities, such as Keeper of the Sydney Markets and Tolls and Keeper of the Pound. Neither was it expected that ex-convict women would become farmers and landholders, stock-keepers and dairywomen and agriculturalists, responsible for their own properties in their own right, or as the wives of convicts or disabled men or as widows; in the eyes of officialdom, the convicted women were suitable only for domestic service.

It was this stigma of convictism with its infamous connotations which clouded any recognition of the nature, diversity and extent of women's work within the developing economy of New South Wales. To the early governors the convict women were a dissolute and refractory group, disobedient and insolent, incapable of reformation. Phillip, Hunter, King and Bligh, and their colonial officials, judged the labour capabilities of the women convicts by moral standards, measuring their 'worthiness' not only in the light of their proven criminality but in accordance with assumptions as to their depraved and dissolute characteristics. Both criminality and immorality therefore impinged on official assessments as to the suitability and ability of the convict women to become a useful part of the colonial workforce.

There were, of course, sufficient cases where this opinion was justified and the complaints to the governors were added evidence of the depravity and irreclaimable infamy of the convict women. John Macarthur wrote to Nicholas Bayly that he 'condoles with the lamentable state of Bayly's family from the infamous conduct of your woman servants':

But you are not singularly unfortunate in this respect, for what with the insolence of the men and obstinacy of the women in my own family I am quite bewildered – remonstrance is useless and I fear changing will be of little avail ... Those now in the Factory are *so bad* that though we are much annoyed Mrs MacArthur submits rather than change ...[1]

That these reports were far outweighed by the testimonials to the good character and industry of most of assigned convict women did not lessen the infamous reputation of drunken, dissolute and disobedient servants. Difficult as it is to imagine John Macarthur 'bewildered' by a convict servant's insolence, this cannot be taken as a typical case. There were, of course, instances where 'unsuitable' women were sent to families who had requested assigned servants. In 1810 Mrs Crossley complained that the woman assigned to her, Ann Powell, 'was pregnant and only fit for the Hospital'; she was replaced by a Newgate woman, Ann Kelly.[2] The case of Ann Horn is far more typical. She had been charged and convicted in her native Essex with Edward Smith, her 'husband'. Both were found guilty of 'burglary in the dwelling house of William Garrett and stealing goods valued at £15', sentenced to death, reprieved, and then transported to New South Wales for life. They were assigned together, and lived at Parramatta until the death of Edward Smith some eight years after their arrival. Ann Horn's colonial employer gave her the following character testimonial: 'I have found her uniformly honest, sober and *very industrious* having supported her sick husband Edward Smith (deceased) during his indisposition of eighteen months and defrayed the cost of a genteel funeral.'[3] The life of assigned servant Ann Horn did not resemble the expected pattern of debauchery, licentiousness and infamous conduct assumed to be characteristic of the convict women.

The evil reputation of the convict working women and their uselessness as labourers in the colony was well-established in the first years of settlement. To Phillip they were 'unsatisfactory abandoned wretches'. That humane man recorded no favourable comment on the application and industry of convicted women such as Susannah Holmes, Eleanor McCabe, Olive Gascoyne, Mary Parker, Hannah Smith, Elizabeth Pulley, or any of the other convict women on that First Fleet who worked with their colonial husbands to ensure a future for themselves and for their children. Nor did he consider those women 'of the better sort' who cohabited with his officers, and whose children were recognised by their 'respectable' fathers, women such as Esther Abrams, Margaret Dawson, Ann Innett and Ann George, all of whom were to become successful women of Botany Bay despite their criminal records and despite – or perhaps aided by – their cohabitation with 'gentlemen'.[4] Hunter found the women in his charge were 'generally worse characters than the men' and urged Portland not to send any more of these 'irreclaimable wretches' to New South Wales. Three years later Hunter recommended that the colonial magistrates be empowered to order corporal punishment in cases where the women convicts continued to be 'refractory and disobedient'.[5] King tried inducements to achieve not only labour but some standards of decency, discipline and morality among the women, offering 'concessions' to the well-behaved.[6] Was the problem simply that there was insufficient employment for women at this time? Or was it that the women themselves were unsuited to colonial needs, possessing either no skills at all or skills totally unsuitable to the colony's needs?

For whatever reason, official comment continued to centre on the uselessness of the labour of women convicts, their lack of any economic value to New South Wales and their continual drain on the colonial expenditure. All complaints were supported directly or indirectly by the 'evidence' of their flagrant immorality. In the same way that contemporaries in Britain had neither expected nor recognised the changing pattern of 'class' at Botany Bay and the emergence of a distinct and distinctive female society based on colonial standards and achievements, so was the role and contribution of colonial women to the economic development of New South Wales misrepresented, glossed over or ignored.

It is a complete distortion of the women's economic role within the colony to consider only the labour of convict women. Ex-convict and free women were to be found at every level of economic society working alone or with husband or partner. It is as erroneous to equate women's labour with convict labour as it is to equate male achievements and failures solely with the labour of the convict men. The girls and women who worked at the direction of government while serving their sentences in no way reflected the position, experiences and opportunities of all colonial women. It was after sentence was served, or after pardon, that the women of Botany Bay had varying degrees of choice as to their occupation, employment or lifestyle in the colony, and the measure of their successes and failures is reflected in the whole fabric of the economic life of New South Wales.

It was the assignment system which initially controlled the labour of most of the convict women. On arrival, the women were either retained by government for Public Labour or assigned to those settlers and officials who requested female servants. Despite the low ratio of women to men, the early governors found that they did not have enough positions to employ the convict women. In 1796 Hunter wrote to Portland:

We have already enough [women] ... We have scarcely any way of employing them ... if we had more work for them it would often be difficult to employ them, for we generally find those of a certain age taken up with the indispensible dutys of nursing an infant.

Some seven months later Hunter reported that:

The vast number of women for whom we have very little work are a heavy weight upon the Store of Government. If we estimate their merit by the charming children with which they have filled the Colony [they] well deserve our care, but it will become a matter for the consideration of Government whether ... children are to continue a burthen on the Public Store.[7]

The problem of increased colonial expenditure to support convict women who were unsuited for or incapable of Public Labour and the additional expense of rationing their children was seen by Hunter, and later by King, as economic difficulties, not as a problem concerning the carrying out of a legal sentence requiring transported women felons to work in penal servitude for the term of their sentences. In 1798 Hunter did attempt to regulate the labour of women assigned as domestic servants. In a Government and General Order of 7 November 1798 Hunter requested 'every Officer or other Housekeeper in the Colony who may have women Servants in their Family to immediately forward to the Judge Advocates Office at Sydney the name of such as they employ in their respective Families.'

The employers were further requested to report when they discharged their women servants from their employ and to forward a 'Character' for their former employee. Employers were advised not to protect any women from Public Labour or to employ any other than those they were permitted to retain by government. The reason for this Order was closely linked with the behaviour of the women convicts:

The Complaints which are daily made to the Governor of the Refractory and disobedient conduct of the Convict women renders it necessary that some steps be taken to make those troublesome Characters more clearly understand the nature of their situations in this Country and the duties which they are liable to be called upon to perform.

A total of eighty-seven women were listed, and their employers named on Hunter's Assignment Report.[8] Incomplete as this list was, it did show clearly that all assigned women were not necessarily 'unfortunate Females . . . given into the possession of such of the Inhabitants, Free Settlers, and Convicts, indiscriminately, as made a demand for them upon the Governor'. Undoubtedly there were abuses, but all assigned women were not necessarily treated as prostitutes by their masters, nor was New South Wales 'an extensive brothel' because of the assignment system of female convicts. Women were assigned to families as well as to single men and assignment frequently led to marriage or 'unblessed unions'. Their 'punishment' by assignment was incomparably less, in almost all cases, than the punishment suffered by those women who remained in Britain to serve their sentences in the notorious and disease-ridden gaols of the Old Country. Normally, the assigned woman in New South Wales was either received as a servant within a respectable household or, where there was no mistress in the household, she became to all intents and purposes her own mistress, her 'labour' frequently being for her own advantage.

Fourteen of the women on Hunter's Assignment Report were described as 'wife' of the man to whom they were technically assigned. These included Mary Parker, wife of John Small, Johanna Mullens, wife of Charles Peat, and Mary O'Brien, wife of George Patfield. These women were still technically 'convicts', for pardons were rarely given to women who married, it being assumed by the authorities that their married state equated with a pardon, or at least a ticket-of-leave. All of these women, and the remainder listed as 'wives', became respectable independent settlers in the colony, raising families in material circumstances which would have been impossible had they remained in Britain.

In addition to the women described as 'wives', many of the women were assigned to men whom they would eventually marry or cohabit with, women such as Mary Phillips and her master, John Pye, Elizabeth Burleigh and Thomas Arndel, Martha Chamberlain and George Best, Margaret Dawson and Surgeon Balmain. Other women were, without doubt, servants within respectable families. Sarah Greggs was nursemaid to the child of Lieutenant Lucas, Sarah Smith was servant to Captain John Macarthur, Ann Hall to Chaplain Johnston [sic], Maria Hensley to Chaplain Marsden. The clerk of the Commissary, captain, quartermaster and sergeants of the New South Wales Corps, lieutenants in the Royal Navy, ex-convict settlers such as Henry Kable and his wife, all could and did apply for women servants to be assigned to them.

The legal basis for assignment was the transference of the rights to the labour of the convicted felon sentenced to penal servitude from government to an individual who, in turn, became responsible for the welfare and maintenance of that servant.[9] Concern over possible abuses by master or servant continued to trouble both the home government and the colonial administration. Given the immoral reputation of the women and the penal nature of the colony, this was not surprising. In 1809 Viscount Castlereagh instructed Macquarie to ensure that the regulation of apprenticed (i.e. assigned) women convicts was strictly enforced to avoid the women 'living indiscriminately, first in one family then in another'. Castlereagh saw this 'general Licence and Want of Restraint' as resulting in 'the worst Tendencies'. Macquarie was to enforce regulations for apprenticeship more strictly for the females than for the males, and to make certain that 'they should not be allowed to dissolve their apprenticeships but for Marriage, which is to be encouraged as much as possible'.[10]

The greatest problem continued to be that the colonial government simply did not need the labour of the convict women and consequently they were simply a drain on the expenditure, returning no useful labour in exchange for their rations and maintenance. In 1802 King had informed the British government of this, and his opinion was echoed by succeeding governors:

[Female Convicts at Public Labour] As most of these are the worse description and totally irreconcilable, being generally the refuse of London, very few of these are useful, except those employed spinning, who are mostly from the country.[11]

Bligh sent regular quarterly returns of the employment of female convicts at Public Labour. In 1807, 149 women were victualled as women at Public Labour for Government, 110 being employed at Parramatta, thirty-five at Sydney, three at Castle Hill and one at the Hawkesbury. Those at Parramatta were mainly employed in the Factory at woollen and linen manufactory (87) or serving as hospital nurses (7) or caring for orphans in the Orphan Institution (3). The largest group in Sydney were servants to officers (8). At Castle Hill, one woman took care of the Government Huts, another 'husked corn and picked weeds', and the third was 'allowed to the Overseer'. The solitary woman at the Hawkesbury was in charge of the Government Hut.[12]

After the arrival of Macquarie as governor, the increasing numbers of convicts transported to New South Wales added to the problem of how to employ the women convicts and, at the same time, reduce colonial expenditure. Macquarie's solution was an increasing dependence on the assignment system so that most women's introduction to labour in the colony was as domestic servants to private households. Table 9.1 indicates the numbers of women in need of employment and the proportion retained for government service between 1814 and 1820. It is based on Macquarie's reports.

Table 9.1   Convict women assigned or retained by Government, New South Wales, 1814-20

Year	Number Arrived	Number Retained by Government	Number Assigned
1814	333	144	189
1815	171	117	54
1816	181	5	176
1817	188	66	122
1818	322	88	234
1819	–	–	–
1820	346	71	275

Source: Bonwick Transcripts (ML), Box 13, p 725.

The women retained by government were mainly those who could work at the Female Factory, spinning and weaving or who had special skills, such as Bridget Kelsh (*Lady Rowena*), a dairymaid from Dublin, who was assigned to the Government Dairy at Parramatta, or Rebecca Hodges (*Lord Wellington*) from Warwick, who was suitable as an assistant at the Female Orphan School, or Harriet Marsh (*Lord Wellington*) who was sent to Emu Plains, but discharged almost immediately as she married the gardener.

The women to be assigned were usually taken to the Female Factory on arrival at Sydney Cove, and assigned from there as quickly as possible. Free and freed colonial women, as well as men, applied for females as their government servants. After the

Francis and Eliza docked in 1815, ten of the nineteen women assigned within three months were assigned to women. Sarah McGrady from Antrim became the indented servant of Elizabeth Cassidy within a week of landing, as did Julia Brien from Dublin, who was assigned to Isabella Curran but shortly after returned to the Factory as unsatisfactory, to be replaced by another woman who was 'not with child'.[13]

It was under Macquarie's administration that the form for indenture of female assigned servants was standardised. By 1815 the Indenture Certificate stipulated that the period of service was to be three years and the employer was bound to

> severally promise and agree as aforesaid to find and provide for such female convict or convicts during that time he or they shall be retained in our said service, good and sufficient meat, drink, washing and lodging and on no account directly or indirectly to part with such female convict or convicts or either of them to any person or persons whatever during the said term of three years.[14]

The women assigned as domestic servants were technically in a better situation than their 'free' counterparts in Britain, being guaranteed accommodation, food and clothing. Of course, if they were unsatisfactory they could be returned to government and face the possibility of punishment. William Cox returned Ann Keogh (*Canada*) because she was 'very often drunk' and had stolen from the household. She was sentenced to six months' confinement in the Factory.[15]

It was after sentence was served or after pardon that the ex-convict women had a wider choice of occupations than those directly connected with domestic service. This choice was open to both single and family women. The most attractive to colonial wives was that of farmer or landholder, either as the recipient of a land grant in their own right or as the wives of convict men ineligible to own land while under sentence of the law. In either case, the free or freed woman was the legal owner of the property, the 'master' of any assigned convict servants, and responsible to government for the land granted. The memorials from these women to the various governors seeking initial or additional grants and associated indulgences, including servants, labourers, cattle, implements and seed, combined with the advertisements and notices for sale of produce, together with the store receipts issued by the Commissariat for goods received, give a clear and as yet unrecognised picture of the role of the freed women and the convict wives within the development of agriculture and grazing in New South Wales. Not all were successful, and land ownership could and did lead to poverty instead of prosperity, and, in a few extreme cases, despair, desolation and suicide. Sarah Lurry who had arrived convict on the *Prince of Wales* petitioned the governor 'two and twenty years later' that she 'had mett with a great misfortune by accident of fire by having the House burnt down and everything destroyed by Thunder & Lightening about nine o'clock in the Evening Day of the monyth Unknown'.

Colonel Paterson took pity on her plight and gave her fifty acres of land to support 'her in her Old Days'.[16] Mary Jones was not so fortunate. Her husband was 'a labouring man ... under the necessity of going up country to seek a living' leaving her with 'a family of nine little children incapable of seeking a livelihood', so she returned to Sydney Town where she was 'under the necessity of paying a considerable weekly rent for a dwelling, to answer which demand, herself and the little ones are often without bread to eat'. Recommended as 'deserving of pity' by William Cowper, Macquarie noted on the petition that she and 'four of her children will be victualled for six months as objects of public charity'.[17] What became of the other five children is unknown.

Ann Davis, who had been tried in Gloucester in 1788 and transported on the *Lady Juliana*, was unsuccessful in her petition that her grant of 'eighty acres of Land for Cultivation' promised her by the late Lieutenant-Governor be confirmed, despite her good character and large family. Was it that the petition stressed she needed confirmation of the grant because 'she had the misfortune of lossing [sic] her eyesight in this Colony upward of thirteen years'? Four years after this plea she was recorded in the 1814 Muster as 'a blind woman, on Charity', with four children. By 1822 she had overcome her disability – and her poverty – to a certain extent by marrying ex-convict Simon Mould of Parramatta.[18]

For the women who settled the bush there was in all probability no consciousness or prior awareness of the possible hardships, isolation and need for self-dependence which would surround the lives of so many of the free and freed women who became the 'bush' women of the outer settlements of New South Wales. That so many did face such great difficulties and succeed, even at the lowest levels of economic independence, was an achievement beyond any that could have been prophesied on the basis of their former lifestyles in Great Britain.

The rewards could be simply independence, or far greater.

Mary Oliver, convicted in Kent in 1787 and transported on the *Mary Ann/Lady Juliana*, married the man to whom she was assigned as housekeeper, Royal Marine Alexander McDonald, and settled with him on land at the Field of Mars. In July 1806 she wrote to the daughter she had left behind in England, advising her to secure free passage for herself and family and join her mother at Botany Bay:

My Dear Barbara ... my dear Chield,
... here you will have from the Governor of this Place one hundred acres of land forever and two men to cleare and work your ground and all kinds of Stock for yourself and family with the two men that will be given to you will be maintained by Government foir Eighteen months. [here] my Dear is the most healthful country in all the Globe for there is nothing that grows in a hot or Cold Country but comes to the Greatest perfection here for Instance one acre of Wheat will produce Forty to Fifty Bushels of wheat and as to fruit no country can equal it, and our Cattle is far beyond in size and Meat to your finest Cattle in England.

This 'convict' woman had done very well for herself as a settler's wife and was able to send presents to her daughter 'as a small Token of her husband's friendship, Ten Pounds Stirling, a Gold Ring and a Necklace, etc'. Her letters pictured the opportunities which could be found by the industrious – and the fortunate.[19] Were such reports received in Britain with the scepticism which greeted Arthur Phillip's account of his administration when he returned on the *Atlantic* in June 1793? The *Public Advertiser* (London) printed the following report:

When the *Atlantic* left New South Wales, the Colony was in a most promising state, upwards of 1500 acres were in the highest cultivation. A specimen of the Wheat and Barley His Excellency General Phillip has brought home, equals any in England; the Indian Corn was expected to be so productive as to remove any apprehension of a future scarcity. Further accounts of this settlement, which seem rather descriptive of the ancient Arcadia, than of a place of retreat for men under punishment of the laws. In a word, the description is so extravagantly poetical as to exceed all belief.

Despite continuing scepticism in Britain – and despite understandably glowing reports from colonial settlers anxious for their British families to join them – New South Wales, although certainly no 'ancient Arcady', could and did offer economic opportunities for women which 'exceeded belief'.

One of the many convict wives who greatly improved their position in the colony was Rosetta Madden who accompanied her convict husband, Edward Madden, on the *Hillsborough* in 1799. They were both from Lancaster, and, unhappily, Madden died on the voyage to New South Wales. She then married another convict, Henry Marsh, and was once again widowed and left 'with three Fatherless children and unprotected'. Rosetta Marsh 'most Respectfully' petitioned Macquarie for additional pasture land:

she has maintained and educated [her fatherless children] by the most persevering industry . . . and is now possessed of a considerable number of horse & cattle breeding Mares and other stock.

. . . she purchased a farm for the accommodation of her stock which she found inadequate to the pasture ground required for her increasing stock and having nothing in view but the eventual benefit of her children she represented her case to Colonel Paterson who, in consideration of her Industry . . . granted to her one hundred and fifty acres of Pasture Land with a view still further to encourage . . . her Industry.

Rosetta Marsh told Macquarie 'of her unremitting attention to her family . . . her persevering industry'. Was it these meritorious characteristics which led to her third marriage to wealthy ex-convict Samuel Terry early in 1810?[20]

Mary Sarjant secured her farm as a freed woman in her own right. She arrived on the *Glatton*, having been sentenced to transportation for life at Stafford in 1801, received a conditional pardon for good behaviour in 1803, and an absolute pardon in 1804. In September 1813 she petitioned Macquarie for an official Deed of Grant for the land she had been given and which she had cultivated and improved 'on the Hawkesbury Road':

Memorialist is now in occupation of the Land [and] has erected buildings and had a large quantity of timber felled and burnt off and is fully intended to proceed in Cultivating the Farm. Your Excellency will of course believe that Memorialist has been at a Vast Expense as small Buildings cost a deal of Money. Memorialist feels herself in some measure injured by not holding in her possession any Kind of security for the Land – she has made two or three applications.

The petition was referred to the Surveyor-General Meehan and the ex-convict woman received her title deeds which no doubt eased her 'injured feelings'.[21]

Not all women petitioners were as literate as Mary Sarjant,

and not all could afford the services of a professional letter-writer. These disadvantages, however, did not prevent or discourage petitions to the governor, obviously written with great difficulty, such as that of Jane Trotter. Jane Trotter was sentenced to seven years' transportation at Northumberland in 1793 and transported on the *Indispensable*. In 1810 she petitioned Macquarie:

The Humble pitition of Jane Trotter most Respectfully Sheweth:
... to yor Excellecy is pitioner came to this Colony in the Ship *Indisspenceable* with Capt. Wilkinson going fourteen years and during this time Bihaved Meself upright and Honnost and mentade a Lifehod by my Industry.

is Honour Colonal Patterson has been plased to grant me thirty acers of Land for to support me in me old days. In hopes that your Excellency will be plased to regrant the same and I will be Ever in Duty Bound Oged. your Honnors Well fare.

Jane trotter free woman got no indulgence from Government ... arrived in the country I have been this 14 years.

Jane Trotter kept her land for her support in her 'old years', but she also doubly insured this support by living with James Ryan, a butcher who had arrived on the *Sugar Cane*.[22]

Rachel Tounkes, who had been sentenced to seven years' transportation at Warwick in 1790, was first assigned to Captain Munroe when she arrived on the *Mary Ann*. Before her sentence was up, she married fellow-convict John Liquorish, who had arrived on the *Barwell* in 1797 and received a conditional pardon shortly afterwards. Rachel Tounkes petitioned 'Lachlan MacQuarrie Esq' for additional land grants:

Yr Petitioner was marryed to John Liquorish settled near Toongabbie & by the help of God with her industry & care & her Husbands has procured them a very comfortable living. And as Yr Petitionr has been in the Colony upwards of Twenty Five Years & is known by most of the Gent.n in the Colony to have an undoubted character for sobriety & Honesty, having never before she was married or since ever done anything unbecoming a Person in any of Her situations yr. Petitionr therefore casts herself at your Excellency's feet Hopes that you will take it into consideration the length of time she has been here & grant her a farm as neither your Petitionr. nor Her Husband has ever been troublesome or even asked for any Land untill now. Your Excellency's compliance with the above request will for Ever Oblige.
  ... Mrs Rachel Tounkes (now Liquerish) [*sic*]

The request was not granted. Macquarie himself noted on the Memorial: 'This application is out of time and contrary to regulations. Besides it is contrary to the Governors to give Land to . . . a Woman.' Despite this, the man and wife continued 'their industry and care' and enlarged their holdings to some 200 acres at Seven Hills, ensuring the continuance of their 'comfortable living'.[23]

Hannah Taylor was one of the women who did receive land grants before Macquarie's decision that women were ineligible to apply for land. She had arrived on the *Lady Juliana*, probably convicted at Warwick, and was sent from Sydney to Norfolk Island, where her husband died. She then returned to Sydney, and 'His Honor Colonel Paterson was pleased to grant [her] Thirty Acres of Land at Prospect' on the recommendation of Captain Piper. In 1811 she petitioned Macquarie to confirm the grant 'by which she would be able to secure herself of an home for the remainder of her Life'. Possibly because the request was simply for the confirmation necessary after the Interregnum which followed the deposition of Governor Bligh, Hannah Taylor received her title deeds to Paterson's grant.[24]

Among the volume of applications to Macquarie for the confirmation of land grants and leases approved after the Bligh rebellion were many from women who feared loss of livelihood or loss of dwelling and property if they did not receive the necessary 'papers' to ensure their legal possession of their premises or property. Many were ex-convict women, and their memorials not only stress their good and honest conduct (as might be expected) but indicate the ways in which they had obtained their 'honest livelihoods' since their arrival as convicted felons. Few described their working lives as graphically as did Ann Kennedy, who had arrived on the *Experiment* sentenced to seven years' transportation:

The Lieutenant-Governor gave her leave to obtain her livelihood on her own [that is, she was not assigned] which she has done with Thomas O'Neale in an honest industrious way at 103 Pitt Street Sydney. She has a child and is now on a small farm two miles from Sydney.[25]

Most simply stressed that they 'had behavd meself upright', as did Mary Morris, convicted in Cork City in 1796 and transported on the *Britannia*, or Martha Jones who wrote that she

[had] a family and now much advanced in years my Husband also far advanced, notwithstanding his failure in Strength & etc He is still the

support of his House ... Memorialist has become a Housekeeper for these five and twenty years in this Colony, and never has had the conduct of the family called to answer the least impropriety of conduct.[26]

Ex-convict women married to prisoners for life were frequently successful in their applications for land grants where their good characters could be proved beyond question. There is no evidence of hesitation on the part of the wife to apply for the maximum indulgences once the husband was assigned to her, or had obtained a ticket-of-leave, that she needed the labour of her husband to assist with her property. Apart from the wording and spelling, there is little difference in the petitions of the ex-convict wives and those of the free wives of prisoners of the Crown. Mary McMahon wrote to Macquarie that she

is a number of years on the Colony and that she and her husband John Hogan a prisoner for life has behived themselves sober and just and honest and always worked hard to acquire a living for our selves and a helpless family of children petitioners Husband leasing no land of their own or obliged to take twenty acres of standing timber for five years clearing ...

The wording and expression of this petition must have made it very difficult for Macquarie to decipher, but the sense seemed to be the strong injustice this woman felt that she and her husband must clear five acres of heavily timbered ground and then leave the land for another family to cultivate while they moved on to the next uncleared five acres:

wary [weary?] of life caused petitioner to address his Honor Colonel Paterson with the state of her case for which thru his Honours goodness was pleased to grant Petitooner sixty acres of forest land for a residence for Petitoners husband and four children her grant she caused to be plaese into the Secretary's Office ...

She then requested that 'the grant be sanctioned and confirmed as soon as possible', and added that she 'hopes and prays that you will be graciously pleased to free John Hogan the father of her children at the first opportunity'. Nor was this all that this ex-convict woman asked. She requested that all papers be sent to Patrick Hynes, first being left for him to collect 'with Edmund Redmond on the Rocks Sydney as we live in a remote part of the Country where there is no resource of newspapers or general orders'. This petition – which was successful – was certainly not written by a woman who was reluctant to stand up for her rights, not did she consider that she was in any way a 'victim' of society except that the labour of herself and her husband in clearing timberland should be for their own benefit, not for the benefit of others who would then be granted the cleared land to cultivate. In her opinion, the rights of herself and her convict husband were as justified as those of any free or freed family. Whatever economic successes this 'convict' family gained at Botany Bay were directly attributable to the endeavours and enterprise of the ex-convict wife who had been prepared to labour with her husband for the benefit of their family.[27]

Sophia Tull had arrived free with her husband, Mr Marchant, and 'he in a short time after our arrival here, horrid to me to relate, was cruelly murdered'. Governor Bligh 'ordered me two cows ... and I have no doubt that had His Excellency been here I should have had the cows as a gift'. Colonel Johnstone [sic] insisted on her paying for the cows, so she applied to Macquarie. Macquarie's decision is unknown, but several years later she again wrote to the governor, this time on behalf of her second husband, Richard Reed, 'an exile for seven years'. Richard Reed was no ordinary criminal, according to his wife: 'from his demeanour from the time he lost his liberty and on board the Capt. did him the favour to recommend and single him from the other men to his Excellency'. Macquarie told the Captain to leave Reed's name with him and 'he would not forget him'. Alas, with all his preoccupations, Macquarie quite neglected to do anything at all for the unfortunate prisoner Richard Reed, so his good wife wrote tactfully but even more forcefully than in the case of her two 'gift' cows·

I cannot but think [His Excellency] will acquiesce with my request for an unfortunate Man when he does me the honor for a moment to reflect it is a Wife who pleads for her Husband, on my Honour, Sir, I would not advance an introduction permit me to say, he is very practical, very industrious indeed he is a man blest with rectitude of conduct, I am confident will always meet the approbation of His Excellency on his benevolence I rely ...

How such a paragon became a convicted felon is not explained, but Macquarie assented to her plea and the husband was released to his wife.[28]

The letters and petitions sent to Macquarie by both ex-convict and free women show clearly the close involvement of family women in land ownership and development in New South Wales. Isabella Roe, who arrived as Isabella Manson alias Smith on the *Lady Juliana*, sentenced to seven years' transportation at Middlesex in 1788, wrote to Macquarie for confirmation of her husband's land grant and for additional government servants to assist with the farm during her husband's indisposition. They had suffered 'heavy losses at the Hawkesbury ... my wheat being all destroyed at the last inundation' and her husband, 'whose industry was well known ... was confined to bed'. She found herself in such a distressing situation that she required the services of a government man (Mick Higgins who had formerly been assigned to her by Colonel Foveaux), and she requested that her children be victualled from the Stores as she was 'totally destitute of dried provisions'. She concluded with this prayer, that His Excellency's approval of her petition would be

An Act of Charity and for so benevolent a deed that the Almighty may shower down his choicest blessings on your Excellency and Families Heads and for which Memorialist and her unfortunate Family as in duty will every pray ...

How could Macquarie refuse such a supplicant? Isabella Roe, formerly convicted London thief, received her sixty acres, her specified government man, the rations for her children and, it would seem, her blessings rained on the governor and his family.[29]

Elizabeth Buckner had come with her convict husband on the *Pitt*, and in 1810 petitioned Macquarie that she had 'four small children and had always behaved herself in an honest and becoming manner'. She, too, had lost eleven acres of wheat as a result of the floods at the Hawkesbury and had applied to Colonel Paterson for assistance. That good man had given her an order for one hundred acres in the District of Prospect, and she requested that Macquarie have the grant confirmed 'in consideration of her losses and large family and never having received any indulgence from Govt. before'. The land was granted and she and her family settled at Prospect, her husband obtaining a conditional pardon some time after 1814.[30]

The number of women who, in their own right, obtained leases for land on which to build houses, conduct businesses, buy and sell, is shown in the number of confirmations requested for leases which had been granted prior to the arrival of Governor Macquarie and which had to be surrendered to government, then regranted or confirmed in accordance with that governor's proclamation issued shortly after his arrival. Some were from women described as the 'better sort' of convicts, others of more dubious reputation. In August 1817 Ann Robinson (*Lady Penrhyn*) begged 'Permission to state Unto your Excellency that some time back I craved your consideration ... with a renewal of my lease'. She had no difficulty in having the lease renewed for fourteen years, for her character in the colony was irreproachable; irreproachable, that is to the former Governor King who had been her de facto husband after her arrival in 1788. As the wife of ex-convict Richard John Robinson (*Scarborough*) – she was married shortly before King returned to the colony as governor – she had contributed to the family fortunes by obtaining a wine and spirit licence in 1809. Her husband was Superintendent of the Government Mills, so the family were well-established in the colony. Ann Innett-Robinson, however, was one of the few successful ex-convict women who finally left the colony to settle once again – although in far better economic circumstances – in their native land in the 1820s, for she returned to the village of Droitwich [*sic*] in Worcestershire from which she had been transported over thirty years previously. Whether she was influenced by the possibility of reunion with her first two sons who had accompanied their father, the then Lieutenant King, when he returned with Governor Phillip, is unknown.[31]

Many of the women who requested leases confirmed in their own names were those who had scarcely owned the very clothes they wore when committed for trial in Britain. Mary Gotham, tried and convicted in Stafford in 1801, wrote to Macquarie in 1810 that she 'has been seven years in this Colony and always conducted herself in an honest industrious & becoming manner since her first arrival': 'That your Petitioner having by her industry built herself a house in Upper Pitt Row which William Paterson then Lieutenant Governor was pleased to grant a lease of for fourteen years.'

She now requested confirmation of her title to the house and land. That Mary Gotham could own a house through the results of her own industry was in itself an indication of the opportunities for economic advancement available to both single and married ex-convict women. How she had obtained the finance is unknown. In both 1806 and 1814 she was described as a single woman, but her title to the lease was only confirmed after the obligatory official investigation of her character which showed that there was no evidence to suggest she had improved her living standards in any improper or immoral way.[32]

The cost of building a house in Sydney was substantial. Mary Marborough, native-born, paid 'Eighty Pounds sterling money' for the purchase of a house, No 22 Military District.[33] Elizabeth Giles who had arrived convict on the *Lady Juliana* and had since 'supported an unblemished character' had

> purchased a House situated on the Rocks of Nathaniel Miller for the sum of One Hundred Pounds ... and other improvements and additions has put her to a further expense of two Hundred and Thirty Pounds making the whole amount of purchase 350 pounds

Where she had obtained this very considerable sum is unknown. Was it her ownership of the house and her obvious ability to acquire capital which led to her marriage to ex-convict carpenter George Woodford who, after their marriage, changed his profession from carpenter to the more respectable 'upholsterer'?[34]

Women were traditionally involved in brewing, and had been since medieval times.[35] In New South Wales it was not unusual for a woman to be both brewer and victualler and involved in the distilling of spirits, in addition to running taverns, inns, public houses, Flash Houses licensed to retail beer and spirits. In New South Wales all licences to brew, distil and sell had to be approved by the governor, and the applicant had to be 'of good character'. This could be a drawback for free or freed women married to convicts, as in the case of Hannah Morley (*Speke*). D'Arcy Wentworth, Superintendent of Police, refused to renew her liquor licence on the grounds that her convict husband Joseph (*Surprize*) was a drunkard. Hannah Morley, free by servitude, wrote to Macquarie petitioning him to overrule this decision for

> she was in debt, as she had just erected a house suitable for a public house and if her licence was not granted she would become poverty-stricken and she could not repay the debt and she had six small children.

Macquarie granted the licence – on condition the husband was barred from the licensed premises, and she continued to run her public house until at least 1828, by which time it would appear her husband had reformed his ways. Joseph Morley, not his wife, was then the licensed publican in Pitt Street, Sydney.[36] The problems of alcohol in the colony differed from those in

Britain, first because of the need to control its sale and prevent abuses from overindulgence among convicts, soldiers, officials and settlers; second, because of the need to import spirits, legally or illegally; third, because of the difficulties in preventing illicit stills and the sale of both beer and spirits without licence. Given the expectations of 'convict' characteristics, there was, to the colonial officials, an obvious and imperative need to prevent the ready availability of alcohol in any form in the colony. In October 1792 David Collins recorded that, after a licence had been issued for the sale of porter, 'spirits found their way among the people, and much intoxication was the consequence':

Several of the settlers, breaking out from the greatest restrain to which they had been subject, conducted themselves with the greatest impropriety, beating their wives, destroying their stock, trampling on and injuring their crops in the ground, and destroying each other's property. One woman, having claimed the protection of the magistrates, the party complained of, a settler, was bound over to the good behaviour to two years . . . Another settler was at the same time set an hour in the stocks for drunkenness . . . [37]

The quality of the spirits available was not considered in relation to the effects of its consumption, although several deaths were directly attributed to 'over-indulgence'. In March 1793 'a stout healthy young woman', Martha Todd (arrived convict *Mary Ann*), 'fell victim to a dysenteric complaint which seized her after drinking too freely of the pernicious spirits which had been lately introduced into the colony'. 'A good sober man', James Hatfield, died in the same way 'after partaking intemperately of the American rum'.[38]

'A fondness for spirituous liquors' was often the official reason for the failure of a settler and his wife to establish themselves on their grants of land. Burn and his wife, according to the Judge-Advocate, 'were too fond of spirituous liquors to be very industrious'. Burn had lost an eye when he was splitting paling for government before his sentence was served. That this may have lessened his ability to work – or increased his need to 'drown his sorrows' – was not considered.[39]

Collins also saw depravity in the way in which a convict settler mourned the untimely death of his wife. The 'rascally Williams' had buried her at his doorstep after she had drowned with their baby in the flooded river; he would sit every night, pouring two glasses of spirits – one for him and one to pour on her grave – for, he said, 'she loved it so in life'. To David Collins this was evidence of the degradation and depravity of those convict settlers[40] – a depravity which continued to plague the governors of New South Wales.

Women who retailed spirits could be involved in the criminal life of New South Wales, either by selling without a licence, illegally distilling, or using their licensed premises for gaming, disorderly houses, or by adding to their income by acting as receivers of stolen goods. Not all were as conscientious as Mrs Mary Alroy of Brickfields, 'a woman of decent appearance', who appeared in court with her child on behalf of her husband who had been convicted of selling spirits without a licence. The shock of his trial had caused 'a derangement of [her] mind and she pleaded for the release of her erring husband into her custody'.[41] The case of Mrs Johnston was more typical of dishonest innkeepers. Mrs Johnston kept a public house in Harrington Street, Sydney and was convicted of receiving stolen goods: 'the conduct of this woman Johnston ... was reprobated [sic] in very severe terms' by the judge and her liquor licence withdrawn.[42] Most women publicans, tavernkeepers and innkeepers were not involved in criminal activities, or, if they were, they escaped the notice of the law. They were well aware that the continuance of their businesses depended on their own reputation and on the good name of their premises. Women deprived of licences on grounds they considered unjust or unwarranted were not hesitant to complain to the governor that the Superintendent of Police had unfairly refused to grant or renew a liquor or spirit licence. Alice Flyn, who claimed to have been 'improperly excluded' from the renewal of her licence by D'Arcy Wentworth, Superintendent of Police – 'she was of proven good character and ran an honest house' – had her licence as a victualler restored to her after her plea to Macquarie. It would appear that D'Arcy Wentworth took his responsibilities seriously, despite his having no aversion to public houses – or female proprietors – as at least three other 'licensed' women publicans successfully appealed to Macquarie against his refusal to renew their licences. These women were two free wives of convicts, Mrs Isaac Moss and Mrs Ann Whittaker, and ex-convict singlewoman Mary Plowright (*Indispensable*).[43]

The *Sydney Gazette* regularly published the names of men and women granted licences for any trade. The lists show the variety of civil conditions of the female applicants as well as the different types of licences which were granted to women. In 1809 Ann Trotter, who had come to the colony on the *Queen* as the free wife of Sergeant Jamieson of the New South Wales Corps, was granted a wine and spirit licence. Ann Robinson, who had arrived convict in 1788 as Ann Innett, also received her wine and spirit licence, as did Rosetta Marsh and Elizabeth Graham. Elizabeth Graham had come free to the colony about 1798, and was a widow with eight children to support when she petitioned for a wine and spirit licence in 1810. She wrote to the governor that 'her husband was a prisoner. She supported her family by her own industry ... her husband had been a licensed victualler'.[44]

In 1810 ex-convict Mary Reibey was granted a liquor licence, Mary Redman (*Atlas*) was granted a beer licence for her premises in Chapel Row, Sarah Wood (*Glatton*), proprietor of the Waterman's Arms at the Rocks, received her beer licence, as did Phebe Waldron of Windmill Row, Jane Muckle of Back East Row, and Elizabeth Mack 'of back of the Hospital'.[45]

By the 1820s almost every street of Sydney Town had at least one public house, tavern or inn of which the proprietor was a woman. Hannah Pawley retailed spirits at the Blue Post in Cambridge Street; Mrs Jones kept a public house 'on the Race Course'; Mrs Hill, formerly of Hills Tavern Hyde Park, leased the Rose and Crown Inn at Castlereagh Street; Mrs McCabe was proprietor of a public house in Market Street; Catherine Clarkson was licensed to retail spirits at the Woodman in Hunter Street; Elizabeth Marr (formerly Driver) had the Star and Garter in Castlereagh Street; Catherine Doyle retailed spirits at the Jolly Sailors in Harrington Street; Esther Hand ran the Golden Fleece in George Street, and numerous women were licensed to sell beer, ale and spirits. These were only a few of the colonial women who were involved in selling liquor in the colony as a means of livelihood.[46]

The free and freed wives of convicts could and did seek licences to sell beer, ale and or spirits in their own names, even when the convict husband was assigned to them and worked at another trade. Mary Whitfield (*Northampton*) complained to Governor Brisbane that the licence she had been given was being illegally used by Daniel Cooper:

She is a free woman [free by servitude] and occupies a house by the sign of the old Manchester Arms on the corner of Park and George Streets. Her husband is a prisoner [employed as a blacksmith]. Daniel Cooper was given the licence on her behalf to vend spirits, but he has been doing so in his own house thus depriving her of her business. She is paying rent of £80 per annum [to Cooper] ... she wants the licence for herself as it was intended.[47]

This ex-convict businesswoman was granted her petition and traded successfully in her own name at her rented premises while her convict husband added to their income by his work as a blacksmith.

Another ex-convict publican was Jane Bennet (*Friends*), married to convict John Nixon (*Eliza*), a prisoner for life. He was a butcher by trade and she had requested that he be assigned to her but 'fears her application has been mislaid'. She described her work as a colonial publican when she repeated her request to the governor that her husband be released to her:

She has been in the colony ten years, the last three of which she has kept a respectable licensed Public House in York Street... The licence for this house expired yesterday and she must quit her business for one which will require the constant attendance of her husband. She was given permission to have him assigned to her when this first licence expired.

The testimonials to her good character and to the 'worthiness' of her husband were written by John Dunmore Lang, by her own former employer, by her convict husband's employer, and by the Commissary Department. Dunmore Lang strongly recommended husband and wife: 'they both attend Scots Church regularly'. Her former employer, Mrs Harrington, vouched that she was 'a very decent woman when in her service', and both former employers of her husband [his assigned masters] testified that 'he behaved himself extremely well'. Mrs Nixon's request was granted, and she became the licensee of new and larger premises. Her husband was assigned to her, and continued his trade as a butcher for the benefit of both – and possibly for the benefit of those patrons who ate the 'saddle of mutton' or 'rabbit pies' served in the parlour of the new public house in Kent Street.[48]

Although 'previous good character' was technically obligatory for successful application for spirit, liquor or beer licences, there were infrequent occasions when certain incidents in the colonial life of a woman applicant might have been thought sufficient to refuse a licence. Lydia Astell, the twenty-five-year-old daughter of Eleck Etherington and his wife Hannah, née Robley, of Cobham, Surrey, was convicted at the Sussex Assizes of March 1819 for 'feloniously having a forged note in her possession ... with feloniously disposing of and putting away a forged £5 note with intent to defraud the Bank of England'. A native of Berkshire, she was described as '5'3" tall, dark brown hair, hazel grey eyes', by trade a mantua-maker and a shoe binder. Transported on the *Janus*, both she and fellow-convict Mary Long became pregnant on the voyage. They were both assigned shortly after arriving at the Parramatta Factory, despite 'being near their time'. Lydia and Mary applied for passes and for permission to visit the *Janus* before it left for England. The father of Lydia's child, John Hodges, 'would visit her parents which will be a great consolation for them and a satisfaction to me'. Shortly after the child was born, Lydia married Thomas Barnes (*Coromandel*) at St John's, Parramatta. By 1825 she had joined in partnership with Charles Williams, and held a licence for the Macquarie Tavern in Pitt Street, Sydney. In 1829 Thomas Barnes became Police Constable at Bathurst, and later was appointed a Gaoler at Bathurst Gaol. Lydia Barnes sought and received licences for the Trafalgar Inn on Bathurst Road, Honeysuckle Flat, and the Golden Fleece at Bathurst, the notoriety she had received over the official charges of prostitution brought against the officers of the *Janus* obviously overlooked.[49]

The behaviour of the convict husband of a licensee continued to come under scrutiny. Thomas Buxton, a brewer by trade, was transported for life on the *Tottenham* in 1818. In 1820 he was joined by his free wife and family, and she applied for and received a licence for a public house, and was successful in having her husband assigned to her. In 1826 she almost lost the licence when her husband was convicted on a charge of disrespectful and improper behaviour towards the Superintendent of Police when inspecting a public house for which the licence had been granted the previous year in the name of his wife.[50] In most cases where the free wife held the licence and the husband did not have a trade connected with brewing, distilling or innkeeping, it was the wife who was directly responsible for the running of the business. Additionally, if there were irregularities or complaints, it was the wife who was reprimanded, indicted, or had to show cause why the licence should not be revoked. Conversely, if there were offences against the business or the proprietors of the employees, it was the wife who must take action in the colonial courts. Elizabeth Lear, the proprietor of a 'butcher's shop and a victualling house known by the sign of the City of London Arms in Pitt Street', charged a light-fingered patron, Cornelius Mahoney, with the theft of six shillings and sixpence-halfpenny in May 1825. Mahoney, a convict for life (*Hoogly*) was then fifty-eight years old and 'an invalid'. He was, however, found guilty, and ordered to make restitution to Mrs Lear. Elizabeth Jackson, the proprietor of the Jolly Waterman, was charged with 'suspicion of having stolen goods on her premises' in January 1825, but was acquitted after giving evidence that the stolen goods had been brought to her house by the thief, and that she had no knowledge of him or of his criminal activities. Thomas Parsons, accused of theft from licensee Mrs Redmond, pleaded the offence was committed 'when I had got a glass too much', but this did not influence the verdict of the Court that he was guilty and that Mrs Redmond, despite the infirmities of her elderly husband, was in no way to blame for his crime.[51]

When the British background of most of the women who became involved in the liquor trade in New South Wales is considered, their adaptability to entirely new 'work' situations becomes apparent. Most of these women had no previous experience with brewing, distilling or running public houses or taverns before their arrival in New South Wales. Most began with the disadvantage of 'bad character' as convict women. They needed not only to secure the licence, but to have the finance to set up house, pay lease, rent or purchase, equip and maintain their premises, and control their staff of government servants or free labourers. In addition, they had to petition – sometimes again and again – to have convict husbands assigned to them as their servants and, at the same time, those who were women with children had the normal responsibilities and cares associated with raising their families. That so many were successful, that they showed no hesitation in 'going to law' if they felt they were injured in any way, in appealing against decisions made which were unfavourable to their business interests, even if these decisions came from the Superintendent of Police himself, underlines the great differences which existed between their former lifestyles in Britain and their lives in New South Wales as free or freed women. The changes were directly attributable to their positive responses to the opportunities these enterprising women found at Botany Bay.

Elizabeth Killett was one example of the successful 'convict' businesswomen of New South Wales. She was tried in Suffolk in 1800 at the age of nineteen, and transported to Botany Bay on the *Nile*. She married John Gray two years later. In 1818 her husband, the assistant to the Clerk of the Market in Sydney, was drowned. The *Sydney Gazette* reported 'He was much respected as an old inhabitant of the Colony, and has left a wife and seven children to lament his premature destiny'. Three weeks later his son, John Gray, was appointed to his father's position. By the next year his widowed mother was 'Lessee of Tolls of the Sydney Market' and continued to hold a spirit licence. In 1820 she petitioned Macquarie for a continuation of her licence: 'she is the person who at present holds the Market at Sydney together with the Market House, Licensed for the Accommodation of Settlers and Others'. This ex-convict woman received her Spirit and Beer Licence for the Macquarie Arms in George Street, as well as being appointed Poundkeeper. As Clerk of the Market she was responsible for public notices for alteration of market days and for the payment to the Police Fund for Market Duties, often in excess of £150. Elizabeth Killett/Gray was one of the ex-convict women of Sydney Town to become vitally involved in, and responsible for, economic ventures in New South Wales.[52]

Women at Botany Bay became directly involved in almost all of the activities concerning trade and commerce in the colony. Shopkeepers such as Mrs Bodenham, the wife of a Land and Estate Agent in Sydney, advertised regularly in the colonial newspapers:

Mrs Bodenham respectfully announced that she will open this day, Ladies and Childrens Leghorn Bonnets of the very finest quality. Ladies kid, black and white gloves, Childrens cambric gloves, worked collars, a few English silks, etc . . . also selling a variety of furniture . . .

Unhappily, this was one 'female' business venture which did not succeed; Mrs Bodenham was forced to retire within a few months 'due to her long and continued illness'. She sold her business, which was 'under the Patronage and Sanction of Mrs Darling', to a married couple, Mr and Mrs Christopher Wright. Mrs Broadbent advertised on a more modest scale that she sold general goods, including clothing. Mrs Mary Dillon, who had arrived as a convict on the *Aeolus*, set up shop as a milliner while a ticket-of-leave woman. Her business expanded during her first two years' trading and she moved to larger premises in George Street, only to be declared insolvent twelve months later. Free and freed women sold a variety of goods: Mrs Dockrell of 68 George Street, 'opposite the market', advertised clothing, books, tea, tobacco, gunpowder and pepper; Mrs Jones 'dealt in ladies wear and furniture from her house'; Mrs Nightingale, 'a Native Girl' and a widow, described herself as 'a dealer' at the age of nineteen. Madame Josephina Rens was more ambitious, advertising the opening of her 'shop of fashionable clothes from Paris' she traded from the house of Mrs Jones; Mrs Smith of 21 Castlereagh Street, Sydney, was a stationer; Mrs Stuart of Brickfield Hill sold 'ladies wear and groceries'; while Mrs Weavers of 19 Pitt Street was 'in business with her mother, Mrs Reynolds'.[53]

It was not only the town women who became deeply involved in trade and commerce. The women from the outer settlements and from 'up country' advertised, sold or tendered their produce. Mrs Frankland of Vineyard Farm at Hunter's River gave notice 'of Agistment available'. Eliza Cheetom, a farmer of Windsor, tendered for 300 bushels of wheat at the Commissariat at six shillings and ninepence; Sarah Cobcroft, another Windsor farmer, tendered for 100 bushels at seven shillings; Elizabeth Corkshill, Hawkesbury farmer, tendered for 50 bushels of wheat at seven shillings; Mary Cupitt, Windsor farmer, tendered for 100 bushels at six shillings and sixpence; Ann Frall, Hawkesbury farmer, for 80 bushels at seven shillings; Elizabeth Jones, farmer at Windsor, tendered for 100 bushels at six shillings, eleven pence and three farthings. All the tenders from these women were accepted by the Commissariat.[54]

Jane Codd was a successful 'convict' dairywoman. She had been sentenced at Heverford in West Pembroke in June 1788 and arrived on the *Mary Ann* in 1791. By 1796 she had received a land grant at Bulnaming, had planted four acres of maize, owned ten pigs and eight goats, and was supporting herself offstores. In 1806 she was living with Edward Edwards who had arrived convict on the *Royal Admiral*, and by 1814 she was described as his wife. She continued to build up her dairy herds, and after her death in November 1826 the following advertisement appeared in the *Australian*:

FOR SALE

Mrs Jane Codd (deceased), Dairywoman of George Street Sydney. A Herd of 21 Milch Cows of the First Description, part of the well-known milking herd of the late Mrs Jane Codd . . . and now vested in her legal representatives.

Sgd. D'Arcy Wentworth,
Trustee

From convicted thief to well-known colonial dairywoman had been an unexpected development in the life of Jane Codd, an enterprising and hard-working woman of Botany Bay.[55]

The variety and diversity of women's occupations in the colony appeared endless. There were schoolmistresses such as Mrs Kingsmill; seminaries for 'female education' run by women such as Mrs Robertson; boarding schools for young ladies, some of which were limited to ten genteel pupils, as was that managed by Mrs James of 76 George Street. Mrs Geoffrey Eager advertised her Seminary for the Instruction of Young Ladies: 'Subjects in which instruction will be given: English Grammar,

Ancient and Modern History, Geography (with the use of the Globes), and needle Work'. Mrs Eager also advertised stores, sheds and cellars to let under her Seminary, these being unnecessary for her own business.[56]

There seemed no end to the businesses in which colonial women were engaged. Mary Ann Whitfield, who had arrived in the colony as a three-year-old on the *Britannia* with her convict mother, placed the following advertisement in the *Australian* in October 1824:

having removed to the house in George-Street, lately occupied by T. Harper, and known by the sign of the Cumberland Arms, where she intends carrying on a ready money-trade; and begs to inform the public that she will sell good rum at 13 shillings and sixpence per gallon, best tea at six shillings per pound, sugar at sixpence per pound, tobacco at five shillings and sixpence.

Mary Whitfield, who lodged in Sydney with that enterprising shopkeeper and dealer, Elizabeth Jones, continued in the liquor trade, but became known as a businesswoman who 'gave no tick', all transactions being on a 'ready-cash' basis only.[57]

Other women combined trades; Mrs Rogers, of 7 King Street, sold clothing from her premises, advertised 'a large consignment of farming equipment for £150', and also let 'Lodgings genteely furnished'. She described herself as a shopkeeper. Mrs E. S. Milton, widow, of Princes Street, not only provided meals 'and other services', but advertised her convenient location 'nearly opposite the Military Hospital', and begged 'to inform Gents. that she intends continuing the establishment of her late Husband' and become the boarding house proprietor of their premises. Her 'Reasonable Terms – for 'Gents' only' – were £1 10s 0d per week. Mrs Carrick published an announcement that she had commenced in 'the Baking Business, in all its Branches . . . Shipping supplied with bread, fruit, confectionery, etc.'[58]

At a lesser social level, there were barrow-women such as Mrs Leadbeater, who had her stand at Clarence Street Corner and 'sells fruit about the town'. In 1826 she narrowly escaped injury after being knocked over by a recklessly driven horse and cart. There were charwomen like Elizabeth Lambert, nursemaids 'who could support an unimpeachable character', or 'respectable middle-aged women', housemaids 'who can work well at the needle with a good character', laundresses, servants of all types. In all advertisements in the *Sydney Gazette* and later in the *Australian*, the emphasis was on the 'good character' which was an essential prerequisite for employment.[59]

It was the degree to which the women of Botany Bay could and did adapt to the nature, needs and availability of women's work in New South Wales, combined with their suitability to respond to the varied and diverse economic opportunities which were open to colonial women of all civil conditions, which was largely determinative in their responses to colonial life. New South Wales, although certainly no pre-industrial Arcady, was primarily an agricultural-based society during the foundation years, and lacked any of the employment open to women in Great Britain in the factories, mines and mills. The women who came to New South Wales needed traditional skills associated with the work of country women, skills which characterised so many of the women transported from Ireland. For that minority of skilled convict women from Britain or from Ireland who had worked at a trade or craft other than domestic service, there was almost unlimited scope for the industrious and the ambitious. There was a continual shortage of skilled and experienced female labour in the penal colony, especially during the first thirty years of settlement when most of the women had arrived as transported convicts. The dressmakers, the seamstresses, the hatmakers, the mantua-makers, were as much in demand as assigned servants as were the skilled male tradesmen among the convict men. Those women who could brew and bake, sew, knit and spin, make butter and cheese, who were experienced cooks or confectioners, had formerly worked as dairywomen, or even as lady's maid or child's nurse, laundress or 'fine washerwoman', were the most sought after as assigned servants. They were also the ones who had the greatest opportunities after they had become free women.

What was unexpected was that women of no trade, women with no prior skills, women who could neither read nor write but signed their names as 'X', became a part of the successful working women of the penal colony, making their livelihoods at occupations for which they had no prior skill or training. These ex-convicts and the convict wives took on new roles in the colony, and with those new enterprises, they shouldered added responsibilities at all economic levels, and did not hesitate to approach the Governor himself – or the more forbidding Superintendent of Police – to insist on their rights as businesswomen and as family women. It was the determined and forceful approach of these women, so many of whom were from the lowest and most despised class of British society, which established the women of Botany Bay as a forceful part of the economic life and development of England's penal colony.

10
'THE SWORD OF GOD AND GIDEON'

Marriage and morals at Botany Bay

From the Circumstances of the Colonists, and the Numbers that go out leaving their Wives or Husbands in England, and the Disproportion between the Sexes, it must be very difficult to remedy the evil complained of... I trust you will... in every case endeavour to make the Reformation of the Female Convict and her regular Settlement by marriage a Consideration superior to the saving, for any short period, the expense of maintaining her...

—Viscount Castlereagh to Governor Bligh,
Downing Street, 31 December 1807

On Wednesday, 6 February 1788, the convict women were landed at Sydney Cove. For them it was journey's end. It was hot that Wednesday at Sydney Cove, with frequent thundery squalls and lightning storms, the like of which few of the new arrivals had ever known. The women were up at '5 o'clock ... dressed in general very clean ... some amongst them might be said to be well-dressed'. By 6 o'clock they were boarding the longboats which were to row them to shore with the few possessions they had brought with them – or had 'acquired' on the voyage. There was little sign of welcome from their new land. Their tents were not ready to receive them, and there was no protection from the squalls, the terrifying electrical storms, the oppressive and unfamiliar heat. There was, however, welcome from their countrymen, a welcome the respectable diarists and journal-keepers found almost beyond their abilities to describe. There had been little comment on the landing of the first white women, the wives of the Royal Marines, a week or so earlier. But 'the Scenes of Riot and Debauchery that ensued ... after the men got at the women shortly after they landed' were to brand the convict women as the depraved whores of Botany Bay. The arrival of these women polluted the new settlement, for they brought with them all the infamy and evil, all the viciousness and depravity believed to typify their former lives in Britain. 'Licentiousness', wrote Watkin Tench, 'was the unavoidable consequence and their old habits of depravity [began] to appear'.[1]

From this arrival of British 'civilisation' on the shores of Terra Australis, a succession of governors, officials and commentators continued to assume that the female convicts were far more infamous and depraved than the men, 'instigating them to vice and corruption', recreating Sodom and Gomorrah in England's penal colony. Their colonial reputation as damned whores, common prostitutes, infamous and degraded strumpets, was stereotyped from that first day and continued to be based on their immorality, not their criminality. To British and colonial officials they were women without shame or decency, women who would sell their bodies for a tot of spirits or a bottle of grog, who would lie and cheat, entice men to rob and thieve to satisfy their lust, women who plagued every governor, thwarted all attempts by colonial officials to promote marriage and to encourage morality among the inhabitants of Botany Bay.

Such behavioural patterns were expected from criminal women, and agreed with reports and descriptions of women imprisoned in the gaols and bridewells of Britain. Moral control and possible reformation of these 'irreclaimable husseys' was an added responsibility for the governors of New South Wales. The difficulties this involved were recognised in England. In a semi-official letter to the newly appointed governor Lachlan Macquarie, colonial theorist T. W. Plummer gave the following warning about New South Wales:

The temptations to a disorderly life are so many, and the facility for indulging in them so great, that most of the Convicts of every description, being destitute of any powerful motives to industry, abandon themselves entirely to habits of idleness and debauchery...

Plummer added that 'the laxity and depravity of public morals' was increased by the practice of allowing settlers 'to choose... not only as Servants but as avowed objects of intercourse' women from among the newly arrived convicts. This, Plummer warned Macquarie, 'rendered the entire colony little more than an extensive Brothel'.[2]

Plummer's opinions were based on the 'evidence' of Samuel Marsden's 1806 Female Register which was damning to the reputation of the women of Botany Bay. Quoting Marsden's statistics, Plummer told Macquarie that 'about one thousand illegitimate children were in New South Wales', their births the direct result of this disgraceful system of assignment. Marsden had listed all the colonial women as either wives or concubines, their children as legitimate or illegitimate (see Table 10.1).[3]

Table 10.1 Summary of Chaplain Marsden's Female Register

Total number of women bond or free in N.S. Wales	1430
Total children	1832
Number of free women married in England	148
Number of free women from England married in N.S. Wales	29
Number of married convict women	217
Number of married free women who have children	125
Number of married free women from England who have no children	32
Number of married convicts who have children	125
Number of married convict women who have no children	90
Number of children belonging to the free married women	468
Number of children belonging to the married convict women	339
Free women from England not married	33
Total number of free women from England	210
Number of convict women who have no children	642
Number of convict women who have children – married and unmarried	572
Number of children belonging to the married and unmarried convicts	1364
Total number of natural children	1025

Note: There is a discrepancy: 125 married convict women with children + 90 without children = 215. Marsden's total of married convict women: 217.

Marsden's description 'concubine' included common-law and de facto relationships. Women such as Ann Parker and Elizabeth Berry, both transported on the *Glatton* in 1803, were described as concubines. Ann Parker was a fifteen-year-old Londoner, convicted of stealing and tried at Middlesex Sessions. By 1806 she was living with W. Hembridge, a sawyer, and in 1814 with Kennedy Murray (*Pitt*), a landholder, and their two children. In 1822 she was a widow with three more Murray children, living on fifteen acres she had purchased at Windsor. From about 1822 she had medical problems supposedly resulting from epilepsy. Nevertheless she was consistently described as a happy, healthy woman. She died at the age of seventy-five, and was buried at All Saints' Church, Parramatta.

Elizabeth Berry, who was known as Jessie, was born in Stevenage in Hertfordshire about 1778, and remained there until sentenced to transportation for seven years. Her trial papers record rather enigmatically that she was tried 'for having an unchristian attitude'. Within some three weeks of arriving at Port Jackson, Jessie was assigned as a domestic servant to Sergeant Charles Whelan. From then until 1810, when she married the good sergeant at St Philip's, Sydney, her lifestyle may have appeared a case history for that pattern of immorality believed to result from that ' "indiscriminate" assignment of convict women to single men' so deplored by Plummer and Marsden. Whether the marriage was prompted by the sergeant's position as a member of Macquarie's personal bodyguard is unknown, but Whelan remained with Macquarie until the governor returned to England. Jessie, the concubine of 1806, became 'the wife of a soldier' in the 1814 Muster, her marriage not only making an honest woman of her – if somewhat belatedly – but conferring respectability as a family woman of Botany Bay.[4]

Ann Parker and Elizabeth Berry are only two of the numerous cases where Marsden's description 'concubine' created an entirely erroneous impression of the lifestyles of the colonial women. An analysis of all the women on the Chaplain's Female Register showed that some had been married in the colony prior to 1806, others married the men with whom they had lived in de facto relationships, others simply remained all their lives in the same 'unblessed union'. Sarah Bellamy (*Lady Penrhyn*) was the de facto wife of James Bloodsworth until his death. Was it that he already had a legal wife and a large family in England which prevented a legal colonial marriage? Why Elinor McDonald (*Queen*) remained the de facto wife of Jonathan Griffiths is unknown, but their relationship lasted until her death. Mary Bergen (*Sugar Cane*) had five illegitimate children to Sergeant Andrew Field, with whom she was living in 1806. In 1814 she was described as 'Mrs Field', wife of Sergeant Andrew Field (*Pitt*). Hannah Mullens (*Lady Penrhyn*) had married Charles Peat on 22 January 1788 – to Marsden, she was a concubine. Catherine Corrigan (*Queen*) had married William Hall/Hull, a soldier in the New South Wales Corps on 23 May 1795. In Marsden's Register she was a concubine with one illegitimate child. Other women were unlikely concubines, even after allowance for the healthy climate of New South Wales: Elizabeth Bird (*Lady Penrhyn*) was sixty-two years old. Others, married in England or Ireland, who bore colonial children, were recorded as concubines. The lives of most of these women after they had served their sentence bore no relationship at all to the connotations of 'concubine', nor did their family lifestyles agree with assumption that New South Wales was simply a vast brothel.

Some colonial or de facto relationships may have been the result of previous legal marriages in Britain. Ann Colpitts (*Lady Penrhyn*) was described at her trial in England as 'the wife of Thomas Colpitts'. Was this why she cohabited with Private John Colethread of the Royal Marines during the first few years they were in the colony and did not marry? Their first child, John, was christened on 8 January 1789 and buried three months later. Their second child, also named John, was christened on 2 May 1790. John Colethread did not return to England with his Company, but remained in New South Wales as a settler. Neither did he marry Ann Colpitts. On 25 September 1791 she married Thomas Smith. Two years later Colethread consoled himself by marrying convict Elizabeth Catherine Mooney, their first child, Gracey, being baptised in 1800. Marsden listed Catherine Mooney as a married woman with five children, but noted in the margin: 'not married'. His reasoning is unknown.

The uncritical acceptance of Marsden's Female Register as indicative of the characters of the 'convict' women by the British government, by commentators such as Sydney Smith and theorists like Plummer, evidenced a complete unawareness of the entirely different social conditions of New South Wales, the redefined features which characterised the nature of female society, and the lack of any perception of factors which acted against, rather than promoted, colonial marriages. These 'hindrances' to respectability were all combined in the eyes of the British officials to show the flagrant disregard for moral standards by the colonial women whose 'respectability' could only be measured by their status as legal wives. Every governor was given explicit instructions to encourage marriage as the chief means of promoting respectability and reformation. Only one suggested that this might not be the only appropriate way to 'reclaim' these unfortunate women.

In August 1806 King wrote to Castlereagh that 360 couples had been married since 1800: 'It certainly would be desirable if marriage were more prevalent, as every encouragement is given for their entering into that state'. He added:

As the will of the individuals ought, in this instance to be free, I cannot say that I ever approved of a proposed plan to lock all the females up who are not married until they are so fortunate as to obtain husbands ... [were this followed] instead of marriage being respected it would become a mere act of convenience to withdraw them from their confinement, exclusive of the impracticability of preventing men having access to them, by art or violence . . .

There were many arguments, King told Castlereagh, which 'might be used against compelling the women to marry beyond their own inclinations'. One of these was that many had living husbands in Britain.[5] King also wrote to London that most of the women of 1806 were 'self-supporting' and no charge to the colonial administration for themselves or for their children. There were 1412 female convicts on the mainland of New South Wales in August 1806: of these '1,216 are of no expense to the public, being married or living with free people of all description, and with those who from good behaviour hold tickets-of-leave'.[6]

King certainly held no brief for those 'troublesome, irreclaimable women', but his comments in favour of their ability to support themselves were as disregarded as were his arguments against enforced marriage. Marsden had listed the names of 217 convict women who were legally married among the 1412 living in New South Wales. That was sufficient 'evidence' for Britain to accept that New South Wales had remained a place of 'Riot and Debauchery' since the first landing of the convict women in February 1788.

In December 1807 Castlereagh instructed the next naval governor, William Bligh:

You appear to be sensible of the Importance of promoting the Increase of Marriage in the Colony . . . I trust you will . . . in every case endeavour to make the Reformation of the Female Convict and her regular Settlement by marriage a Consideration superior to the saving, for any short period, the expense of maintaining her.[7]

Was this a direct rejection of King's suggestion that the women be 'not locked up' until married? In May 1809 Castlereagh repeated these instructions to the new governor, Macquarie: 'Marriage is to be encouraged as much as possible'. Macquarie acted on this instruction almost as soon as he arrived. One of the first Government and General Orders of his administration legislated against cohabitation by imposing legal disabilities on any woman who lived with a man outside legal wedlock. Such a woman could not inherit the property or possessions of the man with whom she lived. There was no allowance for injustice or hardship in cases where the colonial 'possessions' had been accumulated by the enterprise and industry of both man and woman, or where a free woman had obtained land or licence which reverted to the de facto convict husband after he had served his sentence or had been pardoned. The inheritance of a widow, legal or de facto, could include land and stock, houses and buildings, shops and public houses, licences and leases, interests in trade, commerce and shipping. The de facto widow could face considerable economic loss as a direct result of living in an unlawful union. Macquarie's 'legislation' sought to enforce morality and respectability, as evidenced in legal marriage. This was deterrence to immorality by fear of punishment, and deprivation not of liberty but of material independence. It followed the same theory that fear of physical punishment could reduce crime, and fear of material loss could induce matrimony.[8]

Did this affect longstanding relationships? It is not known if Macquarie's Order had any influence on the decision of women such as Esther Abrams to marry her de facto husband.[9] Women like Mary Marshall (*Lady Penrhyn*) petitioned the governor for legal title to properties and premises left to them in the wills of their deceased partners, often unsuccessfully. Mary Marshall had lived with Robert Sidaway (*Friendship*) since 1788 – they had both been convicted in London where Sidaway had a wife and family. In 1810 Mary Marshall wrote to Macquarie:

Your Petitioner has lived in the colony for twenty-two years, during which time she has lived with Robert Sidaway who died a few months back ... He was baker to the troops ... He had a lease of premises in Sydney which he left to her in his will.

Whether or not she retained the lease is unknown, but in the Muster of 1814 she was recorded as a publican of Sydney.[10]

Macquarie's Order made no allowance for those Irish Catholic women whose special circumstances often precluded colonial marriage. To Marsden they had been concubines. To Macquarie they, too, must evidence outward respectability by entering 'the married state'. More Irish women were married when convicted than were the women from England, and this was a major deterrent to colonial marriage. Some Catholic women did marry in the colony according to the rites of the Church of England and some, married or not, had their colonial children baptised by the colonial chaplains. For many, however, there was no alternative to an 'unblessed union', and they simply declared themselves man and wife in the sight of God and waited for the arrival of a priest of their faith to legalise their union.[11] To colonial officials these women were simply concubines and their children illegitimate. Women such as Ann Byrne show the inaccuracy of this description, the distortions implied by the connotations of 'convict concubine'.

Ann Byrne was convicted in Dublin in 1800 and transported on the *Rolla* in 1803. Also on the *Rolla* was Owen McMahon, convicted at Westmeath at the age of twenty-four. Ann became his de facto wife, and in 1804 their first child, Bartholomew, was baptised at Parramatta by Chaplain Marsden. By 1806 this 'concubine' and Owen McMahon had another illegitimate child, and a third, Owen, was born in 1809. In 1810 Owen McMahon left the colony on a sealing voyage, never to return. Three years later Ann had another illegitimate child, fathered by Richard Gilbert, whom she married at St Philip's Church, Sydney, in February 1815. The family life of Ann Gilbert and her husband evidences the lack of any prejudice against Ann's former de facto relationship, or any rejection of her illegitimate children. Gilbert, who had been a private in the New South Wales Corps, (*Salamander* 1791) received his first land grant at the Field of Mars. By 1814 he was a landholder at Lane Cove, where he lived with Ann and their family until her death in January 1842 at the age of sixty-one. He adopted McMahon's children, writing to Governor Brisbane in 1824 asking for a land grant for his stepson John McMahon, and selling his own land to his other stepson, Owen McMahon. His stepdaughter, Mary McMahon, married a convict, Jaspar Morley, in 1825 and Gilbert assisted them to obtain a land grant of 60 acres near the family property. The colonial life of Ann Byrne, as concubine for seven years to McMahon and as wife to Gilbert for twenty-seven years, did not in any way conform to the expected promiscuous and depraved behaviour of a convict woman. Rather did it typify the pattern of family women of Botany Bay, both as de facto and as legal wife.

Among the women designated as concubines by Marsden were those who later married their de facto husbands. Mary Consadine, born in Ennis, County Clare, was transported on the *Rolla* in 1803. By 1806 she had two illegitimate children to convict John Masterton, transported in 1800, from Staffen in County Kildare, for political offences. The two were married in 1807 at St John's, Parramatta, and had five more living children. After her husband's death in the early 1830s Mary Masterton lived with their daughter at Woolloomooloo, then married an ex-convict, James Lownes, in 1833. At her death in 1849 she was described as Mary Consadine. The colonial life of this family woman was not in accordance with the connotations of 'concubine'.[12]

Marriage was to remain the symbol of colonial respectability among the women of Botany Bay and the incidence of legal marriage in the colony the yardstick by which the reformation of the convicted women was measured. How accurate were these assumptions which emphasised the immorality of the colonial women? Were they simply based on the British reputation of criminal, lower-class women, which was the antithesis of all the attributes expected from women in contemporary society – chastity, sobriety, pity, compassion and gentleness? Were expectations of immorality heightened because these women *were* criminal women living within a criminal society? Why did it remain almost unrecognised that, in most cases, their colonial lives did not conform to that expected pattern of depravity and vice, and bore little, if any, resemblance to the lives they had lived in their native country before conviction, and none at all to the months or years they had spent as prisoners in Britain? Did these outcast women, as so many of their contemporaries believed, choose to live in illicit relationships, cohabit without shame, move from man to man as need, necessity or inclination prompted? Or was it that their bodies, as women's bodies, were the only economic commodity that they could offer New South Wales? Was it only by the exploitation of their sexuality that they could survive in a convict colony?

How did convict women such as Lydia Monroe and Sarah Wise fit this pattern? Lydia Monroe had been born to Sarah and Alexander Monroe at the British Lying-In Hospital in London in October 1767. At the age of nineteen she was sentenced to transportation with Ann Forbes at the Surrey Lent Assizes at Kingston-on-Thames:

Ann Forbes late of the Parish of Saint Olave within the borough of Southwark in the county of Surrey, and Lydia Monroe late of the same, spinster, on the 28th day of October . . . [did steal] ten yards of printed cotton of the value of 20 shillings of the goods and chattels of James Rollinson in the shop of the said James Rollinson . . .

Both were sentenced to be hanged, but reprieved at the end of the Sessions. Lydia Monroe sailed for New South Wales on the *Prince of Wales* three weeks after she had been sentenced to death. In New South Wales she became the de facto wife of Andrew Goodwin, who had been sentenced at the age of twenty-eight for stealing 'two hundred poundsweight of lead value

20 shillings, the property of Thomas Wells'. Three years after his trial Goodwin was transported on the *Scarborough*. Lydia Monroe was not backward in protecting her virtue at Botany Bay. In September 1788, as she bathed with another convict, Elizabeth Cole, she was attacked by William Boggis who 'attempted to have connection with her'. Her screams brought assistance; Boggis was apprehended, and received 100 lashes.

The first child of Leticia [*sic*] Munroe and Andrew Goodwin, Mary Goodwin, was baptised on 19 July 1789. They were married eight months later, shortly before they left for Norfolk Island, both signing with their mark. They lived at Norfolk Island for nineteen years, rearing another seven children and increasing the size of their farms by grant and purchase. Their successes at the penal settlement bore no resemblance to the expectations of the lifestyles of 'the scum of British gaols'.[13]

Sarah Wise had been born at Amphney in Gloucestershire in 1769, where she was tried and convicted in July 1795. She was transported on the *Indispensable* and sent to Norfolk Island, where she met John Roberts, a private in the New South Wales Corps who had arrived on the *Britannia* in 1791. There is no record of a marriage, but Sarah Wise accompanied Private Roberts to his posts at Sydney and at Parramatta and again to Norfolk Island, and finally to Sydney, where Sarah remained until her death on 22 May 1850 at the age of eighty. She was buried in the same grave at Devonshire Street as her daughter-in-law, Sophia Charlotte Roberts, and Sophia's mother. The inscription read:

> Mrs Sarah Roberts
> who departed this life May 22 1850
> Aged 80 years

In death 'Concubine' Sarah Wise had gained the respectability of a married family woman.[14]

The distortions which surround accounts and interpretations of the role of women in early colonial society become increasingly apparent from a study of the individual and collective lives of the women at Botany Bay. To appreciate the nature of the colonial society in which they lived, two major characteristics must be clearly understood. One is the unique ratio of women to men, the other the diversity and complexity of female society.

The population of the convict colony of New South Wales was predominantly, overwhelmingly, male from the first day of settlement. Women were to remain a far smaller minority among the colonial inhabitants than they were in contemporary

258 *The Women of Botany Bay*

Britain, or had been in the North American colonies. Figure 10.1 indicates the ratio of men to women in New South Wales during the first forty years of white settlement, as accurately as remaining population statistics allow.[15]

Figure 10.1   Ratio of men to women, New South Wales, 1788–1828

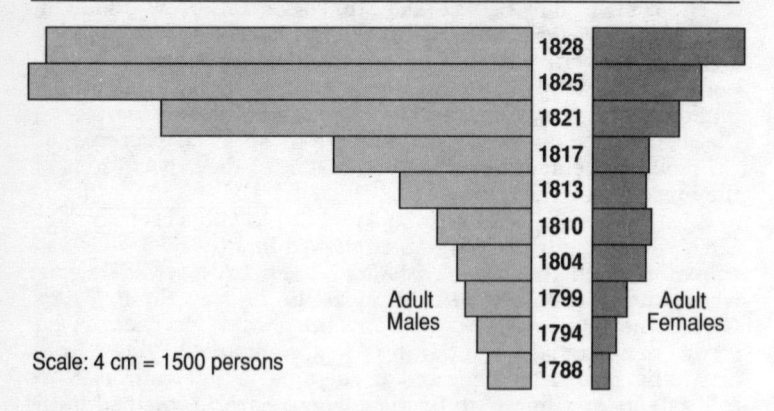

Adult Males │ 1828 │ Adult Females
1825
1821
1817
1813
1810
1804
1799
1794
1788

Scale: 4 cm = 1500 persons

Source: Returns of the Settlement, Victualling Lists, Musters of Population (Mainland), New South Wales Census for 1828.

Closely linked with the ratio of women to men was the distribution of women among the various social and economic levels of society which showed the diversity of their civil conditions. Most of the men had arrived as convicts, but, from January 1788, there were very clear distinctions of rank, class and position among the male inhabitants. Almost all the women who arrived in 1788 shared the same class origins, whether they were prisoners or the wives of the Marines. The sole representative of 'genteel women' was the Chaplain's bride, Mary Johnson, who was joined in 1790 by Elizabeth Macarthur. The female population continued to be predominantly composed of women who had arrived as convicts, and it was not until 1828 that the adult free women, that is, those who had arrived unconvicted or who had been born in the colony, almost equalled in number the women who had arrived as convicts. As married women were to be found among all civil conditions, belief in the 'respectability of the married state' applied to all colonial women, free, freed, native-born or unconvicted. Figure 10.2 indicates the civil condition of the women of Botany Bay and shows clearly the inaccuracy of describing the colonial women as 'convict' women.[16]

Figure 10.2 Civil condition of women in New South Wales, 1788–1828

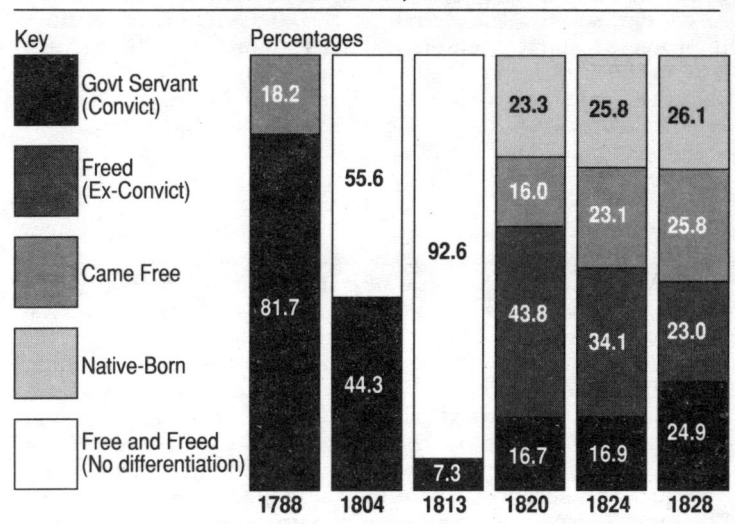

Key	1788	1804	1813	1820	1824	1828
Govt Servant (Convict)	18.2			23.3	25.8	26.1
Freed (Ex-Convict)		55.6		16.0	23.1	25.8
Came Free			92.6	43.8	34.1	23.0
Native-Born	81.7	44.3				24.9
Free and Freed (No differentiation)			7.3	16.7	16.9	

Source: Portia Robinson, 'The first forty years: women and the law', in *In Pursuit of Justice*, J. Mackinolty & H. Radi (eds), Sydney, 1979.

Note: Figures are approximate; owing to the incomplete nature of contemporary records and the possibility of inaccuracies, it is only possible to suggest numbers of women in the various civil condition categories.

It was not only contemporaries who assumed that colonial women could be accurately described as 'convict' women and who believed that immorality was 'encouraged' by the small proportion of women to men. The Australian feminist writers of the mid-twentieth century had little difficulty in accepting uncritically the 'evidence' of contemporaries, which supported both the promiscuity of the 'convict' women and their sexual exploitation as 'objects of gratification' for the men. Evidence such as Chaplain Marsden's Female Register, his observations on the Female Convicts in 1815, and again his evidence to Commissioner Bigge, all gained credence to support the argument that colonial conditions, both social and economic 'fostered whores, not wives' at Botany Bay.[17] The feminist interpretations, heavily veiled in twentieth-century feminist philosophies and theories, attempted to give a base to the presumed degraded position of women in Australian society. These first women, the 'victims of victims', unprotected and vulnerable, forced to submit to the pent-up frustration and aggression of the male convicts, had no choice but to become the prostitutes of New South Wales. What other economic opportunities were available, argued the feminists, in a male-dominated society in need of women as sexual partners?

This argument seeks to excuse the assumed immorality of Australia's first white women settlers. It loses its validity by its very basis: that colonial society was 'convict', with all the connotations this implied, and that its women were 'convict'. It takes no account of either the social or economic developments in the colony, nor of changes in the transportation and assignment system, nor in the 'official' reception and management of newly arrived convicts, nor of the changes in nature, origins and numbers of women arriving in New South Wales during the transportation period. Above all, this argument shows no recognition of, or investigation into, the emergence of a new structure of class among the women, nor the growth of a diverse and complex social and economic hierarchy among the 'convict' women. The importance of civil condition remains unremarked. The emphasis is on women as sexual objects, not as working women or as family women. Such an argument needed heavy and uncritical reliance on the opinions of contemporaries such as Chaplain Marsden rather than a critical and analytical investigation into the realities of colonial life for all the women who had arrived as convicts.

It was Marsden's personal antipathy to Lachlan Macquarie which indirectly added to the 'evidence' of the sexual exploitation of convict women. Marsden sought to discredit the Governor by showing that he had not provided adequate shelter or protection for the women sent to the Factory at Parramatta, either directly on arrival or returned to await reassignment. With no 'official' accommodation provided, these women, who should have been securely housed in the Factory, were allowed to find their own accommodation in the town of Parramatta, and given 'time off' from government labour to seek private employment to pay for their lodgings. This was the same system which had been customary for the male convicts in both Sydney and Parramatta before the building of the convict barracks. Men under sentence continued to be allowed to 'sleep out' while working for government, and those with free wives in the colony often lived as 'employed men' rather than as convicts under sentence of the law.

For the women of Parramatta it was a different story. Such laxity was not accepted as a privileged 'indulgence', but as an inducement to prostitution and 'loose living'. Marsden described these women as 'Unhappy Objects' forced to prostitute themselves in order to obtain the basic necessities of life, for there were no opportunities to obtain honest work as domestics or as servants. Marsden's opinions as to the immorality at Parramatta were supported by men such as John Macarthur, who told Bigge:

I seldom go into the Town, and I avoid all unnecessary intercourse with the inhabitants; The lower classes are reported to be disorderly; – and they always were so – but I cannot think that they are worse than might be expected under the system of indulgence to Convicts upon which this Colony has been established . . . [18]

'Evidence' from contemporaries, whether official, semi-official, or private letters, reports or comments, has been almost exclusively selective, biased, prejudiced by 'class' attitudes, influenced by the convict origins of New South Wales and almost entirely concerned with the assumed depravity, degradation and infamy of convicts in a convict colony. Evidence such as the opinions – even the 'statistics' of officials such as Marsden – has gained credence and even authority by its repetitive and uncritical use by a long line of ill-assorted literary and historical bedfellows. The very real contribution of women, as single women, as working women and as family women, has been completely overshadowed by the concentration on their sexual roles in the colony. That convict and ex-convict women were among the rich and the poor, the employers, the employed and the unemployed; that 'respectability' to them and to their peers was not dependent on 'the married state' but on their material standing, was not recognised. Women such as Elizabeth Beckwith, transported from her native Devon on the *Wanstead* showed the 'respectability' they had gained in the colony by being able to write to relatives in England and offer to share their new-found economic independence. Elizabeth Beckwith wrote to her brother, a labourer at His Majesty's Docks at Plymouth, that she was now free by servitude and had 'a spot of ground' sufficient to support him, his wife and daughter if they could get free passage from the government.[19]

Beatrice McLeod, transported in 1818, wrote to the Colonial Secretary in 1828 reminding him that she had applied for land in 1822 when her sentence had expired and 'had received reply that if she acquired stock she could have land'. She now had forty head of cattle, so requested that the land promised be given her so she could establish herself as a settler. Respectability came to this 'convict' woman through the acquisition of land and stock.[20]

The distinction between convict and ex-convict, overlooked by most contemporaries and ignored by many historians, was not simply a semantic one. The economic and social opportunities, advantages and disadvantages, restriction and freedom of movement, of individual choice of occupation or district of residence, even permission to marry, were all dependent on civil condition, differing for women who were prisoners of the Crown and women who were free by pardon or by servitude. Convict status could and did prevent reunion of families, separate husbands and wives and, in some cases, actually deter marriage. Thomas Moore, 'a correct and obedient soldier', wrote to Governor Darling that his wife, a convict servant to Colonel Morrisset, 'was willing at first to go with the Colonel from Sydney to Norfolk Island, but now wants to be with her husband'. When this request was refused 'the correct soldier' petitioned that he be sent to Norfolk Island to be with his wife. If not, could she not be sent back to him in Sydney? Both requests were refused.[21]

It was because she was a convict woman that Margaret McDonald was unsuccessful in her petition to have her husband reassigned to her. She and her husband, Alexander McDonald, had been tried and convicted together 'at the same time and place' in Edinburgh, and both sentenced to transportation for fourteen years. The man arrived on the *Asia* in 1820, the wife two years later on the *Providence*. The husband was first assigned to Captain Irvine of Minto, then transferred after two weeks to William Howe of the same district. His wife went first to the Female Factory, as was customary, and was then assigned to Mr Howe so that she could rejoin her husband. Mr Howe did not want the wife and family, so they were sent to a Mr Edwin Forbes for six months as assigned servants. Mr Forbes, a more kindly man than Howe, arranged for the husband to be sent to another Scot, John McIntyre, who allowed convict husband and convict wife to set up house on their own land. When this 'indulgence' was discovered by Captain Rossi, Alexander was ordered back to the Prisoners' Barracks at Sydney for reassignment. The wife then petitioned the governor to send her husband back and reunite the family 'so cruelly separated'. Desirable as marriage was, the colonial authorities rejected the appeal and convict husband and convict wife were reassigned to masters in different parts of the colony: 'Acceptance of this Petition could establish a precedent which may hereafter prove embarrassing to Government inasmuch as both parties are convicts and the Petitioner is now actually a convict at large.'[22]

The liberties allowed convict women decreased with the development of the penal colony into a free society. Phillip, Hunter, King, Bligh and Macquarie accepted to varying degrees that convict women need not be strictly confined or directed to Public Labour, so long as they were subject to control by the administration and subject to punishment and/or loss of privileges for any infraction of regulations. Financially, it was beneficial to the colonial expenditure if the convict women were supported by the masters or mistresses to whom they were assigned, or by the men with whom they cohabited or married, or by their own endeavours as working women. After the report and recommendations of Commissioner Bigge, however, there was far stricter supervision, direction, and even confinement, of the women who arrived in the 1820s. From that time, the distinction between the life of a convict and that of an ex-convict became more marked, but both groups continued to be referred to by their respectable contemporaries as convicts and their perceived roles within colonial society were affected by the connotations of immorality and promiscuity surrounding that word.

For the women themselves, their contribution to the nature and characteristics of the emerging 'Australian' society was vitally linked with their femininity, that is, as women within colonial society. This did not imply that they were the 'damned whores of Botany Bay', nor did the vast disproportion between the sexes mean that the typical or average woman of Botany Bay was a bedraggled harlot. Would it not be more accurate to argue that the lack of wives for 75 per cent or more of the colonial men affected the nature of male society to a far greater degree than the small proportion of women influenced the nature of female society? Where did immorality lie in a colony in which most males had no opportunity of finding a colonial wife as a legal or de facto partner, where most men were unable to assume the normal and expected role of men in society, that is, the role of husband and father, protector of and provider for the family? The moral standards of colonial men, however, did not assume the significance of the lack of moral standards believed to exist among the women in a male-dominated settlement.

It was not the abandoned convict woman, forced to sell her favours for her economic survival, who was the normal unit of colonial society. It was the single unattached male, the man without a female partner. Without doubt there were women and girls who exploited their sexuality, traded on their femininity as the way to establish themselves in the colony. Was this more exceptional, more reprehensible than the similar lifestyle 'forced' upon many of the women of Britain's lower orders? Did the immorality of the prostitutes of New South Wales exceed that of the girls from Newgate who had made their living in the courtyards, alleyways and back rooms of London by 'servicing' their clients for threepence – and adding to their income by lifting the watch or pocketbook at the same time? The extent of prostitution in Britain was deplored by contemporary British society, but did not damn that society as depraved and vicious. That women from the same class, the same social origins – with the added stigma of conviction for major felonies – plied their trade at Botany Bay was accepted as typical and expected depraved behaviour by 'convict' women.

The concern caused by the alarming increase of prostitution in London itself was reported in the *Freeman's Journal* of November 1817:

A numerous and respectable meeting took place in the Egyptian Hall, Mansion House, London, for the purpose of checking the increase of prostitution in the city. There has been a great increase in the number of brothels, in three parishes in the eastern suburbs, for example, there are 360 houses of ill-fame and some 3,000 wretched women ...

Such a situation, even the existence of thousands of women who lived by prostitution, did not imply basic depravity within London society as did prostitution in the convict colony of Botany Bay.

In the following December a letter to the editor of the *Freeman's Journal* proposed a remedy for this increasing social evil:

Let every man reform one person, that is, himself ... As a moral agent, the unhappy delinquent whom you would inhumanely hire to criminal indulgence, ought to have kept her chastity inviolate, but the infringement of that chastity does not render a repetition of the crime less atrocious ... [23]

'The sword of God and Gideon' 265

The 'reformers' of Botany Bay society were not so charitable to the 'unhappy delinquents'. Was it that their criminality enhanced their immorality and both crime and promiscuity made them less deserving 'objects of pity' than those 'wretched women' of London who lived by selling their bodies?

Marsden agreed on one point with the colonial governors: the solution to the immorality of the convict women was matrimony:

It is of great consequence to their happiness and usefulness that they should be married; because if they are not they will have no regular Residence, but must spend a vagrant, wandering and vicious life to the end of their days.[24]

This emphasis on marriage as the road to respectability took no account of the women who preferred to gain economic independence without a male partner. To some of the transported women, legal or de facto marriages held no appeal. Margaret Catchpole summed up the attitude of these women when she wrote to her uncle in England: 'There is a fine young man a-courting me, but I am not for marrying'.[25] Sarah Bird was another enterprising working woman who preferred to work alone, although she was atypical in that she chose a male 'friend' to live with her from time to time, not as part of her economic enterprises. This almost led to her death, as one of her former lovers returned at night and 'slit her throat from ear to ear'. He was hanged, and she recovered to continue her activities as a colonial businesswoman.[26]

Neither did all colonial widows feel the need to remarry to maintain either their respectability or their economic independence. Mary Reibey, the best-known example of a woman who took on her deceased husband's business interests and succeeded in her own right, was not unique. At all levels of society, widows, legal or de facto, became the 'master' of farms, managed businesses from blacksmiths to butchers, became publicans, innkeepers, dealers, traders, shopkeepers, 'masters' of the Pound or the local markets, and did not hesitate to ask the governor for assistance in the form of additional assigned servants, extra land grants or renewal of licences or leases in their own name.

Mary Johnson (*Canada*) wrote to the governor that her husband had erected many buildings in Sydney. After his death she was left with four children to support. Her husband had received a grant of forty acres at the Punch Bowl and as she had continued farming their property, supporting her four convict servants, she felt that she was entitled to an extension of this grant. Mary Larkham petitioned for 'land anywhere but not to [*sic*] remote for her twenty head of cattle and the sixty cattle, which belonged to her son, John. She told the governor that she was now a widow and had lived respectably in the colony for twenty-eight years, 'twenty-five of which she had been free by servitude'. Elizabeth Marr, widow of John Driver, petitioned in 1810 for the renewal of her late husband's three land grants and the 'eighty-two rods granted him by Colonel Foveaux in Chapel Row [now Castlereagh Street]. She and her husband had lived in a house at the latter and spent money to improve it'. Lucy Neale, the widow of James Neale, wrote in 1821 that her husband had been given land at Kurrajong at Richmond. Since his death she had cultivated it and made improvements: 'felled nine acres of timber, three acres of which are ready for the planting of maize. She has erected a dwelling house where she and her children reside'. Her petition was granted.[27]

All widows, of course, were not so independent. Ann Bevin petitioned the governor for assistance in 1822:

She had arrived free to join her husband who was a prisoner. He died in 1820 when he fell off the roof of the Judge Advocate's house where he was working. She was now fifty-five years old and in her present advanced and feeble age wanted to be placed on Government stores until her death.

Mary Barnett petitioned in 1822 that she was free by servitude and had been left a widow with two young children, the oldest about four years and the other 'a mere infant'. She wanted a convict assigned to her:

John Rowlings, a prisoner now a labourer at the Brickfields and a distant relative to the petitioner has protected the petitioner's house since her husband's decease, but is unable to do so from the long hours of Government labour.[28]

The widows who requested assistance, either from necessity or to maintain their economic independence did not conform to the expected degraded behavioural patterns of women alone in a convict colony.

Neither the social nor the economic condition of New South Wales was static during the transportation period. Changing conditions, expansion of population, diversity of opportunity, all affected the lives of the colony's women. It did not, however, affect official attitudes towards them to any significant degree. From the first day of settlement Phillip set the pattern for encouraging marriage and discouraging 'illicit relationships' among the women, assuring the convict men 'that if they attempted to get into the women's tents at night there were positive orders for firing upon them'. It was not only from the convict men that the women needed 'protection', for a few days after this warning a carpenter, a sailor and 'a Boy belonging to the *Prince of Wales*' were found in the women's tents. Surgeon Bowes described their punishment:

They were drummed out of the camp with the Rogue's March playing before them, and the boy had petticoats put upon him. They all had their hands tyed behind 'em. The anarchy and confusion which prevails throughout the camp and the audacity of the Convicts, both men and women is arrived at such a pitch as not to be equalled, I believe, by any set of villains in any other part of the Globe.

Second Lieutenant Ralph Clark hoped that this incident would be 'a warning to them from coming into the whore's camp: I would call it by the name of Sodom, for there is more sin committed in it than in any other part of the world.'

That neurotic lieutenant was himself to become a part of that 'sin', fathering a daughter to one of those whores, and giving the name of his wife 'his dearest Betsey' to his bastard daughter.[29]

The conditions in that first camp, the uncertainty of knowing whether the colony would be successfully established, and what was to become of the settlers, added to the temporary nature of the settlement rather than acting as an incentive to establish lasting relationships. Incentive in the form of land grants, with additional land for wife and children was the most effective way by which the governors could encourage marriage. In later years the incentive of tickets-of-leave for women who married before their sentences were expired and the assigning of married convicts to their free or freed wives or husbands were all practical measures aimed primarily at the encouragement of morality and the reformation of manners thought so desirable and necessary among the convict women.

This belief that marriage among the convicts promoted respectability and decreased licentiousness and promiscuity remained central to all official and semi-official attitudes towards the convict women. In 1821 Reverend Cowper told Commissioner Bigge that he believed 'that the present Disproportion of women in New South Wales' was a principal cause of crime and 'that many evils arise from the great deficiency of their number': 'I think that from the want of the Happiness, or Domestic attachment, that arises from the marriage state, the Convicts are induced to pursue various modes of Dissipation, that leads to evil.'

In 1819 Reverend Cartwright had expressed similar opinions, informing the Commissioner that 'marriage improved the Morals of the convicts'. This was shown, he believed, by the extent to which the married convicts 'despite the irregularity in their own lives, were anxious to educate their children'.[30]

John Macarthur held a contrary opinion, believing the convict women too debased to have any good influence on the men they married. In reply to Bigge's question: 'Are any of your servants married?' Macarthur answered: 'Only Six – and I dread their becoming so, the Convict women are generally so depraved, and are the cause of so much disorder.'[31]

Despite Macarthur's poor opinion of the convict women, the colonial authorities continued to be increasingly convinced that matrimony was the only road to respectability. As the actual numbers of convict and ex-convict women increased and their proportion among colonial women decreased, it became more and more essential that they conform to the accepted standards of behaviour in a 'free' society. Despite the number of marriages, despite the evidence of long-lasting de facto relationships, their immorality remained their paramount characteristic in the eyes of officialdom.

For the first century and a half of European settlement the promiscuity of the wanton women of Botany Bay was condemned, deplored, damned and highlighted as indicative of the convict inhabitants of England's convict colony. From the mid-twentieth century, the assumed behaviour of these women was excused and exploited. The outrage of the feminist historians was clearly linked with an attempt to establish a historical basis for the presumed 'low self-image' of modern Australian women. More disastrous in its worldwide impact, however, was the recent rehashing of this same impressionistic evidence in 1987, stressing the sexual exploitation of women on that 'Fatal Shore' of misrepresentation of Australia's origins as an individual society.

The women of Botany Bay did not hold themselves 'in low esteem', nor were they the exploited cast-off mistresses and whores, the passive 'victims' of a male-dominated society. Within the new definitions of respectability which they themselves created in the colony, their morality was expressed not necessarily by legal marriage but by economic independence, gained in the colony either through their own efforts or as wives. It was these same convict and ex-convict women who were primarily responsible for the new structure of female society which emerged at Botany Bay, based on colonial conditions, standards and achievements, resulting in a class system which differed entirely from that in Britain. Women who married or formed de facto relationships were a far greater part of this new society, far more influential in shaping its nature and characteristics than those girls and women who became the street women of The Rocks, continuing the lifestyles so many had known before transportation. It was the family women who were most influential in determining the characteristics of the 'respectable' women of Botany Bay.

11
'SHE SANG HER TOIL AND TROUBLE'

Family women of Botany Bay

Thankful for having herself and children placed on Stores ... but not having a Protector she finds it very difficult to make ends meet as House rent and firing are so dear ... Her husband was removed to Port Macquarie for Government Service ... she requests he be returned ...

—Memorial of Susannah Jones, convict's wife per *Broxbornebury*, 1815, married 22 years, 3 children. Petition granted, husband 'to sleep out of Barracks'

Marriage in New South Wales differed markedly from marriage in Britain, especially in the extent of control and involvement by government and in the altered significance of 'the married state' for both men and women. Given the peculiar nature of the penal administration, it was to be expected that marriage in the colony would be an official concern of the government. Applications for permission to marry had to be submitted to the governor, as did all requests that a convict partner to the marriage be either granted a ticket-of-leave or assigned to the free wife or husband. Such an indulgence was not automatic, either in the case of colonial 'convict' marriages or where the free wife or husband came from Britain to rejoin the convicted partner. Where such a request was refused, either on the grounds of the government's need for the man's skills or because of known bad character of one of the parties, the convict would either continue as a government servant for the full term of servitude or be granted the lesser indulgence of 'sleeping out of Barracks'. Whatever the decision, it was the ultimate responsibility of the colonial governor to determine whether a family should live together or not while one partner was under sentence of the law.

It was also the governor's responsibility to determine whether two convicts could marry before the expiration of their sentences, whether they should be permitted to live as man and wife after such a marriage, and whether or not a man and wife transported together should be reunited by assignment to the same master or mistress. It was as a result of these many official decisions that the governor became more and more deeply involved in the day-to-day lives of the colonial families. It became increasingly customary for either partner to appeal to the governor for advice or assistance not only in times of hardship, misadventure or accident but to arbitrate where there were 'family' disagreements, arguments or problems resulting from the unacceptable behaviour of one of the parties. The memorials and petitions from colonial women to the governor were concerned with all aspects of their colonial marriages, and provide an insight into the darker side of the lives of these family women of Botany Bay. While not typical of the experiences of the majority of the family women in the colony, this evidence in which the women themselves 'sing their toil and trouble' adds to the re-creation of the whole life of the colony during the first forty years of white settlement.

The significance of marriage in New South Wales differed in many aspects from marriage in Britain, partly as a result of the class origins of most of the settlers and partly as a result of the unique nature of the colony. Attitudes to and expectations from marriage in Britain were closely linked with class. Among the 'respectable' ladies of the upper and middle classes of Britain, and even among the daughters of well-to-do tradesmen and farmers, there were few socially acceptable alternatives to 'a good marriage'. The unmarried daughters of the gentry could either become dependents in the households of married relatives, or seek employment as companions or governesses. Without independent means, many of these unmarried gentlewomen lived hidden lives of exploited drudgery and poverty in order to maintain their social respectability.

For the women of the lower orders, marriage was frequently neither necessary nor desirable unless there was a religious motive, as with many of the women of Ireland. Those women who had been married at the time of their trials were familiar with the many problems, deprivations, even abject poverty, which was the lot of most of the working-class wives and the wives of the unemployed or the unemployable in their own country. For the Irishwomen there were the added difficulties of raising the numerous children with which their marriages were so frequently blessed. For both English and Irish, childbearing was rarely more than a brief interruption to a life of drudgery and toil, a continuous struggle to maintain, but not improve, life. Married women laboured not only as domestics but increasingly in the mines, the mills and the factories, receiving a small proportion of a man's wage for hours of unremitting toil. In England Betty Harris gave evidence to a Select Committee on Mines, describing how she worked as a 'drawer', that is, she drew a cart which was strapped to her legs, crawling through the narrow, dark and wet tunnels of the mine pulling coal to the shaft where it would be lifted above ground. She worked six and a half days a week and found it most difficult when she was pregnant, which, she said, was hardest for all the women drawers – babies were often born in the lay-bys and then placed on the cart so that little time was lost from work. Marriage did not bring economic security, 'respectability' or even the prospect of a more comfortable life to the Betty Harrises of England.[1]

As most of the women of New South Wales had arrived convict, sharing the same class origins of the lower orders of Britain, they were familiar with the advantages and drawbacks of legal marriage in their native land. So, too, were most of the free wives who followed their convicted husbands to Botany Bay. In New South Wales these women found an entirely different situation, where marriage was equated with respectability and was actively encouraged by the administration with the prospect of indulgences, material benefits, and even release from government service. It is probable that at least some of the colonial marriages resulted from economic motivation. David Collins recorded that there were an unexpected number of marriages celebrated in the first months of settlement and commented on the possible reason for this 'outbreak of morality':

It was soon observed with satisfaction that several couples were announced for marriage; but on strict scrutinizing of the motive it was found in several instances to originate in an idea, that married people would meet with various little comforts and privileges that were denied those in the single state.

Despite these misgivings, no marriage applications were rejected, 'except where it was clearly understood that either of the parties had a husband or wife living at the time of their leaving England'.[2]

The colonial authorities were well aware that a colonial marriage could impinge on a pre-existing British marriage, but made no allowances for this in the general condemnation of de facto or common-law alliances, many of which did end in lawful wedlock. Common-law wives, however, could and did petition the governor for indulgences or for assistance. Sarah May petitioned for permission to accompany William Judd when he was ordered to Port Macquarie, as 'she has been cohabiting with him'. Mary Ann Holford appealed against the order to remove convict Joshua Armstrong from Sydney to Bathurst, as 'he is her only means of support'.[3] Elizabeth Mason, sentenced to death at the age of twenty-two in Gloucester, was reprieved and transported on the *Friendship* for fourteen years. In the colony she became the de facto wife of James Squires, by whom she had one son and seven daughters. Squires had left a wife, two sons and a daughter in England, and Betty Mason and James Squires did not marry in the colony, nor did Squires try to have his English family rejoin him, despite economic success as a brewery and tavern owner at Kissing Point.[4] An unnamed ex-convict woman who cohabited with Chief Constable Jennings was less fortunate. Reverend Marsden gave evidence to Commissioner Bigge that Jennings had two children by the woman, with whom he cohabited at Parramatta before his lawful wife, from whom he had been separated for seven years, arrived in New South Wales. After she came to him at Parramatta, Jennings 'furnished the other woman with the means to live and return to England and her friends . . . [unhappily] she was hung for some crime . . . Jennings died from a broken heart some time after the woman quitted him.'[5] The case of Jennings and his two 'wives' was not typical, but was used by Marsden to highlight the problems of colonial marriage and morality where a previous lawful union existed in Britain.

Was it the existence of husbands in Britain which prevented so many colonial marriages? Motivation cannot be determined, but there were numerous instances where marriage followed years of cohabitation. Was this the result of knowledge – or belief – in the death of the British partner, or was the colonial marriage simply the result of necessity for respectability, possibly for the husband to maintain his position in the colony, or to be eligible to petition for additional land grants?

The experiences of Ann Taylor were typical of many of the women who married after years of living in a de facto relationship. Ann Taylor, also known as Nancy, had been born in Birmingham in 1775, the daughter of Thomas Taylor and his wife Sarah Haywood. In 1796 she married John Price, and two years later was sentenced to death for shoplifting. Reprieved, she was imprisoned in Staffordshire until she sailed on the *Earl Cornwallis* in 1800, transported for life to Botany Bay. She was accompanied by her baby daughter, Elizabeth Price, but what became of her young husband is unknown. In New South Wales she lived with a soldier, Joseph Baylis, by whom she had three children before their marriage on 25 June 1810 at St Philip's, Sydney. In all, the Baylises had nine living children, settling firstly at Castlereagh and then at Windsor. Ann Baylis died after accidentally drinking poison in December 1827. 'Oh Joe,' she said, 'I'm so sick I am sure I shall die.' Her bereaved husband erected an expensive and ornate tombstone over her grave at St Matthew's Church of England, Windsor, and, at his death in March 1855 – he did not remarry – he was brought back to Windsor as he requested, to lie beside his 'dear wife'.[6] 'Concubine' she may have been to the authorities during her first decade in New South Wales, but the pattern of her colonial life was not that of a degraded and abandoned whore but of a respectable married woman of good reputation.

There was another aspect of colonial marriage which received little comment – or encouragement – from either British or colonial authorities. This was the problem of married convicts being convicted and transported together to Botany Bay. Where there were children of these marriages, it became an urgent problem for the convicted parents. Sophia and William Phillips were among the minority of fortunate 'convict' families permitted to bring their children with them to exile in New South Wales. The couple, married in Birmingham, were tried in Warwick in 1819 'for being in possession of forged and counterfeited banknotes knowing them to be counterfeit'. Both were found guilty, and sentenced to fourteen years' transportation. Their eldest son, who had been apprehended with them, was awaiting trial for 'feloniously disposing of a forged banknote', and his parents petitioned Lord Sidmouth from Portsmouth in October 1819, requesting

that their children may accompany them to Botany Bay. Sarah, 16, Emma 10, Jemima 8, John 5, Caroline 3, Ann an infant. If they remain behind they will be brought up in the care of persons connected with your Petitioners and in habits dangerous to their morals and to Society in general ... [the Father also urges that his eldest son be transported with them].

The mother, Sophia, was transported on the *Janus* in 1819 with her children, the father following on the *Coromandel* in 1820. In 1828 they were living in Sydney, both government servants, the wife working as a laundress, the husband as labourer. Five of their English children were with them and two more colonial-born, while the eldest boy was a convict in an Iron Gang. Sophia lived in Sydney until her death in 1873 at Surry Hills.[7]

Why families convicted together were not encouraged to remain together in the colony is difficult to understand within the context of the continual official emphasis on marriage among

'She sang her toil and trouble' 277

convicts being the solution to the prevalence of 'immoral habits'. That Sophia Phillips was 'disposed of to her husband' in 1822, that their family remained independent of government support, that neither parents nor children became a part of the criminal society of Botany Bay, was all evidence of the beneficial influence of the 'married state', but did not unduly influence decisions as to whether married convicts would be permitted to live together as man and wife in the colony.

An unsuccessful application was made to the governor in 1817 by Mary Moen (*Friendship*), the convict wife of a ticket-of-leave man. The wife was in the Factory and, as a convict herself, not eligible to apply to have her husband assigned to her. She attempted to overcome this with the following argument:

She was tried at Berwick upon Tweed on 24 July 1816 with her husband ... and convicted of uttering. They were both sentenced to transportation for life. She requested an absolute pardon from the governor on the grounds that the sentence passed upon the husband is also applied to a married wife for the same offence is not in accordance with British laws when both husband and wife are participants except in cases of treason and murder.

Her application was unsuccessful. She had been described by the surgeon of the *Friendship* as 'a good mother [she was accompanied by her male child] but of a blasphemous and bad disposition'. Aged twenty-two on arrival, she served her sentence not as a convict wife but as a needlewoman at the Parramatta Factory.[8]

Sarah Meagher was more fortunate. Transported two years after her marriage, her husband joined her and received a ticket-of-leave. Sarah petitioned the governor for a specific land grant:

[She] has been married to William Meagher for five years. He came on the *Three Bees* and now has a ticket-of-leave. [He had previously been employed in the Lumber Yard at Parramatta]. He cuts grass in the neighbourhood of Kissing Point and brings it to Sydney. They live in a small house on unlocated [*sic*] land alongside the Lane River and chiefly rocks. They have cleared about three acres and request a grant of the nearby barren land.[9]

Although married convicts found little official encouragement to live as man and wife, the reverse was often the case where one of the parties was free or freed by servitude. Applications for husbands to be given tickets-of-leave or to be assigned to their 'free' wives were normally received with approval by the colonial administrators, provided the good character of both parties was assured and provided that the services of the man were not needed by government. This was one way in which morality could be promoted while the government received the added benefit of not being obliged to provide support for either the convict or his family. Wives who applied for their husbands as assigned servants or as ticket-of-leave men were from all civil conditions: women who had served their own sentences or who had been pardoned, wives who had followed convict husbands to New South Wales – with or without the assistance from government – and native-born and came-free women who had married convict men. In all cases, the character of both was considered but the encouragement of marriage by the prospect of obtaining a ticket-of-leave was believed a strong inducement to morality. This practice did not meet with the approval of all colonial officials. Commissioner Bigge asked the Reverend Cartwright: 'Do you approve of the System of encouraging Marriage by giving Tickets of Leave to Married Convicts as soon as they enter into that state without reference to their former crimes?' Cartwright replied: 'Certainly not, as it would be making an holy Institution subservient to the vilest purposes which is frequently done in this Colony.'[10]

Applications to have convict husbands assigned to their colonial wives became more and more numerous. Rejection of these petitions continued to be based either on the skill of the man being required by government or on the lack of 'proven good character' of either husband or wife. Ann Evans (*Friendship*), a free woman who had followed her husband to New South Wales after he had been transported on the *Neptune*, wrote to the colonial secretary saying that she had two children 'for whom she was unable to provide' and that her husband, a prisoner for life, 'had been employed as a carpenter at the Government Lumber Yard' since his arrival in New South Wales. She included testimonials to their good characters: Robert Cooper's recommendation for the husband, Charles Evans, testified that he had 'conducted himself very much to my satisfaction'; John Redman wrote that 'Ann Evans has been in my employ for twelve months and has conducted herself faithful and honest'. Three other recommendations came from gentlemen in the colony, including Reverend Cowper. The skills of Charles Evans, however, were too necessary to the Lumber Yard to allow his release to his wife: 'The husband of the Petitioner is a Cabinet Maker and in the present state of the Public Works he cannot be spared.' This recommendation by Captain Dumaresq was accepted by the colonial secretary, and the application refused. He was, however, granted 'the privilege of sleeping out of Barracks'.[11]

The wife of Thomas Egan (*Mangles*) was also refused permission to have her husband assigned to her, although she wrote, 'His sentence has nearly expired and his character is irreproachable ... [I am] shortly to be brought to bed.' Thomas Egan, as a stonecutter, was too valuable to be released from government service, but he, too, continued to be granted the privilege of 'sleeping out' of Barracks.[12]

Wives were not reluctant to contest decisions of the administration. Charlotte Dick managed to have forty-eight persons of proven respectability sign her Memorial on behalf of her husband.[13] Ann Kerr wrote repeatedly. She succeeded in having her husband, to whom she had been married for eighteen years, brought back to Sydney from Port Macquarie where he was a Prisoner of the Crown, but she was unable to gain a ticket-of-leave for him, although she wrote that he was 'well-recommended ... they have three growing children and [wish] to prepare them for some business'. Receiving no answer, she petitioned again, and was told her 'request cannot be complied with at present'. She then sent a long explanatory letter, for her husband's 'character has been good since his return [to Sydney] and her character has been supported and laid before His Excellency':

If my character is blemished as it is represented it is something singular that the law has not called me to order this ten years and upwards so as I have stated I defy the Colony, I have brought my children up clean and respectable and imbibed good habits. I only want the labour of my husband to relieve me out of the most extreme distress ...

A third petition in which she 'wished to vindicate her own and her husband's character' admitted that she had sold spirits without a licence during his absence: 'I have been ten years and upwards a resident of Sydney and five of that in the house I now occupie [*sic*] opposite the Commissariat Store'. She requested permission to vindicate herself. Was her 'poverty and distress' exaggerated? In her petition of March 1827 she explained she was

a resident housekeeper of Sydney ten years and more ... a Dealer in General to sell Tea, Sugar, Candles, Soap and Tobacco, old or new cloathes bought, sold and exchanged ... Twelve months ago she bought a pair of trowsers from a seaman ... they proved to be stolen ... she stood trial but was acquitted.

In all, she made six applications on behalf of her husband, and all were refused because she had stood trial for that theft. All her protestations were in vain. Instead of rejoining his wife in Sydney, the husband was sent to Newcastle 'to paint the Church'.[14] Ann Kerr had showed little of that passive attitude of a helpless 'victim' of colonial society. Rather was she strident and persistent in her attempts to gain what she considered 'her rights' to have her convict husband assigned to her as her government servant for the remainder of their lives.

The numerous applications by wives for the assignment of their convict husbands not only emphasise the extent of family life within the colony but provide a 'first-hand' picture of the problems, difficulties, hopes and ambitions of many of these married women facing a new lifestyle which differed in almost every aspect from that with which they had been familiar in Britain. Furthermore, the responses of the colonial administration to the individual petitions are illustrative of the attitudes and expectations of colonial officialdom towards 'convict' marriages and family life. Without doubt, the petitions of the wives need critical assessment for, as with all pleas for indulgences or assistance, their cases were framed in the most appealing manner. The decisions of the governor or the colonial secretary frequently provide a less embellished view of the circumstances of both convict husband and petitioning wife. One feature emerges very clearly: the direct effects on family life which resulted from the unique nature of the administration of the penal colony. That women – and men – could and did petition the government for assistance in times of distress was quite contrary to any practice in Britain. The wives and children of imprisoned or transported men had no alternative to any form of assistance in England except the parsimonious charity of their local parish, and there was no expectation that any government department would advise or assist in times of marital difficulties. In New South Wales the reverse was the case, for all settlers, convict and free, had the right to petition the governor, and the well-being of the colony and its inhabitants was his direct responsibility.

The free wives who obtained government permission to follow convict husbands, to New South Wales expected that they would rejoin those husbands, who would then provide support and protection. This was not always the case. Although permission to travel to New South Wales had been granted, the wife had to apply formally after her arrival for the convict husband to be assigned to her or for him to be granted a ticket-of-leave in order to support his family. Such applications were not invariably or immediately granted. Although it was the express policy of both the British and the colonial governments to encourage the marriage of convict women, it was not so firm a policy to encourage and assist the reunion of British families of men under sentence in New South Wales. The determinative in England was primarily the expense this involved, both for the British government and for the colonial expenditure. In the colony itself one of the major considerations continued to be the possible value of a skilled man's labour to government, and this could and did take precedence over the economic needs of his family. The free wife who had faced that long and dangerous voyage in the expectation that she would resume married life could find herself alone, the only indulgence granted her being permission for her convict husband 'to sleep out of Barracks'. Where even this was denied, the wife would sometimes petition specifically that her husband 'be allowed to come home from the Prisoners' Barracks'.

Convict wife Mary Pearce arrived in New South Wales in 1816, her passage paid by the British government so that she could rejoin her husband who had been transported on the *Lady Castlereagh*. He was overseer of the Government Bricklayers and, she claimed, capable of supporting his family if he were granted a ticket-of-leave. The request was refused, and he remained a prisoner for life employed by government. The official reason was that 'he is an excellent workman but a drunken dissipated character and would probably be best left where he was than to his own propensities'. There was no reunion for Mary Pearce and her convict husband.[15]

Ellen Sewell arrived on the *Northampton* in 1815 and found that she must petition for 'her husband George Sewell to be put off Government Stores to earn a living for the family, or the family would have to be victualled'. She had five British-born children, aged between thirteen and three. The husband was eventually assigned to her and, after he had received a conditional pardon, the family settled as landholders at Sutton Forest. Had it not been for the persistence of the wife, followed by the 'proven industrious good character' of both, George Sewell would have remained a prisoner of the Crown.[16]

Catherine Donough and her husband were not so fortunate. The wife came free on the *Thames* to find that the convict husband was not in Sydney but assigned as a shepherd 'upcountry'. Her application to have his services transferred to her, or permission given her to go to him, was refused because his master, John Atkinson, told the colonial secretary that the man 'had no means of supporting his family as he was always out with his master's flocks'.[17] Margaret Byrne, who travelled on the same ship as Catherine Donough, was another free wife who found that her convict husband was unable to join her after her arrival at Sydney. She petitioned the governor that she needed him assigned to her 'as she had no means of supporting herself and their three children'. It was fortunate for this convict family that the husband was assigned to Mr Wiltshire, who assisted the petition by testifying that the man had been his servant since his arrival and he had had no cause to make any complaint of his conduct. The Superintendent of Convicts also testified that 'he knew nothing prejudicial to his character ... so presumed he was a steady and useful person'. Byrne was assigned to his wife.[18]

The civil condition of the wife of a convict appeared to have little influence on the decision to grant or withhold assignment of married men. Ann Robertson had arrived convict on the *Janus*, sentenced to seven years' transportation. In 1821 she married prisoner-for-life George Tallentyre, the overseer of the No. 2 Quarry Gang. Freed by servitude and with one child, she petitioned for her husband to be assigned to her. The refusal was explained by Captain Dumaresq: 'Tallentyre is paid for his situation and is allowed to sleep out of Barracks'. Ann Robertson had to be content with this small indulgence.[19] Mary Ann McDade was another freed-by-servitude woman who married a convict, then attempted to have him assigned to her. She married Henry Bacon at St Luke's Church, Liverpool, while he was an assigned servant to James Meehan. She pleaded with the governor that, because Meehan objected to the transference of her husband's assignment, 'she was in great distress which may probably be the cause of becoming an outcast of society'. It was many years before she managed to have Meehan's objections overruled. In 1828 Ann McDade and her husband were together, working for Anne Hollis of the Upper Neptune.[20] Mary Sellers had come free on the *Friendship* in 1818, and was married on 22 May 1822 by Mr Cowper to Thomas Scarr, who had arrived convict on the *Morley* in 1817. In 1826 she petitioned that he be assigned to her as he was then fifty-four years old. He had held a ticket-of-leave and had worked at his trade as a brewer in Newcastle, but the ticket was recalled when he was convicted of selling spirits without a licence and he was returned to Sydney and reassigned as overseer of lime at Market Wharf. The petition was unsuccessful.[21] Native-born Mary Barret was quite unable to obtain permission for her convict husband to be assigned to her. John Barret had been transported for life on the *Guildford*, and they had one child when she petitioned that he be granted a ticket-of-leave. The request was refused after his employer, the superintendent of the Pennant Hills Sawing Establishment, informed the governor that 'John Barret, the husband of the petitioner, is not equal to the support of his wife, child and himself, after performing his task at the Government Sawing Establishment.' Captain Dumaresq added that Barret was 'inclined to be troublesome previously to his marriage'.[22] Whether he reverted to 'troublesome behaviour' after being denied permission to live with his wife and child is unknown.

Expense was always a consideration to the authorities and where a refusal of a petition clearly indicated that wife and family would become an encumbrance to the colonial expenditure, this could and did influence decisions, all other qualifications being satisfactory. Mary Jones, who arrived on the *Jupiter*, faced the unexpected experience of arriving in New South Wales in the expectation of rejoining her husband and, instead, finding herself destitute. Her husband, John Jones, transported on the *Hadlow*, was overseer of carpentry for the government settlement at Bathurst and the free wife had to find some means of maintaining herself and her children in Sydney. Her plea was successful, and Jones was eventually reassigned to his wife and able to support his family adequately by working as a 'free' carpenter in Sydney.[23]

Other free wives were not so fortunate, and were forced to spend long periods separated from convict husbands. Mrs Thomas (Mary Ann Easterbrook) requested that the services of her convict husband be transferred to her from his master, Hannibal MacArthur. MacArthur was willing to release his assigned servant to his wife, but not until he could be replaced by someone as capable of running his watermill. As such skills were at a premium in the colony, Ann Thomas had to continue to maintain herself until the replacement was found.[24] Sarah Hill arrived with her four children on the *Providence* in 1822. A year later she was still requesting that her husband become her assigned servant.[25] The difficulties faced by these family women while waiting for their husbands to be assigned to them are detailed in petitions for assistance from the governor. Apart from the usual request to be placed on stores and victualled by the government, these free wives would request land, cattle or servants to assist them earn their livelihood and support their children. Elizabeth McConolly wrote to the governor that she 'is a free woman and has lived in the Colony for eight years. She has three small children ... her husband is a smith and is assigned to Mr Bowman. She requested land to build a home because rents are so high.' Unhappily for Elizabeth McConolly, her request was refused as 'no land is available'.[26]

Catherine Slater petitioned that 'she had come to relieve the grief of her husband a constable in the District of Melville' – he possessed a ticket-of-leave. She had four children, and she requested a grant of land because it was 'her husband who was one of those who had captured the bushranger James Dowdell'. Doubtless the land would have eased her grief at separation from her husband, but she received no reward and remained with her children as a shopkeeper in Sydney.[27] Matilda Fisk petitioned 'for land on which to graze her cattle as she had four children to support'. She was unsuccessful.[28] Honora Flynn was more successful. She had married Patrick Flynn in 1811 and, after his conviction, had followed him to New South Wales with their three children. On arrival she demanded that her husband be assigned to her before she left the ship. Not only did she obtain her husband's services, but by 'proven industry' he received a conditional pardon and a land grant of 40 acres. After his death she again petitioned the governor, this time that her 'late husband's allotted land be located at the Hunter's River or other suitable place'. Honora Flynn was one of the more determined of the convict wives and her persistence and determination achieved respectability for her 'convict family'.[29]

Other convict wives sought to maintain themselves by asking for assigned servants to act as labourers or skilled workers. Margaret Cooper asked first for a grant of land for her support, and then 'an order for the employment of her husband, George Cooper' to work that land.[30] Mrs Margaret Bunker wrote to Macquarie in 1812, reminding him that in 1810 he had promised her 'more assistance to carry on her farm, and requested that she be given at least one more man to replace the one who had absconded'. She renewed her request a week later, and was successful in obtaining her 'government man'.[31] How Ann Davis expected to manage her farm is not known – she sought confirmation from Macquarie in 1810 of the 50 acres which had been granted to her by Paterson because 'she has five children and is blind'.[32]

Good character was essential for the success of applications, even for the free wives who came to the colony. Bridget Farraugher arrived in New South Wales to join Murty Farraugher, transported on the *Mangles*, and found that he was assigned to Mr Acres at Seven Hills. Being unable to support herself and her three children 'without her husband's exertions', she applied immediately to the governor, sending her petition from the ship as it lay in Sydney Harbour. The success of this petition owed a great deal to the support of colonial official Mr Hely, who testified that

He knew the Petitioner in Ireland ... he considers her one of the most respectable applicants of this class. She resided on the Estate of Hely's relatives at Farm Castle County Mayo the Estate of Lindsey Backnall. Her conduct was marked by the strictest propriety since her husband's conviction and transportation.

This petition was granted. The wife became a tenant farmer at Illawarra, and her husband was assigned to her as her labourer.[33]

Applicants were well aware of the necessity of 'supporting a good character', whatever their colonial circumstances might be. When Jane Jackson – who had arrived as an Irish convict from Wicklow on the *Experiment* in 1809 – petitioned that her husband be assigned to her, she informed the governor that she was a respectable 'widow with some property', having been previously married. She had married Jackson, her second colonial husband, 'with the governor's permission and his master's approbation'.[34]

Was it the lack of proof of good conduct which led to the refusal of Mary Hartford's petition? She had arrived convict on the *Providence*, and in 1822 married convict James Clarke (*Malabar*), a tinman who had been in the employment of government since his arrival. The wife pleaded that he be assigned to her for her support as she had 'lost the sight of one of her eyes and the other was severely afflicted with opthalma [sic]'. Mr Hely refused the petition, 'as the husband already sleeps out of Barracks ... he cannot see a reason for a departure from Regulations'.[35] Margaret Johnston (*Janus*) was another wife who found that physical infirmities were of little concern to the government when determining whether or not to assign a convict to his wife. She pleaded that she was 'almost deaf and blind ... unable to do anything for myself and entreated that her husband [John Simple] may be assigned to her to take care of her'. She had been convicted in County Tyrone in 1819, and was freed by servitude at the time of her petition. What became of her is unknown, but her husband remained a government servant separated from his wife.[36]

Assignment of convict husbands was not without its problems for the wives who became their husbands' 'masters'. Some of the difficulties were simply the result of inefficient official administration, some the result of domestic differences, and some the ironic result of the success of the 'joint labour' of husband and wife which led to the request for further 'indulgences'. When native-born Eleanor Crozier married convict Evan Evans, he was assigned to her immediately after their wedding. The local magistrate at Parramatta, Dr Douglas, neglected to register the assignment, so that four years later Evans was recalled by the Penrith magistrates and ordered 'to be sent to the Principal Superintendent of Convicts at Sydney' for reassignment as there was no record of his assignment to his wife. Eleanor Evans successfully petitioned the governor for his return: 'by their combined industry they had acquired some property and lived on a rented farm at Evan'. Would the result have been so satisfactory if the pair had not been so industrious?[37] Joseph Fernee who was transported for life on the *Indian*, married Mary Clare, a freed-by-servitude convict from the *Providence*. Governor Macquarie had given him 'a note of permission for a ticket-of-leave', and he had mistaken this for the actual ticket. Some sixteen years later – during which time he had lived as a technically free man – he lost his General Pass and applied for its replacement. No record was found that he had received a ticket-of-leave, so he was returned to the Convict Barracks. His wife petitioned the governor, and his former master testified that Macquarie had granted the note of permission and that Fernee 'was an industrious character'. He added, however, that 'his wife was addicted to inebriated habits'. Despite this, a ticket-of-leave was formally granted and the convict husband returned to his family.[38]

On occasion, it was the action of the wife which led to the return of an assigned husband to government. In almost all of these cases, the wife eventually petitioned for the return of her husband. Elizabeth Carver had lived with her assigned husband for three years:

the Petitioner unfortunately having had a few words with her husband, Robert Carver [arrived convict 1817] ... she was induced to leave his house and sought the protection of a friend, the Petitioner's intention was at the time to return to her husband, but during the unfortunate period, a woman by the name of Bowyer gave information at the Police Office that the Petitioner's husband was at large without authority ...

This domestic misunderstanding had a happy ending – Carver was returned to his 'affectionate wife'.[39]

Convict wives showed little hesitation in requesting that the government provide them with 'conveyance' to their husbands when those convicts were assigned or sent away from Sydney. In Britain, the free wives of transported men were expected to make their own way at their own expense to the convict ship when they received permission to travel to New South Wales. In Sydney, however, women such as Charlotte Dixon (Mrs Thomas) petitioned: 'she wishes conveyance for herself and children to the Derwent to join her husband and also to be victualled from Government until then.' She had arrived on the *Indefatigable* with two small children and no means of support, and needed to reach her husband, unaware that he had been sent to the Derwent. The commander of the ship 'attests to her good conduct on the voyage', and the Dixon family were sent on to the Derwent – eventually.[40]

Anne Keith requested the governor to provide her 'with a conveyance to get her to the Hunter River' where her husband was overseer at Mr Winder's farm: 'She is in a delicate state of health and ... she is not able to support herself. Her husband is able to support her but has not sent her any support and she wants to find out the reason for his unkind treatment of her.' Whether or not the government helped her travel to her 'unkind husband' is unknown, but three years later she was working as a laundress in Liverpool Street, Sydney, supporting her five-year-old daughter Mary. There was no trace of the erring John Keith.[41]

Katherine Jackson was not so anxious to have her husband with her, requesting instead that the governor order him to support her and make compensation to her for her sufferings on account of his unpardonable behaviour:

her husband had turned her from her residence forlorn upon the world to obtain her own livelihood. He has been cohabiting with a female prisoner, Mary Montague, who is a Government servant ... and resides in a Public House.

This wife had no doubt that the governor would intervene on her behalf, and her expectations were justified.[42]

Wives of all civil conditions showed little hesitation in applying to the governor to solve their marriage difficulties. Maria Jennings had been married in Scotland about 1805. Her husband was transported for life on the *Anne* in 1809, and was granted a ticket-of-leave, which he held for nine years before being deprived of it. His wife, to whom he was assigned, had had 'no cause for complaint ... until two weeks ago':

> a difference [then] arose between Petitioner and her husband ... she complained and he was returned to the Convict Barracks. She now begs to have her husband restored to her as she is in a declining state of health and unable to work for her support.

The husband of twenty-two years was restored to his wife, and they continued living together until his death in 1828.[43]

Where the government recalled an assigned husband as punishment for misconduct or infringement of regulations, the wife petitioned for his return, usually for economic reasons, but also on the grounds of humanity. Maria Harebut (*Maria*) pleaded that her husband's only offence had been 'harbouring a runaway orphan boy' and that they were both of good character. The appeal was successful and the pair remained living together, the husband supporting his wife by working as a labourer.[44] Sarah Bellinger, native-born, had been married nine years to John Bellinger who had been assigned to her until he 'assaulted a constable and represented himself a free man'. He was recalled as punishment and sent to work in the government Garden Gang. She requested that he be forgiven and returned to her for the sake of the support and care of their three children.[45]

In the domestic dispute between Patrick McBride (*General Hewitt*) and his wife Anne Griffiths, it was the wife who was sent to the Factory. McBride petitioned the governor:

> they had quarrelled and she was taken to Court where in the heat of passion she uttered confessions derogatory to her own feelings as a female and to your Memorialist as a man ... She has repented and he wants her sent back to him for the sake of their infant child ...

Upon official investigation the application was refused, not even the welfare of the infant being sufficient concern to override the bad characters of the parents. The petition was endorsed by the colonial secretary that the woman was not to be returned to the husband because he had allowed her to become a prostitute. She should be assigned 'to the interior' and he was 'a man of bad character'. Was this decision influenced by the fact that the woman was still a convict under sentence and, although married, was 'a known prostitute', the characteristic expected of convict women?[46]

Woman such as Mary Hite petitioned the governor when 'she

had difficulties with her husband'; Eleanor Watt complained of 'her husband's ill-treatment of her'; Ann Coleman told the governor that her husband had deserted her, leaving her to support three small children, so she requested that prisoner Thomas Williams, a baker, be released to her. He had worked for her previously and would now assist her in her troubles. The husband, Edward Coleman, cross-petitioned that Williams had been cohabiting with his wife.[47] This was yet another of the decisions of Solomon which were the responsibility of the colonial governor.

Mary Ann Kelly, who had come free on the *Mariner* was so incensed by the behaviour of her husband that she assaulted him – and was forgiven.[48] All colonial husbands were not so forgiving. Mary Smith, the wife of prisoner Neal Smith, sought permission to join her convict husband at Port Macquarie, but was charged with 'improper conduct with a man called Tiffen' and refused permission because of her 'misconduct'. She petitioned a second time and her husband, when questioned, claimed she was living in an 'improper association' with a man called Swan. He was, however, anxious for her to join him and petitioned to this effect.[49] The husband of Mary Roberts simply accused his wife of adultery when she formed 'an improper connection', and requested assistance from the governor.[50] James Devonport petitioned that 'his wife is acquainted with a James Smith and she has made away with your Memorialist's property'. He wanted the governor to punish her and return her to him.[51] Complaints by husbands were not frequent and were far outnumbered by those from wives. The significance of these petitions lay in their appeal to the governor to right domestic wrongs.

The greatest problem for most of the convict wives of all civil conditions continued to be achieving the assignment of their husbands or the granting of a ticket-of-leave which would enable the man, while still a convict, to live with and support his family. Those petitions to the governor which gave evidence of industry and some material success in the colony were more likely to receive favourable approval. Elizabeth Lee, the native-born wife of convict James Donohue, petitioned for a ticket-of-leave for her husband, 'a respectable and honest young man':

he arrived ... on the *Fanny* and has conducted himself in an honest and correct manner during the whole of his adversity. [I was] married at Sydney and have a young family and am inured from a moral principle to do my duty to my child and myself and place confidence in Your Excellency's humanity and feeling towards [my] unfortunate husband.

The petition was successful, and the convict husband, a ropemaker, was assigned to his wife, until his death in 1826. The following year she married Benjamin Baker by whom she had another eight children. She survived the second husband by ten years, and was buried beside him at Rookwood Cemetery in 1878, a colonial woman of proven 'moral principle'.[52]

The skill of the convict – if not retained for government – could assist an application by the wife for it was evidence that the man had the ability to support his family. Joseph Lee, who had been convicted at Warwick in 1818, was assigned to his wife, Elizabeth Bason, after he had petitioned that she was a free woman with one child and he was a weaver, so could be taken off stores as he was capable of supporting his family.[53] Mary McMahon used the 'fruits of their industry' to apply for a land grant and for her husband's freedom:

She and her husband had no land of their own but have cleared timber for five years. They now have sixty acres for themselves and their children but it is forest land. She requests that the land be re-leased and her husband freed.[54]

The governor was not only petitioned to assist with moral problems arising from colonial marriages, he was also asked to intervene in moral disputes arising from the existence of a prior marriage in Britain contracted by one of the partners. Elizabeth Mitchell (*Lord Melville*), who held a ticket-of-leave, was to marry William Freeman 'but found he had a daughter and wife living in England'. They had cohabited for more than five years when Freeman was sent to Van Diemen's Land as clerk to Thomas Sylde, the Clerk of the Peace, and so they were separated. Elizabeth Mitchell had herself left a daughter in England when she was transported. She wrote to the colonial secretary that she had 'made sure the daughter was skilled with her needle so that she could earn a living by it'. The daughter, Hannah, had been refused permission to come to the colony a number of times but 'had contrived to arrive with a good story, the passage money of £60 was paid by William Freeman'. The mother soon saw 'a criminal propensity in her daughter . . . for a time William Freeman cohabited with both mother and daughter' so the mother left: She petitioned the governor to send her daughter out of the colony'. Unhappily the result of this petition is unknown.[55]

It was another moral, as well as administrative, problem for the colonial administration when a wife petitioned for permission to accompany or join a convict-husband sent by government to another settlement. In most cases – as with Sarah Acton and Mary Cotton – the wives were granted permission if both were of known good character and usually if the husband could support the wife. Sarah Hamilton wrote to Macquarie of the great difficulties which followed the loss of a husband sentenced to another district:

She is the wife of Samuel Hamilton who gave evidence at the trial of Thomas Condon and because of too much grog varied in his depositions and was sent to Newcastle for two years as punishment. [She] is left to support the children by her own endeavours and is in distress. She has been obliged to part with many necessaries when lately ill and incapable of earning . . .

Mrs Hamilton received more than she expected – the humane governor pardoned the husband and returned him to his family.[56]

Not all colonial marriages were happy ones, nor were all wives dutiful and faithful. Domestic differences could lead to notices of separation being inserted in the colonial press, or, even worse, notices giving warning that a husband would not be responsible for his wife's debts, or a wife for her husband's. Some separations were amicable. When William Chalker and his wife agreed to separate, he provided for her well, but the articles of separation specified that he would retain his horse, 'Miss Sprightly'.[57] More disagreeable were the public complaints that a wife had 'absconded', leaving the husband with an infant or young child 'deprived of natural maternal affection'. The husband usually added that this action by his wife was 'without just cause', and advertised that he would not be responsible for her debts. Unfaithfulness was usually the reason, and this could be forgiven. Convict Mary Mazzagora (*Mary Anne*) was accused of misconduct with William Innis, but her husband later requested the government to relieve her from the Factory into his custody, for he preferred to have her with him, and forgave her her alleged misconduct.[58] Patrick Farley was of the same forgiving disposition; he first laid an official charge against his wife for misconduct, and after she was tried and convicted withdrew the charge and told the court 'he was now willing to have her returned'.[59] Typical of the notices of absconded wives was that of J. Moss: 'who will not be responsible for any debts . . . Any person found harbouring her . . . will be prosecuted with the utmost rigour of the law.'[60]

When the social origins of the inhabitants of New South

Wales are considered, and it is recognised that, in Britain, common-law marriages were not unusual among the lower classes, the small percentage of 'absconded wives' and 'deserting' husbands was unexpected. It may have been that the close involvement of the colonial authorities, especially the governor himself, in the everyday lives of the men and women of Botany Bay acted as a restraint. The erring wife or husband knew that appeal could be made to the authorities where there was cause to complain of unlawful, immoral or dishonest conduct. Such an appeal could lead to a wife being sent to the Factory, an assigned husband returned to government. For the women of the colony, life as a 'free' wife was far preferable to that of a worker confined in the Female Factory. For the men, assignment to a wife was a far better prospect and infinitely more preferable to the chain gang or to work as a shepherd in the outer settlements.

It had been unexpected that the colonial governor would become directly involved in the domestic lives of the inhabitants of Botany Bay. Problems of immorality were expected by both British and colonial authorities, but there was little awareness of the domestic difficulties which would face free wives who came to New South Wales to join convicted husbands, little awareness of the problems for colonial families where one or both partners had arrived as convicts, where one was still an assigned servant, or in the service of government. To these convict and ex-convict settlers and their families, the solution to all their problems rested with the authorities, for it was the governor who had the ultimate authority, who had the power to grant or to withhold indulgences, who regulated all aspects of life and labour in the colony. It was to him that they looked for redress and for the solution of their domestic and family problems.

CONCLUSION
'THE WOMEN OF BOTANY BAY'

... persons who have passed through every graduation of vice and mercy – but now transformed into careful purse-keeping housewives ...

—Barbra Diaper, Sydney, *Australian*, April 1825

The settlement of New South Wales was directly influenced by the English transportation system, and the inhabitants of that colony, free or convicted, were indirectly affected by all the assumptions and connotations which surrounded that infamous word 'convict'. To contemporaries, Botany Bay had begun purely and simply as a *convict* colony, a distant penal camp established halfway across the globe, far from the influences of all polite, genteel and civilised society. It was established for the punishment, maintenance and possible reformation of British felons 'of the darkest description', no longer welcome to the independent and proudly free United States of America. These men and women were accepted without question as felons who were incorrigible, recalcitrant, incapable of reformation, decency or morality. They were the dregs and outcasts of the despised criminal classes of Britain and Ireland, unfit to remain with decent men and women. With such inhabitants, how could Botany Bay be linked with any achievements, successes, economic or social progress? It was, and it remained in British eyes, 'a land of convicts and kangaroos', where the very children born to those depraved parents inherited the hideous taint of criminality, and in turn passed this dominant characteristic on to their children and to their children's children for succeeding generations.

It was completely unrecognised by contemporaries or by later generations of commentators that the land of Australia was itself a major determinative in influencing and shaping the society which was to develop as 'Australian'. Nor was it recognised that the men, and especially the women, who had been banished to that land would not necessarily remain the despised, abandoned and worthless objects they had been in Britain, that the land and the needs and opportunities found in New South Wales would lead to the formation of a new class of Britishers, men and women who had accepted the challenges offered in and by the new colony. Successes or failures, these men and women were the first of that new race, the Australians.

The settlement began with transplanted Britishers, but the land to which so many of them were banished was as distinct from the lands of England, Ireland, Scotland and Wales as were the convicted settlers from those who had come free to the colony. It was because of and not in spite of the convictism which dominated the structure of the population, the development of the economy, the shaping of society, its attitudes and values that the new society emerged from the penal colony of Botany Bay. Admittedly, there was the nucleus of a second society based on the traditional English hierarchical and deferential structure from the first day of settlement: the carefully guarded society of the untainted, the unconvicted, the 'free objects', the came-free who would eventually distinguish themselves as 'the pure merinos', 'the exclusives', their pride and their prejudices, their standards and values resting unshakeably on their 'difference' as 'free and respectable'. These men and their women and children remained transplanted Britishers, in almost every case attempting to recreate 'Another Britannia' in this new world, a Britannia based solely on the accepted standards and social definitions of the Old Country. Few had any recognition or awareness that there was a new society struggling for expression in a land which had remained as isolated from and untouched by European cultures as it had from the diseases and evils of 'civilised' European society.

The 'pure merinos' were very much in the minority at Botany Bay; vocal, powerful, authoritative, but a minority. It was not to be their colonial experiences which were to establish the germs of a distinctive Australian society, which were to determine traits and characteristics which became typical and recurring throughout the first two centuries of European settlement, languishing almost unnoticed for the first century, resurrected, misinterpreted and distorted according to prevailing fashions and theories in the next. Almost unconsciously and certainly without spoken recognition, new values and new standards emerged within the first thirty years or so and were evident in the colonial definitions of respectability, position, authority. The ex-convict colonists and their families, adapting as pioneers, outgrew the old and accepted definitions of England, outgrew the traditional class distinctions. Assuredly, New South Wales remained a convict society if that society were defined on the basis of the class origins of most of the inhabitants. It was not, however, a convict society if the definition were based on contemporary British assumptions and connotations of that description. To Britain, there was only one class in her penal colony, the convict class, most of whom had originated from the poorest and worst criminal elements in Britain and Ireland. It was completely overlooked that the convicts and the ex-convicts did not necessarily become colonial criminals nor did they form a homogeneous and all-embracing 'convict class' in New South Wales. Instead, they became part of a new framework of class distinctions which developed as a direct response to the varying and diverse roles of the convict and ex-convict settlers within the economic development of New South Wales. These distinctions were firmly and almost exclusively based on colonial economic achievement, self-advancement, enterprise and industry found among men and women who had been transported or had come to join convict husbands and wives. The economic successes, whether achieved as individuals, as married or de facto couples, or as family groupings, may have been no greater than that of Hannah Murray and Thomas Stone who proudly recorded that they 'owned one cattle and ten acres'. It may have been far less, returning a bare subsistence, providing meagre independence, and it may have been far greater, leading to the enjoyment of lifestyles which would have been the envy of many of Britain's gentry. It was all, however great, however small, infinitely more than could have been achieved had the ex-convict or his or her family remained in their native land. This new 'class structure' was most marked and yet least recognised among the women convicts. They had arrived as one class, the damned whores of the criminal haunts of Britain. They found their own levels in the economic strata of convict society. They lived and worked within a class structure which barred no woman, took no account of proven criminality, paid no heed to assumptions of infamy, degradation and depravity. Their stepping-stone to colonial respectability was economic achievement, self-dependence, enterprise, initiative and colonial honesty. And work. The only irremovable barrier was the artificial division of society created by the 'pure merinos' intent on preserving the purity and respectability of their 'untainted' state in accordance with prevailing standards in Britain. But colonial society had been born from the structure and nature of the penal settlement, bred by the transportation system and nurtured by the nature of the land itself. It was not the ladies of New South Wales but the women of Botany Bay, the despised 'convicts' and convict wives, who became such a vital and integral part of every level of their Australian society.

Many of these women became the first white women of the Australian bush, not from choice but from necessity. They were women who could and did adapt to the realities of a pioneering life in a strange and unknown environment where, even to the country women of Britain and Ireland, 'nature seemed reversed'. It was a land in which flood, fire and drought vied with each other to push the new settlers from their farms, where snakes and spiders and dust and heat brought fear and exhaustion, where the unimaginable labour of felling trees and digging out huge stumps before crops could be sown seemed endless, where family life meant life in isolation, where a child could be born and die and leave no record, where even the comfort of church or priest was denied, and where the company of other women was infrequent and uncertain. Under such conditions these bush women came to know that they must develop self-reliance, self-sufficiency, independence, resources and skill, for the alternative could lead to failure, sickness and even death for themselves and for their families. Children who were lost, or wandered away, who were burned or scalded in accidents, hurt by misadventure, sick or ailing with the summer flux, with infant disorders, with sickness or worse, all must be attended to by the mother, for in so many cases no other help was at hand.

Mary Long was one of these women. She arrived on the *Lady Juliana* in 1790 and settled on the land with convict James Ward, who had been transported the same year. Their land grant was in the then-isolated South Creek district. By 1812 they had developed their property sufficiently for themselves and their three children to be self-supporting. The youngest was barely a year old when James Ward died suddenly from snakebite, and Mary Long was left alone to manage the property and raise her family. Her successes as a widow were unremarked in colonial records.[1] Irishwoman Catherine Barry was another convict woman who typified the determination of these exiled 'refuse' of the Old Country to adapt and succeed in their adopted homeland. Catherine Barry was transported on the *Sugar Cane* in 1793, and married James Dunn, who had been transported in the same year. They settled on a sixty-acre grant at Portland Head, 'an outlying settlement'. In 1806 two of their young children were killed when 'a tree felled by an assigned servant fell on them'. In 1810 they were living with their remaining children in 'a stone cottage', cultivating their land. By 1814 these two ex-convicts had thirty acres under cultivation, and by 1821 they had added another property at Cumberland Reach, two miles down the river from their original grant. This 'convict' family remained on their properties until their deaths, Catherine Barry living with her married daughter after her husband was drowned in a flooded river. She died at the age of eighty-seven, by which time she had been a respected resident and family woman of the Hawkesbury District for fifty-seven years. She was buried at her own request beside her husband at Sackville Reach.[2] Neither Catherine Barry nor Mary Long, nor any of the family farming women of the bush whom they represented, gained any place as pioneers in the legends and histories of their adopted country, a land to which they themselves had given so much. Successful and respected in their own lifetimes, succeeding generations saw them and their 'convict' contemporaries shrouded in the degraded mists of convictism.

The women from the towns and townships fared little better than their bush sisters in gaining recognition in the history or the mythology of Australia. The most well-known exception, Mary Reibey, gained her subsequent fame as the widow of an officer, and her wealth and economic interests in the colony rivalled those of almost any 'Gentleman'. She was, however, a convict woman and the importance of this to Mary Reibey herself is evident in her attempt to escape this stigma by describing herself after she returned from a visit to England as 'Mary Reibey, Came Free, *Mariner*, 1821'. Most of her contemporaries, even widows like successful Elizabeth Grey, remained unacknowledged, their successes and enterprise in taking on the business interests of their late husbands completely disregarded.

The really forgotten women of Botany Bay have been the convict wives, those women who pleaded successfully for free passage to 'be a consolation and a comfort' to transported husbands in their exile and punishment, women whose convict husbands pleaded with colonial and British authorities that 'they could not sleep at nights for thinking of their poor distresses' and begged that wives and children be sent to them at Botany Bay. The lives and achievements, the sorrows and the failures of these free women became as great a part of the beginnings of Australian society as were the sufferings and anxieties of the husbands from whom they had been exiled. For these men, the knowledge that the colony could offer benefits and living standards so far in excess of the poverty and deprivation in which they knew their families were living, added to the punishment of their banishment. Josiah Godber, a transported machine-breaker, wrote to his dearest wife Rebecker [*sic*] not only of his distress but of the life they could lead together in New South Wales if she could join him:

I have said befoore my Dear Wife what would I Give to here from you they Say that absence and Length of Time will whare the thoughts of one another from our minds but my Dear wife if I could but wonse moore Injoy your Company all the Powers on Earth should not Part us O my Deare To think that wee have lived To Gether so maney years and the Tourn a Sunder at Last it all moost Destracts mee when I think of it my dear ...
I am very well of for a prisoner Government man To one Master Dixson a marchant and milnor Hee hath a Larg mill gose by a Steam Enguine I Dress flour for you and has Done ever since I came my alowance is Seven pounds flour and Seven pounds of Beef or Poark and Seven shillings that is my weeks allowance and a very good one for a Prisoner I have my Lodgins and Cloaths To find out of it but I have ... as good Lodgins as any in the Town ... my Dear I could like to have you with mee and be Happy ...[3]

Was it descriptions such as these sent back by convict men and women to relatives in Britain which so greatly encouraged their families to do their utmost to rejoin them, or was it simply a means of escape from starvation and indescribable poverty which caused so many convict wives to come and 'comfort' their husbands 'in their great afflictions'? Mary Cassidy of Clonmel was so desperate to bring her children to join her husband at Botany Bay that she herself became a convict. In 1826 'Mary Cassidy pleaded guilty to a theft which she said she had committed with the hope of being sent to Botany Bay and of joining her husband to whom that fate was assigned last year'.[4]

The convict wives arrived in the colony expecting to be supported and protected by their husbands. Few were daunted when they found that they must petition the governor to have their husbands assigned to them, that they must become the 'master' of the household, they must apply for land, for servants, for indulgences, for licences. It was their positive responses to this entirely new family situation, their strident and repeated demands to the colonial authorities for their rights, for assistance, for advice, which contributed so greatly to the characteristics of the emerging Australian female identity. As the bush women and the townswomen needed the qualities of self-reliance and determination, so did those wives who had accepted banishment and exile. It was the strength and often strident and vocal determination which added so greatly to their 'domestic' influence on family life in the colony and, in many cases, changed entirely the roles and expectations of wives in New South Wales. Convict wives could be even more determined than the convict women to demand from the colonial authorities attention, redress, indulgences or any form of assistance of which they felt in need.

Almost all the achievements of the women of Botany Bay died with them, held only in the remembrances of their families. There was, however, one isolated and exceptional comment made by a correspondent of the *Australian*, whose letters were published in April 1825. Barbra Diaper and her brother, Richard, came to the colony after Barbra's disappointing love affair. The brother set up as a wholesale draper in Sydney. His discussions with his sister, and their opinions of many aspects of the colony, were printed as letters to the editor. Barbra was an outspoken and literate woman. The first letter was a satirical commentary on the supposed effects of the temperance movement in New South Wales. A week later, the Bigge Report was criticised as 'no more or less than a parcel of old washerwoman's chatter'. This was followed by observations on Sydney's Thursday Markets:

In another part of the Market you will find groups of hale and jocular looking butter and egg women – probably persons who have passed through every gradation of vice and misery – but now transformed into careful purse keeping housewives:– the women have made the money here, at least, laid the foundation for all that followed.[5]

This free migrant woman and her brother saw the women of Botany Bay in a different light from almost all of their 'respectable' contemporaries. It was a limited recognition of their achievements for it did not include those women who may have reached a far higher level of economic or domestic success than the 'egg and butter' women. Nor was there any recognition of the very real contribution of the colony's family women or pioneer women. The Diapers did, however unwittingly, sum up concisely the real contribution of the women of Botany Bay to Australian society, for these were the women who 'laid the foundation for all that followed'.

ABBREVIATIONS

AEHR	*Australian Economic History Review*
ANU	Australian National University (Canberra)
AONSW	Archives Authority of New South Wales
ARGS	Australian Research Grants Scheme (Federal Government)
BM	British Museum (London)
BT	Bonwick Transcripts (ML)
Co	County (Ireland)
CO	Colonial Office (London)
COD	Copy of Archives Document (AONSW)
Col Sec	Colonial Secretary (Sydney)
CSIL	Colonial Secretary In Letters (Sydney)
GD	Gaol Delivery
HE	His Excellency
HM	His Majesty
HO	Home Office (London)
H of C	House of Commons
HRA	*Historical Records of Australia*
HRNSW	*Historical Records of New South Wales*

HS	*Historical Studies*
JRAHS	*Journal of the Royal Australian Historical Society*
MGR	Middlesex Gaol Record
ML	Mitchell Library (Sydney)
MURG	Macquarie University Research Grant
NL	National Library
OBSP	*Old Bailey Sessions Papers*
OP	Official Papers (Dublin)
PC	*Privy Council*
PD	*Parliamentary Debates*
PMS	Petition in Mitigation of Sentence
PP	*Parliamentary Papers*
PP&C	Prisoners' Petitions and Cases (Dublin)
PRO	Public Record Office (London)
QS	Quarter Sessions
RN	Royal Navy
RO	Record Office
RSSS	Research School of Social Sciences (ANU, Canberra)
SMH	*Sydney Morning Herald*
SPO	State Paper Office (Dublin)
T	Treasury Papers (London)

Civil conditions (as used by contemporaries)

AP	Absolute Pardon
BC	Born in the Colony
C	Convict
CB	Colonial Born
CF	Came Free
F	Free (no indication of free or freed)
FS	Free by Servitude
GS	Government Servant (Convict)
CP	Conditional Pardon
EC	Emancipated Convict
EX-C	Ex-Convict
P	Prisoner of the Crown (Convict)
TL	Ticket-of-leave

Notes
All abbreviations of proper names and given names, districts, towns, occupations and official positions are as used by contemporaries.
  All spellings may be variant.

NR   No response.

NOTES

Sources for criminal and trial proceedings are not included in the notes for all individual women. Trial date and trial place for all transported women is included in 'Women Transported to New South Wales' (List A: Women transported from England, 1788–1827; List B: Women transported from Ireland, 1791–January 1828).

Sources for Ships' Indents from which individual data has been obtained are listed on pp xii-xiv. Sources for Surgeons' Reports: Guide to Convict Records in AONSW (No 14, 1981), p 294ff.

Where information is from a source not readily accessible or previously unknown, this is noted in the appropriate reference.

Women are identified by ship of arrival (where known) in the text and in the Index to Women. Ship of arrival is included in List A and List B so that trial details for individual women may be easily established. Note that, although a list of major aliases is included, spellings of both names and places are variant and that dates and other details may vary. Some women and men claim to have arrived in New South Wales on ships other than those on which they were listed and at dates which contradict the ships' indents. Others may claim to have arrived on two or more ships. Women who married, or changed their name in the colony, were difficult to trace in their home countries or to identify by correct ship of arrival. Lists A and B include these 'problem women' but no attempt is made to list every alias and variant spelling of all the transported women.

I am indebted to all family researchers and local historical societies in Australia, Great Britain and Ireland who contributed personal research on individual women who were transported during the first forty years of European settlement of New South Wales. All these 'convict' women may not have been mentioned individually in the text but every one has played some part in re-creating the whole picture of the role of women at Botany Bay. Regrettably, it is not possible to thank all the descendants within the limitations of space in this volume, but among the contributors of personal family research were:

B. Adams, S. Ahern, J. Alford, H. Allsop, I. & B. Anderson, S. Anderson, N. Asperey, N. Aston, W. Atkinson, F. Attewell, H. Babauta, E. Bale, E. Ball, D. Barker, K. Barker, G. Barnett, H. Barr, R. Bassett, E. Bate, F. Bate, C. Baxter, L. & D. Baxter, P. Beard, L. Bedwin, P. Bell, B. Bellingham, E. Bennett, R. Bennett, M. Bertoli, A. Billington, M. Bird, J. Birrell, J. Black, J. Black Snr, B. Blackwell, E. Boulton, J. Bourne, M. Bowler, F. Boys, S. Brackenbury, P. Bradley, B. Bragge, J. Brayshaw, I. Brennan, P. Britt, J. Broome, E. Brown, M. Brown, Y. Browning, B. Buckley, J. Buckley, H. Buitendam, G. Bundy, V. Byrne, C. Byrnes, J. Cahill, B. & S. Campbell, K. Campbell, U. Campbell, W. Canty, K. Cape, M. Carey, G. Cargeeg, W. & C. Carlon, L. Carrington, M. Carty, G. Cashman, J. Chalmers, D. Champion, G. Chappell, C. Churches, C. Cleary, K. Cleverly, M. Clougher, F. Cockle, M. Coker, B. Coleman, S. Collier, M. Collins, J. Commons, S. Connelly, B. Cook, K. Cooke, P. & B. Cooke, V. Coote, V. Cornell, C. Cosgrove, W. Cowley, E. Cox, N. Cregan, G. Crockett, L. Cross, D. Crowther, B. Crutchett, S. Cryer, B. Cunningham, N. Cunningham, J. Curnoe, W. Cuthill, H. Dalton, E. Daly, R. Darvall, V. Date, H. Davis, L. Davis, Lee Davis, M. Davison, E. Dawes, J. Dawes, J. Dawson, B. Dickenson, J. Dickenson, E. Dickey, J. Dillon, J. Domjen, J. Donaldson, P. Donovan, T. Doolan, J. Down, G. Doyle, D. Drevins, K. Eccleston, N. Eckford, F. Edmonds, C. Edwards, J. Edwards, B. Elder, D. Ellerman, J. Ellicott, B. Ellis, P. Ellis, F. Embrey, D. Emmingham, Y. Englert, D. Evans, W. Evans, G. Evendon, N. Farleigh, K. & R. Farrell, K. Ferguson, M. Ferrier, E. Finn, A. Flanagan, D. Flood, B. Forbes, B. & B. Forbes, C. Foster, E. Foster, J. Fry, B. Futcher, D. & M. Garland, V. Garner, C. Garrard, K. Gaut, D. Gleeson, P. Goard, D. Godden, A. Godfrey, J. Godsall, L. Goldstone, C. Goodland, K. Greenhalgh, R. Griffiths, S. Griffiths, K. Grose, A. Gugler, W. Gullock, D. Gunner, R. Guy, D. Haggarty, V. Hagger, A. Hainsworth, L. Hanks, L. Hardie, T. Hardy, P. Haren, W. Harper, B. Harrison, J. Harrison, P. Harrison, D. Hartley, M. Hawke, W. Haymet, J. Hazelton, K. Heinrich, K. Hely, K. Henderson, L. Hewson, B. Hilyard, D. Hobbs, G. Hocking, Z. Hodgkinson, R. Hogg, A. Holden, S. Holley, M. Hope-Catan, B. Horsley, S. Hort, E. Hughes, B. Hunt, J. Hunter, A. & P. Hurley, R. Huxley, J. Ireland, T. Ireton, P. Irvin, V. Ivory, W. Jamison, F. Jarvis, C. Jeffery, L. Jeffries, A. Jeffs, H. Jenkins, M. Johnson, R. Johnston, L. Jones, J. Jorgenson, F. Judge, V. & N. Keen, J. Kelynack, M. Kendall, R. Kent, J. Keyssecker, J. Keywood, N. Kissall, E. Kitchen, J. Knight, J. Kok, M. Kretchmer, S. & M. Lake, K. Larbalestier, F. Larkham, S. Lavarack, J. Lee, L. Lee, K. Lenthall, E. Leyer, L. Lister, E. Lustig, M. Madison, J. Major, A. Mann, G. March, B. Mariani, E. Marjoram,

B. Marsh, E. Marshall, B. Martin, M. Martin, S. Martin, L. Mason, R. Mathews, J. Mathieson, J. McArthur, D. McCaffrey, N. McCormack, G. McCrae, E. McCutcheon, G. McDonald, I. McDonald, J. McDonald, N. McGuire, F. McKenzie, P. McKey, J. McLachlan, D. McLennan, N. McLennan, J. McLeod, N. Meadley, R. Meaker, K. Meredith, K.B. Meredith, B. Metham, E. Middleton, L. Millington, M. Monley, P. & S. Mooney, J. Moore, R. Moore, M. Morgan, H. Morris, N. Morrissey, M. Morrow, D. & S. Muir, G. Mulheron, M. Mullins, R. Mulvenna, J. Murphy, L. Murray, A. Mutch, L. Newman, G. Nicholas, L. Nilson, S. Nilsson, F. Nolan, W. Oats, M. O'Brien, J. O'Shea, R. Owens, G. Packman, D. Page, J. Page, H. Parker, D. Pattman, M. Pearce, A. Pearson, D. Pedersen, M. Pegler, M. Pember, P. Perkins, B. Peters, L. Pinch, B. Pittman, J. Pollock, D. Powell, J. Power, J. & S. Power, N. Power, J. Priestley, J. Purdon, P. Quick, A. Quinlan, W. Quinlivan, J. Quinnell, J. Rainer, M. Redding, N. Reedy, H. Reichenbach, N. Reynolds, B. Rice, F. Richardson, K. Richardson, J. Riley, M. Ring, V. Rixon, N. Robbins, M. Robertson, J. & J. Robinson, W. Robinson, B. Ross, J. Rowatt, J. Rowe, N. Rowe, C. Ryan, J. Ryan, L. Sabine, J. Sainsbury, V. Sansom, B. Scanlen, N. Schreiber, B. Scott, L. Scott, C. Searle, J. & B. Shaw, H. Shearman, B. Shearwood, R. Shepherd, R. & H. Shepherd, P. Shoring, R. Shurmer, D. Skenridge, M. Smeaton, B. Smith, J. Smith, M. Smith, R. Smith, W. & A. Smith, A. Souter, D. Spencer, M. Spicer, E. Spilsbery, J. Stacey, C. Stark, B. Stevenson, S. Stevenson, D. Stiff, K. Stokes, M. Stralow, M. Sutton, L. Swadling, M. Swift, S. Swords, R. Taafe, D. Taaffe, R. Tallentire, P. Tancred, M. Tattam, M. Teece, M. Ternovy, F. Thomas, L. Thomas, C. Thompson, K. Thompson, R. Thompson, V. Thompson, W. Thompson, S. Thomson, K. Tipping, S. Tracey, H. Treadgold, M. Treloar, J. Triffitt, M. Troy, J. Turner, M. Upfold, D. Usher, W. Vacher, W. van den Bossche, A. Van Wienan, J. Vidgen, A. Voisey, J. Waddington, J. Waldie, Z. Waldon, A. Walker, C. Walker, G. Walker, E. Waller, G. Ward, M. Ward, L. Wareham, J. Warner, R. Warnock, J. Warren, E. Waters, R. Watkins, J. Watmuff, J. Watt, A. Watts, L. Watts, K. Webb, D. Webster, L. Weier, J. Westmore, J. White, S. White, C. Whitehead, K. Whittaker, P. Wilcox, M. Willcocks, A. Williams, E. Williams, P. Williams, S. Williams, O. & B. Williamson, L. Wines, K. Wiseman, F. Witcom, D. Woodburn, G. Woodfull-Eades, R. Wright, E. Wyse, S. Yates, M. Young, A. Yuille.

CHAPTER 1: 'GUESTS OF HIS MAJESTY'

1   For discussion of the continuing historical debate on the settlement of New South Wales in 1788, see Ged Martin (ed), *The Found-*

ing of Australia: The Argument about Australia's Origins, Sydney 1978. See also Frank Clarke, 'The reasons for settlement in 1788', in *Norfolk Island and Its First Settlement 1788-1814*, Sydney 1988.

2   Richard Johnson, born 1755(?) at Weldon, Yorkshire, died 1827; appointed Chaplain to New South Wales, 24 Oct 1786; married Mary Burton, Dec 1786; Chaplain to New South Wales 1788-1800; for biography see Neil K Mackintosh, *Richard Johnson, Chaplain to the Colony of New South Wales*, Sydney 1978; for Johnson's opinions on the convicts, see 'Johnson Letters to Fricker', ML Ms; Revd Richard Johnson to Governor John Hunter, *HRA* 1, III, p 432ff; see also Revd Richard Johnson, *An Address to the Inhabitants of the Colonies Established in New South Wales and Norfolk Island*, London 1794; facs ed, Adelaide 1963.

   Samuel Marsden, born 1764 at Farsley, Yorkshire, died 1838; married Elizabeth Fristan 1793; Assistant Chaplain to New South Wales 1794-1800, Chaplain 1800-18; for biography see A T Yarwood, *Samuel Marsden, the Great Survivor*, Melbourne 1977; for Marsden's opinions of the convicts see J R Elder (ed), *The Letters and Journals of Samuel Marsden, 1765-1838*, Dunedin 1932; Marsden Papers 1794-1857, ML; see C M H Clark, *A History of Australia*, vol 1, Melbourne 1962, ch 6 'Convicts and the faith of our fathers'.

3   See David Collins, *An Account of the English Colony in New South Wales*, London 1798, Sydney 1975 ed, B H Fletcher (ed); also Lt-Gov Grose to Henry Dundas, 19 Apr 1793, *HRA* 1, I, p 427.

4   Portia Robinson, 'The first forty years, women and the law', in *In Pursuit of Justice*, J Mackinolty and Heather Radi (eds).

5   Letters of Elizabeth Macarthur in S M Onslow (ed), *Some Early Records of the Macarthurs of Camden*, Sydney 1973: 'having no female friend to bend my mind to – not a single woman' p 29; note that Mary Johnson, the chaplain's wife, was in New South Wales at this time but 'from her conversation' Mrs Macarthur 'derived neither pleasure nor profit'; 'Our little circle has been of late quite brilliant' with the arrival of King's wife, the wives of Grose and Paterson and the wife of Captain Parker of the *Gorgon*, p 42; see also Hazel King, *Elizabeth Macarthur and Her World*, Sydney 1980.

6   For the wives who accompanied the Royal Marines, see 'A List of Persons who have been Victualled from His Majesty's Stores commencing the 26th day of February 1788, with the Births, Deaths and Discharges to 17th November 1788', T1/688, ML, and Portia Robinson, 'The victualling list', *SMH* 13, 15, 16 & 17 Dec 1980.

7   Russel Ward, *The Australian Legend*, Melbourne 1958; note that Ward's most recent work, *Finding Australia: The History of Australia to 1821*, Melbourne 1987, does much to correct this oversight.

8   Robert Hughes, *The Fatal Shore*, London 1986; see review article by

Portia Robinson, 'The shock of the old, Robert Hughes's convict mythology', in *The Age Monthly Review*, Melbourne, vol 7, no 2, June 1987; also Portia Robinson, 'Relocating the criminal class', review of *The Fatal Shore* in the *Sunday Tribune* (Dublin), 18 Oct 1987.

9   For concentration of settlement within the Cumberland Plain, see Portia Robinson, *The Hatch and Brood of Time: A Study of the First Generation of Native-born White Australians*, Melbourne 1985, ch 4 'The nature of the times deceas'd'; see also T M Perry, *Australia's First Frontier*, London 1965, ch 5; Macquarie's Diary, 2 Feb & 23 Apr 1818, ML; W C Wentworth, *Statistical, Historical and Political Description of the Colony of New South Wales*, London 1819, facs ed Adelaide 1978, ch 1 'Settlements of New Holland'.

10 For scholarly accounts of the social and economic conditions familiar to these late eighteenth and early nineteenth century women, see M Dorothy George, *London Life in the Eighteenth Century*, London 1925; Derek Jarrett, *England in the Age of Hogarth*, Avon 1974; James Walvin, *English Urban Life 1776-1851*, Essex 1984; Roy Porter, *English Society in the Eighteenth Century*, London 1982; Robert Kee, *The Most Distressful Country*, London 1983; William Nolan (ed), *Tipperary History and Society*, Dublin 1985; Kevin Whelan (ed), *Wexford History and Society*, Dublin 1987.

11 Willan, *Reports on the Diseases in London*, London 1801, p 225, cited in George, *London Life...*, p 95.

12 Maitland, *History of London*, London 1756, cited in ibid, p 95; see also Report from the Committee of the House of Commons on the State of Mendicity in the Metropolis 1814-15, House of Commons III.

13 Based on reports of trials at Middlesex Sessions and London Gaol Delivery, 1785-1827; Margaret Kennedy was not transported although sentenced to 7 years; she remained in Newgate Prison. Evidence in the trial of Ann Wakelin, reported in the *Times* (London), 2 July 1806, shows the prevalence of destitute women to join 'the guardians of the night': 'Ann Wakelin gave all her money and clothing to Rebecca Pile in return for having her fortune told; Rebecca then advised her to "strip [her employer's] child, pawn the clothes, forsake her friends and go on the town" '.

14 John Aiken, *A Description of the Country from 30 to 40 miles around Manchester*, London 1795, ch 4, cited in Walvin, *English Urban Life...*, p 18; see also the case of Margaret Southern (*Experiment*) 'singlewoman, late of the Parish of Manchester', found guilty of stealing in 1803; born in Manchester, she was 19 when convicted and may have been one of the first convict women to be housed in the Parramatta Female Factory. QS Order Book 1803, Lancashire

Notes (Chapter 1) **309**

RO; information from J K Bishop, County Archivist and descendant of Ada Cutbush.

15 Ellen Fraser (*Prince of Wales*), alias Redchester, 'singlewoman' (tried with William Fraser (*Charlotte*) labourer), guilty of theft of cloth, etc, 7 years, QS Manchester, Lancashire RO; St Phillip's Register for sons John and Daniel; she died in the colony 18 Nov 1840 at Concord, aged 76; information from John Moore. Isabella Oldfield (*Friendship*), 'singlewoman from Manchester', tried with Thomas Oldfield (*Friendship*) labourer, for 'stealing three pieces of cloth'; she died at Sydney, aged about 27, on 17 Mar 1789; Lancashire RO; information from John Jarvis. Sarah McCormick (*Friendship*), 'singlewoman of Manchester', guilty of stealing 'two pieces of gold'; Lancashire RO. Jane Parkinson (*Lady Penrhyn*) died on the passage to New South Wales; see *Journal of Arthur Bowes*, ML.

16 Walvin, *English Urban Life* . . ., p 19: 'Manchester was only the most shocking example of a phenomenon that came to characterize plebeian domestic life throughout England'. Walvin stresses that, 'for literally millions of English people . . . the formative domestic experiences . . . were shaped by the unquestionably impoverished conditions of the urban home', p 20.

17 For time lapse between date of trial and date of arrival in New South Wales, see 'Women transported to New South Wales', Lists A & B. For conditions in British prisons, see John Howard, *The State of Prisons, 1777*, London 1929 ed; for conditions for women prisoners, see Russell P Dobash, R Emerson Dobash and Sue Gutteridge, *The Imprisonment of Women*, Oxford 1986, chs 1, 2 & 3. Note that Elizabeth Hope (*Glatton*) was atypical, being sentenced to transportation at Bristol QS in July 1798 and arriving in New South Wales in March 1803; aged 40 she was 'on orders' for transportation in April 1799, April 1800, April 1801 and April 1802; Bristol RO. For 'sufferings in the gaol', see Petition of Frances Sivier and fellow-prisoners in Horse Monger Lane Gaol, 14 Oct 1826, to Robert Peel, *PC* 1:67, PRO 945 1826 'for serving us stinking meat . . . for inhumanity to Prisoners, by Committing them to the Dark Cell for 3 days for trifling offences'. The notation from Downing Street reads: 'Are there not visiting magistrates for Horse Monger Lane? *If there are* tell this man to make his complaint to them'. For a similar case in Ireland, see Petition from 'We the Poor Prisoners of Trim Geail' [*sic*], OP. 488/31 SPO (Dublin).

18 For sources of Surgeons' Journals, see Guide to Convict Records in AONSW (No 14, 1981) p 294ff.

19 Report on the State of Mendicity in the Metropolis, 1814-15, House of Commons III.

20 Elizabeth Hurley claimed at her trial that she had 'served her

apprenticeship with Mr Salter in the Parish of Ide in this County, since which she hath done no act whatever whereby to gain a settlement', Devon RO; in the 1805 annotated edition of Adam Smith, *The Wealth of Nations*, the editor commented 'there is scarce a poor man in England of forty years of age... who has not in some part of his life felt himself most cruelly oppressed by this ill-contrived law of settlement'; see George, *London Life...*, p 155ff, who argues that 'the vagrancy laws encouraged a perpetual travelling and their effect was probably rather to bring people to London than to remove them from it'. It was possible that women and men convicted as vagrants, or 'sleeping abroad in the open air', would first be punished by imprisonment or whipping and then given a vagrant's pass, and taken by cart from parish to parish under the guard of the local constables until he or she reached his or her own parish. The aim of the vagrancy laws was to remove the cost of beggars and vagrants and persons without settlement from all parishes except their own. For the Lee family, see Winchester Bridewell, 2 Jan 1797, Hampshire RO; Sarah Donnelly (*Mary Ann*), 24, committed to Gosport Bridewell, 23 Mar 1789, brought back to Winchester Bridewell, 4 Apr 1789, for 'returning back to Gosport after she had been legally passed to the parish of Whiteparish, Wiltshire, that being her direct road for Ireland', Winchester RO.

21 Lucy Vaughan, born in the parish of Alderbury, Shrewsbury RO; data from Lois Carrington; see also Ann Moulds (*Lord Melville*), 'incorrigible vagrant', a convict in Lincoln Castle, Ships' Musters 2/8267, reel 2424, piece no 179; see also *Report on the Laws relating to Vagrants*, 1821, IV, H of C.

22 William Smith, 1776, cited in Porter *English Society...*, p 155; 'Extortion, prostitution and drunkenness were routine. Many rotted and died in the feculent conditions – gaol fever took more victims than did justice', ibid.

23 Petition of Robert Harris to Lord Sidmouth, 26 Nov 1819. Harris sentenced to life transportation, Elizabeth to 7 years; Dumfries, Scotland *PC* 1:67 PRO, 1819. See also Petition of Helen Guild, Calton Gaol, Edinburgh, *PC* 1:78 PRO951, 1830, requesting 'with the deepest humility' that 'we be sent abroad to some place as near each other as we can with propriety be sent... you can easily conceive... what pangs the feelings of a wife must suffer, to be torn from an affectionate husband to whom she has been united for nearly Six years'. (Her husband was in the hulks awaiting transportation for the same crime.)

24 Report to Surgeon Arnold of the *Northampton*, June 1815, 4/1732, reel 2160, p 172 AONSW.

25 Under-Secretary Goulburn to Macquarie, 26 Sep 1812, *HRA*, VII, pp 520-1.

26 For one of the few examples, see letter from Henry Hobhouse to Lord Sidmouth, May 1818, re letter from Mr Phippard asking if his wife Eliza Phippard (*William Pitt*) 'is alive and if she is married... a Muster Book lately received from the Colony does not have her listed... Application is to be made to the Governor of New South Wales to see if she is now living'. She had been transported for 7 years in 1805. *PC* 1:67 PRO936 1819.

27 There has been little research into the fate of the children left behind when a parent was transported. One attempt to investigate the problems of juvenile crime is Portia Robinson, 'The desolate boys of Dublin City: juvenile crime and punishment Ireland and New South Wales' in *Ireland and Irish-Australia: Studies in Cultural and Political History*, Oliver Macdonagh and W F Mandle (eds), London 1986. See also list of prisoners delivered from Lancaster Gaol to Deptford for *Lord Melville*: five of the women were accompanied by one child; 2/8267, reel 2422, piece no 149, AONSW. Women who petitioned for their children to accompany them included typical cases such as: Mary Dyel (*Janus*), a 'poor soldier's widow in Nottingham Gaol... unsupported and unprotected mother of 4 small children... guilty of receiving stolen goods... he was killed at Poites [sic] serving with the 45th Reg of Foot... begs [something to be done] to prevent me being torn from my dear children'. The petition of this 31-year-old dressmaker and upholsterer was partly accepted, two of the children accompanied her; *PC* 1, reel 938, piece no 1/67, 15 June 1819. Elizabeth Brooks (*Lord Wellington*) petitioned from Newgate Gaol for her children to accompany her for they would be 'without a friend in the world if deprived of her protection... distress drove her to commit her crime'. There is no record that the children accompanied her; *PC* 1, reel 939/9, piece no 1/67, 25 Jan 1819. There were other women who tried to have their children sent to them after they had been transported: Elizabeth Bellingham (*Midas*) asked that the government send 'Sophia 15 and Harriet 13 who are living at John Peninton's House 25 Dean St Felton Lane London and Robert, 10 and Kezia 4 who are living with their grandmother Hester Allcott in Worcestershire'. The Superintendent of Police to whom she was assigned supported the application: she is 'a woman of good character and conduct and of industrious habits that will enable her to maintain her family without expense to Government'; *CSIL* 4/1112/1, reel 697, AONSW, 13 Feb 1827. A few women returned to England to find their children: Mary Reynolds (*Maria*) petitioned the Secretary of State, she had 'come to England to seek her children of whom she had heard nothing during her absence. She now wishes to return to Sydney with a child aged 11 and wants help to obtain a position of servant to work

her passage. She is 38 years old and in perfect health – and does not suffer from seasickness'; *PC* 1:75, PRO945, 15 May 1826, Mary Reynolds/ Leburn, Liverpool.

28 Petition on behalf of Elizabeth Williams (*Providence*) from W P Brownell, Assistant Overseer of Aston near Birmingham, 2 June 1821, *PC* 1:69, PRO940, 1821.

29 See petition of Thomas Jones, Fish St, Worcester, 17 July 1826, on behalf of his wife, Mary Jones, sentenced for stealing handkerchiefs, 11 Apr 1825: petition signed by the Viscount Derhurst, 4 aldermen, 2 clergymen, one Proctor and several respectable gentlemen, 'all of whom well know that my wife is not of a wicked and depraved disposition ... considering my wretched condition being left with 4 children the eldest 10 ... my wife sailed for New South Wales in July 1825 ... that having received 2 letters from her ... wherein ... after stating her distress of mind and motherly feelings for her Dear Infant Children she sincerely craves that an application may be made to the Government for myself and children to go to her ...' The husband was in error as to the dates: Mary Jones arrived on the *Midas*; the petition was refused. 'It was not in Mr Peel's power to comply with this request', although the Visiting Magistrate and Clergymen testified that 'she has obtained a very comfortable situation in the family of Mr (I think Judge) Stephens and she tells him [her husband] that as Tailors are much wanted there he might ... be allowed to go with his children ...'; *PC* 1:75 PRO945, 1825.

30 Notices in the *Hue and Cry and Police Gazette* (London) frequently identified 'wanted' men and women by their speech; see 28 Feb 1808.

31 *Lancet* 1835, based on London Bills of Mortality; see M C Buer, *Health, Wealth and Population in the Early Days of the Industrial Revolution*, London 1968, pp 30ff.

32 Ibid, ch X, 'The Hospital and Dispensary Movement', pp 126ff.

33 See L L Robson, *The Convict Settlers of Australia*, Melbourne 1965, Appendixes; an analysis of age at time of trial supports this; see Ships' Indents.

CHAPTER 2: 'THE INCREASING DEPRAVITY OF THE AGE'

Individual reference is not given for all data from Settlers or Population, Land and Stock Musters, the 1828 Census of New South Wales and Parish Registers. Sources used were: *Musters:* 1800, 1806, 1811, 1814, 1819, 1820, 1822, 1825 (ML). These were checked, compiled and computed by Portia Robinson and research staff working on Dr Robinson's

Macquarie University and Australian Research Grants Scheme Projects, 1979–87 and by staff and volunteers for the Women of Botany Bay Bicentennial Project (1985–88). *The Census of New South Wales 1828*: Return of the Population of New South Wales according to a Census taken in November 1828, Home Office Papers 10/21-8 and Householders' returns, boxes 47/1238-41, AONSW. This was computed from this source by Anthony Sherrard for Dr Robinson's ARGS Projects (financed by the Federal Government) at Macquarie University Computing Centre commencing January 1981.

I acknowledge with gratitude the initial advice and assistance in the use of the 1828 Census for historical evidence by Dr Jim Waldersee, formerly of the University of Sydney, given to me during my first years as a PhD candidate at the University of Sydney (1978–79) researching *The Hatch and Brood of Time*.

I thank all the men and women who voluntarily assisted with copying, checking and collating Musters and relevant papers and documents for the Women of Botany Bay Project. Among these were: Chris Champion, Wendy Cowley, Betty Ellis, Anne Jarrett, Martin Killian, Mary McAlister, Jean McArthur, Perry McIntyre, Corelli Madden, Pat Mooney, Gwen Noble, Dot Pedersen, Pam Quick, Joy Rainer, Ron Robinson, Joyce and Betty Shaw, and Jill Warren.

1   For scholarly accounts of transportation to the North American Colonies in the 18th century see A G L Shaw, *Convicts and the Colonies*, London 1966, ch 1, and Alan Frost, *Convicts and Empire*, Melbourne 1980, ch 1. In 1717, 4 Geo I c 11; 1719: 6 Geo I c 23; 1743: 16 Geo II c 15 made transportation the punishment for 'robbery, larceny, receiving, burglary and destruction of property'. Shaw concludes that, by the early 1770s, about 1000 convicts a year were transported to North America, most going to Virginia and Maryland; Colquhoun believed that convicts were preferred as labour because 'they generally were more adroit and had better abilities' than the voluntary migrants to America (1797), ibid, p 299.

2   See Ged Martin, 'A London Newspaper on the Founding of Botany Bay. August 1786–May 1787', *JRAHS* 61, 1975, pp 73-90.

3   For a report of petition sent to Lord Sydney by the prisoners on board the hulk *Ceres* awaiting transportation to Botany Bay, see the *Public Advertiser* (London), 31 Oct 1788, Burney Papers, vol 859, BM: 'these prisoners entreated His Lordship's attention to the nature of their respective sentences, and the probability of their not surviving this winter on board the Prison ship ... and prayed the indulgence of being sent to Canada with the first fleet that sails, by which their lives might be preserved ... and their persons sold or disposed of, as His Majesty may see fit, in the new settlements

Notes (Chapter 2)

under Lord Durham'. See also ibid, 25 Aug 1788: '20 convicts removed from Newgate to Woolwich and put on board the hulks there, where they are to remain till the ships are ready to carry them over to Botany Bay'. This indicates an official intention of continuing transportation to Botany Bay.

4 Lord Sydney to the Commissioners of the Treasury, Whitehall, 18 Aug 1786, *HRNSW* 1, pt 2, pp 14-19; for modern interpretations of the significance of this document see Frost, *Convicts and Empire...*, pp 128ff: 'Nepean framed the "Heads" alert alike to satisfy the British public's sense of humanity, and Pitt's rather conflicting desire to increase the nation's strategic capacity in the East and at the same time restrain expenditure'; also C M H Clark, *A History...*, vol 1, ch 4; Ged Martin, 'Economic motives behind the founding of Botany Bay', *AEHR* 16, 1976, pp 128-43.

5 Inquiry into the feasibility of building penitentiaries at home as an alternative to transportation, from the Lord Lieutenant of Ireland to the County Grand Juries, OP, SPO (Dublin); see also 'Report of a Committee of the House of Commons on the problems of transportation', *Journals of the H of C*, vol xl, pp 1161-4. For the first Irish transports to sail from Cork to New South Wales, see Con Costello, *Botany Bay: The Story of the Convicts Transported from Ireland to Australia, 1791-1853*, Dublin 1987. See also letter from George Hamilton to Mr Secretary Hobart for the information of His Excellency acquainting him (under instructions) of his opinion respecting Penitentiary Houses, 20 May 1790, PP&C 91, 17/4, SPO (Dublin).

6 *Public Advertiser* (London), 6 Jan 1784, 23 Mar 1784; see also 27 Nov 1788, 'a young man from the country decoyed into a house in Blackboy Alley near West Smithfield, by 2 women who, having robbed him of a few shillings, he insisted on the money being restored; whereupon a man and a women came into the room, and after violently beating the complainant, dragged him out of the house, and then, assisted by the woman first mentioned, robbed him of a bundle containing shirts, neckcloths, handkerchiefs'; the attackers were later apprehended, the bundle found and returned to the lad, the women sent to the Bridewell, the man to the New Prison. For 'the labouring Man' and similar cases, see *Public Advertiser*, 23 Mar 1784, in Duncan Sprott, *1784*, London 1984, pp 72, 117.

7 Sarah Saunders described in the HO Criminal register PRO2732: 'a fair complexion, brown hair, grey eyes, born Spitalfields, London'; Mary Marshall, case reported in the *Freeman's Journal* (Dublin), 16 Nov 1802, tried before the Recorder of Dublin, sentenced to transportation, no record of arrival as Mary Marshall; Ann Daly (*Marquis Cornwallis*) who attacked Mrs Ormsby in Coles Lane,

Dublin, was seen by Rose Molloy who said that Mrs Ormsby did not immediately complain that she had lost her money but 'appeared very much agitated from the abuse she received from the prisoner'. The money belonged to her husband; 26 June 1794.

8 *Public Advertiser*, 17 May 1788, BM.

9 See Introduction, *The Newgate Calendar*, Sir Norman Birkett (ed), London 1957; note that the editors of the original, *The Malefactors' Register or New Newgate and Tyburn Calendar* (from which cases were selected by Sir Norman) held the firm opinion that 'It is to the low and abandoned women that hundreds of young fellows owe their destruction. They rob, they plunder, to support these wretches. Let it seem cruel that we make one remark ... The execution of *ten* women would do more public service than that of an *hundred* men; for exclusive of the force of example, it would perhaps tend to the preservation of more than an hundred'. The contemporary editors are also referred to 'the encreasing [sic] depravity in the manners of the age'.

10 John Delaney, Bourgeois Bodies/Dead Criminals, England c 1750s–1830s, unpublished paper given to History Seminar, RSSS, ANU (Canberra), 1987, cites the case of Jeremiah Aversham (1795) executed with a flower in his mouth: 'He was afterwards hung in chains on Wimbledon common, and for several months [it was reported], thousands of the London populace passed their Sundays near the spot as if consecrated by the remains of a hero'. Delaney argues that 'for centuries [the body] was the visible target of punishment. The floggings, the brandings, the pillory and executions all revealed the body in degrading circumstances'. See also Dobash, *The Imprisonment of Women ...*, p 23, for whipping of 'idle and lewd women'; for physical and symbolic punishments of women in pre-industrial society, see ibid, pp 16-20; see also contemporary accounts of executions: John Orr of Carrickfergus on his way to execution for the murder of his wife 'conducted himself with that deportment becoming his unhappy situation; and solemnly declared to the Sheriff, previous to mounting the ladder, that he was innocent of the crime for which he was to suffer. He was then launched into eternity and his body was afterwards quartered' (21 Aug 1788). Such mutilations of the body were not confined to legal authorities; E P Thompson in 'The Crime of Anonymity' in D Hay et al, *Albion's Fatal Tree*, Penguin 1975, pp 300-1, cites threats in anonymous letters addressed to 'farmers, dealers' and others in the late 18th and early 19th century: Bideford 1812: 'Your Cakase if any should be found will be given to the Dogs ...'; to a Bideford miller in 1802: 'The Devil will grind your Head to a powder as the mill grinds Corn'; Dumfries 1771: to dealers and others, threats to 'having their

316 *Notes (Chapter 2)*

Houses burnt to the Ground, punished in their Persons in Proportion to the Office they bear, viz. if a Magistrat [*sic*] with Mutilation, and if a Tradesman to have his Ears cut off at the Cross'; Bridgenoth 1801: 'to farmers and millers ... we will cut off their Ears and slit their Noses as a mark that the country will know them'.

11 Patrick Colquhoun, *A Treatise on the Police of the Metropolis*, London 1800 ed, pp 24-5; note that Colquhoun also argued 'Indigence, in the present state of Society, may be considered as a principal cause of the increase in Crimes ... It is in the progress to the adult state, that the infants of parents broken down by misfortunes, almost unavoidably learn, from the pressure of extreme poverty, to resort to devices which early corrupt their morals'. Note that there are no reliable figures for criminal convictions before 1805 when the Home Secretary's Department prepared returns of charges, committals and convictions. In that year, out of a total population of England of 8 331 434, 4527 were tried at the Old Bailey and Assizes; of these 1310 were women. Patrick Colquhoun, *A Treatise on Indigence*, London 1806, p 45. Figures which showed an increase in the number of committals in London, Westminster and the county of Middlesex were compiled in 1812 by Parliamentary Secretary Ryder: 1806: 899, 1807: 1017, 1808: 1110, 1809: 1242, 1810: 1207; *PD* 1/xxi/241, 21 Jan 1812.

12 Elizabeth Fry, a Quaker, was involved in 'benevolent visiting as a means of bringing the message of salvation to the poor', see Dobash, *The Imprisonment of Women* ..., p 41ff; for life and work of Elizabeth Fry see *A Memoir of the Life of Elizabeth Fry with Extracts from her Journal and Letters*, K Fry and E Cresswell (eds), 2 vols, London 1847; Report of the Society for the Reform of Prison Discipline (London), Third Report 1821; Sydney Smith 'Prisons', *Edinburgh Review* 1822; Elizabeth Fry, *Observations on the Siting, Superintendence and Government, of Female Prisoners*, London 1827; F K Procjaska, *Women and Philanthropy in Nineteenth Century England*, Oxford 1980.

13 Third Report, The Society for the Improvement of Prison Discipline ...

14 The Act by which convicts could be transported to New South Wales was 24 Geo III c 56; this amalgamated the various statutes concerned with the transportation of offenders, allowed for the continuance of the hulks as places of detention for those awaiting transportation, revived transportation (the Act of 19 Geo II c 74, for the Temporary Reception of Criminals under Sentence of Transportation needed renewal) and allowed for the King in Council to fix the place of transportation. See Frost, *Convicts and Empire* ... ,

Notes (Chapter 2) **317**

pp 15ff; for crimes denoted Felonies punishable by Deprivation of Life (which could be commuted to transportation) and crimes denoted Single Felonies punishable by Transportation, Whipping, etc., see Colquhoun, *A Treatise* ... pp 436-43. A copy of this may be found in *Contemporary Sources and Opinions in Modern British History*, L Evans and P J Pledger (eds), vol 2, Melbourne 1967, pp 98-103.

15 F X Bruxton, *PD* 1/xxxix/8080180, 2 Mar 1819, H of C.

16 Catherine Rourke, *Freeman's Journal*, 25 Aug 1792: aged 20; *Sydney Gazette*, 15 May 1803: 'Rev James Dixon officiated at the wedding of Henry Simpson and Catherine Rourke'; Simpson was a shipwright, Rourke 'a widow of the Rocks', Dixon 'of the Council of Rome'; Mary Rooney, *Freeman's Journal*, 20 Jan 1812: aged 30, tried Dublin; 1814: wife to Moses Brennan (*Ann*) F, off stores, labourer; 1822: Mary Brennan FS, wife to M Brennan, Appin; 1828: Mary Brennan with husband Moses Brennan CP, settler Appin, 50 acres (35 cleared, 30 cultivated), 5 horses, 36 horned cattle; both Catholics, married at St Phillip's 31 Aug 1813. Jane Fletcher (*Experiment*) also murdered her bastard child and was sentenced to death at Hereford Assizes, 15 Mar 1803; she was more fortunate than Martha Davis and Charlotte Roberts who were 'hanged on Monday 12 April 1802 and let their bodies be delivered to Mr Godfrey Lowe of the City of Bristol, Surgeon, to be dissected and anatomised'. Martha Davis, a widow, was 20, Charlotte Roberts, spinster, 23, both 'convicted of the murder of Richard Davis aged 15 months', Bristol RO. There was compassion at the Cambridge QS for Mary Ann Pritch 'Arraigned on the coroner's inquest for the wilful murder of her new born baby (bastard). The body was found under a mattress, a scarf around the neck, so loose it could not have caused death by choking. The Prisoner was greatly affected, she had only been in the employ of the Duke of Grafton for seven weeks'. Acquitted of murder she was imprisoned 12 months for concealing the truth.

17 Sir James Mackintosh, *PD* 1/xxxix/777-92, 2 Mar 1819, H of C.

18 Robert Peel, *PD* 2/xiv/1220, 9 Mar 1826, H of C; note that excerpts from *PD*, etc., relating to nineteenth-century crime and punishment may be found in *Contemporary Sources and Opinions* ..., vol 2, Evans and Pledger (eds), pp 86-123.

19 Robson, *The Convict Settlers* ..., Appendix 6 (male convicts), Appendix 8 (female convicts).

20 Robert Peel, House of Commons Debates on Consolidated Bills, *PD* 3/xi/952, 27 Mar 1832, H of C.

21 Jeremy Bentham, 'Principles of the Penal Law' in *The Works of Jeremy Bentham*, John Bowing (ed), Edinburgh 1843, vol 1, p 450. Cesare Beccaria, noted penal scientist of the late 18th century, also

argued that: 'If an equal punishment be ordained for two crimes that injure society in different degrees, there is nothing to deter men from committing the greater ... a punishment to be just should not only have that degree of severity which is sufficient to deter others ... Perpetual slavery ... has in it all that is necessary to deter the most hardened and determined'. Cesare Beccaria, *Del Delitti e delle Pene*, 1794, English edition with commentary by Voltaire, 1801.

22 Sophia Brannigan (*Experiment*), *Freeman's Journal*, 13 Aug 1799, at Down Assizes, sentenced 'to be burned in the hand' for stealing wearing apparel; sentenced again at Down Assizes in Mar 1807; in 1814 she was living in Liverpool (NSW), a free woman, off stores, wife to Joseph Davis; Ann/Mary Reed (*Nile*), convicted of felony in 1796: 'let her be burnt in the hand'; this was done Hertford GD, 28 July 1800; Elizabeth Williams (*Sydney Cove*) had been privately whipped; she was 21, a singlewoman from Hollywell in the county of Flint (Wales), convicted at Chester, her behaviour 'bad in prison', she was taken to Portsmouth by the constable and supplied with 'the necessaries' stipulated by the Secretary of State: '2 midgowns, 1 on, 1 off, 4 petticoats, 2 on, 2 off, 4 shifts, 1 on, 3 off, 5 handkerchiefs, 1 on, 4 off, 2 aprons, 1 on, 1 off, 4 caps, 1 on, 3 off, 4 pair of stockings, 1 on, 3 off, 1 yellow wool hat, 2 pairs of shoes, 1 on, 1 off'. Did this new wardrobe in any way compensate for her whipping? Chester RO. Sarah Baxter (*Experiment*), a native of America, had also been whipped and imprisoned for a previous offence; aged 33, singlewoman, she 'behaved well in prison' and was delivered to the hulks at Portsmouth with 4 male prisoners and supplied with '2 spare shifts, 2 spare handkerchiefs, 2 spare pair of stockings and 1 pair of shoes'; listed as alias Susannah Brickell. Chester RO.

23 Penelope or Penwell Mackenzie: Judgement of the Lord Armadale, 'requiring the Magistrates of Aberdeen and Keepers of their Tolbooth to see this Sentence put into Execution as they shall be answerable at their highest peril'. Her crime was 'feloniously stealing and Feloniously carrying away from the Shop of James Gordon Merchant in the Gallow gate of Aberdeen an entire piece of calico', and thefts of a similar nature from stalls at the Market Cross of Aberdeen and other places: JC 11/47, Scottish Record Office, Edinburgh.

24 Petition of Margaret Dunn to the Lord Lieutenant of Ireland, PP&C, Petition 4008, 15 Jan 1812, SPO (Dublin).

25 Petition of the two Mary Lalors to the Lord Lieutenant of Ireland, 21 & 22 Apr 1801, PP&C no 706, SPO (Dublin): for full account, see Portia Robinson, 'Convict colleens', *Good Weekend*, *SMH*, 17 Mar 1983. There were, of course, executions which did not arouse pity

from officials or the public: The *Public Advertiser* reported the execution of Doreen Kelly, a brothel-keeper 'in the vaults of whose whore-house in Copper Alley (London) five bodies of murdered gentlemen were found ... She was burned almost alive among the groans and ecercrations of the people', 27 Aug 1788; the same edition reported the trial of a woman for assisting in a rape in the County of Roscommon (Ireland) 'who went to bed to a young lady, at a house where they were both visitors together, and held the lady down while the brother of the former perpetrated the crime'; both escaped death 'through the extreme delicacy of the prosecutrix' – she married the brother. The witch of Leeds was not so fortunate: 'Mary Bateman, the reputed witch of Leeds, was tried on Friday the 17th March last before Mr Justice Lawrence and Mr Justice LeBlanc for the wilful murder of Mary Perigo of Gramby near Leeds by poison, as mentioned in a former *Hue and Cry*. Guilty, to be executed and her body to the surgeons.' *Hue and Cry and Police Gazette* (London), 1 Apr 1809, BM.

26 Petition of Bridget Hennegan to His Grace the Duke of Richmond, Lord Lieutenant of Ireland, 20 Apr 1809, PP&C, SPO (Dublin), Petition 1235. Ribbonism: secret organisation developing from the Whiteboy movement; 'men assembled by night with white shirts over their clothes', in the early 1800s they called themselves 'Thrashers'; 'Ribbonmen tended to become the generic term for the secret-society phenomenon' in nineteenth-century Ireland, as 'Whiteboys had done in the eighteenth'; all were 'secret oathbound organizations of a rather primitive nature in which the swearing of an oath (often forcibly extracted) was an important part of the ritual ... their rough justice included ham-stringing of cattle ... levelling of houses ... burning of barns ... sending threatening letters ... even savage tortures inflicted on offenders against the code ... branding of flesh ... cutting off of small pieces of the ear', see Kee, *The Most Distressful Country* ... , p 25.

27 Mary Watkins (*Broxbornebury*) tried with her son Thomas, 24, for the 'wilful murder of John Gwilliam', reported at length in *Pugh's Hereford Chronicle*, 18 Mar 1811; Watkins, a flax spinner, was accused by her son in his Gallows Speech: '[he] had been initiated to the perpetration of crimes, and bred up in idleness, ignorance and dishonesty, by the wretched parent whose peculiar province it was to have taught him his duties to mankind, a sense of religion and morality of conduct'. Mary was respited and sentenced to transportation on the evidence of that son who repeatedly asserted her innocence of the actual murder.

28 Petition of Catherine Kit to HE the Marquis Cornwallis, Lord Lieutenant of Ireland, Jan 1799, PP&C, SPO (Dublin), petition 1799/172, written from the Bridewell of Cork.

Notes (Chapter 2)

29 I am indebted to Rebecca and Russell Dobash (Stirling University) for the following reference: Henry Mayhew and John Binney, *The Criminal Prisons of London and Scenes of Prison Life*, London 1862, pp 285-6.

30 John Howard, *The State of the Prisons*, London 1777, 1929 ed, p 217.

31 Revd F Archer, Inspector General of Prisons (Dublin), 'Observations relative to the adoption of Regulations proposed by Lord Sidmouth with respect to the Selection of Convicts for transportation', 11 Feb 1815, OP/439/5, SPO (Dublin). Note that the Revd Archer appears as both Foster and Forster in contemporary sources.

32 Petition of Elizabeth Boyle to the Lord Lieutenant of Ireland, from Londonderry, 24 Oct 1804, PP&C, SPO (Dublin) (from Stranorlar Parish Co Donegal, in Londonderry Gaol, sentenced to 7 years' transportation for robbery).

33 Journal of Surgeon Robert Harding, 'of my attendance on the Convicts here and at the Cove . . . ', 7 June 1805-14 Sep 1805, SPO (Dublin).

34 Sydney Smith, 'gaols are a place of punishment'; see Dobash, *The Imprisonment of Women . . .* p 38; see also Ernest Rhys (ed), *Selections from Sydney Smith*, London 1922; and N C Smith (ed), *Selected Letters of Sydney Smith*, Oxford, 1981.

35 Petition of Eliza Brown to the Lord Lieutenant of Ireland: 'now confined in His Majesty's Gaol at Phillipstown, King's County [Dun Laoghaire] . . . hopes yr Honour will . . . send her of to Bottaney Bay', 28 July 1820, PP&C, SPO (Dublin).

36 *Public Advertiser*, 15 June 1793, Burney Papers, vol 859, BM.

37 Plummer to Macquarie, 4 May 1809, *HRNSW* 7, p 120; for another contemporary opinion, see G B Worgan in a letter to his brother Richard sent from Sydney Cove, 12 June 1788: 'The greater part of the women convicts are a shocking abandoned set . . . in short they are a vile pack of Baggages continually violating all Laws and disobedient to all Orders', ML Ms p 19.

38 Phillip to Sydney, 12 Mar 1787, *HRNSW* 1, pt 2, pp 56-7; an unidentified source quotes Phillip as writing: 'If you do not do as I ask, for God's sake let the world know that I asked'. For one example of the ill-equipped First Fleet, see Phillip to Sydney, Santa Cruz, 5 June 1787, *HRNSW* 1, pt 2, pp 106-7, requesting ammunition, etc., for the garrison and clothing for the women 'to be sent out by the first ship'.

39 Phillip to Grenville, 17 July 1790, *HRNSW* 1, pt 2, p 361: 'Many of those helpless wretches who were sent out in the first ships are dead . . . The sending out of the disordered and helpless helps clear the gaols, and may the parishes from which they are sent'.

40 Elizabeth Hayward (*Lady Penrhyn*); see *Some Letters of the Rev*

Richard Johnson ..., pt 1; see also John Cobley, *Sydney Cove 1789-90*, vol 2, Sydney 1963, p 11.

41 Phillip to Grenville, 5 Nov 1791: 'convicts landed ... not so sickly as those brought out last year, the greatest part of them so emaciated so worn out by long confinement, or want of food, that it will be long before they recover their strength and which many of them will never recover.' *HRNSW* 1, pt 2, p 538.

42 Revd F Archer, 'Observations ...', SPO (Dublin).

43 Dorothy Handland, alias Gray (*Lady Penrhyn*), aged 82, 'an old clothes woman' or dealer, tried at the Old Bailey Sessions commencing 22 Feb 1786 and convicted of 'wilful and corrupt perjury in her evidence at the trial of William Till', *OBSP*, 1785-86, trial no 318, pp 487 & 489. Note that Robert Hughes in *The Fatal Shore*, p 73, erroneously claims: 'in a fit of befuddled despair, she was to hang herself from a gum tree at Sydney Cove, thus becoming Australia's first recorded suicide'. Romantic as this may sound, Dorothy Handland behaved so well in the colony that a subscription was taken up and she sailed for England on the *Kitty* in 1794; see Collins, *An Account* ..., p 244; Handland arrived at Cork on 5 Feb 1794 and was noted by the Navy Board; see J B Cleland, 'The Old Woman from Botany Bay', *JRAHS*, vol 43, pt 3, 1947, pp 137-9. For Mary Parker and Jane Shaw, 'invalids ... of tender constitution', see petition of High Sheriff of Devon from Exeter Gaol that they 'receive the consideration of Government', *PC* 1:67, PRO938, Feb 1819.

44 For Mrs Bartlett, see petition from James Whatman, surgeon, to Lord Sidmouth, 30 May 1819: 'Mrs Bartlett confined in HM prison Maidstone (Kent) is in ill-health – removal from it would tend materially to her recovery'; petition from her son S Bartlett, 30 May 1819, pleading to have his mother 'mitigated from prison she is so ill', *PC* 1:67, PRO938, 1819.

45 Elizabeth Birkett petitions: from Ludgate (prison surgeon), *PC* 1:67, PRO938, 3 May 1819; from Nottingham Police Office, 1 May 1819; from Sam White, Police Officer at Woolwich; from Mr Creagh (*Lord Wellington*) to Henry Hobhouse of the Navy Office, 19 October 1819.

46 Papers re 13 female convicts, *PC* 1:67, PRO938, 15 Sep 1819: Elizabeth Dunham (Middlesex), 'jury found her insane', Preston House of Correction re 'The Condemning of Old Women in the Gaol', Preston Lancashire, *PC* 1:67, PRO938, 30 Mar 1819, report from surgeon supported; aged from 56-76; 9 had previous convictions (Catherine Evans, 64, had 5 previous convictions; Mary Stambles, 73, 'had been transported before').

47 Grand Jury of the County of Warwick: 16 females 'sentenced 12 months ago and still confined ... This causes great inconvenience ... the average time females sentenced to transportation re-

322 *Notes (Chapters 2-3)*

main in the County Gaol is nearer twelve months', H Vemely, Foreman of the Grand Jury of the County of Warwick to Lord Sidmouth, 3 Apr 1819, *PC* 1:67, PRO938, 1817. Note that from time to time pleas for mitigation of sentence for transportation were made by women claiming to be 'subject to fits'. See petition of Mary Haigney in County Galway Gaol 'committed at a very young age for stealing clothes under the influence of her mother ... Pleads she is subject to fits of convulsions and prays pardon from sentence of 7 years transportation'. PP&C, 9 Nov 1818, SPO (Dublin).

48 See List A (Women Transported from England) and List B (Women Transported from Ireland) to compare date of trial with date of arrival in New South Wales.

49 Navy Office to Lord Sidmouth, 18 May 1819, *PC* 1:67, PRO938, 1819.

CHAPTER 3: 'THE REFUSE OF LONDON'

1 Walvin, *English Urban Life* ... , p 16; for detailed account of 'London Immigrants and Emigrants' see George, *London Life* ..., ch 3; note that seasonal migration to London included women who came to work in London's market gardens, walking from North Wales and Somerset and returning home on foot in the autumn, having earned five to seven shillings a week, ibid p 145; see also T Baird, *Report on the Agriculture of Middlesex*, 1793, p 21, and Sir Phillips, *A Morning's Walk from London to Kew*, 1817, p 225, ibid, pp 354-5: 'They consist for the most part of Shropshire and Welsh girls, who walk to London in droves at this season to perform this drudgery ... Their remuneration for this is unparalleled slavery ... For beauty, symmetry and complexion that are not inferior to the nymphs of Arcadia ... Their morals too are exemplary'.

2 For examples of Irish women tried at London/Middlesex, see 'List of Prisoners 28 April 1792 to 28 Sept 1793 in HM Gaol of Newgate', HO 26/56PRO2752. Typical examples from Old Bailey/Middlesex trials included: widows such as Mary Walker (*Midas*), a seamstress from Ireland with two children, and Margaret Varlow (*Midas*) with two children, whose husband 'fell at Waterloo'; she came from County Antrim and 'milks, makes butter and cheese'; married women such as Sophia Stephenson (*Mary*), a maid of all work from Armagh, 'child dead, bridge of nose broken', and Mary Quinion (*Mary*) from Tipperary, with three children, her husband in Ireland, she 'milks, makes butter and cheese', or Margaret Dwyne (*Midas*), a laundress from Cork whose husband was a labourer at Deptford (she 'suffered severe seasickness'); singlewomen such as Mary Blake (*Mary Anne*), servant from Cork who had 'lost three upper

teeth', or Maria Smith (*Midas*), laundrymaid from Dublin with an eighteen-month-old child (she suffered from epilepsy), or Frances Shannon (*Mary Anne*), dressmaker from Armagh, an eighteen-year-old with 'fair, pale complexion, brown hair and blue eyes'.

3 George, *London Life*..., pp 142-5; note William Blackstone, *Commentaries*, 1, p 127, cited in ibid p 354: 'The spirit of liberty is so deeply implanted in our constitution and rooted even in our very soil, that a slave or negro, the moment he lands in England, falls under the protection of the law and so far becomes a freeman, though the master's right to his services may possibly still continue'. Free or not, negroes, lascars and other coloured peoples were subject to the criminal law of England. I am indebted to Dr Ian Duffield of the University of Edinburgh for information on black men and women living in Britain in this period.

4 *Public Advertiser*, Burney Papers, vol 859, BM: 1 Nov 1788; John P Halliday and Mary Oakes, *Hue and Cry and Police Gazette*, 31 Jan 1801; *Public Advertiser*, Aug 1788.

5 Susannah, sentenced Middlesex Sessions commencing 16 Sep 1795, aged fifteen, sentenced to seven years, *OBSP*, 8 Dec 1794-Dec 1795, FM4/7160, roll 15, ML. Clara Ward arrived on the *Campbell Macquarie* on 7 Jan 1812; she had been convicted at Fort William, Bengal, and sentenced to seven years' transportation; all that is known about her is that she received a ticket-of-leave (no 521) and a certificate of freedom before her seven years were served; Sophie was 'a negress', a native of Madagascar, who had been sentenced to life transportation at Port Louis, Isle of France, in Sep 1823; she arrived on the *Ann*, 30 Jan 1825, at the age of twenty; a former servant, she was described as '5'¼", copper colour complexion, black hair and eyes, lips thick, nose broad, scar under right ear'; she received a conditional pardon (no 231) on 1 Feb 1845. See 'Chronological List of convicts from places other than the United Kingdom 1807-1826', pp 104-111, CO 207/1 PRO57.

6 Notice re Ann Harrison (*Indispensable*), 'escaped from Gloucester County Gaol on 28 Nov. She has a stealing conviction, native of Liverpool, 28-30 years of age, 5 feet 5 inches, corpulent, scar on her forehead, hazel eyes, dark brown hair, dark complexion'. *Hue and Cry and Police Gazette*, 26 Dec 1807; 'Reward for Ann Harrison, wen on her left thigh, speaks with a broad Lancashire dialect', ibid, 6 Feb 1808.

7 von Archenholtz, *Picture of England*, cited in George, *London Life*..., p 76.

8 Colquhoun, *A Treatise on the Police*..., pp 352-3; note that Colquhoun also estimated that, at the end of the 18th century in London, 'above twenty thousand miserable individuals of various

classes, who rise up every morning without knowing how... they are to be supported during the passing day, or where, in many instances they are to lodge on the succeeding night', ibid, p 33.

9   J M Beattie, 'The pattern of crime in England, 1600–1800', *Past and Present*, 62, 1974, pp 47-95; see also J M Beattie, 'The criminality of women in eighteenth century England', *Journal of Social History*, 72, 1975, pp 80-116.

10   Based on trial proceedings of women sentenced to death or transportation at London/Middlesex Sessions, 1785-1827, and Petitions in Mitigation of Sentence sent to the Secretary of State, Downing St London (Privy Council Papers mainly unbound). For example, petition of Elizabeth Brooks (*Lord Wellington*) from Newgate Gaol, 25 Jan 1815, requesting that her children be transported with her for they would be 'without a friend in the world if deprived of her protection... distress drove her to commit her crime which has brought her to this situation'. *PC* 1:67, PRO938/9.

11   *The Times*, 30 Sep 1808.

12   For the wives and children of transported men, see ch 7, 'A great and bitter grief'.

13   Elizabeth Surman, case cited in André Parreaux, *Daily Life in England in the Reign of George III*, transl Carola Congreve, London 1969.

14   Colquhoun, *A Treatise on the Police...*, p 324; see also Report on the State of Mendicity in the Metropolis, 1814-15, III and 1816, V (*Committees of the House of Commons printed by order of the House*); Colquhoun, *A Treatise on Indigence...*, 1806, p 281ff.

15   Ann Baker (*Indispensable*); for her 'victim', see *The Memoirs of James Hardy Vaux*, N McLachlan (ed), London 1964.

16   Note that, with no reliable criminal statistics before 1805, the public relied on newspaper reports for accounts of crimes as an indication of the incidence and nature of offences.

17   For contemporary account see Parreaux, *Daily Life...*; Willan, *Diseases in London...*; note that at the beginning of the 19th century 'the poor quarters of London are indicated by the places where typhus cases were to be expected', George, *London Life...*, p 94ff; Ann Barrington, charged with theft, said in defence, 'I lodge by myself. I have no fastenings to the door, it is sixpence a week, and under the straw and hay which I had to lay on these things were found', Jan 1787, ibid, p 101; Margaret King told the court, 'I was out all day at hard labour... I had been begging all that day'; she paid ninepence a week for 'lodging... in a sort of room where there was a sort of bed which she shared with a woman who carried chips to sell', ibid, p 100; see also Malcolm, *Anecdotes of the Manners and Customs of London*, 1808, pp 160ff, and George, *London*

Notes (Chapter 3) **325**

Life..., p 117: 'If any person is born with any defect or deformity or maimed by fire or other casualty, or any inveterate distemper which renders them miserable objects, their way is open to London, where they have free liberty of showing their nauseous sights to terrify people and force them to give money to get rid of them.'

18 For trial of Sarah Townsend, see *OBSP*, 10 Apr 1783; for Mrs Ward, see the *Public Advertiser*, 12 Aug 1788, Burney Papers, vol 859, BM; for servant assaulted and similar cases, see ibid.

19 Agnes Vallance (*Indispensable*) had two colonial-born children, Thomas (b 9 Mar 1797) and William (b 18 June 1799) Smith, father Thomas Smith; 24 Jan 1800, she received an Absolute Pardon 'In consequence of her good conduct and decent deportment... on the recommendation of Thomas Smyth and several officers of the Colony' 4/4486, p 5, reel 800.

20 See, for example, Letters from John Pearson and Family to Jane Murray and Family 1799-1826, RO York; also *Public Advertiser*, 9 Aug 1793, 'Several highway and footpad robberies have lately been committed on the road between Esher, Cobham and Surrey'.

21 Crimes by London/Middlesex women included prostitution, highway robbery, accosting in the street, coining and uttering and pickpocketing. See *OBSP* (ML) HOCR & M'sex GR (AONSW).

22 *The Times*, 22 Aug 1810: Elizabeth Hinchcliff (*Minstrel*), 'a girl of fourteen, committed for attempting to poison Ann Parker her mistress... The prisoner admitted to putting some arsenic into tea pots. She is reported to have said if her mistress died she would have all her clothes'. Another case of callous disregard for employers was that of Diana Lovell, 'charged with stealing [£58 in notes, 4 guineas in gold] from William Wilcocks in the parish of St John the Evangelist. She was nurse to his wife for four weeks when wife and infant died... She was searched in her lodgings at Peter Street Soho... Guilty'. *The Times*, 2 July 1812.

23 *Morning Herald*, 15 Apr 1828. I am indebted to John Delaney (RSSS, ANU) for this example and for sources and data on public executions in England.

24 *The Times*, 26 June 1788. Note that the following year there was a brief mention in *The Times* of 'six female convicts that preferred death to transportation to Botany Bay'. No account of their execution has been found. *Times*, 12 June 1789. In Dublin, 31 Aug 1795, the execution of Sarah Delany was reported (she had assisted a man in the rape of a twelve-year-old girl): 'Between 12 and 1 o'clock this unfortunate woman was called from her cell in the prison to meet her ignominious fate; a summons she obeyed with more fortitude than expected from her sex'. *The Times*, 31 Aug 1795.

25 Note that the *Daily Register* was renamed *The Times* in 1788; I am

indebted to John Delaney for this case.
26 *Morning Advertiser*, 18 Feb 1818.
27 Sydney Smith, cited in Dobash, *The Imprisonment of Women...*, p 38.
28 Elizabeth Anderson: *Sydney Gazette*, 2 Mar 1816, report of Coroner's Inquest at the Hawkesbury 'on the body of John Anderson who had been inhumanely murdered the night before'; his wife was committed to the county gaol, 22 June 1816; Macquarie's warrant, 18 July 1817; execution: *Sydney Gazette*, 20 July 1816. For the fear of dissection see Peter Lindebaugh, 'The Tyburn Riot Against the Surgeons', in *Albion's Fatal Tree...*, p 69ff; for an account of the ritual preceding execution, see ibid, p 67; note that neither 'the Crown (which granted the bodies of condemned felons to the Physicians and the Surgeons) nor the legislature (which strengthened the law by royal grants) regarded the dissection of felons from the standpoint of science... They were motivated by... the anticipation of dishonour to the "Scum of the People"', ibid, p 73. Women sentenced to death in Scotland also heard that 'after her execution [the Court] ordains her body to be delivered to Doctor... Lecturer on Anatomy... in the College of Aberdeen to be by him publicly dissected and anatomised in terms of the said Act'. This was the sentence passed on Helen Duncan, accused of murdering her husband James Reid at Aberdeen, 16 Apr 1816; found guilty by a 'plurality of voices she... was to be taken from the said Tolbooth [where she had been fed only on bread and water] to the common place of execution... once there to be hanged by the neck upon a Gibbet by the hands of the Common Executioner until she be dead... all her moveable goods and gear to be Escheat and Inbrought to His Majesty's use', Scottish Record Office (Edinburgh), JC 11/55. Helen Duncan/Reid was fortunate in having that sentence commuted. She arrived in New South Wales on the *Lord Melville*.

CHAPTER 4: 'THE GODS GO A-BEGGING'

1 J J Gurney, *Notes on a Visit to Some of the Prisons...*, London 1819, p 153; I am indebted to Rebecca and Russell Dobash (Stirling University) for references to women's prisons and places of confinement.
2 Based on trials of women sentenced to death or transportation, OB and Middlesex Sessions 1785-1827, HO Criminal Registers, ML; examples are numerous: Maria Tate, 30 (*Experiment*), uttering counterfeit money (had already spent a year in New Prison,

Clerkenwell for similar offence), 'I was very much intoxicated'; Eliza Pleasant, 25 (*Maria*), stealing watch and key from her lodging-house keeper, 'I was intoxicated'; note that Ann Lloyd, 37 (*Northampton*), had been a maidservant for six weeks, discharged for insobriety, she returned and stole household goods worth 43 shillings; see also *Public Advertiser*, 6 Aug 1783, report of 'woman charged with setting fire to an apartment' in St Giles: 'It appeared to be an accident on the part of the woman, she being very much intoxicated and having burnt a great part of her clothes'. Burney Papers, vol 859, BM.

3 Highwaywomen included Mary Murphy, 20 (*Friends*), guilty of the highway robbery of Jonathan Whittaker, 7 yrs; Ann Franklin, 21 (*Friends*), guilty of highway robbery of a watch worth £4 from James Escomba, 7 yrs; Susannah Brown (*Mary Ann*) convicted with Ann Guest and Ann Yardsley, 'felonious assault on John Fogg ... sentenced to death'; Fogg pleaded for mercy for his attackers: 'My Lord, I beg leave to observe that the blow that was made at me was more an act of wantonness than an act of cruelty, for it was not a straight forward blow, it was slanting'; Sarah Bailey, 43 (*Surprize*), assaulted Samuel Evan on the highway and took his watch, 7 yrs; Bridget Bays, 25 (*Wanstead*), guilty of highway robbery of a watch from John Mackin, death commuted to life transportation, charged with Martha Bailey, 24 – death, no record of reprieve; Eleanor Brown, 19 (*Experiment*), highway robbery with 2 male accomplices, of Elizabeth Moore, 'stole stockings out of her hand ... grabbed and held her by her hair', death but recommended for mercy 'because she only held the prosecutrix'; Elizabeth Cope, 20 (*Surprize*), highway robbery of Samuel Milson, '5' 4"', grey eyes brown hair fresh complexion, born London, singlewoman', death, commuted to transportation for life; Matilda Dyer, 33 (*Canada*), highway robbery of money from Benjamin Bird, tried with Ann Kennington, 37 (*Canada*), who 'sold fish for a living', sentenced to death, commuted to life transportation; Mary Hughes, 21 (*Kitty*), robbing James Mann of the highway, 7 yrs: 5' 4¼", hazel eyes, dark brown hair and fair complexion, born Bethnal Green; Elizabeth Powell, 27 (*Royal Admiral*), highway robbery on Cornelius Courtney, death commuted to transportation for life, 5' 3", dark hazel eyes, born Canterbury, singlewoman. *OBSP* and MGR.

4 See Porter, *English Society*..., p 104; for contemporary accounts, see Thomas Turner, *The Diary of a Georgian Shopkeeper*, R W Blencowe & M A Lower (eds), Oxford; L A Clarkson and E M Crawford, *Ways to Wealth, The Cust Family of Eighteenth Century Armagh*, Belfast 1985, p 67ff, 'An Inventory of the goods assets and

effects of the late Mrs Cust . . .' 1794, 'one black bonnett [sic] given to Jenny the maid'.

5 *Morning Herald*, 24 & 26 June 1793, Burney Papers, BM. Similar advertisements appeared in Irish newspapers: Sat, Feb 9 1799, the *Cork Advertiser or Commercial Register*: a cryptic notice inserted by a former employer warned: 'Any Person inclined to hire Elinor Hart . . . who lately lived with me as a servant will act prudently and consult me prior to engaging her'. NL (Dublin).

6 Elizabeth Fry to Samuel Buxton, in Samuel Buxton, *An Inquiry into Whether Crimes and Misery are Produced or Prevented by Our Present System of Prison Discipline*, London 1818, p 122; see also Dobash, *The Imprisonment of Women* . . ., ch 2, 'Penitentiaries for Women'; note Rev John Clay in *The Prison Chaplain: A Memoir of the Rev John Clay BD*, p 81, cited in ibid, p 42, described the visit of a group of American Quakers to Newgate Gaol in 1813; 'they were shocked and sickened . . . by the blaspheming, fighting, dram-drinking, half-naked women'.

7 Gurney, *Notes on a Visit* . . ., p 151, cited in Dobash, *The Imprisonment of Women* . . . pp 43-4; note that Gurney added that 'they were ignorant to the greatest degree, not only of religious truth, but of the most familiar duty and business of life'.

8 Among the women who were tried at London/Middlesex and transported to New South Wales on the *Nile* were: Ann Metcalf, singlewoman from Darlington, Yorkshire: 'guilty of stealing from her master, aged 27, 5′ 8″, fair complexion, red hair, grey eyes'; Susannah Williams, singlewoman from Rochester, Kent: 'guilty of stealing from her master, aged 20, 5′, dark complexion, brown hair, dark hazel eyes'; Mary Murphy/Welsh/Murray, 'wife of Lawrence' from Charlemont, Limerick: 'stealing from her master, aged 23, 5′ 2″, dark complexion, brown hair, grey eyes'; Elizabeth Giles, 'wife of William', from Watford, Hertfordshire: 'stealing several ounces of silk from her master, aged 42, 5′ 6″, fair complexion, brown hair, grey eyes'; Sarah Green, married woman from Manchester: 'stealing from her master, aged 23, 5′ 7″, fresh complexion, brown hair, dark eyes'.

9 Members of Mrs Fry's Ladies Association 'boasted that there had been radical changes in the habits and manners of the women: 'from drunkenness to sobriety, from riot to order, from clamour to quietness, from obscenity to decency'; Dobash, *The Imprisonment of Women* . . ., p 46ff for opinion of Lord Mayor of City of London, p 44ff for 'improvement'. For further discussion of treatment of prisoners see M Ignatieff, *A Just Measure of Pain: The Penitentiary in the Industrial Revolution 1750-1780*, London 1978.

10 See also unpublished MA thesis, Macquarie University: The Ladies

of the *Friendship*, by Janice Roberts, for an analysis of the colonial lives of these women and an assessment of the Surgeon's comments. Note that most were described as 'prostitutes' and few occupations given; there were servants (Mary Smith, 22), laundresses (Jane Barnes, 24), a mantua-maker (Emma Groom, 22), a former farmworker (Mary Sheen, 45), and other occupations.

11 A typical case of child stealing was that of Bridget Cosgrove (*Mary Ann*), who feloniously assaulted Elizabeth (Betsey) Bailey, 'a female infant child under the age of three years, putting her in fear' and taking from her her frock, value 2 shillings, pincloth, value 6d, and cap trimmed with lace, value 6d; the child's father, Thomas Bailey, was a flower-and-herb seller in Covent Garden; neighbours found Mrs Cosgrove in nearby Ruffle Court, undressing the little girl; they put her frock back on her and took the child to her father; Mrs Cosgrove was taken to Bow Street where the child's lace-edged cap was 'found in her bosom ... she was in liquor; she had come up from Dublin with her husband some six years ago. The trial judge asked her "What is to become of the three children you have?" She replied: "My husband took them to some work-house near Covent Garden. I do not know whether my husband has them or not" '. She was transported without her children. Among the child stealers who were sent to Botany Bay were: Mary Wilson (*Surprize*) 63, a London widow 'with light brown hair, grey eyes and fresh complexion'; Sarah Church (*Nile*), 23, a singlewoman from the parish of St Andrew, Holborn, 'for stealing and stripping a child of its apparal'; Ann Beaumont (*Speke*), 22, two previous offences for stealing children's clothes from their persons; Ann Riley (*Northampton*), 36, who pleaded intoxication when sentenced for stealing a hat and handkerchief from a child; Isabella Thompson (*Wanstead*), 34, transported for life for stealing a frock worth 2 shillings from the person of a young child; Jane Brown (*Sydney Cove*) 35, who pleaded innocence to the charge of stripping a child, saying she had 'seven children of my own'. Mary Ann Morey (*Britannia*), 19, 'stealing the clothes from John Thomas's young child'. Mary Cox (*Mary Ann*) wife of Matthew Cox took a child under 6 years from the door of her house at 8 pm. At bedtime, the mother could not find her and a search by neighbours was unsuccessful; the child came back by herself about 9 pm 'stripped of her frock, skirt, and the clasps out of her shoes ... she said a woman took her to Fleet Market and stripped her ... the clothes were later found at the pawnbroker's'.

12 Examples are numerous: Susannah Jones (*Mary Ann*) met Ann Puddiford who had just arrived in London from the country and wanted a lodging; she took her to Mary Carroll (*Mary Ann*) 'who she mistook for a decent woman and asked her for a lodging ... she

took her to Susannah Jones's room and she lost her gown'. Carroll admitted stealing the gown and pawning it after she had been drinking. Elizabeth 'Betsey' Clarke (*Sydney Cove*), 24, and Mary 'Polly' Weston (*Sydney Cove*), 22, were both transported for stealing from Johanna Witts, with whom they lodged; Mary Weston was a married woman, a bookbinder, with a husband 'at sea'; Frances Ebden (*Broxbornebury*), 40, pleaded 'my husband is on board the *Shannon* frigate. I meaned to replace them [the stolen articles] when I got my husband's money'. Elizabeth Evans (*Northampton*), 40, was sentenced to death, commuted to life transportation, for stealing goods and banknotes from fellow lodger William Mason; she 'did washing and needlework'. For conditions in lodging houses in London, see George, *London Life...*, p 94ff: 'a large proportion of the poorer classes in London lived in ready-furnished rooms, paying a weekly rent'; see also T A Murray, *Remarks on the Situation of the Poor in the Metropolis, 1801*, pp 5-6, ibid, p 340.

13 Other examples include: Elizabeth Waring, aged 43, sentenced to 14 yrs transportation (ship NR), whose 16-yr-old son was sentenced to death, Middlesex Sessions commencing 30 Nov 1796; Alice Rawlins, 57, and Abigail Rawlins, 15, both transported for 14 yrs on the *Experiment* (Abigail presumed to have died on the voyage) for receiving stolen goods from three young boys; Mary Linton and Ann East (*Mary Ann*) sentenced for burglary with their husbands; the men were hanged and the women transported. Mary Linton was assigned to James Sommervail (see List of Women Assigned 1798, SZ767, reel 766, pp 155-7 AONSW). Ann East became the 'wife' of John Owen (*Scarborough*) and mother of Sophia Charlotte Owen. Data from E. Cox.

14 Neighbours and shopkeepers, householders and their servants, were alert for 'suspicious characters'; Ann Rogers, 15, and Jane Jones, 17, were both sentenced to death, commuted to transportation (*Broxbornebury*). The beadle saw them with a fowl, looking suspicious; they were taken to the watch-house and searched – the till belonging to a publican was concealed under the girl's checked apron. The publican's maid testified that a window had been broken – the two had climbed on the mews dunghill to get through the window at 7 am. Mary Sullivan (*Broxbornebury*) went into a haberdasher's shop with 2 other women and behaved 'very impatient' – the owner suspected the 3 were companions and turned around and 'saw the prisoner looking very confused'; she laid hold of her apron and found a piece of ribbon – Mary Sullivan said it must have fallen in by accident, but a neighbour testified 'they were very suspicious characters; she was 18 years old. Mary Jones (*Broxbornebury*) went alone to a linen-draper in Covent Gar-

den and, after being served by the shop's boy, left 'walking in a singular manner'. She was brought back, dropped 21 yards of printed calico at the door, and was apprehended and convicted. Note that pickpockets were rarely executed; some worked in pairs; Ann Arnett (*Broxbornebury*), 30, waited at the corner of Haymarket while James Smith, 64, was picking pockets; he gave the handkerchiefs to her 'and she went off and he continued to pick pockets'. She was picked up and searched at the Opera House, and Smith, a known pickpocket, was also caught and transported. There are numerous examples of pickpocketing by prostitutes, although few admitted that they were 'on the town'. An exception was Harriet Haynes (*Sydney Cove*), sentenced to 7 yrs' transportation at the age of 18 for 'stealing money from John Cullen by pickpocketing ... she said she was a prostitute'.

15 Colquhoun, *A Treatise on the Police...*; Beattie, 'The Pattern of Crime...', argues that 'Colquhoun's guess that no more than a tenth of the crimes committed in London at the end of the eighteenth century were eventually indicted is not implausible', p 54, and Colquhoun p 223; see also Manning Clark, *A History...*, vol 1, p 95: 'It has been estimated that in London at the end of the eighteenth century one hundred and fifteen thousand depended on crime for a living'; also Colquhoun, pp 88-90 & 158-9, cited in ibid. David Phillips, *Crime and Authority in Victorian England*, London 1977, pp 208-10, notes the reluctance of some 'victims' of prostitutes to prosecute the following day. Letitia Baker was not so fortunate. She was convicted in 1797 of stealing a tin box from the pocket of the man with whom she was 'going home'. *OBSP*, 30 Nov 1796.

16 William Noah, *Voyage to Sydney in the Ship Hillsborough 1796 and Description of the Colony*, ML Ms (also published Sydney 1978).

17 Other examples include: Eliza Cammell (*Providence*) stole banknotes from seaman William Hughes after allowing him to rest in her room when he became unwell; Matilda Ogle stole money from Charles Mabbely, a Frenchman, she put the money in her mouth when discovered, but later said that she could not have swallowed it because 'I have been lock-jawed these three months'; Sarah Goodwin (*Indispensable*) stole a silver watch, a steel watch chain, a base metal watch key, a pair of men's silk stockings and one shilling and six halfpence from Peter Daley while he was asleep. See *OBSP* (ML) HOCR & MGR (AONSW).

18 For Mrs Fry, see Dobash, *The Imprisonment of Women...*, pp 44-5.

19 Margaret Buckie (*Speedy*), 40, married woman from Birmingham, had been pardoned in 1797 (stealing spoons) 'to look after her family'; in 1798 she was sentenced for stealing wearing apparel. Most

women who were transported for coining, uttering or counterfeiting had previous convictions; Margaret Harrington (*Canada*), 45, 'also known as Peggy Sullivan and said to have a child', had been convicted the previous year of 'being utterer of false counterfeit money' and imprisoned for 1 year; Bridget Joyce (*Wanstead*), 56, had been previously tried and convicted for passing counterfeit money at a rate higher than it looked, ie 2 shillings for 1 shilling.

20 Other cases included: Sarah Draper/Ingram alias Ann Watson (*Britannia*), 7 yrs for stealing a watch, banknotes, etc: 'I have 2 fatherless children to maintain'; Sarah Ward (*Mary Anne*) pleaded, 'I am a servant out of a place; they [man and wife accused with her] had the nursing of my child. I had been in the country and returned that night and slept there that night'. The two accomplices (aged 59) were sentenced to death; Sarah Ward recommended mercy.

21 Petitions (3) to Lord Sidmouth on behalf of Ann Levitt, prisoner confined in Newgate Gaol: 'She had borne an excellent character and has behaved remarkably well since her confinement. She is in my mind a proper object for Royal mercy. She has lived with Mr Turney as cook as well as in several reputable families, and could immediately get employment. She is at present in a bad state of health owing to confinement and anxiety of mind'; also from former employers: 'Request that charitable assistance and kindness be shown Ann Levitt', 29 & 30 May 1821, *PC* 1:69, PRO940.

22 Other women sentenced to death for returning from transportation included: Mary Talbot (*Mary Ann*), evidence was given at her trial in February 1790: 'I know the prisoner, she was convicted in the February Sessions 1788 and sentenced to transportation'. She replied, 'I beg for mercy, having a young child almost starved which suckled at my breast when I was on board. I had little or no provision'. She was 'humbly recommended to mercy by the jury'; she also claimed to be with child and, after sentence of death was passed upon her 'a Jury of Matrons were sworn, who returned a verdict that she was with quick-child, upon which execution of her was stayed'. In 1800 Mary Ann Fielding (*Nile*) was tried for the same offence, her death sentence commuted to life transportation: '25 years old, 5' 3", fair complexion, brown hair, grey eyes, single-woman from Tottenham'.

CHAPTER 5: 'POOR PETITIONERS' OR 'NOTORIOUS OFFENDERS'?

Prisoners' Petitions and Cases are used extensively as evidence for the Irish women sentenced to transportation. Previous use of these records by Dr Robinson includes:

1982 Research in Dublin Castle, commencement of compilation/indexing (ARGS/MURG Projects).

1983 Paper to Ireland–Australia Kilkenny Conference (October, Ireland): Portia Robinson, on 'Colleen to Matilda, Irish convict women transported to New South Wales', subsequently published in *Australia and Ireland Bicentennial Essays*, Colm Kiernan (ed), Dublin 1986.

1984 'Convict Colleens', Portia Robinson in the *Good Weekend, SMH*, pp 1 & 2, 17 Mar 1984. 'Colleen to Matilda Display', public showing of the PP&C petitions at Macquarie University Open Day, 11 Aug 1984, opened by HE Joseph Small, Ambassador for Ireland. Keeper of State Papers brought from Dublin to Macquarie University by Dr Robinson to speak at the annual meeting of the Colleen to Matilda Society on the petitions and papers in the State Paper Office relating to Australia in the transportation period (17 Nov 1984). I gratefully acknowledge the interest of HE Dr P Hillery, President of Ireland; the support and encouragement of HE J Small, former Ambassador for Ireland; HE Sir Peter Lawler, former Ambassador for Australia to Ireland. Thanks to Anne Neary, formerly of the SPO (Dublin), now of Cambridge University, for her continuing guidance and encouragement, and to the SPO staff for all their assistance.

1 Based on analysis of native place and trial place for women transported from England.

2 *Kitty*: references to the *Kitty*'s indents name 16 convict women, 4/4002 AONSW; PRO reel 87, HO 11/1, ML; reel 2423, 2/8265, p 59ff, AONSW – 14 names excluding Elizabeth Davies and Jane Sharp; Shelton to King, PRO4, CO 201/7, no 7, 1792, p 322, gives the following numbers: '10 males, 16 females and 14 Irish females'; the following week 'persons on the *Royal Admiral*: 300 males, 49 females of those 4 are Irish and 10 Scots who had arrived too late on a former occasion' (p 332), the *Kitty* women from Dublin were: Mary Cassidy, 17, Sarah Daly, 23, Martha Dempsey, 22, Ann Short, 17, Catherine Haggarty, 19, Catherine Jackson, 19, Sarah McLean, 20, Rose White, 28, Bridget Bolton, 22, Bridget Fitzpatrick, 18, Catherine Evans, 18, Elizabeth Hyland, 30, Charlotte Stroud, 26, Rose Burk, 22; note re Rachael Davies in letter from D Woodriff on the *Kitty* at Woolwich.

3 William Richards (contractor for the First Fleet) to Nepean, 16 Oct 1792, PRO4, CO 201/7, no 7, pp 283-85; H Martin of the Navy Office (London) to Nepean, 17 Oct 1792, also requests terms of other contractors for taking convicts from Ireland to New South Wales, ibid, p 301; S Hamilton (Dublin Castle) to Nepean, 25 Oct 1792, ibid, pp 318-19.

4 See Mr Shelton to Mr King, 30 Dec 1792: 'he has understood at times when the Irish convicts were sent that particular accounts of their sentences were not sent out with them or indeed bonds or contracts entered into, which he has several times mentioned at the Office', ibid, p 322; *Minerva*: 'A List of Prisoners Embarked on the *Minerva* transport ... at Cork in the Kingdom of Ireland in 1799 and bound for the Colony of New South Wales with the several Occupations, Date & Term of Conviction Age, etc, etc. Characters Explained', OP, SPO (Dublin). A self-transportee was a man or woman who had received permission to transport themselves to New South Wales, thus avoiding criminal conviction. Self-transportation could be 'prayed' by men and women under sentence of death, transportation or confinement in Ireland. If granted, the prisoner paid his/her own passage to the Americas, arriving as a free person. Elizabeth Boyle, 18, of Stranorlar Parish, Co Donegal, a prisoner in the gaol of the City and County of Londonderry, Oct 1804, signed her petition with her mark, and was supported by testimonials that she was 'Descended from Honest respectable Roman Catholick Parents, who were always remarkable for their industry and good conduct'; the Mayor and Sheriffs of Londonderry petitioned on her behalf that 'On account of the age and character of the within Petitioner, & we [suggest] that the Security of His Majesty's Government would not be Misapplied in changing her Sentence to Transportation to America on her giving a Security', PP&C, 1804/865, SPO (Dublin).

5 Downing Street to Dublin Castle, 17 Sep 1819.

6 *Bassingbourne Chronicle*, compiled as part of the *Cambridgeshire Collection of Chronicles*, intro by Mike Petty, Local Studies Librarian, Central Library, Cambridge. I am indebted to Mr Petty for this and other valuable references to the people of Cambridgeshire during this period. Note that the Collection includes *Chronicles*, such as the *Fulbourn Chronicle (1750–1850)* compiled by D G Crane, and the *Littleport Chronicle*, intro Mike Petty.

7 Conspiracy to seize the *Marquis Cornwallis*, Hunter to Portland, 2 Sep 1796, encl, *HRNSW* 3, pp 107, 109: 'the whole [of the Irish convicts] were of the very worst description'; 'that some of the women were concerned in the conspiracy, their part being to convey knives to the men, and to put pounded glass into the messes of the ship's company'; Hunter to Portland, 18 Nov 1796, ibid, p 182 'they [the women] are generally found to be worse characters than the men'.

8 Elizabeth Paterson, Letters to her Uncle, ML Ms.

9 Elizabeth Mulhall, Letter from W W Pole, London, enclosing Captain Read's letter to him from Doonane, 18 Jan 1800, PP&C VI-15-1; see also Portia Robinson, 'Convict Colleens', in *SMH*, 17 Mar 1984

for account of Elizabeth Mulhall. Conclusions regarding the nature of female criminality in Ireland are based on (1) *Colleen to Matilda: Irish Convict Women in New South Wales* (forthcoming) by Portia Robinson, and (2) work in progress, 'Gender and criminality: criminal women and society, Great Britain, Ireland, Western Europe and Australia, 1788–1828' by Portia Robinson.

10 *Freeman's Journal* (Dublin), 7 Jan 1802, Proclamation of 31 Dec 1801.

11 Conspiracy of 1800: I am indebted to Prof E M Johnston for her private papers on this conspiracy; see also James Waldersee, *Catholic Society in New South Wales 1788-1860*, Sydney 1974, pp 6-8; papers relating to the Irish Conspiracy, *HRA* 1, 2, p 575ff: Summary of Proceedings of Inquiry, examination of James Harrold (priest); evidence of James McNally: 'You are not safe in your Bed ... a Plot to overturn the Government by putting Governor King to death and confining Governor Hunter'; for punishment of the plotters, see 'The sense of the matter', ibid, pp 582-3: 'James Harrold be also publickly brought in person as a Culprit and Ordered to Attend and bear Witness of the said several sentences being severely carried into Execution as a peculiar Mark of Infamy and Disgrace'.

12 Waldersee, *Catholic Society...*, p 9, and also cites Patrick O'Farrell, *The Catholic Church in Australia*, p 10.

13 *Morning Star* (Dublin), 10 Mar 1794, NL (Dublin). For examples of atrocities by both sides, see *The Rebellion of 1798* facsimile documents, PRO, SPO (Dublin), for example 'The deposition of Richard Grandy of Ballyshan Co Wexford describing his experiences as a prisoner of the rebels, 23 June 1798, Frazer Ms 1/30', describes 'the massacre of more than one hundred loyalist prisoners at Scullabogue, an abandoned country house near New Ross Co Wexford ... the cause of the killings ... a report that government forces at New Ross were killing all rebel prisoners'; also letter from Joshua Kemmia, Ballina, 25 Sep 1798, describing action against the rebels in Mayo 'when we killed I suppose 4-5000 ... They engaged us [again] for half an hour when such dreadful slaughter took place as is impossible for me to describe'. Frazer Ms 11/89, PRO, SPO (Dublin); letter from Ebenezer Jacob, Deputy Mayor of Wexford, 27 May 1798, describing the defeat of government troops by rebels at Oulart Hill, Rebellion Papers 620/37/178, PRO, SPO (Dublin).

14 Catherine Edwards, born c 1762, tried Dublin, 7 yrs, arrived NSW accompanied by 2-yr-old son John Edwards; married Wickham Yearly/Yarley/Yardley (as Catherine Edwards/Everett) 7 Jan 1796, St John's, witnesses Thomas Browning and Elinor Homan; son Edward born 1 Apr 1794; 1806: Mary Yarley FS widow; 1814: Free, off stores, widow Yarley, Windsor; David Collins, *An Account...*,

Notes (Chapter 5)

Fletcher (ed), pp 54ff, for report of 'a party of Irish convicts abscond' and 'the wretched female'.

15 Elinor McDonald (*Queen*) and Jonathon Griffiths, information from Betty Elder and S Holley; Griffiths mentioned by David Blackburn in Letters, NL Ms (Canberra).

16 Bridget Nowlas/Nowland (*Queen*), CSIL 4/1822, 246, 16 Feb 1810; described by Marsden in his Female Register as 'a concubine with 1 natural female child', she lived with John Everett; additional information from B Harrison.

17 'Convicts under sentence of Death and Transportation' in the Gaols of Ireland; see OP, 439/15, SPO (Dublin).

18 For examples of rations for convicts, see Hunter to Portland, 4 July 1799, *HRA* 1, 11, p 369 (Note): 'Convicts p'r week. – 7 lb. of beef or 4 lb. of pork, 7 lb. of fine flour, 1 pint of rice, 3 pints of pease, 6 ozs. of butter or a proportion of sugar'.

19 Petitions in PP&C, SPO (Dublin): example, Petition of Mary Byrne (*Mariner*), convict in Wexford Gaol 'with three fatherless children the eldest of whom is but seven years old'; PP&C, 1834, no 1002; petition of Mary Prendergast (*Experiment*), in Wicklow Gaol, 16 Oct 1806, 'in a miserable Condition not having one week's perfect health', PP&C, 1808, no 1231; petition of Mary Kibrea (*John Bull*), 'very much impaired her health', PP&C, 1820, no 1503.

20 Petition of Charlotte Kavanagh, 20 Apr 1809, PP&C no 1426, SPO (Dublin); Mary Murphy confined in Gaol of Carlow, 14 May 1812, PP&C no 4034.

21 Margaret Delaney, 21 Oct 1823, PP&C no 1895.

22 Catherine Blake or Black, 5 Nov 1823, PP&C no 1817; the surgeon of the *Almorah* noted: 'has four children with her husband in Dublin'; she was 5' 3" with fair complexion, fair to dark brown hair, grey to hazel eyes, aged 39 when sentenced'; other women who were transported leaving children in Ireland included: Susan Agnew (*Almorah*) 52, 'has three children in Armagh, of weak intellect, 5' 4", fresh fair and freckled complexion, brown hair, grey eyes' – she had stolen a web of linen; Ann Bryan/Byrne (*Almorah*) 28, married, a pickpocket who could 'sew, spin and wash'.

23 Catherine Stafford (*John Bull*) 19 July 1820, PP&C no 1558, SPO (Dublin).

24 Jane Shaw (*Almorah*), Surgeon's Report.

25 See Portia Robinson, 'The desolate boys . . .'

26 There is little available evidence for the few convict women who joined convict husbands, apart from notations on surgeons' journals, that the husband had been transported earlier.

27 See Applications for Permission to Marry, including applications from women who arrived on transports from Ireland; Bridget

Burke (*Woodman*), application Oct 1823 & 5 Dec 1823, 4/1773, pp 24 & 26; Eliza Dougherty (*John Bull*), 5 Dec 1825, 4/1789, p 16; Mary Fitzgerald (*Almorah*), Apr 1824, 4/1786, p 33; see also Marriage Licences, 4/630 & 4/1710; for women who arrived prior to 1800, see parish registers of St John's and St Phillip's, for example Mary Heron (*Boddingtons*) married Samuel Owens, 17 Sep 1792, at St John's, Parramatta; Mary Dunbar (*Sugar Cane*) married John Hackett, 17 Feb 1796; Catherine Burns (*Sugar Cane*) married Thomas Rumbold, 21 Dec 1794, at St Phillip's, Sydney; Mary Brien (*Marquis Cornwallis*) married William Laron, 13 Nov 1798, at St John's; Ann McCabe (*Marquis Cornwallis*) married John Parker, 13 Mar 1796; Catherine Butler (*Britannia*) married Joseph Winlock, 5 May 1798. From the 1820s Father Therry recorded Catholic marriages in New South Wales – see Therry Papers, ML Ms 1810/107, Petitions and Memorials. These mainly relate to convict husbands requesting passages for free wives, such as that of Matthew McGill, 'a good farming man', with a wife and four children aged from 13 and 20 in Kilcurry, Co Louth. Petitions and Memorials 1816-31, pp 107-8.

28 Petition of Mary Coghlan (*Almorah*), 24 Dec 1823, PP&C no 1854, SPO (Dublin).

29 Mary McCarroll, CSIL 4/11121.1, reel 697, 24 Jan 1827, AONSW; Johanna McCarty, CSIL 4/1112.1, reel 697, Nov 1825, AONSW; see also petition of Margaret and Mary Hogan (15), request for passage to join brother, a boy of 10, transported after being found out of his residence after sunset, Co Clare; refused, PC 1:72(2), PRO943.

30 Petition of William Folks/Fowkes for wife Mary Fowkes (*Almorah*), 3 Dec 1823, PP&C no 1945, SPO (Dublin).

31 Petition of Anne Donnelly (removed from Omagh Gaol in Co Tyrone), nd 1822, PP&C no 1650, SPO (Dublin).

32 Petition for Bridget Boddican/Brodican/Prodigan from her husband Daniel, 21 Sep 1801, PP&C no 632, SPO (Dublin).

33 Petition of Mary Murphy, 14 May 1812, PP&C no 4034, SPO (Dublin).

34 Surgeon's Journal, *Brothers*, PRO, reel 3190, ML.

CHAPTER 6: 'STATIONED IN PARADISE'?

1 These papers are to be found in the State Paper Office, Dublin Castle, Dublin. Some have been microfilmed as a Bicentennial gift from the Irish government to Australia. All petitions and references to girls sentenced to death or transportation have been extracted from Prisoners' Petitions and Cases and form part of the evidence on which this chapter is based. All references to women in relevant

338 Notes (Chapter 6)

papers, reports, inquiries, etc, have been cross-checked with lists of women transported from Ireland to New South Wales. Contemporary newspapers from Dublin, Belfast and all counties have supplied both additional data on individuals and information hitherto unknown relating to crimes, sentences, age, physical and character descriptions, etc. Reports and Journals of prison surgeons and of ships' surgeons have supplied contemporary evidence of conditions familiar to the transported women, of health and diet difficulties and, at times, of contemporary 'respectable' assumptions about, and expectations of, the behavioural characteristics of convicted women. The Rebellion Papers of 1798 have provided the background of social and economic conditions familiar to the early transportees; Quarterly Reports of the Adult Female Penitentiary, James Street, Dublin, supplied details of criminal women sentenced to transportation but confined in the penitentiary in Ireland: age, religion, when and where convicted, before whom, crime, sentence, when admitted, how employed, state of health, religious knowledge, industry, moral conduct, how disposed of or discharged, where, when and to whom.

2 Most of the women on the *John Bull* were identified by both native place and trial place: Ann Anderson, country servant from Waterford, was tried in Clare; Mary Browne, washerwoman from Waterford, was tried in Carlow; Mary Byrne, vagrant from Wexford, was tried in Dublin City; Mary Connor, country servant from Meath, was tried in Dublin (she was 'swarthy and pockpitted'); Mary King, country servant from Mullingar, was tried in Dublin ('sallow and rather freckled'); Harriet Scott, from Meath, was tried in Dublin. One was a native of Edinburgh (Jane Maher, 28, 'in town service', guilty of felony of wearing apparel, convicted in Dublin) and one was from Newcastle on Tyne (Matilda Browne, 26, 'sandy pockpitted complexion, sandy hair and hazel eyes ... in town and country service'), convicted in Dublin of felony of wearing apparel. These two were the rare exceptions whose native place was not in Ireland. Among the *Woodman* women was Elizabeth Barry, native of Dublin, a 22-year-old housemaid convicted of stealing money in Dublin. She was described at her trial as 'single but 5 months pregnant (she was later delivered of a large male child), full habit [plump], sanguineous temperament, twice ill on embarkation, pains in side of thorax and seasick on voyage'. All of the *Woodman* women were natives of Ireland, as were those on the *Mariner*.

3 Not all native places were given for women on the *Mariner*, but two were identified as Galway-born: Ann Howard, 20, housemaid, convicted in Clare for larceny: 'tolerable behaviour, fair & freckled'; Sarah McDermott, 24, married, a spinner found guilty of larceny in Leitrim: 'husband a labourer'.

Notes (Chapter 6) 339

4   Comparatively fewer women transported from Ireland were described as 'pockpitted'. On the *John Bull*: Mary Burke, from Lough, '30, swarthy & pitted'; Mary Connor, from Meath, '33, swarthy and pitted'; Catherine Cox, from Dublin, '30, pockpitted'; Celia Cox, Ballymurray, '23, pockpitted'; Sally Cunningham, from Monaghan, '20, little pitted, freckled'; Anne Fitzpatrick, Clownes, '18, pitted'; Catherine Kelly, Cork, '23, pockmarked'; Ann Morrison, from Down, '33, pockpitted'; Elizabeth Moss, 28, from Maryboror, Mary Murphy, 26, from Duncree, Eleanor Nolan, 20, Roscommon, Bridget O'Donnell, 24, Limerick, were all 'pitted'; Rose Richey, 33, from Baltinglass, 'swarthy & pitted'; the remaining 67 women were either 'sallow', 'freckled', 'swarthy', 'fair' and, occasionally, 'ruddy'. The *Mary Anne* which arrived from England five months later disembarked 62 of the 108 women in Sydney: 13 were 'pockmarked', from Liverpool, Plymouth, Suffolk, Stafford, London, Lancaster, Derby. Women from England were either 'ruddy', 'fair', 'pale', occasionally 'florid', and less likely to be freckled.

5   *Freeman's Journal*: Mary Marshall, 16 Nov 1802; Hessy Burke and Elizabeth Murphy, 18 Apr 1822.

6   The petition of the mother of Bridget Burke (*Francis and Eliza*) was rejected on the advice of the Recorder of Dublin that, although her prosecutor forgave her, 'she is not a fit object for mercy ... she is one of those abandoned Prostitutes who infest our streets at night for the purpose of robbing the unwary'. PP&C, 30 July 1814, Petition 4068.

7   See 'The criminality of Dublin Women' in *Colleen to Matilda: Irish Women Transported to New South Wales* (forthcoming). Distress among county women is evident in the critical reading of petitions to the Lord Lieutenant: Elizabeth Catherine Healy, alias Connell, and her husband John Connell were tried together in Cork and sentenced to death for killing seven lambs, the property of the husband's uncle. Confined in Richmond General Penitentiary, the wife pleaded that 'her husband was driven to the deed by poverty only and not for himself alone but in despair at seeing his family wanting food and he was out of employ'. She prayed pardon for her husband 'who had learnt a trade since his confinement', but if he were not pardoned 'she will remain in prison rather than accept her liberty instead of his'. PP&C, 18 Oct 1823, Petition 1860. There were, of course, examples of distress in Dublin. Elizabeth Kane, alias Doyle, in the New Prison, Green Street, sentenced to death for 'endeavouring to pass Bank Notes which had been robbed from the mail coach'; her husband (she had been married 3 weeks) had given her the notes; he had 'suffered the death penalty'. PP&C, 16 June 1800, Petition 476.

8 *Freeman's Journal*: Mary Tyrell, 24 Aug 1802; Margaret Doyle, 24 Aug 1802.
9 Ibid: Mary Dunbar, 31 July 1792.
10 Ibid: Catherine Donnelly, 21 October 1823.
11 Ibid: Elizabeth Jackson, 26 June 1794.
12 Additional evidence may be found in the Quarterly Reports of the Adult Female Penitentiary, OP 373/15, SPO (Dublin). Thirteen women were received into the Penitentiary in 1809, all of whom had been sentenced to 7 years' transportation; aged from 23 to 50, all Catholic, tried before the Recorder of Dublin for theft (unidentified, 4), receiving stolen goods (2), stealing a watch (4), banknotes (1), calico (1), burglary (1); they were employed as: nurse (1), plain work (9), weaving (3); their characters: 'continues subject to fits and very troublesome; Improving in her habits, particularly in her industry; continues quiet and industrious; continues vicious; still a doubtful character tho' apparently much improved; has improved...; quiet but being an old offender cannot be recommended; useful as a Nurse at the hospital.' Why these women were not transported is unknown; their descriptions and crimes were similar to many of the deportees. For the next Quarter's Report, five more names were added. One, Catherine Worthington, 31, 7 yrs, was released to her father in 1812.
13 Recommendations for Pardon for women under sentence for Transportation confined in the Adult Female Penitentiary, Dublin, by the Superintendent, OP, SPO (Dublin).
14 Report of Forster Archer, Inspector General of Prisons, 1815, OP, SPO (Dublin). Note that the name has been transcribed in contemporary records as Foster and Forster. The Report contains lists from all counties headed 'Convicts under Sentence of Death and Transportation in the Gaol of... After Summer Assizes 1815'. OP/43915, SPO (Dublin).
15 Petition of Sarah Geentry, PP&C, 10 Mar 1808, Petition 3969. There were cases where distress was taken into account: Margaret Scott, a convict under sentence of transportation, sent from Derry to Kilmainham Gaol, Dublin, 'appears to be an object for consideration on account of her infant child at her breast... I am of the opinion as there are many other females more fit objects for transportation'. Margaret Scott was confined in the Penitentiary. PP&C SPO (Dublin), 22 & 29 Sep 1810. This was not a typical case; many women were transported without infants or young children.
16 See List B (Women transported from Ireland to New South Wales 1791-Jan 1828) for comparison of trial date with year of arrival in New South Wales.
17 Trial places of women transported from Ireland to New South

Wales: *Freeman's Journal*, Dublin, NSW Biographical Data, Ships' Indents, Musters, 1828 Census, *Sydney Gazette*, CSIL, see also List B.

18 The average age of the women transported from Ireland was a few years older than the average woman transported from England. This is shown in the numbers of married women. The *Mariner* listed husbands of the women being transported; these included a heraldry painter (husband of seamstress Elizabeth Burke, 28), a Dublin victualler (Catherine Byrne/Murphy, 30, nurse), a labourer (Eleanor Coniskey, 28, nursery-housemaid), a pensioner (Mary Dunlevie, 38, seamstress), a Dublin carpenter (Susan Gafney, 36, housemaid), a Dublin gardener (Mary Gernon, 30, seamstress), a Kildare labourer (Rose Hill, 24, baker), a Dublin sailor (Sarah Howard, 19, washerwoman), a Dublin publican (Anne Lang, 27, 'deranged'), a Tipperary labourer (Honora Leary, 36, washerwoman), a Monaghan labourer (Rose McCluffon, 52, spinner), a Dublin servant (Margaret McEvoy, 35), a Co Derry farmer (Elizabeth Moon, one child left behind), a soldier in 91st Reg (Rose Morgan, 24, washerwoman). Unlike earlier deportees, at least nine of these women had husbands who had already been transported to New South Wales.

19 Records of applications for permission to marry, applications for marriage licences, banns published, marriages registered at colonial churches, etc, provide details of women marrying in the colony. After the arrival of Governor Macquarie, a Government and General Order of 22 Dec 1810 established fees for marriages by licence and by banns, but these fees were for free persons only. Macquarie ordered that all chaplains in the colony keep strict records of all ceremonies performed, for both free and convict partners. This granting or withholding of permission to marry to all inhabitants of the colony was the sole responsibility of the governor.

20 Petitions for Maintenance in Bastardy, 1801-14, COD 297/A, Bench of Magistrates 1801-14, AONSW.

21 See Peter Cunningham, RN, *Two Years in New South Wales: A Series of Letters Comprising Sketches of the Actual State of Society in that Colony*, 2 vols, London 1827, reprinted Adelaide 1988, ch 13.

22 *Freeman's Journal*, 17 Apr 1823.

23 Petition of Mary Ryan, PP&C, 2 Apr 1822, Petition 1769. Other women who petitioned for mercy for the sake of their small children included: Mary Byrne (*Mariner*), convicted of stealing 'a few yards of waistcoating which [she came by] honestly in the way of her trade, she being a Hawker of soft goods . . . she has three fatherless children the eldest of whom is but seven years old', PP&C, 23 Oct 1825 (Wexford Gaol), Petition 1002, SPO (Dublin); Elizabeth

Dougherty (*John Bull*) in Downpatrick Gaol, 'five young children one of whom is an infant Nine months old at the breast', PP&C, 19 Aug 1820, Petition 1474; Catherine Stafford (*John Bull*); Mary Clarke (*Woodman*), 10 Aug 1822, PP&C 1630, SPO (Dublin); Margaret Delaney (*Almorah*), 21 Oct 1823, PP&C, 1895, SPO (Dublin).

24 Mary Griffin (*Almorah*), 23 Apr 1823 & 28 Aug 1823, PP&C, 1963/1964, SPO (Dublin).

25 Ann/Mary Connell (*Almorah*), 13 Aug 1823, PP&C, 1863, SPO (Dublin).

26 Margaret Fowkes/Mary Folks (*Almorah*), 3 Dec 1823, PP&C, 1945, SPO (Dublin).

27 Elizabeth French, 16 Apr 1823 & 14 May 1823, PP&C, 1946, SPO (Dublin).

CHAPTER 7: 'A GREAT AND BITTER GRIEF'

1 Catherine Slater, *PC* 1:67, PRO938, 1819; Jane Booth, *PC* 1:68, PRO939, 1820; aged 38, she was the wife of Edward Booth, 43 (*Earl St Vincent*), and petitioned Lord Sidmouth that she and her 5 children be given 'a free passage in any ship bound to New South Wales where the cargo or freight is only women as Petitioner has ever been virtuous'. From Little Bolton, Lancashire, the family arrived in 1829 at Hobart on the *Lady of the Lake*, and then per *Calista* to Sydney. Additional data from Joan Broome. Examples come from England, Scotland and Wales; for example, the wife of Gilbert McLeod of Glasgow, transported 'for his wicked political writings' was described as 'the innocent victim of her husband's bad conduct and a family depending on her makes her more wretched', *PC* 1:69, PRO940, 1821, from 46 Millar St, Glasgow. Petitions from Irish convict husbands for passages for their free wives and children may be found in Therry Papers, ML Ms, 1810/107, C7, reel 808.

2 For the wives who accompanied the Royal Marines in 1787-88, see Portia Robinson, 'The Victualling List', in *SMH*, 15, 16 & 17 Dec 1980; see also TI/688 ML. These were the first white women to land in New South Wales: 28 Jan 1788, 17 wives of the Marines from the *Prince of Wales* landed with their husbands and 14 of their children; 29 Jan 1788, the Marines aboard the *Charlotte* disembarked. Note that at least one of these wives was a convict woman who later married her Marine 'husband' in New South Wales: Maria Nash (Victualling List 251), 'wife' of Pte William Nash, was Maria Haynes, convict, who married William Nash on 13 Feb 1789; her friend, Ann Perry, 'wife' of Sgt William Perry, was married as Ann Scrobie to Sgt Perry on 8 June 1789; Sgt James Scott, husband of

Jane Scott, noted in his diary, 24 Oct 1787, at Capetown: 'I and my wife went on shore with Sgts Dawn and Perry and their wives and Spent the Day very Agreeably; Went to the Company's Gardens and Seen the varios Birds which is as desirable a place as evere I should wish to see'. Diary of James Scott, ML Ms.

3   Mary Harris re Silas Harris, convict on board *Laurel* at Portsmouth, to H Capper Esq, 'has left 6 children to lament his loss', from Castle Street, Salisbury, 2 May 1819, *PC* 1:67, PRO938, 1819; Mary (Sarah) Ashton to Lord Sidmouth from Woolwich, 10 May 1820, *PC* 1:68, PRO939, 1820.

4   Francis Smith alias Gavin to Lord Sidmouth from Downpatrick Gaol, 30 Jan 1819, *PC* 1:67, PRO938, 1819.

5   Zachariah Phillips to Lord Sidmouth from *Justitia* hulk, 23 Mar 1819, petition 'borne by his wife', *PC* 1:67, PRO938, 1819.

6   Terence O'Brien, 29 June 1826, and letter from Downing St, Hays to Hobson, 13 Aug 1826, *PC* 1:74, PRO945, 1826.

7   Jane Ryan from 3 Warbington Street, Portsmouth, 5 Sep 1821, *PC* 1:69, PRO940, 1821.

8   Hannah Yardley to Lord Sidmouth from Wolverhampton, Staffordshire, 14 Dec 1819, *PC* 1:67, 1819.

9   Margaret Street of Radcliffe Bridge near Manchester, Lancashire, 5 Apr 1820, *PC* 1:68, 1820.

10 W A Minton to Robert Peel, for Mrs Garland, *PC* 1:71, PRO941, 1823. *Note:* On 7 April 1821 William Gregory wrote from Dublin Castle to Henry Hobhouse at Downing Street that the Lord Lieutenant of Ireland had received his letter instructing that 'it has been the rule in England not to permit male children above the age of 14 years to proceed to their fathers being convicts in New South Wales and that his Lordship conceives that his Excellency will upon consideration deem it proper that the same rule should apply in Ireland'. Gregory added that boys who were not allowed to join their parents 'would be most disappointed if they could not go now. As there are not many it is hoped that the law will not be enforced in this instance but in future it will be strictly observed'. *PC* 1:69, PRO940, 1821.

11 Ann Schofield of Clapgate, near Rochdale, to Henry Hobhouse Esq, 4 Sep 1821, *PC* 1:69, PRO940, 1821.

12 See Robinson, *The Hatch and Brood of Time* . . . , pp 3-5.

13 Elisha Baker: John Wright, Committing Magistrate, to Robert Peele [*sic*] from Hartford on 13 Feb 1822 re Elisha Baker, *PC* 1:70, PRO941, 1822.

14 William Tidman re Thomas Tatt, convict at Woolwich under sentence of transportation, and petition of wife of Thomas Tatt to Lord Sidmouth, 8 Feb 1819, *PC* 1:67, PRO968, 1819.

344 *Notes (Chapter 7)*

15   John Willmott, 7 Apr 1819, *PC* 1:67, PRO938, 1819; wife Sarah Willmott. Charles Ellis of Sheffield, 14 Aug 1821, *PC* 1:69, PRO940, 1821; wife Rebecca Ellis.

16   John Gamble at York re wife Ann Gamble tried at Durham, *PC* 1:69, PRO940, 1821.

17   Sydney Smith, 'Botany Bay', *Edinburgh Review*, July 1819, Mr Marsden's letter dated July 1815 'to Governor Macquarrie ... given at length in the Appendix to Mr Bennet's book. A more horrid picture of the state of any settlement was never penned'. Smith's review of *Letter to Viscount Sydney...* by the Hon Henry Grey Bennet, London 1819.

18   See ch 11, 'She sang her toil and trouble'; see also Col Sec Letters Received, Lists of Tickets-of-Leave issued 2 July 1810-3 Oct 1814, 4/4427; certificates of conduct and petitions from applicants for tickets-of-leave, etc, 1822-24, 4/1715-7, AONSW.

19   Mary Kette/Kettle, 27 Feb 1830, CSIL 4/2167, no 213; her husband had been transported for life, she arrived to join him in 1823, and her husband was assigned to her, but returned to Government 'for a small offence' in Nov 1826; he lost his ticket of exemption in 1828 when 'he was found in a Public House with a very respectable free gentleman' and was again taken to Barracks. She is afraid he is under threat 'to be sent away because the overseer has taken a dislike to him and is making his life a misery'. Mary McPherson, 26 Feb 1827, 4/7084, AONSW.

20   James Roe, Rector of Newbury, to Lord Sidmouth from Newbury, 12 Jan 1821, re Mrs Wiggins, wife of James Wiggins, *PC* 1:69, PRO940, 1821.

21   William Holland: P Beale from Mayfair to Lord Sidmouth, 19 Aug 1819 & 20 Oct 1819, on behalf of Mrs Holland, *PC* 1:67, 1819; James Knowles: Jno Mawsley to Robert Peele [*sic*], from Bolton, on behalf of Mrs Knowles, 30 Mar 1822, *PC* 1:67, 1822; Elizabeth Brown of Weldon, Wansford, 26 July 1819, re husband David Brown, transported 1812, *PC* 1:67, PRO938, 1819. Other examples include: Samuel Owen: petition of wife Elizabeth Owen of Hull, 18 Mar 1819, *PC* 1:67, PRO938, 1819; Sarah Allen of Weaverham near Warwick, petition on her behalf from John Fear 'wishes to know if the husband transported in 1818 is alive or dead as she has not heard from him', 2 Mar 1819, *PC* 1:67, PRO938, 1819; Rector of Newbury, Berks, re William Cook, reported dead, had arrived at Hobart Town in 1821, 16 Mar 1822 (William Cook was living in Sydney with a wife, FS, and two native-born children by 1828, a brickmaker of Clarence Street); Sarah Pickup of Lancaster wanted to know if her husband Thomas, transported in 1817, was alive or dead, *PC* 1:67, PRO938, 1819.

22 Mary Parish of West Bronwick, Staffordshire, 9 Aug 1819, to Lord Sidmouth, *PC* 1:67, PRO938, 1819.
23 Katherine Evans (*Kitty*): 'a murder was committed by a man on the person of a woman with whom he cohabited. It appeared they had both been intoxicated, and had quarrelled the night preceding and in the morning of the murder Oct 1796', Court of Criminal Jurisdiction, and Cobley, *Sydney Cove* ... vol V, p 105.
24 Edward Collman (*Canada*), 11 Apr 1822, CSIL 4/1762, reel 2190, p 20; 1 Nov 1822, 4/1762, reel 2171, p 39.
25 Barnabas Traynor: petition from Robert Carter, Inspector of Gaol Wicklow, to Lord Sidmouth on behalf of Judith Traynor of Wicklow, 29 Sep 1821, *PC* 1:69, PRO940, 1821.
26 Peter Hinnegan: petition of Cecilia Hinnegan to Viscount Sidmouth, 20 Jan 1820, *PC* 1:69, PRO939, 1820; Richard (Peter) Hicks: petition from Thomas Woods, Littleton, 28 Jan 1820, *PC* 1:68, PRO939, 1820.
27 Grenville to Phillip, 24 Dec 1789, *HRA* 1, I, p 131, 'the numbers of females leaving a great disproportion to that of the males'.
28 See Phillip to Nepean, 1 Mar 1787: 'send ships to the Friendly Islands for the bread-fruit, and, as women will be there procured', *HRNSW* 1, pt 2, p 55.
29 See Phillip to Lord Sydney, 28 Feb 1787, 'Phillip's views on the Conduct of the Expedition and the Treatment of the Convicts': 'it may be best if the most abandoned are permitted to receive the visits of the convicts in the limits allotted to them at certain hours and under certain restrictions; something of this kind was the case in Mill Bank formerly.' ibid, p 52.
30 'The perfect antidote to desire' – the phrase is David Collins'; see Collins, *An Account...*, Fletcher (ed), p 405.
31 29 Oct 1791, T1/703, reel 3554, p 122, note from Lieut Robert Parry Young, Naval Agent: 2 wives accompanied the 282 male and 6 female convicts on the *Albemarle*, 4 wives and 297 male convicts were on the *Admiral Barrington*, 1 wife and 191 male convicts were on the *Matilda*, and there were no wives on the *Britannia*. According to Lieut Young's report, a total of 1149 male convicts were accompanied by 7 wives, one of whom died on the passage.
32 King to Camden, 22 Feb 1806, *HRA* 1, V, p 636: Note '6 children and 2 women wives of State Prisoners Byrn & Dwyer' (*Tellicherry*); Rev Henry Fulton, 28 Oct 1798, Curate of Kilmore and Vicar of Mountsea, Co Tipperary: information sworn before Mr Henry Osborne, Magistrate, 15 May 1797, and a letter re Fulton's Memorial (Memorial not found), PP&C no 77, SPO (Dublin).
33 Celia Cosgrove, CSIL 11 July 1823 4/1772; also *PC* 1:69, PRO940, 1821.

Notes (Chapter 7)

34 Hobart to Lt Col Collins, 7 Feb 1802, *HRA* 1, IV, p 10.
35 Select Committee on Transportation 1812, published in *House of Commons Papers for 1812*, vol ii, Paper no 341: 'the women sent out are of the most abandoned description, and ... in many instances they are likely to whet and encourage the vices of the men'. 'Your Committee think this an additional reason for affording increasing facilities to the wives of male convicts'.
36 Bathurst to Macquarie, 10 Nov 1812, *HRA* 1, VII, pp 539-40.
37 Bathurst to Macquarie, 22 Mar 1813, *HRA* 1, VII, p 696.
38 Ibid; Macquarie to Bathurst, 19 Jan 1814, ibid, p 119; Lieut Jeffries to Macquarie, 10 Jan 1814, ibid, p 123.
39 Macquarie to Bathurst, 7 Oct 1814, *HRA* 1, VIII, pp 296, 309.
40 Bathurst to Macquarie, 11 May 1816, *HRA* 1, IX, p 120.
41 Macquarie to Bathurst, 18 March 1814, *HRA* 1, IX, p 556.
42 Macquarie to Bathurst, 23 May 1817, *HRA* 1, IX, p 412.
43 Macquarie to Bathurst, 7 Oct 1814, *HRA* 1, VIII, p 302; Bathurst to Macquarie, 11 May 1816, ibid, IX, p 120.
44 James Goodlands: from Richard Marshall re wife and children, 24 Apr 1820, *PC* 1:68, PRO939, 1820. Mary Mulligan, *PC* 1:75, PRO945, 1826; Mary Ann Easterbrook, 5 Apr 1824, *PC* 1:71, PRO941, 1823; see also Henry Gauntlett of Berks to Robert Peel re John Wright, 13 Sep 1826, *PC* 1:75, PRO945, 1826: convicted 2 years last March, his wife and eldest son aged 5 wish to join him: 'She is an honest and well-disposed woman, a very good lace-maker ... her husband believes she would earn a considerable sum in the Colony at her lace pillows ... she would be able to teach others'.
45 Ann Humphreys: letter of Edward Rowden, Vicar of Highworth to Lord Sydney, 28 Jan 1820, encl petition of Ann Humphreys, 'he is willing to maintain her and she is very anxious to comply with her husband's wishes', *PC* 1:68, PRO939, 1820.
46 Macquarie to Bathurst, 9 Dec 1817, *HRA* 1, XI, p 543.
47 Re Mrs Ann Davis, wife of Thomas Davis, convict of New South Wales, 21 Feb 1826, *PC* 1:75(1), PRO945, 1826.
48 Mrs Sarah Stanford/Stanfield of Kirkham, Lancaster, *PC* 1:72, PRO943.
49 Sarah Bell: from Dr Edward Trevor (Dublin) to William Gregory, *PC* 1:69, PRO940, 1821 (children aged 11, 7, 5); see also Celia Cosgrove, ibid.
50 Thomas Newman: James Vaughan from Bolton, Parish of Bethnal Green, Lancashire, to Lord Sidmouth on behalf of Harnett: 'This is a most distressing case as there is the wife and 5 small children the eldest under 9 wholly destitute of support with the exception of 3/6 per week from the Parish'. *PC* 1:67, PRO939, 1819.
51 Assistant Overseer of the Parish of Chaveling to Secretary of State,

Home Department, 29 Sep 1826, *PC* 1:74, PRO945, 1826; note also: Charles Barkway, Overseer of the Parish of Fressingfield, Norfolk, a general inquiry 'to enquire if there were any allowance or encouragement for wives and families to go to their husbands in New South Wales', *PC* 1:72, PRO943, 1824.

52 Jane Davis, Plymouth Workhouse, to Lord Sydney re husband James, convicted for sheep stealing, accompanied by a letter from Henry Roberts and a supporting letter from George Eastel, Mayor of Plymouth, 9 Oct 1819, *PC* 1:67, PRO938, 1819.

53 William Walters: petition of Susannah Walters, Fulmodestone, Norfolk, 16 Oct 1819, re her husband William now aboard *Leviathan* hulk for transportation, *PC* 1:67, PRO938, 16 Oct 1819.

54 John Lynch: petition of Mary Lynch, 8 Apr 1824, letter attached, *PC* 1:72, PRO943, 1824 (letter from husband enclosed, dated 6 July 1823).

55 Letters of Josiah Godber to his wife Rebecker, NL Ms (Canberra); he added, 'I am as Comfortable as Posable in my sittewation but my Dear I could like to have you with mee and I should be happy'.

56 Hannah Yardley of Staffordshire, 14 Dec 1812, *PC* 1:67, PRO938, 1819.

57 John Proctor: petition of wife Elizabeth Proctor of Armagh, Ireland, to Lord Sidmouth, 5 Aug 1819, *PC* 1:67, PRO938, 1819; petition of Hannah and Matthew Kirkby of Great Bolton, Lancaster, 13 Sep 1819, *PC* 1:68, PRO938, 1819; Sarah Lawton of Northampton, 4 Apr 1819, *PC* 1:67, PRO938, 1819.

CHAPTER 8: 'WOMEN OF PROVEN GOOD CHARACTER'

1 Daniel Defoe, *A Tour through the Whole Island of Great Britain*, London 1962, p 62; see Robinson, *The Hatch and Brood of Time...*, pp 121-9.

2 Report on the State of Prisons and Prison Discipline, 1820...; Sydney Smith, 'Prisons', in *Edinburgh Review*, 1822; also Samuel Buxton, *An Inquiry into Whether Crime and Misery Are Produced or Prevented by Our Present System of Prison Discipline*, London 1818, BM, and cited in Dobash, *The Imprisonment...*, p 43.

3 Based on an analysis of cases in which women were the defendants, Court of Criminal Jurisdiction, Reports of Proceedings 1788-1825: Schedule of Prisoners Tried; Miscellaneous Criminal Papers 1788-91; Indictments, Informations, Depositions and Related Papers (Sydney) 1817-23; return of 153 convicts who after receiving remission, or after expiration of sentences, had been convicted of a felony in colonial courts, 12 Mar 1810-22 Sep 1823; Reports of crimi-

Notes (Chapter 8)

nals tried in the Court of Criminal Jurisdiction, June-Nov 1820, Feb 1822-Jan 1824; Judgement Book, 22 Feb 1822-11 Feb 1824, AONSW.

4 Elizabeth Wilson (*Sugar Cane*) and Mary Carrol (*Marquis Cornwallis*), *Sydney Gazette*, Mar 1803; Mary Tyrrell (*Rolla*), 8 July 1804; Elizabeth McDuel, 21 Aug 1808; *Sydney Gazette*: Jane Marcus, 16 Sep 1820.

5 *Sydney Gazette*: similar examples are numerous: 26 Feb 1804, 'we feel it our duty upon this doleful occasion [the execution of a young man of comely appearance ... his former character by no means a bad one] to hope that his example may operate upon the wavering mind, and that the awful spectacle may serve as a lasting warning against the prosecution of crime and thereby effectually promote the needs of moral rectitude'; see ibid, 26 Mar 1803, 2 Oct 1803, 27 Apr 1806, 4 May 1806, 12 Oct 1806, 21 Dec 1806, 25 Jan 1807, 5 Apr 1807.

6 Ann Tibbutt, Court of Criminal Jurisdiction, 5/1119, reel 2390, p 30, AONSW.

7 Mary Farrell, Court of Criminal Jurisdiction, 5/1149, reel 2651, p 211, AONSW: *Sydney Gazette*, 24 June, 9 Sep, 18 Nov, 23 Nov 1804.

8 Marianne Wilkinson, recorded by Collins, *An Account ...*, p 363: 'Criminal Court assembled on 7 Nov 1795 when the following persons were tried: viz. Samuel Chinnery [a black] servant to Mr Arndell ... acquitted; Smith and Abraham Whitehouse ... condemned to die [Whitehouse executed 16 Nov]; and two settlers and six convicts, for an assault on one Marianne Wilkinson (attended with like circumstances of infamy as that on Mary Hartley in April last) of which three were found guilty, and sentenced: Merchant, alias Jones, the principal, to receive one thousand lashes; the others, Ladley and Everitt, eight hundred each.' Note that Fletcher comments, 'The Court records show nine men as having been accused, and not eight as Collins indicated', p 601.

9 Mary Hartley, recorded by Collins, *An Account ...*, pp 346-7; the criminal court was convened on 15 May 1795; those charged were: John Anderson and Joseph Marshall, settlers; John Hyams, Joseph Dunstill, Richard Watson and Morgan Bryan, convicts; 'such a crime could not be passed with impunity', and they were tried again on 22 May for assault. See also Court of Criminal Jurisdiction, Minutes of Proceedings, Feb 1788-Dec 1797, pp 420ff.

10 Ann Tuckey (*Glatton*), *Sydney Gazette*, 2 Oct 1808.

11 Elizabeth Jones, letter of Rev Richard Johnson to Joseph Hardcastle, Esq, Treasurer of the Evangelical Society, 26 Aug 1799, in *Some Letters of Rev Richard Johnson*, George Mackness (ed), Dubbo 1954, p 33ff: 'after their conviction I officially visited these three horrid monsters'; Johnson was a friend of the murdered man

Notes (Chapter 8) **349**

and gave a full account of the crime in his letter. See also Court of Criminal Juridsiction, Minutes of Proceedings, 1798-1800, pp 6-13.

12 Elizabeth Roanes, *Sydney Gazette*, 13 Nov 1808; Elizabeth Connor (*Marquis Cornwallis*) was also sentenced to death; convicted of theft she was sentenced 'to be executed tomorrow' but was reprieved. *Sydney Gazette* 12, 19 & 26 June 1808; on 2 Oct 1809 she was again tried, but acquitted of the charge of murder, ibid; Elizabeth Jones was charged with murder, killing her child, 25 Aug & 25 Sep 1808, ibid. They were among the very few women who appeared on either murder or manslaughter charges in the Criminal Court.

13 Mary Grady, found guilty 12 June and executed 19 June 1808, *Sydney Gazette*.

14 Judith Jones, alias Ann Davis, Collins, *An Account...*, p 70: at her execution she admitted that 'she was about to suffer justly, and that an attempt which she had made, when put on her defence, to criminate another person (a woman whose character was so notorious that she hoped to establish her own credit and innocence on her infamy), as well as her plea of pregnancy, were advanced merely for the purpose of saving her life'. With reference to 'the jury of matrons', this was a practice brought from Britain and Ireland; see *Freeman's Journal*, 15 Aug 1800: 'Elizabeth Mulholland was found guilty of the murder of her bastard child, upon her being convicted and being called to receive sentence of death, she pleaded being pregnant. A jury of matrons was sworn and found the verdict of pregnancy whereupon her sentence was respited'.

15 Frances Moreton, reel 2651, X905, AONSW.

16 Simon Taylor and wife Ann Smith, *Australian*, 25 Nov 1834; Collins, *An Account...*, vol 2, pp 145-6, 151, 271, 272: Simon Taylor 'a man who had been considered as one of the few industrious settlers which the colony could boast of'. Collins saw the murder as 'the effect of intoxication... This unhappy man was thoroughly sensible of the enormity of his guilt, and in his last moments admonished the spectators against indulging in drunkenness, which had brought him to that untimely and disgraceful end.

17 Julia Bates, *Australian*, 30 Dec 1824 & 14 Apr 1825; Mrs Bennett, ibid, 16 Dec 1828.

18 Mary Smith, murdered by John Kenny: *Sydney Gazette*, 25 Jan 1807, also Court of Criminal Jurisdiction, 22 Jan 1807, 1149, p 337, AONSW; see also murder of Mary Rowe, 14 Sep 1811, accused John Dunn, alias Donne, Thomas Welch and Anne Wilson, ibid, 1120, p 1, AONSW; murder of Hannah Allen, 21 Feb 1812, accused Thomas Allen, ibid, 1120, p 100; murder of Margaret Finney, 6 Mar 1812, accused John Gould, ibid, 1120, p 116, & 1152, p 475; murder of Mary Connor, 7 May 1812, accused John Hunt, ibid, 1120, p 146.

19 Henry Hacking: R 2651 10 Mar 1802, AONSW; for Hacking see also Collins, *An Account*..., Fletcher (ed): 'Henry Hacking, one of the quarter-masters of the *Sirius*, who, being reckoned a good shot, was allowed to shoot for the officers and the ship's company' (attacked by natives, Sep 1789), pp 66-7; see also pp 365, 398, 321-2.

20 Brisbane to Bathurst, 14 May 1825, HRA 1, II, p 585ff; see also Ritchie, *Punishment and Profit*...

21 Keeper of York Castle, 29 June 1816, 2/8267, reel 2424, AONSW. Note that the Keeper's comments were repeated by the surgeon of the *Lord Melville*. Phillis Gordon, who had stolen bed linen and blankets was a needlewoman; Jane Graham/Wood, a servant, was 'ux Ezekial Graham Wood'; Ann Chapman, a servant; Elizabeth Wales was Elizabeth Walsh on the *Lord Melville*'s indents; Hannah Whiteby was Hannah Whitely or Wilkinson. See also petition re assigned female servants Catherine Bryan and Ellen Clarke, 7 Aug 1822, CSIL 4/1762, reel 2171, p 48: Bryan 'is to be sent back as she is not a fit person. Her appearance is greatly disfigured by cutaneous disease which forbid her being employed near a child'. The women sent so far by the Factory are totally unsuitable 'nothing but evil could be expected' of them and 'one ... a vicious prostitute'. Memorial re Rose Francis, 12 Aug 1826, requesting her husband be assigned to her, Assignment and Employment of Convicts, 4/7084, AONSW: 'Note: Rose Francis name is Ryan ... a woman of abandoned character and as I am informed a public prostitute. She is the wife of Francis a man of colour lately from Port Macquarie'. Petition of Maria Bates for her husband to be returned to her, 11 June 1826, CSIL 4/7084, AONSW, comment: 'This petitioner is a most abandoned prostitute, and has been repeatedly punished by the Bench of Magistrates for her dissolute conduct; her husband had a ticket-of-leave of which he was deprived for keeping a disorderly house over which it appeared he had no control.'

22 Eliza Campbell/Cammell (*Providence*), *Australian*, 17 Feb 1825.

23 Janet Mackellar, murdered by Lot McNamara, *Australian*, 12 Mar 1828; McNamara hanged 17 Apr 1826; Catherine Douglas, murdered by John Clives, alias Malkland, alias McLane, ibid 17 Dec 1826, 10 Feb 1827.

24 In the first case brought before the Court of Criminal Jurisdiction, where a man was convicted of carnal knowledge of a child, the offender was Henry Wright, a marine private: 'indicted for that he not having the Fear of God before his eyes, but being moved and seduced by the instigation of the Devil ... with Force and Arms ... in and upon Elizabeth Chapman, Spinster ... violently and feloniously did make an Assault ... and then and there did ravish and carnally know' a child of eight years who was called to give evidence;

when asked what would happen if she told an untruth, she replied that she would 'Go to the Devil'. (A similar question at a Middlesex trial provoked the reply 'the naughty man will get me'.) Found guilty and sentenced to death, Wright was pardoned and sent to Norfolk Island for life. The Judge Advocate commented: 'This was an offence that did not seem to require an immediate example; the chastity of the female part of the settlement had never been so rigid as to drive men to so desperate an act'. Court of Criminal Jurisdiction, 19 Sep 1789, 1147A, p 141, AONSW; Collins, *An Account...*, Fletcher (ed), p 66. Wright received a conditional pardon on 13 Sep 1796 and returned to the mainland. Col Sec CP 1796, AONSW. Ann McAdams, *Sydney Gazette*, 10 Feb 1825; cases reported in the 1820s included that of Elizabeth Cutter aged nine years, Benjamin Jones accused of 'having committed violence to' was discharged on the grounds of insufficient evidence, *Australian*, 25 Nov 1828.

25 Ann Kennedy, Court of Criminal Jurisdiction, 5/1119, reel 2390, p 69, AONSW.

26 Mrs Ralph: *Australian*, 20 Aug 1828; Mrs New: ibid. Based on records of Court of Criminal Jurisdiction and Benches of Magistrates Proceedings.

27 Examples taken from cases reported in the *Australian*, 1824-28. Note the facetious manner in which most cases were published and the nicknames 'demoiselles of the ton' and 'ladies of the Cyprian tribe' were given. Mrs Goodwin, 23 Apr 1825; Jane Quigley, 9 Feb 1826. The pattern of punishment is evident in cases tried during Macquarie's administration. Typical examples were: Mary Kearns (*Sugar Cane*), 6 months in the Factory for fraudulently obtaining goods to the value of £6 from the warehouses of Lord and Williams, 14 Nov 1812, *Sydney Gazette*, 'with nothing known to detract from her previous respectable character'; Mary Mears (*Experiment*), stealing a cow from the Government herd, 26 Mar 1814, 7 yrs' hard labour; Elizabeth O'Brien, breaking, entering and stealing 20 yards of calico, 'to stand in the pillory at Parramatta on 7 July between 9 o'clock and 10 o'clock in the forenoon for one hour and then to suffer 5 years imprisonment with hard labour', 25 June 1814; note that for a similar crime in that same year in Ireland, Mary Stephens (*Francis and Eliza*) was transported for 7 yrs; see Court of Criminal Jurisdiction, AONSW.

28 *Australian*: Betty Dixon, 13 Jan 1825; Mary Davis, 28 Oct 1828; Mary Scott, 22 Dec 1824; Kitty Connor, 8 Sep 1825; Mary Hartigan, 5 Jan 1826; Sarah Webb, 15 Apr 1826.

29 See B H Fletcher, *Ralph Darling: A Governor Maligned*, Melbourne 1984, for the wife of the governor; see also 'Rules for Female Convicts, 31 Jan 1821: Rules and Regulations for the Management of

the Female Convicts in the new Factory at Parramatta', Bigge Appendix BT Box 26, 6075 ML.

30 James Daly, in Collins, *An Account...*, Dec 1788, pp 38-9: 'The convicts being all assembled for muster, she was directed to stand forward and, her head having been previously deprived of its natural covering'. It was Daly who had pretended to discover gold in Aug 1788. See 'Letters of David Blackburn...'; also Court of Criminal Jurisdiction, 2 Dec 1788, 1147A, p 93.

31 Rosamond Sparrow, in Collins, *An Account...*, p 352; Joseph Hatton, see note by Fletcher ibid, p 598; I am also indebted to Judith Bryce for trial details; Court of Criminal Jurisdiction, 25 Oct 1799, X905, p 389. Note that solitary confinement as a punishment was ordered more frequently from the middle years of Macquarie's administration, reflecting the increase in gaols and places of confinement for both women and men: 18 July 1815, Rosetta Lovatt (*Speke*), 3 months' solitary confinement in the cells at Parramatta Gaol for larceny; Oct 1817, Elizabeth Terrie (*Aeolus*), 3 weeks' solitary for stealing seven pounds of meat from Mr Cribb's butcher shop; 18 Oct 1817, Mary Taylor, convicted of petty larceny, sentenced to a month in solitary confinement 'to reflect on her wickedness', Court of Criminal Jurisdiction, and *Sydney Gazette*.

32 Jane McFae, tried 26 May 1800, X905, reel 2561, p 447, AONSW. The public shaming of women by sentences to pillory or stocks continued in the colony well into the 1820s and beyond: 6 July 1816, Maria Wilson was pilloried 'for keeping a disorderly house in Castlereagh Street, a common nuisance to the neighbourhood'; she stood one hour in the pillory at Sydney Market, was then sent to Parramatta Gaol for 6 months, then to Newcastle for 2 years; 20 June 1818, Mary Carney was transported to Newcastle for 7 years' hard labour for stealing pairs of boots, some clothing and five shillings from Thomas Watkins of King Street; Dec 1818, Elizabeth Finlay, guilty of larceny, sentenced to transportation to Newcastle for 3 years.

33 M J D Roberts, 'The Society for the Suppression of Vice and its Early Critics, 1802-1812', *Historical Journal* 26, 1 (1983). Dr Roberts cites the justification of the publicists when the Society began in 1802, 'a truth too evident to be denied... that vice of late advanced upon us with almost unexampled rapidity'; for scholarly discussion as to why the founders defined vice 'in the way they did', see pp 175-6: 'The vice which the society most deplored can, broadly speaking, be identified as disorderly and culturally rebellious group behaviour'.

34 General orders and proclamations were the only medium of legislation in the colony until after the departure of Macquarie. Macquarie issued general orders and proclamations 'after the manner

of his predecessors... with no thought of the possible consequences of illegality'. In 1815 Judge J H Bent challenged the validity of the Governor's orders and Macquarie complained to Bathurst – see Bent to Macquarie, 2 Oct 1815, encl Macquarie to Bathurst, 20 Feb 1816, *HRA* 1, IX, p 3. Bathurst replied to Bent, 'I have only to observe that the power of the Governor to issue government and general orders, in the absence of all other authority, and the necessity of obeying them, rests on the same foundation on which it has stood since the first formation of the colony', Bathurst to Bent, 11 Dec 1815, *HRA* 1, IV, p 170; see A C V Melbourne, *Early Constitutional Development in Australia*, Oxford 1934, 1972 ed, pp 32-3. These Orders were printed in the *Sydney Gazette*. They had the form of legislation, stating the problem, the remedy and the punishment for non-observance.

35 25 Feb 1788: Charles Clay also brought a bottle of brandy ashore 'for two convicts'; he received 25 lashes; 25 Feb 1788: 'missed' a dozen and a half bottles of wine from his store tent – William Murphy was found very drunk, Cobley, ibid, p 87; note that Ann Davis, the first white woman to be executed 'was found drunk and in possession of some articles taken from Robert Sidaway's house', 14 Nov 1789; she claimed she had been 'with a seaman in the woods who had given her liquor'.

36 For examples of the problems believed to result from over-indulgence, see Collins, *An Account...*, and reports in the *Sydney Gazette* 1803-26 and the *Australian* 1824-28. Reports are also collected and published in Cobley, *Sydney Cove...*, 5 vols; for Ann Farmer, 2 Aug 1788, in Cobley, *Sydney Cove...*, vol 1, p 202. *Australian*: Ann Baker, drunkenness, to the Factory, 20 May 1826; Mary Banks, drunkenness 'for at least the 50th time', to the Factory, 28 Oct 1826; Mrs Esther Bigges charged Mary Scott with drunkenness, 23 Dec 1824; Elizabeth Chambers charged and fined 5 shillings for drunkenness 'in default thereof the elderly matron got a 4 hours standing in the stocks', 23 Apr 1828.

37 Phillip's Commission, *HRA* 1, I, pp 1-2; Phillip's Second Commission, ibid p 2ff; see also Tench, *Sydney's First Four Years...*, p 41ff; Collins, *An Account...*, pp 6-7.

38 Mary Joyce: *Sydney Gazette*, 6 May 1811. Mary Joyce gave evidence at the trial of John McIntosh for the murder of Patrick Ward, 23 Mar 1819: 'I live at Upper Minto in the same house with the prisoner – the house is between Mr McIntosh's and my husband's. Ward had stopped me... I charged him with a robbery and a rape – he took my baby's things from under my arm that I was going to wash... he forcibly possessed himself of my person'. Box 18, 2530 ML.

Notes (Chapter 8)

39 Jane Bayly/McKay: Court of Criminal Jurisdiction, 5/1121, reel 2390, p 347, AONSW.
40 Jane Jones, 1149, reel 2651, p 225, AONSW.
41 Catherine Murphy/Muphy and Bridget Conoboy née Phillips: *Sydney Gazette*, 15 Feb 1811; 1119, reel 2390, p 84; 21 Jan 1810, Memorial 4/1821, no 67(a); 26 Feb 1811, Commutations Warrant 4/7020, no 8.
42 Catherine Elliott: *Australian*, 17 Oct 1827.
43 Anne Campbell (*Louisa*), *Australian*, 22 Aug 1827 & 7 Sep 1827. Examples of fines passed on free persons (Windsor) 1 Jan 1813 to 31 Dec 1813 included: Mary Dignuin (*Atlas*), contempt £1; Ann Embrey, abuse and threats £1; Elizabeth Clarke (*Sydney Cove* or *Speke*), rescue of pigs £2.10.0; Mary Goodwin (*Britannia*), assault 10 shillings; Mary Welsh (*Nile*), rescue of pigs £2, and (2) assaulting a constable £1; Maria Markwell, BC, assault; Sarah Jones (*Speedy*, née Thomas, m 2 June 1811, Windsor), swearing 5 shillings; Jane Surrins, selling spirits without a licence £5; Sarah Sullivan (*Alexander*), harbouring a GS late at night (NR); Sarah Conelly (*Minerva*, née Maloney, m 27 July 1800, Sydney), abuse £2; Bridget O'Brien, drunkenness 5 shillings, and (2) drunkenness £2; Mary Hodley (*Speke*, née Stafford, m 9 Mar 1813, Sydney), rescue of a horse £1; Mary Brown, selling spirits without a licence £30; BT Box 12 193-200 ML.
44 *Australian*: Ann Gatty, 14 Feb 1827 & 23 Apr 1827; Mary Cole, 18 Nov 1824; Elizabeth Piggett, 29 Dec 1825.
45 Mary Dunlevey: *Australian*, 10 May 1826.
46 Sophia Davis (*Midas*) and Mary Ward: examples from court reports regularly published in the *Australian* 1824–28.
47 Henry and Susannah Kable (Susannah née Holmes); Court of Civil Jurisdiction, NSW. Court consisted of David Collins, Chaplain Johnson and Surgeon John White, 1 July 1788; the goods retained by Duncan Sinclair, master of the *Alexander*, were 'a parcel of clothes, books and other items, sent on board the *Alexander* by Mrs Jackson of Somerset. Note also Mary Humm (*Lady Juliana*, née Hook, m 6 Mar 1810, Sydney) brought charges against Joshua Holt, 14 Mar 1812, for 'killing a gamecock, the property of her son'. Holt was her neighbour, and she claimed 'envy of my success in trade beyond himself' as the motive. She signed her accusation with her mark, 5/1153, p 149, AONSW.
48 Catherine Cotton: 6 Oct 1809, CSIL 4/1822, reel 1066, no 273, p 3, AONSW.
49 Mrs Jenkins: *Australian*, 5 Apr 1826 & 21 June 1826.
50 Susan Cooper, 13 Mar 1826, CSIL 4/1792, p 170.
51 *Australian*: Mrs Susannah Raymond, 15 Dec 1825; Clara Parsons,

26 Jan 1826; Mrs Dillon, Jan 1826; Thomas Kinton, July 1826; Catherine Brown, July 1826.

CHAPTER 9: 'A WOMAN IS A WORTHY THING'

1 John Macarthur to Nicholas Bayly, BT Box 13, p 894, 1815; see also N Bayly to Macquarie, 7 June 1818, 'The reasons why I particularly requested to have Jane Barnes (*Lord Melville*) returned to me were that we have not had a woman servant that can, or will, either wash or iron, and she can. She is as infamous as I think it possible for a woman to be, and I am sorry to say that the woman we have now and what we have lately had, are but little better'. BT Box 17 2184.
2 Mrs Crossley, Memorial, 17 Sep 1810, CSIL 4/1725, reel 2158, p 340, AONSW; note that on 31 July 1808 Mrs Crossley advertised for an overseer for her farm, *Sydney Gazette*.
3 Ann Horn, servant of James Bradley: Ann/Harriet, alias Horn/Holmes, petition re ticket-of-leave, 13 Sep 1824, CSIL 4/1716, no 1334, AONSW.
4 Phillip's views on the conduct of the expedition and the treatment of convicts, written before he had seen the women who were to accompany the expedition, *HRNSW* 1, pt 2, p 50ff: 'The women in general I suppose possess neither virtue nor honesty. But there may be some for thefts who still retain some degree of virtue'.
5 Hunter to Portland, 1 Mar 1802, *HRA* 1, III, p 421; King to Hobart, 1 Mar 1804, *HRNSW* 5, pp 330-1;
6 King, 'Present State of HM Settlements on the East Coast of New Holland called New South Wales', 12 Aug 1806, *HRNSW* 6, pp 150-1; see also Foveaux to Castlereagh, 6 Sep 1808, *HRNSW* 6, p 741.
7 Hunter to Portland, 18 Nov 1798, *HRNSW* 3, p 182.
8 Governor Hunter's Assignment List, COD 197, 1798, AONSW. Note that the problem of labour for convict women continued to plague the governors. On 24 June 1820 William Lawson advised Bigge, 'with respect to the female convicts I am of the opinion that those who will not go out to service ought to be left confined to labour in manufacturing blankets, linsey woolsey and course [*sic*] linens for the Government servants, and to have no intercourse with men; this mode of treatment would induce them to go to service, as service, I think, will tend more to Reformation than any other Employment, and they may probably get married and become mothers'. BT Box 23 4537, ML. Compare these conditions and observations with the state of gaols for women in contemporary Britain.
9 Phillip's Additional Instructions, 20 Aug 1789, gave power to the governor to assign the labour of the convicts to 'non commissioned

356 Notes (Chapter 9)

officers and men of the marine detachment or other persons who may become settlers', *HRNSW* 1, pt 2, p 258; see also Government and General Order 11 June 1801, 'The convicts being the servants of the Crown during their term of transportation, their labour is to be invariably appropriated to the public benefit, and reducing the heavy expense of the colony', *HRNSW* 4, p 403.

10 Castlereagh to Macquarie, 14 May 1809, *HRA* 1, VII, p 84.
11 King to Portland, 1 March 1802, *HRA* 1, III, p 424.
12 Bligh to Windham, 31 Oct 1807, *HRA* 1, VI, p 181; preceding governors sent regular quarterly returns of employment of male and female convicts – see appropriate vols of *HRA*.
13 Sarah McGrady, Julia Brien/O'Brian, Col Sec Papers 4/1733, reel 2160, p 15, AONSW.
14 Indenture certificate: example Certificate of Indenture for convicts from *Francis and Eliza* granted as indented servants, 8 Aug 1815, Col Sec Papers 4/1733, reel 2160, p 15, AONSW. Of the 19 convict women listed, 10 were assigned to women; see also Indenture form of female convicts per *Mary Ann*: 'and we severally promise and agree as aforesaid to find and provide for such female convict or convicts during the time she or they shall be retained in our said service, good and sufficient meat, drink, washing and lodging and on no account directly or indirectly to part with such female convict or convicts or either of them to any person or persons whatever during the term of three years'. BT Box 14 1237. (49 of the *Mary Ann* women were privately assigned.)
15 Ann Keogh (*Canada*), BT Box 19, p 1741 ML; a former housekeeper from Dublin, transported for 7 years for stealing tea trays; married William Blake, F, of Liverpool, banns 30 Dec 1820, BT Box 13, ML.
16 Sarah Lurry, Memorials re land 1810, reel 1066, no 199, AONSW.
17 Mary Jones, petition 1 Dec 1816, Col Sec Letters and Petitions received 1816, 4/1736, reel 2161, p 180, AONSW.
18 Ann Davis, Memorials re land, 28 Jan 1810, reel 1066, no 83a, AONSW.
19 Mary Oliver, BT Box 60a, pp 295-8, ML.
20 Rosetta Marsh (CF 1799), Memorials re land 1810, reel 1066, no 209, AONSW; CF *Hillsborough* with convict husband Charles Madden who died on the voyage, then married Henry Marsh who also died; 1806, self-employed; held a wine and spirit licence, 26 Feb 1808; subscribed to the fund for enclosing the Sydney burial ground.
21 Mary Sarjant, Memorials re land, 6 Sep 1813, Col Sec 4/1822A, reel 1066, no 44, AONSW.
22 Jane Trotter, Memorials re land 1810, 4/1822, reel 1066, no 316, AONSW.
23 Rachael Tounkes (*Mary Ann*), Memorials re land 1813-19, Col Sec 4/1822A, reel 1066, no 54, AONSW.

24 Hannah Taylor, incomplete source, 'no 305 12 Jan 1811', AONSW.
25 Ann Kennedy, CSIL 4/1848, p 19, AONSW.
26 Mary Morris/Moran, incomplete source, no '305A'. Martha Jones, 6 Sep 1813, Memorials re land 1813-19, Col Sec 1822A, reel 1066, no 26, AONSW.
27 Mary McMahon, incomplete source, 'no 154', petition is on the same sheet as that of Patrick Hynes and is in his handwriting, 'Jan'ye 29th 1810', AONSW; she received a Deed of Land grant, 5/12 Nov 1808, *Sydney Gazette*.
28 Sophia Tull, 8 Jan 1810, Memorials re land 1810, reel 1066, no 318, AONSW; see also petition of 20 Sep 1819 signed Sophia Read late Tull; she arrived on the *Duke of Portland* 1807, and first worked as a schoolmistress at Parramatta, *Sydney Gazette*, 2 March 1809.
29 Isabella Roe, incomplete source, 'no 286', 'John Roe's Grant and his wife's Petition Rec'd 10th Jany 1810 . . . Granted lease . . . 60 Governor McQuarry', AONSW. Isabella Manson alias Smith (*Lady Juliana*).
30 Elizabeth Buckner (*Pitt*) bore children to Richard Tuckwell, Quarter-Master Sergeant, NSW Corps, and married Patrick Kirk; additional data from Joan Keywood, Nan Farleigh and G Barnette.
31 Ann Robinson, petitions re land, 13 Aug 1817, 4/1822A, reel 1066, no 42; Ann Innett (*Lady Penrhyn*) married Richard John Robinson, 18 Nov 1792 (Robinson, *Scarborough*).
32 Mary Gotham, petitions re land 1810, reel 1066, no 119; received CP, 4 June 1804, Cert of Emancipation, 7 April 1814 (12/120 S).
33 Mary Marborough: nd 4/1822, reel 1066, no 205, 1814: BC wife to a soldier; Mary McDonagh 'in the colony 10 years and by persevering industry has got a comfortable dwelling', CSIL 4/1822, reel 1066, no 240, AONSW; see also 'List of Persons in Sydney who have been convicts and have now become landholders, including those persons on ticket of leave, October 1820': (women included in the District of Sydney): Mary Shipley (née Moore, *Experiment*, FS, m Parramatta, 27 Sep 1804), 60 acres; Jane Roberts (née Longhurst, *Glatton*, FS, m Sydney, 3 May 1810, to innkeeper), 700 acres; Ann Shorter (*Friends*, FS, m Windsor Edward Robinson, 1 March 1813), 200 acres; Mary Reibey (née Haddock, *Royal Admiral*, m Sydney, 6 Sep 1794), 500 acres by grant, 500 acres by purchase. BT 12 series 1, Box 24, pp 5160-5160B, ML.
34 Elizabeth Giles (*Lady Juliana*) married George Woodford (*Duke of Portland*), 15 Nov 1811, at St John's; on 26 June 1808 she advertised her house for sale; on 4 June subscribed to a fund for enclosing the Sydney burial ground, *Sydney Gazette*.
35 For women in medieval brewing see Judith M Bennett, *Women in the Medieval English Countryside: Gender and Household in*

Brigstock before the Plague, Oxford 1987, p 120ff; for medieval women traders see A Abram, 'Women Traders in Medieval London', *Economic Journal* 26 (1916), pp 276-85; Rodney Hilton, 'Women traders in medieval England', *Women's Studies* 11 (1984); Mary Prior, 'Women and the urban economy: Oxford 1500-1800', in *Women in English Society 1500-1800*, Mary Prior (ed), London 1985. I am indebted to Dr John Walmsley for research data for medieval working/family women.

36 Petition of Hannah Morley, publican, CSIL 4/1759 9/1444.
37 Collins, *An Account...*, Oct 1792, p 202.
38 Martha Todd: Collins, *An Account...*, March 1793, p 229.
39 Collins, *An Account...*, Oct 1794, p 331; note also that Collins described the murder of Simon Burn who died with 'sin upon his head of having profaned the Lord's day by rioting and drunkenness'. Burn was buried 'with orgies suitable to the disposition and habits of the deceased, his widow', pp 328-9.
40 Collins, *An Account...*, Charles Williams (Christopher Magee), p 223.
41 Mrs Alroy: Sarah McGouran/McGournan, BC, 1805 m Matthew McElroy/Alroy (Chapman). 1828 census: husband publican York St Sydney. Additional data: M. Stralow.
42 Few women had licences withdrawn; earlier cases were: 1813, Jane Surkins was fined £5 for selling spirits without a licence; Mary Brown, for the same offence, £36, 'but in consequence of her poverty this fine was forgiven': BT Box 12, 'Fines passed on free persons (Windsor) 1 Jan 1813-31 Dec 1813', ML.
43 Alice Flyn, Mrs Isaac Moss, Mrs Ann Whittaker, Mary Plowright. Evidence of D'Arcy Wentworth to Bigge, 23 Nov 1819, in Ritchie, *The Evidence...*, vol 1, p 56.
44 *Sydney Gazette*, 26 Feb 1809, Ann Trotter, Ann Robinson, Rosetta Marsh, Elizabeth Graham; note that Elizabeth Graham received the deed of a land grant, 15 Oct 1808, *Sydney Gazette*.
45 *Sydney Gazette*: 17 Feb 1810, Mary Reibey; 21 July 1810, Mary Redman, Sarah Wood, Phoebe Waldron, Jane Muckle, Elizabeth Mack; for Mary Reibey's own letters see *SMH*, 4 July 1987, and the *Weekend Australian*, 8-9 Feb 1986.
46 Notices/advertisements in the *Australian* 1824-27; see also 'Names of Public Houses in Sydney 1819-': Mary Cullen, George Street; Mary Plowright, 32 Pitt St (*Speed the Plough*); Rachael Wyatt, Pitt St (*Spread Eagle*); Mary Ford, Upper Pitt St (*Seven Stars*); Mary Driver, Clarence St (*York Ranger*); Ann Whittaker, Harrington St (*Labour in Vain*); Alice Flynn, Gloucester St (*St Patrick*); Sarah Waples, Pitt St (*Adam and Eve*); the following women possessed Beer Licences in 1819: (Sydney) Mary Thomas, Clarence St (*Wheat*

Notes (Chapter 9) **359**

Sheaf); Judith Simpson, Pitt St; Elizabeth Cassidy, Gloucester St (*Lord Nelson*); BT 12, series 1, Box 15, 226/267, ML; note 'Mrs Jones kept a public house at the race course', *Australian*, 25 Nov 1824.

47 Mary Whitfield, 20 Nov 1822, 4/1832, reel 1070, no 421, AONSW: Memorial for licence to sell liquor at *Manchester Arms*, corner of Park and George Streets, Sydney, complaint against landlord Daniel Cooper.

48 Jane Bennet, 21 Feb & 22 Feb 1827, 4/7084, reel 588; women who held licences as bakers between 1 Oct 1810 and 30 Sep 1821 included: Mary Driver (CF *Lord Melville*), Park St; Catherine Kennedy (*Canada*), Clarence St; Sophia Bond (née Sophia Parker, widow of Wm Bond), Pitt St; Sarah Whiting (*Aeolus*), York St; among the list of butchers in 1821 were: Elizabeth Tuckwell (née Sidebotham, *Speke*), Pitt St; Frances Wood (*Glatton*), Pitt St; Sarah Whiting (*Aeolus*), York St; BT 12, series 1, Box 15, 271/279, ML. For trial details, where applicable, see Lists A & B. Note also that women were among the suppliers of meat to Govt, eg 2000 lbs of fresh meat received from Mrs Laycock, 4 Sept 1814, BT Box 13, 806.

49 See Inquiry re prostitution of convicts on *Janus*, HRA 1, X, pp 318ff, 325ff.

50 Thomas Buxton and wife, *Australian*, 1826, living in Campbell St, Sydney, in 1828; occupation: brewer.

51 Elizabeth Lear, licensed butcher, *Australian*, 5 May 1825; note that three women were among the List of Butchers in Sydney, 1821: Elizabeth Tuckwell née Sidebotham (*Speke*), widow, married Richard Tuckwell, 2 Feb 1810, at St Phillip's, later received CP, by 1828 housekeeper to Simon Lear, Macquarie St, Sydney; Frances Wood (*Glatton*) of Pitt St, Sydney; Sarah Whiting (*Aeolus*), York St, Sydney, also licensed baker, from Warwick, listed as 'wife to Francis Whiting' in 1814. BT Box 12, ML.

52 Elizabeth Killett: D'Arcy Wentworth Papers, A765, p 27, ML; *Sydney Gazette*, 4 Sept 1818; I am indebted to Lois Sabine for detailed biography of Elizabeth Killett.

53 Mrs Bodenham, Mary Dillon, Mrs Dockrell, Mrs Jones, Mrs Nightingale, Madame Josephina Rens, Mrs Smith, Mrs Stuart, Mrs Weavers: all representative of advertisements in the *Australian* 1824–28. Similar advertisements appeared in the *Sydney Gazette*.

54 Mrs Bodenham, Mrs Broadbent, Mrs Frankland, Mrs Cheetom, Sarah Cobcroft, Elizabeth Corkshill, Mary Cupitt, Elizabeth Jones, Mrs Kingsmill, Mrs Robertson, Mrs James, Mrs Geoffrey Eager, are all representative of the working women who advertised regularly in the *Australian* 1824–28; note that these women also requested government servants: see for example petition of Mary Brady who 'supports herself by keeping a small shop', 7 Upper Kent

360 Notes (Chapters 9–10)

St, Sydney, 18 July 1828: 'she would like Harriet Lather (*Louisa*) as a servant', CSIL 4/6665/4, AONSW.

55 Jane Codd, *Australian*, 14 Oct 1828; note that on 5 June 1808 Mrs Codd was assaulted and robbed; 12 June 1808 she gave evidence against her attacker, *Sydney Gazette*, 12 June 1808.

56 Mrs Kingsmill, Mrs Geoffrey Eager: women advertising educational services in the *Australian*; for earlier notices see the *Sydney Gazette*, eg Mrs Peter Hodges (CF, *Royal Admiral*) 'will instruct young ladies in Reading, Writing and Arithmetic', *Sydney Gazette*, 2 April 1809.

57 Mary Ann Whitfield, *Australian*, 28 Oct 1824.

58 Mrs Rogers, *Australian*, 11 Aug 1825; Mrs E S Milton, 30 Aug 1826.

59 Mrs Leadbeater; note list of Carts Licensed in Sydney 1819 included the names of 3 women: Sarah Watkins (*Canada*), son to 'James' Ellison bapt 5 Feb 1813, St Phillip's; 1828: Sarah Ellison FS, 10 children, with John Ellison (*Albemarle*) publican, Parramatta; Jane Stubbs, Phillip St, Sydney; Mary Greenwood (*Northampton*) Kent St, Sydney, BT Box 12, ML; note women employed as washerwomen included Judith Kelly (*Sydney Cove*), a washerwoman from Dublin, HO/2 PRO60, p 85, 'female convicts 1810–19', AONSW.

CHAPTER 10: 'THE SWORD OF GOD AND GIDEON'

1 Journal of Arthur Bowes, ML Ms, now published as *The Journal of Arthur Bowes Smyth, Surgeon of the Lady Penrhyn 1787–89*, Sydney 1979; Watkin Tench, *Sydney's First Four Years*, L F Fitzhardinge (ed), Sydney 1979; Collins, *An Account...*, Fletcher (ed), Feb 1788; Ralph Clark, Journal 1787–92, typescript & letterbook, ML.

2 Plummer to Macquarie, 4 May 1809, *HRNSW* 7, p 20.

3 See also Robinson, *The Hatch and Brood of Time...* pp 74-7.

4 Ann Parker, convicted at the age of 15 of 'stealing goods from Catherine Martin with whom she lodged', said at her trial that she 'worked as a prostitute in Catherine Martin's house'; additional data from A K Mann and M Sutton; Elizabeth Berry, soldier's wife with 4 children in 1814, additional data from L J Hardie.

5 King to Castlereagh, 12 Aug 1806, *HRNSW* 6, p 151.

6 Ibid.

7 Castlereagh to Bligh, 31 Dec 1807, *HRA* 1, VI, p 202.

8 Castlereagh to Macquarie, 14 May 1809, *HRA* 1, VII, p 84; see also Macquarie's Proclamation promoting marriage, 24 Feb 1810, 7/2655, pp 579-81, AONSW; Macquarie to Castlereagh, encl 4, 30 Apr 1810, Proclamation against immorality and vice, *HRA* 1, VII, pp 278-9.

Notes (Chapter 10) **361**

9   For biography of Esther Abrams see J S Levi & G F Bergman, *Australian Genesis: Jewish Convicts and Settlers 1788–1850*, Melbourne 1974, ch 3, 'The First Lady'; see also Esther Julian, Memorial 4/1822, no 167, nd, asking confirmation from Macquarie for 590 acres of land she had received from Colonel Paterson; 'five and twenty years in the Colony during which time she never received the smallest indulgence from Government'.

10 Mary Marshall: Petition to Macquarie, 15 Jan 1810, Memorials re Land 1810, CS Letters 4/1821, reel 1066, no 210, AONSW.

11 See chapters 5 & 6 for Irish family women transported to NSW; see also Robinson, 'Colleen to Matilda . . .', in *Ireland and Australia . . .*, Kiernan (ed).

12 Ann Byrne and Owen McMahon, additional data from J Curnoe & F Cockle; Mary Consadine/Cusadine, from Noel McGuire. Note Maquarie's reply to Marsden, 19 Feb 1817: 'I am fully as great an advocate for marriage as you can possibly be, both amongst Free Persons and convicts; and it has been my study to promote this useful and holy institution by every means in my power . . . I conceive it to be a measure of too much importance to the peace and future happiness of the parties concerned to be hurried or forced upon them, and therefore the more time they have for consideration, the more likely they are to form a judicious and permanent connection', BT 12, series 1, Box 15, p 1685.

13 Lydia Monroe, additional data from Kevin Richardson and Yvonne Enclert.

14 Sarah Wise, additional data from E Cox.

15 See Robinson, 'The first forty years . . .' in *In Pursuit of Justice . . .*, Mackinolty and Radi (eds).

16 Ibid; also Robinson, *The Hatch and Brood of Time . . .*, ch 3, 'I am not for Marrying'.

17 Miriam Dixson, *The Real Matilda, Women and Identity in Australia 1788 to 1975*, Pelican 1976; see also Patricia Grimshaw, 'Women and the family in Australian history – a reply to *The Real Matilda*', *HS*, vol 18, no 72, Apr 1979, for a critical assessment of *The Real Matilda*. Ann Summers, *Damned Whores and God's Police*, Victoria 1975; see also Robinson, *The Hatch and Brood of Time . . .*, chs 3 & 6, for a reply to the assumption that 'social and economic conditions of the first fifty years . . . fostered whores not wives'. See also Annette Salt, *These Outcast Women*, Sydney 1974, vol 2, in *Macquarie Colonial Papers*, Portia Robinson (gen ed), for a reassessment of the role and influence of the Female Factory.

18 Macarthur to Bigge, nd, in Ritchie, *The Evidence . . .*, vol 2, p 81; see also 'Names of Persons Tried at Parramatta 4 March 1815 to 8 Nov 1817', BT 12, Series 1, Box 12, p 230, ML: Ann Redmond (*Experi-*

ment), rioting, 3 months in Factory; Sarah Barrs (*Wanstead*), stealing wine, 1 month solitary, bread & water and 5 months in Factory; Barbara Sutherland (Sullivan on ship) (*Indispensable*), stealing goods, 3 months hard labour in Factory; Mary Squires (*Broxbornebury*), neglect of work, 3 months in Factory; Ann Tierney, drunkenness, 1 week in cell on bread & water; Mary Flood (*Catherine*), run away, 6 months in Factory; Sarah Ellis (*Minstrel* or *Lord Melville*), run away, ironed & confined in Factory 6 months; Ann Healy (*Indispensable*) v Charles Ivory, claiming support for 2 bastard children, given £1 per week; Jane Hurst (*Minstrel*) & Mary Margerum (*Wanstead*), rioting in Factory, to be chained together for one month. BT 12, series 1, Box 12, 230, ML.

19 Letter of Elizabeth Beckwith to her brother, *PC* 1:69, PRO940, 1821.
20 Memorial of Beatrice McLeod (*Maria*), Nov 1822, CSIL 4/1830, reel 1070, no 237, AONSW.
21 Petition of Thomas Moore to Gov Darling, 15 Oct 1830 & 10 Dec 1830, CSIL 4/2167, reel 2197, AONSW.
22 Memorials of Margaret McDonald, 26 Sep 1826 & 10 Oct 1826, CSIL 4/7084, reel 586, AONSW; note that McDonald was the married name; she was tried and transported as Margaret Smith (*Providence*).
23 *Freeman's Journal*, Nov & Dec 1817.
24 Marsden, 'Observations on the Female Convicts' (attributed to Chaplain Marsden), ML Ms; see M Saclier, 'Sam Marsden's Colony: Notes on a Manuscript in the Mitchell Library, Sydney', *JRAHS*, vol 52, part 2, 1966.
25 Margaret Catchpole, Letters, ML Ms; see also Harold Lingwood's Ms biography of Margaret Catchpole, Shelly Garner Papers (16131A), Battye Library of WA History, Perth.
26 Sarah Bird, *True Briton* (London), 10 Nov 1798, 'Letter of a woman lately transported to Botany Bay to her father', reprinted in *HRNSW* 3, pp 509-10. Additional data from Joy Jorgensen.
27 Memorial of Mary Johnson, 7 Nov 1825, CSIL 4/1842, reel 1079, no 417, AONSW; Lucy Neale: 10 Sep 1809, CSIL 4/1750, reel 2167, pp 152-3; Mary Larkham: 2 Sep 1824, CSIL 4/1838, reel 1075, no 561; Elizabeth Marr: 20 Dec 1810, CSIL 4/1822, reel 1066, no 207.
28 Memorial of Ann Bevin nd 1822, CSIL 4/1763, reel 2172, p 137, AONSW; Mary Barnett: nd 1822, CSIL 4/1763, reel 2172, p 133, AONSW.
29 Ralph Clark, Journal ..., 11 Feb 1788; cited in *Sydney Cove 1788* ... Cobley (ed), p 67.
30 Evidence of Revd William Cowper to Bigge, 23 Jan 1821, in Ritchie, *The Evidence* ..., vol 1, pp 150-1; evidence of Robert Cartwright to Bigge, 26 Nov 1819, ibid, p 157.

31 Evidence of John Macarthur to Bigge, nd, ibid, p 83.

CHAPTER 11: 'SHE SANG HER TOIL AND TROUBLE'

1 Report of Royal Commission on the Labour of Women and Children in Mines and Factories, *PP*, 1842/xvii/163-4, evidence of Betty Harris, drawer, Little Bolton: 'I have drawn till I have had the skin off me: the belt and chain is worse when we are in the family way... I have known many a man beat his drawer. I have known men take liberties with the drawers, and some of the women are bastards'.
2 Collins, *An Account...*, Feb 1788, p 14.
3 Sarah May (*Northampton*), tried at York Assizes in 1814 at the age of 21 and sentenced for 14 years; a former servant, born Yorkshire, she received a ticket-of-leave and cohabited with William Judd, convict, in Sydney until he was sent to Port Macquarie. See also 5 Dec 1818, (PMS) CSIL 4/1855, p 181; Mary Holford petitioned in 1825 that she was unable to pay her debts for 3 months, 25 July 1825, 4/1787, p 48.
4 Elizabeth Mason and James Squires: see evidence of James Squires to Bigge, 29 Dec 1820, Ritchie, *The Evidence...*, vol 1, pp 116-17: 'I have been in this Colony from its earliest establishment and for 30 years I have been a brewer.' Additional data from Mary O'Brien: Squires became a wealthy philanthropist; Elizabeth Mason was the grandmother of the first colonial-born premier of NSW, James Squire Farnell.
5 Evidence of Revd Samuel Marsden to Bigge, 'A Few General Remarks respecting the Convicts', undated, in Ritchie, *The Evidence...*, 2, pp 109-10: in answer to the question 'Have you frequently discovered that women who are married here after their arrival, had husbands in England & that those Husbands join them here after the second marriage?' Marsden replied: 'I have seen several Instances of this kind & one very affecting Instance in a Person named Patrick Emmentter.' He had married a young woman who thought her husband was dead and, on finding him alive and in the colony she had had no choice but to go with the first husband 'and the 2nd Husband has been unhappy ever since'. The case of Constable John Jennings, who died of a broken heart after his lawful wife arrived in the colony and he had to part from his second wife, ibid.
6 Ann Taylor/Baylis(s): I am indebted to Yvonne Browning for biographical data for Ann (Nancy) Taylor; see also *Sydney Gazette*, 1 Jan 1827, for account of events leading to the accidental poisoning of Ann Baylis(s) and her daughter.

7   Petition of Sophia and William Phillips to the Secretary of State, London, Oct 1819, *PC* 1:67.
8   Memorial of Mary Moen, 17 Jan 1831, CSIL 4/2167, reel 2194, no 137, & 4/1740, reel 2163, p 66, AONSW.
9   Memorial of Sarah Meagher, 16 Apr 1822, CSIL 4/1831, reel 1070, no 245.
10 Evidence of Revd Robert Cartwright to Bigge, 26 Nov 1819 in Ritchie (ed), *The Evidence..*, vol 1, p 158.
11 Petition of Ann Evans, 19 May 1826, 4/7084, reel 588, 'Petitions of wives of convicts for their husbands to be assigned to them', AONSW; see also petition of Elizabeth Fogarty (*Mary Ann*) to have her husband John Fogarty (*Atlas*) assigned to her; she had married the former seaman with the Governor's consent (he was 33, she 44), and John Redman of Sydney testified that both had been in his service for 15 months 'and conducted themselves honest sober and attentive'. They married 20 Apr 1818 at St John's; see 'Assignment and Employment of convicts', 04/7184, AONSW; see also petition of Ann Kelly (*Woodman*), married to Patrick Kelly (*Southworth*), both Catholic, Patrick assigned to his brother Edward Kelly of Broken Bay; husband to be transferred to her; permission granted, 4/0784, AONSW; not so fortunate was Mary Kennedy (CF *Thames*), who waited five years for her husband Thomas McGuiggan (*Isabella*) to be reassigned to her from Government, 4/7084, AONSW.
12 Petition of Mrs Thomas Egan, 3 Apr 1826, 4/7084, reel 557, AONSW.
13 Petition of Charlotte Dick, 4/7084, reel 558, AONSW.
14 Petition of Ann Kerr, 4 Sep 1826, 4/7084, reel 558, AONSW.
15 Petition of Mary Pearce, July 1826, 4/7084, reel 558, AONSW.
16 Petition of Ellen Sewell, nd, 4/7084, reel 558, p 32, AONSW (located between Petition, 3 Dec 1815, and Petition, 7/8 Dec 1815).
17 Petition of Catherine Donough, 24 June 1826, 4/7084, reel 558, AONSW.
18 Petition of Margaret Byrne, 15 May 1826, 4/7084, reel 558, AONSW.
19 Petition of Ann Robertson, May 1826, 4/7084, reel 588, AONSW.
20 Petition of Mary Ann McDade, Feb 1826, 4/7084, reel 588, AONSW.
21 Petition of Mary Sellers, 22 July 1826, 4/7085, reel 558, AONSW.
22 Petition of Mary Barret, 20 May 1826, 4/7084, reel 588, AONSW.
23 Petition of Mary Jones, 1 Dec 1816, 4/1736, reel 2161, 'Col Sec Letters & Petitions Received 1816', AONSW.
24 Memorial of Mary Ann Easterbrook – Mrs Thomas, 28 July 1825 & nd Oct 1825, 4/1787, p 56, & 4/1788, p 7. See also letter from James Lancaster, Governor of the Workhouse at Stockhouse Parish, Plymouth, *PC*, 1, reel 942, piece no 1/71, 1823: 'Mary Ann Easterbrook who with her children are chargeable to this Parish having received a letter dated in July last from her husband, one Thomas

Easterbrook a convict, transported to New South Wales and who sailed from this country about October 1820 – in which letter he states himself to be in the service of Mr H McArthur and who says he has written home to solicit a free passage for his wife and children. I have to request Sir that you will be pleased to inform me whether there be any grants from His Majesty's Government for that purpose or, if not, as to the most proper mode of proceeding will be most thankfully received.' Thomas was 50 in 1828, his wife 45, their two sons 15 and 13. Also, petition to Henry Hobhouse, 12 Oct 1819, *PC* 1:67: '[she] has embarked on the *Janus* being sent from Maidstone Gaol ... accompanied by her child James Easterbrook 3 and has most earnestly requested conjunction with her husband ... a biscuit baker at the Victualling Office Deptford for permission to send the child to his father'.

25 Petition of Sarah Hill, nd Apr 1826, 4/7084, reel 558, AONSW.
26 Petition of Elizabeth McConolly, nd 1825, 4/1843, reel 1079, AONSW.
27 Memorial of Catherine Slater, nd 1824, CSIL 4/1839, reel 1076, AONSW. See also petition to join husband (*Larkins* 1817) in Botany Bay, *PC* 1:67, 9 Mar 1819.
28 Memorial of Matilda Fisk, 1822, 4/1829, no 121, AONSW.
29 Petition of Honora Flynn, 19 Apr 1826, 4/7084, & 1829, 4/2167, no 224, & 4/2167, no 90, AONSW.
30 Memorial of Margaret Cooper, nd, Col Sec 4/1829, reel 1069, no 67, AONSW.
31 Memorial of Mrs Margaret Bunker, 20 Jan 1812 & 28 Jan 1812, CSIL 4/1727, reel 21, pp 364-5, 368, AONSW.
32 Memorial of Ann Davis, 28 Jan 1810, 'Memorials re Land', reel 1066, no 83A, AONSW.
33 Petition of Bridget Farraugher, 14 Apr 1826, 4/7084, reel 558, AONSW.
34 Petition of Jane Jackson, 2 Oct 1826, 4/7084, reel 558, AONSW.
35 Petition of Mary Hartford, nd, 4/7084, reel 558, (1826?), AONSW.
36 Petition of Margaret Johnston, 25 July 1826, 4/7084, reel 558, AONSW.
37 Petition of Eleanor Crozier, 29 Sep 1826, 4/7084, reel 557, AONSW.
38 Petition of Mary Clare/Fernee, wife of Joseph Fernee, 10 Nov 1826, 4/7084, reel 558, AONSW.
39 Petition of Elizabeth Carver, 18 Apr 1827, 4/7084, reel 558, AONSW.
40 Memorial of Charlotte Dixon (Mrs Thomas), 29 June 1815, CSIL 4/1733, reel 2160, p 1, AONSW.
41 Memorial of Anne Keith, 1825, CSIL 4/1812, reel 2187, p 163, AONSW.
42 Memorial of Katherine Jackson, 23 Dec 1823, CSIL 4/1773, reel 2176, p 131, AONSW.

366 Notes (Chapter 11)

43 Petition of Maria Jennings, 12 Feb 1827, 4/7084, reel 588, AONSW.
44 Petition of Maria Harebut, 3 Nov 1826, 4/7084, reel 588, AONSW.
45 Memorial of Sarah Bellinger, 20 Feb 1826, CSIL, 4/7084, reel 588, AONSW.
46 Petition of Patrick McBride, husband of Ann Griffiths, 4 July 1831, 4/2167, reel 2194, no 284, AONSW.
47 Petitions of/re: Mary Hite, 1822, 4/1763, p 287; Eleanor Watt, 1822, (PMS) 4/1763, p 281; Ann Coleman, 1824, (PMS) 4/1872, pp 25 & 28, AONSW.
48 Petition of Mary Ann Kelly, 1826, (PMS) 4/1876, p 36, AONSW.
49 Petition of Mary Smith, wife of Neal Smith of Port Macquarie, 7 June 1824, 4/1811, p 117, AONSW.
50 Petition of husband of Mary Roberts, 24 Sep 1823, 4/1772, p 146, AONSW.
51 Petition of James Devonport, 1822 (PMS) 4/1865, p 3, AONSW.
52 Memorial of Elizabeth Lee, wife of James Donohue, nd 1822–23, CSIL 4/1715, AONSW.
53 Memorial of Elizabeth Bason, wife of Joseph Lee, 18 Sep 1826, CSIL 4/1794, reel 2183, p 110, AONSW.
54 Memorial of Mary McMahon, 29 Jan 1810, CSIL 4/1821, reel 1066, no 154, p 1, AONSW.
55 Memorial of Elizabeth Mitchell, wife of William Freeman, 14 Aug 1822, 4/1831, reel 107, no 249, AONSW.
56 Memorial of Sarah Hamilton, 20 Mar 1821, CSIL 4/1862, AONSW.
57 *Sydney Gazette*, 5 July 1807: 'Articles of separation by mutual consent, dated 4 July 1807 ... the wife to have lands, farms, premises etc. except the horse named Miss Sprightly'. Mary Chalker was Mary Kearns (*Sugar Cane*); William Chalker (*Coromandel*) was emancipated by 1806 and owned '65 acres by grant and purchase by rights of wife'. Other cases included: Mrs Ann Morley who cautioned the public not to purchase a property from Joseph Morley, 9, 16 & 23 July 1809; her husband countered with a notice that he would not pay her debts, Nov 1809, *Sydney Gazette*. In 1808 Mrs Mary Pate published notice of separation from her husband; on 4 Sep and 2 Oct 1809, Sarah Reynolds warned the public against accepting Edward Reynolds's security; the husband of Mrs Wall would not be responsible for his debts, 4 June 1808; Catherine White/Mellon absconded with her husband's promissory notes and he cautioned against giving her credit; she then advertised as a mantua-maker & milliner, 12 June 1808, 1 Jan 1809, *Sydney Gazette*.
58 Petition of Mary Mazzagora, Dec 1823, 4/1773, p 120 (re misconduct), & 4 Sep 1826, 4/1794, p 89, AONSW.
59 Petition of Patrick Farley, 1824, (PMS) 4/1872, p 42, AONSW.
60 J Moss, *Australian*, 14 Apr 1825.

CONCLUSION: 'THE WOMEN OF BOTANY BAY'

1 Mary Long: additional data from K. Gaut.
2 Catherine Barry: additional data from NJ Asperey, S Lavarack, F McKenzie and CA Ryan.
3 Mary Cassidy: *Australian*, 9 Dec 1826.
4 Letters of Josiah Godber, NL (Canberra).
5 *Australian*, 28 Apr 1825; see also 14 & 21 Apr 1825: note, 'The Markets are the favourite employment of the Sydney ladies to attend'.

WOMEN TRANSPORTED TO NEW SOUTH WALES

List A. Women transported from England, 1788–1827
    A–1: Women transported
    A–2: Aliases or variant names
    A–3: Women listed on the indents of more than one ship

List B. Women transported from Ireland, 1791–January 1828
    B–1: Women transported
    B–2: Aliases or variant names

These lists give, for the first time, details of every woman transported to New South Wales on ships leaving from Irish and English ports. They are divided alphabetically by name within years of trial and under the ship on which they were transported, and show trial place and trial date where known. For more information about ship and voyage number see the guide to ships in the preliminary pages of this book.

Notes
Convict women were occasionally transported on ships with free passengers or carrying male convicts. The number rarely exceeded two or three and the reasons for their inclusion on that particular ship are unknown. The only evidence by which they may be identified is the musters or the 1828 Census. This information was provided by the women and there is the possibility of error.

F. Archer, Inspector of Prisons, Dublin, wrote in his answer to the accusations of Governor Macquarie that female convicts were on the *Three Bees*. There is no record of these women on the ship's indents; the only remaining record is the 1828 Census.

It is probable that Archer intended to name the *Catherine* which carried Irish women convicts, the *Three Bees* carrying Irish male convicts.

Variant spellings and discrepancies are found throughout these original records. The name listed is that name given on the indents of the transport ship. This has been checked against all known copies of the Ships' Indents held in New South Wales and in Dublin, and counterchecked against trial papers, newspaper reports, surgeons' journals, gaolers' and prison reports where applicable.

There are numerous examples in the Irish contemporary records where no trial date or trial place is given. A listing of women for whom there were no trial dates is given at the end of lists A-1, A-2 and B-1.

NR No response.

* An alias or variant spelling of the name is given in lists A-2 and B-2. All variants of given names are not included.

† The name appears on the indents of more than one ship. The names of the ships are given in list A-3.

LIST A WOMEN TRANSPORTED FROM ENGLAND 1788-1827

A-1 WOMEN TRANSPORTED

1782 TRIAL YEAR

Friendship 1788
BARBER, Elizabeth 16-10-1782; London
HALL, Margaret 04-12-1782; London

1783 TRIAL YEAR

Charlotte 1788
JONES, Margaret 08-03-1783; Launceston
WICKHAM, Mary 02-08-1783; New Sarum

Friendship 1788
DUDGENS*,
  Elizabeth 10-09-1783; London
GARTH*, Susanah 10-09-1783; London
GREEN, Hannah 10-09-1783; London
HART, Frances 10-09-1783; London
POWLEY*, Elizabeth 14-03-1783; Thetford
WARE, Charlotte 10-12-1783; London

Lady Penrhyn 1788
DAVIES*, Sarah 02-08-1783; Worcester
HUMPHRIES*, Mary 10-12-1783; London
LOCK, Elizabeth 26-03-1783; Gloucester

Prince of Wales 1788
WILLIAMS, Frances 02-09-1783; Mold, Flint

1784 TRIAL YEAR

Friendship 1788
HARVEY*, Elizabeth 23-03-1784; Bury
HOLMES*,
  Susannah 19-03-1784; Thetford
McCORMACK*,
  Mary 12-08-1784; Liverpool

Lady Penrhyn 1788
COLLEN*,
  Elizabeth 08-12-1784; London
FOWNES, Margaret 04-08-1784; Salop
GABEL*, Mary 13-01-1784; Southwark
HART, Catherine 08-12-1784; London
TWY(I)FIELD*,
  Ann 04-08-1784; Salop

Prince of Wales 1788
BOULTON, Rebecca 16-07-1784; Lincoln
ELLAM, Deborah 30-08-1784; Chester
HARRISON, Mary 06-03-1784; Lincoln

1785 TRIAL YEAR

Charlotte 1788
JACKSON, Hannah 27-07-1785; Bristol
SMITH, Ann 01-03-1785; Winchester
SMITH, Hannah 05-04-1785; Winchester

Friendship 1788
CLARK, Elizabeth 11-01-1785; Derby
MASON, Betty/
  Elizabeth 23-03-1785; Gloucester
PARKER, Elizabeth 23-03-1785; Gloucester
PARKISON*,
  Jane Ann 21?07-1785; Manchester

Lady Penrhyn 1788
ABELL*, Mary 05-03-1785; Worcester
BELLAMY, Sarah 09-07-1785; Worcester

BIRD, Elizabeth/ Winifred	14-03-1785; Maidstone	GROVES, Mary	09-07-1785; Lincoln
BOULTON*, Mary	12-03-1785; Salop	LAYCOCK, Caroline	NR-04-1785; Westminster
BRANDHAM*, Mary	23-02-1785; London		
COLPITTS*, Ann	20-07-1785?; Durham		
COOPER, Mary	19-07-1785; Worcester	**1786 TRIAL YEAR**	
CRUX*, Jane	14-09-1785; London		
DALTON*, Elizabeth	14-09-1785; London	*Charlotte* 1788	
DAVIES*, Mary	12-03-1785; Salop	BRAUND*, Mary	30-03-1786; Exeter, Devon
FOWLES, Ann/Elizabeth	06-04-1785; London	CAREY, Ann	30-03-1786; Taunton
GASCOIGNE*, Olive/Olivia	05-03-1785; Worcester	CLEAVER*, Mary	04-04-1786; Bristol
		COLE, Elizabeth	20-03-1786; Exeter, Devon
GEORGE, Ann	11-05-1785; London	COOMBES, Ann	30-03-1786; Taunton
GREENWOOD, Mary	13-12-1785?; London	EATON*, Mary	20-03-1786; Exeter, Devon
HAMILTON, Maria	19-10-1785; London		
HARRISON, Mary	19-10-1785; London	FITZGERALD*, Jane	04-04-1786; Bristol
HIPSLEY, Elizabeth	23-02-1785; London	FRYER*, Catherine	20-03-1786; Exeter, Devon
JACKSON*, Jane/Mary	29-06-1785; London		
LANGLEY, Jane	14-09-1785; London	LYNCH, Ann	20-03-1786; Bristol
LAWRENCE, Mary	23-02-1785?; London	MEECH, Jane	20-03-1786; Exeter, Devon
LEE, Elizabeth	23-02-1785; London		
LEONARD, Elizabeth	23-02-1785; London	PHILLIPS, Mary	30-03-1786; Taunton
LOVE, Mary	14-03-1785; Maidstone	POOLE, Jane	19-08-1786; Wells
McCABE*, Eleanor	17?05-1785; London	STEWART, Margaret	28-08-1786; Exeter
MARSHALL, Mary	23-02-1785?; London	*Friendship* 1788	
MITCHELL, Mary	03-10-1785; Kingston	BEARDSLEY*, Ann	05-08-1786; Derby
MORTON, Mary/Ann	23-02-1785; London	EARLY*, Rachel	24-07-1786; Reading, Berks
PARTRIDGE*, Sarah	23-02-1785?; London		
PHYN*, Mary	14-09-1785; London	McCORMICK*, Sarah	04-05-1786; Manchester
PILES, Mary/Sarah	06-04-1785; London	OLDFIELD, Isabella	20-07-1786; Manchester
READ, Ann	20-02-1785?; London	THACKERY*, Elizabeth	05-05-1786; Manchester
SLATER, Sarah/Mary	23-02-1785; London	WATKINS*, Mary	25-04-1786; Cowbridge
SPRIGMORE, Charlotte	19-08?1785; London	*Lady Juliana* 1790	
TURNER*, Mary	05-03-1785; Worcester	KARRAIN*, Eleanor	NR-10-1786; London
WRIGHT, Ann	23-02-1785; London	KEARNON*, Elizabeth	25-10-1786; Middlesex
YATES, Nancy/Ann	09-07-1785; York	ROSE, Mary	NR-03-1786; Lincoln City
Neptune 1790		*Lady Penrhyn* 1788	
SANDWICK, Eleanor	29-07-1785; Cumberland	ADAMS, Mary	13-12-1786; London
WATKINS, Rachael	17-03-1785; Hereford	ALLEN, Mary	25-10-1786; London
WATT, Jane	09-03-1785; Stafford	ALLEN*, Tasmin	25-10-1786; London
		BAKER, Martha	30-08-1786; London
Prince of Wales 1788		BRAND*, Lucy	19-07-1786; London
FIELD, Jane	NR-NR-1785; London	BUNN*, Margaret	26-04-1786; London

BURDS*, Sarah	25-10-1786; London	JONES, Grace	NR-07-1786; Denbighshire
BURKITT*, Mary	20?08-1786; London		
CARROLL, Mary	25-10-1786; London	MORGAN, Martha	04-10-1786; Pembroke
COLE, Elizabeth	26-04-1786; London	NEVE, Margaret	11-01-1786; Cumberland
DAVIDSON*, Rebecca	25-10-1786; London	WILSON, Mary	03-10-1786; Cumberland
DAVIS, Ann	26-04-1786; London		

Prince of Wales 1788

ABRAHAMS*, Esther	30-08-1786; London
BALDWIN*, Ruth	20-08-1786; London
DALY*, Ann	03-10-1786; Cheshire
DIXON, Mary	31-05-1786; London
FARMER, Ann	01-12-1786; London
HERBERT*, Jane/Rose	30-08-1786; London
JOHNSON, Mary	26-04-1786; London
LONG, Mary	25-10-1786; London
MASON*, Susannah	NR-01-1786; London
ROLT, Mary	NR-NR-1786; London
SPENCE, Mary	NR-01?1786; Wigan

DAVIS, Frances	06-03-1786; Chelmsford
DUTTON, Ann	26-04-1786; London
DYKES*, Mary	26-04-1786; London
EVANS*, Elizabeth	13-12-1786; London
FITZGERALD, Elizabeth	13-12-1786; London
GREEN*, Ann	13-12-1786; London
HALL, Elizabeth	18-01-1786; Newcastle
HANDLAND*, Dorothy	22-02-1786; London
HARWOOD*, Esther	20?08-1786; London
HILL, Mary	25-10-1786; London
HUFNELL*, Susan	02-10-1786; Worcester
INETT, Ann	11-03-1786; Worcester
JACKSON, Mary	20-03-1786; London
LEWIS, Sophia	25-10-1786; London
NEEDHAM, Elizabeth	19-07-1786; London
NORTON, Phoebe/Phebe	25-10-1786; London
OSBORNE*, Elizabeth	30-08-1786; London
PARKER, Mary	26-04-1786; London
POWELL, Ann	13-12-1786; London
SANDLIN(E)*, Ann	31-12-1786; London
SMITH, Ann	30-08-1786; London
SPRINGHAM, Mary	25-10-1786; London
THORNTON, Ann	13-12-1786; London
TRIPPETT, Susan	20?08-1786; London
WADE*, Mary	19-07-1786; London
WARD, Ann	13?12-1786; London
WILLIAMS, Mary	22-02-1786; London

1787 TRIAL YEAR

Charlotte 1788

FRASER*, Ellen	NR-01-1787; Manchester

Lady Juliana 1790

ARMSDEN*, Ann	Lent 1787; Kent
ARNOLD, Mary	12-12-1787; Middlesex
ATKINSON, Mary	23-05-1787; Middlesex
AYRES, Elizabeth	24-10-1787; Middlesex
BARNES, Elizabeth	12-09-1787; Middlesex
BEACH, Mary	12-12-1787; Middlesex
BROOKS, Ann	12-12-1787; Middlesex
BROOKS, Jane	12-09-1787; Middlesex
BROWN, Elizabeth	24-10-1787; Middlesex
BUTLER, Mary	12-12-1787; Middlesex
CARROLL, Mary	18-04-1787; London
CARTER, Sarah	11-07-1787; Middlesex
CHAFEY, Mary	11-07-1787; Middlesex
CHAPLIN, Mary	12-12-1787; Middlesex
COWCHER*, Mary	24-10-1787; London
DAVIS, Mary	12-09-1787; Middlesex
DAVIS, Mary	24-10-1787; Middlesex
DAWSON, Jane	12-09-1787; Middlesex
DAWSON*, Mary	23-05-1787; Middlesex
DORSET, Sarah Mary	24-10-1787; London

Neptune 1790

BOND, Mary	19-08-1786; Somerset
EVANS, Sarah	NR-07-1786; Denbighshire
HAWKINS, Elizabeth	07-07-1786; Bedford
JOHNSON, Elizabeth	NR-01-1786; Glamorgan

DOYLE, Ann   Lent 1787; Kent
EMMES*, Ann   12-12-1787; Middlesex
EVERITT*, Ann   Summer 1787; Essex
FARRELL, Elizabeth   23-05-1787; Middlesex
FITZPATRICK, Rose   12-09-1787; Middlesex
FORBES, Jane   12-09-1787; London
FORTESCUE, Ann   Lent 1787; Kent
GALE, Elizabeth   12-09-1787; London
GOSLIN(G),
  Elizabeth   24-10-1787; Middlesex
GRAHAM, Sarah   23-05-1787; Middlesex
HAGAR, Ann   12-09-1787; London
HAYNES, Alice   12-12-1787; London
HENDERSON*,
  Elizabeth   12-09-1787; Middlesex
HOLLOWAY,
  Elizabeth   11-07-1787; London
HOPPER, Elizabeth   12-12-1787; London
HOWARD, Ann   12-12-1787; Middlesex
IVEMAY*, Elizabeth   24-10-1787; Middlesex
JOHNSON*,
  Elizabeth   23-05-1787; London
JONES, Elizabeth   24-10-1787; London
JONES, Hannah   18-04-1787; Middlesex
JONES, Mary   12-09-1787; London
KEMP, Ann   18-04-1787; Middlesex
KIMES*, Mary   18-04-1787; Middlesex
LLOYD, Jane   12-09-1787; Middlesex
LONG, Mary   23-05-1787; Middlesex
McCORMICK, Sarah   NR-09-1787; London
McDONALD,
  Eleanor   12-12-1787; Middlesex
MANNING, Sarah   Lent 1787; Essex
NASH, Mary   23-05-1787; Middlesex
OLIVER†, Mary   Lent 1787; Kent
OWSTON*, Ann   Summer 1787; Surrey
PARRY*, Elizabeth   24-10-1787; Middlesex
PEALING, Hannah   12-12-1787; Middlesex
PENNINGTON,
  Elizabeth   12-09-1787; London
PICKETT, Susannah   12-12-1787; London
POOR, Ann   Lent 1787; Kent
PRICE,   Summer 1787;
  Ann/Elizabeth   Gloucester
RANDALL, Mary   12-12-1787; Middlesex
RICHARDS,
  Elizabeth   NR-08-1787?; Warwick
SANDERS*, Jane   12-12-1787; Middlesex

SIMPSON*,
  Charlotte   24-10-1787; Middlesex
SMITH*, Elizabeth   11-07-1787; Middlesex
STEEL, Ann   12-09-1787; Middlesex
STEEL, Elizabeth   24-10-1787; Middlesex
STEWART, Mary   23-05-1787; Middlesex
STOCKWELL, Ann   Lent 1787; Gloucester
SUTTON, Sarah   24-10-1787; Middlesex
THORNTON,
  Ester/Hester   18-04-1787; Middlesex
TUCK, Mary   24-10-1787; Middlesex
TURNER, Rachael   12-12-1787; Middlesex
VANDEBUS, Jane   12-09-1787; Middlesex
WALKER, Mary   23-05-1787; Middlesex
WATSON*, Elizabeth   23-05-1787; London
WILLIAMS*, Mary   24-10-1787; Middlesex
WILMOT, Catherine   Lent 1787; Essex
WOOD, Ann   24-10-1787; Middlesex
WOOD, Margaret   NR-04-1787; London
YEOMAN(S), Ann   12-09-1787; Middlesex
YOUNG, Sarah   11-07-1787; Middlesex

Lady Penrhyn **1788**
ALLEN*, Mary   10-01-1787; London
ANDERSON,
  Elizabeth   10-01-1787; London
BECKFORD,
  Elizabeth   10-01-1787; London
BRUCE, Elizabeth   10-01-1787; London
COOK*, Charlotte   10-01-1787; London
DAWSON, Margaret   10-01-1787; London
DICKENSON, Mary   05-01-1787; Southwark
HALL*, Sarah   10-01-1787; London
HAYWARD*,
  Elizabeth   10-01-1787; London
HENRY, Catherine   10-01-1787; London
LEVI*, Amelia   09-01-1787; Southwark
MARSHALL,
  Mary Elizabeth   10-01-1787; London
MARTIN, Ann   09-01-1787; Southwark
MULLENS*, Hannah   10-01-1787?; London
PARRY, Sarah   10-01-1787?; London
ROSSON*, Isabella   10-01-1787; London
SMITH, Catherine   10-01-1787; London
SMITH, Mary   10-01-1787?; London

Mary Ann **1791**
ROBERTS, Jane   01-10-1787; Devon

374 *List A-1*

***Neptune* 1790**
BATHER, Mary	09-04-1787; Chester
CARR, Susan	19-07-1787; Bedford
COOKSEY*, Mary	14-03-1787; Stafford
COUSINS, Mary	04-10-1787; Lincoln
CRAGG, Mary	02-10-1787; Yorkshire
DONNOLLY, Sarah	28-07-1787; York
DRURY†, Elizabeth	10-07-1787; Lincoln
GILL, Amelia	10-03-1787; York
LINSLEY*, Elizabeth	11-01-1787; York
RISAM, Elizabeth	16-04-1787; York
THOMPSON, Jane	04-10-1787; York?
WHITLAM†, Sarah	10-07-1787; Lincoln
WILLIS, Sarah	21?07-1787; York

***Prince of Wales* 1788**
ALLEN, Sussanah	18-04-1787; London
AULT, Sarah	21-02-1787; London
BLANCHETT*, Susan/nah	02-04-1787; Kingston
BONNER, Jane	18-04-1787; London
DARNELL*, Margaret	18-04-1787; London
DUNDAS, Jane	18-04-1787; London
FLARTY, Phebe/Phoebe	21-02-1787; London
FORBES, Ann	02-04-1787; Kingston
GREEN, Mary	18-04-1787; London
HOLLOGIN, Elizabeth	18-04-1787; London
HUGHES*, Frances Ann	06?03-1787; Lancaster
JOHNSTON, Catherine	18-04-1787; London
KENEDY*, Martha	02-04-1787; Kingston
LARA, Flora	NR-02-1787; London
MARRIOTT, Jane	18-04-1787; London
MATHER, Ann	18-04-1787; London
MATHER*, Mary	18-04-1787; London
MITCHCRAFT, Mary	09-04-1787; Kingston
MUNRO, Lydia	02-04-1787; Kingston
PARSLEY, Ann	21-02-1787; London
PINDER, Mary	13-01-1787; Lincoln
SCOTT, Elizabeth	21-02-1787; London
SMITH, Ann	18-04-1787; London
SMITH, Catherine	18-04-1787; London
TAYLOR, Sarah	02-04-1787; Kingston
THOMAS, Elizabeth	NR-01-1787; Wigan
WAINWRIGHT*, Ellen	NR-01-1787; Preston
YOUNGSON, Elizabeth	06?03-1787; Lancaster

1788 TRIAL YEAR

***Lady Juliana* 1790**
ABORROW, Ann	Summer 1788; Surrey
ANDERSON, Mary	07-05-1788; Middlesex
ANSELL, Mary	10-09-1788; Middlesex
ATKINS, Violetta	25-06-1788; Middlesex
BARNSLEY, Elizabeth	27-02-1788; Middlesex
BARRY*, Ann	10-09-1788; Middlesex
BATEMAN, Mary	07-05-1788; Middlesex
BONE*, Ann	10-12-1788; Middlesex
BRADY, Ann	25-06-1788; Middlesex
BROWN, Grace	27-02-1788; London
BROWN, Sarah Sophia	10-09-1788; Middlesex
CARTER, Elizabeth	10-09-1788; Middlesex
CAVENAUGH, Mary	02-04-1788; London
CLAPTON, Ann	10-12-1788; London
CLAYTON, Mary	02-04-1788; Middlesex
COTTEREL(L), Elizabeth	02-04-1788; Middlesex
CURTIS, Esther	10-12-1788; Middlesex
DANIELS, Martha	10-09-1788; Middlesex
DAVIS, Ann	NR-NR-1788; Gloucester
DAVIS, Deborah	NR-07-1788; Kent
DEAN*, Elizabeth	NR-NR-1788; Warwick
DOWLING, Mary	10-12-1788; Middlesex
FLANNEGAN*, Mary	02-04-1788; Middlesex
FROST, Frances	Summer 1788; Exeter, Devon
GALLAND, Ann	10-12-1788; Middlesex
GEE*, Hannah	27-02-1788; London
GIBSON, Ann	23-06-1788; London
GILES, Elizabeth	25-06-1788; Middlesex
GITTOS, Mary	10-09-1788; Middlesex
GOLDSMITH, Elizabeth	25-06-1788; Middlesex
GOMER, Sarah	10-09-1788; London
GOSLING, Mary	NR-03-1788; Warwick
HANDYMAN*, Ann	25-06-1788; Middlesex

HARDING, Amelia	22-10-1788; Middlesex	SULLEY, Elizabeth	07-05-1788; Middlesex
HEYLAND, Catherine	02-04-1788; Middlesex	TALBOT, Dorcas	25-06-1788; Middlesex
		TALBOT, Mary	27-02-1788; Middlesex
HODDY, Rachael	25-06-1788; Middlesex	TAYLOR, Sarah	10-09-1788; Middlesex
HOOK, Mary	07-05-1788; Middlesex	THOMSON*, Elizabeth	NR-07-1788; Northumberland
HOUNSUM, Catherine	07-05-1788; Middlesex	TILLEY, Elizabeth	NR-02-1788; Gloucester
HOUSE, Sarah	07-05-1788; Middlesex	WHEELER*, Ann	27-02-1788; Middlesex
JOHNSON, Matilda	10-12-1788; Middlesex	WHITTAKER, Jane	07-05-1788; Middlesex
JONES, Ann	27-02-1788; London	WILLIAMS, Margaret	NR-02-1788?; Somerset
JONES, Elizabeth	07-05-1788; Middlesex		
JONES, Lydia	27-02-1788; Middlesex	WILLIAMS, Phoebe	02-04-1788; Middlesex
JONES, Sarah	27-02-1788; Middlesex	WILLIAMS*, Jane	09-01-1788; Middlesex
KELLY, Sarah	23-06-1788; London	WILSON, Mary	10-09-1788; Middlesex
LEICESTER, Elizabeth	09-01-1788; Middlesex	WILSON, Sarah	09-01-1788; London
		WINSPEAR, Mary	02-04-1788; Middlesex
LEICESTER, Isabella	09-01-1788; Middlesex	WISHAW, Elizabeth	10-09-1788; Middlesex
LEWIS, Mary	25-06-1788; Middlesex		
LYONS, Sarah	23-06-1788; London	***Neptune 1790***	
MADDOCKS*, Grace	09-01-1788; Middlesex	ANTONY*, Mary	14-03-1788; Norfolk
		BARKER*, Ann	10-10-1788; Suffolk
MANSON*, Isabella	27-02-1788; Middlesex	BARNETT†, Martha	24-07-1788; Lancaster
MARSH, Ann	NR-NR-1788; London	BRADLY*, Betty	18-08-1788; Chester
MARSH, Charlotte	10-12-1788; London	BROWNE*, Kezzia	09-10-1788; Gloucester
METCALF(E), Elizabeth	22-10-1788; London	CHADDERTON†, Mary	24-03-1788; Lancashire
MORGAN, Ann	23-06-1788; London	CLARKE, Magaret	NR-04-1788; Radnor
MORGAN*, Margaret	09-01-1788; Middlesex	CODD†, Jane	16-01-1788; Haverford West
MORTIMORE, Susannah	Spring 1788; Exeter	CROWLEY, Catherine	30-07-1788; Stafford
OAKLEY, Mary	10-12-1788; Middlesex	DALE†, Rosina	08-03-1788; Lincoln
ROBERTS, Sarah	09-01-1788; London	EDWARDS, Elizabeth	26-01-1788; Suffolk
ROSTER, Elizabeth	09-01-1788; London		
ROWNEY, Hannah	10-09-1788; London	GRIGGS, Sarah	13-10-1788; Kent
SHAKESPEARE, Elizabeth	10-09-1788; Middlesex	HANDLEY, Frances	12-03-1788; Stafford
		HEATHCOTE, Rebecca	18-08-1788; Chester
SIMPSON, Mary	09-01-1788; London		
SMITH, Isabella	Lent 1788; Kent	LITHERBY*†, Elizabeth	Lent 1788; Devon
SMITH, Mary	09-01-1788; London		
SMITH, Sarah	02-04-1788; Middlesex	LYNCH*, Alice	24-03-1788; Monmouth
SMITH*, Elizabeth	27-02-1788; Middlesex	MASSEY*†, Betty	16-10-1788; Manchester
STEWART, Margaret	Lent 1788; Kent	MAYO, Elizabeth	20-03-1788; Hereford
STEWART, Susannah	09-01-1788; Middlesex	PRINCE, Hannah	09-03-1788; Chester
		SMITH, Ann	08-03-1788; Worcester
STOKES, Ann	NR-03-1788; Warwick	SOUTH, Elizabeth	20-03-1788; Hereford
STRINGER, Elizabeth	NR-03-1788; Gloucester	WHEELER, Ann	27-01-1788; Middlesex
		WILLIAMS, Mary	19-07-1788; Monmouth

1789 TRIAL YEAR

Lady Juliana 1790

ACTON, Sarah	14-01-1789; Middlesex
BARNES, Mary	Lent 1789; Kent
BRYANT, Ann	Lent 1789; Kent
CARTER, Margaret	22-04-1789; Middlesex
CLARK(E), Catherine	Lent 1789; Kent
FLAVEL(L), Ann	NR-03-1789; Gloucester
GREGORY, Sarah	Lent 1789; Hertford
HANNAWAY†, Ann	14-01-1789; Middlesex
HARDYMAN, Elizabeth	22-04-1789; Middlesex
HIGGINS*, Mary	14-01-1789; Middlesex
HOUNSET(T), Mary	14-01-1789; Middlesex
HUNT, Susannah	NR-03-1789; Suffolk
ISRAEL, Maria	22-04-1789; Middlesex
JOHNSON, Mary	25-02-1789; Middlesex
JONES, Mary	22-04-1789; Middlesex
MICHAEL, Sarah	22-04-1789; Middlesex
MULLENDEN*, Mary	NR-03-1789; Chelmsford
NATCHELL*, Sarah	NR-04-1789; London
READ, Mary	NR-04-1789; Middlesex
REID, Mary	25-02-1789; Middlesex
RILEY, Elizabeth	Lent 1789; Kent
ROBINSON, Elizabeth	22-04-1789; Middlesex
ROCH, Ann	22-04-1789; Middlesex
THOMAS, Ann	22-04-1789; Middlesex
WADE, Mary	14-01-1789; Middlesex
WATERS, Jane	14-01-1789; Middlesex
WATSON, Eleanor	Lent 1789; Surrey
WHITE, Catherine	Lent 1789; Kent
WHITING, Jane	14-01-1789; Middlesex
WILLIAMS, Mary	Lent 1789; Kent

Mary Ann 1791

CARLETON, Hannah	09-12-1789; Middlesex
COLLIN, Mary	09-12-1789; Middlesex
DONNE(A)LLY*, Sarah	14-07-1789; Hampshire
EVANS, Sarah	29-09-1789; Worcester
HOLMES, Margaret	09-12-1789; Middlesex
HUGHES, Elizabeth	08-08-1789; Warwick
HUTCHINSON, Ann	09-12-1789; Middlesex
HUTCHINSON, Mary	09-12-1789; Middlesex
JOHNSON, Elizabeth	09-12-1789; Middlesex
JONES, Mary	05-03-1789; Hampshire
KINGSFORD, Ann	05-03-1789; Hampshire
McDOUGALL, Elizabeth	09-12-1789; Middlesex
MOSELEY, Elizabeth	25-03-1789; Derby
NEVERS, Hester	Summer 1789; Gloucester
PHILLIPS, Mary	08-08-1789; Warwick
PRANGLEY, Elizabeth	14-07-1789; Wiltshire
RICHARDS, Rebecca	13-06-1789; Bristol City
RUSSELL, Mary	09-12-1789; Middlesex
SPRIGS, Isabella	08-08-1789; Northumberland
STACEY, Alice	NR-NR-1789; Durham
STACEY, Barbara	NR-NR-1789; Durham
STUBBINS, Mary	30-07-1789; Nottingham
TOOME, Jane	08-08-1789; Warwick
TWIGG, Ann	30-03-1789; Worcester
WELCH, Elizabeth	09-12-1789; Middlesex
WESTON, Elizabeth	08-08-1789; Warwick
WICKS, Ann	08-12-1789; Middlesex
WILLIAMS, Catherine	NR-04-1789; Breconshire
WILLIS, Ann	13-01-1789; Hampshire
WOOLLEY, Jane	08-08-1789; Shrewsbury

Neptune 1790

BAKER, Elizabeth	03-08-1789; Surrey
BATES, Martha	28-10-1789; Middlesex
BEILBY, Elizabeth	14-03-1789; York
BRAY*†, Susannah	22-04-1789; Middlesex
BROWN, Martha	05-10-1789; Essex
BROWN†, Mary	16-03-1789; Lincoln
BUTLER, Mary	09-09-1789; Middlesex
CACUTT*, Ann	13-08-1789; Stafford
CALLAHAN*, Margaret	08-07-1789; Middlesex
CAREY, Ann	03-08-1789; Norfolk
CARTER, Elizabeth	14-03-1789; York
CHIPPENHAM*, Rebecca	09-09-1789; Middlesex
DAVIS, Elizabeth	28-10-1789; London
DELL†, Elizabeth	24-04-1789; Berkshire
DESMONT*, Mary	09-09-1789; Middlesex
DONNOVAN, Mary	09-09-1789; Middlesex

EDWARDS, Jane	28-10-1789; Middlesex		*Pitt* 1792	
ELLEY, Jane	28-10-1789; London		WARD, Mary	15-01-1789; Westmoreland
FLANNAGAN†, Mary	08-07-1789; Middlesex			
FLOOD, Rose	09-09-1789; Middlesex		**1790 TRIAL YEAR**	
FROST, Mary	19-03-1789; Norfolk			
GODWIN, Elizabeth	17-03-1789; Hereford		*Bellona* 1793	
GOTT, Ellen	03-08-1789; Lancashire		NEWMAN, Jane	07-06-1790; Devon
GREGORY, Mary	08-07-1789; Middlesex		*Indispensable* 1796	
GRIFFITHS, Ann	28-10-1789; Middlesex		MOORE, Mary	17-09-1790; Middlesex
HARBOUR, Jane	30-10-1789; Hants.			
HAWKINS, Hannah	13-08-1789; Stafford		*Mary Ann* 1791	
IRELAND, Elizabeth	06-10-1789; Kent		ALLEN, Elizabeth	26-07-1790; Norfolk
JONES, Elizabeth	03-08-1789; Lancashire		ASKER, Elizabeth	08-12-1790; Middlesex
JONES, Margaret	09-09-1789; Middlesex		BARNES, Sarah	03-01-1790; Middlesex
JONES, Mary	28-10-1789; Middlesex		BARTLAM, Sarah	23-03-1790; Warwick
JONES, Mary	30-10-1789; Middlesex?		BLIGH, Ann	14-04-1790; Middlesex
JOY, Ann	06-10-1789; Kent		BRIGHT, Bridget	27-10-1790; Middlesex
JUSTIN, Mary	04-03-1789; Buckinghamshire		BROWN, Mary	19-07-1790; Kent
			BROWN, Susannah	08-12-1790; Middlesex
LEARY, Mary	28-10-1789; Middlesex		BURDOCK, Ann	23-03-1790; Warwick
McDONAUGH, Mary	19-10-1789; Portsmouth		BURKE, Ann	06-03-1790; Worcester
MANLOVE, Sarah	14-03-1789; York		BUTCHER, Mary	24-02-1790; Middlesex
MARTIN, Mary	09-09-1789; Middlesex		CAMPBELL, Ann	27-10-1790; Middlesex
MEREDITH, Ann	02-02-1789; Worcester		CAREY, Ann	18-01-1790; Avon
MERRYFIELD, Ann	16-07-1789; Devon		CARTY*, Bridget	26-05-1790; Middlesex
MITCHELL, Mary	09-09-1789; Middlesex		CHAPMAN, Isabella	23-03-1790; York
MORGAN, Mary	08-08-1789; Shrewsbury		CHESSELL, Sarah	15-09-1790; Middlesex
MULLOY*, Jane	09-09-1789; Maidstone		CLOSE, Elizabeth	15-09-1790; Middlesex
NAGGS, Elizabeth	27-07-1789; Kent		COOL*, Susan	14-07-1790; Essex
PHILLIPS, Sarah	08-07-1789; Middlesex		COOLEY, Sarah	14-04-1790; Middlesex
RICE, Elizabeth	09-09-1789; Middlesex		COSGROVE, Bridget	14-04-1790; Middlesex
RYMES, Elizabeth	28-10-1789; Middlesex		COX, Mary	26-05-1790; Middlesex
SMITH, Elizabeth	08-07-1789; Middlesex		DAVIS, Eleanor	07-07-1790; Middlesex
SMITH, Sarah	21-04-1789; Essex		DOWDING, Rachael	15-09-1790; Middlesex
STULTZ, Mary	28-10-1789; Middlesex		DYER, Susannah	24-02-1790; Middlesex
THOMPSON†, Mary	19-03-1789; Lincoln		EAST, Ann	24-02-1790; Middlesex
TUCKER, Mary	28-10-1789; London		EDWARD, Mary	19-03-1790; Hereford
WADE†, Elizabeth Ann	08-07-1789; Middlesex		FRANKLIN, Ann	27-10-1790; Middlesex
WALTERS, Mary	28-10-1789; Middlesex		GITTENS*, Sarah	15-01-1790; Shrewsbury
WHITE, Ann	28-10-1789; Middlesex		GUEST, Ann	08-12-1790; Middlesex
WHITE, Mary	26-08-1789; Surrey		GUY, Ann	15-09-1790; Middlesex
WILCOCK, Ann	19-04-1789; Lincoln		HAMILTON, Elizabeth	08-12-1790; Middlesex
WILLIAMS, Catherine	26-08-1789; Surrey		HARPER, Ann	23-03-1790; Warwick
WOOD, Elizabeth	09-09-1789; Middlesex		HARRIS, Catherine	NR-01-1790; Westmoreland
WOOLLEY, Sarah	28-10-1789; London		HAWKINS, Mary	08-12-1790; Middlesex

HIPWELL, Mary	27-10-1790; Middlesex	WELSH*, Mary	19-01-1790; Gloucester
HUMPHRIES, Elizabeth	23-03-1790; Warwick	WHITFIELD, Johanna	Epiphany 1790; Exeter
JACKSON, Ann	08-12-1790; Middlesex	WILKINSON, Hannah	27-10-1790; Middlesex
JARMY, Ann	26-07-1790; Norfolk	WILKINSON, Mary Ann	27-10-1790; Middlesex
JOHNSON, Mary	27-10-1790; Middlesex	WILLIAMS, Alice	15-09-1790; Middlesex
JONES, Martha	15-09-1790; Middlesex	WILLIAMS, Lydia	23-03-1790; Yorkshire
JONES, Mary	29-07-1790; Hereford	WILLIAMS, Margaret	18-02-1790; Surrey
JONES, Sophia	08-12-1790; Middlesex	WILSON*, Jemima	24-02-1790; Middlesex
LEE, Elizabeth	NR-01-1790; Lancashire	WINN, Hannah	14-04-1790; Middlesex
LEESON, Hannah	27-10-1790; Middlesex	WOODWARD, Jane	11-03-1790; Nottingham
LINTON, Mary	24-02-1790; Middlesex		
McKENZIE, Maria	15-09-1790; Middlesex		
MASON, Elizabeth	14-04-1790; Middlesex		
METCALF, Ann	08-12-1790; Middlesex		
MITCHELL, Betty	06-03-1790; Wiltshire		

Pitt 1792

ATKINSON, Ann	08-12-1790; Middlesex
BURTON, Rachael	14-01-1790; Cornwall
COOK, Maria Ann	27-10-1790; Middlesex
FARRELL, Lydia	21-07-1790; Stafford
HOUSE, Mary	07-03-1790; Essex
KIRK, Sarah	07-10-1790; Lancashire
PARSONS, Mary	11-03-1790; Dorset
SWAIN, Mary	25-03-1790; Somerset
WHEATLEY, Hannah	07-03-1790; Essex
WRIGHT, Elizabeth	18-01-1790; Norfolk

MOONEY, Catherine	14-07-1790; Essex
MORRIS, Elizabeth	05-04-1790; Gloucester
MURPHY, Ann	05-10-1790; Surrey
MUSKETT, Mary	NR-01-1790; Middlesex
NEWLAND, Mary Ann	26-05-1790; Middlesex
PARKER, Eleanor	13-01-1790; Middlesex
PARKER, Mary	27-10-1790; Middlesex
PENLARRICK, Phoebe	01-08-1790; Devon
PIGG, Sarah	03-03-1790; Hertford
POTTER, Mary	Epiphany 1790; Devon
POWELL, Elizabeth	29-07-1790; Hereford
PROBERT, Hannah	23-03-1790; Warwick
RAMSAY, Bella	06-08-1790; Cumberland
SMITH, Ann	Michaelmas 1790; Exeter
SPARROW, Ann	13-04-1790; Yorkshire
SPARROW, Rose	13-04-1790; Yorkshire
STANTON, Elizabeth	19-03-1790; Hereford
STEVENSON, Jane	31-07-1790; Northumberland
STEWARD*, Elizabeth	06-03-1790; Worcester
TALBOT, Mary	08-12-1790; Middlesex
TAYLOR, Ann	08-12-1790; Middlesex
TAYLOR, Jane	11-03-1790; Nottingham
TODD, Martha	24-02-1790; Middlesex
TOMKINS, Ann	29-07-1790; Hereford
TONKS, Rachael	23-03-1790; Warwick
TROTTER, Jane	14-04-1790; Middlesex
TURNER, Ann	05-10-1790; Surrey
WATTS, Mary	27-10-1790; Middlesex

1791 TRIAL YEAR

Albemarle 1791

CAVE, Elizabeth	16-02-1791; Middlesex
FROST*, Sarah	16-02-1791; Middlesex
GORMAN, Mary	16-02-1791; Middlesex
GRIFFIN, Ann	16-02-1791; Middlesex
OZELAND, Elizabeth	16-02-1791; Middlesex
SMITH, Sarah	16-02-1791; Middlesex

Kitty 1792

CHAMBERS, Elizabeth	26-10-1791; Middlesex
CLOUGH, Elizabeth	26-10-1791; Middlesex
DAVIES, Elizabeth	20-08-1791; Carmarthen
FLINN, Mary	26-10-1791; Middlesex
GARDNER, Sarah	14-09-1791; Middlesex
GULLIVER, Elizabeth	14-09-1791; Middlesex
HANSTEAD, Bridget	20-07-1791; Middlesex
HUGHES, Mary	26-10-1791; Middlesex

List A-1

JONES, Mary 14-09-1791; Middlesex
MATTHEWS, Ann 26-10-1791; Middlesex
MATTHEWS,
  Elizabeth 20-07-1791; Middlesex
NAIRN*, Susannah 26-10-1791; Middlesex
PEARSON, Ann 20-07-1791; Middlesex
SHARP, Jane 14-09-1791; Middlesex
WALDEN, Sarah 14-09-1791; Middlesex

Mary Ann 1791
BLACKWELL,
  Elizabeth 12-01-1791; Middlesex
CARROLL, Mary 12-01-1791; Middlesex
HUDDER, Priscilla 12-01-1791; Middlesex
JONES, Susannah 12-01-1791; Middlesex
MacGENNIS, Sarah 12-01-1791; Devon
MILLS, Sarah 12-01-1791; Middlesex
SMITH, Ann 12-01-1791; Middlesex
STILLS, Sarah 12-01-1791; Middlesex

Pitt 1792
ASPLANDS, Miah 05-05-1791; Lincoln
BROOKE, Ann (Jnr) 19-03-1791; Warwick
BROOKE, Ann (Snr) 19-03-1791; Warwick
BROWN, Mary 13-01-1791; Kent
BRYANT, Catherine 08-06-1791; Middlesex
BULL, Eleanor 05-03-1791; Worcester
COLLINS, Eleanor 13-04-1791; Middlesex
COWLEY, Judith 23-03-1791; Gloucester
CUMMINS,
  Elizabeth 07-06-1791; Middlesex
DICKENS, Mary 11-04-1791; Middlesex
FISHER, Hannah 13-04-1791; Middlesex
FORD, Ann 09-03-1791; Stafford
GLOSSOP*, Ann 28-03-1791; Pool
HAYES, Ann 23-03-1791; Surrey
HAYES, Ann 03-05-1791; Southampton
HERNYMAN, Betty 26-03-1791; Somerset
HUGO, Mary Ann 13-01-1791; Cornwall
JONES, Mary 09-05-1791; Lancashire
KELLY, Eleanor 23-03-1791; Surrey
KING, Ann 13-04-1791; Middlesex
LINCH, Mary 13-04-1791; Middlesex
MARTIN, Mary 13-01-1791; Kent
MIELL, Diana 10-03-1791; Dorset
MORSE, Ann 23-03-1791; Gloucester
MUNDAY, Jane 13-04-1791; Middlesex
NEWLAND, Ann 13-04-1791; Middlesex
OWEN, Mary 02-06-1791; Middlesex

PARTRIDGE, Mary 16-02-1791; Middlesex
RICHARDS,
  Margaret 13-04-1791; Middlesex
SELWYN, Elizabeth 23-03-1791; Gloucester
SHRIEVE, Elizabeth 05-03-1791; Worcester
SMITH, Mary 15-01-1791; Lancashire
SMITH*, Mary 13-04-1791; Middlesex
WALKER, Elizabeth NR-05-1791; Derby
WATKINS, Jane 05-03-1791; Wiltshire
WOOD, Jane 20-01-1791; Lancashire
YATES, Elizabeth 09-03-1791; Stafford

Royal Admiral 1792
BOLLARD*,
  Susanna 06-08-1791; Worcester
BURT(ALL)*, Sarah 07-09-1791; Glamorgan
CAHALL, Sarah NR-09-1791; Middlesex
COOPER, Ann 06-08-1791; York
DAVIES†, Rachel 20-08-1791; Carmarthen
GRAHAM, Mary Jul/Sep 1791; Middlesex
GREEN, Mary 11-08-1791; Nottingham
GUEST, Charlotte 06-08-1791; Worcester
HADDOCK*, Mary 24-08-1791; Stafford
HOOLEY, Mary 15-09-1791; Cheshire
KIRK, Mary 18-07-1791; York
METCALFE,
  Margaret 06-08-1791; Yorkshire
MORSE, Ann 03-03-1791; Gloucester
O'BRIEN†, Mary 22-08-1791; Devon
REVELL, Frances 03-10-1791; Northumberlnd
SCOTT, Ann 06-08-1791; York
SMITH, Mary 14-07-1791; Lincoln
THOMAS†, Betty 22-08-1791; Exeter
THOMAS, Mary 22-08-1791; Devon
VILES, Ann 16-08-1791; Somerset
WATTS, Anne/Jane 24-08-1791; Stafford

Surprize 1794
WILSON, Mary 20-07-1791; Middlesex

1792 TRIAL YEAR

Bellona 1793
BONG*, Sarah 23-05-1792; Middlesex
BUCKLEY,
  Catherine 23-05-1792; Middlesex
DUNSTAN, Jane NR-07-1792; Middlesex

GRECIAN*, Mary
Ann   NR-05-1792; Middlesex
HARDY*, Esther
Jane   NR-05-1792; Middlesex
MASON, Sarah   NR-07-1792; Middlesex
MATTHEWS,
Elizabeth   NR-05-1792; Middlesex
PULSON*, Sarah   NR-07-1792; Middlesex
RANDALL, Mary   NR-05-1792; Middlesex
STEVENS, Lydia   NR-07-1792; Middlesex
WARBURTON*,
Hannah   NR-05-1792; Middlesex

Britannia 1798
COLE, Mary   30-07-1792; Devon

Indispensable 1796
LEWIN, Rebecca   19-07-1792; Lancashire
SIMPSON, Eleanor   11-07-1792;
                      Northumberland

Royal Admiral 1792
COX, Ann   27-03-1792; Warwick
FOWLER, Ann   17-03-1792; Shropshire
FUDGE*, Priscilla   28-03-1792; Gloucester
HARDING, Elizabeth   27-03-1792; Warwick
HIGGINSON, Sarah   27-03-1792; Warwick
HOLLOWAY†, Ann   10-01-1792; Hampshire
HOOTON*, Jane   01-03-1792; Hertford
HOY, Jane   12-01-1792; Horsham
JENKIN*, Mary   16-01-1792; Glamorgan
KENDALL, Mary   10-01-1792; Berkshire
LOVERIDGE,
Priscilla   05-03-1792; Berkshire
LOVERIDGE*, Mary   05-03-1792; Berkshire
MARCH, Winney   NR-NR-1792; NR
POWELL, Elizabeth   NR-02?1792; Middlesex
SMITH, Sarah   28-03-1792; Gloucester
SPRINGATE, Mary   21-03-1792; Kent
STEVENS, Frances   11-01-1792; Middlesex
TATE, Sarah   NR-NR-1792; NR
TERRY, Elizabeth   NR-03?1792; Middlesex
WALKER*,
Elizabeth   21-03-1792; Surrey
WELLS, Mary   19-03-1792; Yorkshire
WILSON, Ann   NR-NR-1792; NR
WILSON*, Margaret   11-01-1792;
                      Northumberland
WRAY, Harriott   NR-03?1792; Middlesex

Surprize 1794
AYRES, Sarah   02-10-1792; Surrey
FOWLES*, Mary   12-12-1792; Middlesex
HARRIS, Mary   12-09-1792; Middlesex
HARRISON,
Elizabeth   12-09-1792; Middlesex
HARRISON, Mary   12-09-1792; Middlesex
JONES, Sarah   12-09-1792; Middlesex
MARSHALL,
Margaret   12-09-1792; Middlesex
ROLFE*, Jemima   12-09-1792; Middlesex
STURDY*, Louisa   12-09-1792; Middlesex
WILSON*, Jane   02-10-1792; Surrey

William 1794
SMITH, Maria   12-09-1792; Middlesex

1793 TRIAL YEAR

Britannia 1798
FOGARTY, Margaret   07-04-1793; Bristol
JONES, Elizabeth   17-03-1793; Hereford
POWELL, Hannah   28-07-1793; Hereford

Indispensable 1796
ANDERSON,   08-10-1793;
Margaret   Southampton
BENTLEY, Susannah   16-09-1793; Middlesex
BULLER, Elizabeth   11-11-1793; Middlesex
CHAPLIN*, Ann   14-03-1793; Stafford
COOK, Elizabeth   24-01-1793; Salford
ELLIOTT, Martha   12-01-1793; Cumberland
HALL, Mary   11-04-1793; New
                      Hereford
HOBSON, Hannah   19-07-1793; Yorkshire
HUGHES, Sarah   21-01-1793; Salford
HUGHES*, Anne   08-10-1793; Denbeigh
JONES, Anne   15-01-1793; Denbeigh
JONES, Mary   15-01-1793; Denbeigh
LAMBE, Ann   15-04-1793?; Middlesex
LIDDIARD, Sarah   09-03-1793; Wiltshire
LOWLE, Hester   06-04-1793; Gloucester
PEARCE, Sarah   07-03-1793; Wiltshire
ROBSON, Isabel   27-07-1793;
                      Northumberland
STEWARD, Elizabeth   12-01-1793; Cumberland
THOMPSON*, Jane   11-07-1793;
Bell   Northumberland

TROTTER, Jane	27-07-1793; Northumberland	MARSHALL, Martha	31-10-1793; Middlesex
TURNER, Sarah	24-01-1793; Salford	MERCHANT, Elizabeth	25-05-1793; Middlesex
WEIR, Mary	18-07-1793; Northumberland	NEWTON*, Sarah	31-10-1793; Middlesex
		OWENS, Catharine	11-09-1793; Middlesex
		PAGE, Mary	04-12-1793; Middlesex

Nile 1801

LEWIS, Mary	06-04-1793; Merioneth

Surprize 1794

		PRICE, Elizabeth	16-07-1793; Surrey
		RANDALL, Sarah	04-12-1793; Middlesex
		SIMMONS*, Ann	20-02-1793; Middlesex
BAKER*, Lydia	15-01-1793; Surrey	SMITH, Sarah	10-04-1793; Middlesex
BANKS, Ann	30-10-1793; Middlesex	STEVENSON, Elizabeth	12-12-1793; Middlesex
BAYLEY*, Sarah	20-02-1793; Middlesex	TAYLOR, Ann	20-02-1793; Middlesex
BIDWELL, Judith	31-10-1793; Middlesex	THORN, Ann	31-10-1793; Middlesex
BIGGS, Elizabeth	25-05-1793; Middlesex	TOWNSEND, Sarah	10-04-1793; Middlesex
BLANEY, Mary	30-10-1793; Middlesex	TURNER, Catherine	04-12-1793; Middlesex
BREWER†, Elizabeth	04-12-1793; Middlesex	WIGGINS*, Jane	12-12-1793; Middlesex
BURGESS, Mary	12-12-1793; Middlesex		
BURLEY, Sarah	30-10-1793; Middlesex		
BURN, Susannah	20-02-1793; Middlesex		

1794 TRIAL YEAR

CAMPBELL, Margaret	10-04-1793; Middlesex	*Britannia* 1798	
CARTER, Elizabeth	12-12-1793; Middlesex	HORE, Joanna	17-03-1794; Devon
CARTER*, Mary	11-09-1793; Middlesex	*Indispensable* 1796	
CAVE, Mary	31-10-1793; Middlesex	BAILEY, Jane	04-03-1794; Southampton
CAVER*, Ann	26-06-1793; Middlesex		
CLIFFORD, Sarah	30-10-1793; Middlesex	BAKER, Ann	04-06-1794; Middlesex
COPE, Elizabeth	11-09-1793; Middlesex	BARNARD, Ann	16-07-1794; Middlesex
DAVIS*, Mary	11-09-1793; Middlesex	BERRY, Margaret	04-03-1794; Southampton
DAWSON, Ann	20-02-1793; Middlesex		
EMERY, Susannah	04-12-1793; Middlesex	BINNS, Hannah	10-02-1794; Middlesex
FINDALL*, Hannah	25-05-1793; Middlesex	BIRD, Sarah	16-07-1794; Middlesex
FORD, Elizabeth	20-02-1793; Middlesex	BISCOE*, Catherine	16-07-1794; Middlesex
GILES, Mary	10-04-1793; Middlesex	BROWN, Mary	22-01-1794; Salford
GOODALL, Mary	11-09-1793; Middlesex	BURKE, Mary	16-07-1794; Middlesex
HICKEY, Catherine	30-10-1793; Middlesex	BUTLER, Elizabeth	11-11-1794; Middlesex
HIGGINS*, Jane	11-09-1793; Middlesex	CHEESEMAN*, Mary	17-09-1794; Middlesex
HINES, Sarah	25-05-1793; Middlesex	CORBET*, Sarah	16-08-1794; Northumberland
ISON, Jane	20-02-1793; Middlesex		
JENNINGS, Mary	30-10-1793; Middlesex		
JOHNSON, Catharine	10-04-1793; Middlesex	COX, Elizabeth	08-12-1794; Middlesex
		DALLISON, Margaret	16-07-1794; Middlesex
JONES, Catharine	30-10-1793; Middlesex	DUNCAN*, Jane	04-03-1794; Southampton
JONES, Mary	25-05-1793; Middlesex		
JONES, Mary	20-02-1793; Middlesex	ELDRIDGE*, Sarah	16-09-1794; Middlesex
KIRBY, Mary	30-10-1793; Middlesex	EVETT, Elizabeth	26-03-1794; Surrey
LANGFORD*, Sophia	10-04-1793; Middlesex	FISHBOURN, Martha	30-04-1794; Middlesex
LAWFORD, Sarah	11-09-1793; Middlesex		
MARCH, Mary Ann	20-02-1793; Middlesex		

GOODWIN, Sarah 16-09-1794; Middlesex
HACKER, Esther 30-04-1794; Middlesex
HARRIS, Elizabeth 14-01-1794; Wiltshire
HILL, Elizabeth 08-03-1794; Lincoln
HOLLAND, Mary 26-03-1794; Surrey
HUTCHINS,
 Elizabeth 17-09-1794; Middlesex
LESAGE, Louisa 17-09-1794; Middlesex
LLOYD, Ann 04-06-1794; Middlesex
LLOYD, Rose 17-09-1794; Middlesex
LOCKHART, Ann 04-06-1794; Middlesex
LONG, Elizabeth 01-05-1794; Hampshire
McCARTHY,
 Margaret 17-09-1794; Middlesex
MATTINGLY, Mary 26-03-1794; Surrey
MOORE, Bridget
 Ann 18-08-1794; Surrey
MORRIS, Elizabeth 15-10-1794; Lancashire
MULLETT, Mary 29-07-1794; Hampshire
PICK, Jane 02-08-1794; Yorkshire
POOLE, Mary 15-08-1794; Sussex
PURFIT, Frances 17-09-1794; Middlesex
ROBINSON,
 Elizabeth 26-03-1794; Surrey
ROGERS, Sarah 30-03-1794; Stafford
SIMPSON, Judith 11-11-1794; Middlesex
SMITH, Susannah 30-04-1794; Middlesex
SPENCER, Esther 17-09-1794; Middlesex
THOMAS, Elizabeth 17-09-1794; Middlesex
THORPE, Mary NR-07-1794; Middlesex
WALKER, Ann 17-09-1794; Middlesex
WALTERS, Phoebe 19-08-1794; Gloucester
WATSON, Margaret 04-06-1794; Middlesex
WILLIAMSON,
 Sarah 15-07-1794; Berwick
WILSON, Ann 02-05-1794; Middlesex
WOODHOUSE, Mary 30-04-1794; Middlesex
WRIGHT, Hannah 01-05-1794; Stafford
YOUNG, Elizabeth 04-03-1794; Hampshire

Surprize 1794
McCARTY, Ann 15-01-1794; Middlesex

1795 TRIAL YEAR

Britannia 1798
CETTY*, Elizabeth 08-08-1795; Somerset
CODY, Catherine 08-01-1795; Westminster
COLEMAN, Sarah 27-07-1795; Devon
COOPER*, Mary 07-08-1795; Surrey
HARDING, Margaret 18-03-1795; Kent
JONES, Ann 01-08-1795; Salop
LEATHER, Sarah 12-10-1795; Lancashire
TAYLOR, Ann 20-05-1795; Middlesex
TAYLOR, Mary 13-01-1795; Middlesex
VICKERY, Elizabeth 08-08-1795; Somerset
WILLIAMS, Eleanor 01-07-1795; Middlesex
WISE, Mary 23-12-1795; Middlesex
YATES, Ann 13-01-1795; Middlesex
YATES, Nancy 14-10-1795; Lancashire

Indispensable 1796
ARCHER, Ann 15-04-1795; Middlesex
ARMSTRONG, Mary 15-04-1795; Cumberland
BERRY, Sarah 25-03-1795; Stafford
BROWN, Elizabeth 20-01-1795; Lincoln
BROWN, Hannah 20-01-1795; Lincoln
BURKETT,
 Elizabeth 01-07-1795; Middlesex
BURROWS*, Alice 20-05-1795; Middlesex
CHAMBERLAIN,
 Martha 01-07-1795; Middlesex
CLARK, Ann 15-04-1795; Middlesex
CLARKE, Elizabeth 05-08-1795; Stafford
COX, Margaret 16-09-1795; Middlesex
COX, Mary 20-05-1795; Middlesex
CRANMER, Frances 01-07-1795; Middlesex
CROOKE, Elizabeth 18-07-1795; Yorkshire
DARKE*, Sarah 11-03-1795; Gloucester
DONALD, Mary 15-04-1795; Cumberland
EDMONDS,
 Catherine 01-07-1795; Middlesex
EDWARDS,
 Elizabeth 13-01-1795; Denbeigh
EVANS, Amelia 20-05-1795; Middlesex
FIELDING, Mary
 Ann 01-07-1795; Middlesex
FISHER, Sarah 16-07-1795; Southwell
FITZGERALD, Mary 16-09-1795; Middlesex
HAINSLEY,
 Elizabeth 14-01-1795; Nottingham
HAINSLEY, Maria 14-01-1795; Nottingham
HARRISON,
 Elizabeth 15-04-1795; Middlesex
HAWKINS, Ann 14-01-1795; Middlesex
HOLMAN, Eleanor 20-05-1795; Middlesex
KING, Frances 13-07-1795; Hampshire
LUNN, Hester 05-08-1795; Stafford

McNEAL, Judith	15-04-1795; Northumberland	*Nile* 1801	
McVITIE, Hannah	13-07-1795; Cumberland	GREGORY, Sarah	01-03-1796; Hampshire
MANN, Sarah	11-03-1795; Gloucester	SMITH, Sarah	07-08-1796; Portsmouth
MARCHANT, Mary	18-02-1795; Middlesex	*Speedy* 1800	
PEALTHORPE, Martha	14-01-1795; Middlesex	BASDEN, Sarah	07-10-1796; Sussex
PERCIVAL, Jane	13-04-1795; Middlesex	BURRELL, Martha	12-01-1796; Bristol
ROBINSON, Mary	20-05-1795; Middlesex	FITZJOHN, Catherine	26-10-1796; Middlesex
ROY*, Ann Judith	01-07-1795; Middlesex		
SALVEL, Elizabeth	14-01-1795; Middlesex		

1797 TRIAL YEAR

SHILDON, Margaret	13-01-1795; Yorkshire
SIMS, Sarah	30-05-1795; Middlesex
SLADE, Sarah	18-02-1795; Middlesex
SMITH, Mary	20-05-1795; Middlesex

Britannia 1798

ALLEN, Elizabeth	12-07-1797; Middlesex
ATKINSON, Betty	11-10-1797; Lancaster
BACON, Elizabeth	25-04-1797; Surrey
BAKER, Letitia	20-09-1797; Middlesex
STOCKER, Margaret	20-05-1795; Middlesex
THOMPSON, Ann	22-07-1795; Gloucester
VALANCE, Agnes	16-09-1795; Middlesex
WARNER, Sophia	20-05-1795; Middlesex
WILMOT, Elizabeth	15-04-1795; Middlesex
WISE, Sarah	22-07-1795; Gloucester
WRIGHT, Elizabeth	18-04-1795; Lincoln
BEER, Ann	15-03-1797; Kent
BEER, Elizabeth	15-03-1797; Kent
BENNETT, Elizabeth	26-04-1797; Middlesex
BERRY, Mary	25-04-1797; Lancaster
BEST*, Sarah	06-12-1797; Middlesex
BRIANT*, Mary	31-05-1797; Middlesex
BROOKS, Elizabeth	03-10-1797; Essex
BRYAN, Mary	12-07-1797; Middlesex
BUCKLEY, Mary Cath.	12-07-1797; Middlesex

1796 TRIAL YEAR

Britannia 1798

BAKER, Ann	02-06-1796; Middlesex
BERRY, Mary	25-04-1796; Lancashire
BROWN, Mary	14-09-1796; Middlesex
BROWN, Mary	02-12-1796; Middlesex
CARTER, Sarah	14-03-1796; Devon
CAWTHORN*, Mary	14-09-1796; Middlesex
CHEETHAM*, Ann	12-07-1796; Surrey
EDWARDS, Martha	17-03-1796; Hereford
HESSELL, Jane	22-07-1796; Sussex
HIDE*, Mary	21-03-1796; Warwick
PALMER, Margaret	12-03-1796; Salop
TRACEY, Ann	02-12-1796; Middlesex
WILLIAMS, Mary	21-03-1796; Bristol
WOOD, Ann	20-01-1796; Lancashire

CARTER, Eleanor	25-10-1797; Middlesex
CLARK, Mary	25-10-1797; Middlesex
CORDELL*, Mary	11-01-1797; Middlesex
CRESWELL, Mary	13-08-1797; Hereford
CRESWELL, Susannah	13-08-1797; Hereford
CROCKER, Ann	15-02-1797; Middlesex
DILLON, Ann	12-07-1797; Middlesex
DRAPER*, Sarah/Ann	12-07-1797; Middlesex
EDWARDS, Margaret	25-03-1797; Salop
FERGUSON*, Frances	20-08-1797; Surrey
FORD, Mary	26-04-1797; Somerset
GARNETT, Susannah	08-03-1797; Essex
GREEN, Ann	02-03-1797; Surrey
GRIFFITHS, Elizabeth	10-07-1797; Bristol
HALL, Ann	26-04-1797; Middlesex

Earl Cornwallis 1801

ANDERSON, Martha	06-10-1796; Northumberland
BADGER, Charlotte	09-07-1796; Worcester
TOOLE, Ann	05-03-1796; Yorkshire

HENDRICH,
Susannah 20-08-1797; Surrey
HILL, Sarah 10-07-1797; Bristol
HODGES*,
Mary/Susannah 25-10-1797; Middlesex
HULME, Elizabeth 25-03-1797; Lancaster
HUNT*, Sarah 15-03-1797; Kent
JACKSON, Sarah 30-11-1797; Middlesex
JOHNSON, Mary 26-04-1797; Middlesex
JOHNSON, Sarah 25-10-1797; Middlesex
KELSALL, Elizabeth 11-10-1797; Lancaster
KENNEDY, Ann 26-10-1797; Middlesex
LEWIS, Elizabeth 11-01-1797; Middlesex
McCANN*, Sarah 20-09-1797; Middlesex
MEATH, Elizabeth 20-09-1797; Middlesex
MOORE, Elizabeth 06-12-1797; Middlesex
MOREY, Mary Ann 25-10-1797; Middlesex
NICHOLSON, Alice 11-10-1797; Lancaster
O'CONNOR,
Elizabeth 26-04-1797; Middlesex
PATTEN, Mary 10-01-1797; Salop
POTTS, Ellen 03-05-1797; Lancaster
ROCHFORD, Ann 11-01-1797; Middlesex
SEMPLE, Jennett 03-05-1797; Lancaster
SHEPHERD,
Catherine 26-10-1797; Middlesex
SMITH, Mary 20-09-1797; Middlesex
SMITH, Mary 03-10-1797; Devon
SMITH*, Mary 26-04-1797; Middlesex
STIRLING,
Elizabeth 31-05-1797; Middlesex
THOMAS, Rebecca 26-04-1797; Somerset
THOMPSON*, Ann 12-07-1797; Middlesex
THOMPSON*, Sarah 20-08-1797; Surrey
VALENCE, Mary 06-12-1797; Middlesex
WARBURTON, Rose 01-05-1797; Lancaster
WILLIAMS*, Mary 31-03-1797; Hereford
WOOD, Mary 15-03-1797; Kent
WRIGHT*, Sarah 20-08-1797; Surrey

Earl Cornwallis 1801
BOARDMAN,
Elizabeth 11-09-1797; Chester
FRANKLIN, Mary 25-04-1797; Chester
LEATHERLAND,
Sarah 25-04-1797; Chester
SPENCE, Hannah 29-07-1797; Yorkshire
WILLIAMS*, Mary 21-03-1797; Hereford

Nile 1801
BEYNON, Margaret 23-03-1797; Glamorgan
DAVID, Ann 28-03-1797; Glamorgan

Speedy 1800
GUILE, Mary 20-09-1797; London

1798 TRIAL YEAR

Britannia 1798
BROWN*, Sarah 10-01-1798; Middlesex
MORETON, Ann 10-01-1798; Middlesex
POWELL, Mary 10-01-1798; Middlesex

Earl Cornwallis 1801
APPLEYARD,
Audrey 05-10-1798; Lincoln
ASHMAN,
Susannah 04-04-1798; Bristol
BAKER, Ann 16-04-1798; Devon
BOWDEN, Mary Michaelmas 1798; Devon
COPSEY, Ann 16-07-1798; Berkshire
ELTIS, Isabella 04-10-1798; Northumberland
HALL, Hannah 21-07-1798; Worcester
HATESBY*, Mary 10-10-1798; Lancaster
HILL, Sarah 21-07-1798; Worcester
HONELL, Mary Easter 1798; Devon
HURLEY, Elizabeth Summer 1798; Devon
JONES*, Elizabeth 24-03-1798; Shropshire
LAYLAND, Sarah 21-07-1798; Worcester
MEEKS, Sarah 20-03-1798; Hereford
MUGFORD, Sarah Michaelmas 1798; Devon
OAKLEY, Elizabeth 31-07-1798; Hereford
OBRENSHAW,
Margaret 28-03-1798; Stafford
PRICE, Nancy 28-03-1798; Stafford
RICHMOND, Mary
Jane 10-03-1798; Yorkshire
SHESTON,
Elizabeth 31-03-1798; Warwick
SLY*, Elizabeth 21-07-1798; Wiltshire
TAYLOR, Elizabeth 05-10-1798; Lincoln
TWYNHAM, Mary 16-07-1798; Berkshire
WALKER, Ellen 10-07-1798; Lancashire
WICK, Ann 30-07-1798; Norfolk

Glatton 1803
HOPE, Elizabeth	09-07-1798; Bristol
MODE, Isabella	12-10-1798; Dover
SHELTON, Susannah	04-07-1798; London

Nile 1801
BARKER, Sarah	21-03-1798; Suffolk
CARNE, Jane	05-12-1798; London
PINE, Sarah	05-12-1798; London
RICHARDS, Sarah	27-03-1798; Glamorgan

Speedy 1800
ATKINS, Mary	04-07-1798; London
BAKER, Sarah	12-09-1798; London
BATTERSBY, Margaret	24-10-1798; Middlesex
BUCKIE, Margaret	12-09-1798; Middlesex
BUTLER, Mary	21-03-1798; Kingston
CHADDICK, Ann	03-03-1798; Reading
CLARK, Sarah	30-07-1798; Guildford
EVANS, Mary	04-07-1798; Middlesex
FALKNER, Elizabeth	02-10-1798; Guildford
FLARENAUGH, Elizabeth	04-07-1798; Middlesex
GRANT, Elizabeth	27-02-1798; Surrey
HARDCASTLE, Hannah	24-10-1798; London
HASTEN, Elizabeth	23-07-1798; Maidstone
HERBERT, Catherine	04-03-1798; Reading
HILL, Martha	30-07-1798; Guildford
JENNINGS, Maria	23-05-1798; Middlesex
LAHEY, Catherine	12-09-1798; Middlesex
LAWRENCE, Sarah	12-09-1798; London
PATTERSON, Jane	18-04-1798; Middlesex
PIAKA, Mary	27-02-1798; Surrey
SEXTON, Sarah	18-04-1798; Middlesex
SHAY, Mary	27-02-1798; Surrey
SIDNEY, Ann	12-09-1798; Middlesex
SMITH, Elizabeth	04-07-1798; Middlesex
SMITH, Elizabeth	16-07-1798; Hertford
SOUTH*, Ann	12-09-1798; Middlesex
STATHAM, Elizabeth	NR-12-1798; Middlesex
THOMAS, Sarah	24-10-1798; Middlesex
THOMPSON, Margaret	18-04-1798; London
TILLOT, Sarah	18-07-1798; Essex
TURNER, Sarah	14-02-1798; Middlesex
WARD, Elizabeth	02-10-1798; Guildford
WILLIS, Sarah	12-09-1798; Middlesex
WOOD, Sarah	24-10-1798; Middlesex

1799 TRIAL YEAR

Earl Cornwallis 1801
ARMSTRONG, Sarah	17-01-1799; Northumberland
BOTT, Sarah	17-01-1799; Stafford
BRODDIE, Catherine	20-03-1799; Bristol
CONNELL, Catherine	14-01-1799; Bristol
CRADDOCK, Dinah	24-07-1799; Stafford
FOGG, Ann	24-07-1799; Lancaster
HILL, Ann	11-09-1799; Middlesex
HOGGARD, Frances	14-03-1799; Dorset
HOLLETT, Jane	18-03-1799; Surrey
HOPKINS, Sarah	15-03-1799; Norfolk
JENNINGS, Charlotte	11-09-1799; Middlesex
JOHNS, Hannah	03-04-1799; Bristol
JONES, Mary	12-08-1799; Chester
JONES, Sarah	18-03-1799; Surrey
LEADBETTER, Sarah	16-10-1799; Lancaster
McENTIRE*, Eleanor	11-09-1799; Middlesex
PARKER, Alice	06-07-1799; Wiltshire
PARKER, Lydia	02-04-1799; Dorset
PLAYER, Ann	09-03-1799; Wiltshire
PUGH, Ann	16-07-1799; Hereford
ROBERTSON, Helen	08-04-1799; Stirling
ROBINSON, Sarah	08-10-1799; Chester
SPINKS, Jane	09-03-1799; Wiltshire
STEVENS, Mary	28-03-1799; Somerset
STEWARD, Mary	10-07-1799; Gloucester
TAYLOR, Betty	09-03-1799; Wiltshire
VOLLER, Elizabeth	15-07-1799; Southampton
WATTS, Betty	19-03-1799; Hereford

Glatton 1803
GROVER, Martha	14-01-1799; Hampshire

Nile 1801
DOUGLAS, Susannah	11-09-1799; London

FORDHAM, Sarah 30-10-1799; Middlesex
GREEN, Sarah 11-09-1799; Middlesex
MUCKLE, Jane 16-07-1799; Durham
PRICE*, Sarah NR-03-1799; Hampshire
SOMERVILLE, Ann 15-07-1799; Newcastle
WILSON, Elizabeth 30-10-1799; Middlesex

Speedy 1800
BOWMEND, Mary 09-01-1799; Middlesex
BROWN, Elizabeth 03-04-1799; Middlesex
BROWN, Elizabeth 11-03-1799; Maidstone
CLARKE, Ann 03-04-1799; Middlesex
COLETON, Elizabeth 09-01-1799; London
GARNHAM, Mary 09-01-1799; London
GOODWIN, Ann 15-07-1799; Maidstone
HARRISON, Susannah 08-05-1799; Middlesex
HILLAR, Mary 19-06-1799; Middlesex
KING, Sarah 22-07-1799; Croydon
LILLEY, Elizabeth 15-01-1799; Guildford
THOMAS, Mary 03-04-1799; Middlesex
THOMAS, Sarah 19-06-1799; Middlesex
UNDERHILL*, Mary 03-04-1799; Middlesex
WHALEY, Sarah 22-07-1799; Croydon

1800 TRIAL YEAR

Earl Cornwallis 1801
BARRETT, Elizabeth 30-04-1800; Lancashire
BIDDLE, Mary 22-01-1800; Lancashire
BOWDEN, Mary 01-03-1800; Berkshire
CARR, Jane 08-03-1800; York
CROUCH, Elizabeth 19-02-1800; London
DAVIS, Maria 25-03-1800; Lancaster
DAVISON, Elizabeth 24-04-1800; Northumberland
DENTON, Mary 25-03-1800; Lancaster
EDWARDS, Elizabeth 09-07-1800; London
EDWARDS, Mary 19-07-1800; Devon
GANTHONY, Mary 14-07-1800; Bristol
HICKS, Elizabeth 17-03-1800; Devon
HOWARD, Elizabeth 30-04-1800; Lancaster
HUNT, Hannah 14-07-1800; Bristol
JOHNSON, Alice 30-04-1800; Lancashire
JUSTIN, Ann 04-03-1800; Southampton
PHILLIPS, Elizabeth 12-03-1800; Gloucester
POUNDS, Frances 10-03-1800; Kent
POUNDS, Philadelphia 10-03-1800; Kent
PRICE, Elizabeth 09-07-1800; London
PRUCK, Elizabeth 07-03-1800; Worcester
REYNOLDS, Esther 22-01-1800; Lancashire
ROBSON, Mary 09-07-1800; London
SCOLTOCK, Elizabeth 09-07-1800; Middlesex
SHADDICK, Susanna 17-03-1800; Devon
SHEPLEY, Mary 22-01-1800; Lancashire
SPENCER, Ann 09-07-1800; London
STOWE, Elizabeth 27-01-1800; Yorkshire
THOMPSON, Mary 28-05-1800; London
TRAPNELL, Sarah 14-07-1800; Bristol
TUTTON, Ann 05-02-1800; Bristol
WHITESIDE, Elizabeth 24-04-1800; Lancashire
WILLS*, Elizabeth 09-07-1800; Middlesex

Experiment 1804
GILLETT, Christian 22-07-1800; Hampshire
OWEN, Catherine 20-08-1800; Pembroke

Glatton 1803
BOUGH, Elizabeth 19-02-1800; Middlesex
BRIMBLE*, Mary 03-12-1800; Bristol
CLEMENTS, Ann 28-05-1800; Middlesex
HOLLAND, Charlotte 30-07-1800; Gloucester
TUCKEY, Ann 03-03-1800; Northampton
WHITE, Elizabeth 16-01-1800; Nottingham
WILLIAMS, Eleanor 02-08-1800; Monmouth

Nile 1801
BECKWITH, Mary 09-07-1800; Middlesex
BECKWITH, Mary (Jnr) 09-07-1800; Middlesex
BIRKS*, Emma 13-08-1800; Stafford
BLAKE, Ann 29-10-1800; Middlesex
BROWNLOW, Ann 23-10-1800; Oxford
BRYNE, Mary 29-10-1800; Middlesex
CAMM, Jane 03-12-1800; Middlesex
CATCHPOLE, Margaret 31-07-1800; Suffolk
CHAPMAN, Sarah 15-10-1800; York
CHURCH, Sarah 09-07-1800; London
COLESFORD, Ann 19-02-1800; London
DAVIS, Catherine 28-05-1800; Middlesex
DEMPSTER, Mary 15-10-1800; Newcastle

EDWARDS, Harriott 22-03-1800; Cornwall
FIELDING, Mary
  Ann 09-07-1800; Middlesex
GORDON, Sarah 29-10-1800; Middlesex
HASLEN*, Sarah 05-03-1800; Essex
HAWKINS, Amelia 14-07-1800; Colchester
HOW*, Mary 15-01-1800; Middlesex
JOHNSON, Mary 09-07-1800; London
KILLETT, Elizabeth 31-07-1800; Suffolk
KIRTON*, Elizabeth 09-10-1800; Northumberland
LAURENCE*, Esther 17-09-1800; London
METCALF, Ann 03-12-1800; London
MILLER, Ann 29-10-1800; Middlesex
MILLER, Margaret 03-12-1800; Middlesex
MOORE, Elizabeth 03-12-1800; Middlesex
NORMAN, Lydia 05-03-1800; Essex
OAKES, Mary 03-12-1800; Middlesex
OKIE, Catherine 19-02-1800; London
PEACH, Mary 23-07-1800; Lancashire
PRIESTLY, Sarah 14-07-1800; Colchester
REED, Mary 28-07-1800; Hertford
RICE, Ann 29-10-1800; London
ROBERTSON,
  Margaret 22-07-1800; Hampshire
ROSS, Mary 23-09-1800; Middlesex
RYAN*, Margaret 17-01-1800; York
SAGUS*, Elizabeth 15-10-1800; Newcastle
SANDALL, Ann 06-10-1800; Kingston
SHAW, Elizabeth 26-07-1800; Worcester
SMITH, Charlotte 17-09-1800; London
SMITH, Elizabeth 15-01-1800; Middlesex
SMITH, Mary 28-05-1800; London
SMITH, Mary 09-07-1800; Middlesex
SMITH, Mary 29-10-1800; Middlesex
SMITH*, Mary 09-07-1800; Middlesex
SULS, Elizabeth 15-01-1800; Middlesex
THOMPSON,
  Elizabeth 23-07-1800; Lancashire
TITLEY, Elizabeth 22-03-1800; Shropshire
TUNSTALL, Phoebe 17-09-1800; Middlesex
WALKER, Charlotte 15-01-1800; London
WARD, Elizabeth 17-09-1800; Middlesex
WELCH*, Mary 03-12-1800; Middlesex
WHIDDICK, Hannah 16-08-1800; Somerset
WILLIAMS,
  Charlotte 11-08-1800; Surrey
WILLIAMS,
  Elizabeth 01-12-1800; Middlesex
WILLIAMS, Hannah 14-08-1800; Carmarthen
WILLIAMS, Mary 16-08-1800; Somerset
WISE, Margaret 22-07-1800; Hampshire
WOOTTEN*,
  Betty/Elizabeth 26-07-1800; Wiltshire
WOOTTON*, Ann 26-07-1800; Wiltshire

1801 TRIAL YEAR

Experiment 1804

CAHUSAC, Elizabeth 10-03-1801; Essex
CRAIG, Elizabeth 18-02-1801; Middlesex
DANIEL*, Martha Spring 1801; Carmarthen
DANIELS, Mary 22-07-1801; Essex
DAVIES, Mary 15-07-1801; Pembroke
FOX, Elizabeth 02-01-1801; Lancashire
HILL, Jane 28-03-1801; Somerset
JAMES*, Sophia 18-08-1801; Pembroke
LAWRENCE, Mary 01-04-1801; Pembroke
LLOYD, Ann NR-09-1801; Carmarthen
MOORE, Mary 27-07-1801; Kent
PORTER, Betty NR-08-1801; Somerset
PURL, Martha NR-08-1801; Somerest
SALT, Mary Summer 1801; Cornwall
TREASURE,
  Deborah NR-08-1801; Somerset

Glatton 1803

ABBSOLM, Esther 16-04-1801; St Albans
BAKER, Betty 22-07-1801; Lancashire
BERRY, Elizabeth 05-03-1801; Hertford
BILL, Mary 11-03-1801; Salop
BOOTLESTON*,
  Sarah 25-07-1801; Salop
BOYLE, Mary Ann 20-05-1801; Middlesex
CLARK, Susannah 02-03-1801-; Hampshire
COPLEY, Eleanor 07-03-1801; York
COULTER, Mary 21-07-1801; Lancashire
CUNNINGHAM,
  Mary 28-10-1801; Middlesex
DAVIES, Margaret 15-08-1801; Glamorgan
DAVIS, Mary 19-03-1801; Hereford
DEAN, Mary 15-04-1801; Middlesex
DENNEY, Bridget 03-08-1801; Surrey
DOVORANE, Juliet 01-07-1801; Middlesex
DUNNING, Mary 28-03-1801; Somerset

388 List A-1

EDDIS, Mary	28-10-1801; Middlesex	MORT, Mary	22-07-1801; Lancashire
EVANS, Mary	25-07-1801; Salop	MURPHY, Elizabeth	28-10-1801; Middlesex
FORBES, Catherine	20-05-1801; Middlesex	OSBORNE,	
GARDNER, Jannet	13-04-1801; Cumberland	Catherine	22-04-1801; Lancashire
GARDNER, Maria	11-05-1801; Bristol	OWENS, Catherine	19-08-1801; Denbigh
GIBBS, Ann	15-07-1801; Somerset	PALMER, Mary	28-03-1801; Somerset
GILES, Margaret	01-07-1801; Middlesex	PALMER, Mary	01-07-1801; Middlesex
GILL, Ann	16-09-1801; Middlesex	PARKER, Ann	01-07-1801; Middlesex
GOLDING, Martha	14-07-1801; Gloucester	PEWTERS,	
GOTHAM, Mary	11-03-1801; Stafford	Constance	28-03-1801; Somerset
GREEN, Charlotte	27-07-1801; Kent	PHILLIPS, Elizabeth	28-10-1801; Middlesex
GRIFFITHS, Ann		PHILLIPS, Margaret	03-08-1801; Monmouth
Hawkes	06-03-1801; Worcester	PICK, Sarah	05-08-1801; Gloucester
GRIFFITHS, Mary	13-08-1801; Montgomery	PRICHARD*, Mary	03-08-1801; Monmouth
		RHYND, Jane	01-07-1801; Middlesex
HAMBLETON, Ann	22-07-1801; Lancashire	RICHARDS,	13-08-1801;
HAYES, Mary	20-05-1801; Middlesex	Margaret (Snr)	Montgomery
HAYNES, Sarah	05-08-1801; Gloucester	ROBERTS, Susan	15-04-1801; Middlesex
HAYWARD*,		ROBERTS, Susanna	22-07-1801; Stafford
Hannah	02-03-1801; Hampshire	ROBINSON,	
HEMMINGS,		Elizabeth	01-08-1801; Warwick
Elizabeth	25-03-1801; Gloucester	ROGERS, Ann	22-04-1801; Lancashire
HILL, Mary	28-10-1801; Middlesex	ROSE, Mindred/	
HOLLOWAY, Mary	05-08-1801; Gloucester	Mary	16-09-1801; Middlesex
HOLMSLEY*, Mary	12-01-1801; Yorkshire	RUGG, Mary	05-10-1801; Exeter
HORRS*, Mary	13-01-1801; Lancashire	SANDERS, Sarah	01-07-1801; Middlesex
HOWELL, Jane	16-03-1801; Kent	SANDLE, Mary	28-03-1801; Somerset
HUDDLESTONE,		SARGENT*, Mary	22-07-1801; Stafford
Ann	07-03-1801; Yorkshire	SHAKESHAFT,	
HUGHES, Jane	16-09-1801; London	Mary	25-07-1801; Salop
HUNTER, Hannah	25-03-1801; Surrey	SHAW, Elizabeth	01-07-1801; Middlesex
ILES, Elizabeth	05-08-1801; Gloucester	SINGLETON, Sarah	23-12-1801; Dover
JOBBER*, Sarah	15-04-1801; Middlesex	SMITH, Mary	25-03-1801; Surrey
JONES, Jane	28-03-1801; Somerset	STANLEY,	
KEEN, Mary	20-05-1801; London	Elizabeth	13-07-1801; Hampshire
LEATH, Elizabeth	07-10-1801; Norfolk	THOMAS, Mary	23-03-1801; Monmouth
LESTER, Sarah	02-12-1801; Middlesex	THOMAS*, Mary	13-04-1801; Cumberland
LEWIS, Elizabeth	06-03-1801; Worcester	TURNER, Elizabeth	07-03-1801; York
LOCK*, Agnes	28-03-1801; Somerset	VOLLER, Ann	02-03-1801; Hampshire
LONG, Ann	02-12-1801; Middlesex	WEBB, Sarah	02-03-1801; Hampshire
LONGHURST, Jane	11-07-1801; Surrey	WOOD, Sarah	06-03-1801; Norcorton
MANLEY, Hannah	28-03-1801; Somerset	YOUNG, Ellen	09-10-1801; Nottingham
MANSELL, Grace	16-03-1801; Devon		
MANVELL, Elizabeth	14-07-1801; Sussex	*Nile* **1801**	
		APPLETON*, Jane	16-01-1801; Reading
MANVELL, Letty	14-07-1801; Sussex	CHIDWORTH,	
MIDDLEBROOK,		Elizabeth	25-03-1801; Gloucester
Ann	11-03-1801; Stafford	EWEN, Jane	14-01-1801; London
MILLS, Mary	15-08-1801; Lancashire	GENNETT, Martha	12-01-1801; Bristol
		GIBBS*, Elizabeth	14-01-1801; Middlesex

GILES, Elizabeth	14-01-1801; Middlesex	JONES, Elizabeth	01-04-1802; Somerset
HODGES, Mary	18-02-1801; Middlesex	KELSO, Elizabeth	27-10-1802; London
HORRS*, Ellen	13-01-1801; Lancashire	LEWIS, Margaret	04-10-1802; Oxford
KEEFE, Elizabeth	14-01-1801; London	MORGAN, Ann	02-06-1802; Middlesex
KINNESLEY*, Sarah	13-01-1801; Surrey	MOUNTFORD, Elizabeth	20-03-1802; Salop
MARTIN, Margaret	12-01-1801; Bristol	NUTTALL, Mary	21-07-1802; Lancashire
MATTHEWS, Rachel	18-02-1801; Middlesex	PERRY, Mary	NR-10-1802; Westminister
RIGBY, Catherine	13-01-1801; Surrey	PROSSER, Elizabeth	15-09-1802; Middlesex
SCOTT, Mary	14-01-1801; Middlesex	QUINLAND, Judith	27-10-1802; Middlesex
SKINNER, Mary	06-04-1801; Bristol	RADSHAW, Margaret	01-12-1802; Middlesex
SMITH, Mary	12-01-1801; Hampshire	RAVENSCROFT, Hannah	15-09-1802; Middlesex
WHITEBREAD*, Sarah	18-02-1801; Middlesex	RAWLINS, Abigail	26-04-1802; Bristol
WILLIAMS, Jane	12-01-1801; Gloucester	REES, Margaret	13-01-1802; Monmouth
WILLIAMS, Susannah	14-01-1801; Middlesex	RISLEY, Maria	09-08-1802; Surrey

William Pitt 1806

DUNDAS, Carolin Julia	07-04-1801; Avon	ROBINSON, Mary	11-10-1802; Surrey
MADDOCKS, Hannah	16-03-1801; Devon	SMITH, Ann	30-03-1802; Breconshire
		SMITH, Ann	28-04-1802; Middlesex
		SMITH, Martha	01-12-1802; Middlesex
		SMITH, Mary	28-04-1802; Middlesex
		SMITH, Mary	01-12-1802; Middlesex
		SMITH, Sarah	25-08-1802; Carmarthen

1802 TRIAL YEAR

		SWAN, Mary	14-07-1802; Middlesex

Experiment 1804

		TANDY, Sarah	16-02-1802; Surrey
ABRAHAMS, Mary	09-08-1802; Surrey	TIMMIS, Sarah	21-08-1802; Somerset
ALLEN, Mary	12-07-1802; Lancaster	TODD, Grace	01-04-1802; Somerset
ATKIN, Mary	15-07-1802; Nottingham	WILLIAMS, Alice	20-08-1802; Glamorgan
BAXTER*, Sarah	21-04-1802; Cheshire	WILLOWS, Mary	11-01-1802; Leicester
BLAKE, Ann	01-12-1802; Middlesex	WILMOTT, Jane	15-01-1802; Hampshire
BOWATER, Mary	20-03-1802; Salop	WILSON, Rebecca	13-10-1802; Newcastle
BROMLEY, Ann	03-05-1802; Surrey	WINTER, Ann	27-10-1802; Middlesex
BROUGHTON, Margaret	29-04-1802; Lancashire		

Glatton 1803

BROWN, Eleanor	10-08-1802; Durham	BATES, Eleanor	11-01-1802; Cumberland
CASHMAN, Sarah	14-07-1802; Middlesex	BILTON, Charlotte	01-02-1802; York
COLEMAN*, Norah	12-07-1802; Hampshire	CHAPMAN, Ann	05-05-1802; Lancashire
COWELL, Ann	14-07-1802; Middlesex	CHAPMAN, Susannah	19-07-1802; Surrey
DICKSON, Elizabeth	20-03-1802; Salop	COULTER, Elizabeth	29-04-1802; Lancashire
DOOLEY, Mary	13-10-1802; Lancashire	DIXON, Ann	13-01-1802; Middlesex
DRING, Frances	14-07-1802; Middlesex	GRANGER, Mary	06-03-1802; Yorkshire
EDWARDS, Hannah	07-10-1802; Portsmouth	GROUNDHIE, Sophia	28-04-1802; Middlesex
FIELD, Sarah	27-07-1802; Hampshire	HODGE, Elizabeth	26-04-1802; Exeter
GOODWIN, Ann	14-08-1802; Warwick	HOWARD, Hannah	28-04-1802; Middlesex
HILL, Elizabeth	11-10-1802; Devon	HUGHES, Mary	08-03-1802; Hertford
HILL, Hannah	25-03-1802; Stafford		
HOWE, Margaret	09-08-1802; Surrey		
JONES, Eliza	28-04-1802; Middlesex		

HUTCHESON,
Elizabeth   20-03-1802; Norfolk
MARTIN, Mary   28-04-1802; Middlesex
MITCHENOR*,
Mary   13-01-1802; Middlesex
MORE, Mary   17-02-1802; Middlesex
SMITH, Susannah 17-02-1802; Middlesex
STAPLES, Amy   13-01-1802; Middlesex
STOKES, Elizabeth 23-03-1802;
                 Westmoreland
WARD, Mary   17-02-1802; Middlesex
WELDON, Mary   28-04-1802; Middlesex
WIGGINS, Sarah   14-01-1802; Oxford

Sydney Cove **1807**
WARDROP, Agnes   16-09-1802; Glasgow

William Pitt **1806**
ELLIS, Mary   20-03-1802; Shropshire
SMITH, Martha   31-07-1802; Yorkshire

1803 TRIAL YEAR

Experiment **1804**
ABEL, Mary   24-03-1803; Warwick
ALLEN, Ann   12-07-1803; Derby
ARNOLD, Sarah   05-02-1803; Wilts
ATHERLEY, Sarah 06-08-1803; Warwick
BARNFYLDE,
Elizabeth   05-01-1803; Exeter City
BELL, Sarah Ann 14-09-1803; Middlesex
BLUNDELL, Sophia 06-07-1803; Middlesex
BRADWELL, Ann   27-04-1803; Lancaster
BROWN, Eleanor   06-07-1803; Middlesex
BROWN, Mary   06-07-1803; Middlesex
BROWN, Sarah   26-10-1803; London
CABLE, Mary   19-04-1803; Essex
CAHILL, Mary   20-04-1803; London
CARY, Catherine 26-10-1803; London
COPPOCK, Mary   13-01-1803; Oxford City
CURTIS, Esther   19-07-1803; Liverpool
DAVIS, Sarah   20-04-1803; Middlesex
DAVIS, Sarah   26-10-1803; Middlesex
DIGGINS, Ann   20-04-1803; Middlesex
DUGGAN, Margaret 19-03-1803; Lancaster
ELLIS*, Mary   18-04-1803; Hants
EVANS, Margaret 08-08-1803; Surrey
FARRELL, Sarah   16-02-1803; Middlesex
FLETCHER, Jane   15-03-1803; Hereford
GRAHAM, Ann   23-07-1803; Hants

GRIFFITHS, Raihel 11-04-1803; Carmarthen
GUYSE, Elizabeth 24-07-1803; Worcester
HARCOURT, Sarah 20-04-1803; London
HARRIS, Rose   Lent 1803; Cornwall
HOLLINGSWORTH,
Elizabeth   16-02-1803; London
HOLMES, Rebecca 24-03-1803; Warwick
HOOPER, Mary   27-07-1803; Gloucester
HUDSON, Martha   23-04-1803; York
HUNT, Elizabeth 20-04-1803; Middlesex
JACKSON, Frances 20-04-1803; London
JONES, Ann   11-01-1803; Salop
JONES, Margaret 03-04-1803; Brecon
KELLY, Mary   14-03-1803; Kent
KING, Charlotte 09-03-1803; Essex
MARY, Catherine 23-07-1803; Hants
MASON, Mary   02-04-1803; Bristol
MASON*, Margaret 19-03-1803; Lancaster
MATTHEWS, Mary   21-03-1803; Surrey
MEARS, Mary   10-10-1803; Surrey
MEREDITH*,
Elizabeth   02-04-1803; Bristol
MORLEY, Martha   13-01-1803; Nottingham
MORRIS, Martha   19-03-1803; Salop
MOSS, Mary   20-01-1803; Lancaster
MURRALL*, Mary   11-01-1803; Salop
PAGE, Mary   05-03-1803; Worcester
REFFIN, Ann   11-03-1803; Nottingham
RONNES, Elizabeth 06-07-1803; Middlesex
SOUTHERN,
Margaret   27-04-1803; Lancaster
STARMER, Ann   19-07-1803;
                 Northampton
SULLIVAN, Mary   26-10-1803; Middlesex
TATE, Maria   06-07-1803; Middlesex
TAYLOR, Elizabeth 19-03-1803; Salop
TAYLOR, Elizabeth 20-04-1803; Middlesex
THEW, Hannah   14-09-1803; London
TRANE, Martha   18-07-1803; Surrey
WALWORTH,
Hannah   19-01-1803; Lancaster
WARE, Elizabeth 06-07-1803; Middlesex
WEST, Hannah   05-03-1803; Worcester
WHITE, Catherine 19-07-1803; Hants
WHITEHEAD,
Elizabeth   20-04-1803; Middlesex
WICKER, Elizabeth 19-04-1803; Essex
WILLIAMS,
Catherine   19-01-1803; Lancaster

WILLIAMS,
Elizabeth   11-07-1803; Hants
WILLIAMS, Hannah   24-03-1803; Suffolk
WILSON, Elizabeth   19-07-1803; Liverpool
YARMOUTH,
Hannah   06-08-1803; Newcastle

William Pitt **1806**
ADAMS, Mary   06-10-1803; Portsmouth
BUTTERWORTH,
Jane   20-08-1803; Lancaster
COTTAM, Elizabeth   07-10-1803; Berkshire
DAVIS, Elizabeth   04-10-1803; Bristol
DUCK, Ann   13-03-1803; Gloucester
GARNER, Lucy   20-07-1803; Lancaster
HEWITT, Jane   15-04-1803; Chester
KING, Mary   12-10-1803;
                      Northumberland
LOWRIE, Mary   06-08-1803;
                      Northumberland
ROBINSON,
Elizabeth   11-10-1803; Lancaster
ROBINSON, Rachael   20-07-1803; Lancaster
SCHOLEFIELD,
Alice   12-10-1803; Lancaster
SHEIN*, Ann   18-07-1803;
                      Buckinghamshire
SHERRARD, Alice   26-10-1803; Middlesex
SIDEWELL, Isabella   06-08-1803;
                      Northumberland
SIMMONDS, Sophia   03-10-1803;
                      Southhampton
STAGG*, Ann   05-03-1803; Buckingham
THOMPSON, Ann   20-07-1803; Lancaster

1804 TRIAL YEAR

Alexander **1806**
MOSS, Sarah   10-10-1804; Lancashire

Sydney Cove **1807**
STEWART, Christian   07-05-1804; Glasgow

William Pitt **1806**
ALLEN, Frances   28-07-1804; Warwick
ARMSTRONG,
Eleanor   12-03-1804; Kent
BARTLETT,
Elizabeth   26-07-1804; Dorset
BENT, Diana   13-03-1804; Hereford

BRICE, Catherine   11-08-1804; Somerset
BROWN,
Hannah/Mary   09-01-1804; Wiltshire
BURBRIDGE,
Elizabeth   12-03-1804; Kent
BURNETT, Mary   05-12-1804; Middlesex
CALDER, Ann   24-09-1804; Inverness
CLAYTON, Eliza   30-07-1804; Devon
CLOTHIER, Hannah   02-10-1804; Gloucester
CONNER, Mary   10-04-1804; Lancashire
CONWAY, Hannah   10-04-1804; Lancashire
DAVIS, Mary   05-12-1804; Middlesex
EPTON, Ann   25-07-1804; Lincoln
EVANS, Matilda   07-04-1804; Avon
FLEMING, Mary   06-03-1804; Hampshire
FRAZIER, Catherine   29-03-1804; Lancashire
GEER, Mary   28-07-1804; Sussex
GIBBINS, Ann   24-03-1804; Worcester
GIBSON*, Hannah   12-04-1804;
                      Northumberland
GOODAIRE, Ruth   13-03-1804; York
GRACE, Catherine   25-10-1804; Cheshire
GRAY, Margaret   28-04-1804; Grampian
HALL, Sarah   05-12-1804; Middlesex
HARRIS, Ann   05-12-1804; Middlesex
HARRIS, Elizabeth   12-03-1804; Kent
HAYNES, Ann   24-07-1804; Hereford
HAYNES*, Ann   11-04-1804; Middlesex
HICK, Johanna   12-07-1804; York
HODGSON, Eve   11-08-1804; Lancashire
HOWSTER, Mary   11-01-1804; Middlesex
HUGHES, Ann   29-03-1804; Lancashire
IRELAND, Elizabeth   23-07-1804; Kent
JACKSON, Ann   09-01-1804; Cumberland
JOHNSON, Ann   05-12-1804; Middlesex
JONES, Catherine   17-03-1804; Shropshire
KELLY, Ann   24-10-1804; Middlesex
LANCASTER,
Martha   13-03-1804; York
LEES, Mary   29-03-1804; Lancashire
McCARTY, Ann   15-02-1804; Middlesex
MacKINTOSH, Ellen   29-03-1804; Lancashire
MacNAMARA, Mary   14-04-1804; Gloucester
MERCER, Mary   24-10-1804; Middlesex
MORGAN, Jane   24-03-1804; Worcester
OAKLEY, Mary   06-03-1804; Hampshire
OSBORN, Catherine   04-10-1804; Hampshire
OWEN, Jane   28-03-1804;
                      Montgomery

PALMER, Hannah 05-12-1804; Middlesex
PHIPARD, Eliza 03-08-1804; Dorset
PLEASE, Susannah 11-08-1804; Somerset
PRICE*, Ann 16-07-1804; Surrey
RALPH, Ann 26-03-1804; Warwick
RAYCRAFT, Mary 03-12-1804; Middlesex
RILEY, Rose 06-03-1804; Hampshire
ROBINSON, Jane 13-03-1804; Yorkshire
ROGERS, Mary 28-07-1804; Shropshire
RUMBOLD*, Sarah 05-12-1804; Middlesex
RUSSELL, Elizabeth 21-07-1804; Wiltshire
SABIN, Rose 12-03-1804; Kent
SMITH*, Elizabeth 03-10-1804; Cumberland
STRATTON, Mary 06-08-1804; Cornwall
THOMPSON*, Ann 21-03-1804; Surrey
TURNBULL, Mary 03-10-1804; Cumberland
VAUGHAN, Lucy 28-07-1804; Shropshire
WHILEY, Sarah 11-04-1804; Middlesex
WHITE, Sarah 28-07-1804; Northumberland
WIDDUP, Susanna 13-03-1804; Yorkshire
WILLIAMS, Elizabeth 28-07-1804; Warwick
WILLIAMS, Jane 14-04-1804; Gloucester
WILLIAMS, Susan 13-03-1804; Hereford
WISE, Martha 20-04-1804; Dorset
WOOD, Mary 18-10-1804; Middlesex
WOODS, Elizabeth 04-08-1804; Breconshire
YORK, Mary 09-07-1804; Gloucester
YOUNG, Ann 20-04-1804; Aberdeen
YOUNG, Euphemia 20-04-1804; Aberdeen

1805 TRIAL YEAR

Alexander 1806
BARNES*, Isabella 29-05-1805; Middlesex
BELLAS, Mary 27-07-1805; York
BERRY, Mary 24-04-1805; Middlesex
BRAZIER, Anne 09-03-1805; Wiltshire
BRIANT, Sarah 29-05-1805; Middlesex
BROOKS, Elizabeth 23-01-1805; Lancaster
BUFFY, Elizabeth 23-01-1805; Lancaster
BULMER, Ann 27-07-1805; York
BURKETT, Mary 18-07-1805; York
CARTER, Elizabeth 17-08-1805; Somerset
CARTEY, Mary 18-09-1805; Middlesex
CHEDLEY, Sarah 28-03-1805; Somerset
CHILDS, Mary 14-08-1805; Surrey
CLARKE, Mary 10-07-1805; Middlesex
CURTIS, Jane 18-09-1805; Middlesex
DUNN, Elizabeth 14-10-1805; Surrey
GREADY, Catherine 24-04-1805; Middlesex
HAMMETT, Mary 17-08-1805; Somerset
JOHNSON, Margaret 27-07-1805; York
JOHNSON, Mary 09-01-1805; Middlesex
JONES, Mary Ann 18-09-1805; Middlesex
KELLY, Catherine 29-05-1805; Middlesex
KNIGHT, Grace 28-03-1805; Somerset
LEA*, Sarah 10-07-1805; London
LONGDON, Elizabeth 16-10-1805; York
LUKE, Martha 18-09-1805; Middlesex
MARNEY, Mary 24-04-1805; Middlesex
MERRIMAN, Esther 29-05-1805; London
MILES, Catherine 14-08-1805; Surrey
MILLER, Mary 27-05-1805; Middlesex
OGDEN, Martha 01-05-1805; Lancaster
PARSONS, Ann 18-03-1805; Devon
PETERSON, Elizabeth 26-03-1805; Lancaster
POOR, Mary 04-03-1805; Surrey
PORTER, Diana 16-08-1805; Surrey
REASON, Rebecca 24-04-1805; Middlesex
RICH, Elizabeth 17-08-1805; Somerset
RICHES, Elizabeth 14-08-1805; Surrey
SCOTT, Jane 24-04-1805; Middlesex
SIBURY, Sarah 14-08-1805; Surrey
SLATER*, Sarah 18-09-1805; Middlesex
SOWDEN, Mary 18-09-1805; Middlesex
SULLIVAN, Sarah 24-04-1805; Middlesex
SYMONS, Elizabeth Michaelmas 1805; Devon
TAYLOR, Ann 18-09-1805; Middlesex
TAYLOR, Elizabeth 10-07-1805; Middlesex
WEBB, Ann 23-01-1805; Lancaster

Speke 1808
KENWORTHY, Betty 24-08-1805; Lancaster

Sydney Cove 1807
ANSTEE*, Elizabeth 10-10-1805; Bucks
ATKINS*, Sarah 30-10-1805; Middlesex
ATKINSON, Mary 16-10-1805; Lancaster
BALDWIN, Ann 30-10-1805; Middlesex
BERRY, Margaret 24-04-1805; Middlesex
BURTON, Ann 09-03-1805; Lincoln
CAMPBELL, Mary 15-01-1805; Lancaster
COCK*, Ann 17-08-1805; Salop

CRAIG, Jean	03-05-1805; Glasgow	PERCY*, Ann	29-05-1805; Middlesex
FRANCIS, Ann	05-03-1805; Southampton	ROCK, Margaret	15-01-1805; Lancaster
		STEDLING, Mary	21-02-1805; Middlesex
GLOVER, Ann	10-08-1805; Warwick	SURINGHAM, Barbara	18-03-1805; Norfolk
HOLWARD*, Ann	04-12-1805; Middlesex		
JENNER, Esther Jane	09-12-1805; Middlesex	TUES, Jane	09-01-1805; London
		WADE, Mary	16-01-1805; Somerset
McGOWAN, Mary	15-01-1805; Lancaster	WILSON*, Mary	27-03-1805; Surrey
McLEOD*, Catherine	04-09-1805; Edinburgh		
MARKLAND, Ellen	22-07-1805; Lancaster		

1806 TRIAL YEAR

Aeolus 1809

MEAD, Margaret/Mary	30-10-1805; Middlesex
MUNTON, Elizabeth	05-08-1805; Norwich
MURPHY*, Margaret	17-04-1805; Chester
NEAL*, Mary/Betty	09-09-1805; Chester
NOCK, Susannah	17-08-1805; Salop
PAPPS, Sarah	18-09-1805; London
PORTER*, Sarah	18-07-1805; Cambridge
RILEY, Margaret	18-09-1805; Middlesex
ROBERTSON, Agnes	27-04-1805; Stirling
SULLIVAN, Ann	30-10-1805; Middlesex
TODD, Elizabeth	04-12-1805; Middlesex
TODD, Harriet	04-12-1805; Middlesex
WALLACE, Bridget	15-01-1805; Lancaster
WATERS, Ann	30-10-1805; Middlesex
WATTS, Catherine	09-09-1805; Chester
WHITAKER, Mary	08-10-1805; Derby
WILLIAMS, Elizabeth	17-04-1805; Chester
WILSON*, Agnes	27-04-1805; Stirling
WOODCOCK, Elizabeth	27-08-1805; Gloucester

MURRAY*, Betty/Elizabeth	08-05-1806; Perth
NANTIN, Elizabeth	06-10-1806; Southampton

Speke 1808

BALLARD, Mary	17-09-1806; Middlesex
BENTLEY*, Maria/Hannah	13-08-1806; Stafford
BERRY, Elizabeth	23-07-1806; Lancaster
BROUGHTON, Susannah	02-07-1806; London
DALEY, Mary	29-10-1806; Middlesex
DOYLE, Martha	02-07-1806; Middlesex
GREEN, Maria	28-07-1806; Kent
HILKIN, Sarah	13-08-1806; Stafford
HIRON, Sarah	09-08-1806; Warwick
HODGSON, Jane	14-07-1806; Lancaster
HOTCHKISS*, Jane	17-07-1806; Rutland
LANE, Ann	21-07-1806; Surrey
LEWIS, Mary	06-10-1806; Bristol
LLOYD, Elizabeth	17-09-1806; Middlesex
RAFTRY*, Jane	17-09-1806; Middlesex
RAGAN, Margaret	21-05-1806; London
RAILTON, Hannah	29-10-1806; Middlesex
ROSS, Ann	03-12-1806; Middlesex
RUSSELL, Mary	09-08-1806; Salop
WILLIAMS, Ann	03-12-1806; Middlesex

William Pitt 1806

BARNES*, Susannah	15-01-1805; Dorset
BLACK, Jane	17-01-1805; Northumberland
BOARD, Elizabeth	21-02-1805; Middlesex
HAMILTON*, Catherine	21-02-1805; Middlesex
HUTCHINSON, Mary	15-01-1805; Surrey
JENKINSON, Mary	21-02-1805; Middlesex
McLAUGHLIN, Sarah	21-02-1805; London
MEDCALF, Priscilla	18-01-1805; Norwich
MURRAY, Ann	15-01-1805; Surrey
ODEN, Mary	22-04-1805; York
PAGET, Elizabeth	24-04-1805; Middlesex

Sydney Cove 1807

BARRETT, Ann	15-01-1806; Middlesex
BLAKE, Sarah	21-05-1806; Middlesex
BOYD, Mary Ann	17-03-1806; Kent
BRACHER, Mary	17-07-1806; Wiltshire
BRELSFORD, Susannah	16-07-1806; Newcastle
BROWN, Jane	21-03-1806; London

BROWN, Mary Ann	17-09-1806; Middlesex	NUNN, Jane	21-05-1806; Middlesex
BROWNENT, Elizabeth	17-09-1806; London	O'BRIAN, Margaret	21-05-1806; Middlesex
BURCHEM, Mary	15-01-1806; Middlesex	PARKER*, Ann	28-07-1806; Devon
BURKE, Hannah	16-04-1806; Middlesex	PEARCE*, Ann	16-04-1806; Middlesex
BURN, Mary	26-03-1806; Surrey	PITCHER, Sarah	17-09-1806; Middlesex
BUTCHER, Ann	17-09-1806; Middlesex	PULLEN, Mary	15-01-1806; Middlesex
CARTY*, Nelly	21-05-1806; Middlesex	RASBERRY, Elizabeth	02-07-1806; London
CLARKE, Elizabeth	16-04-1806; Middlesex	ROBERTSON*, Katharine	28-07-1806; Edinburgh
COLLINGWOOD, Mary	15-01-1806; Middlesex	ROSCHINSKY, Charlotte	15-07-1806; Southampton
CONNOR, Mary	24-03-1806; Warwick	RUSSELL, Bridget	16-04-1806; Middlesex
DUNCAN, Sarah	13-10-1806; Surrey	RUSSELL, Eleanor	17-09-1806; Middlesex
EDLESTON, Sally	19-03-1806; Lancaster	SAXTON, Mary	03-03-1806; Berkshire
EDMUNDS, Hannah	24-03-1806; Warwick	SHAW, Juliet	15-01-1806; Middlesex
EMMETT, Eleanor	17-09-1806; Middlesex	SINGLE, Ann	17-04-1806; Cambridge
EVANS, Ann	29-10-1806; Middlesex	SMITH, Maria	17-03-1806; Devon
FAGAN, Elizabeth	15-07-1806; Somerset	STANBURY, Ann	13-01-1806; Devon
FERRIDAY, Jane	22-03-1806; Salop	TYLER, Ann	02-07-1806; Middlesex
FISHER, Charlotte	07-08-1806; Surrey	UREN, Ann	22-03-1806; Cornwall
FUSSELL, Charlotte	15-01-1806; Somerset	WESTON, Mary	16-04-1806; Middlesex
GRAY, Elizabeth	17-04-1806; Cambridge	WILSON, Ann	19-04-1806; Lancaster
GREEN, Ann	16-01-1806; York	WORRALL, Sarah	13-01-1806; Leicester
GREEN, Ann	11-08-1806; Norfolk		
GREENSLADE, Jenefer	22-03-1806; Cornwall		
GREGORY, Martha	24-03-1806; Warwick		

1807 TRIAL YEAR

Aeolus 1809

GRIFFITHS, Elizabeth	21-05-1806; Middlesex	ANDERSON, Jane	15-07-1807; Northumberland
GRUBB, Charlotte	15-01-1806; Middlesex	ARKINSTALL, Elizabeth	16-01-1807; Stafford
HALL, Sarah	28-07-1806; Kent	ARNETT, Elizabeth	09-10-1807; York
HARRIS, Hannah	21-07-1806; Northampton	AUSTIN, Susannah	17-07-1807; Norfolk
HAYNES, Harriet	17-09-1806; Middlesex	BENNETT, Phebe	16-07-1807; Wiltshire
HAYWARD, Sarah	17-09-1806; Middlesex	BOOR, Tabitha	23-03-1807; Warwick
HINES, Maria	24-03-1806; Warwick	CLARK, Mary	22-07-1807; Essex
HOWELL, Mary	29-10-1806; Middlesex	COBB, Elizabeth	14-01-1807; Middlesex
KELLY, Judith	17-09-1806; Middlesex	DOLEMAN, Mary	25-03-1807; Stafford
KILLICK, Ann	04-03-1806; Southampton	DUFFEY*, Mary	16-09-1807; Middlesex
LEADER, Ann	07-08-1806; Surrey	EDLIN, Mary	15-01-1807; Bucks
LEE, Mary	08-03-1806; York	HANCOX, Mary	11-07-1807; Worcester
LITTLEWOOD, Ann	13-01-1806; Lincoln	HARDING, Mary	16-07-1807; Nottingham
MacGWYER, Mary	14-04-1806; Gloucester	HATHERLEIGH, Mary	21-03-1807; Cornwall
McNALTY, Catherine	17-09-1806; Middlesex	HEATH, Dorothy	25-03-1807; Stafford
MARSHALL, Maria	04-03-1806; Southampton	HICKEY, Catherine	27-07-1807; Kent
MATHUM, Isabella	19-03-1806; Lancaster	JONES, Ann	18-03-1807; Lancaster
MURRAY, Esther	16-04-1806; London		

JONES, Esther 08-08-1807; Lancaster
KELL, Mary 21-01-1807; Lancaster
KILLICK, Martha 18-03-1807; Suffolk
LASCELLES, Sarah 27-07-1807; Kent
MARTIN, Lydia 11-07-1807; Worcester
MINIKIN, Mary 21-01-1807; Lancaster
NAYLOR, Elizabeth 11-04-1807; York
NIGHTINGALE, Ann 15-04-1807; Lancaster
PEARSALL, Mary 11-07-1807; Worcester
PELHAM, Sarah 05-03-1807; Hertford
RIDGWAY, Ann 18-03-1807; Lancaster
SMITH, Ann 22-07-1807; Essex
STOREY, Margaret 08-04-1807; Cumberland
WARWICK, Mary 05-03-1807; Hertford
WHITE, Elizabeth 18-07-1807; Wiltshire
WHITE, Jane 15-04-1807; Lancaster
WHITING, Sarah 23-03-1807; Warwick
WOMACK, Jane 11-04-1807; York
WYNNE, Elizabeth 25-07-1807; Warwick

Canada 1810
ROBINSON,
  Elizabeth 20-07-1807; Lancaster
WESTCOTT, Jane 27-07-1807; Devon

Indispensable 1809
PHILLIPS, Mary 07-10-1807; Norfolk

Speke 1808
ALDERSON, Hannah 11-07-1807; York
BARBER, Mary 03-04-1807; Suffolk
BARKER, Mary 13-05-1807; London
BARNETT*,
  Fanny/Ann 07-03-1807; Wiltshire
BEAUMONT, Ann 16-09-1807; Middlesex
BERRY, Ann 08-04-1807; Middlesex
BIRD, Frances 23-03-1807; Warwick
BRAY, Harriet 11-01-1807; Bristol
BRIGGS, Ann 13-04-1807; Suffolk
BROWN, Ann 09-10-1807; York
BRYAN, Margaret 01-07-1807; Middlesex
BUCKLE*, Mary 18-03-1807; Suffolk
BURKE, Elizabeth 28-10-1807; Middlesex
CHALLENOR,
  Eleanor 21-01-1807; Lancaster
CHAPMAN, Mary 28-10-1807; Middlesex
CLARK, Elizabeth 01-07-1807; Middlesex
CLARKE, Elizabeth 16-09-1807; Middlesex
CLARKSON, Isabella 16-09-1807; Middlesex
CLEMENTS, Sophia 08-10-1807; Cambridge
COURSER*,
  Georgiana 13-01-1807; Surrey
CUNNINGHAM,
  Ellen 06-01-1807; Liverpool
CUNNINGHAM,
  Mary 06-01-1807; Liverpool
DAVISON, Elizabeth 07-04-1807; York
DUDLEY, Elizabeth 16-09-1807; Middlesex
DUFFELL, Ann 11-07-1807; York
ELRIDGE*,
  Elizabeth 16-03-1807; Sussex
FRY, Jane 16-07-1807; Wiltshire
GILL, Ann 28-10-1807; Middlesex
GILL*, Elizabeth 16-09-1807; Middlesex
GREEN, Mary 20-07-1807; Surrey
HALL, Eleanor 08-04-1807; Cambridge
HAVILAND, Hester 13-07-1807; Gloucester
HOLMES, Margaret 16-09-1807; Middlesex
HOPKINS, Maria 11-07-1807; Worcester
HOPKINS, Mary 18-03-1807; Surrey
HOPKINS, Sarah 11-07-1807; Worcester
JOINER, Elizabeth 08-04-1807; Middlesex
JONES, Ann 01-07-1807; London
KELLY, Mary 18-03-1807; Surrey
KINMAN, Elizabeth 07-03-1807; Wiltshire
LAMB, Mary 04-03-1807; Oxford
LAVENDER,
  Caroline 18-02-1807; London
LIGHTLY, Judith 18-02-1807; Middlesex
LOVELL*, Rosie 08-04-1807; London
McCARTY, Mary 13-05-1807; London
McCOLLISTER,
  Rose 06-01-1807; Liverpool
MURRAY, Mary 08-04-1807; Middlesex
NEALE, Elizabeth 13-01-1807; Gloucester
NEALE, Mary 28-10-1807; Middlesex
NEWBERRY, Mary 18-02-1807; Middlesex
NEWMAN, Alice 23-03-1807; Kent
PRINCE, Mary 18-02-1807; Middlesex
ROBERT, Ann 07-03-1807; Worcester
ROGERS, Mary 12-03-1807; Dorset
SHACKLE, Elizabeth 12-03-1807; Dorset
SIDEBOTHAM,
  Elizabeth 01-07-1807; London
SIMMONDS,
  Rebecca 02-12-1807; Middlesex
SIMONS, Ann 01-07-1807; Middlesex
SIMPSON, Hannah 13-05-1807; Middlesex
SINGER, Dinah 23-03-1807; Kent

SMITH, Elizabeth	14-01-1807; Middlesex	MEREDITH, Elizabeth	02-04-1808; Warwick
SMITH, Elizabeth	14-07-1807; Somerset	MOORE, Mary	24-03-1808; Surrey
SMITH*, Elizabeth	01-07-1807; Middlesex	PICKETT, Mary	11-01-1808; Devon
STACEY, Elizabeth	14-01-1807; London	PORCH, Susannah	02-04-1808; Somerset
STAFFORD, Mary	08-04-1807; Middlesex	PRICE, Susannah	25-04-1808; Bristol
STEVENS, Hannah	01-07-1807; Middlesex	QUICK, Susanna	02-04-1808; Somerset
SWAYNE, Elizabeth	04-03-1807; Oxford	RENNETT, Susan	14-03-1808; Kent
SWINNEY, Hannah	08-04-1807; Middlesex	SEARL, Rebecca	25-04-1808; Devon
THOMAS, Margaret	28-10-1807; London	SHEERING*, Mary	13-01-1808; Middlesex
TREE, Mary	16-03-1807; Sussex	SIMMONS, Martha	07-03-1808; Essex
TURNER, Frances	16-09-1807; London	TERRY, Elizabeth	24-03-1808; Surrey
WADE, Elizabeth	08-04-1807; Cambridge	TRUMAN, Susannah	06-04-1808; Middlesex
WHITMORE, Elizabeth	13-05-1807; Middlesex	WHALES, Mary	06-04-1808; Bristol
WRIGHT, Mary	07-03-1807; York		

1808 TRIAL YEAR

Aeolus 1809

ALLEN, Ann	16-03-1808; Lancaster
BAKER, Sarah	13-01-1808; Middlesex
BARNES, Charlotte	16-03-1808; Dorset
BARTLETT, Sophia	02-05-1808; Surrey
BOOTH, Elizabeth	06-04-1808; London
BUTLER, Elizabeth	16-03-1808; Dorset
CARROL, Mary	08-03-1808; Southampton
CARROL*, Mary	13-01-1808; Middlesex
DAWSON, Mary	20-01-1808; Lancaster
DOLAN, Mary	16-03-1808; Lancaster
DYER, Fanny	12-03-1808; Wiltshire
ENDACOTT, Mary	25-04-1808; Devon
FAGAN, Hannah	16-03-1808; Lancaster
GRACE, Ann	06-04-1808; Middlesex
GULLEY, Martha	02-04-1808; Warwick
HOLTON*, Ann	08-02-1808; London
HORGAN, Mary	06-04-1808; Bristol
JOHNSON, Mary	13-01-1808; Middlesex
JOHNSON, Mary	06-04-1808; London
JONES, Maria	06-04-1808; Middlesex
LAKE, Sarah	25-04-1808; Devon
LINAM, Margaret	13-01-1808; Middlesex
McGEE, Mary	06-04-1808; London
MANDEVILLE, Elizabeth	06-04-1808; Middlesex
MARLBOROUGH, Elizabeth	05-03-1808; York
MEADOWS, Mary	25-04-1808; Devon

Canada 1810

ADAMSON, Ann	27-04-1808; Northumberland
CONNELL, Elizabeth	26-10-1808; Middlesex
COOPER, Ann	28-06-1808; London
DAVIS, Mary	08-08-1808; Kent
DUCKWORTH, Sarah	12-10-1808; Lancaster
EVANS, Jane	27-03-1808; Kent
HALL, Elizabeth	28-04-1808; York
HUBIE, Ann	30-07-1808; York
JAMES, Mary	27-08-1808; Glamorgan
MITCHELL, Betty	04-05-1808; Lancaster
MOORE, Mary	01-08-1808; Hertford
PARKER, Mary Ann	30-11-1808; London
PINCHES, Elizabeth	06-10-1808; Stafford
PORTER, Hannah	27-03-1808; Kent
POWELL, Ann	01-06-1808; London
POWELL, Mary	15-07-1808; Berkshire
RILEY, Ann	06-08-1808; Devon
STANLEY, Hannah	27-03-1808; Kent
THOMPSON, Mary	27-03-1808; Kent
VICKERS, Isabella	16-03-1808; Lancaster
WATKINS, Elizabeth	14-09-1808; Middlesex
WEBB, Mary	30-11-1808; Middlesex
WILSON*, Bridget	21-07-1808; Lancaster

Friends 1811

McDONALD, Margaret	29-04-1808; Glasgow
McKAY*, Catherine	22-03-1808; Edinburgh

Indispensable 1809

ALDRIDGE, Elizabeth	18-07-1808; Surrey
ALLISON, Jane	07-10-1808; York City
BURGESS*, Sarah	01-06-1808; Middlesex
CRAWFORD, Sarah	18-02-1808; Middlesex
CRUMP, Mary	13-08-1808; Warwick
DALE, Mary	14-09-1808; Middlesex
DAVID*, Mary	05-04-1808; Brecon
DAVIS, Margaret	14-09-1808; Middlesex
DAVIS, Martha	13-01-1808; Middlesex
DAY, Jane	01-06-1808; Middlesex
DINSDALE, Elizabeth	30-07-1808; York
EADES, Susannah	14-09-1808; Middlesex
EDWARDS, Sarah	01-06-1808; Middlesex
FINLAND, Ann	13-07-1808; London
FOSTER, Mary	14-09-1808; Middlesex
FOWLER, Ann	26-10-1808; Middlesex
GAGAN, Hannah	01-06-1808; Middlesex
GEE, Mary	30-11-1808; London
HAINES, Mary	11-07-1808; Middlesex
HARDY, Mary	06-04-1808; Middlesex
HARRISON, Ann	15-08-1808; Norfolk
HARTLEY, Charlotte	06-10-1808; York
HEALEY, Ann	14-09-1808; Middlesex
JENNINGS, Catherine	10-02-1808; Middlesex
JENNINGS, Mary	13-07-1808; Middlesex
KETTLE, Sarah	01-06-1808; London
KITE, Rose	13-07-1808; Middlesex
LEWIS, Mary	01-06-1808; Middlesex
LINNING, Mary	29-04-1808; Berwick
McKENZIE, Sarah	14-09-1808; Middlesex
MANN, Catherine	14-09-1808; Middlesex
MILLER, Mary	01-06-1808; Middlesex
MOODEY, Frances	26-10-1808; Middlesex
MORRIS, Jane	06-04-1808; London
OAKES, Susannah	06-10-1808; Nottingham
PHILLIPS, Sarah	13-08-1808; Warwick
PLOWRIGHT, Ann	04-08-1808; Nottingham
SPENCER, Frances	01-06-1808; Middlesex
STARTIN, Elizabeth	13-08-1808; Warwick
THOMPSON, Elizabeth	26-10-1808; Middlesex
TYSON, Isabella	25-04-1808; York
WARD, Mary	05-03-1808; York
WARD, Sarah	26-10-1808; Middlesex
WILDGRASS, Ann	05-10-1808; Norfolk
WILDGRASS, Judith (Jnr)	05-10-1808; Norfolk
WILDGRASS, Judith (Snr)	05-10-1808; Norfolk
WOOD, Charlotte	13-07-1808; Middlesex

Speke 1808

HINCKS, Elizabeth	13-01-1808; Middlesex
MITCHELL, Jane	11-01-1808; Bristol
ROUTLEDGE, Eleanor	12-01-1808; Surrey

1809 TRIAL YEAR

Canada 1810

ANDREWS, Ann	22-07-1809; Wiltshire
BAILEY, Elizabeth	13-04-1809; York
BARNETT, Mary	19-07-1809; Lancaster
BATES, Mary	28-06-1809; London
BEAMOND, Mary	23-03-1809; Salop
BEESON, Susannah	20-09-1809; Middlesex
BENNETT, Elizabeth	20-03-1809; Devon
BIRD, Margaret	28-06-1809; Middlesex
BLISS, Elizabeth	02-08-1809; Gloucester
BOLTON, Jemima	22-07-1809; Huntingdon
BROWN, Eleanor	20-09-1809; London
BUNTING, Alice	12-04-1809; Middlesex
CAPON, Martha	31-07-1809; Norfolk
CAREY, Mary Ann	20-03-1809; Devon
CATHERINE, Eleanor	12-04-1809; Northumberland
CLARK, Mary	13-02-1809; Middlesex
CLARK, Mary	20-09-1809; Middlesex
CLARKE, Ann	03-04-1809; Lancaster
CLEAVES, Susannah	24-07-1809; Lancaster
CLEMENT, Catherine	10-04-1809; Chester
COHEN, Mary	28-06-1809; London
COLE, Frances	12-04-1809; Middlesex
DRAKE, Mary Ann	12-07-1809; Suffolk
DYER, Matilda	20-09-1809; Middlesex
EATON, Ann	20-04-1809; Nottingham
FARRALL, Mary	28-06-1809; Middlesex
FLAMSTON, Elizabeth	01-11-1809; Middlesex
FULLER, Mary	01-04-1809; Somerset
GIBSON, Mary	26-07-1809; Essex

GOLDSMITH,
  Mary Ann   20-09-1809; Middlesex
GOODMAN, Ann   20-09-1809; Middlesex
HARRINGTON,
  Margaret   11-01-1809; Middlesex
HEDDY, Hannah   02-03-1809; Surrey
HEWSON, Martha   20-09-1809; Middlesex
HORSLEY, Ann   12-04-1809; Middlesex
HUDSON, Frances   31-07-1809; Kent
HUNTER, Margaret   12-04-1809;
                     Northumberland
JENNINGS, Mary   09-08-1809; Surrey
KELLY, Ann   15-02-1809; Middlesex
KENNINGTON, Ann   20-09-1809; Middlesex
KERSHAW, Mary   05-10-1809; York
KNIGHT, Hannah   10-01-1809; Gloucester
LATTIMER, Mary   12-04-1809; Cumberland
LAWS, Hannah   20-09-1809; London
LINES, Catherine   20-09-1809; Middlesex
McCORMACK,
  Isabella   23-03-1809; Salop
McGUIRE, Margaret   28-06-1809; Middlesex
MANNING, Mary   06-03-1809;
                     Northumberland
MARTIN, Mary   09-10-1809; Surrey
MAYFIELD*, Mary   13-04-1809; Nottingham
MURRAY, Jane   03-10-1809; Huntingdon
MURRAY, Mary   13-02-1809; Middlesex
NEWBERRY, Mary   01-11-1809; Middlesex
NEWMAN, Mary   28-06-1809; London
NEWTON, Ann   12-04-1809; Middlesex
O'HARA, Mary   07-03-1809;
                     Southampton
OGLE, Mary   03-10-1809; York
PALLISTER,   12-04-1809;
  Elizabeth   Northumberland
PARKER, Harriet   10-07-1809; Somerset
PARKER, Mary   28-06-1809; London
PARKS, Ann   19-04-1809; Lancaster
PRESTON, Mary   20-09-1809; Middlesex
RICHMOND,
  Elizabeth   03-10-1809; York
ROACH, Elizabeth   01-11-1809; London
ROBERTS, Charlotte   28-06-1809; Middlesex
ROBERTS, Margaret   23-03-1809; Salop
SHADWELL, Ann   23-03-1809; Lancaster
SHARPES, Mary   06-12-1809; Middlesex
SLADE, Sarah   09-01-1809; Somerset
SMITH, Ann   01-11-1809; Middlesex
SMITH, Elizabeth   13-04-1809; York
SMITH, Jane   17-04-1809; Surrey
SMITH, Louisa   12-04-1809; Middlesex
SMITH, Mary   01-11-1809; London
SULLIVAN, Mary   20-09-1809; Middlesex
TAYLOR, Ann   09-10-1809; Surrey
TAYLOR, Nancy   13-07-1809; York
THOMAS, Ann   28-03-1809; Glamorgan
THOMAS, Mary   20-09-1809; Middlesex
TILLETT, Sarah   02-10-1809; Colchester
TUTTON, Elizabeth   09-01-1809; Somerset
TYLER, Harriet   23-03-1809; Suffolk
TYSO, Ann   11-03-1809; Gloucester
WALFORD, Ann   11-04-1809; Worcester
WALSH, Eleanor   10-07-1809; York
WATKINS, Sarah   12-01-1809; Kent
WEBBER, Elizabeth   29-07-1809; Devon
WILBY, Margaret   20-09-1809; Middlesex
WILLIAMS, Jane   01-11-1809; Middlesex
WILLIAMS, Sarah   03-10-1809; York
WILMOT, Elizabeth   17-05-1809; Middlesex
YATES, Sarah   28-06-1809; London

Friends 1811
BROWN, Mary   11-01-1809; Middlesex
CARBERRY, Jane   15-08-1809; Stafford
DAVIS, Sarah   08-12-1809; Middlesex
GOLSBY, Rebecca   01-11-1809; Middlesex
HARVEY, Elizabeth   06-12-1809; Middlesex
NORMAN, Mary   12-04-1809;
                     Northampton
SHORTER, Ann   08-12-1809; Middlesex
WRIGHT, Rachel   25-01-1809; Edinburgh

Indispensable 1809
ASHBY, Ruth   10-01-1809; Warwick
BROWN, Mary   11-01-1809; Middlesex
COLEMAN, Ann   11-01-1809; Norfolk
GEORGE, Sarah   11-01-1809; Middlesex
GRENVILLE, Ann   11-01-1809; London
HOWE, Mary   12-01-1809; Nottingham
KEELE, Ann   10-01-1809; Surrey
NODES, Maria   11-01-1809; Middlesex
POULTNEY,   10-01-1809; Warwick
  Elizabeth
REDDY, Susannah   11-01-1809; Norfolk
ROBINSON,
  Hannah   10-01-1809; Warwick
SKIDDAY, Hannah   11-01-1809; Middlesex
SULLIVAN, Barbara   10-01-1809; Surrey

1810 TRIAL YEAR

Broxbornebury 1814
TERRET, Ann 01-05-1810; Gloucester

Canada 1810
BIRD, Mary 09-01-1810; Surrey
COTTERELL, Ann 10-01-1810; London
SMITH, Elizabeth 09-01-1810; Surrey

Friends 1811
BATSON, Ann 18-07-1810; London
BAXTER, Ann 11-01-1810; Northumberland
BELLARS, Amelia 21-02-1810; Middlesex
BINGHAM, Emelia 17-01-1810; Lancaster
BOLTON, Caroline 18-08-1810; Surrey
BOLTON, Mary 18-08-1810; Middlesex
BOONE, Elizabeth 11-04-1810; London
BRICE, Jane 19-09-1810; Middlesex
BROWN, Elizabeth 05-12-1810; Middlesex
BROWNING, Mary 11-04-1810; Middlesex
BRYANT, Mary 19-09-1810; Middlesex
BRYANT, Mary 05-12-1810; Middlesex
BURGESS, Mary 10-07-1810; Surrey
BURN, Ann 16-07-1810; Middlesex
CALLAGHAN, Mary 18-07-1810; Middlesex
CARTHY, Mary 19-09-1810; London
COWANS, Margaret 25-08-1810; Northumberland
DIXON, Jane 02-05-1810; Cumberland
DRISCOLL, Catherine 19-09-1810; Middlesex
DUFF, Janet 23-04-1810; Glasgow
DURANT*, Elizabeth 06-06-1810; Middlesex
EVANS*, Ann/Nancy 11-01-1810; Montgomery
FIELD, Lydia 05-12-1810; Middlesex
FITZGERALD, Margaret 11-04-1810; Middlesex
FLINN, Eleanor 19-09-1810; Middlesex
FRANKLIN, Ann 19-09-1810; Middlesex
FRENCH, Mary 11-04-1810; Middlesex
FUSSELL, Sarah 31-10-1810; London
GAGE*, Susan 30-04-1810; Essex
GAMBLE, Esther 18-07-1810; Middlesex
GOFF, Joanna 05-03-1810; Southampton
GRAHAM, Sarah 02-05-1810; Cumberland
HALL, Ann 09-10-1810; Hertford
HALL*, Elizabeth 24-08-1810; Kent
HODGSON, Elizabeth 24-03-1810; Lancaster
HOLLAND, Elizabeth 28-03-1810; Surrey
HOPKINS, Lucy 10-03-1810; Wiltshire
HUGHES, Margaret 21-02-1810; Middlesex
IRWIN, Mary 21-08-1810; Durham
JACKSON, Ann 12-07-1810; Worcester
JAMES, Mary 28-03-1810; Surrey
JONES, Elizabeth 02-05-1810; Cumberland
JONES, Mary 31-10-1810; London
JONES, Sarah 06-06-1810; London
JUKES, Ann 29-03-1810; Warwick
KEAN, Elizabeth 16-07-1810; Surrey
KEEP, Sarah 06-06-1810; Middlesex
KERSHAW, Elizabeth 17-01-1810; Lancaster
KINGSTON*, Hannah 03-03-1810; Bucks
KITE, Mary 06-06-1810; Middlesex
KOLP, Ann 21-02-1810; Middlesex
LONGFIELD, Mary 18-07-1810; Middlesex
MacDONALD, Mary 21-02-1810; Middlesex
MAY, Sarah 21-02-1810; Middlesex
MURPHY, Mary 18-07-1810; Middlesex
OSBOURN, Ann 28-03-1810; Surrey
PAYNE, Elizabeth 31-10-1810; London
PENDEGRASS*, Bridget 19-09-1810; Middlesex
RICKABY, Ann 18-07-1810; Middlesex
ROBINSON, Margaret 06-06-1810; London
ROBY, Mary 11-01-1810; Lancaster
ROSCOE, Elizabeth 17-07-1810; Lancaster
ROWE, Martha 28-03-1810; Surrey
RYLEY, Ann 06-06-1810; Middlesex
SANDERS, Mary 19-09-1810; Middlesex
SHADWELL, Mary 05-12-1810; Middlesex
SHEARMAN, Mary 31-10-1810; London
SMITH, Elizabeth 11-04-1810; Middlesex
SMITH, Mary 11-04-1810; Middlesex
SMITH, Sarah 17-07-1810; Lancaster
ST. LEDGER, Sarah 19-03-1810; Devon
TAYLOR, Hannah 31-10-1810; London
TAYLOR, Mary 03-05-1810; Hertford
THOMPSON, Elizabeth 02-05-1810; Northumberland
VERNOR, Biddy 19-03-1810; Kent

WALKER, Ann	05-12-1810; Middlesex		**1811 TRIAL YEAR**	
WARDLE, Ann	02-05-1810; Northumberland		***Broxbornebury* 1814**	
WHITE, Maria	20-08-1810; Kent		BANFORD, Martha	07-08-1811; Essex
WHITELOCK, Hannah	11-04-1810; Middlesex		LANE, Ann	30-10-1811; Middlesex
WILLIAMS, Eleanor	06-06-1810; Middlesex		WATKINS, Mary	18-03-1811; Hereford
WILMOT, Mary	03-05-1810; Hertford		***Friends* 1811**	
WILSON, Mary	11-04-1810; Middlesex		BOWBRICK, Sarah	15-01-1811; Surrey
WILSON, Sarah	02-05-1810; Cumberland		CLARK, Louisa	15-01-1811; Surrey
WYATT, Susan	16-08-1810; Suffolk		JEFFRIES, Mary	09-01-1811; Middlesex
			KNOWLES, Sophia	09-01-1811; London
***Minstrel* 1812**			WELCH*, Mary Ann	09-01-1811; Middlesex
BELL, Mary	04-10-1810; Portsmouth			
BROOKSHAW, Susannah	10-09-1810; Lancaster		***Minstrel* 1812**	
CHITTLEBOROUGH, Margaret	31-10-1810; Middlesex		ABBEY, Mary	23-01-1811; Norfolk
			ALDRIDGE, Ann	04-03-1811; Surrey
CLARKE, Catherine	09-05-1810; Lancaster		ATKINS, Mary	27-03-1811; Surrey
			ATKINS, Sarah	10-07-1811; London
CRACK, Bridget	22-03-1810; Suffolk		ATKINSON, Elizabeth	30-10-1811; London
DINSDALE, Mary	10-03-1810; York City		BAILEY, Sarah	09-01-1811; Middlesex
FRANKLINGTON, Sarah	10-09-1810; Lancaster		BARKER, Amelia	16-10-1811; York
			BEATON, Mary	18-09-1811; Middlesex
GRAVES, Hannah	31-08-1810; Cumberland		BELL, Mary	09-03-1811; York City
HARDCASTLE, Frances	08-08-1810; York City		BLANDY, Sarah	30-10-1811; Middlesex
			BRAY, Mary	18-03-1811; Suffolk
HAYWOOD, Margaret	22-08-1810; Stafford		BROWN, Judith	18-09-1811; London
			BUCKLEY, Elizabeth	16-10-1811; Lancaster
HINCHCLIFF, Elizabeth	19-09-1810; Middlesex		BUCKLEY, Mary	08-10-1811; Chester
			BUTCHER, Elizabeth	04-12-1811; Middlesex
LLOYD, Sarah	28-08-1810; Kent		CARR, Jane	28-03-1811; Somerset
ROBINSON, Mary	04-10-1810; Cambridge		CARROLL, Ann	10-07-1811; Middlesex
SEARLE, Sarah	24-08-1810; Sussex		CLARKE, Mary	03-04-1811; Middlesex
STINSON, Jane	18-07-1810; London		COCKBURN, Margaret	18-07-1811; Hexham
TILLEY, Jane	18-08-1810; Salop		COCKING, Jane	18-09-1811; Middlesex
WALLWORK, Mary Ann	10-10-1810; Lancaster		COLEMAN, Sarah	04-12-1811; London
			CONNOR*, Catherine	30-10-1811; Middlesex
WITHERINGTON, Elizabeth	09-05-1810; Lancaster		COOMBS, Agnes	18-09-1811; Middlesex
			CORFIELD, Diana	25-04-1811; Salop
***Northampton* 1815**			CREED, Ruth	15-07-1811; Somerset
BAILLIE, Elizabeth	24-09-1810; Dumfries		CUMSON*, Elizabeth	17-01-1811; Stafford
INGLIS*, Jane/Janet	14-09-1810; Glasgow		DALLY, Eleanor	18-03-1811; Kent
			DAVIS, Sarah	18-09-1811; Middlesex
INGLIS*, Margaret/Cath	14-09-1810; Glasgow		DAVIS*, Mary Ann	18-09-1811; Middlesex
			DEWSE*, Catherine	09-01-1811; Middlesex
			DIDSBURY, Elizabeth	16-07-1811; Chester
			DUNCLEY, Frances	20-09-1811; Middlesex

ELLIS, Sarah	15-07-1811; Lincoln	SMITH, Mary	03-04-1811; London
ELVIN, Jane	18-09-1811; London	SMITH, Mary	29-05-1811; London
FIDLER*, Diana	10-07-1811; Middlesex	SMITH, Mary	18-09-1811; Middlesex
GIBBON, Louisa	29-05-1811; Middlesex	STONE, Sarah	10-07-1811; London
GREEN*, Sarah	18-09-1811; Middlesex	THORPE, Mary	18-09-1811; London
GROOM, Susannah	20-02-1811; London	WALTERS, Margaret	29-05-1811; Middlesex
HALLIDAY, Jane	09-01-1811; Middlesex	WATTS, Georgiana	27-03-1811; Surrey
HANELL, Elizabeth	29-05-1811; Middlesex	WHISTON, Eliza	03-04-1811; London
HARROP, Elizabeth	23-03-1811; Lancaster	WHITE, Ann	09-03-1811; Gloucester
HARVEY, Catherine	04-12-1811; Middlesex	WHITE, Harriet	29-05-1811; Middlesex
HAYCOCK, Charlotte	10-08-1811; Warwick	WILLIAMS, Ann	29-05-1811; Middlesex
HAYES, Mary	10-07-1811; London	WILSON, Jean/Jane	14-01-1811; Cumberland
HELEN, Mary	18-09-1811; Middlesex	WISE, Eleanor	20-02-1811; London
HENNESSEY, Elizabeth	03-04-1811; Middlesex	WISE, Sarah	10-07-1811; London
HILLIER, Ann	31-07-1811; Gloucester	WOOD, Louisa	18-09-1811; Middlesex
HURST, Jane	15-07-1811; Lincoln	WOODHEAD, Ann	23-03-1811; Lancaster
IRWIN, Sarah	30-10-1811; London	WRIGHT, Maria	04-12-1811; Middlesex
KELLY, Ann	18-09-1811; Middlesex	YATES, Elizabeth	18-09-1811; Middlesex
KING, Elaine	18-09-1811; London		

Wanstead 1814

ARLOW, Mary	14-01-1811; Bristol
BLACK, Jane	06-08-1811; Hereford
HARLOW*, Sarah	14-01-1811; Bristol
HEALE, Ann	15-07-1811; Devon
HUBBERT, Ann	14-08-1811; Stafford
PATTERSON*, Charlotte	25-04-1811; Glasgow
SMITH*, Margaret	19-09-1811; Glasgow
TIDDY, Hannah	15-07-1811; Devon
WILLIAMS, Elizabeth	09-09-1811; Stirling

KING, Mary	18-09-1811; Middlesex
LAREY, Eleanor	18-09-1811; Middlesex
LEVI, Hannah	10-07-1811; London
LINDSAY, Sarah	16-01-1811; Newcastle
LUCAS, Mary	04-03-1811; Surrey
McDONALD, Ann	23-03-1811; Norfolk
MASON, Mary	27-03-1811; Surrey
MILLS*, Jane	18-09-1811; Middlesex
MITCHELL, Martha	27-03-1811; Surrey
MORRIS*, Susanna	18-09-1811; Middlesex
MORRISON, Ann Maria	27-03-1811; Surrey
MOULD, Eleanor	16-01-1811; Newcastle
MURPHY, Margaret	01-04-1811; Warwick
NESBITT, Ann	09-01-1811; Middlesex
OVERETT, Elizabeth	20-02-1811; Middlesex
PAYNE, Ann	30-10-1811; London
PEARCE, Elizabeth	09-03-1811; Gloucester
POWELL, Mary	03-04-1811; London
PRICE, Mary	31-07-1811; Gloucester
READY, Elizabeth	23-01-1811; Lancaster
REYNOLDS, Rebecca	18-09-1811; Middlesex
ROACH*, Catherine	03-04-1811; London
ROBERTS, Eliza	29-05-1811; Middlesex
ROGERS, Susannah	15-01-1811; Lincoln
ROWLAND, Betty	23-01-1811; Lancaster
SCOTT, Catherine	16-01-1811; Newcastle
SHIPLEY, Mary	29-05-1811; Middlesex

1812 TRIAL YEAR

Broxbornebury 1814

ALLEN, Sarah	28-10-1812; Middlesex
ANDERSON, Isabella	22-01-1812; Lancaster
BAKER, Sarah	16-09-1812; Middlesex
BEST, Ann	22-01-1812; Lancaster
BLAKE, Eleanor	01-07-1812; Middlesex
BRUCE, Mary	16-09-1812; Middlesex
CHAMBERS, Eleanor	13-05-1812; Middlesex
CLARKE, Ann	02-12-1812; Middlesex
CUNNINGHAM, Margaret	21-03-1812; Lancaster
DAID, Mary Ann	16-09-1812; Middlesex

ENTWISTLE,
  Martha   21-03-1812; Lancaster
FEARN, Hannah   30-03-1812; Warwick
GIBSON, Elizabeth   24-10-1812; Derby
GREAVES, Mary   21-03-1812; Lancaster
GRIFFITHS,
  Elizabeth   13-05-1812; Middlesex
HARRIS, Mary   28-10-1812; Middlesex
HOLLOWAY,
  Elizabeth   14-01-1812; Gloucester
HORN*, Harriot
  Arin   09-03-1812; Essex
HYATT, Elizabeth   30-03-1812; Warwick
JANSON, Bella   21-03-1812; Lancaster
JONES, Elizabeth   24-10-1812; Derby
JONES, Jane   01-07-1812; Middlesex
JONES, Mary   16-09-1812; Middlesex
JONES, Priscilla   23-03-1812; Sussex
KING, Elizabeth   16-09-1812; Middlesex
KINGSMORE,
  Sophia   23-03-1812; Sussex
LALLAMONT,
  Susannah   01-07-1812; London
LORD, Ann   21-03-1812; Lancaster
MAJOR, Amelia   13-05-1812; Middlesex
PARSONS, Ann   16-03-1812; Devon
PROCTOR,
  Margaret   15-04-1812; Lancaster
ROGERS, Ann   01-07-1812; Middlesex
ROGERS, Mary   16-09-1812; Middlesex
ROWLEY, Ann   30-03-1812; Warwick
SMITH, Sarah   02-12-1812; Middlesex
SQUIRES, Mary   16-09-1812; Middlesex
SULLIVAN, Mary   13-05-1812; London
SULLIVAN,
  Susannah   13-05-1812; London
TOMLINSON, Alice   09-04-1812; Lancaster
WALLIS, Ellis   01-07-1812; Middlesex
WHITE, Jane   21-03-1812; Lancaster

Minstrel 1812
ATHERTON, Louisa   19-02-1812; Middlesex
BAGGS, Mary   15-01-1812; Middlesex
BONE, Sarah   19-02-1812; Middlesex
BROWN, Jane   15-01-1812; Middlesex
CARROLL, Mary   15-01-1812; London
DONKINS, Mary   15-01-1812; Newcastle
DRUCE, Sarah   15-01-1812; Middlesex
LEE, Eleanor   30-03-1812; Surrey
PEARCE,
  Teresa/Elizabeth   30-03-1812; Surrey
ROACH, Margaret   15-01-1812; Middlesex
RYAN, Mary   15-01-1812; Middlesex
SLATER, Sarah   15-01-1812; Middlesex
THORPE,
  Charlotte Jane   19-02-1812; Middlesex

Wanstead 1814
BANKS, Mary   01-07-1812; Middlesex
BARBER, Mary   28-10-1812; Middlesex
BARRS, Sarah   28-10-1812; Middlesex
BAYS, Bridget   28-10-1812; Middlesex
BECK, Mary   08-04-1812; London
BEST, Mary   13-05-1812; Middlesex
BLACK, Mary   28-10-1812; London
BOWYER(S), Sarah   28-10-1812; Middlesex
BRADLEY, Charlotte   16-01-1812; York
CAWTHORNE,
  Elizabeth   16-07-1812; Nottingham
CHIDLOW,
  Elizabeth   29-07-1812; Stafford
COATES, Sarah   15-07-1812; Gloucester
COVERLEY, Maria   28-10-1812; Middlesex
CRONE, Jane   14-10-1812;
                        Northumberland
CROSBIE, Elizabeth   21-12-1812; Edinburgh
DANIEL, Ann   15-07-1812;
                        Northumberland
DUGGLEBY, Judith   06-10-1812; York
FALKERD*, Jane   23-07-1812; Suffolk
FIELD, Martha   13-01-1812; Bristol
FOSKEW, Sarah   08-04-1812; London
GILBERT, Bassano   06-10-1812; Huntingdon
GRAHAM, Margaret   16-09-1812; Middlesex
HEARSON, Hannah   28-10-1812; London
HOBLEY, Elizabeth   01-08-1812; Somerset
HUGHES, Martha   02-12-1812; Middlesex
HUR(L)STON*,
  Mary   05-08-1812; Kent
HUTCHINS*, Mary   05-10-1812;
                        Southampton
JACKWAY*, Martha   14-07-1812; Gloucester
JONES*, Ann
  Elizabeth   23-03-1812; Caernarvon
LE SURF(E),
  Elizabeth   02-12-1812; Middlesex
LEVERTON*, Mary   23-03-1812; Leicester
LINDSAY, Elizabeth   02-12-1812; Middlesex

LONGUST, Sarah	16-09-1812; Middlesex	CARPENTER, Mary	01-12-1813; London
LUDDAM*, Ann	28-03-1812; Gloucester	CLARKE, Maria	27-10-1813; Middlesex
MacDEMAW, Ann	02-12-1812; Middlesex	CLOUGH, Ann	13-10-1813; Lancaster
McDONALD, Sarah	02-12-1812; Middlesex	COOK, Elizabeth	15-09-1813; Middlesex
McDOUGAL, Jane	14-10-1812; Northumberland	COOPER, Lucy	07-04-1813; Middlesex
		DANIEL, Margaret	19-04-1813; Carmarthon
McGINNIS, Margaret	01-07-1812; Middlesex	DANNET*, Jane/Ann	07-08-1813; Devon
MARJORAM, Mary	18-03-1812; Suffolk	DAVIES, Mary	11-10-1813; Lancaster
MORAN, Eliza	13-05-1812; Middlesex	DEERING, Sarah	14-07-1813; London
MURRAY, Hannah	14-10-1812; Lancaster	DUNN*, Judith	17-08-1813; Norfolk
OGLE, Christobel	16-07-1812; Nottingham	EBDEN, Frances	15-09-1813; Middlesex
OWEN, Ann	16-09-1812; Middlesex	ENTWISTLE, Ann	04-09-1813; Lancaster
PALMER, Mary/Margaret	16-09-1812; London	FLINTOFT, Sarah	31-07-1813; York
		GARNER, Maria	04-09-1813; Lancaster
PHILIP, Mary	08-10-1812; Northumberland	GIBBARD, Sarah	03-03-1813; Oxford
		GORDON, Margaret	19-08-1813; Northumberland
PHIPPS, Elizabeth	16-09-1812; Middlesex	GREEN, Susannah	14-07-1813; Middlesex
PRICE, Mary	28-10-1812; Middlesex	GREGORY, Henrietta	15-09-1813; Middlesex
RIDER, Mary	16-09-1812; Middlesex	HAMILTON, Ann	07-04-1813; London
SAGE, Frances	28-10-1812; Middlesex	JENKINS, Elizabeth	15-09-1813; Middlesex
STEWARD, Sarah	28-10-1812; Middlesex	JENNINGS, Ann	14-07-1813; Middlesex
THOMPSON, Isabella	16-09-1812; Middlesex	JONES, Susannah	11-08-1813; Leicester
THORPE, Ellen	22-08-1812; Lancaster	KEAN, Catherine	01-12-1813; Middlesex
TOMLIN, Elizabeth	05-08-1812; Kent	KITSON, Jane	02-08-1813; Hertford
WATSON, Catherine	28-10-1812; London	LAWRENCE, Mary	04-08-1813; Dorset
WILKIN, Margaret	08-04-1812; Northumberland	LUMMES*, Ann	15-09-1813; Middlesex
		McCARTHY*, Mary	01-12-1813; Middlesex
		McKENNELL, Margaret	15-09-1813; Middlesex
1813 TRIAL YEAR		MALE, Elizabeth	11-03-1813; Stafford
		MALONEY, Mary	14-07-1813; Middlesex
Broxbornebury 1814		MAY, Charlotte	14-07-1813; Middlesex
ADAMS, Sarah	15-09-1813; Middlesex	MELLING, Mary	19-07-1813; Lancaster
ARNETT, Ann	14-07-1813; Middlesex	MUERS, Alice	19-08-1813; Northumberland
ATKINS, Louisa	19-07-1813; Surrey		
BAKER, Elizabeth	15-09-1813; Middlesex	MURPHY, Catherine	19-07-1813; Surrey
BAKER*, Mary/Cath	14-07-1813; Middlesex	MURPHY, Norah	02-06-1813; Middlesex
BARKWORTH, Elizabeth	18-08-1813; Kent	PEARCE*, Charlotte	02-06-1813; Middlesex
		PERKINS, Mary	23-02-1813; London
BARNES, Catherine	03-05-1813; Lancaster	PHILLIPS, Isabella	14-07-1813; Middlesex
BARROW, Peggy	04-09-1813; Lancaster	PRICE, Elizabeth	15-09-1813; Middlesex
BEADLE, Elizabeth	14-07-1813; London	ROBINSON, Jane	30-03-1813; Warwick
BLADES, Esther	31-07-1813; York	ROBSON, Alice	29-04-1813; Northumberland
BLAND, Isabella	14-07-1813; Northumberland		
		ROWE, Ann	14-07-1813; Middlesex
BROWN, Hannah	14-07-1813; Middlesex	RUBY, Mary	27-10-1813; Middlesex
BRYANT, Catherine	15-09-1813; Middlesex	RUTH, Jane	02-06-1813; Middlesex

SHARMAN, Ann	01-09-1813; Norfolk	GORE, Sophia	20-03-1813; Norfolk
SMITH, Ann	15-09-1813; Middlesex	GREEN, Mary	13-03-1813; Nottingham
SMITH, Hannah	17-02-1813; Middlesex	HARRISON, Elizabeth	20-03-1813; Lancaster
SMITH, Mary	17-02-1813; Middlesex	HUGHES, Martha	20-03-1813; Lancaster
SMITH*, Ann	31-07-1813; Lincoln	INNES, Ann	17-02-1813; Middlesex
SMITH*, Mary	27-10-1813; Middlesex	IRELAND, Elizabeth	20-01-1813; Lancaster
STEPHENS, Mary	14-07-1813; London	ISSOTT, Sarah	06-03-1813; York
STONE*, Margaret	11-10-1813; Lancaster	JENNINGS, Elizabeth	29-03-1813; Warwick
SWEENEY, Clara	15-09-1813; Middlesex	JONES, Ann	31-03-1813; Gloucester
SYMONS, Elizabeth	29-04-1813; Northumberland	JONES, Elizabeth	07-04-1813; Middlesex
TAYLOR, Mary	03-05-1813; Lancaster	JONES, Mary	17-02-1813; London
THOMAS, Ann	11-10-1813; Surrey	JOYCE, Bridget	07-04-1813; Middlesex
THOMAS, Elizabeth	21-08-1813; Somerset	LAMB, Hannah	11-01-1813; Somerset
THORN*, Sarah	27-10-1813; Middlesex	LANGWITH, Ann	15-01-1813; Lincoln
WEST, Sarah	07-04-1813; London	LATHAM, Elizabeth/Esther	20-03-1813; Lancaster
WHEELER, Mary	01-12-1813; London	LETTERMAN*, Catherine	29-03-1813; Warwick
WHITE, Mary	15-09-1813; Middlesex	LEVENS, Frances	15-03-1813; Kent
WHITING, Sarah	12-07-1813; Somerset	McLAUGHLIN, Elizabeth	29-03-1813; Surrey
WILSON, Ann	28-04-1813; Northumberland	MORRIS, Mary	29-03-1813; Warwick

***Mary Anne* 1816**

FALKINER, Mary	01-12-1813; Middlesex	NORTON, Elizabeth	10-01-1813; Lancaster
WHITEHOUSE, Mary	14-08-1813; Warwick	O'FLERTY, Letitia	29-03-1813; Warwick
WILLIAMS, Ann	31-07-1813; Worcester	PANNETT, Sarah	07-04-1813; Middlesex

***Northampton* 1815**

AYNSLEY, Jane	Easter 1813; Northumberland	PARKIN, Elizabeth	06-03-1813; York
CORBETT, Sarah	31-07-1813; Worcester	PEDLAY, Martha	29-03-1813; Warwick
WILLIAMS*, Ann	27-10-1813; Middlesex	POTTER*, Elizabeth/Anne	01-03-1813; Southampton

***Wanstead* 1814**

ASHCROFT, Margaret	10-01-1813; Lancaster	QUAIL*, Elizabeth	18-01-1813; Lancaster
ASHWELL, Sarah	29-03-1813; Warwick	ROBERTS, Mary	02-06-1813; London
BECKWITH, Elizabeth	15-03-1813; Kent	SKELTON, Sarah	29-03-1813; Surrey
BULL, Mary	07-04-1813; Middlesex	SMITH, Jane	17-02-1813; London
CHANDLER, Phoebe	10-04-1813; Bristol	SMITH, Jane	07-04-1813; Middlesex
CLARKE, Mary	17-03-1813; Salop	SMITH, Martha	29-03-1813; Warwick
COOK, Hannah/Alice	31-03-1813; Gloucester	SMITH*, Susan	25-01-1813; Norfolk
DAVIS, Elizabeth	15-03-1813; Kent	STARTIN, Sarah	29-03-1813; Warwick
DEWHURST, Elizabeth	20-03-1813; Lancaster	TOMLINSON, Eleanor	13-01-1813; Middlesex
DRAYTON, Sarah Ann	13-01-1813; Middlesex	WARD, Catherine	07-04-1813; Middlesex
DUNCAN, Sarah	01-03-1813; Surrey	WEBB, Mary	29-03-1813; Surrey
		WHITE, Mary	17-02-1813; London
		WILLIAMS, Lucy	20-03-1813; Lancaster
		WILMOT*, Elizabeth	25-03-1813; Cornwall
		WOODFORD, Harriett	13-01-1813; London
		WRIGHT, Esther	20-03-1813; Lancaster

WRIGHT,
  Mary Elizabeth   29-03-1813; Surrey
WRIGLEY, Alice   20-01-1813; Lancaster

1814 TRIAL YEAR

Broxbornebury 1814
MILLARD, Judith   14-01-1814; Hertford

Lord Melville 1817
BEVATT, Mary   20-04-1814; Middlesex
NICHOLLS, Barbara   25-05-1814; Middlesex

Mary Anne 1816
ANDREWS, Ann   30-11-1814; Middlesex
BEARD, Eleanor   30-07-1814; Devon
BROWN, Christiana   18-10-1814; Essex
CHAPMAN, Jane   05-03-1814; Lancaster
CHUDLEIGH,
  Elizabeth   19-03-1814; Devon
CLEMENTS, Jane   30-11-1814; Middlesex
DIGBY, Jane   17-10-1814; Somerset
DOWN, Mary   19-03-1814; Devon
FLEMING, Anne   05-03-1814; Lancaster
FREAR, Catherine   30-11-1814; Middlesex
GETTY, Jane   31-08-1814; Lancaster
GOOSE, Eliza   26-10-1814; Middlesex
GREEN, Elizabeth   30-11-1814; Middlesex
GUY, Betty   26-10-1814; Lancaster
HALLARD*, Ann   29-12-1814; Kent
HASTY, Mary   11-08-1814; Northumberland
HICKEY, Ann   14-09-1814; Middlesex
HUNTINGDON,
  Mary   11-11-1814; Lancaster
JONES, Elizabeth   14-09-1814; Middlesex
KEATING, Sarah   14-09-1814; Middlesex
LUSCOMB*, Mary   30-11-1814; Middlesex
MALLARD,
  Elizabeth   30-11-1814; London
MARTIN, Hannah   30-11-1814; London
MAYNE, Mary   18-10-1814; Devon
MOLYNEUX, Ann   31-08-1814; Lancaster
OATES, Mary   11-08-1814; Northumberland
PRICE, Phoebe   29-08-1814; Chester
RILEY, Catherine   30-11-1814; Middlesex
RILEY, Frances   02-01-1814; Lancaster
ROCHLEY, Sarah   29-08-1814; Chester

RUSSELL, Mary   30-11-1814; Middlesex
SHAW, Elizabeth   11-11-1814; Lancaster
STANLEY*,
  Charlotte   30-11-1814; Middlesex
STEWART*, Rosa   11-08-1814; Northumberland
TAYLOR, Elizabeth   11-08-1814; Northumberland
WALKER, Ann   30-11-1814; Middlesex
WILKINSON,
  Frances   26-10-1814; London
WOOD, Jane   26-10-1814; Middlesex

Northampton 1815
ABSOLOM, Mary   11-07-1814; Southampton
ARGENT, Susannah   24-10-1814; Surrey
BAILEY, Ann   06-07-1814; Middlesex
BARNARD, Mary   03-03-1814; Hertford
BARTON, Rebecca   23-03-1814; Suffolk
BAXTER*, Margaret   22-04-1814; Perth
BELL, Mary   20-04-1814; Middlesex
BERRIDGE*, Ann   12-01-1814; Middlesex
BERRIDGE*,
  Eleanor   Michaelmas 1814; Northampton
BLAKE, Susannah   19-07-1814; Southampton
BOWERS, Jemima   06-07-1814; Middlesex
BRAZELEY,
  Susannah   20-04-1814; Middlesex
BRITT*, Elizabeth   30-07-1814; Devon
BROADFIELD*,
  Sarah   14-09-1814; Middlesex
BROWN, Hannah   16-02-1814; Middlesex
BRYAN, Margaret   20-04-1814; Middlesex
BUCKLEY, Alice   27-04-1814; Lancaster
CARMAN, Sophia   19-10-1814; Norfolk
CARTER, Mary   23-03-1814; Suffolk
COMBE, Mary   16-02-1814; Middlesex
CRASTON*, Sarah   14-09-1814; Middlesex
CROUCH, Sophia   26-10-1814; Middlesex
DIAS, Rebecca   06-07-1814; Middlesex
DOBSON*, Esther   14-09-1814; Middlesex
DOWNS, Ann   31-08-1814; Lancaster
ENGLAND, Mary   16-02-1814; Middlesex
EVANS, Elizabeth   20-04-1814; Middlesex
FERGUSON*, Esther   14-09-1814; Middlesex
FINDLATER, Agnes   27-04-1814; Glasgow
FITZGERALD, Mary   06-07-1814; Middlesex

406 List A-1

FRENCH, Ann	19-03-1814; Devon
GIBBS, Elizabeth	20-04-1814; Middlesex
GIBBS, Elizabeth	26-10-1814; Middlesex
GRANVILLE*, Catherine	30-07-1814; Devon
GRAY*, Mary	17-02-1814; Middlesex
GREENROD*, Mary	24-10-1814; Surrey
GRIFFITH, Margaret	05-04-1814; Glamorgan
GUTSELL, Fanny	21-03-1814; Sussex
HALWORTH, Mary	12-03-1814; Huntingdon
HANDAL, Mary	28-07-1814; Nottingham
HATFIELD, Amelia	25-05-1814; Middlesex
HATHAWAY, Mary	13-01-1814; Stafford
HEAD, Jane	17-10-1814; Hertford
HILL, Elizabeth	31-03-1814; Somerset
HOSTE, Jane	05-03-1814; Lancaster
HUMPHREYS, Jane	05-03-1814; Lancaster
HUTCHELL*, Jane	19-03-1814; Devon
JOHNSON, Elizabeth	24-10-1814; Surrey
JOHNSON, Rose/Rosetta	24-03-1814; Surrey
LANGRIDGE, Mary	14-03-1814; Kent
LANTAFF, Ann	12-03-1814; Huntingdon
LANTAFF, Elizabeth	12-03-1814; Huntingdon
LAWSON, Sarah	07-03-1814; Essex
LEONARD, Mary	25-05-1814; Middlesex
LLOYD, Ann	06-07-1814; Middlesex
McGAVIN*, Mary	28-04-1814; Glasgow
McINTYRE, Maria	01-08-1814; Kent
MACK*, Katherine	25-08-1814; Kent
MARKS, Harriot	06-07-1814; London
MASCALL, Mary	26-10-1814; Middlesex
MAY, Sarah	23-07-1814; York
MORRIS, Sarah	01-08-1814; Kent
MUNRO, Eleanor/Helen	12-01-1814; Middlesex
NEAVETT*, Elizabeth/Mary	18-04-1814; Somerset
NOBLE, Ann	19-03-1814; Devon
NORTON, Hannah	07-04-1814; Warwick
O'NEAL, Sarah	22-03-1814; Nottingham
PARSONS, Martha	10-01-1814; Somerset
PATTEN, Jane	11-08-1814; Northumberland
PAUL, Ann	31-08-1814; Lancaster
PEARCE, Jane	06-07-1814; Middlesex
PERRY, Mary	26-10-1814; Middlesex
RICE, Eleanor	20-04-1814; Middlesex
RILEY, Ann	25-05-1814; Middlesex
ROBERTS, Ann	01-08-1814; Kent
ROBERTS, Esther	06-08-1814; Warwick
ROBERTS, Maria	05-03-1814; Lancaster
ROBERTSON*, Elizabeth	10-01-1814; Cumberland
RUBEN, Catherine	06-07-1814; Middlesex
RYAN, Margaret	14-09-1814; Middlesex
SHIPP, Elizabeth	09-08-1814; Norfolk
SHURWEL*, Elizabeth	21-10-1814; Berkshire
SHURWEL*, Sarah	21-10-1814; Berkshire
SIMMONS, Sarah	14-09-1814; Middlesex
SLADEN, Rachael	31-08-1814; Lancaster
SMITH, Ann	26-10-1814; London
SMITH, Catherine	16-02-1814; London
SMITH, Mary	26-10-1814; London
TURNER*, Ann	16-02-1814; Middlesex
TURNER, Mary	17-01-1814; York
WARD*, Ann/Hannah	21-04-1814; York
WATLING, Ann	20-04-1814; Norwich
WATSON, Sarah	14-09-1814; Middlesex
WEBB, Frances	06-07-1814; Middlesex
WHITE, Mary	20-04-1814; London
WILLIAMS, Eliza	20-04-1814; Middlesex
WILLIAMS, Mary	20-04-1814; Middlesex
WILLIAMSON, Mary	23-04-1814; York
WILSON, Frances	12-01-1814; London
WILTSHIRE, Ann	12-03-1814; Wiltshire
WRIGHT, Elizabeth	20-04-1814; Middlesex

1815 TRIAL YEAR

Friendship 1818

BURRELL*, Elizabeth	05-04-1815; Northumberland

Lord Melville 1817

BARRELL, Jane	16-10-1815; Bristol
BEVAN, Jane	07-04-1815; Bristol
BROWN, Frances	25-04-1815; Lancaster
BROWN, Susan	31-01-1815; Lancaster
BUTLER*, Alice	25-10-1815; Lancaster
BUTLER, Ann	06-12-1815; Middlesex
CARTER, Mary	13-09-1815; Middlesex
CHAPMAN, Ann	17-10-1815; York
CLARE, Mary	06-12-1815; Middlesex
CLARK, Ann	17-01-1815; Norfolk
CROWTHER, Mary	25-10-1815; Lancaster

CUNNINGHAM, Elizabeth	25-03-1815; Lancaster	BROWN, Elizabeth	11-03-1815; Lincoln
DAVIE, Jean	28-09-1815; Glasgow	BUDGE, Elizabeth	10-01-1815; Surrey
DUGGINS, Jane	13-09-1815; Middlesex	BURRELL, Ann	11-03-1815; Lincoln
ELLIS, Sarah	15-07-1815; Huntingdon	CLARKE, Mary	21-06-1815; Middlesex
GILBRITH, Mary Ann	17-10-1815; Devon	CLEMENTS, Ann	01-04-1815; Somerset
GRANT, Elizabeth	27-09-1815; Aberdeen	COLLINS, Ann	21-06-1815; Middlesex
GREEN, Ann	06-12-1815; Middlesex	CROFTON, Elizabeth	21-06-1815; Middlesex
HINES, Phebe	01-04-1815; Warwick	CROUCH, Ann	11-01-1815; Hertford
HOLMES, Mary	15-07-1815; Nottingham	EMMOTT, Mary	15-02-1815; Middlesex
HULMES, Ann	31-01-1815; Lancaster	EVANS, Mary	21-06-1815; Middlesex
JOHNSON, Frances	14-07-1815; Lincoln	FRAYLEY, Ann	21-06-1815; Middlesex
JONES, Hannah	13-09-1815; Middlesex	GREEN, Hannah	21-06-1815; Middlesex
LEONARD, Caroline	21-06-1815; Middlesex	GRIFFIN, Mary	11-03-1815; York
LOGAN, Eleanor	25-10-1815; Middlesex	HEASMAN, Phillis	05-04-1815; Middlesex
McKENZIE, Hannah	20-07-1815; Nottingham	HETHERALL, Elizabeth	21-06-1815; Middlesex
MALLETT, Mary	13-03-1815; Suffolk	HEWETT, Isabella	10-01-1815; Surrey
MAYNE, Mary	17-10-1815; Devon	HULL, Mary	06-03-1815; Essex
PARSONS, Elizabeth	13-09-1815; Middlesex	HUTTEN*, Margaret	12-01-1815; Southampton
POLLITT, Margaret	19-07-1815; Lancaster	JOHNSON, Hannah	11-01-1815; Middlesex
REYNOLDS, Sarah	06-12-1815; Middlesex	JONES, Elizabeth	05-04-1815; London
ROSS, Martha	13-09-1815; Middlesex	LAMBERT, Elizabeth	11-01-1815; Middlesex
SKINNER, Elizabeth	13-09-1815; Middlesex	LINCOLN, Elizabeth	11-03-1815; Lincoln
SPRUCE, Ann	13-09-1815; Norfolk	McMAHON*, Mary	30-03-1815; Chester
STILES, Ann	25-03-1815; Norfolk	MALES, Eleanor	02-03-1815; Hertford
STONEHAM, Mary	06-12-1815; Middlesex	MAZAGORA, Mary	01-04-1815; Warwick
TAYLOR, Ann	06-12-1815; Middlesex	MEADE, Jane	05-01-1815; Middlesex
THOMPSON, Isabella	07-11-1815; Lancaster	MEREDITH, Jane	20-03-1815; Devon
TOWNS*, Martha	25-03-1815; Lancaster	MILLER, Mary Ann	11-01-1815; Middlesex
WALSH, Elizabeth	02-08-1815; York	NELSON, Jane	21-06-1815; Middlesex
WATERMAN, Mary Ann	25-03-1815; Lancaster	OSMOND*, Caroline	05-04-1815; Middlesex
WILLIAMS, Ann	18-01-1815; Lancaster	PERREY, Sarah	15-02-1815; Middlesex
WORTHINGTON*, Agnes/Nancy	30-09-1815; Glasgow	POWIS, Ann	11-03-1815; Worcester
YOUNG, Elizabeth	05-04-1815; London	RADFORD, Ann	16-01-1815; Devon
		ROBINSON, Elizabeth	05-04-1815; London

Maria 1818

PHILLIPS, Mary Ann	13-09-1815; Middlesex

Mary Anne 1816

BEARANCE, Elizabeth	20-03-1815; Devon
BEARANCE, Rebecca	20-03-1815; Devon
BLAKE, Mary	11-01-1815; Middlesex
BROUGH, Margaret	21-03-1815; Salop

RUSH, Eleanor	05-04-1815; Middlesex
SALT, Hannah	16-03-1815; Stafford
SHANNON, Frances	17-03-1815; Nottingham
STALLARD, Elizabeth	09-01-1815; Somerset
STALLARD, Mary	09-01-1815; Somerset
STEPHENSON, Ann	10-01-1815; Lancaster
SUPPLE, Mary	25-03-1815; Kent
THOMAS, Mary	18-01-1815; York
THOMAS, Mary	21-06-1815; Middlesex
TOZER, Agnes	20-03-1815; Devon

TURNER, Frances 25-03-1815; Surrey
TURNER, Margaret 01-04-1815; Warwick
VICKERY, Joanna 21-06-1815; Middlesex
WALLACE,
 Catherine 05-04-1815; London
WARD, Jane 17-03-1815; Nottingham
WARD, Sarah 15-02-1815; Middlesex
WATSON, Mary 05-04-1815; Middlesex
WATSON, Mary 11-01-1815; Middlesex
WHITTAKER,
 Martha 11-01-1815; London
WILKINSON,
 Elizabeth 09-01-1815; Durham
WILLIAMS,
 Elizabeth 11-01-1815; Middlesex
WOOLLEY,
 Elizabeth 01-04-1815; Warwick

1816 TRIAL YEAR

Friendship 1818

ARMSTRONG, Sarah 21-08-1816; Cumberland
BARNS, Jane 13-07-1816; Middlesex
BEAL, Jane 17-07-1816; Northampton
BLAKER, Grace 18-09-1816; London
BRIDGE, Mary 31-08-1816; Lancaster
BROWN, Jane 18-09-1816; Middlesex
BUXTON, Mary 23-10-1816; York
CAFFRY, Mary Ann 18-09-1816; Middlesex
CARTER, Maria 23-07-1816; Lincoln
COURTNEY, Maria 24-07-1816; Berwick
DUDLEY, Ann 12-08-1816; Warwick
DUFFY, Margaret 24-07-1816; Berwick
EUDEN*, Rosannah 16-01-1816; York
GARVA*, Harriet 18-09-1816; Middlesex
GILBERT, Sarah 29-05-1816; Middlesex
GORDON, Sarah 31-08-1816; Lancaster
GRANGER, Jane 15-08-1816; Northumberland
GUNTON, Elizabeth 17-07-1816; Northampton
HASSALL, Sarah 31-08-1816; Lancaster
JACKSON, Mary 01-08-1816; Stafford
JARVIS, Hannah 13-08-1816; Norfolk
LEGGETT, Elizabeth 22-07-1816; Nottingham
LIGHTHARNESS,
 Amelia 13-08-1816; Norfolk
MARSHALL, Sarah 24-07-1816; Lancaster
MOEN*, Mary 24-07-1816; Berwick
MORGAN, Ann 31-08-1816; Brecon
NOWLAND, Frances 04-12-1816; Middlesex
OLIVER, Barbara 10-08-1816; Durham
PERKINS, Elizabeth 15-07-1816; Bristol
QUANTRELL,
 Elizabeth 15-10-1816; Norfolk
RANDALL, Sarah 05-08-1816; Kent
ROBERTS, Elizabeth 12-08-1816; Warwick
ROBINSON, Sarah 23-10-1816; Lancaster
SELLAIRS, Margaret 21-08-1816; Cumberland
SHEEN, Mary 18-09-1816; Middlesex
SIBLEY, Frances 18-09-1816; Middlesex
SIMKIN, Ellen 23-03-1816; Lancaster
TILLING, Ann 18-09-1816; Middlesex
WALKER, Maria 19-07-1816; Salop
WILSON*, Frances 17-10-1816; York

Lord Melville 1817

AIRYMAN, Mary 08-01-1816; Bristol
ALLEN, Mary Ann 23-03-1816; Lancaster
ARNOLD, Sarah 22-04-1816; Bristol
ASHBY, Esther 01-04-1816; Warwick
BANE, Elizabeth 07-04-1816; Bristol
BANNISTER,
 Elizabeth 10-01-1816; Middlesex
BARNES, Jane 23-03-1816; Lancaster
CHANDLER,
 Elizabeth 03-04-1816; London
CHATTELS, Ann 22-04-1816; Bristol
COLLINS*, Harriet 29-05-1816; Middlesex
CONWAY, Bridget 29-05-1816; Middlesex
COOPER, Maria 07-03-1816; Hertford
CORNWELL, Mary 12-03-1816; Cambridge
CROSS, Jane 29-05-1816; Middlesex
DAVIS, Ann 08-01-1816; Bristol
DAVIS, Mary 29-05-1816; Middlesex
DODD(S)*, Hannah 17-04-1816; Chester
DUNCAN, Mary 17-04-1816; Chester
DUNN, Elizabeth 06-04-1816; Bristol
DUNN, Jane 08-01-1816; Bristol
ENGLAND, Jane 14-02-1816; Middlesex
EVANS, Ann 17-04-1816; Chester
FORDICE, Elizabeth 29-05-1816; London
GORDON, Phillis 29-04-1816; Devon
GREENWOOD,
 Martha 22-04-1816; Bristol
HALL, Sarah 28-03-1816; Surrey

HALLIWELL, Sarah	23-03-1816; Lancaster
HARDY*, Sarah	29-05-1816; Middlesex
HARVEY, Elizabeth	10-01-1816; Middlesex
HAYSELDEN, Elizabeth	10-01-1816; Middlesex
HENSHAW, Mary	17-04-1816; Chester
HILL, Margaret	29-05-1816; Middlesex
JONES, Mary	10-01-1816; Middlesex
LUSBY*, Caroline	09-03-1816; Lincoln
McCARTHY, Margaret	03-06-1816; Middlesex
MacKAY, Elizabeth	03-04-1816; London
MATTHEWS*, Elizabeth	06-04-1816; Bristol
MAY, Margaret	13-01-1816; Nottingham
MOULDS, Ann	02-05-1816; Lincoln
NEWMAN, Susannah	03-04-1816; Middlesex
O'HARA*, Mary	03-05-1816; Glasgow
PRIMER, Sarah	17-01-1816; Lancaster
REID*, Helen	16-04-1816; Aberdeen
ROBINS, Sophia	03-04-1816; Gloucester
SADLER*, Esther	19-03-1816; Worcester
SCOTT, Mary	11-05-1816; Edinburgh
SCOTT*, Mary	27-04-1816; Ayshire
SMITH, Ann	14-02-1816; Middlesex
SOUL, Elizabeth	29-05-1816; Middlesex
TINNY*, Susan	11-03-1816; Edinburgh
TURNER, Esther	30-03-1816; Somerset
TURVEY, Mary Ann	01-04-1816; Warwick
WHITELY*, Hannah	29-04-1816; York
WOOD*, Jane	03-04-1816; Gloucester
YOUNG*, Christian(a)	03-05-1816; Glasgow

***Maria* 1818**

NICKSON, Ann	16-04-1816; Chester
STOKES, Sarah	09-03-1816; Worcester

1817 TRIAL YEAR

***Friendship* 1818**

ADCOCK, Mary	26-03-1817; Leicester
ATKINSON, Ann	22-01-1817; Lancaster
BARFOOT, Amay	27-03-1817; Surrey
BRADY, Elizabeth	08-03-1817; Lincoln
BRODIE, Elizabeth	26-04-1817; Glasgow
BUCKLEY, Mary Ann	27-02-1817; Lancaster
CAIN, Mary	26-04-1817; Glasgow
CHANDLER, Sarah	NR-04-1817; Radnor
COTSWORTH, Mercy	22-04-1817; Lincoln
COURTNEY, Susannah	16-04-1817; Middlesex
COX, Sarah Ann	13-01-1817; Bristol
CRAMPTON*, Hannah	08-03-1817; York
DAVIS, Mary	14-03-1817; Nottingham
EGINTON*, Mary	01-04-1817; Warwick
FINCHAM, Mary	15-01-1817; Middlesex
GRIFFIN*, Sarah	18-04-1817; Nottingham
GROOM, Emma	16-04-1817; Middlesex
GUEST, Ruth	20-01-1817; Lancaster
HOOPER, Rebecca	14-01-1817; Devon
HOPKINS, Sarah	12-04-1817; Bristol
HORTON, Ann	01-04-1817; Warwick
HUME, Jean	16-04-1817; Glasgow
JACKSON, Ann	16-04-1817; Middlesex
JENNISON, Ann	17-04-1817; York
JOHNSON, Mary	19-03-1817; Devon
JONES, Jane	20-01-1817; Lancaster
JONES, Margaret	05-04-1817; Denbighshire
JONES, Mary	22-03-1817; Lancaster
KENNICOTT, Ann	13-01-1817; Bristol
LANG, Jean (Snr)	25-04-1817; Glasgow
LANG, Margaret	22-01-1817; Lancaster
LANG*, Jean (Jnr)	25-04-1817; Glasgow
LENNY, Mary	03-03-1817; Southampton
MacDONALD*, Jean/Jane	19-04-1817; Perth
McGINNIS, Elizabeth	15-01-1817; London
MASON, Susannah	21-04-1817; Norfolk
MEARES, Lucy	12-04-1817; Bristol
NEAT, Harriet	13-01-1817; Bristol
NORTH, Sarah	13-01-1817; Bristol
OSBORNE*, Catherine	01-04-1817; Warwick
PATRICK, Elizabeth	13-01-1817; Bristol
PLUMMER, Sarah	19-03-1817; Devon
RICHARDS, Sophia	12-04-1817; Bristol
ROGERS, Jane	24-03-1817; Sussex
ROSS, Ann	22-01-1817; Lancaster
SHARPE, Mary	22-01-1817; Lancaster
SMILES, Mary	16-04-1817; Northumberland

410 List A-1

SMITH, Mary	15-01-1817; Middlesex
STEWART, Helen	30-04-1817; Inverness
STOCKHAM, Mary	14-04-1817; Devon
THIRKILL, Isabella	08-03-1817; York
VALLANCE, Hannah	20-03-1817; Derby
WELCH, Catherine	22-01-1817; Lancaster
WHELDON, Ann	14-03-1817; Nottingham
WILLIAMS, Mary	15-01-1817; Middlesex
WRIGHT, Hester	13-01-1817; Bristol
YATES, Margaret	13-03-1817; Stafford

Maria 1818

ALMOND, Elizabeth	22-07-1817; Lancaster
BANKS, Mary	14-10-1817; Huntingdon
BOWDEN, Elizabeth	14-01-1817; Devon
BRAMWELL, Charlotte	17-07-1817; Lancaster
BRITTAIN, Mary	19-07-1817; York
BROWN, Hannah	13-10-1817; Warwick
BUCKLEY, Mary	21-05-1817; Middlesex
BUCKLEY, Mary	21-10-1817; Lancaster
BURNET, Euphemia	17-09-1817; Perth
CASSIDY, Judith	27-08-1817; Lancaster
CHAMBERS, Mary	17-09-1817; Middlesex
CLEGG, Ann	22-07-1817; Lancaster
DOCKER, Sarah	02-08-1817; Warwick
FOSTER*, Jane	13-10-1817; Cumberland
GASH, Martha	18-07-1817; Nottingham
HARDACRE, Catherine	27-08-1817; Lancaster
HEALEY, Betty	27-08-1817; Lancaster
HOWARTH, Mary	21-10-1817; Lancaster
JOHNSTON, Mary	15-01-1817; Middlesex
LYNCH, Eleanor	13-08-1817; Surrey
McCARTHY, Joanna	12-04-1817; Bristol
McLEOD, Beatrix	14-07-1817; Edinburgh
MOORE, Elizabeth	04-08-1817; Lancaster
NORMAN, Mary	29-07-1817; Stafford
PHILLIPS, Harriet	03-12-1817; Middlesex
REYNOLDS, Elizabeth	08-03-1817; Wiltshire
REYNOLDS, Mary	17-04-1817; Lancaster
ROBERTS, Mary	Summer 1817; Caernarvon
SLEIGH, Harriet	15-01-1817; Middlesex
SMITH, Ann	17-07-1817; York
TAYLOR, Betty	22-07-1817; Lancaster
TAYLOR, Elizabeth	17-07-1817; York
THOMPSON, Maria	03-12-1817; Middlesex
THORNLEY, Ann	04-10-1817; Lancaster
WALKER, Caroline	16-01-1817; Cambridge
WATKINS, Margaret	12-08-1817; Monmouth
WESTLEY, Ann	15-01-1817; Middlesex
WILCOCK, Alice	27-08-1817; Lancaster
WILD*, Betty	27-08-1817; Chester
WILLIAMS, Mary	Summer 1817; Caernarvon
WILLIAMS, Mary	03-12-1817; Middlesex
WOMOCK, Jane	19-03-1817; Salop
YOUNG, Mary	16-08-1817; Cumberland

1818 TRIAL YEAR

Janus 1820

DYEL, Mary	22-10-1818; Nottingham
HILL, Jean	01-10-1818; Glasgow
HUGHES, Mary	13-03-1818; Montgomery
LOVETT, Elizabeth	28-03-1818; Warwick
MILLER, Elizabeth	06-08-1818; Surrey
WAIN, Lucy	13-03-1818; Nottingham
WARD, Sarah	09-09-1818; Middlesex

Lord Sidmouth 1823

SCOTT, Charlotte	28-03-1818; Somerset

Lord Wellington 1820

ALLEN, Elizabeth	20-07-1818; Surrey
ANDERSON, Margaret	21-07-1818; Lancaster
BAMFORD, Elizabeth	28-03-1818; Warwick
BAMFORD, Rebecca	28-03-1818; Warwick
BASON, Elizabeth	06-05-1818; Middlesex
BAYLEY, Mary	28-03-1818; Warwick
BERRY, Eliza	21-03-1818; Lancaster
BLAKEMORE, Mary	13-07-1818; Montgomery
BRADNEY, Mary	28-03-1818; Warwick
BROOKS, Elizabeth	09-09-1818; Middlesex
BROWN, Mary	28-10-1818; Middlesex
BRYANT, Catherine	28-10-1818; Middlesex
CARR, Jane	21-03-1818; Lancaster
CRAWFORD, Mary	21-10-1818; Northumberland
DALEY, Elizabeth	21-03-1818; Lancaster
DICKINS*, Ann	25-07-1818; Warwick

DOWNES, Clarissa Ward	06-05-1818; Middlesex	ROBERTSON*, Catherine	15-07-1818; Edinburgh
ENO, Elizabeth	07-03-1818; Lincoln	SAUNDERS, Ellen	23-07-1818; Stafford
FAHRLAND, Mary	02-03-1818; Southampton	SHAW, Jane	16-03-1818; Devon
		SIZER, Mary Ann	29-04-1818; Norfolk
FRISBY*, Elizabeth	22-10-1818; Northampton	SMITH, Ann	21-07-1818; Lancaster
		SMITH, Ann	02-12-1818; Middlesex
GILBERT, Hannah	09-09-1818; London	SMITH, Maria	17-06-1818; Middlesex
GRANT*, Ann	16-07-1818; Northumberland	SMITH, Mary	27-07-1818; Durham
		STEELE, Mary	21-03-1818; Lancaster
GREEN, Lydia	09-09-1818; London	TERRIER*, Catherine	08-06-1818; Edinburgh
HAGUE, Sarah	03-08-1818; York		
HANCOCK, Elizabeth	23-03-1818; Leicester	TOMKISSON, Elizabeth	23-10-1818; Salop
HARTNETT, Mary	28-10-1818; Middlesex	TRELIVING, Elizabeth	16-03-1818; Devon
HEYLIN, Mary	07-08-1818; Cumberland		
HILTON, Elizabeth	21-03-1818; Lancaster	WADDLE, Letitia	15-08-1818; Lancaster
HINES, Amelia	28-03-1818; Warwick	WARD, Ann	21-03-1818; Lancaster
HITCHCOCK, Hannah	26-09-1818; Derby	WARD, Mary	19-10-1818; Durham
		WILKES, Maria	09-09-1818; Middlesex
HODGES*, Rebecca	28-03-1818; Warwick	WILLIAMS, Jane	09-09-1818; Middlesex
HOLMES, Sarah	16-03-1818; Devon	WILSON, Jane	06-08-1818; Surrey
JACKSON, Ann	09-09-1818; Middlesex	WINGFIELD, Elizabeth	17-06-1818; London
JONES, Elizabeth	09-09-1818; Middlesex		
JONES, Maria	NR-04-1818; Montgomery	WINN, Elizabeth	02-03-1818; Southampton
JONES, Mary	23-07-1818; Stafford	WOLSENHALL, Sarah	01-03-1818; Surrey
KENNEDY, Margaret	01-10-1818; Glasgow		
LAPAGE, Ann	30-03-1818; York	*Maria* 1818	
LINNEGAR, Mary	28-03-1818; Warwick	ALDRIDGE, Elizabeth	01-04-1818; Middlesex
McDONALD, Effey	21-03-1818; Lancaster		
MARSH, Harriet	09-07-1818; Southampton	ASHLEY, Ann	15-01-1818; York
		BRYANT, Hannah	14-01-1818; Middlesex
MILLER, Mary	09-07-1818; Southampton	CAUSER*, Matilda	14-01-1818; Stafford
		CHILD, Ann	12-01-1818; Durham
MITCHELL, Elizabeth	07-08-1818; Cumberland	COSGROVE, Susannah	20-01-1818; Lancaster
MOORES, Elizabeth	21-03-1818; Lancaster	CRAWFORD*, Mary	16-01-1818; Nottingham
NOWLAND*, Mary Ann	21-07-1818; Lancaster	DOUBLE, Elizabeth	14-01-1818; London
		FORSHAW, Mary	20-01-1818; Lancaster
ORTON*, Sarah	23-03-1818; Leicester	GILDERSLEEVES, Mary	14-01-1818; Middlesex
PHILLIPS*, Susannah	17-03-1818; Devon		
		GILLES, Mary	14-01-1818; Middlesex
PRIOR, Elizabeth	12-03-1818; Dorset	HUGHES, Elizabeth	12-01-1818; Salop
REED, Mary Ann	17-06-1818; London	HUMPHREYS, Margaret	14-01-1818; Middlesex
RENOWDON, Jenny	27-07-1818; Devon		
RICHARDS, Rachel	28-03-1818; Warwick	O'HARA, Rose	14-01-1818; Middlesex
ROBERTS, Mary	21-03-1818; Lancaster	PILKINGTON, Ann	14-01-1818; Middlesex

PINK*, Ann   18-02-1818; Middlesex
PLEASANT,
  Elizabeth   14-01-1818; London
SHAW, Mary   01-04-1818; Middlesex
TAYLOR, Jane   07-03-1818; Worcester
THOMAS, Rosannah   07-03-1818; Worcester

1819 TRIAL YEAR

Janus 1820
ASTELL, Lydia   24-03-1819; Sussex
BEVAN, Esther   07-07-1819; Middlesex
DALEY, Mary   26-05-1819; Middlesex
EASTERBROOKE,
  Mary   15-03-1819; Kent
GRAHAM, Jean   29-04-1819; Glasgow
GRIFFITHS,
  Mary Ann   21-04-1819; London
HORNE, Mary   02-08-1819; Kent
HOWLETT, Mary   07-08-1819; Warwick
IRVING, Isabella   01-04-1819; Cumberland
LONG, Mary   26-04-1819; Lancaster
MORRIS, Christina   21-04-1819; Middlesex
MUNDAY, Ann   21-04-1819; Middlesex
ORR, Mary   01-04-1819; Cumberland
PHILLIPS, Sophia   07-08-1819; Warwick
ROBERTSON, Ann   01-05-1819; Glasgow
SEFTON, Ellen   18-01-1819; Lancaster
TAVENER,
  Susannah   21-04-1819; Middlesex
WOOD, Ann   21-04-1819; Middlesex

Lord Wellington 1820
ARNOLD, Ann   17-02-1819; London
CHAMBERS,
  Elizabeth   13-01-1819; London
CLOWES, Sarah   29-03-1819; Surrey
DUNNING*, Sarah   12-01-1819; York
GORMAN, Catherine   29-03-1819; Surrey
JELLEY, Mary   11-01-1819; Leicester
McCORMICK, Mary   20-03-1819; Lancaster
McWILLIAMS, Mary   11-01-1819; Cumberland
MILES, Catherine   01-03-1819; Suffolk
MOORE, Elizabeth   03-03-1819; Oxford
PARSONS, Margaret   13-01-1819; Stafford
POOLE, Mary   29-03-1819; Surrey
SMALLMAN, Ann   17-02-1819; Middlesex
SMITH, Elizabeth   29-03-1819; Surrey

Morley 1820
ASTON, Lucy   06-03-1819; Worcester
BAKER, Jane   21-08-1819; Gloucester
BROWN, Jane   24-07-1819; Lincoln
BROWN, Mary   07-07-1819; London
BURNETT, Margaret   22-04-1819; Aberdeen
CONNOR, Eleanor   15-09-1819; London
CROFT, Mary Ann   27-10-1819; Middlesex
DAVIS, Emma   27-10-1819; Middlesex
DILLING*, Eliza   27-10-1819; London
DUNKEY, Elizabeth   15-09-1819; Middlesex
HALL, Ann   12-07-1819; Somerset
HARRIS, Sarah   15-09-1819; Middlesex
HICKMAN, Mary   14-08-1819; Somerset
HOLTON, Ann   NR-12-1819; Surrey
JOHN*, Mary   18-10-1819; Bristol
KELLY, Mary   18-10-1819; Devon
LEESON, Catherine   14-08-1819; Somerset
LEWIS, Ann   07-07-1819; Middlesex
McGREGOR,
  Christian   28-04-1819; Perth
MITCHELL, Sarah   01-12-1819; Middlesex
NIXON, Eliza   NR-10-1819; Surrey
PEACOCK, Maria   24-07-1819; Essex
PUGH, Ann   07-09-1819; Brecon
SEWARD*,
  Ann Jemima   02-08-1819; Devon
STRACHAN*, Isabel   29-09-1819; Aberdeen
STRATH, Susan   27-04-1819; Perth
SWATMAN, Esther   01-12-1819; Middlesex
SWATMAN, Sarah   01-12-1819; Middlesex
TATE, Johanna   02-08-1819; Devon
TAYLOR, Mary   01-09-1819; Lancaster
TOMLINSON, Mary   25-10-1819; Lancaster
WHITE, Elizabeth   27-03-1819; Somerset
WILLIAMS, Maria   01-12-1819; London
WILSON*, Jean   27-04-1819; Perth

1820 TRIAL YEAR

Lord Sidmouth 1823
JENNINGS,
  Elizabeth   28-06-1820; Middlesex
WRIGHT, Sarah   13-09-1820; Middlesex

Mary Anne 1822
ANDERSON,
  Elizabeth   23-10-1820; Lancaster

CAMPBELL, Mary	23-10-1820; Lancaster		CAMMELL, Eliza	17-05-1820; Middlesex
JACKSON, Mary	23-10-1820; Lancaster		CARTER, Sarah	28-06-1820; Middlesex
QUIN, Catherine	23-10-1820; Lancaster		CLARKE, Mary	03-10-1820; Lancaster
SHARMAN, Elizabeth	24-07-1820; Norfolk		CLIFTON, Ann	25-10-1820; Middlesex
THOMPSON, Louisa	13-08-1820; Lincoln		CLOUSLEY, Elizabeth	12-04-1820; Middlesex
			CORBYN, Sarah	25-10-1820; London

Morley 1820

BROMLEY, Sarah	28-02-1820; Southampton
CAMPBELL, Catherine	18-01-1820; Isle of Man
CLAPHAM, Ruth	04-03-1820; York
COCKSHALL, Elizabeth	10-03-1820; Nottingham
CURTIS, Ann	17-02-1820; Middlesex
DOWNES, Sarah	17-01-1820; Lancaster
DUNCAN, Elizabeth	20-03-1820; Lancaster
HALL, Ann	12-01-1820; Middlesex
HARRISON*, Jane	10-03-1820; Nottingham
HEARD*, Mary	17-02-1820; London
HESKETCH, Jane	05-04-1820; Chester
HEWITT, Esther	12-01-1820; Middlesex
HOUGH, Mary	05-04-1820; Chester
JOHNSON, Susan	18-01-1820; Norfolk
JONES, Mary	17-01-1820; Lancaster
KELLY, Mary	12-01-1820; London
KING, Mary	23-03-1820; Surrey
MARTIN, Catherine	12-01-1820; London
MYERS, Judith	23-03-1820; Surrey
OLDHAM, Margaret	17-01-1820; Lancaster
OWEN, Browning	23-03-1820; Surrey
PARKER, Jane	10-01-1820; Cumberland
RANDALL, Mary	17-02-1820; London
REDGREAVE, Elizabeth	23-03-1820; Surrey
ROGERS, Margaret	20-03-1820; Lancaster
RUDGE*, Prudence	11-01-1820; Gloucester
SPINKS, Ann	27-03-1820; Warwick
TENNANT, Sarah	NR-01-1820; Surrey
TRUEMAN*, Sarah	14-01-1820; Salop
WELCH, Ann	28-02-1820; Southampton
WILLIAMS, Sarah	23-03-1820; Surrey
WILSON, Jane	23-03-1820; Surrey

Providence 1822

BOSSAND, Mary	27-03-1820; Warwick
BURNHAM, Elizabeth	25-10-1820; Middlesex
CREW*, Esther	23-08-1820; Chester
DENHAM, Elizabeth	06-12-1820; Middlesex
DILLOW, Susan	25-10-1820; Middlesex
DOORS, Mary	13-09-1820; Norfolk
GIBSON, Ann	06-12-1820; Middlesex
HALLAM, Charlotte	18-10-1820; Stafford
HARTFORD, Mary	29-07-1820; Sussex
HARVEY, Maria	13-09-1820; Middlesex
HERBERT, Rachael	25-10-1820; London
HEWSTER, Sarah	28-06-1820; Middlesex
HUGHES, Mary	13-09-1820; London
JENKINS, Ann	13-09-1820; Middlesex
JONES*, Jane	06-11-1820; Lancaster
LOWE, Elizabeth	12-04-1820; Middlesex
LUDAM, Hannah	13-07-1820; York
MORRIS, Mary	28-06-1820; Middlesex
NEVILLE, Mary	31-01-1820; Lancaster
ROBINSON, Mary	12-04-1820; Middlesex
SMITH, Elizabeth	12-04-1820; Middlesex
SMITH, Margaret	16-03-1820; Edinburgh
SMITH, Mary	12-04-1820; Middlesex
THORN, Louisa	12-04-1820; Middlesex
WALKER BIRD, Mary	06-12-1820; London
WILLIAMS, Elizabeth	20-07-1820; Stafford
WINGFIELD*, Jane	06-12-1820; Middlesex
WOODWARD, Mary Ann	06-12-1820; Middlesex

1821 TRIAL YEAR

Lord Sidmouth 1823

BELL, Mary Ann	06-06-1821; London
BOWDEN, Mary	07-04-1821; Bristol
CROMPTON, Ann	29-01-1821; Lancaster
JACKSON, Ann	05-12-1821; Middlesex
JENKINS, Ann	05-12-1821; Middlesex
JONES, Catharine	24-10-1821; Middlesex
KINSEY, Elizabeth	05-12-1821; Middlesex
KNIGHT, Cordelia	06-06-1821; Middlesex

414 List A-1

LOWE, Mary	16-07-1821; Lancaster
PALMER, Mary	24-10-1821; Middlesex
POOLE, Ann	25-08-1821; Somerset
RIGBY, Hannah	02-10-1821; Lancaster
ROGERS, Jane	11-01-1821; Lancaster
SIMPSON, Elizabeth	11-10-1821; Nottingham
SMITH, Ann	12-09-1821; London
SMITH, Sarah	05-12-1821; London
TAYLOR, Mary	22-10-1821; Lancaster
TRAVIS, Elizabeth	18-10-1821; Nottingham
WILLIAMS, Mercy	07-04-1821; Bristol

Mary 1823

ALLEN, Ann	10-07-1821; Worcester
GAYS, Mary	10-01-1821; Middlesex
QUINION, Mary	05-12-1821; Middlesex

Mary Anne 1822

AMOS, Elizabeth	12-09-1821; Middlesex
AUSTIN, Sarah	06-06-1821; Middlesex
BENJAMIN, Phoebe	12-09-1821; Middlesex
BEST*, Elizabeth	19-03-1821; Devon
BRIDGE, Jane	24-03-1821; Lancaster
BRITLEY, Jane	12-09-1821; Middlesex
BROOKS, Elizabeth	31-03-1821; Somerset
BROOKS, Martha	19-03-1821; Devon
BRYAN, Catherine	12-09-1821; Middlesex
CARTER, Jane	06-06-1821; Middlesex
CATTIN*, Elizabeth	18-08-1821; Warwick
CLARKE, Elizabeth	06-06-1821; London
DAVIES, Elizabeth	12-09-1821; Middlesex
DOWD, Matilda	12-09-1821; Middlesex
EASTERBROOK, Maria	11-08-1821; Devon
EDYVEAN, Elizabeth (Jnr)	24-03-1821; Cornwall
GRAY, Frances	06-06-1821; London
HINCHLEY, Margaret	23-07-1821; Lancaster
HOLDER, Mary	12-09-1821; Middlesex
HOLLAND, Harriet	06-06-1821; Middlesex
HORROCKS, Esther	07-05-1821; Lancaster
IRVIN, Sarah	30-08-1821; Cumberland
JOHNSON, Sarah	06-06-1821; London
JOHNSTON, Elinor	18-07-1821; Middlesex
KAYE, Ruth	04-08-1821; York
KELSEY, Margaret	03-05-1821; York
KING, Lavinia	13-08-1821; Norfolk
McCARTY, Ellen	12-09-1821; Middlesex
McGILVRAY*, Isabella	20-09-1821; Glasgow
MANSELL, Phoebe	11-07-1821; Stafford
MIARES, Clementine	29-03-1821; Surrey
MONTAGUE, Elizabeth	07-03-1821; Oxford
NEWLAND, Mary Ann	06-06-1821; London
PAYNE, Lucy	18-07-1821; Middlesex
PHILLIPS, Ann	21-03-1821; Salop
PIMBLOTT*, Mary	24-03-1821; Middlesex
PRINCE, Sarah	30-07-1821; Southampton
RAWLINGS, Elizabeth	26-03-1821; Hereford
READING, Sarah	06-06-1821; Middlesex
RUMSBY, Ann	16-05-1821; Norfolk
SLATER, Mary	07-05-1821; Lancaster
SMITH, Isabella	06-06-1821; London
SMITH, Mary	06-06-1821; Middlesex
SMITH, Mary Ann	11-07-1821; Northumberland
STALKER, Mary	19-07-1821; London
STEWART, Sarah	06-06-1821; Middlesex
STINTON, Elizabeth	12-09-1821; Middlesex
SULLIVAN, Catherine	12-09-1821; Middlesex
SULLIVAN, Mary Ann	24-10-1821; Middlesex
TAYLOR, Matilda	16-07-1821; Lancaster
THORNE, Charlotte	06-06-1821; Middlesex
TURNER, Ann	24-10-1821; Middlesex
WALTON, Mary	23-08-1821; Northumberland
WHALLEY, Elizabeth	23-07-1821; Lancaster
WILSON, Catherine	30-08-1821; Lancaster
WILSON, Mary	08-09-1821; Chester
WOOTTON, Mary	11-04-1821; Chester

Providence 1822

BELL*, Hannah	02-05-1821; Stafford
BROWN, Sarah	09-01-1821; Surrey
CULL, Ann	31-03-1821; Warwick
DAVIS, Mary	31-03-1821; Warwick
HARRIS, Elizabeth	05-03-1821; Southampton
HARTNET, Mary	11-04-1821; Middlesex

JOHNSON, Elizabeth 14-02-1821; Middlesex
LAMBERT, Rebecca 12-01-1821; Sussex
MacLEOD, Judith 03-03-1821; Northumberland
MAHONEY, Eleanor 10-01-1821; Middlesex
POTTER*, Janet 12-03-1821; Edinburgh
SMITH, Mary Ann 11-04-1821; Middlesex
TRIMNELL, Elizabeth 31-03-1821; Warwick
WHITE, Ann 11-04-1821; Middlesex
WILKINSON, Matilda 11-04-1821; Middlesex

1822 TRIAL YEAR

Brothers 1824
CARMAN*, Elizabeth 23-10-1822; Mansion House
GARDNER*, Lydia 22-07-1822; Worcester
ROBINSON, Sarah NR-04-1822; Chester

Lord Sidmouth 1823
ANDERSON, Janet 08-07-1822; Edinburgh
BILLINGS*, Ann 16-04-1822; Gloucester
BRIDGES, Elizabeth 17-01-1822; Kent
BROWN, Jane 20-02-1822; Middlesex
BUDD, Mary 22-05-1822; Middlesex
CAPPS, Elizabeth 03-07-1822; Middlesex
DAM, Epsaby 18-04-1822; Lincoln
DAVIES, Rachael 03-04-1822; Gloucester
DOVE, Mary 15-03-1822; Nottingham
FERRIS, Christiana 20-02-1822; Middlesex
GARDNER, Sarah 02-03-1822; Northumberland
HEARTNELL, Elizabeth 15-04-1822; Bristol
HEATHER, Mary 03-07-1822; Middlesex
KING, Charlotte Bird 21-01-1822; York
LARKIN, Bridget 15-04-1822; Cumberland
PARFITT, Elizabeth 14-01-1822; Somerset
PHILLIPS, Elizabeth 15-04-1822; Bristol
ROGERS, Sophia 30-03-1822; Warwick
SEEKINS, Mary 03-07-1822; Middlesex
SHERRATT, Martha 03-07-1822; Middlesex
SMITH, Charlotte 09-01-1822; Middlesex
WILSON, Eleanor 17-07-1822; Northumberland
WITNEY, Ann 03-07-1822; Middlesex
WORDEN, Eliza 22-04-1822; Surrey
YOUNG*, Elizabeth 16-04-1822; York

Mary 1823
AARONS, Rachael 21-10-1822; Lancaster
ANDERSON, Mary 11-09-1822; Middlesex
AYNSLEY, Jane 16-10-1822; Northumberland
BATEMAN, Sarah 11-09-1822; Middlesex
BRANSTON, Ann 02-03-1822; Northampton
BROWN, Ann 23-10-1822; Middlesex
CALLOW*, Mary 30-07-1822; Norfolk
COWELL, Mary 27-08-1822; Castle Rushen
DALEY, Eleanor 02-12-1822; Surrey
DARKE, Elizabeth 28-07-1822; Devon
DUDDRIDGE, Mary 13-07-1822; Bristol
FINNEGAN, Elizabeth 04-02-1822; Lancaster
FURNESS, Rebecca 20-07-1822; Norfolk
HARGREAVES, Ellen 23-03-1822; Lancaster
HATTON, Ellen 22-07-1822; Lancaster
HEALEY, Margaret 22-04-1822; Lancaster
HEWSON, Jane 11-12-1822; Essex
HOUGH, Mary Ann 22-07-1822; Lancaster
IRONS, Hannah 14-10-1822; Worcester
JARVIS*, Mary 17-09-1822; Glasgow
JOHNSON, Sarah 23-10-1822; Middlesex
LOWDEN, Deborah 11-03-1822; Essex
McPHAIL, Euphemia 16-09-1822; Glasgow
MORRIS, Elizabeth 16-12-1822; Kent
MURPHY, Margaret 23-10-1822; Middlesex
NEWMAN, Ann 16-12-1822; Kent
PERRY, Sarah 23-10-1822; Middlesex
PHILLIPS, Dorothy 25-07-1822; Stafford
PHILLIPS, Sarah 25-07-1822; Stafford
POWELL, Ann 09-03-1822; Worcester
QUAYLE*, Jane 27-08-1822; Castle Rushen
SALTER, Mary 20-02-1822; Middlesex
SAUNDERS, Ann 13-07-1822; Bristol
SMITH, Catherine 22-07-1822; Lancaster
SMITH, Elizabeth 04-12-1822; Middlesex
STEPHENSON, Sophia 04-12-1822; Middlesex
TURNER, Caroline 02-12-1822; Surrey

416 List A-1

WEBB, Eliza	30-12-1822; Surrey
WELDING, Mary	20-07-1822; Worcester
WEST, Sarah	11-09-1822; Middlesex
WINTERBOTTOM, Sarah	17-07-1822; Stafford
WISE, Harriet	11-09-1822; Middlesex

1823 TRIAL YEAR

Brothers 1824

ALVEY, Charlotte Ann	10-09-1823; Newgate
BAILEY, Sarah	25-06-1823; Newgate
BENSON, Elizabeth	25-05-1823; Newgate
BIGGS, Catherine	24-06-1823; Newgate
BOYLE, Margaret	02-04-1823; Lancaster
CEFENDER*, Jane	05-04-1823; Chester
CLARKE, Esther	NR-04-1823; Newgate
DAY, Sarah	25-06-1823; Newgate
FRAZER, Sophia	NR-04-1823; Newgate
HANNING, Bridget	10-09-1823; Newgate
HELPS, Mary Ann	10-09-1823; Newgate
HUTCHINS*, Hannah	15-06-1823; Newgate
KEEFE, Catherine	05-03-1823; Horsemonger Lane
LEECH, Eleanor	08-04-1823; Newgate
McMANUS, Catherine	NR-07-1823; Liverpool
MEADOWS, Ellen	04-04-1823; Lancaster
MULLEN, Ann	20-01-1823; Manchester
NORRIS, Ann	NR-04-1823; Newgate
PALMER, Mary Ann	25-06-1823; Newgate
REASON, Ann	08-04-1823; Newgate
RILEY, Catherine	08-04-1823; Newgate
RUSSELL, Ann	05-04-1823; Warwick
RYAN, Catherine	03-03-1823; Horsemonger Lane
SHAW, Martha	NR-06-1823; Newgate
SHEENE, Kitty	24-05-1823; Newgate
SMITH, Mary	08-04-1823; Newgate
STRANGE, Mary Ann	24-05-1823; Newgate
THORN, Mary	10-09-1823; Newgate
TWELBRIDGE, Sarah	NR-07-1823; Leicester
UNDERHILL, Mary Day	15-04-1823; Warwick
WHEATLEY, Jane	24-09-1823; Newgate
WILLIAMS, Fanny	21-05-1823; Newgate
WILLIAMS, Mary	24-05-1823; Newgate
WILLIAMS*, Sarah/Elizabeth	18-03-1823; Shrewsbury
WILSON, Amelia	10-09-1823; Newgate
WILSON*, Ann/Hannah	03-03-1823; Horsemonger Lane

Grenada 1825

BEACH, Mary	26-07-1823; Warwick
BELLAMY, Sarah	26-07-1823; Warwick
BEVAN, Elizabeth	22-10-1823; Middlesex
BROWN, Elizabeth	03-12-1823; Middlesex
COURTNEY*, Susan/Elizabeth	10-09-1823; Middlesex
GIBBONS, Mary	03-12-1823; Middlesex
HITCHMAN, Sarah	10-09-1823; Middlesex
HOLME, Hannah	14-10-1823; Cumberland
JOHNSON, Mary Ann(a)	03-12-1823; Middlesex
KENNEDY, Mary	10-09-1823; Middlesex
LAWSON, Johanna	03-12-1823; Middlesex
LLOYD, Isabella	03-12-1823; Middlesex
PARTRIDGE, Mary (Snr)	29-03-1823; Lancaster
PATTERSON, Betsey	14-10-1823; Cumberland
PRICE, Mary	10-09-1823; Middlesex
READ, Elizabeth	03-12-1823; Middlesex
ROACH, Mary	03-12-1823; Middlesex
RYMER, Ann	03-12-1823; Middlesex
THOMSON*, Mary	21-07-1823; Lancaster
WILKINSON, Elizabeth	21-07-1823; Lancaster
WILLIAMS, Caroline	22-10-1823; Middlesex
WRIGHT, Ann	03-12-1823; Middlesex

Mary 1823

BALDWIN, Elizabeth	05-03-1823; Durham
BRIDGER, Sarah	11-04-1823; Middlesex
CURTIS, Ann	13-01-1823; Worcester
DOWLING, Martha	19-02-1823; Middlesex
FORD, Elizabeth	15-01-1823; Middlesex
FORD, Hannah	15-01-1823; Middlesex
HEANEY, Eleanor	03-02-1823; Lancaster
MEREDITH, Mary	15-01-1823; Middlesex
OLDFIELD, Ann	19-02-1823; Middlesex
OSBORN, Ann	17-03-1823; Nottingham
PRICE, Elizabeth	15-01-1823; Middlesex
RIX, Maria	15-01-1823; Middlesex

SHAW, Elizabeth 17-01-1823; Hertford
STEWARD, Elizabeth 15-01-1823; Middlesex

***Midas* 1825**
CURRAN, Mary 20-10-1823; Manchester

1824 TRIAL YEAR

***Grenada* 1825**
BAKER, Elizabeth 18-02-1824; Middlesex
BARRATT, Sarah 27-03-1824; Warwick
BEECHY, Isabella 03-06-1824; Middlesex
BENNETT, Maria 18-02-1824; Middlesex
BENSON, Isabella 18-02-1824; Middlesex
BIRD, Sarah 04-03-1824; Cumberland
BLAKE, Jane 18-02-1824; Middlesex
BOLTON*, Mary 26-04-1824; Warwick
BRADSHAW, Mary 07-04-1824; Middlesex
BRYAN, Margaret 14-01-1824; Middlesex
CARTY, Catherine 07-04-1824; Middlesex
COANS, Sarah 07-04-1824; Middlesex
COXHEAD, Rosina 14-01-1824; Middlesex
CRABTREE*,
 Elizabeth 01-04-1824; Surrey
DARBY, Ann 07-04-1824; Middlesex
DRISCOLL,
 Catherine 18-02-1824; Middlesex
FITZGERALD,
 Elizabeth 07-04-1824; London
FOX, Sarah 03-06-1824; Middlesex
GAINHAM, Sarah 14-01-1824; Middlesex
GATES, Ann 03-06-1824; Middlesex
GILL, Elizabeth 27-03-1824; Warwick
GILL, Mary 27-03-1824; Warwick
GRAHAM, Alice 13-01-1824; Cumberland
GRAY, Mary 14-01-1824; Middlesex
HARDING, Mary 14-01-1824; Middlesex
HEATOCK*, Ellen 10-03-1824; Lancaster
HOUSE, Mary 27-03-1824; Warwick
HUDSON, Mary Ann 07-04-1824; Middlesex
JONES, Jane 03-06-1824; Middlesex
JONES, Mary 03-06-1824; Middlesex
JOWETT, Martha 19-01-1824; Lancaster
KELLY, Margaret 14-01-1824; Middlesex
KENT, Ann 14-01-1824; Middlesex
LEE, Mary 03-06-1824; Middlesex
LEEVIS, Mary 07-03-1824; Warwick
LEONARD, Eleanor 07-04-1824; Middlesex
LEPPARD*,
 Charlotte 07-04-1824; Middlesex
LEWIS, Mary Ann 18-02-1824; London
McNAMARA, Mary 03-05-1824; Lancaster
MASON, Mary 19-01-1824; Lancaster
MAYERS, Martha 19-01-1824; Lancaster
MILFORD,
 Sarah Amelia 18-02-1824; Middlesex
MOORE, Jane 18-02-1824; London
RUSSELL, Mary 14-01-1824; Middlesex
SAMMERS, Maria 27-03-1824; Warwick
SAVAGE, Amelia 15-07-1824; Middlesex
SHAW, Hannah 27-03-1824; Warwick
SHAW, Lydia 27-03-1824; Warwick
SMITH, Mary 03-06-1824; Middlesex
STRIKES, Mary 14-01-1824; Middlesex
SUTTON, Ann 12-01-1824; Warwick
TAYLOR, Caroline 03-06-1824; Middlesex
THURSFIELD,
 Louisa 27-03-1824; Warwick
WATSON, Mary 03-06-1824; London
WEBB, Mary 18-02-1824; Middlesex
WELCH*, Hannah 07-04-1824; Middlesex
WILLIAMS, Maria 14-01-1824; Middlesex
WOOD*, Sarah 14-01-1824; Middlesex
WOOLLEY, Jane 27-03-1824; Warwick

***Grenada* 1827**
ROBINSON, Mary 08-11-1824; Liverpool

***Henry* 1825**
GATTEN, Elizabeth 22-04-1824; Kent
JEFFERSON, Jane 02-02-1824; Lancaster

***Louisa* 1827**
CAMPBELL,
 Margaret 01-10-1824; Glasgow

***Midas* 1825**
ADAMS, Ann 10-11-1824; Edinburgh
ANGUS, Janet 16-04-1824; Perth
BAKER, Jane 23-10-1824;
 Horsemonger Lane
BARNES, Sarah NR-03-1824; Suffolk
BURK, Mary 02-11-1824; London
CROSS, Ann 20-10-1824; Stafford
DAVIES, Mary 24-10-1824; Liverpool
DAVIS, Sophia 28-10-1824; London
DWYNE, Margaret 13-01-1824;
 Horsemonger Lane

418 List A-1

FLORENCE, Ann	19-07-1824; Manchester	HILL, Louisa	NR-04-1825; London
GREENLEES*, Janet	30-04-1824; Glasgow	JONES, Mary	10-04-1825; Worcester
HAILEY, Margaret	27-12-1824; Kingston	KERSLAKE, Ann	11-04-1825; Devon
HAY, Hannah	15-09-1824; London	McPHERSON, Mary	01-02-1825; Liverpool
JEFFERIES, Ann	28-10-1824; London	MESSER*, Elizabeth	NR-01-1825; London
JEFFERIES, Hannah	19-10-1824; Dorchester	MONTAGUE, Mary	17-03-1825; Exeter
MILNE, Jane	01-12-1824; London	O'DONNELL, Mary	11-01-1825; Chester
MORGAN, Mary	26-08-1824; Monmouth	POTTS, Martha	16-04-1825; Stafford
MUNRO, Ruth	30-10-1824; London	PROVEN, Lionel (?)	01-05-1825; Glasgow
PHILLIPS, Elizabeth	18-10-1824; Exeter	ROBINSON, Mary	29-03-1825; Warwick
PICKERS, Letitia	NR-09-1824; London	ROBINSON*, Catherine	01-05-1825; Liverpool
RUSSELL, Margaret	27-09-1824; Glasgow	SANSOM, Elizabeth	12-03-1825; Nottingham
RYCROFT, Mary Ann	09-12-1824; London	SIDDALL, Ellan	18-04-1825; Manchester
SMITH, Elizabeth	01-02-1824; Kirbey	SMITH, Lucy	10-01-1825; Cambridge
VARLOW*, Margaret	NR-10-1824; London	SMITH, Maria	06-04-1825; London
WEAVER, Mary	20-10-1824; Stafford	SMITH, Mary	17-01-1825; London
WHITTINGTON*, Elizabeth	03-12-1824; London	SMITH*, Maria Ann	17-02-1825; London
		SNOOK, Mary	NR-03-1825; Somerset
		UNWIN, Ann	08-04-1825; Hampshire

***Princess Charlotte* 1827**

GRAHAM*, Mary	09-11-1824; Edinburgh

WALKER, Hannah	17-01-1825; Manchester
WALKER, Mary/Margaret	14-01-1825; London
WHITE, Ann	13-01-1825; Sussex
WILLIAMS, Eleanor	Summer 1825; Caernarvon
WILSON, Mary	17-02-1825; London
WILSON, Mary Ann	07?-04-1825; London

1825 TRIAL YEAR

***Grenada* 1827**

ANTROLRY*, Hannah	18-07-1825; Manchester
CRAGGS, Isabella	03-07-1825; Durham
HODGE, Hannah	18-07-1825; Chelmsford
McEVOY, Jane	08-12-1825; London
MOORE, Mary	27-10-1825; London
RICE, Mary	01-08-1825; Liverpool
RYLAND, Ann	03-12-1825; Chelmsford
SMITH, Elizabeth	08-12-1825; London
WADE, Ann	27-10-1825; London

***Louisa* 1827**

DUGGAN, Sarah	27-10-1825; London
SULLIVAN, Judith	27-10-1825; London

***Midas* 1825**

ALLANSON, Maria	18-04-1825; Manchester
BELLINGHAM, Elizabeth	05-03-1825; Worcester
COLSON, Ann	30-05-1825; Horsemonger Lane
DALE, Mary	10-01-1825; Cambridge
DALEY, Margaret	NR-03-1825; Horsemonger Lane

***Princess Charlotte* 1827**

DUGGAN, Sarah	19-12-1825; Edinburgh

1826 TRIAL YEAR

***Grenada* 1827**

ALLEN, Maria	15-02-1826; London
ARCHER, Eliza	27-03-1826; Maidstone
ARCHER, Sophia	27-03-1826; Maidstone
BARKER, Emma	22-06-1826; London
BARNETT, Susan	12-01-1826; London
BOWKER, Betty	17-07-1826; Manchester
BROOKS, Elizabeth	20-03-1826; Exeter
BUCKLEY, Ann	10-04-1826; Lancaster
CARROLL, Ann	10-04-1826; Lancaster
CLARKE, Susan	29-03-1826; Gloucester
CLARKE*, Catharine	06-04-1826; London
CLAY, Maria	13-01-1826; Nottingham
COCHRANE, Catherine	02-01-1826; Middlesex

COLLINS, Eleanor	24-06-1826; London	SMITH*, Sarah	13-01-1826; Nottingham
COLLINS, Margaret	16-01-1826; Manchester	STODDARD, Hannah	03-01-1826; Derby
COOK, Louisa	06-04-1826; Hull	SULLIVAN, Mary	06-04-1826; London
DARTON, Elizabeth	03-04-1826; Exeter	THOMPSON, Elizabeth	11-05-1826; London
DEEBLE, Bridget	NR-03-1826; Launceston		
DIXON, Ann	11-05-1826; London	THOMPSON, Mary Ann	16-01-1826; Manchester
DREWITT, Elizabeth	17-07-1826; Manchester		
EVANS, Margaret	06-04-1826; Bristol	TROEMANATS*, Emma	12-01-1826; London
FARRAN, Ann	17-07-1826; Manchester		
FISHER, Sarah	25-03-1826; Warwick	VALANCE, Catharine	11-05-1826; London
GANNON, Mary	22-06-1826; London	WADLEY, Elizabeth	04-03-1826; Worcester
HARRIS, Mary	15-01-1826; London	WEBBER, Mary Ann	19-07-1826; Exeter
HOGUE, Mary	13-01-1826; Nottingham	WELSH, Elizabeth	02-01-1826; Maidstone
HOLDEN, Elizabeth	29-03-1826; Gloucester	WELSH, Mary	20-02-1826; London
HOLLROYD, Mary Ann	16-07-1826; Manchester	WESTWOOD, Mary	10-07-1826; Warwick
		WHALE, Ann	25-07-1826; Warwick
HULBERT, Prudence	13-01-1826; Nottingham	WILLIAMS, Sarah	17-07-1826; Manchester
JACKSON, Ann	22-02-1826; London	WILLSON, Mary	25-03-1826; Warwick
JACKSON, Margaret	17-07-1826; NR		
JACKSON, Susannah	10-04-1826; Lancaster	***Harmony* 1827**	
JAMES, Eliza	12-01-1826; London	BARTRIP, Susan	07-12-1826; Hertford
JOHNSON, Mary Ann	07-07-1826; Manchester	BIRCHLEY, Mary	16-10-1826; Worcester
		BLOXHAM, Rebecca	19-07-1826; Leicester
JONES, Selina	06-04-1826; Bristol	BODENHAM, Sarah	16-10-1826; Worcester
LUDLOW, Sarah	27-03-1826; Maidstone	BRENNETT*, Isabella	23-10-1826; Lancaster
MacKAY, Elizabeth	16-01-1826; Liverpool		
McKENZIE, Mary	10-04-1826; Liverpool	BROWN, Ann	21-12-1826; Surrey
McMAHON, Mary	19-02-1826; London	COFFIN, Sarah	28-08-1826; Southwark
MEAD, Eleanor	23-02-1826; Durham	DAVIES, Mary	18-08-1826; Pembroke
MORGAN, Elizabeth	12-02-1826; London	DAWSON, Charlotte	21-10-1826; Lincoln
MUSHENS, Sarah	23-02-1826; Durham	DOYLE, Mary Ann	19-10-1826; Nottingham
NICHOLLS, Eleanor	06-04-1826; London	DUDDELL, Mary	12-10-1826; Leicester
NICHOLLS, Elizabeth	06-04-1826; London	EDWARDS, Mary	01-08-1826; Maidstone
		ENTWISLE, Ann	16-08-1826; Lancaster
PARKER, Mary	10-01-1826; Exeter	GARDINER, Ann	16-10-1826; Warwick
PEARCE, Ann Sarah	22-02-1826; London	HICKSON, Sabina	20-10-1826; Stafford
PEARSON, Betty	07-03-1826; Lancaster	HINDLE, Mary	16-08-1826; Lancashire
PRIOR, Mary	12-01-1826; London	HUBBERT, Martha	23-10-1826; Linclon
PRITCHARD, Hannah	16-01-1826; Manchester	JONES, Elizabeth	03-08-1826; Gloucester
		KENSEY, Caroline	10-07-1826; Essex
PRITCHARD, Sarah	06-04-1826; Bristol	KNOTT, Mary Ann	19-12-1826; Surrey
REEVES, Maria	22-07-1826; Coventry	LOWE, Mary	13-10-1826; Lincoln
REGAN, Mary	20-02-1826; London	McDONALD, Esther	14-12-1826; Surrey
SEEWARD, Margaret	NR-07-1826; Exeter	McQUEEN, Mary	21-10-1826; Lincoln
		MILLS, Sarah	16-10-1826; Worcester
SHAW, Catherine	19-02-1826; London	MORAN, Mary	20-10-1826; Shrewsbury
SILK, Ann	25-07-1826; Warwick	OXLEY, Mary	21-12-1826; Southworth
SMITH, Isabella	28-03-1826; Maidstone	PARKER, Elizabeth	03-08-1826; Gloucester
SMITH, Mary	10-07-1826; Warwick	PARTRIDGE, Susan	03-08-1826; Gloucester

SIMPSON, Elizabeth	16-10-1826; Shrewsbury		ELLIS, Rachel	12-12-1826; London
TAYLOR, Elizabeth	21-12-1826; Surrey		FARRELL*, Janet	30-09-1826; Glasgow
THOMPSON, Mary	21-10-1826; Stafford		FLINN, Margaret	03-09-1826; Glasgow
WILLIAMS, Margaret	18-07-1826; Shrewsbury		FOX, Hannah	07-12-1826; London
WOODS, Jane	16-10-1826; Warwick		GILES, Mary Ann	07-12-1826; London
WOODS, Sarah	21-12-1826; Surrey		GRANT*, Helen	27-12-1826; Edinburgh
WOODWARD, Ann	19-07-1826; Leicester		GREEN, Eleanor	14-09-1826; London
WRIGHT, Naomi	10-07-1826; Essex		GREEN, Emma	12-12-1826; London

Louisa 1827

CAMERON*, Jean	30-10-1826; Glasgow
CARROLL, Ann	23-10-1826; Lancaster
GARNER, Ann	17-10-1826; Knutsford
HEYWOOD, Ann	17-10-1826; Knutsford
LOVELL, Sapy	13-07-1826; Bury
PEACOCK, Amelia	17-10-1826; Knutsford
ROBERTSON*, Sarah	21-09-1826; Stirling
TELFORD, Ann	23-10-1826; Lancaster
WILLIAMS, Sarah	03-04-1826; Bristol

Princess Charlotte 1827

ARMSTRONG, Catherine	14-09-1826; London
ATKINSON, Sarah	06-11-1826; Doncaster
BARNETT*, Euphemia	20-09-1826; Perth
BASSETT, Emma	07-12-1826; Middlesex
BLAKE, Ann	08-12-1826; Middlesex
BROWN, Elizabeth	26-10-1826; Middlesex
BROWNE, Mary	14-09-1826; London
BRUCE*, Rose	20-04-1826; Perth
CAMPBELL, Helen	25-04-1826; Aberdeen
CAMPBELL*, Mary	06-09-1826; Inverary
CANE, Julia	24-10-1826; London
CARTER, Elizabeth	14-09-1826; London
CHAMBERS, Sarah	14-09-1826; London
CONDON, Mary	14-09-1826; London
COSTELLO, Elizabeth	14-09-1826; London
COX, Mary	07-12-1826; London
DAVIS, Charlotte	23-10-1826; London
DAVIS, Mary	14-09-1826; London
DAVIS, Mary	28-10-1826; London
DESLEY*, Margaret	11-12-1826; Edinburgh
DOUGLASS*, Elizabeth	25-09-1826; Glasgow
EDWARDS, Eliza	14-09-1826; London
ELLIOTT*, Ann	06-11-1826; Edinburgh
HAMLEY*, Catherine	14-09-1826; London
HARRNETT*, Ellen	23-10-1826; London
HOPE, Jean	07-11-1826; Edinburgh
HUTCHINSON, Ann	22-07-1826; Dochairn
INGLIS*, Jean	27-12-1826; Edinburgh
JARVIS, Sarah	14-09-1826; London
JENKINS, Susannah	07-12-1826; London
JONES, Louisa	12-12-1826; London
KEEFE, Margret Mary	07-11-1826; Surry
KELLY, Anne	26-07-1826; Newcastle
KELLY, Catherine	07-12-1826; London
LAMOND*, Mary	25-09-1826; Glasgow
LAWSON*, Violett	18-12-1826; Edinburgh
LEWIS, Mary Ann	26-10-1826; London
LIPPARD, Mary	14-09-1826; London
LLOYD*, Elizabeth	24-03-1826; Caernarvon
LUNN, Mary Ann	07-12-1826; London
McDONALD, Sarah	06-08-1826; Newcastle
McGILP, Susan	27-12-1826; Edinburgh
MELSAM*, Susan	14-09-1826; London
MILL, Elizabeth	20-09-1826; Perth
MILLER, Elizabeth	20-09-1826; Perth
MORRIS, Sarah	26-10-1826; London
MULLAGHAN, Sarah	18-10-1826; Leeds
MURPHY, Catherine	14-09-1826; London
MURPHY, Hannah	14-09-1826; London
MURRAY*, Helen	16-09-1826; Aberdeen
NICHOLSON, Harriet	06-11-1826; Doncaster
PARMENTIER, Catherine	14-09-1826; London
PATRICK, Frances	26-10-1826; London
ROBERTSON, Margaret	30-09-1826; Glasgow
SCOTT, Mary	12-12-1826; London
SHIRRESS*, Margaret	16-09-1826; Aberdeen
SMITH, Eliza	07-12-1826; London
SMITH, Martha	14-09-1826; London

SMITH, Sarah	14-09-1826; London	HAMMOND, Susanna	13-02-1827; London
SMITH*, Elizabeth	28-10-1826; London	HARRIS, Mary	10-01-1827; Bristol
STREET, Eleanor	14-09-1826; London	HARRISON, Charlotte	13-01-1827; London
THORNTON, Elizabeth	28-10-1826; London	HUGHES, Mary	15-02-1827; London
URQUHART, Catherine	15-09-1826; Aberdeen	KANE, Margaret	15-02-1827; London
VAUGHAN*, Mary/Sarah	30-09-1826; Glasgow	KIRK, Isabella	18-01-1827; London
WALKER, Ellen	26-06-1826; London	LLOYD, Susannah	25-01-1827; Manchester
WALKER*, Mary	27-12-1826; Edinburgh	MacMAHON, Elizabeth	15-01-1827; Manchester
WARNER, Mary	14-09-1826; London	MARTIN, Mary	15-01-1827; Manchester
WESTWATER, Ann	11-12-1826; Edinburgh	MILLINGTON, Martha	06-01-1827; Maidstone
WILLIAMS, Charlotte	26-10-1826; London	MILLWOOD, Elizabeth	15-01-1827; Leicester
WILLSON, Eliza	28-10-1826; London	MUMBORD*, Mary	15-02-1827; London
WILLSON*, Elizabeth	25-09-1826; Glasgow	MURPHY, Margaret	17-02-1827; London
WILLSON*, Mary/Anne	24-10-1826; London	POLLARD, Ellen	10-01-1827; Preston
YEALEY, Sophi	12-12-1826; London	ROBERTS*, Eleanor	17-02-1827; London
		ROBINSON, Catherine	13-01-1827; London
1827 TRIAL YEAR		SMITH, Catherine	09-01-1827; Bristol
		SMITH, Elizabeth	15-03-1827; Nottingham
***Grenada* 1827**		SMITH, Mary	17-02-1827; London
CONROY, Ann	16-01-1827?; London	STROUD, Margaret	06-01-1827; Woolwich
		TROUTT, Sarah	08-01-1827; Wells
***Harmony* 1827**		UPCROFT, Sarah	24-03-1827; Norfolk
ADDISON, Elizabeth	NR-02-1827; London	WARHURST, Elizabeth	15-01-1827; Manchester
BALFOUR, Ann	15-01-1827; Berwick	WELSH, Mary Ann	15-01-1827; Manchester
BARRETT, Ellen	10-01-1827; Preston	WELSH, Rosanna	15-01-1827; Manchester
BENNETT, Ann	15-02-1827; London	WEST, Hannah	13-01-1827; London
BROWNE, Eliza	19-02-1827; London		
BRYANT, Hannah	08-01-1827; Bath	***Louisa* 1827**	
BUTTERWORTH, Ann	10-01-1827; Preston	ALLISON, Catherine	05-05-1827; Glasgow
CHAMBERLAIN, Sarah	16-02-1827; London	BARBER, Hannah	07-06-1827; London
		BARCLAY, Margaret	27-05-1827; Glasgow
COCKHEAD, Mary	13-01-1827; London	BETT*, Ann	25-04-1827; Glasgow
COLEMAN, Sophia	15-02-1827; London	BOWDEN, Catherine	16-07-1827; Lancaster
COLEY, Ann	03-01-1827; Lewes	BRETT, Jane	12-07-1827; London
COUNTER, Judith	04-01-1827; Salisbury	BRIERLY, Ruth	15-01-1827; Lancaster
DAVIES, Elizabeth	15-01-1827; Manchester	BROWN, Eliza	12-07-1827; London
ELLAM, Margaret	15-01-1827; Manchester	BROWN, Mary	01-06-1827; London
GOULDING, Margaret	19-02-1827; London	BROWN*, Sarah	12-07-1827; London
		BURKE, Hannah	12-07-1827; London
GRATTON, Ann	19-02-1827; London	CAMPBELL, Ann	28-04-1827; Stirling
HAGUE, Elizabeth	15-01-1827; Manchester	CHRISTMAS, Elizabeth	07-06-1827; London

422 List A-1

CLAYTON, Mary Ann	30-04-1827; Lancaster
DAVIS, Mary	24-03-1827; Bristol
DEANE, Eliza	12-07-1827; Hastings
DICKENSON*, Mary	12-07-1827; Hull
DRISCOL, Julia	01-06-1827; London
DRYNAN, Ellen	01-06-1827; London
DURRANT*, Ann	17-04-1827; Aberdeen
ELLIOTT, Mary	12-07-1827; London
FARISH, Alice	09-01-1827; Chester
FOX*, Hannah	12-07-1827; Montgomery
FRAZER, Maria	12-07-1827; London
GOLDIE*, Ann	07-05-1827; Glasgow
GRAHAM, Mary	12-07-1827; London
HARMAN, Elizabeth	01-06-1827; London
HARRISON, Esther	28-04-1827; Lincoln
HARROP, Mary Ann	09-07-1827; Chester
HIGGS, Caroline	24-04-1827; Bristol
HITCHENS, Lydia	09-07-1827; Chester
JOHNSON, Ann	14-04-1827; Chester
JONES, Mary	10-04-1827; Manchester
JUDD, Mary Ann	19-03-1827; Kent
KELLY*, Priscilla	20-04-1827; Ayr
KERR*, Isabella	05-03-1827; Edinburgh
KEVAN*, Mary	12-07-1827; London
LARTHER, Harriet	12-07-1827; Middlesex
LIVINGSTONE, Elizabeth	04-05-1827; Glasgow
LYONS, Catherine	12-07-1827; Middlesex
McALLISTER*, Rose	05-05-1827; Glasgow
McCAWLEY, Mary	12-07-1827; London
McCREA*, Mary	07-05-1827; Glasgow
McKIMMON, Sarah	05-05-1827; Glasgow
MANBY*, Ann	07-05-1827; Glasgow
MEAN, Mary Ann	23-03-1827; Cambridge
MILLER*, Mary	07-05-1827; Glasgow
MORIN, Mary	25-04-1827; Lancaster
MUIRHEAD, Mary	05-03-1827; Edinburgh
MURHENS, Jane	02-03-1827; Durham
MURPHY, Nancy	17-03-1827; Edinburgh
NANCE, Ann	25-03-1827; Cornwall
NEWMAN, Venus	07-06-1827; London
OLD, Mary Ann	30-04-1827; Lynn
OPENSHAW, Mary	10-03-1827; Lancaster
OYDEN, Esther	12-07-1827; Montgomery
PALLAN, Mary	20-04-1827; Ayr
PARKINS, Lucy	14-04-1827; Chester
PARRY, Margaret	09-07-1827; Chester
POPE, Avis	01-06-1827; London
RADFORD, Sarah	27-03-1827; Exeter
RAGAN, Norah	01-06-1827; London
RYAN, Margaret	07-06-1827; London
SHILLING, Eliza	05-07-1827; Surrey
SMITH, Ann	02-03-1827; Durham
SMITH, Jane	01-03-1827; Durham
SMITH, Jane	30-04-1827; Lancaster
SMITH, Lydia	24-04-1827; Bristol
SMITH, Martha	13-03-1827; Salisbury
THOMAS, Eliza	29-07-1827; Exeter
THOMPSON, Maria	09-07-1827; Cambridge
WILLIAMS, Ann	12-07-1827; Middlesex
WILLIAMS, Jane	27-04-1827; Kent
WILLIAMS*, Mary	30-04-1827; Lancaster
WRIGHT, Hannah	09-01-1827; Chester
YATES, Mary	30-04-1827; Lancaster
YELLOP, Ann	07-06-1827; Middlesex

***Princess Charlotte* 1827**

CLIFTON, Mary	10-01-1827; London
EDDISON, Mary	08-01-1827; Leeds
GORDON, Anne	10-01-1827; London
GRAYSON, Mary Ann	08-01-1827; Yorkshire
SUTTON, Clara	11-01-1827; London
WELDON, Jane	09-01-1827; Surrey

NO RESPONSE ON TRIAL YEAR

***Brothers* 1824**
WRAY*, Elizabeth	Penrith

***Canada* 1810**
CONNOR, Catherine	NR

***Friendship* 1818**
ROBERTSON, Elizabeth	NR

***Grenada* 1827**
CLARKE, Hannah	NR
COLLINTON, Harriet	NR
KIRKHAM, Olive	NR
OGBORN, Elizabeth	NR
WILLIAMSON*, Jane	NR

Kitty 1792
BOULTON, Bridget	Dublin
BURK, Rose	Dublin
CASSIDY, Mary	Dublin
DALY, Sarah	Dublin
DEMSEY, Martha	Dublin
EVANS, Catherine	Dublin
FITZPATRICK, Bridget	Dublin
HAGGERTY, Catherine	Dublin
HYLAND, Elizabeth	Dublin
JACKSON, Catherine	Dublin
McLEAN, Sarah?	Dublin
SHORT, Ann	Dublin
STROUD?, Charlotte	Dublin
WHITE, Rose	Dublin

Lady Juliana 1790
ANSTEY†, Mary Ann	Warwick
BARLOW*, Mary	Warwick
BAXTER, Susannah	Warwick
BOLTON*, Hannah	Warwick
BRAMMER*, Mary	Nottingham
CARTER, Mary	Berkshire
COOK, Elizabeth	Warwick
COTTLE, Mary	Somerset
COUSENS, Mary	Lincoln
CROSS*, Mary	Warwick
CUMBERLAND, Sarah	Nottingham
DAVIDSON, Mary	Northumberland
DOUGLAS, Elizabeth	Warwick
DRING, Ann	Nottingham
DRING, Sarah	Warwick
ELLIS, Jane	Liverpool
EMMANS, Elizabeth	Berkshire
FIDOE, Alice	Bristol
FIDOE, Elizabeth	Bristol
FIDOE, Jane Elizabeth	Bristol
GRIFFIN, Elizabeth	Devon
HARPER, Ann	Somerset
HILL, Ann	Gloucester
LAMMERMAN, Mary	Northumberland
MILLEDGE*, Susannah	Bristol
MOODY, Elizabeth	Bristol
NEWTON, Mary	Warwick
PEASLEY, Hannah	Somerset
PROUD, Martha	Warwick
RUSSELL, Mary	Warwick
SANEY*, Elizabeth	Bristol
SCOTT, Eleanor	Northumberland
SMITH, Hannah	Warwick
SMITH, Margaret	Liverpool
SMITH, Rebecca	Devon
STUBBS, Susannah	Warwickshire
TUFT, Mary	Warwick
VERRINER*, Sarah	Wiltshire
WARREN, Mary	Warwick
WHEELDEN, Jane	Derby
WILLOCK, Ann	Lincoln
YOUNG, Ann	Northumberland

Lady Penrhyn 1788
EATON, Martha	NR

Neptune 1790
ROBERTS, Jane	NR

Princess Charlotte 1827
COUTTS, Maria	NR

Prince of Wales 1788
BINGHAM*, Elizabeth	London
PIPKIN, Elizabeth	London

Royal Admiral 1792
ALLEN†, Margaret	Middlesex
CASE*†, Ann	Lancashire
HOLMES, Ann	NR
HYLAND, Elizabeth	NR
WOODHOUSE, Mary	Middlesex

A-2 *Aliases or Variant Names*

Surname, First Name(s) *ALIAS*	Ship
ABELL, Mary *TILLEY*	*Lady Penrhyn* 1788
ABRAHAMS, Esther *ABRAM*	*Prince of Wales* 1788
ALLEN, Mary *CONNER*	*Lady Penrhyn* 1788
ALLEN, Tasmin *BODDINGTON*	*Lady Penrhyn* 1788
ANSTEE, Elizabeth *ANSTEY*	*Sydney Cove* 1807
ANTONY, Mary *ANTON*	*Neptune* 1790
ANTROLRY, Hannah *ANTROBERY*	*Grenada* 1827
APPLETON, Jane *WAY, Mary*	*Nile* 1801
ARMSDEN, Ann *HARMSDEN*	*Lady Juliana* 1790
ATKINS, Sarah *SHEARMAN*	*Sydney Cove* 1807
BAKER, Lydia *GILBERT*	*Surprize* 1794
BAKER, Mary/Cath *McCAWLEY*	*Broxbornebury* 1814
BALDWIN, Ruth *BOWYER*	*Prince of Wales* 1788
BARKER, Ann *BAKER*	*Neptune* 1790
BARLOW, Mary *PARDOE*	*Lady Juliana* 1790
BARNES, Isabella *RANKELION*	*Alexander* 1806
BARNES, Susannah *LEE, Hannah*	*William Pitt* 1806
BARNETT, Euphemia *BUCHANAN*	*Princess Charlotte* 1827
BARNETT, Fanny/Ann *RIBB*	*Speke* 1808
BARRY, Ann *BERRY*	*Lady Juliana* 1790
BAXTER, Sarah *BRICKELL*	*Experiment* 1804
BAXTER, Margaret *REEKIE*	*Northampton* 1815
BAYLEY, Sarah *BAILEY*	*Surprize* 1794
BEARDSLEY, Ann *BAIZLEY*	*Friendship* 1788
BELL, Hannah *TOMLINSON*	*Providence* 1822
BENTLEY, Maria/Hannah *SMITH*	*Speke* 1808
BERRIDGE, Ann *BURRIDGE*	*Northampton* 1815
BERRIDGE, Eleanor *BURRIDGE*	*Northampton* 1815
BEST, Elizabeth *McVALY*	*Mary Anne* 1822
BEST, Sarah *CATAPODI*	*Britannia* 1798

Surname, First Name(s) *ALIAS*	Ship	Surname, First Name(s) *ALIAS*	Ship
BETT, Ann		BRITT, Elizabeth	
FARRELL	Louisa 1827	*BRETT/MOODY*	Northampton 1815
BILLINGS, Ann	Lord Sidmouth	BROADFIELD, Sarah	
PRINCE/DAVIS	1823	*GILLINGHAM*	Northampton 1815
BINGHAM, Elizabeth	Prince of Wales	BROWN, Sarah	
MOORING	1788	*WILSON*	Britannia 1798
BIRKS, Emma		BROWN, Sarah	
VERNON	Nile 1801	*FLOWERS*	Louisa 1827
BISCOE, Catherine		BROWNE, Kezzia	
BRISCOE	Indispensable 1796	*BROWN, Kezia*	Neptune 1790
BLANCHETT, Susan/		BRUCE, Rose	Princess Charlotte
Susannnah	Prince of Wales	*McKENZIE*	1827
BLANCHARD	1788	BUCKLE, Mary	
BOLLARD, Susanna	Royal Admiral	*OLLEY*	Speke 1808
BALLARD	1792	BUNN, Margaret	
BOLTON, Hannah		*BOURN*	Lady Penrhyn 1788
MOORE	Lady Juliana 1790	BURDS, Sarah	
BOLTON, Mary		*BURDO/PURDUE*	Lady Penrhyn 1788
BOULTON	Grenada 1825	BURGESS, Sarah	
BONE, Ann		*JONES*	Indispensable 1809
SMITH	Lady Juliana 1790	BURKITT, Mary	
BONG, Sarah		*BURKETT, Martha*	Lady Penrhyn 1788
BOND/BONO	Bellona 1793	BURRELL, Elizabeth	
BOOTLESTON, Sarah		*LEVESTON*	Friendship 1818
BEETLESON	Glatton 1803	BURROWS, Alice	
BOULTON, Mary		*BOROUGHS*	Indispensable 1796
BOLTON	Lady Penrhyn 1788	BURT(ALL), Sarah	Royal Admiral
BRADLY, Betty		*PHILLIPS, Jenny*	1792
BRADLEY	Neptune 1790	BUTLER, Alice	
BRAMMER, Mary		*RUSSELL*	Lord Melville 1817
BRAMWELL	Lady Juliana 1790		
BRAND, Lucy		CACUTT, Ann	
WOOD	Lady Penrhyn 1788	*CALCUT*	Neptune 1790
BRANDHAM, Mary		CALLAHAN, Margaret	
BRA(E)NHAM	Lady Penrhyn 1788	*CALLAGHAN*	Neptune 1790
BRAUND, Mary		CALLOW, Mary	
BRAND	Charlotte 1788	*CARLOW*	Mary 1823
BRAY, Susannah		CAMERON, Jean	
GAY	Neptune 1790	*BROWN*	Louisa 1827
BRENNETT, Isabella		CAMPBELL, Mary	Princess Charlotte
BRENNAN	Harmony 1827	*McDONALD*	1827
BRIANT, Mary		CARMAN, Elizabeth	
BRIAN	Britannia 1798	*CANNAN*	Brothers 1824
BRIMBLE, Mary		CARROL, Mary	
TAYLOR	Glatton 1803	*MITCHELL*	Aeolus 1809

Surname, First Name(s) *ALIAS*	Ship	Surname, First Name(s) *ALIAS*	Ship
CARTER, Mary *McCARTY*	Surprize 1794	COOKSEY, Mary *JONES/BURNE*	Neptune 1790
CARTY, Bridget *McCARTY*	Mary Ann 1791	COOL, Susan *COOT*	Mary Ann 1791
CARTY, Nelly *BARRETT*	Sydney Cove 1807	COOPER, Mary *CHAPMAN*	Britannia 1798
CASE, Ann *KEYS*	Royal Admiral 1792	CORBET, Sarah *CORBIE*	Indispensable 1796
CATTIN, Elizabeth *CATTELL*	Mary Anne 1822	CORDELL, Mary *CORDELLE*	Britannia 1798
CAUSER, Matilda *CAWSAR*	Maria 1818	COURSER, Georgiana *BARRINGTON*	Speke 1808
CAVER, Ann *CAVERON*	Surprize 1794	COURTNEY, Susan/ Elizabeth *JONES*	Grenada 1825
CAWTHORN, Mary *CRAWTHORNE*	Britannia 1798	COWCHER, Mary *CHRISTMAS*	Lady Juliana 1790
CEFENDER, Jane *SERGISSON*	Brothers 1824	CRABTREE, Elizabeth *MADDOCKS*	Grenada 1825
CETTY, Elizabeth *KEWER*	Britannia 1798	CRAMPTON, Hannah *HAMMOND*	Friendship 1818
CHAPLIN, Ann *CHAPLAIN*	Indispensable 1796	CRASTON, Sarah *CURTON*	Northampton 1815
CHEESEMAN, Mary *CHEESEHAM*	Indispensable 1796	CRAWFORD, Mary *WRIGHT*	Maria 1818
CHEETHAM, Ann *ELKIN*	Britannia 1798	CREW, Esther *JONES*	Providence 1822
CHIPPENHAM, Rebecca *CHIPPERHAM*	Neptune 1790	CROSS, Mary *DAVIDSON*	Lady Juliana 1790
CLARKE, Catharine *PITT*	Grenada 1827	CRUX, Jane *CREEK*	Lady Penrhyn 1788
CLEAVER, Mary *CLEVER*	Charlotte 1788	CUMSON, Elizabeth *MIDDLETON, Mary/ SIM, Sarah*	Minstrel 1812
COCK, Ann *CORK*	Sydney Cove 1807		
COLEMAN, Norah *KEELMAN*	Experiment 1804	DALTON, Elizabeth *BURLEY*	Lady Penrhyn 1788
COLLEN, Elizabeth *COLLEY*	Lady Penrhyn 1788	DALY, Ann *WARBURTON*	Prince of Wales 1788
COLLINS, Harriet *HILL*	Lord Melville 1817	DANIEL, Martha *DAVID*	Experiment 1804
COLPITTS, Ann *COLEPITS*	Lady Penrhyn 1788	DANNET, Jane/Ann *WILLIAMS*	Broxbornebury 1814
CONNOR, Catherine *BURKE*	Minstrel 1812	DARKE, Sarah *DRAKE*	Indispensable 1796
COOK, Charlotte *COOKE*	Lady Penrhyn 1788	DAVID, Mary *PHILIP*	Indispensable 1809

List A-2

Surname, First Name(s) *ALIAS*	Ship
DAVIDSON, Rebecca *DAVISON*	Lady Penrhyn 1788
DAVIES, Mary *DAVIS*	Lady Penrhyn 1788
DAVIES, Sarah *DAVIS/ASHLEY*	Lady Penrhyn 1788
DAVIS, Mary *HAINES*	Surprize 1794
DAVIS, Mary Ann *SALE*	Minstrel 1812
DAWSON, Mary *BRAY*	Lady Juliana 1790
DEAN, Elizabeth *DEANE*	Lady Juliana 1790
DESLEY, Margaret *DUGGAN*	Princess Charlotte 1827
DESMONT, Mary *DISMON*	Neptune 1790
DEWSE, Catherine *MUNNINGS*	Minstrel 1812
DICKENSON, Mary *DIXON*	Louisa 1827
DICKINS, Ann *DIGGINS*	Lord Wellington 1820
DILLING, Eliza *DILLON/HORGAN*	Morley 1820
DOBSON, Esther *FERNANDEZ*	Northampton 1815
DODD(S), Hannah *FORSTER*	Lord Melville 1817
DONNE(A)LLY, Sarah *WELCH*	Mary Ann 1791
DOUGLASS, Elizabeth *HASSAM*	Princess Charlotte 1827
DRAPER, Sarah/Ann *INGRAM/WATSON*	Britannia 1798
DUDGENS, Elizabeth *DUDGEON*	Friendship 1788
DUFFEY, Mary *GRAYLEY*	Aeolus 1809
DUNCAN, Jane *ROBINSON*	Indispensable 1796
DUNN, Judith *THOMPSON*	Broxbornebury 1814
DUNNING, Sarah *DUNHILL*	Lord Wellington 1820

Surname, First Name(s) *ALIAS*	Ship
DURANT, Elizabeth *WILLIAMS*	Friends 1811
DURRANT, Ann *BROWN*	Louisa 1827
DYKES, Mary *DICKS*	Lady Penrhyn 1788
EARLY, Rachel *HARLEY*	Friendship 1788
EATON, Mary *SHEPHERD/SHEPHARD*	Charlotte 1788
EGINTON, Mary *EGERTON*	Friendship 1818
ELDRIDGE, Sarah *ALDRIDGE*	Indispensable 1796
ELLIOTT, Ann *ALEXANDER*	Princess Charlotte 1827
ELLIS, Mary *CONNOLLEY*	Experiment 1804
ELRIDGE, Elizabeth *EVRIDGE*	Speke 1808
EMMES, Ann *HEMS/J'AMMS*	Lady Juliana 1790
EUDEN, Rosannah *HUDEN*	Friendship 1818
EVANS, Ann/Nancy *WATTERS*	Friends 1811
EVANS, Elizabeth *JONES*	Lady Penrhyn 1788
EVERITT, Ann *EVERED*	Lady Juliana 1790
FALKERD, Jane *FALKARD*	Wanstead 1814
FARRELL, Janet *DOHERTY, Rose*	Princess Charlotte 1827
FERGUSON, Frances *GROSVENOR/FOX*	Britannia 1798
FERGUSON, Esther *CHERRY*	Northampton 1815
FIDLER, Diana *SCHULTZ*	Minstrel 1812
FINDALL, Hannah *TINDALL*	Surprize 1794
FITZGERALD, Jane *PHILLIPS*	Charlotte 1788

428 List A-2

Surname, First Name(s) *ALIAS*	Ship
FLANNEGAN, Mary *FLANAGAN*	*Lady Juliana* 1790
FOSTER, Jane *FORSTER*	*Maria* 1818
FOWLES, Mary *FOULES*	*Surprize* 1794
FOX, Hannah *DAINTY*	*Louisa* 1827
FRASER, Ellen *REDCHESTER*	*Charlotte* 1788
FRISBY, Elizabeth *CLITHERO*	*Lord Wellington* 1820
FROST, Sarah *WALKERALS*	*Albemarle* 1791
FRYER, Catherine *PRIOR*	*Charlotte* 1788
FUDGE, Priscilla *WILLIAMS, Elizabeth*	*Royal Admiral* 1792
GABEL, Mary *GAMBOLL*	*Lady Penrhyn* 1788
GAGE, Susan *NOON*	*Friends* 1811
GARDNER, Lydia *GARDENER*	*Brothers* 1824
GARTH, Susanah *GOUGHT/GRATH*	*Friendship* 1788
GARVA, Harriet *GARVEY*	*Friendship* 1818
GASCOIGNE, Olive/Olivia *GASCOIN*	*Lady Penrhyn* 1788
GEE, Hannah *TEASDALE/TEESDALE*	*Lady Juliana* 1790
GIBBS, Elizabeth *BIGNALL*	*Nile* 1801
GIBSON, Hannah *FENWICK/FRANKLIN*	*William Pitt* 1806
GILL, Elizabeth *FANE*	*Speke* 1808
GITTENS, Sarah *GITTINS*	*Mary Ann* 1791
GLOSSOP, Ann *GLASSOP*	*Pitt* 1792
GOLDIE, Ann *HUGHES*	*Louisa* 1827

Surname, First Name(s) *ALIAS*	Ship
GRAHAM, Mary *FRASER*	*Princess Charlotte* 1827
GRANT, Ann *RUTHERFORD*	*Lord Wellington* 1820
GRANT, Helen *HUGHES*	*Princess Charlotte* 1827
GRANVILLE, Catherine *GLENFIELD*	*Northampton* 1815
GRAY, Mary *CARNEY*	*Northampton* 1815
GRECIAN, Mary Ann *GREGSON*	*Bellona* 1793
GREEN, Ann *COWLEY/COWLY*	*Lady Penrhyn* 1788
GREEN, Sarah *CLAYTON*	*Minstrel* 1812
GREENLEES, Janet *WILSON*	*Midas* 1825
GREENROD, Mary *GREENWOOD*	*Northampton* 1815
GRIFFIN, Sarah *GRIFFINS*	*Friendship* 1818
HADDOCK, Mary *BURROWS, James*	*Royal Admiral* 1792
HALL, Elizabeth *ALLEN*	*Friends* 1811
HALL, Sarah *HAMMOND*	*Lady Penrhyn* 1788
HALLARD, Ann *BROWN*	*Mary Anne* 1816
HAMILTON, Catherine *HAMBLETON*	*William Pitt* 1806
HAMLEY, Catherine *HARNLEY*	*Princess Charlotte* 1827
HANDLAND, Dorothy *HANDLYN/GREY*	*Lady Penrhyn* 1788
HANDYMAN, Ann *HARDIAMAN*	*Lady Juliana* 1790
HARDY, Esther Jane *HARDING*	*Bellona* 1793
HARDY, Sarah *SULLIVAN*	*Lord Melville* 1817
HARLOW, Sarah *ARLOW*	*Wanstead* 1814
HARRISON, Jane *JONES*	*Morley* 1820

Surname, First Name(s) *ALIAS*	Ship	Surname, First Name(s) *ALIAS*	Ship
HARRNETT, Ellen *HARMETT*	*Princess Charlotte* 1827	HORRS, Ellen *STORRS*	*Nile* 1801
HARVEY, Elizabeth *HERVEY/HARVY*	*Friendship* 1788	HORRS, Mary *STORRS*	*Glatton* 1803
HARWOOD, Esther *HOWARD*	*Lady Penrhyn* 1788	HOTCHKISS, Jane *HOTCHKIN*	*Speke* 1808
HASLEN, Sarah *HASLER*	*Nile* 1801	HOW, Mary *HOWEL/HOWET*	*Nile* 1801
HATESBY, Mary *KATESBY*	*Earl Cornwallis* 1801	HUFNELL, Susan *HUFNALL*	*Lady Penrhyn* 1788
HAYNES, Ann *FOSS*	*William Pitt* 1806	HUGHES, Anne *ROBERTS*	*Indispensable* 1796
HAYWARD, Elizabeth *HAWARD*	*Lady Penrhyn* 1788	HUMPHRIES, Mary *HUMPHREYS*	*Lady Penrhyn* 1788
HAYWARD, Hannah *HEYWOOD*	*Glatton* 1803	HUNT, Sarah *AUTT*	*Britannia* 1798
HEARD, Mary *DAVIS*	*Morley* 1820	HUR(L)STON, Mary *PAYNE*	*Wanstead* 1814
HEATOCK, Ellen *EATOUGH*	*Grenada* 1825	HUTCHELL, Jane *LIAS*	*Northampton* 1815
HENDERSON, Elizabeth *ANDERSON*	*Lady Juliana* 1790	HUTCHINS, Hannah *HUTCHINGS*	*Brothers* 1824
HERBERT, Jane/Rose *RUSSELL, Jenny*	*Prince of Wales* 1788	HUTCHINS, Mary *HUTCHENS*	*Wanstead* 1814
HIDE, Mary *BLUNN, Sarah*	*Britannia* 1798	HUTTEN, Margaret *BRUCE*	*Mary Anne* 1816
HIGGINS, Jane *HUGGINS*	*Surprize* 1794	INGLIS, Jane/Janet *KIDD/ALLAN*	*Northampton* 1815
HIGGINS, Mary *HARROLD*	*Lady Juliana* 1790	INGLIS, Jean *MARSHALL*	*Princess Charlotte* 1827
HODGES, Mary/ Susannah *ROBINSON*	*Britannia* 1798	INGLIS, Margaret/Cath *WILSON*	*Northampton* 1815
HODGES, Rebecca *HODGETTS*	*Lord Wellington* 1820	IVEMAY, Elizabeth *IVENAY*	*Lady Juliana* 1790
HOLMES, Susannah *HOLMS*	*Friendship* 1788	JACKSON, Jane/Mary *ROBERTS, Esther*	*Lady Penrhyn* 1788
HOLMSLEY, Mary *HELMSLEY*	*Glatton* 1803	JACKWAY, Martha *JACKAWAY*	*Wanstead* 1814
HOLTON, Ann *PLAYFAIR*	*Aeolus* 1809	JAMES, Sophia *JONES*	*Experiment* 1804
HOLWARD, Ann *HALWARD*	*Sydney Cove* 1807	JARVIS, Mary *NIMMO/LAMB*	*Mary* 1823
HOOTON, Jane *HOOTEN*	*Royal Admiral* 1792	JENKIN, Mary *JENKINS*	*Royal Admiral* 1792
HORN, Harriot Arin *HOLMES*	*Broxbornebury* 1814		

Surname, First Name(s) *ALIAS*	Ship	Surname, First Name(s) *ALIAS*	Ship
JOBBER, Sarah *JONES*	Glatton 1803	LEPPARD, Charlotte *LEOPARD*	Grenada 1825
JOHN, Mary *ST.JOHN*	Morley 1820	LETTERMAN, Catherine *LATTIMORE*	Wanstead 1814
JOHNSON, Elizabeth *LEE*	Lady Juliana 1790	LEVERTON, Mary *LEWISPON*	Wanstead 1814
JONES, Ann Elizabeth *PARRY*	Wanstead 1814	LEVI, Amelia *LEVY*	Lady Penrhyn 1788
JONES, Elizabeth *EVANS*	Earl Cornwallis 1801	LINSLEY, Elizabeth *LINDEY*	Neptune 1790
JONES, Jane *LINBECK*	Providence 1822	LITHERBY, Elizabeth *STRATTON*	Neptune 1790
KARRAIN, Eleanor *KERVEIN*	Lady Juliana 1790	LLOYD, Elizabeth *OWEN*	Princess Charlotte 1827
KEARNON, Elizabeth *PRICE*	Lady Juliana 1790	LOCK, Agnes *LOCKE*	Glatton 1803
KELLY, Priscilla *WEYMESS*	Louisa 1827	LOVELL, Rosie *LOVETT*	Speke 1808
KENEDY, Martha *KENNEDY*	Prince of Wales 1788	LOVERIDGE, Mary *HORNSBY*	Royal Admiral 1792
KERR, Isabella *GREGG/KEER*	Louisa 1827	LUDDAM, Ann *LEARDHAM*	Wanstead 1814
KEVAN, Mary *McAULIFFE*	Louisa 1827	LUMMES, Ann *LOMAS*	Broxbornebury 1814
KIMES, Mary *POTTEN*	Lady Juliana 1790	LUSBY, Caroline *COULBECK*	Lord Melville 1817
KINGSTON, Hannah *BAKER/MOSS*	Friends 1811	LUSCOMB, Mary *MILLER*	Mary Anne 1816
KINNESLEY, Sarah *KINNERSLEY*	Nile 1801	LYNCH, Alice *DAVIS*	Neptune 1790
KIRTON, Elizabeth *WALKER*	Nile 1801	McALLISTER, Rose *CAMPBELL*	Louisa 1827
LAMOND, Mary *LAMONT*	Princess Charlotte 1827	McCABE, Eleanor *McCAVE*	Lady Penrhyn 1788
LANG, Jean (Junior) *MORRISON*	Friendship 1818	McCANN, Sarah *LLOYD/BEVAN*	Britannia 1798
LANGFORD, Sophia *LAWFORD*	Surprize 1794	McCARTHY, Mary *MACARDING*	Broxbornebury 1814
LAURENCE, Esther *LAWRENCE*	Nile 1801	McCORMACK, Mary *McCORMICK*	Friendship 1788
LAWSON, Violett *McKAY*	Princess Charlotte 1827	McCORMICK, Sarah *CORNWALL*	Friendship 1788
LEA, Sarah *LEE*	Alexander 1806	McCREA, Mary *SHANKS*	Louisa 1827
		MacDONALD, Jean/Jane *PEDAN/DUNLOP*	Friendship 1818

Surname, First Name(s) *ALIAS*	Ship	Surname, First Name(s) *ALIAS*	Ship
McENTIRE, Eleanor *McINTIRE*	Earl Cornwallis 1801	MOEN, Mary *MOON*	Friendship 1818
McGILVRAY, Isabella *RHIND*	Mary Anne 1822	MORGAN, Margaret *JONES, Mary*	Lady Juliana 1790
McGAVIN, Mary *NICOL*	Northampton 1815	MORRIS, Susanna *NORRIS*	Minstrel 1812
MACK, Katherine *DALTON*	Northampton 1815	MULLENDEN, Mary *MULLENDON*	Lady Juliana 1790
McKAY, Catherine *SUTHERLAND*	Friends 1811	MULLENS, Hannah *MULLINS*	Lady Penrhyn 1788
McLEOD, Catherine *BAIRD*	Sydney Cove 1807	MULLOY, Jane *MALLOY*	Neptune 1790
McMAHON, Mary *JOHNSON*	Mary Anne 1816	MUMBORD, Mary *McGRATH*	Harmony 1827
MADDOCKS, Grace *MADDOX*	Lady Juliana 1790	MURPHY, Margaret *CRAWFORD*	Sydney Cove 1807
MANBY, Ann *WABES*	Louisa 1827	MURRALL, Mary *MURRELL*	Experiment 1804
MANSON, Isabella *SMITH*	Lady Juliana 1790	MURRAY, Betty/ Elizabeth *BAILLIE*	Aeolus 1809
MASON, Margaret *MOORE*	Experiment 1804	MURRAY, Helen *LAMB*	Princess Charlotte 1827
MASON, Susannah *GIBBS*	Prince of Wales 1788		
MASSEY, Betty *MERSEY*	Neptune 1790	NAIRN, Susannah *NAON/TALBOT*	Kitty 1792
MATHER, Mary *MARTIN*	Prince of Wales 1788	NATCHELL, Sarah *MITCHELL*	Lady Juliana 1790
MATTHEWS, Elizabeth *HARTLEY*	Lord Melville 1817	NEAL, Mary/Betty *ASKINS*	Sydney Cove 1807
MAYFIELD, Mary *TRAVIS*	Canada 1810	NEAVETT, Elizabeth/ Mary *BARBER*	Northampton 1815
MELSAM, Susan *WILSON*	Princess Charlotte 1827	NEWTON, Sarah *GOWER*	Surprize 1794
MEREDITH, Elizabeth *HARE*	Experiment 1804	NOWLAND, Mary Ann *KNOWLAND*	Lord Wellington 1820
MESSER, Elizabeth *MERCER*	Midas 1825		
MILLEDGE, Susannah *MILLER*	Lady Juliana 1790	O'HARA, Mary *QUIGLEY*	Lord Melville 1817
MILLER, Mary *HOLMES*	Louisa 1827	ORTON, Sarah *HORTON*	Lord Wellington 1820
MILLS, Jane *GROVES*	Minstrel 1812	OSBORNE, Catherine *OSBORN*	Friendship 1818
MITCHENOR, Mary *MITCHINER*	Glatton 1803	OSBORNE, Elizabeth *JONES*	Lady Penrhyn 1788

Surname, First Name(s) *ALIAS*	Ship	Surname, First Name(s) *ALIAS*	Ship
OSMOND, Caroline		PULSON, Sarah	
HORNSBY/WATSON	*Mary Anne* 1816	*POULSON*	*Bellona* 1793
OWSTON, Ann			
HOUSTON	*Lady Juliana* 1790	QUAIL, Elizabeth	
		QUAYLE	*Wanstead* 1814
PARKER, Ann		QUAYLE, Jane	
WILLCOCKS	*Sydney Cove* 1807	*COWELL*	*Mary* 1823
PARKISON, Jane Ann			
PARK(IN)ENSON/		RAFTRY, Jane	
PARTINGTON/		*HOLDEN*	*Speke* 1808
MARSDEN, Anne	*Friendship* 1788	REID, Helen	
PARRY, Elizabeth		*DUNCAN*	*Lord Melville* 1817
PERRY	*Lady Juliana* 1790	ROACH, Catherine	
PARTRIDGE, Sarah		*MURPHY*	*Minstrel* 1812
ROBERTS	*Lady Penrhyn* 1788	ROBERTS, Eleanor	
PATTERSON, Charlotte		*ROBINSON*	*Harmony* 1827
SCOTT	*Wanstead* 1814	ROBERTSON, Catherine	*Lord Wellington*
PEARCE, Ann		*DUDGEON*	1820
SMITH/JORDAN	*Sydney Cove* 1807	ROBERTSON, Elizabeth	
PEARCE, Charlotte	*Broxbornebury*	*ROBINSON*	*Northampton* 1815
HOPKINS	1814	ROBERTSON, Katharine	
PENDEGRASS, Bridget		*STEWART*	*Sydney Cove* 1807
SMITH, Betty	*Friends* 1811	ROBERTSON, Sarah	
PERCY, Ann		*ANDERSON*	*Louisa* 1827
CURETON	*William Pitt* 1806	ROBINSON, Catherine	
PHILLIPS, Susannah	*Lord Wellington*	*SIVINBURN*	*Midas* 1825
VEAL	1820	ROLFE, Jemima	
PHYN, Mary		*WEBB, Mary*	*Surprize* 1794
FINN	*Lady Penrhyn* 1788	ROSSON, Isabella	
PIMBLOTT, Mary		*LAWSON*	*Lady Penrhyn* 1788
COLLINS	*Mary Anne* 1822	ROY, Ann Judith	
PINK, Ann		*TAYLOR*	*Indispensable* 1796
SIMPSON	*Maria* 1818	RUDGE, Prudence	
PORTER, Sarah		*BROWN*	*Morley* 1820
HURSTON	*Sydney Cove* 1807	RUMBOLD, Sarah	
POTTER, Elizabeth/Anne		*RUMBLE*	*William Pitt* 1806
WILSON	*Wanstead* 1814	RYAN, Margaret	
POTTER, Janet		*DUNN*	*Nile* 1801
SMITH	*Providence* 1822		
POWLEY, Elizabeth		SADLER, Esther	
PULLY	*Friendship* 1788	*BARTON*	*Lord Melville* 1817
PRICE, Ann		SAGUS, Elizabeth	
REEVES	*William Pitt* 1806	*MITCHELL*	*Nile* 1801
PRICE, Sarah		SANDERS, Jane	
PEARCE	*Nile* 1801	*NORRIS*	*Lady Juliana* 1790
PRICHARD, Mary		SANDLIN(E), Ann	
RICHARDS	*Glatton* 1803	*PATTENS/BRETTON*	*Lady Penrhyn* 1788

Surname, First Name(s) *ALIAS*	Ship	Surname, First Name(s) *ALIAS*	Ship
SANEY, Elizabeth *SENEY*	Lady Juliana 1790	SMITH, Mary *MACKLIN*	Pitt 1792
SARJENT, Mary *SARJANT*	Glatton 1803	SMITH, Mary *WARNER*	Britannia 1798
SCOTT, Mary *McPHILAMY*	Lord Melville 1817	SMITH, Sarah *CLARKE*	Grenada 1827
SEWARD, Ann Jemima *STEWARD*	Morley 1820	SMITH, Susan *CROW/WITTON*	Wanstead 1814
SHEERING, Mary *METCALF*	Aeolus 1809	SOUTH, Ann *ARCHER*	Speedy 1800
SHEIN, Ann *SHEINEY*	William Pitt 1806	STAGG, Ann *WOODWARD*	William Pitt 1806
SHIRRESS, Margaret *SHIRIFFS*	Princess Charlotte 1827	STANLEY, Charlotte *MILLER*	Mary Anne 1816
SHURWEL, Elizabeth *SHERWEL*	Northampton 1815	STEWARD, Elizabeth *COMPSON*	Mary Ann 1791
SHURWEL, Sarah *SHERWEL*	Northampton 1815	STEWART, Rosa *LOWDEN*	Mary Anne 1816
SIMMONS, Ann *SIMMONDS*	Surprize 1794	STONE, Margaret *BURGESS*	Broxbornebury 1814
SIMPSON, Charlotte *HALL*	Lady Juliana 1790	STRACHAN, Isabel *BURNET*	Morley 1820
SLATER, Sarah *MORGAN*	Alexander 1806	STURDY, Louisa *HURDY*	Surprize 1794
SLY, Elizabeth *REDFORD*	Earl Cornwallis 1801	TERRIER, Catherine *STEWART*	Lord Wellington 1820
SMITH, Ann *WARDLE*	Broxbornebury 1814	THACKERY, Elizabeth *THACKEY*	Friendship 1788
SMITH, Elizabeth *BELCHER*	Speke 1808	THOMAS, Mary *RAY*	Glatton 1803
SMITH, Elizabeth *BELLATT*	Princess Charlotte 1827	THOMPSON, Ann *ATKINS, Catherine*	William Pitt 1806
SMITH, Elizabeth *CARR*	Lady Juliana 1790	THOMPSON, Ann *BRUCE*	Britannia 1798
SMITH, Elizabeth *FUE/FREE*	Lady Juliana 1790	THOMPSON, Jane Bell *BAILEY*	Indispensable 1796
SMITH, Elizabeth *MITCHINSON*	William Pitt 1806	THOMPSON, Sarah *McFIE*	Britannia 1798
SMITH, Margaret *MILLER*	Wanstead 1814	THOMSON, Elizabeth *THOMPSON*	Lady Juliana 1790
SMITH, Maria Ann *JOHNSON, Ann*	Midas 1825	THOMSON, Mary *THOMPSON*	Grenada 1825
SMITH, Mary *CRAWFORD/MADDEN*	Broxbornebury 1814	THORN, Sarah *THORNTON*	Broxbornebury 1814
SMITH, Mary *HALL*	Nile 1801	TINNY, Susan *TILLY*	Lord Melville 1817

Surname, First Name(s) *ALIAS*	Ship	Surname, First Name(s) *ALIAS*	Ship
TOWNS, Martha *METCALF, Betty*	Lord Melville 1817	WHEELER, Ann *WHELLER*	Lady Juliana 1790
TROEMANATS, Emma *TRUEMAN*	Grenada 1827	WHITEBREAD, Sarah *GRIFFITHS*	Nile 1801
TRUEMAN, Sarah *FREEMAN*	Morley 1820	WHITELY, Hannah *WILKINSON*	Lord Melville 1817
TURNER, Ann *AKERS*	Northampton 1815	WHITTINGTON, Elizabeth *WHITTINGHAM*	Midas 1825
TURNER, Mary *WILKES*	Lady Penrhyn 1788	WIGGINS, Jane *YOUNG*	Surprize 1794
TWY(I)FIELD, Ann *DAWLEY/DAWLY*	Lady Penrhyn 1788	WILD, Betty *WYLDE*	Maria 1818
UNDERHILL, Mary *UNDREL*	Speedy 1800	WILLIAMS, Ann *Harkett*	Northampton 1815
VARLOW, Margaret *BURFES*	Midas 1825	WILLIAMS, Jane *VICARS*	Lady Juliana 1790
VAUGHAN, Mary/Sarah *WATSON/DEVLIN*	Princess Charlotte 1827	WILLIAMS, Mary *HALKS*	Louisa 1827
VERRINER, Sarah *VERRINDER*	Lady Juliana 1790	WILLIAMS, Mary *JONES*	Britannia 1798
WADE, Mary *COCKLANE/COCKRAN*	Lady Penrhyn 1788	WILLIAMS, Mary *JONES*	Earl Cornwallis 1801
WAINWRIGHT, Ellen *ECCLES, Esther*	Prince of Wales 1788	WILLIAMS, Sarah/Elizabeth *ELLIOTT*	Brothers 1824
WALKER, Elizabeth *ALLEN*	Royal Admiral 1792	WILLIAMSON, Jane *COWEN*	Grenada 1827
WALKER, Mary *McNULTY*	Princess Charlotte 1827	WILLS, Elizabeth *WELLS*	Earl Cornwallis 1801
WARBURTON, Hannah *WALTON*	Bellona 1793	WILLSON, Elizabeth *WHITTINGTON*	Princess Charlotte 1827
WARD, Ann/Hannah *FOSTER*	Northampton 1815	WILLSON, Mary/Anne *PIPE*	Princess Charlotte 1827
WATKINS, Mary *WATKINGS*	Friendship 1788	WILMOT, Elizabeth *WILMOTT*	Wanstead 1814
WATSON, Elizabeth *DAVIS*	Lady Juliana 1790	WILSON, Agnes *LAWRIE*	Sydney Cove 1807
WELCH, Hannah *WELSCH*	Grenada 1825	WILSON, Ann/Hannah *ASKER/ASKEW*	Brothers 1824
WELCH, Mary *MURPHY*	Nile 1801	WILSON, Bridget *JACKSON*	Canada 1810
WELCH, Mary Ann *RIX*	Friends 1811	WILSON, Frances *MILLER/MILNER*	Friendship 1818
WELSH, Mary *SIMPSON*	Mary Ann 1791	WILSON, Jane *SCALAN*	Surprize 1794

Surname, First Name(s) *ALIAS*	Ship	Surname, First Name(s) *ALIAS*	Ship
WILSON, Jean *BROWN*	*Morley* 1820	WOOTTON, Ann *WOOTTEN*	*Nile* 1801
WILSON, Jemima *WASTER*	*Mary Ann* 1791	WORTHINGTON, Agnes/Nancy *WITHERINGTON*	*Lord Melville* 1817
WILSON, Margaret *WILLSON*	*Royal Admiral* 1792	WRAY, Elizabeth *WREAY*	*Brothers* 1824
WILSON, Mary *WHITE*	*William Pitt* 1806	WRIGHT, Sarah *SQUIRE*	*Britannia* 1798
WINGFIELD, Jane *WOOD*	*Providence* 1822		
WOOD, Jane *GRAHAM*	*Lord Melville* 1817	YOUNG, Christian(a) *EWING*	*Lord Melville* 1817
WOOD, Sarah *BARKER*	*Grenada* 1825	YOUNG, Elizabeth *CHAPMAN/JONES*	*Lord Sidmouth* 1823
WOOTTEN, Betty/ Elizabeth *WOOTTON*	*Nile* 1801		

A-3 Women Listed on the Indents of More Than One Ship

1787 TRIAL YEAR

DRURY, Elizabeth	*Neptune* and *Lady Juliana*
OLIVER, Mary	*Lady Juliana* and *Mary Ann*
WHITLAM, Sarah	*Neptune* and *Lady Juliana*

1788 TRIAL YEAR

BARNETT, Martha	*Neptune* and *Mary Ann*
CHADDERTON, Mary	*Neptune* and *Mary Ann*
CODD, Jane	*Neptune* and *Mary Ann*
DALE, Rosina	*Neptune* and *Lady Juliana*
LITHERBY, Elizabeth Stratton	*Neptune* and *Mary Ann*
MASSEY, Betty	*Neptune* and *Mary Ann*

1789 TRIAL YEAR

BRAY, Susannah	*Neptune*, *Mary Ann* and *Lady Juliana*
BROWN, Mary	*Neptune* and *Mary Ann*
DELL, Elizabeth	*Neptune* and *Lady Juliana*
FLANNAGAN, Mary	*Neptune* and *Mary Ann*
HANNAWAY, Ann	*Lady Juliana* and *Neptune*
THOMPSON, Mary	*Neptune* and *Lady Juliana*
WADE, Elizabeth Ann	*Neptune* and *Pitt*

1791 TRIAL YEAR

DAVIES, Rachel	*Royal Admiral* and *Kitty*
O'BRIEN, Mary	*Royal Admiral* and *Bellona*
THOMAS, Betty	*Royal Admiral* and *Bellona*

1792 TRIAL YEAR

HOLLOWAY, Anne	*Royal Admiral* and *Bellona*

1793 TRIAL YEAR

BREWER, Elizabeth	*Surprize* (2) and *Indispensable* (1)

NO RESPONSE ON TRIAL YEAR

ALLEN, Margaret	*Royal Admiral* and *Bellona* (*Bellona* trial date: 26.10.1791)
ANSTEY, Mary Ann	*Lady Juliana* and *Mary Ann* (*Mary Ann*, trial date: 23.03.1790)
CASE, Ann	*Royal Admiral* and *Bellona* (*Bellona* trial date: 18.07.1791)

List B Women Transported from Ireland 1791–January 1828

B–1 *Women Transported*

1788 TRIAL YEAR

Queen 1791
SLATER, Ann   NR-NR-1788; Dublin

1789 TRIAL YEAR

Queen 1791
NOWLAS*, Bridget   NR-NR-1789; Dublin

1790 TRIAL YEAR

Boddingtons 1793
CHRISTY, Jane   NR-08-1790; Antrim

Queen 1791
BOULTON*, Ann   NR-NR-1790; Dublin
BRAZILL*, Sarah   NR-NR-1790; Waterford City
BRENNAN*, Sarah   NR-NR-1790; Dublin
CLERK*, Anne   NR-NR-1790; Queens County
CONNOR, Mary   NR-NR-1790; Dublin
CORRIGAN, Catherine NR-NR-1790; Dublin
DAVIDSON, Mary   NR-NR-1790; Armagh
DAVIS, Mary   NR-04-1790; Dublin City
EDWARDS, Catherine NR-NR-1790; Dublin
HEALLY*, Mary   NR-NR-1790; Limerick City
HERON, Mary   NR-NR-1790; Dublin
INNIS, Mary   NR-NR-1790; Dublin
McDONALD, Elinor   NR-NR-1790; Dublin
McDONNELL*, Bridget NR-NR-1790; Armagh
MANDEVILLE, Mary   NR-NR-1790; Kilkenny
MARLOW, Marcia   NR-NR-1790; Dublin
SMYTH, Mary   NR-NR-1790; Dublin
STEPHENSON, Margaret NR-NR-1790; Armagh
WHELAN, Mary   NR-NR-1790; Dublin

Sugar Cane 1793
DOLAN, Margaret   NR-09-1790; Dublin
DOOLAN, Mary   NR-09-1790; Dublin
SMITH, Anne   NR-07-1790; Dublin
STROUD, Hester   NR-03-1790; Dublin

1791 TRIAL YEAR

Boddingtons 1793
BRIEN, Mary   NR-04-1791; Dublin
CAMPBELL, Mary   NR-08-1791; Co Down
CARTHY, Mary   NR-04-1791; Waterford
CORE, Nancy   NR-08-1791; Donegal
CUNNINGHAM, Mary   NR-08-1791; Armagh
CURRAN, Mary   NR-04-1791; Dublin
CURRY, Eleanor   NR-08-1791; Donegal
FITZGERALD, Elizabeth NR-08-1791; Cavan
HAMILTON, Margaret NR-08-1791; Cavan
HERON, Mary   NR-10-1791; Dublin

438 *List B-1*

KELLY, Ann	NR-04-1791; Queens County
LYNCH, Julianna	NR-04-1791; Cork
MAGUIRE*, Margaret	NR-04-1791; Monaghan
McDONNELL, Flora	NR-04-1791; Antrim
McLEAN, Catherine	NR-10-1791; Dublin

Sugar Cane 1793

BERGEN, Mary	NR-08-1791; Co Cork
BRADY, Elinor	NR-09-1791; Cork
BRYAN, Eleanora Mary	NR-04-1791; Co Waterford
BURNES, Catherine	NR-08-1791; Co Cavan
CONDRON, Catherine	NR-08-1791; Co Cork
CONNOLLY, Bridget	NR-09-1791; Co Westmeath
FARRELLY, Anne	NR-04-1791; Co Cavan
FLINN, Mary	NR-04-1791; Cork
JACKSON*, Elizabeth	NR-04-1791; Co Limerick
McARTHY*, Elinor	NR-04-1791; Cork
MOONEY*, Margaret	NR-05-1791; Dublin
MORAN, Elizabeth	NR-09-1791; Co Westmeath
REGAN, Rose	NR-04-1791; Co Cavan
REILLY*, Rosanna	NR-06-1791; Dublin
SHEY, Ann	NR-08-1791; Co Cork
SULLIVAN, Joanna	NR-09-1791; Cork
WAIR, Mary	NR-NR-1791; Dublin
WILSON, Elizabeth	NR-11-1791; Dublin

1792 TRIAL YEAR

Boddingtons 1793

CONNOR, Mary	NR-08-1792; Queens County
DAVERAN, Alice	NR-03-1792; Dublin
MALOWNEY, Margaret	NR-04-1792; Carlow
POOR, Margaret	NR-04-1792; Carlow

Sugar Cane 1793

BARRY, Catherine	NR-04-1792; Cork
BRIEN, Catherine	NR-10-1792; Dublin
BRIEN*, Mary	NR-03-1792; Dublin
BURNE, Mary	NR-07-1792; Dublin
DUNBAR, Mary	NR-07-1792; Dublin
ESLIN, Bridget	NR-09-1792; Dublin
FINNIGAN*, Mary	NR-08-1792; Dublin
HARTLEY, Mary	NR-NR-1792; Dublin
HENDERSON, Margaret	NR-01-1792; Dublin
HOPKINS, Mary	NR-07-1792; Dublin
HUGHES, Mary	NR-09-1792; Dublin
IVORY, Mary	NR-10-1792; Dublin
KEARNS, Mary	NR-06-1792; Dublin
KELLY, Alice	NR-08-1792; Dublin
KIERNAN, Catherine	NR-06-1792; Dublin
LEONARD, Rose	NR-01-1792; Dublin
LODGE, Mary	NR-07-1792; Dublin
McNAMARA*, Ann	NR-04-1792; Dublin
MALONE, Catherine	NR-04-1792; Dublin
MOONEY*, Margaret	NR-08-1792; Dublin
MORGAN*, Rose	NR-08-1792; Co Antrim
MORRISON, Margaret	NR-04-1792; Cork
MURRY*, Eleanor	NR-04-1792; Cork
O'HARA, Jane	NR-08-1792; Dublin
PIKE, Sarah	NR-04-1792; Dublin
RIEBY*, Mary	NR-01-1792; Dublin
RODNEY*, Mary	NR-07-1792; Dublin
ROE, Mary	NR-04-1792; Co Clare
ROURKE, Catherine	NR-08-1792; Dublin
SHIEL, Catherine	NR-03-1792; Dublin

1793 TRIAL YEAR

Marquis Cornwallis 1796

ALLICOT, Elinor	NR-03-1793; Limerick
BURN, Sarah	NR-11-1793; Dublin
DANFORD, Susanna	NR-11-1793; Dublin City
DILLON, Elizabeth	NR-08-1793; Dublin
FOX, Maria	NR-08-1793; Dublin
GORMAN, Ann	NR-01-1793; Dublin
HAYES, Margaret	NR-08-1793; Wexford
HOWE, Elinor	NR-07-1793; Dublin
KELLY, Maria	NR-03-1793; Dublin
LAWLER, Elinor	NR-08-1793; Limerick
MORAN, Maria	NR-12-1793; Dublin
NEIL, Catherine	NR-12-1793; Dublin
NEWMAN, Mary	NR-09-1793; Cork
QUIN, Margaret	NR-NR-1793; Tyrone
WALKER, Jane	NR-03-1793; Dublin
WARREN, Bridget	NR-05-1793; Dublin City

WILLARD*,
Henrietta   NR-01-1793; Dublin

1794 TRIAL YEAR

Britannia 1797
BRYAN, Mary	Summer 1794; Cork City
GRAHAM, Jane	Spring 1794; Sligo

Marquis Cornwallis 1796
BAKER, Catherine	NR-03-1794; Louth
BRIEN, Mary	NR-03-1794; Cork
BURKE, Honora	NR-03-1794; Tipperary
BURN*, Margaret	NR-10-1794; Dublin
CANE, Mary	NR-07-1794; Dublin
CARROLL, Mary	NR-08-1794; Dublin
CONNELL*, Elinor	NR-03-1794; Cork
CONNOR, Elizabeth	NR-NR-1794; Westmeath
DALY, Ann	NR-11-1794; Dublin
ELLIS, Maria	NR-05-1794; Dublin
FARRELL, Catherine	NR-03-1794; Limerick
FARRELL, Sarah	NR-02-1794; Dublin
FITZGERALD, Mary	NR-03-1794; Cork
GREGAN*, Maria	NR-07-1794; Dublin
HAYES, Maria	NR-03-1794; Dublin
JACKSON, Elizabeth	NR-11-1794; Dublin
KENNEDY*, Judith	NR-03-1794; Cork
McCABE, Ann	NR-04-1794; Dublin
McKEARMAN, Catherine	NR-08-1794; Kings County
MURPHY, Ann	NR-08-1794; Dublin
POWER, Mary	NR-12-1794; Dublin
POWNDEN, Catherine	NR-06-1794; Dublin
ROCHE, Mary	NR-08-1794; Dublin
SCOTT, Margaret	NR-07-1794; Dublin
SWEENEY, Mary	NR-03-1794; Cork
TALLON, Mary	NR-10-1794; Dublin
WALPOLE, Elizabeth	NR-03-1794; Co Westmeath

1795 TRIAL YEAR

Britannia 1797
BUTLER, Catherine	NR-07-1795; Dublin City
FINN, Sarah	NR-07-1795; Dublin City
HAMILTON, Ann	NR-08-1795; Dublin City
HORISH, Ann	NR-10-1795; Dublin City
JONES, Elinor	NR-07-1795; Dublin City
LYNCH, Mary	NR-07-1795; Dublin City
MAHON, Mary	NR-12-1795; Dublin City
RAFFARTY, Elizabeth	NR-10-1795; Dublin City
SHEEHAN, Mary	Summer 1795; Limerick
SMYTH, Mary	NR-10-1795; Dublin City

Marquis Cornwallis 1796
ANNESLEY, Maria	NR-02-1795; Dublin
BARTLEY*, Elizabeth	NR-02-1795; Dublin
BIRMINGHAM, Ann	NR-05-1795; Dublin
BUTLER, Mary	NR-06-1795; Dublin City
BYRNE, Ann	NR-04-1795; Dublin
CAFFREY, Elizabeth	NR-06-1795; Dublin
CAFFREY, Mary	NR-02-1795; Dublin
CARR, Elizabeth	NR-07-1795; Dublin
COLLINS, Catherine	NR-03-1795; Limerick
COLLINS, Honora	NR-03-1795; Kerry
FAY*, Ann	NR-05-1795; Dublin
FLANNAGAN, Maria	NR-04-1795; Dublin
HANLY, Mary	NR-05-1795; Dublin
HERTCHY, Mary	NR-03-1795; Cork
HICKEY, Bridget	NR-03-1795; Tipperary
HUGHES, Judith	NR-08-1795; Dublin
KENNEDY, Mary	NR-03-1795; Cork
McCARTY, Margaret	NR-04-1795; Dublin
McMAHON, Margaret	NR-01-1795; Dublin
McNALLY, Maria	NR-06-1795; Dublin
MALTON*, Catherine	NR-04-1795; Dublin
MURPHY, Catherine	NR-03-1795; Cork
O'DONNELL, Bridget	NR-07-1795; Dublin
REILY, Mary	NR-11-1795; Dublin
RICHARDSON, Ann	NR-05-1795; Dublin
RYAN, Ann	NR-03-1795; Tipperary

SULLIVAN,
  Catherine   NR-04-1795; Dublin
SULLIVAN, Honora   NR-03-1795; Cork

Rolla 1803
WALSH, Jane   NR-NR-1795;
                   Westmeath

1796 TRIAL YEAR

Britannia 1797
ANDERSON, Mary   NR-04-1796; Dublin City
BLEADS, Jane   NR-07-1796; Dublin City
BRIEN, Judy   NR-07-1796; Dublin City
BRUEN, Ann   NR-11-1796; Dublin City
COLLIGAN, Sarah   NR-04-1796; Dublin City
COLLINS, Catherine NR-07-1796; Dublin City
CULLEN, Bridget   NR-09-1796; Dublin City
DEASE, Mary   NR-01-1796; Dublin City
FANE, Mary   NR-04-1796; Dublin City
FOSTER, Mary   NR-01-1796; Dublin City
FOY, Margaret   NR-04-1796; Dublin
HALL, Rose   NR-07-1796; Dublin City
JACKSON, Sarah   NR-09-1796; Dublin City
KEALY*, Abby/Anny NR-11-1796; Dublin City
LANGAN, Mary   NR-01-1796; Dublin City
LOYDE, Ann   NR-11-1796; Dublin City
McCARTY, Catherine NR-07-1796; Dublin City
McDERMOT, Mary   NR-01-1796; Dublin City
MAHER, Jane   NR-04-1796; Dublin City
MOONEY, Margaret   NR-03-1796; Dublin City
MORAN, Mary   NR-08-1796; Cork City
MURPHY, Margaret   NR-03-1796; Dublin City
MURPHY, Mary   NR-09-1796; Dublin City
NOWLAN, Esther   NR-11-1796; Dublin City
RAFFERTY, Margaret NR-01-1796; Dublin City
ROBINSON, Mary   NR-09-1796; Dublin City
SAVAGE, Ann   NR-04-1796; Dublin City
SMYTH, Catherine   NR-03-1796; Dublin City
SMYTH, Mary   NR-09-1796; Dublin City
TALLON, Mary   NR-11-1796; Dublin City
THOMAS, Mary   NR-02-1796; Dublin City
THOMSON, Jane   NR-03-1796; Dublin City
UPTON, Mary   NR-05-1796; Dublin City

Minerva 1800
KELLY*, Anne   NR-11-1796; Dublin

1797 TRIAL YEAR

Hercules 1802
MORAN, Ann   Summer 1797; Meath

Minerva 1800
ANDERSON, Betty   NR-02-1797; Dublin
ANDREWS, Elizabeth NR-02-1797; NR
COGAN, Margaret   NR-04-1797; Cork City
COLLINS, Mary   NR-02-1797; Dublin City
CUMING*, Mary   NR-02-1797; Dublin City
DONAGHUE, Mary   NR-04-1797; Co Cork
DUNN, Mary   NR-02-1797; Dublin
FITZGERALD, Catherine NR-03-1797; NR

FLYNN*, Mary	NR-02-1797; Dublin City
HUTCHINSON, Ann	NR-02-1797; NR
MALONY*, Bridget	NR-02-1797; Dublin City
MALONY*, Sarah	NR-04-1797; Dublin
MONKS, Francis	NR-03-1797; NR
SMITH*, Mary	NR-02-1797; NR

1798 TRIAL YEAR

Minerva 1800
BROWN, Ann	NR-02-1798; Dublin City
CLARK*, Eleanor	NR-09-1798; Co Cork
DALY, Celia	NR-05-1798; Dublin City
DORAN, Mary	NR-05-1798; Dublin City
DURHAM, Mary	NR-05-1798; Dublin City
KIDD, Catherine	NR-03-1798; Limerick
MacDONALD*, Ann	NR-05-1798; Dublin City
READY, Ann	NR-03-1798; Limerick

1799 TRIAL YEAR

Hercules 1802
FAVIOL*, Ann	Spring 1799; Louth
HARVEY, Margaret	Summer 1799; Tyrone

Minerva 1800
CONOLLY*, Mary	NR-08-1799; Cork
FITZGERALD, Honoria	NR-08-1799; Cork

Rolla 1803
BARRY, Mary	NR-04-1799; Kerry

1800 TRIAL YEAR

Atlas 1802
DELANY, Ann	Spring 1800; Queens County
DIGNUM, Mary	NR-11-1800; Dublin City
DOYLE, Mary	Summer 1800; Carlow
LACY, Mary	Spring 1800; Limerick
MARTIN, Jane	Spring 1800; Waterford
MULHALL, Elizabeth	Summer 1800; Kilkenny
MULKEEN, Bridget	Summer 1800; Mayo
NOWLAND, Ann	Summer 1800; NR
RYAN, Mary	Spring 1800; Clare
SHEE, Mary	NR-09-1800; Waterford
SMITH*, Ann	Spring 1800; Louth
TARLTON, Rebecca	Summer 1800; Carlow

Hercules 1802
BASS, Mary	NR-11-1800; Dublin City
CONORTY*, Mary	Lent 1800; Antrim
DILLANY, Alice	NR-11-1800; Dublin City
FIELDING, Elizabeth	NR-10-1800; Dublin City
HAMILTON, Margaret	Lent 1800; Antrim
HARRINGTON, Mary	NR-11-1800; Dublin City
KAVANAGH, Margaret	Summer 1800; Meath
McCANNOF, Mary	Summer 1800; Down
McLEAN, Mary	NR-09-1800; Dublin City
PRODIGAN*, Bridget	NR-11-1800; Dublin City
STRATFORD, Mary	NR-12-1800; Dublin City
SULIVAN, Ann	NR-12-1800; Dublin City

Rolla 1803
BROWNE, Elizabeth	NR-12-1800; Dublin City
BYRNE, Ann	NR-NR-1800; Dublin City
McDANIEL, Catherine	NR-08-1800; Carlow
MURPHY, Catherine	NR-04-1800; Carlow
MURPHY, Mary	NR-08-1800; Cork City
QUIN, Mary/ Margaret	NR-04-1800; Co Down
RYAN, Mary	NR-NR-1800; Clare

1801 TRIAL YEAR

Atlas 1802
CONNOR, Mary	NR-07-1801; Dublin City
COOKE, Elizabeth	NR-07-1801; Dublin City
DEAN, Mary	Spring 1801; Waterford
DONALLY*, Eliza	Spring 1801; Tipperary
DOWLING, Eliza	Summer 1801; Kildare
DOWLING, Winifred	Summer 1801; Kildare
FITZGERALD, Catherine	NR-06-1801; Dublin City
FITZGERALD, Elen	Spring 1801; Waterford
FITZPATRICK, Mary	Spring 1801; Waterford
GRAHAM, Mary Ann	Spring 1801; Cork City
LAWLER*, Mary	Spring 1801; Tipperary
McCOURTNEY, Catherine	NR-06-1801; Dublin City
McNAMARY, Elizabeth	Spring 1801; Tipperary
NEWIN, Martha	NR-07-1801; Dublin City
PHILLIPS, Bridget	NR-07-1801; Dublin City
REDMOND, Mary	Spring 1801; Co Waterford

Hercules 1802
CAMBWELL, Margaret	NR-07-1801; Dublin City
DAVIS, Eleoner	NR-04-1801; Dublin City
DUN, Mary	NR-09-1801; Dublin City
ENGLISH, Mary	NR-09-1801; Dublin City
KELLY, Ann	Spring 1801; Dublin City
MORGAN, Margaret	NR-06-1801; Dublin City
MURPHY*, Catherine	NR-04-1801; Dublin City
NUGENT, Elizabeth	NR-01-1801; Dublin City
RIALLY, Ann	NR-07-1801; Dublin City
TURLEY, Mary	NR-09-1801; Dublin City

Rolla 1803
BYRNE, Bridget	NR-08-1801; Meath
CARTER, Catherine	NR-04-1801; Longford
COLLINS, Catherine	NR-08-1801; Cork City
CUSADINE, Mary	NR-NR-1801; Clare
GARETHY, Rose	NR-07-1801; Dublin
HURLEY*, Catherine	NR-08-1801; Tipperary
McENTEE, Mary	NR-08-1801; Meath
MAGILL, Ann	NR-08-1801; Tipperary
MOLLOY, Mary	NR-04-1801; Clare
PLUMLAND*, Matty	NR-06-1801; Dublin City
POWER, Mary/ Cathrine	NR-04-1801; Cork City

1802 TRIAL YEAR

Rolla 1803
BOLTON, Elinor	NR-04-1802; Kildare
DOYLE, Ann	NR-03-1802; Dublin City
DOYLE, Margaret	NR-08-1802; Dublin City
GOLDING, Margaret	NR-05-1802; Dublin City
HIGGINS*, Mary	NR-08-1802; Dublin City
HONNER, Mary	NR-04-1802; Kings County
HUGHES, Jane	NR-06-1802; Dublin City
KELLY, Mary	NR-04-1802; Meath
LAUGHLIN, Catherine	NR-04-1802; Kilkenny
NORRIS, Catherine	NR-08-1802; Dublin City
READ*, Elinor	NR-03-1802; Dublin City
ROE, Judith	NR-03-1802; Dublin City
RYAN, Hester	NR-03-1802; Dublin City

List B-1

SCULLY, Catherine	NR-04-1802; Drogheda
TYRREL, Bridget	NR-08-1802; Dublin City

***Tellicherry* 1806**

BRADSHAW, Mary	NR-09-1802; Dublin City
HINCHEY, Catherine	NR-NR-1802; Limerick City

1803 TRIAL YEAR

***Tellicherry* 1806**

BARRY, Mary	NR-01-1803; Dublin City
BRADY, Catherine	NR-06-1803; Dublin City
COOKSEY, Sarah	NR-10-1803; Dublin City
FINNIS, Catherine	NR-10-1803; Dublin City
FORBES, Ann	Spring 1803; Londonderry
HAYES, Margaret	NR-NR-1803; Clare
KELLY, Margaret	NR-10-1803; Dublin City
McLAUGHLIN, Catherine	NR-01-1803; Dublin City
MOLLOWNY, Honora	NR-NR-1803; Limerick City
RICE, Mary	NR-01-1803; Dublin City
SHANLEY, Anstice	NR-10-1803; Dublin City
SHEA, Bridget	NR-NR-1803; Limerick City

1804 TRIAL YEAR

***Experiment* 1809**

CONNOLLY, Margaret	NR-08-1804; Co Down

***Tellicherry* 1806**

BEGLEY*, Mary	Spring 1804; Monaghan
BURKE, Eleanor	NR-01-1804; Dublin City
BYRNE, Mary	NR-03-1804; Dublin City
COOPER, Eliza	NR-08-1804; Dublin City
GOUGH, Mary	NR-05-1804; Dublin City
GRADY, Mary	NR-NR-1804; Kerry
HILL, Catherine	NR-01-1804; Dublin City
KENNEDY, Mary	NR-01-1804; Dublin City
LAMB, Mary	NR-09-1804; Dublin City
LEESON*, Catherine	NR-NR-1804; Limerick City
LEONARD, Eleanor	NR-NR-1804; Limerick City
McMAHON, Bridget	NR-07-1804; Armagh
MATHEWS, Ann	NR-05-1804; Dublin City
O'BRIEN, Margaret	NR-01-1804; Dublin City
SHANNON, Mary	NR-12-1804; Dublin City
SMITH, Mary	NR-01-1804; Dublin City

1805 TRIAL YEAR

***Experiment* 1809**

LAMB, Rose	NR-12-1805; Dublin City
REILY, Mary	NR-12-1805; Co Dublin

***Tellicherry* 1806**

FAGAN*, Mary	Spring 1805; Westmeath
JOHNSON, Bridget	NR-02-1805; Dublin City
JOHNSON, Mary	Spring 1805; Co Meath
McNULTY, Mary	NR-06-1805; Dublin City
TYRRELL, Elinor	Spring 1805; Co Meath

1806 TRIAL YEAR

Experiment 1809
BAIRD, Mary	NR-08-1806; Armagh
BRYAN, Mary	NR-07-1806; Cork City
CLARK*, Mary	NR-10-1806; Dublin City
CONNOR*, Eleanor	NR-11-1806; Dublin City
CURRAN, Catherine	NR-07-1806; Cork City
DORAN, Mary	20-01-1806; Dublin City
GRADY, Mary	NR-07-1806; Cork City
MADDER, Sarah	NR-03-1806; Cork City
MESKILL, Margaret	NR-03-1806; Clare
SPARKS, Honoria	NR-07-1806; Cork City
WARD*, Anne	NR-12-1806; Dublin City
WILSON, Anne/ Sarah	NR-08-1806; Armagh

1807 TRIAL YEAR

Experiment 1809
BRANNAGAN, Sophia	NR-03-1807; Co Down
BROWN*, Mary	NR-07-1807; Dublin City
BURN*, NR	NR-04-1807; Dublin City
BURN, Catherine	NR-06-1807; Dublin City
CARR*, Anne	NR-12-1807; Dublin City
CARTY, Barbara/ Elizabeth	NR-06-1807; Dublin City
COLLINS, Anne	NR-08-1807; Armagh
COX, Catherine	NR-03-1807; Co Dublin
DOWLAND*, Ann	NR-05-1807; Dublin City
FARRELL, Anne	NR-03-1807; Meath
FARRELL, Margaret	NR-11-1807; Dublin City
FINLAY, Elizabeth	NR-03-1807; Monaghan
HATCH, Catherine	NR-01-1807; Dublin City
HOGAN, Margaret	NR-09-1807; Limerick City
JOHNSTON, Mary	NR-03-1807; Co Fermanagh
KELLY*, Mary	NR-05-1807; Dublin City
KENNEDY, Anne	NR-02-1807; Dublin City
PRENDERGAST*, Mary	NR-03-1807; Wicklow
TRACY, Mary	NR-02-1807; Dublin City

Providence 1811
BULLEN, Bridget	NR-08-1807; Limerick City
CARR, Hester	NR-01-1807; Dublin City
CHURCH, Elizabeth	NR-10-1807; Dublin City

1808 TRIAL YEAR

Experiment 1809
BRYAN, Bridget	NR-03-1808; Cork City
BRYAN, Margaret	NR-03-1808; Cork City
BURN, Ann	NR-08-1808; Meath
BURN*, Eleanor	NR-07-1808; Dublin City
CLARK, Mary	NR-01-1808; Dublin City
CONNOLLY, Anne	26-01-1808; Dublin City
DAVIS, Elizabeth	NR-09-1808; Dublin City
DOWD, Anne	NR-01-1808; Dublin City
DOYLE, Anne	NR-08-1808; Kilkenny
ERWIN*, Maria	NR-03-1808; Dublin City
EUSTACE, Catherine	NR-11-1808; Dublin City
KENNA, Mary	NR-07-1808; Dublin City
LEHY, Julia	NR-08-1808; Dublin City
LEONARD, Anne	NR-02-1808; Dublin City
McKENSIE, Sarah	NR-10-1808; Dublin City
McLEAN, Mary	NR-08-1808; Monaghan

MAY, Jane	NR-07-1808; Wicklow
MOORE*, Mary	NR-11-1808; Dublin City
MULLEN, Anne	NR-03-1808; Monaghan
REDMOND, Anne	NR-05-1808; Dublin City
REDMOND, Mary	NR-11-1808; Dublin City
REILLY, Catherine	NR-07-1808; Wicklow
SAUNDERS, Mary	NR-11-1808; Dublin City
SEARY, Elizabeth	NR-10-1808; Dublin City
TIERNEY, Anne	NR-04-1808; Dublin City
WILLIAMSON*, Jane	NR-09-1808; Dublin City

***Providence* 1811**
BRYAN, Margaret	NR-08-1808; Co Carlow

1809 TRIAL YEAR

***Archduke Charles* 1813**
FEARNS, Catherine	NR-NR-1809; Dublin City

***Providence* 1811**
BUCKLEY*, Catherine	NR-03-1809; Cork City
BYRNE, Anne	NR-03-1809; Dublin City
BYRNE, Catherine	NR-06-1809; Dublin City
BYRNE, Margaret	NR-04-1809; Dublin City
COLLOGAN, Anne	NR-02-1809; Dublin City
CONOLLY, Mary	NR-02-1809; Dublin City
FAHEY, Honora	NR-08-1809; Galway Town
GAREVAN, Mary	NR-05-1809; Dublin City
GLEESON, Mary	NR-08-1809; Kings County
GLYNN, Elizabeth	NR-03-1809; Co Tipperary
HENNESSEY, Catherine	NR-03-1809; Co Limerick
KAVENAGH, Bridget	NR-04-1809; Dublin City
KELLY, Mary	NR-04-1809; Dublin City
KIRK, Martha	NR-06-1809; Dublin City
McEVATT, Bridget	NR-04-1809; Dublin City
MULHOLLAND, Mary	NR-06-1809; Dublin City
NEIL, Elinor/ Hannah	NR-06-1809; Dublin City
QUINN, Bridget	NR-06-1809; Dublin City
QUINN, Mary	NR-03-1809; Co Meath

1810 TRIAL YEAR

***Archduke Charles* 1813**
DUNN, Martha	NR-NR-1810; Dublin City
EYRES, Sarah	NR-NR-1810; Dublin City
FARRELL, Mary	NR-NR-1810; Dublin City
HAVENAGH*, Mary	NR-NR-1810; Dublin City
NIXON, Sarah	NR-NR-1810; Co Armagh
SHARKEY, Frances	NR-NR-1810; Dublin City

***Catherine* 1814**
SMITH*, Mary	NR-01-1810; Dublin City

***Providence* 1811**
BROWNE, Catherine	NR-08-1810; Dublin City
CARROLL, Catherine	NR-07-1810; Dublin City
CAVENAGH, Elinor	NR-08-1810; Dublin Co
CUMMINS, Mary	NR-08-1810; Co Galway
DOGHERTY, Margaret	NR-08-1810; Dublin City
DONOVAN, Margaret	NR-08-1810; Co Cork
DOYLE, Elinor	NR-08-1810; Co Dublin

DRISCOLL, Mary   NR-08-1810; Co Cork
GLINN, Catherine   NR-03-1810; Co Antrim
LYONS, Mary   NR-03-1810; Limerick City
McDERMOTT, Bridget   NR-01-1810; Dublin City
MURPHY, Honora   NR-08-1810; Cork City
POWER, Mary   NR-08-1810; Co Tipperary
QUINLAN, Judith   NR-08-1810; Limerick City
SHEEHAN, Mary   NR-08-1810; Co Cork
SULLIVAN, Ellinor   NR-03-1810; Co Cork

1811 TRIAL YEAR

Archduke Charles **1813**
BROWNE, Catherine   NR-NR-1811; Dublin City
BUCKLEY*, Mary   NR-NR-1811; Limerick City
CHARLETON, Mary   NR-NR-1811; Collonaghan
COLLINS, Mary   NR-NR-1811; Co Dublin
CONNOR, Mary   NR-NR-1811; Dublin City
CUNNINGHAM, Mary   NR-NR-1811; Collonaghan
DOHERTY, Elizabeth   NR-NR-1811; Co Down
DOHERTY*, Catherine   NR-NR-1811; Co Armagh
DOYLE, Mary   NR-NR-1811; Dublin City
FAGAN, Anne   NR-NR-1811; Dublin City
FERNS, Mary   NR-NR-1811; Dublin City
FISHER, Catherine   NR-NR-1811; Dublin City
FITZGERALD, Susan   NR-NR-1811; Collonaghan
FLYNN*, Catherine   NR-NR-1811; Dublin City
GRIMES, Letty   NR-NR-1811; Dublin City
HOLLAND, Ellinor   NR-NR-1811; Cork City
KELLY*, Mary   NR-NR-1811; Dublin City
KENNY, Rose   NR-NR-1811; Dublin City
LARKIN, Sarah   NR-NR-1811; Co Louth
LEE, Judith   NR-NR-1811; Dublin City
LYSAGHT, Mary   NR-NR-1811; Limerick City
McCLORINAN, Jane   NR-NR-1811; Co Down
McDONAGH, Mary   NR-NR-1811; Sligo
McDONALD, Catherine   NR-NR-1811; Collonaghan
McDONNELL, Margaret   NR-NR-1811; Co Longford
McGRANIGAN, Letitia   NR-NR-1811; Co Tyrone
McMULLEN, Catherine   NR-NR-1811; Co Westmeath
MAGUIRE, Mary   NR-NR-1811; Dublin City
MATHEWSON, Ellinor   NR-NR-1811; Co Down
MURPHY, Elizabeth   NR-NR-1811; Kilkenny City
O'BRIEN, Jane   NR-NR-1811; Dublin City
PHILIPS, Mary   NR-NR-1811; Dublin City
READY, Jane   NR-NR-1811; Co Tipperary
WILEY*, Susan   NR-NR-1811; Dublin City

Catherine **1814**
COATES, Catherine   NR-11-1811; Dublin City
HUTCHINSON, Elizabeth NR-03-1811; Co Tyrone
HYNDS*, Mary   NR-08-1811; Dublin City
MAGUIRE, Eleanor   NR-06-1811; Dublin City
MURRAY, Jane   NR-03-1811; Dublin City

Francis & Eliza **1815**
O'BRIEN*, Ann   NR-06-1811; Dublin City

WHITE, Mary
  Bridget   NR-05-1811; Dublin
                   City

1812 TRIAL YEAR

Archduke Charles 1813
AUSTIN, Mary   NR-NR-1812; Dublin
                  City
CONNELL,
  Catherine   NR-NR-1812; Cork City
HICKEY, Ann   NR-NR-1812; Dublin
                  City
HOEY, Mary   NR-NR-1812;
                  Co Wexford
KEINAN, Catherine NR-NR-1812; Dublin
                  City
KELLY*, Mary   NR-NR-1812; Dublin
                  City
LEARY, Margaret   NR-NR-1812; Cork City
ROONEY, Mary   NR-NR-1812; Dublin
                  City
SHEA, Jane   NR-NR-1812; Co Cork
STRINGER, Maria   NR-NR-1812; Dublin
                  City
TWOHIGG, Hannah   NR-NR-1812; Cork City

Catherine 1814
AHERN, Catherine NR-08-1812;
                  Co Kerry
BARNES, Elizabeth NR-08-1812; Dublin
                  City
BOYLAN, Mary   NR-04-1812; Dublin
                  City
BRYAN, Rose   NR-08-1812; Co Cork
BYRNE, Ann   NR-10-1812; Dublin
                  City
BYRNE*, Mary   NR-12-1812; Dublin
                  City
CAFFRAY, Ann   NR-07-1812; Dublin
                  City
CARROLL, Ann   NR-08-1812;
                  Co Armagh
CLEARY,
  Elizabeth   NR-08-1812; Cork City
COLE, Honora   NR-08-1812; Limerick
                  City
ENGLISH, Mary   NR-10-1812; Dublin
                  City
FARRELL, Mary   NR-10-1812; Dublin
                  City
FITZGERALD, Mary NR-08-1812;
                  Co Limerick
FLOOD, Mary   NR-10-1812; Dublin
                  City
FRAINE, Ann   NR-03-1812; Co Tyrone
GILMOR*, Mary   NR-07-1812; Co Mayo
GREEN, Ann/   NR-03-1812; Dublin
  Margaret   City
HUDSON, Mary   NR-08-1812; Co Cork
HUGHES, Alice   NR-08-1812;
                  Co Armagh
JONES, Ann   NR-05-1812; Dublin
                  City
KEATINGE*, Eliza NR-07-1812; Dublin
                  City
KELLY, Catherine NR-10-1812; Dublin
                  City
KELLY, Mary Ann   NR-10-1812; Dublin
                  City
KILROY, Bridget   NR-07-1812; Co Meath
KING*, Elizabeth NR-08-1812; Co Cork
KIRK, Catherine   NR-10-1812; Dublin
                  City
LYNCH, Catherine NR-08-1812; Limerick
                  City
McARDLE, Mary   NR-10-1812; Dublin
                  City
McDERMOTT, Ann   NR-12-1812; Dublin
                  City
McDONNELL,
  Catherine   NR-07-1812; Co Tyrone
MOORE, Ann   NR-07-1812; Dublin
                  City
MURPHY, Alice   NR-08-1812; Dublin
                  City
MURPHY, Mary   NR-08-1812; Cork City
NIXON, Catherine NR-08-1812;
                  Co Monaghan
O'BRIEN, Catherine NR-08-1812;
                  Co Armagh
POWER, Mary   NR-11-1812; Dublin
                  City
QUIN*, Margaret   NR-03-1812; Co Antrim
QUINN, Margaret   NR-07-1812; Co Mayo
QUINN*, Elinor   NR-08-1812;
                  Co Wicklow
READ, Mary   NR-03-1812; Co Mayo

448 List B-1

RORKE, Ann	NR-06-1812; Dublin City	HAND, Bridget	NR-03-1813; Co Armagh
SCOTT, Sarah	NR-08-1812; Co Monaghan	HANLON, Mary	NR-03-1813; Co Louth
		HAYES*, Anne	NR-08-1813; Limerick City
SHERIDAN, Rose	NR-07-1812; Co Longford	HICKEY, Ellen	NR-04-1813; Cork City
SMITH, Ann	NR-03-1812; Co Tyrone	HOLLOWAY, Ann	NR-09-1813; Dublin City
SWAINE, Alice	NR-06-1812; Dublin City	JOHNSTON, Eleanor	NR-07-1813; Dublin City
THORNTON, Ellen	NR-03-1812; Co Galway	JUDGE, Bridget	NR-03-1813; Co Kildare
WALSH, Rose	NR-08-1812; Dublin City	KAVANAGH, Mary	NR-05-1813; Dublin City
WILSON, Margaret	NR-03-1812; Co Antrim	KAVENAGH, Jane	NR-09-1813; Dublin City

***Francis & Eliza* 1815**

McEVOY, Elizabeth	NR-10-1812; Dublin City

KELLY, Margaret	NR-02-1813; Dublin City

1813 TRIAL YEAR

		KELLY, Mary	NR-04-1813; Dublin City

***Catherine* 1814**

AHERN, Honor	NR-04-1813; Cork City	LOFTUS, Catherine	NR-09-1813; Dublin City
BALDWIN, Margaret	NR-09-1813; Cork City	McINTIRE, Mary	NR-09-1813; Cork City
BRADY*, Susan	NR-06-1813; Dublin City	MORAN*, Mary Ann	NR-03-1813; Dublin City
BRENNAN, Mary Ann	NR-09-1813; Dublin City	MURPHY, Alice	NR-03-1813; Co Kilkenny
CLARKE, Mary Ferns	NR-03-1813; Dublin City	NEWPORT, Ann	NR-07-1813; Dublin City
CODEHY, Margaret	NR-03-1813; Co Kilkenny	NOBLE, Isabella	NR-03-1813; Co Longford
CONNELL, Ann	NR-08-1813; Dublin City	O'HEAR, Mary	NR-03-1813; Co Down
		QUINN, Catherine	NR-05-1813; Dublin City
COUGHLAN, Catherine	NR-06-1813; Dublin City	QUINN, Jane	NR-06-1813; Dublin City
CURBY, Mary	NR-06-1813; Dublin City	READ, Elizabeth	NR-02-1813; Dublin City
DUNN, Mary Ann	NR-03-1813; Dublin City	SMITH, Ann	NR-05-1813; Dublin City
EDEN, Mary Ann	NR-03-1813; Co Kilkenny	SMITH, Elizabeth	NR-05-1813; Dublin City
EGAN, Catherine	NR-08-1813; Dublin City	STEWART, Jane	NR-03-1813; Co Kilkenny
GERAN, Catherine	NR-03-1813; Co Limerick	WALLACE, Jane	NR-06-1813; Dublin City
GRIFFIN, Teresa	NR-08-1813; Dublin City	WHEELER, Jane	NR-09-1813; Cork City
HAMILTON*, Elinor	NR-05-1813; Dublin City	WHITE, Mary	NR-03-1813; Co Kilkenny

Francis & Eliza **1815**

BRAY*, Catharine	NR-01-1813; Dublin City
BROWN, Mary	NR-NR-1813; Dublin City
BURKE, Bridget	NR-10-1813; Dublin City
BUTLER, Mary	NR-11-1813; Dublin City
BYRNE*, Catherine	NR-09-1813; Dublin City
BYRNE*, Margaret	NR-12-1813; Dublin City
CAVANAGH*, Catherine	NR-10-1813; Dublin City
GRAHAM, Isabella	NR-09-1813; Dublin City
HARRINGTON, Mary	NR-12-1813; Dublin City
HEALY, Elizabeth	NR-10-1813; Dublin City
HYLAND, Margaret	NR-11-1813; Dublin City
KINGSMILL*, Catherine	NR-12-1813; Dublin City
McLOGHLIN*, Rose	NR-08-1813; Co Tyrone
MAXWELL, Jane	NR-10-1813; Dublin City
ROE*, Margaret	NR-12-1813; Dublin City
ROONEY, Honora	NR-11-1813; Co Dublin
RYAN, Mary	NR-08-1813; Kilkenny City
SMITH, Catherine	NR-08-1813; Co Down
STEPHENS*, Mary	NR-10-1813; Dublin City
WALSH, Bridget	NR-08-1813; Co Sligo

1814 TRIAL YEAR

Alexander **1816**

FOLEY, Agnes	NR-10-1814; Dublin City
KELLY, Margaret	NR-10-1814; Dublin City
McCLEAN, Rose	NR-10-1814; Dublin City
McEVOY, Elizabeth	NR-12-1814; Dublin City
MURPHY, Eleanor	NR-12-1814; Dublin City
OGLE*, Catherine	NR-12-1814; Dublin City
STOTT*, Mary	NR-12-1814; Dublin City
THORPE, Catherine	NR-12-1814; Dublin City

Canada **1817**

FLYNN, Catherine	NR-10-1814; Dublin City
MULLENS, Ann	NR-04-1814; Dublin City

Francis & Eliza **1815**

ARMSTRONG, Catherine	NR-08-1814; Co Armagh
BARRETT, Honora	NR-03-1814; Cork City
BERRY*, Mary	NR-NR-1814; Co Kildare
BOYLE, Catherine	NR-08-1814; Dublin City
BRIEN*, Julia	NR-02-1814; Dublin City
BRYAN, Mary	NR-08-1814; Cork City
BYRNE*, Ann	NR-07-1814; Dublin City
BYRNE*, Bridget	NR-03-1814; Co Wexford
CAMPBELL, Margaret	NR-03-1814; Dublin City
CANDLER*, Mary	NR-03-1814; Co Wexford
CARDEN, Mary	NR-03-1814; Kilkenny City
CASEY, Mary	NR-03-1814; Cork City
CONNOR, Mary	NR-07-1814; Co Kildare
CULLEN*, Ann	NR-09-1814; Dublin City
DENIGAN, Frances	NR-07-1814; Co Longford
EMERSON*, Ann	NR-05-1814; Dublin City
FARREL*, Mary/Bridget	NR-03-1814; Cork City
FITZGIBBON, Mary	NR-08-1814; Cork City

450 *List B-1*

FLANIGAN*, Mary	NR-09-1814; Dublin City
GODFREY, Mary	NR-05-1814; Dublin City
HYLAND, Bridget	NR-07-1814; Co Kildare
KINAHAN*, Ann	NR-08-1814; Dublin City
KIRWAN, Alice	NR-09-1814; Dublin City
McCONNEL, Charlotte	NR-03-1814; Co Tyrone
McCONNEL*, Elizabeth	NR-08-1814; Co Armagh
McGRADY, Sarah/Cicily	NR-03-1814; Co Antrim
McGUIRE, Mary	NR-03-1814; Co Armagh
MITCHELL, Margaret	NR-03-1814; Co Wexford
MULLOON, Mary	NR-07-1814; Co Roscommon
NEVILLE*, Marcella/Priscilla	NR-08-1814; Dublin City
O'NEAL*, Catherine	NR-08-1814; Co Antrim
PEW*, Catherine	NR-02-1814; Dublin City
REED*, Rose	NR-03-1814; Co Tyrone
ROURKE, Bridget	NR-07-1814; Co Roscommon
RYAN*, Ann	NR-07-1814; Dublin City
SHEARON, Ann	NR-08-1814; Co Armagh
SHERIDAN, Catherine	NR-07-1814; Dublin City
SMITH, Elizabeth	NR-07-1814; Co Sligo
STAFFORD, Margaret	NR-07-1814; Dublin City
THOMPSON, Jane	NR-08-1814; Dublin City
THOMSON, Susan	NR-07-1814; Dublin City
THORPE, Mary	NR-04-1814; Dublin City
WALKER*, Matilda	NR-03-1814; Dublin City
WILSON, Ann	NR-03-1814; Co Down

1815 TRIAL YEAR

Alexander **1816**

ASPILL, Elizabeth	NR-02-1815; Dublin City
BARNETT, Catherine	NR-08-1815; Dublin City
BARNETT, Mary	NR-08-1815; Dublin City
BEATY, Angelica	NR-03-1815; Dublin City
BECKETT, Ann	NR-01-1815; Dublin City
BENNETT, Ann	NR-08-1815; Dublin City
BLAKE, Judith	NR-05-1815; Dublin City
BRADSHAW, Mary	NR-02-1815; Dublin City
BROWN, Elizabeth	NR-07-1815; Co Armagh
BROWN*, Mary	NR-09-1815; Dublin City
BURKE, Judith	NR-03-1815; Cork City
BYRNE*, Catherine	NR-01-1815; Dublin City
CAHILL*, Mary Ann	NR-05-1815; Dublin City
CARR, Mary	NR-01-1815; Dublin City
CARTY*, Bridget	NR-03-1815; Limerick City
CHAMBERS, Judith	NR-03-1815; Co Wexford
CLARKE, Catherine	NR-03-1815; Cork City
CONNELL, Bridget	NR-03-1815; Cork City
CONNOR, Isabella	NR-01-1815; Dublin City
CONWAY, Johanna	NR-03-1815; Limerick City
D'ARCY, Ann	NR-08-1815; Dublin City
ELLIS, Ann	NR-08-1815; Co Tipperary
EUSTACE, Catherine	NR-01-1815; Dublin City
FARRELL, Ann	NR-05-1815; Dublin City

Name	Reference
FEGAN, Martha	NR-01-1815; Dublin City
FENNESSY, Margaret	NR-03-1815; Co Tipperary
FOSTER, Ann	NR-01-1815; Dublin City
GOFF, Catherine	NR-08-1815; Drogheda
HAMILTON, Mary	NR-02-1815; Dublin City
HUNTER*, Isabella	NR-03-1815; Co Down
HURLEY, Bridget	NR-08-1815; Co Louth
JOHNSTON, Mary	NR-02-1815; Dublin City
KEELY, Maria	NR-01-1815; Dublin City
KELLY, Bridget	NR-02-1815; Dublin City
KELLY, Catherine	NR-02-1815; Dublin City
KELLY, Eleanor	NR-05-1815; Dublin City
KELLY, Judith	NR-06-1815; Dublin Co
KELLY, Margaret	NR-02-1815; Dublin City
KELLY, Mary	NR-03-1815; Co Westmeath
KENNEDY, Ann	NR-06-1815; Dublin City
KENNEDY, Bridget	NR-03-1815; Co Tipperary
KENNEDY, Mary	NR-08-1815; Kings County
KINSELA*, Eleanor/Ellen	NR-03-1815; Co Carlow
LAMB, Bridget	NR-04-1815; Dublin City
McCLUSKY*, Phoebe/Pheby	NR-01-1815; Dublin City
McEVOY, Eleanor	NR-01-1815; Dublin City
McGUINESS, Ann	NR-08-1815; Drogheda
McKEON, Ann	NR-08-1815; Co Meath
McNALLY, Elizabeth	NR-03-1815; Dublin City
MAGARRY, Ann	NR-04-1815; Dublin City
MAGUIRE, Abigal	NR-08-1815; Dublin City
MAGUIRE, Maria	NR-08-1815; Dublin City
MARTIN, Mary	NR-01-1815; Dublin City
MULLEN, Mary	NR-07-1815; Dublin City
MURPHY, Johanna	NR-03-1815; Cork City
MURRAY, Mary	NR-06-1815; Co Dublin
MURRAY*, Mary	NR-03-1815; Dublin City
PERRY, Margaret	NR-08-1815; Co Meath
POWELL, Mary	NR-08-1815; Dublin City
POWER, Mary	NR-01-1815; Dublin City
REDMONDS, Mary	NR-09-1815; Dublin City
ROCHFORT*, Mary	NR-03-1815; Cork City
ROCK, Mary	NR-01-1815; Dublin City
SAVAGE, Mary	NR-05-1815; Dublin City
SMITH, Mary	NR-05-1815; Dublin City
WALES*, Martha	NR-08-1815; Co Down
WALSH, Bridget	NR-03-1815; Co Wexford
WARD, Ann	NR-07-1815; Dublin City
WATSON, Ann	NR-01-1815; Dublin City
WEBB, Hester	NR-02-1815; Dublin City
WILLS*, Catherine	NR-08-1815; Co Meath

Canada 1817

Name	Reference
BASS*, Ann	NR-11-1815; Dublin City
BIRMINGHAM, Elizabeth	NR-11-1815; Dublin City
BRADY, Elinor	NR-11-1815; Dublin City
BROWN*, Bridget	NR-11-1815; Dublin City
BYRNE, Judith	NR-12-1815; Dublin City
CODY, Elinor	NR-11-1815; Dublin City

452 *List B-1*

CUMMINS, Margaret	NR-10-1815; Dublin City
DOOLAN, Mary	NR-11-1815; Dublin City
DOYLE, Jane	NR-08-1815; Dublin City
FOLEY, Mary	NR-12-1815; Dublin City
FURLONG, Mary	NR-11-1815; Dublin City
HARNEY, Clarissa	NR-10-1815; Dublin City
JOHNSON, Mary	NR-10-1815; Dublin City
KELLY, Catherine	NR-10-1815; Dublin City
KELLY, Christina	NR-12-1815; Dublin City
LEONARD, Ann	NR-11-1815; Dublin City
McDONOUGH, Catherine	NR-10-1815; Dublin City
MURRAY, Mary	NR-10-1815; Dublin City
MURRAY*, Bridget	NR-10-1815; Dublin City
O'NEIL*, Mary Ann	NR-05-1815; Dublin City
WALSH, Jane	NR-08-1815; Dublin City.
WATERS, Mary	NR-11-1815; Dublin City
WOODCOCK, Margaret	NR-11-1815; Dublin City

1816 TRIAL YEAR

Canada 1817

BARNS, Ann	NR-06-1816; Dublin City
BELL, Eliza/ Ann	NR-03-1816; Drogheda Town
BOLAND, Ann	NR-08-1816; Co Cork
BYRNE*, Elizabeth	NR-11-1816; Dublin City
CONNOR, Mary	NR-09-1816; Co Tipperary
DIXON, Ellen	NR-08-1816; Galway
DOYLE, Elizabeth	NR-01-1816; Dublin City
DUNN, Catherine	NR-12-1816; Dublin City
FITZGERALD, Mary	NR-08-1816; Co Cork
FITZPATRICK, Catherine	NR-03-1816; Dublin City
GREEN, Ann	NR-01-1816; Dublin City
GREEN, Catherine	NR-08-1816; Dublin City
HALEY, Margaret	NR-08-1816; Co Roscommon
HALLOGAN, Ellen	NR-05-1816; Dublin City
HAMILTON, Ann	NR-03-1816; Co Antrim
HART, Catherine	NR-03-1816; Co Mayo
HUGHES*, Ann	NR-09-1816; Dublin City
IVIS, Mary	NR-09-1816; Cork City
KANE, Sarah	NR-03-1816; Co Antrim
KEARNEY, Susan/ Julian	NR-03-1816; Co Cork
KEATING, Bridget	NR-08-1816; Kilkenny City
KEATING, Sarah	NR-03-1816; Kilkenny City
KELLY, Ann	NR-08-1816; Kilkenny City
KELLY, Mary Ann	NR-07-1816; Dublin City
KENNA, Ann	NR-03-1816; Cork City
KENNA, Juliana	NR-08-1816; Co Kerry
KENNEDY, Catherine	NR-07-1816; Dublin City
KEOGH, Ann	NR-01-1816; Dublin City
KEOGH, Margaret	NR-11-1816; Dublin City
KESLING*, Ann	NR-03-1816; Co Leitrim
KILFOILE*, Margaret	NR-03-1816; Co Carlow
KILLEHER, Mary	NR-03-1816; Cork City
LOONEY, Ellen/ Eleanor	NR-09-1816; Cork City
McDERMOTT, Honora	NR-08-1816; Co Mayo
McKENNA*, Ann	NR-03-1816; Co Donegal

McNALLY, Bridget — NR-03-1816; Co Mayo
McNALLY, Winifred — NR-03-1816; Co Mayo
MULLINS*, Margaret — NR-03-1816; Londonderry
MURPHY, Margaret — NR-09-1816; Cork City
NEALE, Mary (Jnr) — NR-07-1816; Dublin City
NEALE, Mary (Snr) — NR-07-1816; Dublin City
NEALE*, Catherine — NR-08-1816; Dublin City
NESBITT, Mary — NR-08-1816; Dublin City
NEWBY, Mary — NR-09-1816; Dublin City
O'HARA, Ann — NR-02-1816; Dublin City
O'NEIL, Margaret — NR-03-1816; Dublin City
O'NEIL, Sarah — NR-03-1816; Co Antrim
O'REILLY, Ann — NR-10-1816; Dublin City
PRENDERGAST, Catherine — NR-08-1816; Co Carlow
QUINN, Margaret — NR-07-1816; Co Dublin
REILLY, Mary — NR-03-1816; Dublin City
REYNOLDS, Mary Margaret — NR-03-1816; Dublin City
RONAN, Mary — NR-09-1816; Dublin City
RYAN, Mary — NR-08-1816; Co Meath
SCULLY, Margaret — NR-02-1816; Dublin City
SHARKEY, Ann — NR-01-1816; Dublin City
SHEA, Mary — NR-08-1816; Co Cork
STEWART, Mary — NR-01-1816; Dublin City
SULLIVAN, Hannah — NR-03-1816; Cork City
TARMITTY, Ann — NR-08-1816; Co Down
TOBIN, Catherine — NR-08-1816; Co Cork
WALSH, Elinor — NR-08-1816; Co Kilkenny
WHOLOGAN, Margaret — NR-05-1816; Dublin City

Elizabeth **1818**
DRISCOLL, Elizabeth — NR-03-1816; Co Cork
FITZGIBBON, Mary — NR-03-1816; Cork City

1817 TRIAL YEAR

Elizabeth **1818**
BERGIN, Margaret — NR-08-1817; Co Kilkenny
BESSONETT, Eleanor — NR-07-1817; Dublin City
BOURKE, Mary — NR-07-1817; Dublin City
BRANAGAN, Elinor — NR-03-1817; Antrim
BRIEN, Ellen — NR-03-1817; Co Cork
BROWNE, Anne — NR-07-1817; Dublin City
BUTLER, Anne — NR-03-1817; Tipperary
CARROLL, Mary — NR-06-1817; Dublin City
CASEY, Julia — NR-07-1817; Dublin City
CLOAKEY, Mary — NR-08-1817; Antrim
COOGAN, Elinor — NR-03-1817; Wicklow
CORRIGAN, Mary — NR-11-1817; Co Dublin
COULTER, Margaret — NR-03-1817; Down
CRAWFORD, Mary — NR-08-1817; Down
CURRAN*, Anne — NR-08-1817; Down
DALY, Anne — NR-06-1817; Dublin City
DONNELLY, Anne — NR-07-1817; Monaghan
DOOLY, Ellen — NR-08-1817; Cork City
ELLIS, Mary — NR-06-1817; Dublin City
FLAHERTY, Ellen — NR-03-1817; Meath
FREEL, Madge — NR-08-1817; Londonderry
GRIFFITH*, Anne — NR-08-1817; Meath
HAYES, Sarah — NR-08-1817; Cork City
HICKEY, Sarah — NR-03-1817; Limerick City
HORRAGAN, Mary — NR-08-1817; Cork City
HUGHES, Elizabeth — NR-07-1817; Dublin City
JENNINGS, Mary — NR-08-1817; Sligo
JOHNSON, Susan — NR-03-1817; Cork City
KELLY, Margaret — NR-12-1817; Dublin City

KELLY, Sarah   NR-12-1817; Co Dublin
KEON*, Bridget   NR-09-1817; Dublin City
LINEHAM, Mary   NR-03-1817; Co Cork
LITTLE, Anne   NR-03-1817; Dublin City
LOWRY, Mary   NR-08-1817; Kings County
LYNCH, Bridget   NR-03-1817; Cork City
McCAFFRY, Elizabeth   NR-08-1817; Cavan
McDONALD, Mary   NR-03-1817; Queens County
McEVOY, Mary   NR-11-1817; Dublin City
McGREIRRY*, Margaret   NR-08-1817; Cork City
McILROY*, Martha   NR-08-1817; Down
McKEON*, Catherine   NR-09-1817; Dublin City
MAHONY, Catherine   NR-08-1817; Cork City
MARSHALL, Judith   NR-07-1817; Kildare
MASSEY, Margaret   NR-07-1817; Kildare
MASTERSON, Margaret   NR-08-1817; Co Galway
MAWKING*, Mary   NR-08-1817; Antrim
MILLER, Catherine   NR-02-1817; Dublin City
MORGAN, Margaret   NR-08-1817; Antrim
MURPHY*, Catherine   NR-02-1817; Dublin City
MURTAGH, Rose   NR-08-1817; Meath
NOWLAN, Anne   NR-02-1817; Dublin City
O'HARA*, Mary   NR-03-1817; Antrim
QUIGLEY, Jane   NR-08-1817; Londonderry
RAFFERTY, Mary   NR-03-1817; Westmeath
REDMOND, Elinor   NR-12-1817; Dublin City
REILLY, Anne   NR-02-1817; Dublin City
REILLY, Catherine   NR-03-1817; Cavan
ROCHFORD, Margaret   NR-08-1817; Cork City
RYAN, Anne   NR-08-1817; Cork City
RYAN, Catherine   NR-12-1817; Co Dublin
SCANNELL, Margaret   NR-08-1817; Cork City
SHERLOCK, Mary   NR-11-1817; Dublin City
THOMSON, Catherine   NR-02-1817; Dublin City
USHER*, Mary   NR-08-1817; Kings County
WALSH, Mary   NR-03-1817; Queens County
WILLOUGHBY, Mary   NR-03-1817; Monaghan

Janus **1820**
WILSON, Sarah   Lent 1817; Queens County

Lord Wellington **1820**
GIBSON, Sarah Jane   NR-08-1817; Antrim

1818 TRIAL YEAR

Elizabeth **1818**
AHERN, Honora   NR-03-1818; Cork City
ARMSTRONG, Anne   NR-03-1818; Antrim
BROWNE, Mary Anne   NR-06-1818; Dublin City
BRYAN, Margaret   NR-03-1818; Dublin City
CAMPBELL, Margaret   NR-03-1818; Longford
CARROLL, Mary   NR-03-1818; Drogheda
CONNOLLY, Bridget   NR-05-1818; Dublin City
CORCORAN, Margaret   NR-03-1818; Longford
CRAWLY*, Honora   NR-03-1818; Co Cork
CULLEN, Anne   NR-03-1818; Dublin City
CULNANE, Catherine   NR-03-1818; Mayo
FANNING, Mary   NR-06-1818; Dublin City
FOX, Hannah/ Sarah   NR-03-1818; Kings County
GAHAN, Elizabeth   NR-02-1818; Dublin City
GARVIN, Elizabeth   NR-03-1818; Fermanagh

GLEESON, Ellen/
  Eleanor   NR-03-1818; Tipperary
JACOB, Mary   NR-03-1818;
                         Co Kilkenny
KEATING, Anne   NR-03-1818; Kildare
KELLY, Mary   NR-03-1818; Antrim
LILLYS, Mary   NR-04-1818; Dublin
                         City
McCARTHY,
  Catherine   NR-03-1818; Clare
McCUE, Honor   NR-03-1818; Tipperary
McDERMOTT,
  Elizabeth   NR-03-1818; Longford
McINTIRE, Isabella   NR-03-1818; Antrim
McLOUGHLIN, Anne   NR-03-1818; Antrim
MAGRATH, Catherine   NR-05-1818; Dublin
                         City
MAHER, Elizabeth   NR-05-1818; Dublin
                         City
MARRIN, Margaret   NR-03-1818; Monaghan
PIDGEON, Catherine   NR-03-1818; Carlow
REID, Elizabeth   NR-03-1818; Longford
RYAN, Margaret   NR-03-1818; Co Cork
STANTON*, Mary   NR-03-1818; Mayo
WALSH, Catherine   NR-03-1818; Clare

Janus 1820
MURPHY, Rose   Summer 1818;
                         Monaghan

Lord Wellington 1820
BALFE, Mary   01-09-1818; Dublin City
BARRY, Mary/   Summer 1818; Cork
  Margaret   City
BURKE, Mary   Summer 1818;
                         Roscommon
BURKE*, Judith   Summer 1818;
                         Tipperary
BUTLER, Eleanor   NR-11-1818; Co Dublin
CASHMAN,   Summer 1818; Cork
  Elizabeth   City
COURTNEY, Mary   NR-11-1818; Co Dublin
DINAN, Ellen   Summer 1818; Cork
                         City
DOWLING, Bridget   Summer 1818;
                         Co Kilkenny
FORAN, Elizabeth   25-08-1818; Dublin City
FORD, Mary   Summer 1818; Sligo
GRADY, Catherine   Summer 1818; Cork
                         City

HENDERSON,
  Elizabeth   Summer 1818; Cavan
HENDERSON,
  Susan   Summer 1818; Cavan
HORAN, Ann   25-08-1818; Dublin City
KEEFE, Margaret   Summer 1818;
                         Wexford
KELLY, Alice   25-08-1818; Dublin City
LANGIN, Mary   Summer 1818; Mayo
LYONS, Mary   Summer 1818; Clare
MADDIGAN,   Summer 1818;
  Catherine   Co Limerick
NASH, Mary   Summer 1818; Cork
                         City
PURLEY, Ann   18-12-1818; Dublin City
REDDY, Mary   Summer 1818; Cork
                         City
SULLIVAN, Mary   Summer 1818; Cork
                         City
TAYLOR, Maria   18-12-1818; Dublin City

1819 TRIAL YEAR

Almorah 1824
DUNN, Ellen   03-08-1819; Waterford

Janus 1820
BARRETT, Johanna   Lent 1819; Cork City
EAKIN*, Ruth   Lent 1819; Kildare
JOHNSTON, Mary/
  Margaret   Lent 1819; Tyrone
KENNEDY*,
  Margaret   Lent 1819; Westmeath
LEAHY, Johanna   Lent 1819; Cork City
MOLLOY, Ellen   NR-08-1819; Dublin
                         City
O'BRIEN, Mary   Lent 1819; Down
REILLY, Mary   Summer 1819; Mayo
SAVAGE, Catherine   Lent 1819; Louth
WHELAN, Anne   NR-03-1819; Dublin
                         City
WHITE, Mary   Lent 1819; Cork City

Lord Wellington 1820
BARRETT, Catherine   Lent 1819; Cork City
BRIEN*, Margaret   Lent 1819; Cork City
CRONE*, Elizabeth   Lent 1819; Cork City
DUGGAN, Catherine   Lent 1819; Cork City
DUNNE, Joanna   Lent 1819; Cork City

List B-1

McCARTHY,
  Margaret Mary   Lent 1819; Cork City
MOORE, Margaret   Lent 1819; Cork City
MURPHY, Mary   Lent 1819; Cork City

***Woodman* 1823**
JOYCE, Ann   Summer 1819;
                   Co Limerick

1820 TRIAL YEAR

***Almorah* 1824**
ARMSTRONG, Jane   NR-08-1820; Co Down
MARUM, Catherine   NR-03-1820; Waterford
RYAN, Mary   01-11-1820; Dublin

***John Bull* 1821**
NEILL, Catherine   02-04-1820; Cork City
O'NEILL*, Mary   NR-08-1820; Clare
STAFFORD,
  Catherine   NR-04-1820; Cork City

***Woodman* 1823**
BATEMAN, Eleanor/ Summer 1820;
  Ellen   Co Tipperary
CONNOR, Catherine Lent 1820;
                   Co Tipperary
CURRAN, Judith   Summer 1820;
                   Antrim
HOGAN, Julian/   Summer 1820;
  Judith   Co Kerry
KIRBY, Honora   Summer 1820;
                   Co Clare.
McLAUGHLIN,
  Catherine   Lent 1820; Co Kilkenny
WARD, Judith   Summer 1820;
                   Co Monaghan
WARREN, Margaret   Summer 1820;
                   Co Tipperary

1821 TRIAL YEAR

***Almorah* 1824**
COLLIGAN, Ellen   NR-07-1821; Longford
O'REILLEY, Ann   10-12-1821; Dublin
WALKER, Catherine 18-12-1821; Dublin
WARD, Ann   NR-03-1821; Wexford

***John Bull* 1821**
O'NEILL*, Mary   NR-03-1821; Limerick
                   City

***Woodman* 1823**
BENNETT*, Mary   Summer 1821; Cork
                   City
BOURKE, Bridget   27-10-1821; Dublin City
BRENNAN, Anne   02-10-1821; Dublin City
BUCKLEY, Mary   Summer 1821; Cork
                   City
BURKE, Bridget   Summer 1821;
                   Co Longford
BURKE, Mary   Summer 1821;
                   Co Waterford
BYRNE, Margaret   29-11-1821; Dublin City
CAIRNS, Mary   17-09-1821; Co Sligo
CARBERY, Ellen   08-12-1821; Dublin City
COGHLAN, Mary   Lent 1821; Co Cork
COURTNEY, Bridget Lent 1821; Co Cork
DOGHERTY, Bridget Summer 1821;
                   Co Antrim
DOWNEY, Mary   Summer 1821;
                   Co Down
FITZGERALD,
  Eleanor   Lent 1821; Co Cork
GARRAGHAN, Mary   NR-09-1821;
                   Co Monaghan
GILSHEENAN, Mary   NR-09-1821;
                   Co Monaghan
GORDON, Harriet   18-12-1821; Dublin City
HEENY*, Ellen   16-10-1821; Dublin City
HURLEY*, Mary   Lent 1821; Co Cork
KEEFFE, Johanna   NR-09-1821; Cork City
KEENAN, Grace   Summer 1821;
                   Co Cavan
LANE, Johanna   Lent 1821; Co Cork
LARKIN*, Margaret Lent 1821;
                   Co Tipperary
McCARTHY, Mary   Summer 1821; Cork
                   City
McDERMOTT*, Ann   14-09-1821; Dublin City
MAHONY, Mary   Summer 1821; Cork
                   City
MOORE, Margaret
  Mary   16-10-1821; Dublin City
NEAL, Elizabeth   Spring 1821; Cork City
NORTON, Catherine Lent 1821; Co Cork

PHELAN, Eleanor	Summer 1821; Kilkenny City	BROWNE, Catherine	Summer 1822; Limerick City
PRESTON, Margaret	16-10-1821; Dublin City	BURKE, Bridget	30-08-1822; Dublin City
REED*, Mary	Spring 1821; Cork City	BURKE, Margaret	Summer 1822; Cork City
REYNOLDS, Catherine	Summer 1821; Co Longford	BURKE*, Hessy/ Esther	16-04-1822; Dublin City
RING, Mary	Spring 1821; Cork City	BYRNE, Lucy	26-11-1822; Dublin City
ROBISON, Margaret	08-09-1821; Co Louth	BYRNE, Mary	29-06-1822; Dublin City
SHERLOCK, Ellen	Lent 1821; Co Cork	CALLAGHAN, Mary	Spring 1822; Cork City
SMITH, Rose	16-03-1821; Co Fermanagh	CARROLL, Margaret	26-11-1822; Dublin City
STEWART, Eliza	16-10-1821; Dublin City	CASEY, Honora	Spring 1822; Cork City
STEWART, Mary	Summer 1821; Co Antrim	CLERK, Mary	Summer 1822; Armagh
SULLIVAN, Honora	Summer 1821; Co Cork	COGHLAN, Mary	06-09-1822; Dublin City
WALSH, Ann	16-10-1821; Dublin City	COURTNEY, Elizabeth	20-11-1822; Dublin City
WHEELER, Sarah	16-10-1821; Dublin City	DALTON, Anne	26-04-1822; Dublin City
		DAVIS, Bridget	Summer 1822; Co Clare

1822 TRIAL YEAR

		DELAHUNT, Mary	20-09-1822; Dublin City
***Almorah* 1824**		DUANNY*, Bridget	Summer 1822; Co Mayo
CONNELL*, Ann	NR-08-1822; Cork		
FITZGERALD, Bridget	12-07-1822; Dublin	DUFFY, Elizabeth	Lent 1822; Co Cavan
GIBBONS, Mary	NR-08-1822; Co Mayo	HART, Mary	Summer 1822; Co Cork
GORDON, Elizabeth	NR-02-1822; Dublin	HAYES, Margaret	Summer 1822; Co Waterford
HALLORAN*, Margaret	NR-08-1822; Waterford	KELLY, Catherine	20-07-1822; Dublin City
HANNON, Alice	NR-08-1822; Limerick	KENNELLY, Mary	Summer 1822; Co Clare
HARVEY, Ann	NR-07-1822; Maryborough	KIRWAN, Catherine	Summer 1822; Co Leitrim
HARVEY, Mary	NR-07-1822; Queens County	KIRWAN*, Mary Ann	Summer 1822; Co Leitrim
HAUGHTON, Eliza	15-10-1822; Dublin	LEDWIDGE, Elizabeth	30-08-1822; Dublin City
KEOHANE, Catherine Judith	NR-04-1822; Cork	LEE, Winifred	Summer 1822; Co Leitrim
MEARY*, Margaret	NR-NR-1822; Co Tyrone	LONG, Catherine	Spring 1822; Cork City
WHITE, Catherine	NR-04-1822; Cork	McDERMOTT*, Johanna	Spring 1822; Co Tipperary
***Mariner* 1825**		McILVEE*, Mary	Summer 1822; Antrim
BYRNE*, Catherine	NR-09-1822; Dublin City	MALLAN, Sarah	Spring 1822; Co Armagh
TANGNEY, Mary	NR-08-1822; Kerry	MORRISON, Mary/ Mary Ann	Lent 1822; Co Down
***Woodman* 1823**		MURPHY, Elizabeth/ Eliza	16-04-1822; Dublin City
AHERN, Judith	Summer 1822; Cork City	NUGENT, Frances	20-11-1822; Dublin City
BARRY, Elizabeth	30-08-1822; Dublin City	QUIN*, Catherine	Lent 1822; Co Kildare

SULLIVAN, Mary   Summer 1822;
                      Co Kerry
SWEENY, Catherine   Summer 1822; Co Cork
THOMPSON, Abigail   Lent 1822; Co Down
WADE, Mary   27-07-1822; Dublin City
WHELAN*, Eliza   17-04-1822; Dublin City

1823 TRIAL YEAR

Almorah 1824
AGNEW, Susan   Easter 1823; Co Down
ANDERSON, Ann   NR-07-1823;
                      Maryborough
BEDFORD, Ann   26-03-1823; Cork
BLACK*, Catherine   14-01-1823; Co Dublin
BOURKE, Penelope   NR-08-1823; Galway
BRIAN*, Margaret   01-04-1823; Cork
BRYAN*, Ann   NR-03-1823;
                      Maryborough
BURKE, Mary   06-03-1823;
                      Co Kilkenny
BYRNE, Elizabeth   24-09-1823; Dublin
BYRNE*, Margaret   22-11-1823; Dublin City
CAMPBELL, Ellen   NR-03-1823; Antrim
CARROLL, Ann   25-03-1823;
                      Maryborough
CARROLL, Bridget   26-07-1823; Limerick
                      City
CARROLL, Catherine   09-09-1823; Dublin
CARROLL, Eleanor   Spring 1823;
                      Maryborough
CHESTER, Mary   10-10-1823; Dublin
COGLAN*, Mary   26-07-1823; Limerick
                      City
COLLINS, Harriott   01-08-1823; Dublin City
CONDRON,
  Elizabeth   NR-02-1823; Dublin
CROWLEY, Bridget   25-03-1823; Cork
CROWLEY, Judith   25-03-1823; Cork
CUNNINGHAM, Ann   15-10-1823; Dublin City
DELANEY, Margaret   15-07-1823; Cork
DELEA, Ann   29-03-1823; Cork
DILLON, Catherine   20-05-1823; Dublin
DONLEY*, Catherine   29-10-1823; Dublin
DOYLE, Rose   06-03-1823; Drogheda
FITZGERALD, Mary   Spring 1823; Kilkenny
FITZPATRICK, Ann   04-03-1823; Drogheda
FOWKES, Mary   15-04-1823; Cork

FRENCH, Elizabeth   NR-03-1823; Mullingar
GORMON*, Johanna   NR-03-1823; Co Clare
GRIFFIN*, Mary   NR-03-1823; Co Kerry
HARTIGAN, Mary   NR-04-1823; Limerick
                      City
HEANEY, Mary   11-03-1823; Monaghan
JENNINGS, Ann   NR-08-1823; Cork
KANE, Rose   NR-03-1823; Antrim
KAVANAGH, Mary   20-05-1823; Dublin
KEARNEY,
  Margaret   20-05-1823; Dublin
KELLY, Rose   NR-03-1823; Leitrim
KELLY*, Margaret   12-04-1823; Dublin
KENNA*, Ellen   26-03-1823; Cork
KENNEDY, Bridget   NR-03-1823;
                      Maryborough
LEAHY*, Cathrine/
  Mary   NR-04-1823; Cork City
LEARY, Ann   26-03-1823; Cork
McCARTHY, Mary   Spring 1823; Cork
McCONNELL, Ann   NR-03-1823;
                      Downpatrick
McDANIEL*, Ann   NR-02-1823; Dublin
McGARRY, Bridget   10-06-1823; Dublin
McGRADY,
  Catherine   15-03-1823; Co Armagh
McGUIRE*, Ann   07-03-1823; Dundalk
MANGAN*,
  Catherine   26-07-1823; Meath
MANLY, Catherine   NR-03-1823; Cork
MASTERSON, Judith   07-04-1823; Dublin
MAY, Margaret   09-09-1823; Dublin
MONEYHAN*,
  Johanna   05-08-1823; Tralee
MOORE, Elizabeth   10-06-1823; Dublin
MOORE, Mary   06-03-1823; Drogheda
MORIARTY,
  Margaret   NR-03-1823; Co Kerry
MULLIGAN, Mary   16-07-1823; Cork
MURPHY, Jane   14-01-1823; Co Dublin
NASH, Bridget   Summer 1823;
                      Co Clare
PENDERGAST, Ann   NR-03-1823; Co
                      Carlow
PENDERGAST,
  Catherine   NR-03-1823; Kilkenny
REDDY, Mary   15-10-1823; Dublin
REEVES, Margaret   Spring 1823; Limerick
                      City

REILLEY*, Bridget	NR-03-1823; Downpatrick		*Elizabeth* 1828	
REILLEY*, Margaret	22-08-1823; Dublin		MEEHAN, Bridget	NR-08-1824; Tyrone
RIELLY, Bridget	22-08-1823; Dublin		MURPHY, Anne	NR-12-1824; Dublin
ROGAN, Catherine	15-03-1823; Co Armagh		*Lady Rowena* 1826	
RYAN, Mary	NR-05-1823; Limerick		McCARTHY, Rose	NR-08-1824; Limerick City
SAVAGE, Ellen	15-07-1823; Cork City		McKENNA, Margaret	NR-08-1824; Cavan
SCOTT, Elizabeth	Summer 1823; Downpatrick		*Mariner* 1825	
SHAW, Jane	03-05-1823; Dublin		ARMSTRONG, Catherine	21-03-1824; Down
SHEEHAN, Ellen	16-07-1823; Cork City		BAIRD, Margaret	21-07-1824; Dublin City
SHEEHAN*, Bridget	NR-08-1823; Tralee		BERGEN, Anne	15-03-1824; Limerick City
SHORT, Margaret	29-07-1823; Downpatrick		BOAMANN*, Sarah/ Sally	NR-08-1824; Tyrone
SMITH, Bridget	NR-01-1823; Dublin		BROOKWELL*, Marianne	NR-10-1824; Dublin City
SMYTH, Ann	04-03-1823; Co Monaghan		BURKE, Ellen	20-08-1824; Dublin City
STERNE, Jane	03-05-1823; Dublin		BYRNE, Ann	28-09-1824; Dublin City
STEWART, Bridget	NR-03-1823; Antrim		CAULFIELD*, Mary	26-10-1824; Dublin
TOOKES, Mary	Easter 1823; Galway		COGHLAN, Anne	05-08-1824; Queens County
TOOLE, Margaret	22-11-1823; Dublin		COLEMAN, Rose	NR-05-1824; Dublin City
WALSH, Ann	14-05-1823; Dublin		CONISKEY*, Eleanor	10-08-1824; Fermanagh
WALSH*, Catherine	NR-08-1823; Cork		CONNORS*, Mary	NR-03-1824; Clare
Lady Rowena 1826			CONWAY, Sarah	19-01-1824; Dublin City
CONNORS, Mary	23-07-1823; Limerick City		DELAHUNT, Mary Ann	30-11-1824; Co Dublin
Mariner 1825			DERBY*, Anne	09-08-1824; Kildare
BYRNE, Mary	14-07-1823; Wexford		DILLON*, Anne	06-06-1824; Dublin City
HICKSON, Eliza	28-09-1823; Dublin City		DONOVAN, Margaret	17-08-1824; Cork City
LEARY, Honora	14-07-1823; Wexford		DRAPER, Mary	02-08-1824; Dublin City
McKENNA, Margaret	NR-07-1823; Cavan		DREW, Ellen	09-11-1824; Co Dublin
RYAN, Honor	25-11-1823; Dublin City		DRISCOLL, Catherine	17-08-1824; Cork City
			DUGGAN, Grace	18-05-1824; Dublin City
1824 TRIAL YEAR			DUNLEVIE, Mary	10-01-1824; Dublin
Almorah 1824			DUNN, Ellen	12-08-1824; Antrim
DRISCOLL, Mary	06-01-1824; Dublin		DWYER, Bridget/ Biddy	14-03-1824; Limerick City
RYAN, Mary	12-01-1824; Westmeath		FARRELL, Mary	28-09-1824; Dublin City
Brothers 1827			FOSTER*, Mary Anne	04-04-1824; Dublin City
BROWNE, Catharine	NR-07-1824; Dublin		FOX, Lucy/ Louisa	09-07-1824; Dublin City
BUTCHER, Caroline	23-03-1824; Antrim		GAFNEY, Susan	17-02-1824; Dublin City
HUGHES, Mary	NR-08-1824; Galway		GERNON, Mary	NR-03-1824; Dublin
STEVENS, Rosanna	11-12-1824; Dublin			
WALL, Catherine	NR-03-1824; Naas			

460 List B-1

GODFREY, Mary	10-08-1824; Tipperary
GORMON, Anne	09-07-1824; Dublin City
GORMON, Mary	04-05-1824; Dublin City
GUDDIS*, Mary	NR-08-1824; Armagh
HAMILTON, Mary	28-09-1824; Dublin City
HAMILTON, Mary Jane	09-03-1824; Monaghan
HAYDON, Rosanna	30-04-1824; Dublin City
HAYES, Ellen	NR-04-1824; Cork City
HEYBURN, Elizabeth	02-08-1824; Antrim
HILL, Rose	05-08-1824; Monaghan
HOGAN, Bridget	NR-03-1824; Wicklow
HORNBY, Caroline	20-01-1824; Dublin City
HOURIGAN, Eleanor	28-09-1824; Limerick City
HOWARD, Anne	NR-03-1824; Clare
HOWARD, Sarah	20-08-1824; Dublin City
HYDE, Elizabeth	24-08-1824; Dublin City
JACKSON*, Margaret	22-04-1824; Dublin City
JOHNSTONE, Margaret	22-04-1824; Dublin City
KEARNS, Mary	04-09-1824; Dublin City
KEATING, Margaret	02-08-1824; Dublin City
KELLIHER, Honora	03-04-1824; Cork City
KELLY, Bridget	NR-03-1824; Clare
KELLY, Catherine	19-03-1824; Dublin City
LANG, Anne	28-09-1824; Dublin City
LEONARD, Alice	NR-08-1824; Donegal
LUNGAIN*, Catherine	20-08-1824; Londonderry
McARDLE*, Margaret	01-09-1824; Dublin City
McCABE(RS)*, Mary	12-03-1824; Armagh
McCARTHY, Frances	08-10-1824; Dublin City
McCLELLAND, Mary	16-08-1824; Down
McCLUFFON*, Rose	03-08-1824; Monaghan
McDERMOTT, Sarah	17-03-1824; Leitrim
McDONALD, Mary	08-03-1824; Monaghan
McEVOY, Margaret	20-01-1824; Dublin City
McMANUS, Margaret Mary	NR-08-1824; Donegal
MAGUIRE, Catherine	21-07-1824; Dublin City
MAGUIRE, Margaret	12-08-1824; Antrim
MALONE, Bridget	27-07-1824; Dublin City
MARTIN*, Hannah	30-11-1824; Co Dublin
MARTIN, Margaret	23-03-1824; Monaghan
MATTHEWS, Anne	06-10-1824; Dublin City
MATTHEWS, Marianne	08-10-1824; Dublin City
MELLISH, Anne	NR-02-1824; Antrim
MOON*, Elizabeth	12-08-1824; Antrim
MOORE, Eleanor	15-03-1824; Limerick City
MORGAN, Rose	12-08-1824; Antrim
MORROSSEY, Mary	01-08-1824; Tipperary
MURDOCK, Sarah	12-03-1824; Armagh
MURPHY, Julia	19-05-1824; Dublin City
NEVIN, Mary	19-03-1824; Dublin City
NICHOLSON, Elizabeth	21-03-1824; Down
NOWLAN, Catherine	NR-08-1824; Carlow
O'CONNELL*, Frances	02-04-1824; Cork City
PIGGOTT, Elizabeth	06-12-1824; Co Dublin
QUAIL, Anne	02-08-1824; Dublin City
READ*, Mary	21-04-1824; Dublin City
ROCHE, Hannah	22-05-1824; Dublin City
RYAN*, Mary	23-06-1824; Dublin City
SCREEN, Mary	17-03-1824; Antrim
SHANAGHAN*, Elizabeth	10-08-1824; Tipperary
SHEPPARD, Harriet	08-05-1824; Dublin City
SMILEY, Ellen	16-08-1824; Down
SPILLANE, Catherine	NR-04-1824; Cork City
STEWART, Frances	12-04-1824; Antrim
SULLIVAN, Letitia	25-07-1824; Leitrim
SWIFT, Catherine	06-06-1824; Dublin City
TAYLOR, Anne	19-01-1824; Dublin City
TOOHEY, Ceciley	06-08-1824; Mayo
WALSH, Mary	27-08-1824; Dublin City

1825 TRIAL YEAR

Brothers 1827

ALLISON, Isabella	27-03-1825; Armagh
BIRNEY, Mary	NR-08-1825; Monaghan
BRADY, Mary	NR-08-1825; Clare
BRYAN*, Mary	28-03-1825; Kilkenny
BURKE, Julian/ Judith	03-08-1825; Tralee
BYRNE, Ann	18-08-1825; Dublin
BYRNE, Catherine	11-07-1825; Wexford
BYRNE, Mary	14-05-1825; Dublin

CAMPBELL, Mary	NR-08-1825; Belfast	MINCHIN, Catherine	NR-03-1825; Queens County
CARROLL, Ann	21-12-1825; Dublin	MONKS, Judith	15-12-1825; Dublin
COLLINS, Ellen	17-07-1825; Cavan	MURPHY, Jane	24-11-1825; Dublin
CRAMSIL, Sarah	17-03-1825; Antrim	MURPHY, Mary	18-10-1825; Dublin
CREEVY, Mary	31-12-1825; Dublin	MURRAY, Margaret	05-10-1825; Dublin
DAY, Mary Ann	31-12-1825; Dublin	NICHOLSON, Elizabeth	13-11-1825; Dublin
DEEHAN*, Esther	23-03-1825; Londonderry	O'BRIEN, Alice	NR-03-1825; Limerick
DELANEY, Mary	26-08-1825; Dublin	O'BRIEN, Honora	03-08-1825; Kerry
DICKSON, Bridget	13-11-1825; Dublin	PEPPARD, Honora	23-07-1825; Limerick
DOYLE, Maria	03-10-1825; Dublin	PRIM, Bridget	11-07-1825; Wexford
FAIRBROTHER, Mary	14-07-1825; Wicklow	RALPH, Ann	03-10-1825; Dublin
FINNEGAN, Judith	03-08-1825; Kerry	RELIAN, Mary	03-08-1825; Kerry
FITZPATRICK, Sarah	25-10-1825; Dublin	SAVAGE, Bridget	15-12-1825; Dublin
		SLATTERY, Mary	23-07-1825; Limerick
FOLEY, Eleanor	22-03-1825; Londonderry	SMITH, Bridget	28-NR-1825; Dublin
FOY, Jane	03-10-1825; Dublin	STEWART, Ann Mary	24-03-1825; Londonderry
GORDON, Mary	NR-08-1825; Waterford	SULLIVAN, Mary	03-08-1825; Kerry
HALPIN, Mary	23-07-1825; Limerick	SULLIVAN*, Honora	03-08-1825; Kerry
HANLON, Amelia	24-11-1825; Dublin	TAAFE, Jane	26-10-1825; Dublin
HASSEY, Mary	NR-03-1825; Monaghan	VEARLEY, Ann	26-10-1825; Dublin
HUGHES, Catherine	13-11-1825; Dublin		

Elizabeth **1828**

DONNELLY, Sally	06-08-1825; Armagh

Lady Rowena **1826**

JOHNSON*, Elizabeth	22-08-1825; Dublin
JOHNSON*, Mary	NR-07-1825; Fermanagh
KEARNES, Bridget	NR-03-1825; Naas
KEARNES, Elizabeth	11-10-1825; Dublin
KEEFE, Margaret	28-10-1825; Dublin
KELLS, Matilda	29-12-1825; Dublin
KELLY, Ann	NR-11-1825; Dublin
KELLY, Mary	28-11-1825; Dublin
KENNEDY, Mary	03-07-1825; Roscommon
LAMB, Catharine	21-12-1825; Dublin
LARKIN, Margaret	27-03-1825; Clonmell
LYNCH, Mary	16-03-1825; Waterford
McCORMICK, Mary	22-03-1825; Londonderry
McCORMICK, Rose	NR-03-1825; Antrim
McLOUGHLIN, Ann/Ellen	04-03-1825; Longford
McMAHON, Mary	27-03-1825; Clonmell
McNAMARA, Margaret	23-07-1825; Limerick
MEEHAN, Jane	25-03-1825; Mayo

BIRD, Catherine	17-08-1825; Dublin City
BIRMINGHAM, Mary	13-05-1825; Dublin City
BLAKE, Maria	07-07-1825; Dublin City
BOYD, Margaret	NR-07-1825; Antrim
BOYLE, Catherine	17-03-1825; Tipperary
BYRNE*, Cath/Mary Ann	08-08-1825; Dublin City
CAMPBELL, Margaret	04-08-1825; Dublin City
CARROLL, Ellen	25-03-1825; Cork City
CARROLL, Ellen	NR-08-1825; Cork
CARROLL, Mary	09-08-1825; Cork City
CARROLL, Mary	02-01-1825; Dublin City
CLARKE, Margaret	03-05-1825; Dublin City
CONNORS, Ellen	NR-08-1825; Cork
COTTER, Anne	NR-08-1825; Cork
COUGHLAN, Elizabeth	17-08-1825; Cork City
CROAK, Honora	NR-03-1825; Cork
CURTIN, Anne	10-08-1825; Cork City
DALY, Mary	29-07-1825; Limerick City

462 List B-1

DARCY, Margaret	16-02-1825; Dublin City	McNAMARA, Bridget	NR-07-1825; Dublin City
DAVIS, Anne	03-02-1825; Dublin City		
DAVIS, Ellen	07-07-1825; Dublin City	MADDEN, Mary	09-08-1825; Clare
DAY, Ellen	18-03-1825; Kerry	MAGUIRE, Mary Ann/Jane	NR-02-1825; Dublin City
DIGNAM, Mary	03-05-1825; Dublin City		
DONOHOE, Jane	08-03-1825; Dublin City	MAHONY, Abigail	09-08-1825; Cork City
DREW*, Anne	NR-03-1825; Cork City	MAHONY, Bridget	NR-03-1825; Cork
DRISCOLL, Mary	NR-08-1825; Cork	MAHONY, Catherine	NR-03-1825; Cork
DUGGAN, Catherine	NR-08-1825; Cork City	MEEHAN, Mary	23-07-1825; Limerick City
ERIN, Anne	13-12-1825; Dublin City		
FARRELL*, Mary	15-07-1825; Roscommon	MOONEY, Mary Anne	NR-06-1825; Dublin City
FIELD, Elizabeth	09-08-1825; Cork City	MURPHY, Mary	12-08-1825; Cork City
FINN, Catherine	17-03-1825; Cork City	MURPHY*, Margaret	09-08-1825; Cork City
FITZGERALD, Mary	NR-08-1825; Cork	NAUGHTON, Ellen	09-03-1825; Limerick City
FITZPATRICK, Honora	18-08-1825; Kilkenny	NESBITT*, Susan	04-08-1825; Dublin City
FRAYNE, Mary	04-02-1825; Dublin City	NOWLAN*, Catherine	22-11-1825; Dublin City
FREEL*, Sarah	NR-04-1825; Londonderry	NUGENT, Anne	07-07-1825; Dublin
		NUGENT, Catherine	22-04-1825; Dublin City
GAVIN, Catherine	09-03-1825; Limerick City	O'BRIEN, Mary Anne	08-04-1825; Dublin City
		PERCIVAL, Julia	07-07-1825; Dublin City
GREEN*, Eliza	08-04-1825; Dublin City	REA, Johanna	NR-03-1825; Cork
HADDOCK, Charlotte Mary	04-02-1825; Dublin City	READ*, Anne	04-08-1825; Dublin City
		REDMOND, Eleanor	23-03-1825; Dublin City
HANNON*, Mary	29-07-1825; Limerick City	REGAN*, Caroline	18-03-1825; Kerry
		REILLEY, Johanna	NR-03-1825; Cork
HARVEY, Eliza	18-06-1825; Dublin City	REILLEY, Mary	NR-03-1825; Cork
HOLMES, Hester	13-05-1825; Dublin City	REYNOLDS, Elizabeth	04-08-1825; Dublin City
HUGHES, Mary	23-04-1825; Dublin City	RICE, Catherine	NR-03-1825; Cork
HURLEY, Mary	NR-03-1825; Cork	ROBERTS*, Jane	23-07-1825; Limerick City
JACKSON*, Margaret	01-03-1825; Dublin City		
JONES, Eleanor	08-03-1825; Dublin City	RYAN, Bridget	NR-02-1825; Dublin City
KEARNEY, Bridget	17-08-1825; Dublin City		
KEARY, Mary	16-07-1825; Dublin City	SHANAGHAN, Mary	18-08-1825; Kerry
KEEFE, Honora	NR-08-1825; Cork	SHEA, Margaret	17-08-1825; Cork City
KELLY, Eliza	03-04-1825; Dublin City	SINGLETON*, Mary	NR-03-1825; Down
KELLY, Judith	20-11-1825; Dublin City	SMITH, Eliza	NR-03-1825; Down
KELLY, Margaret	09-02-1825; Dublin City	SMITH*, Anne	04-08-1825; Dublin
KELLY, Margaret	03-05-1825; Dublin City	SULLIVAN, Honora	17-08-1825; Cork City
KELLY*, Julia	09-02-1825; Dublin City	WALSH, Anne	06-05-1825; Dublin City
KELSH*, Bridget	23-11-1825; Dublin City	WALSH, Margaret	17-03-1825; Tipperary
LEDWICK*, Eliza	03-11-1825; Dublin City	WILLIAMSON, Jane	04-08-1825; Dublin City
LEONARD*, Bridget	17-08-1825; Dublin City	WILSON*, Anne	22-08-1825; Dublin City
LYONS, Bridget	03-05-1825; Dublin City		
McMAHON, Margaret	23-07-1825; Limerick City	*Mariner* **1825**	
		QUINN, Margaret	NR-01-1825; Dublin

1826 TRIAL YEAR

Brothers 1827

BARRY, Ellen	30-07-1826; Cork
BARRY, Mary	Easter 1826; Down
BLAKE, Anne	30-07-1826; Cork
BOURKE*, Margaret	05-03-1826; Wicklow
BOURNE, Ellen	10-03-1826; Fermanagh
BRAZIL, Bridget	22-07-1826; Dublin
BROWNE, Ellen	10-03-1826; Fermanagh
BUTTLER, Mary Ann	18-03-1826; Kilkenny
CALLAGHAN, Elizabeth	17-03-1826; Antrim
CARROLL, Anne	29-04-1826; Dublin
CARTHY, Honora	22-03-1826; Antrim
CLARKSON, Lydia	10-01-1826; Dublin
COFFEY, Eleanor	05-07-1826; Dublin
COLLINS, Maria	26-06-1826; Dublin
CONNELL, Mary	06-08-1826; Cork
CRANNAVAN, Mary	25-03-1826; Carlow
CULLEN, Anne	NR-02-1826; Dublin
CURRY, Elizabeth	26-03-1826; Londonderry
DEEN, Peggy	20-07-1826; Kerry
DELANEY, Anne/Mary	03-04-1826; Dublin
DEVANEY, Anne	22-07-1826; Dublin
DONAGHY, Mary	22-03-1826; Antrim
DONEVAN, Mary	26-03-1826; Cork
DONOHUE, Anne	01-03-1826; Dublin
DONOHUE, Mary	01-03-1826; Dublin
DOWNING, Mary	20-07-1826; Kerry
DOYLE*, Esther	27-07-1826; Dublin
DUNOVAN, Catherine	04-03-1826; Wexford
FEARY, Ann	22-03-1826; Donegal
FIELD, Catherine	06-08-1826; Cork
FITZPATRICK, Bridget	08-03-1826; Cavan
FITZPATRICK, Catherine	08-03-1826; Cavan
FLINN, Catherine	NR-08-1826; Cavan
FRAZER, Anne	22-03-1826; Antrim
GALLAGHER*, Mary	30-03-1826; Dublin
GRIFFIN, Mary	09-03-1826; Limerick
HARRINGTON*, Matty	26-03-1826; Londonderry
HARRIS, Catherine	06-08-1826; Cork
HICKEY, Ellen	06-08-1826; Cork
JACKSON, Mary	09-03-1826; Limerick
KEBLEY, Joanna	28-07-1826; Cork
KEEFE, Catharine	25-05-1826; Dublin
KEEFE, Mary	09-03-1826; Limerick
KELLY, Anne	02-06-1826; Dublin
KELLY, Nancy	11-03-1826; Fermanagh
KELLY*, Mary	30-03-1826; Dublin
LARKINS, Catharine	08-03-1826; Cavan
LINEHAN, Mary	29-07-1826; Cork
McALUONE, Ellen	11-03-1826; Fermanagh
McARDILE, Bridget	15-02-1826; Dublin
McCAFFEREY, Sarah	20-02-1826; Dublin
McGEE, Catherine	29-03-1826; Down
McGOWRAN, Abagail	13-02-1826; Dublin
McMAHON, Anne	NR-03-1826; Dundalk
McNAMARA, Ellen	08-03-1826; Clare
MAHONEY, Mary	29-03-1826; Cork
MATHEWS, Susan	29-03-1826; Down
MEEKIN, Elizabeth	15-02-1826; Dublin
MEIGHAN*, Sarah	17-03-1826; Monaghan
MOLLOY, Eleanor	NR-06-1826; Dublin
MURPHY, Ellen	30-07-1826; Cork
NEILE, Bridget	NR-07-1826; Carlow
NICHOL, Jane	17-03-1826; Monaghan
O'BRIEN, Catherine	27-04-1826; Dublin
O'BRIEN, Honora	09-03-1826; Limerick
O'HARA, Isabella	11-03-1826; Fermanagh
RAMSEY, Ellen	22-03-1826; Antrim
REARDON, Honora	06-08-1826; Cork
REGAN, Mary	28-03-1826; Cork
REYNOLDS, Margaret	NR-03-1826; Dublin
ROBINSON, Elizabeth	27-06-1826; Dublin
RONAYNE*, Mary	26-03-1826; Cork
ROSS*, Ann	NR-08-1826; Monaghan
RYAN, Catharine	26-03-1826; Cork
SADLER, Mary Martha	29-05-1826; Dublin
SAVAGE, Mary	NR-03-1826; Armagh
SHANNAHAN, Mary	29-07-1826; Cork
SHEA, Catharine	NR-08-1826; Cork
SHEA, Judith	29-03-1826; Cork
SHEA, Mary	NR-08-1826; Cork

464 List B-1

SHELTON, Bridget	09-03-1826; Limerick	SWEENY, Lucinda	NR-07-1826; Donegal
SMITH, Margaret	17-03-1826; Monaghan	THOMPSON,	
SMITH*, Ann	10-03-1826; Fermanagh	Catherine	24-08-1826; Tipperary
TWIGG, Martha	27-04-1826; Dublin	WALLACE, Hannah	14-07-1826; Down

Elizabeth 1828

ATKINS, Mary Ann	14-07-1826; Queens County

1827 TRIAL YEAR

Elizabeth 1828

BROWN, Ann	06-09-1826; Dublin
BURKE, Mary	28-09-1826; Dublin
CARR, Margaret	30-12-1826; Dublin
CONNOLLY, Mary	23-03-1826; Mayo
CONNOR, Mary	25-03-1826; Cork
CURRY, Anne	02-08-1826; Dublin
DOWNES, Mary Ann	10-11-1826; Dublin
DOYLE*, Mary	NR-06-1826; Dublin
DRISCOLL, Eleanor	NR-03-1826; Limerick
EARELY, Ann	25-09-1826; Dublin
FAHY, Bridget	24-08-1826; Tipperary
FANNING, Eleanor	02-08-1826; Dublin
FLANNAGAN, Mary	24-10-1826; Dublin
GODFREY, Margaret	14-03-1826; Limerick
GOGARTY, Catherine	06-03-1826; Drogheda
GRIFFIN, Mary	02-04-1826; Cork
HARRINGTON, Mary	25-03-1826; Cork
HENRY*, Rose	NR-03-1826; Meath
HICKIE, Mary	14-03-1826; Limerick
HOARE, Catherine	19-03-1826; Kerry
KEELY, Instatia	17-04-1826; Waterford
KELLY, Ellen	05-04-1826; Dublin
KEOGH, Eliza	11-11-1826; Dublin
McCOY, Anne	NR-08-1826; Cork
MAHER, Sarah	04-08-1826; Dublin
MEALEY, Mary	06-10-1826; Dublin
MITCHELL, Mary	17-07-1826; Antrim
MOORE, Mary	04-08-1826; Dublin
MURPHY, Margaret	NR-03-1826; Monaghan
MURRAY, Margaret	17-04-1826; Waterford
NEALE, Catherine	29-07-1826; Cork
NEILLE, Honora	14-03-1826; Limerick
O'DEA, Ellen	14-03-1826; Limerick
PORTER*, Sarah	NR-08-1826; Tipperary
ROCK, Ann	17-03-1826; Kings County
ROWE, Aliza	27-10-1826; Dublin
SMITH, Eleanor	NR-06-1826; Dublin
AUSTIN, Mary	05-10-1827; Dublin
BARRINGTON, Eleanor	27-03-1827; Dublin
BLANEY*, Margaret	27-03-1827; NR
BOLLISTY*, Mary	13-03-1827; Westmeath
BRYAN, Margaret	13-06-1827; Limerick
BUCKLEY, Mary	16-03-1827; Limerick
BURKE, Ellen	02-04-1827; Cork
BUTLER, Catherine	25-03-1827; Kilkenny
BYRNE, Elizabeth	09-03-1827; Wicklow
BYRNE, Judith	13-03-1827; Westmeath
BYRNE, Mary	13-03-1827; Wexford
CARPENTER, Elizabeth	06-03-1827; Dublin
CARROLL, Catherine	13-03-1827; Wexford
CARROLL, Margaret	13-03-1827; Wexford
CARROLL, Mary	13-03-1827; Wexford
CHAMBERS, Sarah	17-07-1827; Limerick
COBB, Eleanor	17-03-1827; Kings County
COBB, Letitia	17-03-1827; Kings County
COGHLAN, Bridget	02-03-1827; Kilkenny
COGHLAN, Honor	29-03-1827; Queens County
CONNELL, Ellen	21-03-1827; Tipperary
CONNOR*, Mary	12-04-1827; Dublin
CONNORS, Catherine	15-04-1827; Tipperary
COURTNEY, Mary	12-04-1827; Dublin
COURTNEY, Sarah	NR-02-1827; Dublin
CUMMINS, Sarah	17-07-1827; Limerick
DANAGHER, Hannah	16-03-1827; Limerick
DELANY, Margaret	10-04-1827; Dublin
DOGHERTY, Catherine	08-03-1827; Longford
DOGHERTY, Mary	16-03-1827; Londonderry
DORMER, Eleanor	NR-03-1827; Waterford

List B-1

DOWLING*, Catherine	28-03-1827; Wicklow	LEARY, Mary	13-03-1827; Wexford
DOYLE, Mary	24-03-1827; Kilkenny	LONG*, Mary	17-03-1827; Leitrim
DUMAN*, Sarah	14-07-1827; Leitrim	LYNCH, Catherine	27-03-1827; Dublin
DWYER, Mary	01-04-1827; Tipperary	McANNALLY, Alice	15-03-1827; Louth
EGAN, Eleanor	NR-04-1827; Cork	McASPERIT, Ann	14-03-1827; Fermanagh
EMMERSON, Mary	12-04-1827; Dublin	McCARTHY, Honora	02-04-1827; Cork
FALLON, Rose	NR-03-1827; Derry	McCORMACK, Margaret	10-03-1827; Dublin
FIELDS, Margaret	12-04-1827; Cork	McCORMICK, Mary	12-02-1827; Dublin
FIELDS, Mary	10-04-1827; Cork	McDONNELL, Anne	05-11-1827; Dublin
FLOOD, Ellen	10-04-1827; Dublin	McEVOY, Clare	15-05-1827; Dublin
GARTLAND*, Isabella	17-03-1827; Meath	McGIVERN, Anne/ Margaret	14-07-1827; Armagh
GASKIN, Mary	06-03-1827; Dublin	McGLADE, Sarah	14-03-1827; Fermanagh
GAWLEY, Mary	12-07-1827; Limerick	McGRATH, Honora	31-03-1827; Tipperary
GIBBON, Mary	17-03-1827; Westmeath	McINAHENY*, Bridget	19-07-1827; Clare
GIBBONS, Bridget	12-05-1827; Dublin		
GIBBONS, Mary Anne	12-05-1827; Dublin	McREDMOND, Margaret	15-04-1827; Tipperary
GORMAN, Elizabeth	27-03-1827; Queens County	MAHER, Mary	10-01-1827; Dublin
		MALONY, Margaret	05-11-1827; Dublin
GRANT, Catherine	29-03-1827; Antrim	MANION*, Catherine	17-03-1827; Kings County
GRAY, Mary	14-02-1827; Dublin		
GREENE, Anne	08-03-1827; Louth	MARTIN, Sarah	13-07-1827; Armagh
HALPIN, Ann	15-02-1827; Dublin	MEANY, Mary	22-03-1827; Waterford
HANLEY, Tereas	17-04-1827; Dublin	MITCHELL*, Mary	NR-03-1827; Londonderry
HANLON, Catherine	10-04-1827; Cork		
HARRINGTON, Margaret	22-08-1827; Waterford	MOORE, Catherine	12-04-1827; Dublin
		MORRIS, Mary	15-03-1827; Louth
HEALY, Ellen	NR-04-1827; Cork	MULCAHY, Mary	16-03-1827; Limerick
HENEY*, Mary	17-03-1827; Kings County	MULLALLY, Mary	22-08-1827; Waterford
		MULLALY, Mary	22-03-1827; Waterford
HIGGINS, Honor	17-03-1827; Galway	MULLIGAN, Catherine	26-02-1827; Dublin
HOGAN, Margaret	14-03-1827; Limerick		
HOLMES, Catherine	12-04-1827; Dublin	MURPHY, Anne	NR-04-1827; Kildare
IRWIN, Margaret	07-07-1827; Dublin	MURPHY, Annstatia	27-03-1827; Kilkenny
JOHNSON, Bridget	30-05-1827; Dublin	MURPHY, Ellen	11-04-1827; Cork
KEEFE, Ann	22-03-1827; Waterford	MURRAY, Bridget	02-04-1827; Cork
KELLY, Anne	05-08-1827; Waterford	NOONE, Mary	08-03-1827; Longford
KELLY, Bridget	12-03-1827; Drogheda	NORTON, Catherine	17-04-1827; Dublin
KELLY, Elizabeth	29-03-1827; Antrim	NOWLAN, Anne	29-03-1827; Antrim
KELLY, Mary	04-08-1827; Dublin	O'BRIEN, Eliza	07-07-1827; Dublin
KELLY, Mary	10-08-1827; Dublin	PAGE, Eliza	18-05-1827; Dublin
KENNY, Elizabeth	10-08-1827; Dublin	PHELAN*, Mary	22-03-1827; Queens County
KEOGH, Margaret	16-03-1827; Limerick		
KIELY, Mary	31-03-1827; Tipperary	POWER, Ellen	29-03-1827; Tipperary
KIRBY, Mary	02-04-1827; Cork	POWER, Margaret	15-03-1827; NR
LAWLESS, Mary	05-05-1827; Dublin	QUIGLEY, Hannah	NR-03-1827; Londonderry
LAWLOR, Catherine	02-04-1827; Carlow		

QUINN, Anne 12-03-1827; Fermanagh
RAFTER, Catherine 05-08-1827; Waterford
REGAN, Mary 05-08-1827; Waterford
REILLEY, Anne 20-03-1827; Dublin
RENOHAN, Catherine 17-03-1827; Kings County
ROBINSON, Marianne 09-03-1827; Dublin
ROSSITER, Eleanor 14-03-1827; Wexford
ROURKE, Mary 09-07-1827; Clare
RUSSELL, Anne NR-02-1827; Dublin
RYAN, Catherine 24-03-1827; Kilkenny
RYAN, Mary 14-03-1827; Wexford
RYAN, Mary 15-04-1827; Tipperary
SAUNDERS*, Catherine 22-03-1827; Waterford
SCOTT, Mary NR-08-1827; Waterford
SCOTT, Sarah NR-03-1827; Monoghan
SCULLY*, Mary 01-04-1827; Tipperary
SHEA, Mary 15-05-1827; Dublin
SHEA*, Ellen 01-04-1827; Tipperary
SHERRIDAN, Elizabeth 06-03-1827; Dublin
SHIERLEY, Harriet 27-03-1827; Kilkenny
SLATTERY, Mary 14-03-1827; Limerick
SMITH, Eliza 10-04-1827; Cork
STEENSON, Margaret 25-03-1827; Monaghan
SULLIVAN, Margaret 02-04-1827; Cork
TAFFE, Mary 17-03-1827; Louth
WALSH, Honora 10-04-1827; Cork
WALSH, Judith NR-04-1827; Kildare
WARREN, Johanha NR-04-1827; Cork
WELLSON, Ellen 19-07-1827; Londonderry
WELSH, Mary 03-04-1827; Tipperary
WHELAN, Alley 24-03-1827; Kilkenny
WINTERS, Anne 07-07-1827; Dublin

NO RESPONSE ON TRIAL YEAR

Almorah 1824
McKEE, Margaret Londonderry

Anna 1801
BRENAN*, Catherine NR
BUCKLY, Bridget NR

CASSINS, Ann NR
CLAFFY, Catherine NR
DINAHY*, Mary NR
FLINN, Elizabeth NR
FLYN, Judith NR
GALLAGHER, Elizabeth NR
HICKEY, Catherine NR
LAWLER, Mary NR
LEWINS*, Mary NR
LYNCH, Anastasia NR
McNALLY, Mary NR
MADDEN, Mary NR
MOONEY, Margaret NR
MOORE, Elinor NR
QUINLAN, Mary NR
QUINN, Jane NR
QUINN, Mary NR
RIGNEY, Mary NR
WATSON, Ann NR
WELSH, Eleanor NR
WILSON, Margaret NR
WOODS, Elizabeth NR

Archduke Charles 1813
KEARNEY, Mary Co Tipperary

Britannia 1797
ANDERSON, Mary Dublin

Brothers 1827
DALEY, Elizabeth Down
DONNELLY, Catherine NR
McCARTHY, Margaret NR
RYAN, Mary NR
TREEL, Mary Margery Londonderry
WILLSON, Elizabeth NR

Canada 1817
EDRINGTON*, Elizabeth Armagh

Catherine 1814
CARTER, Mary Dublin City
KAVENAGH, Mary Dublin City

Elizabeth 1828
CONNORS, Bridget Clare

Francis & Eliza 1815
SHERIDAN, Catharine	Dublin City
WATSON*, Elizabeth	Dublin City

John Bull 1821
ANDERSON, Ann	Clare
BRADY, Ann	Armagh
BRADY, Mary	Co Dublin
BRENNAN, Margaret/Mary	Dublin City
BROWNE, Alice	Monaghan
BROWNE, Elizabeth	Kings County
BROWNE, Mary	Carlow
BROWNE, Matilda	Dublin City
BURKE, Mary	Dublin City
BUTLER, Sarah	Monaghan
BYRNE, Jane	Dublin City
BYRNE, Mary	Dublin City
BYRNE*, Eliza	Queens County
CAMPBELL, Susanna	Down
CARROL, Margaret	Dublin City
CLARKE, Eleanor	Dublin City
CLARKE*, Ann	Down
CONNOR, Mary	Dublin City
COONEY, Sarah	Antrim
COX, Catherine	Dublin City
COX, Celia	Roscommon
CUNNINGHAM, Sally	Cavan
DIXON, Ann	Kings County
DOGHERTY*, Elizabeth	Down
DONNELLY, Margaret	Antrim
DOWNS*, Mary	Dublin City
DOYLE, Mary	Down
EVANS, Ann	Dublin City
FARLEY*, Jane	Cavan
FINLAY, Margaret	Antrim
FITZPATRICK, Anne	Monaghan
GEOGHEGAN, Bridget	Carlow
GERRAGHTY, Bridget	Roscommon
HAMILTON, Jane	Monaghan
HENRY, Frances	Dublin City
HINES, Mary	Westmeath
KANE, Ann	Westmeath
KEENAN, Eleanor	Longford
KELLY, Catherine	Cork City
KERRIGAN, Bridget	Roscommon
KIBREA, Mary	Westmeath
KING, Mary	Dublin City
LOUGHLAN, Eleanor	Antrim
LOUGHLIN, Margaret	Limerick City
LUNNY, Bridget	Roscommon
McAULAY, Margaret	Antrim
McCUE, Mary	Clare
McDONNELL, Rose	Antrim
McMAHON*, Mary	Louth
MAHER, Jane	Dublin Co
MITCHELL*, Jane	Mayo
MOORE, Catherine	Dublin City
MOORE, Mary	Down
MOORE, Mary	Queens County
MORAN, Mary	Galway
MORRISON, Ann	Down
MOSS, Elizabeth	Kings County
MURPHY, Mary	Tyrone
NICHOLSON*, Jane	Antrim
NOLAN, Eleanor	Roscommon
O'DONNEL, Bridget	Limerick City
O'HARA, Bridget	Louth
PATTERSON*, Ann	Antrim
RAGAN, Mary	Roscommon
REILLY, Margaret	Dublin City
RICHEY, Rose	Dublin City
ROE*, Bridget	Clare
ROURKE, Elinor	Roscommon
RYAN, Ann	Carlow
SCOTT, Harriet	Dublin City
SMITH*, Mary	Antrim
TUCKER, Eleanor	Kildare
WADE, Maria	Monaghan
WARD, Ann	Down
WASON*, Susannah	Antrim
WILSON, Elizabeth	Down

Lady Rowena 1826
BYRNE, Mary	Dublin City
MURRAY, Ellen	Dublin City

Mariner 1825
BELLY, Frances	Monaghan
COLLINS, Ann	Tipperary

WALSH, Mary   Tipperary
WILLIAMSON,
  Mary Ann   Cork City
WILSON, Mary Ann   Leitrim

***Providence* 1811**
CONNOLLY,
  Catherine   Dublin City
FITZPATRICK,
  Catherine   NR

***Queen* 1791**
DEVEREUX,
  Catherine   Dublin
PLUNKETT, Mary   Dublin

***Rolla* 1803**
FLAHERTY,
  Winifred   Clare

***Woodman* 1823**
CORCORAN,
  Lester/Nessy   Co Kilkenny
FOLEY, Bridget   Co Sligo
MOORE, Catherine   Co Cork

B-2 ALIASES OR VARIANT NAMES

Surname, First Name(s) *ALIAS*	Ship
BARTLEY, Elizabeth *BENTERLEY/ BERKELEY*	Marquis Cornwallis 1796
BASS, Ann *KING*	Canada 1817
BEGLEY, Mary *BAGLEY*	Tellicherry 1806
BENNETT, Mary *BARRETT*	Woodman 1823
BERRY, Mary *DOYLE*	Francis & Eliza 1815
BLACK, Catherine *BLAKE*	Almorah 1824
BLANEY, Margaret *BLAMY*	Elizabeth 1828
BOAMANN, Sarah/Sally *BRENNAN/BANON*	Mariner 1825
BOLLISTY, Mary *BOLLASTY*	Elizabeth 1828
BOULTON, Ann *DOGHERTY*	Queen 1791
BOURKE, Margaret *ROURKE*	Brothers 1827
BRADY, Susan *BRIEN*	Catherine 1814
BRAY, Catharine *ROGERS*	Francis & Eliza 1815
BRAZILL, Sarah *BROZOL/BRASIL*	Queen 1791
BRENAN, Catherine *BRENNAN*	Anna 1801

Surname, First Name(s) *ALIAS*	Ship
BRENNAN, Sarah *HOWE*	Queen 1791
BRIAN, Margaret *BRIEN/BRYAN*	Almorah 1824
BRIEN, Julia *O'BRIAN*	Francis & Eliza 1815
BRIEN, Margaret *BRYAN*	Lord Wellington 1820
BRIEN, Mary *BURN*	Sugar Cane 1793
BROOKWELL, Marianne *BROCKNALL*	Mariner 1825
BROWN, Bridget *WILSON*	Canada 1817
BROWN, Mary *GROVE*	Experiment 1809
BROWN, Mary *KIRK*	Alexander 1816
BRYAN, Ann *BYRNE*	Almorah 1824
BRYAN, Mary *MURPHY*	Brothers 1827
BUCKLEY, Mary *CUFF*	Archduke Charles 1813
BUCKLEY, Catherine *CONNOR*	Providence 1811
BURKE, Hessy/Esther *ROURKE*	Woodman 1823
BURKE, Judith *DRISCOLL*	Lord Wellington 1820
BURN, Margaret *BURNE*	Marquis Cornwallis 1796

Surname, First Name(s) *ALIAS*	Ship	Surname, First Name(s) *ALIAS*	Ship
BURN, NR *GILMORE*	Experiment 1809	COGLAN, Mary *COCKLIN/COGHLIN*	Almorah 1824
BURN, Eleanor *BOIN*	Experiment 1809	CONISKEY, Eleanor *DOLANN*	Mariner 1825
BYRNE, Eliza *GILLASLEY*	John Bull 1821	CONNELL, Ann *CONNOR*	Almorah 1824
BYRNE, Elizabeth *ROSS*	Canada 1817	CONNELL, Elinor *SULLIVAN*	Marquis Cornwallis 1796
BYRNE, Catherine *BURNS*	Francis & Eliza 1815	CONNOR, Eleanor *DWYER*	Experiment 1809
BYRNE, Ann *BURNS*	Francis & Eliza 1815	CONNOR, Mary *McGRATY*	Elizabeth 1828
BYRNE, Bridget *BURN*	Francis & Eliza 1815	CONNORS, Mary *O'CONNOR*	Mariner 1825
BYRNE, Margaret *BURNS*	Francis & Eliza 1815	CONOLLY, Mary *CONNELLY*	Minerva 1800
BYRNE, Mary *BOYNE*	Catherine 1814	CONORTY, Mary *CONNAUGHTY*	Hercules 1802
BYRNE, Catherine *BURN*	Alexander 1816	CRAWLY, Honora *CROWLY*	Elizabeth 1818
BYRNE, Catherine *MURPHY*	Mariner 1825	CRONE, Elizabeth *CROHAN*	Lord Wellington 1820
BYRNE, Margaret *BOYLE*	Almorah 1824	CULLEN, Ann *CURREN*	Francis & Eliza 1815
BYRNE, Cath/Mary Ann *EGGLESTONE*	Lady Rowena 1826	CUMING, Mary *CUMMING*	Minerva 1800
CAHILL, Mary Ann *DELANEY/DELANY*	Alexander 1816	CURRAN, Anne *QUINN*	Elizabeth 1818
CANDLER, Mary *CHANDLER*	Francis & Eliza 1815	DEEHAN, Esther *QUIGLEY*	Brothers 1827
CARR, Anne *HINCHLEY*	Experiment 1809	DERBY, Anne *DARBY*	Mariner 1825
CARTY, Bridget *CASSIDY*	Alexander 1816	DILLON, Anne *CLARKE*	Mariner 1825
CAULFIELD, Mary *FITZGERALD*	Mariner 1825	DINAHY, Mary *DENAHY*	Anna 1801
CAVANAGH, Catherine *DOGHERTY*	Francis & Eliza 1815	DOGHERTY, Elizabeth *JOHNSTON*	John Bull 1821
CLARK, Eleanor *WHELAN*	Minerva 1800	DOHERTY, Catherine *AIRLY*	Archduke Charles 1813
CLARK, Mary *CLEARY*	Experiment 1809	DONALLY, Eliza *DANIEL*	Atlas 1802
CLARKE, Ann *COOLEY*	John Bull 1821	DONLEY, Catherine *DONNLEY*	Almorah 1824
CLERK, Anne *MURPHY/CLEARY*	Queen 1791	DOWLAND, Ann *DOLLAND*	Experiment 1809

Surname, First Name(s) *ALIAS*	Ship	Surname, First Name(s) *ALIAS*	Ship
DOWLING, Catherine		FREEL, Sarah	
HENNESSY	*Elizabeth* 1828	*DOGHERTY*	*Lady Rowena* 1826
DOWNS, Mary			
DAWNES	*John Bull* 1821	GALLAGHER, Mary	
DOYLE, Esther		*LIPSEY*	*Brothers* 1827
LEESON	*Brothers* 1827	GARTLAND, Isabella	
DOYLE, Mary		*GERNON*	*Elizabeth* 1828
DEMPSEY	*Elizabeth* 1828	GILMOR, Mary	
DREW, Anne		*GILMAN*	*Catherine* 1814
CAMPBELL	*Lady Rowena* 1826	GORMON, Johanna	
DUANNY, Bridget		*PATERSON*	*Almorah* 1824
DEVANNY	*Woodman* 1823	GREEN, Eliza	
DUMAN, Sarah		*GREENE*	*Lady Rowena* 1826
JOHNSTON	*Elizabeth* 1828	GREGAN, Maria	*Marquis*
		CROGHAN	*Cornwallis* 1796
EAKIN, Ruth		GRIFFIN, Mary	
EGAN	*Janus* 1820	*SULLIVAN*	*Almorah* 1824
EDRINGTON, Elizabeth		GRIFFITH, Anne	
HITHERS	*Canada* 1817	*GRIFFIN*	*Elizabeth* 1818
EMERSON, Ann	*Francis & Eliza*	GUDDIS, Mary	
EMMERSON	1815	*GADDES/GADDIS*	*Mariner* 1825
ERWIN, Maria			
KELLY	*Experiment* 1809	HALLORAN, Margaret	
		HORRAGAN	*Almorah* 1824
FAGAN, Mary		HAMILTON, Elinor	
NAGLE	*Tellicherry* 1806	*GOFF*	*Catherine* 1814
FARLEY, Jane		HANNON, Mary	
HART	*John Bull* 1821	*KARMON/RANNON*	*Lady Rowena* 1826
FARRELL, Mary		HARRINGTON, Matty	
CLYNCH	*Lady Rowena* 1826	*HARRIGAN*	*Brothers* 1827
FARREL, Mary/Bridget	*Francis & Eliza*	HAVENAGH, Mary	*Archduke Charles*
CONWAY	1815	*DOGHERTY*	1813
FAVIOL, Ann		HAYES, Anne	
FARROL/MARTIN	*Hercules* 1802	*MAGRATH*	*Catherine* 1814
FAY, Ann	*Marquis*	HEALLY, Mary	
FOY	*Cornwallis* 1796	*GILL*	*Queen* 1791
FINNIGAN, Mary		HEENY, Ellen	
FINNEGAN	*Sugar Cane* 1793	*HENRY*	*Woodman* 1823
FLANIGAN, Mary	*Francis & Eliza*	HENEY, Mary	
FLANNAGHAN	1815	*HINEY*	*Elizabeth* 1828
FLYNN, Catherine	*Archduke Charles*	HENRY, Rose	
DART	1813	*GARLAND*	*Elizabeth* 1828
FLYNN, Mary		HIGGINS, Mary	
FLINN	*Minerva* 1800	*TYRRELL*	*Rolla* 1803
FOSTER, Mary Anne		HUGHES, Ann	
FORSTER	*Mariner* 1825	*STEPHENS*	*Canada* 1817

472 List B-2

Surname, First Name(s) *ALIAS*	Ship
HUNTER, Isabella *DAVIDSON*	Alexander 1816
HURLEY, Catherine *HARE*	Rolla 1803
HURLEY, Mary *MURLEY*	Woodman 1823
HYNDS, Mary *CARNEY*	Catherine 1814
JACKSON, Elizabeth *DEA*	Sugar Cane 1793
JACKSON, Margaret *FARRELL*	Mariner 1825
JACKSON, Margaret *ROONEY*	Lady Rowena 1826
JOHNSON, Elizabeth *WELSH*	Brothers 1827
JOHNSON, Mary *BRADY, Bridget*	Brothers 1827
KEALY, Abby/Anny *ALEY*	Britannia 1797
KEATINGE, Eliza *KANE*	Catherine 1814
KELLY, Anne *HALLEY/HOLLEY*	Minerva 1800
KELLY, Julia *ROMAY/MALLONE*	Lady Rowena 1826
KELLY, Margaret *ANDERSON*	Almorah 1824
KELLY, Mary *ANDERSON*	Archduke Charles 1813
KELLY, Mary *CARROL*	Experiment 1809
KELLY, Mary *CARTY*	Archduke Charles 1813
KELLY, Mary *KENNY*	Brothers 1827
KELSH, Bridget *KEANE*	Lady Rowena 1826
KENNA, Ellen *HINNA*	Almorah 1824
KENNEDY, Judith *FITZGERALD*	Marquis Cornwallis 1796
KENNEDY, Margaret *DIGNUM*	Janus 1820
KEON, Bridget *SMITH*	Elizabeth 1818

Surname, First Name(s) *ALIAS*	Ship
KESLING, Ann *CARROLLY*	Canada 1817
KILFOILE, Margaret *KILFAY*	Canada 1817
KINAHAN, Ann *KINNAGHAN*	Francis & Eliza 1815
KING, Elizabeth *ROSS*	Catherine 1814
KINGSMILL, Catherine *NEALE*	Francis & Eliza 1815
KINSELA, Eleanor/Ellen *KENSELAGH*	Alexander 1816
KIRWAN, Mary Ann *WARD*	Woodman 1823
LARKIN, Margaret *LARKINS*	Woodman 1823
LAWLER, Mary *LAWLOR*	Atlas 1802
LEAHY, Cathrine/Mary *LEAHEY*	Almorah 1824
LEDWICK, Eliza *LEDWICH*	Lady Rowena 1826
LEESON, Catherine *GLEESON, Kitty*	Tellicherry 1806
LEONARD, Bridget *DOYLE*	Lady Rowena 1826
LEWINS, Mary *LEWENS*	Anna 1801
LONG, Mary *LAING*	Elizabeth 1828
LUNGAIN, Catherine *LANGAIN*	Mariner 1825
McARDLE, Margaret *McARDELL*	Mariner 1825
McARTHY, Elinor *DONOVAN, Mary*	Sugar Cane 1793
McCABE(RS), Mary *SHERRETON*	Mariner 1825
McCLUFFON, Rose *McQUITTAN*	Mariner 1825
McCLUSKY, Phoebe/Pheby *McCUSKY*	Alexander 1816

Surname, First Name(s) *ALIAS*	Ship	Surname, First Name(s) *ALIAS*	Ship
McCONNEL, Elizabeth *CONNOLLY*	*Francis & Eliza* 1815	MAWKING, Mary *MAWKINNY*	*Elizabeth* 1818
McDANIEL, Ann *BILLEN, Ellen*	*Almorah* 1824	MEARY, Margaret *MEARS*	*Almorah* 1824
McDERMOTT, Ann *DONALDSON*	*Woodman* 1823	MEIGHAN, Sarah *DEENEY*	*Brothers* 1827
McDERMOTT, Johanna *McDONEL*	*Woodman* 1823	MITCHELL, Jane *ENGLAND*	*John Bull* 1821
MacDONALD, Ann *McDONOUGH*	*Minerva* 1800	MITCHELL, Mary *McDADE*	*Elizabeth* 1828
McDONNELL, Bridget *McDONALD*	*Queen* 1791	MONEYHAN, Johanna *MOYNEHAN*	*Almorah* 1824
McGREIRRY, Margaret *McGREEVY*	*Elizabeth* 1818	MOON, Elizabeth *HARKIN*	*Mariner* 1825
McGUIRE, Ann *MAGUIRK*	*Almorah* 1824	MOONEY, Margaret *KELLY*	*Sugar Cane* 1793
McILROY, Martha *McILBERRY*	*Elizabeth* 1818	MOONEY, Margaret *SHILLING*	*Sugar Cane* 1793
McILVEE, Mary *McDONA*	*Woodman* 1823	MOORE, Mary *ARCHER*	*Experiment* 1809
McINAHENY, Bridget *McMANARA, Mary*	*Elizabeth* 1828	MORAN, Mary Ann *MOORE*	*Catherine* 1814
McKENNA, Ann *McKARRAN*	*Canada* 1817	MORGAN, Rose *MOGGARITY*	*Sugar Cane* 1793
McKEON, Catherine *ECHLIN*	*Elizabeth* 1818	MULLINS, Margaret *MILLING*	*Canada* 1817
McLOGHLIN, Rose *McLAUGHLIN*	*Francis & Eliza* 1815	MUPHY, Catherine *MURPHY*	*Hercules* 1802
McMAHON, Mary *PIERCE*	*John Bull* 1821	MURPHY, Catherine *KELLY*	*Elizabeth* 1818
McNAMARA, Ann *GRANT*	*Sugar Cane* 1793	MURPHY, Margaret *SULLIVAN*	*Lady Rowena* 1826
MAGUIRE, Margaret *MURPHY*	*Boddingtons* 1793	MURRAY, Bridget *WALL*	*Canada* 1817
MALONY, Bridget *MALONE*	*Minerva* 1800	MURRAY, Mary *BARRET*	*Alexander* 1816
MALONY, Sarah *MULLOWNY*	*Minerva* 1800	MURRY, Eleanor *BROWNE*	*Sugar Cane* 1793
MALTON, Catherine *MELTON*	*Marquis Cornwallis* 1796	NEALE, Catherine *HICKEY*	*Canada* 1817
MANGAN, Catherine *COLEMAN*	*Almorah* 1824	NESBITT, Susan *REYNOLDS*	*Lady Rowena* 1826
MANION, Catherine *MARMION*	*Elizabeth* 1828	NEVILLE, Marcella/ Priscilla *PENDERGAST*	*Francis & Eliza* 1815
MARTIN, Hannah *JENNINGS*	*Mariner* 1825		

Surname, First Name(s) *ALIAS*	Ship
NICHOLSON, Jane	
DONNELLY	John Bull 1821
NOWLAN, Catherine	
MASON	Lady Rowena 1826
NOWLAS, Bridget	
ROSSITER	Queen 1791
O'BRIEN, Ann	Francis & Eliza
GRAHAM	1815
O'CONNELL, Frances	
OSBURNE	Mariner 1825
O'HARA, Mary	
O'HARE	Elizabeth 1818
O'NEAL, Catherine	Francis & Eliza
O'NEIL	1815
O'NEIL, Mary Ann	
McMANUS	Canada 1817
O'NEILL, Mary	
NEALE	John Bull 1821
O'NEILL, Mary	
NEALE	John Bull 1821
OGLE, Catherine	
OAKS	Alexander 1816
PATTERSON, Ann	
DOHERTY	John Bull 1821
PEW, Catherine	Francis & Eliza
PUGH	1815
PHELAN, Mary	
WHELAN	Elizabeth 1828
PLUMLAND, Matty	
PLUMLEY	Rolla 1803
PORTER, Sarah	
MALONY	Elizabeth 1828
PRENDERGAST, Mary	
FARRELL	Experiment 1809
PRODIGAN, Bridget	
BRANNIGAN	Hercules 1802
QUIN, Catherine	
KIRWAN	Woodman 1823
QUIN, Margaret	
GOURLY	Catherine 1814
QUINN, Elinor	
RYDER	Catherine 1814

Surname, First Name(s) *ALIAS*	Ship
READ, Anne	
SMITH	Lady Rowena 1826
READ, Elinor	
RAY	Rolla 1803
READ, Mary	
CLARKE	Mariner 1825
REED, Mary	
READ	Woodman 1823
REED, Rose	Francis & Eliza
READ	1815
REGAN, Caroline	
CAREY	Lady Rowena 1826
REILLEY, Bridget	
RIELLY	Almorah 1824
REILLEY, Margaret	
RIELLEY	Almorah 1824
REILLY, Rosanna	
KELLY	Sugar Cane 1793
RIEBY, Mary	
REILY	Sugar Cane 1793
ROBERTS, Jane	
DWYER	Lady Rowena 1826
ROCHFORT, Mary	
ROCHFORD	Alexander 1816
RODNEY, Mary	
ROONEY	Sugar Cane 1793
ROE, Bridget	
ROWE	John Bull 1821
ROE, Margaret	Francis & Eliza
ROWE	1815
RONAYNE, Mary	
RONAN	Brothers 1827
ROSS, Ann	
MULLEN	Brothers 1827
RYAN, Ann	Francis & Eliza
BRYAN	1815
RYAN, Mary	
DRAKE	Mariner 1825
SAUNDERS, Catherine	
LINDEN	Elizabeth 1828
SCULLY, Mary	
McGUIRE	Elizabeth 1828
SHANAGHAN, Elizabeth	
SHANNON	Mariner 1825
SHEA, Ellen	
MURPHY	Elizabeth 1828

Surname, First Name(s) *ALIAS*	Ship	Surname, First Name(s) *ALIAS*	Ship
SHEEHAN, Bridget *KELLY/WELSH*	*Almorah* 1824	WALES, Martha *McELROY*	*Alexander* 1816
SINGLETON, Mary *JOHNSTON*	*Lady Rowena* 1826	WALKER, Matilda *LARACY*	*Francis & Eliza* 1815
SMITH, Ann *FERGUSON*	*Brothers* 1827	WALSH, Catherine *LOUGHAN/LANGA*	*Almorah* 1824
SMITH, Ann *LENNON/LENNAN*	*Atlas* 1802	WARD, Anne *KIRWAN*	*Experiment* 1809
SMITH, Anne *GIBNEY*	*Lady Rowena* 1826	WASON, Susannah *WARSON*	*John Bull* 1821
SMITH, Mary *COLLINS*	*John Bull* 1821	WATSON, Elizabeth *SHEA*	*Francis & Eliza* 1815
SMITH, Mary *FLAHARTY*	*Minerva* 1800	WHELAN, Eliza *WHEELAN*	*Woodman* 1823
SMITH, Mary *LEESON*	*Catherine* 1814	WILEY, Susan *FARRELL*	*Archduke Charles* 1813
STANTON, Mary *REILLY*	*Elizabeth* 1818	WILLARD, Henrietta *VILLERS*	*Marquis Cornwallis* 1796
STEPHENS, Mary *SMITH*	*Francis & Eliza* 1815	WILLIAMSON, Jane *BULGER, Mary*	*Experiment* 1809
STOTT, Mary *FOY*	*Alexander* 1816	WILLS, Catherine *WELLS*	*Alexander* 1816
SULLIVAN, Honora *DURREEN/SHEA*	*Brothers* 1827	WILSON, Anne *WILLSON*	*Lady Rowena* 1826
USHER, Mary *MURTAGH*	*Elizabeth* 1818		

INDEXES

Women Mentioned in the Text

Notes
1 The entries at one name may refer to more than one woman.
2 For details of trial places, trial years and ships of arrival, see Lists A and B.

Abrams, Esther, 220, 254, 361
Acton, Sarah, 291
Adams, Sarah, 97
Agnew, Susan, 334
Ainsley/Aynsley, Jane, 24
Allen, Elizabeth, 72
Allen, Hannah, 349
Allen, Jasmin, 56
Allen, Sarah, 344
Alroy/McElroy, Mary, 238, 358
Anderson, Ann, 338
Anderson, Elizabeth, 79, 326
Anderson, Martha, 29
Anderson, Mary, 147
Angus, Janet, 20
Arnett, Ann, 331
Ashton, Mary (Sarah), 158-9, 343
Asker, Elizabeth, 29
Astell/Barnes, Lydia, 240-1
Aynsley/Ainsley, Jane, 24

Bailey, Martha, 327
Bailey, Sarah, 123, 327
Baker, Ann, 72, 324, 353
Baker, Elizabeth, 97
Baker, Letitia, 331
Baker, Sarah, 65
Ball, Agnes, 61
Banks, Mary, 353
Barnes, Isabella, 90
Barnes, Jane, 89, 329, 355

Barnes, Sarah, 93
Barnes/Astell, Lydia, 41
Barnett, Mary, 266, 362
Barret, Honora, 116
Barret, Mary, 283, 364
Barrett, Anne, 83
Barrington, Ann, 324
Barrs, Sarah, 362
Barry, Catherine, 297-8, 367
Barry, Elizabeth, 338
Barry, Mary, 146
Bartlett, Mrs, 59, 321
Bason, Elizabeth, 74, 290, 366
Bateman, Mary, 319
Bates, Julia, 201, 349
Bates, Maria, 350
Baxter, Sarah, 318
Baylis/Taylor, Ann (Nancy), 275-6, 363
Bayly/McKay, Jane, 213, 354
Bays, Bridget, 327
Beaumont, Ann, 329
Beckford, Elizabeth, 59
Beckwith, Elizabeth, 261, 362
Bedford, Ann, 50
Bell, Frances, 141
Bell, Sarah, 180, 346
Bellamy, Sarah, 251
Bellinger, Sarah, 288, 366
Bellingham, Elizabeth, 311
Bennet/Nixon, Jane, 240, 359
Bennett, Mrs, 201

476

Women Mentioned in the Text

Bergen, Mary, 251
Berry, Ann, 83
Berry, Elizabeth (Jessie), 251, 360
Best, Sarah, 70
Bevin, Ann, 266, 362
Bidon, Jane, 146
Bigges, Esther, 353
Bird, Elizabeth, 251
Bird, Sarah, 265, 362
Birkett, Elizabeth, 59, 321
Blake, Ann, 83
Blake, Catherine, 117, 336
Blake, Eleanor, 83
Blake, Mary, 322
Blake, Susannah, 25
Boddican/Brodican/Prodican, Bridget, 122, 337
Bodenham, Mrs, 243, 359
Bolton, Bridget, 333
Bolton/Boulton, Rebecca, 56, 172
Bond, Sophia, 359
Booth, Elizabeth, 95
Booth, Jane, 156, 342
Boulton/Bolton, Rebecca, 56, 172
Bowen, Ann, 202-3
Bowman, Mary, 48
Bowsted, Hannah, 59
Bowyer, Sarah, 95
Boyle, Elizabeth, 52, 320, 334
Boyle, Margaret, 123
Brady, Catherine, 138
Brady, Mary, 359
Brannigan, Sophia, 48, 318
Brazeley, Susannah, 24
Brennan, Mary, 317
Brennan, Sarah, 112
Brickell, Susannah, 318
Brien, Julia, 226, 356
Brien, Mary, 337
Broadbent, Mrs, 243, 359
Brodican/Boddican/Prodican, Bridget, 122, 337
Brooks, Elizabeth, 311, 324
Brooks, Sarah, 92
Brown, Catherine, 216, 355
Brown, Eleanor, 327
Brown, Eliza, 53-4, 320
Brown, Elizabeth, 139, 166, 344
Brown, Jane, 329
Brown, Mary, 72, 75-6, 133, 354, 358
Brown, Susannah, 327
Browne, Catherine, 130
Browne, Mary, 338
Browne, Matilda, 338
Bryan, Catherine, 350

Bryan, Margaret, 99
Bryan, Mary, 116
Bryan, Mary Ann, 119
Bryan/Byrne, Ann, 336
Bryant, Esther, 123
Bryant, Hannah, 78
Buckie, Margaret, 331
Buckley, Mary, 92
Buckner, Elizabeth, 234, 357
Bunker, Margaret, 284, 365
Bunting, Alice, 91
Burk, Rose, 333
Burke, Bridget, 130, 337, 339
Burke, Elizabeth, 83, 341
Burke, Hessy, 133, 339
Burke, Mary, 131, 339
Burkett, Elizabeth, 18
Burleigh, Elizabeth, 223
Burn, Bridget, 149
Burne, Jane, 45
Burns, Catherine, 337
Burns, Margaret, 149
Burroughs, Alice, 75
Burton, Mary, 307
Butler, Ann, 98
Butler, Catherine, 337
Buxton, Mrs, 241, 359
Byrne, Ann, 147, 255, 361
Byrne/Bryan, Ann, 336
Byrne, Bridget, 146
Byrne, Margaret, 133-4, 282, 364
Byrne, Mary, 336, 338, 341
Byrne/Murphy, Catherine, 341

Caffry/Coffrey, Mary Ann, 88
Cammell, Eliza, 331, 350
Campbell, Anne, 214, 354
Campbell, Eliza, 204, 350
Campbell, Ellen, 120
Carney, Mary, 352
Carney/Gray, Mary, 34
Carrick, Mrs, 245
Carrol, Mary, 137, 193, 348
Carroll, Bridget, 120
Carroll, Mary, 133, 329-30
Carter, Catherine, 146
Carty, Mary, 73
Carver, Elizabeth, 286-7, 365
Casey, Mary, 116
Cassidy, Elizabeth, 226, 359
Cassidy, Mary, 299, 333, 367
Catchpole, Margaret, 265, 362
Cavanough, Margaret, 23
Chalker, Mary, 366
Chamberlain, Martha, 223

Chambers, Elizabeth, 353
Chambers, Mary, 78
Chandler, Sarah, 88
Chapman, Ann, 203, 350
Chapman, Elizabeth, 350
Charlton, Mary, 148
Cheetom, Eliza, 244, 359
Church, Sarah, 90, 329
Clare/Fernee, Mary, 286, 365
Clarke, Ann, 76
Clarke, Elizabeth, 354
Clarke, Elizabeth ('Betsy'), 91, 330
Clarke, Ellen, 350
Clarke, Mary, 84, 342
Clarkson, Catherine, 239
Clements, Catherine, 21
Clements, Jane, 83
Clifford, Sarah, 93
Coak, Elizabeth, 134-5
Cobcroft, Sarah, 244, 359
Codd, Jane, 244, 360
Coffrey/Caffry, Mary Ann, 88
Coghlan/Coglan, Mary, 120, 337
Cole, Elizabeth, 257
Cole, Mary, 214, 354
Collins, Mary, 84
Coleman/Collman, Ann, 167-8, 289, 366
Colethread, Elizabeth Catherine, 252
Colpitts, Ann, 252
Conelly, Sarah, 354
Coniskey, Eleanor, 341
Connell, Ann/Mary, 120, 152-3, 154, 342
Connell, Elizabeth Catherine, 339
Connelly, Bridget, 193
Connor, Eleanor, 98
Connor, Elizabeth, 349
Connor, Kitty, 207, 351
Connor, Mary, 112, 338-9, 349
Conoboy, Bridget, 213, 354
Consadine/Cusadine, Mary, 146, 255, 361
Cook, Elizabeth, 89
Cooper, Lucy, 89
Cooper, Margaret, 284, 365
Cooper, Susan, 216, 354
Cope, Elizabeth, 327
Corkshill, Elizabeth, 244, 359
Corrigan, Catherine, 251
Cosgrove, Bridget, 329
Cosgrove, Celia, 173, 345, 346
Cotton, Catherine, 215, 354
Cotton, Mary, 291
Cowden, Sarah, 100-1
Cox, Catherine, 53, 339
Cox, Celia, 339

Cox, Margaret, 70
Cox, Mary, 329
Cranmer, Frances, 45
Crossley, Mrs, 220, 355
Crozier, Eleanor, 286, 365
Cullen, Mary, 358
Cunningham, Sally, 339
Cupitt, Mary, 244, 359
Curran, Isabella, 226
Curtis, Jane, 73
Cusadine/Consadine, Mary, 146, 255, 361
Cutter, Elizabeth, 351

Daly, Ann, 41, 314
Daly, Sarah, 333
Darling, Eliza, 207, 243
Darnall/Darnell, Margaret, 22-3, 105
Daugherty, Elizabeth, 140
Davidson, Mary, 114
Davies, Elizabeth, 333
Davies, Rachael, 333
Davis, Ann, 227, 284, 346, 356, 365
Davis/Jones, Ann/Judith, 200, 349, 353
Davis, Jane, 181, 347
Davis, Martha, 317
Davis, Mary, 206, 351
Davis, Sophia, 214-15, 318, 354
Davison, Rebecca, 56, 57
Dawson, Margaret, 220, 223
Dean, Mary, 90
Delaney, Margaret, 117, 336, 342
Delany, Sarah, 325
Dempsey, Martha, 333
Devereux, Catherine, 114
Diaper, Barbra, 300
Dick, Charlotte, 279, 364
Diguin, Mary, 354
Dillon, Mrs Mary, 214, 216, 243, 355, 359
Dixon, Betty, 206, 351
Dixon, Charlotte, 287, 365
Dockrell, Mrs, 243, 359
Donahoe, Elizabeth, 366
Donnelly, Anne, 121-2, 337
Donnelly, Catherine, 136, 340
Donnelly, Sarah, 310
Donough, Catherine, 281-2, 364
Doolan, Mary, 141
Dougherty, Eliza/Elizabeth, 337, 342
Douglas, Catherine, 204, 350
Downes, Rosetta, 173
Doyle, Catherine, 239
Doyle, Elizabeth, 339
Doyle, Margaret, 135, 146, 340
Doyle, Martha, 95
Draper/Ingram, Sarah, 332

Women Mentioned in the Text

Drayton, Sarah Ann, 97
Driscoll, Elizabeth, 142
Driver, Mary, 358, 359
Driver/Marr, Elizabeth, 239, 266, 362
Duffie/Duffy, Margaret, 89
Dunbar, Mary, 136, 337, 340
Duncan, Helen, 326
Dunham, Elizabeth, 321
Dunlevey, Mary, 214, 341, 354
Dunn, Margaret, 48, 49, 318
Durant, Mary, 95
Durrant, Ann, 31
Dwyne, Margaret, 322
Dyel, Mary, 311
Dyer, Matilda, 327

Eager, Mrs Geoffrey, 244-5, 359-60
East, Ann, 330
Easterbrook, Mary Ann, 283, 346, 364-5
Ebden, Frances, 330
Edwards, Catherine, 112, 113
Edwards/Everett, Catherine, 335
Edwards, Hannah, 20
Edwards, Mary, 21
Egan, Mrs Thomas, 279, 364
Elliott, Catherine, 214, 354
Ellis, Ann, 140
Ellis, Elizabeth, 95
Ellis, Rebecca, 164, 344
Ellis, Sarah, 362
Ellison, Sarah, 360
Embrey, Ann, 354
Emmett, Eleanor, 98
Evans, Amelia, 75
Evans, Ann, 20, 278, 364
Evans, Catherine, 321, 333
Evans, Elizabeth, 21, 330
Evans, Katherine, 167, 345
Everett/Edwards, Catherine, 335
Eyres, Sarah, 147

Farmer, Ann, 211, 353
Farraugher, Bridget, 285, 365
Farrel, Mary, 116
Farrell/Farrel, Ann/Nancy, 53
Farrell, Mary, 194-6, 348
Fennessy, Mary, 140
Fergusson, Ellen, 53
Fernee/Clare, Mary, 286, 365
Field, Mary, 251
Fielding, Mary Ann, 332
Finlay, Elizabeth, 352
Finney, Margaret, 349
Fisk, Matilda, 284, 365
Fitzgerald, Mary, 337

Fitzgerald, Susan, 148
Fitzgibbon, Mary, 142
Fitzjohn, Catherine, 99
Fitzpatrick, Anne, 339
Fitzpatrick, Bridget, 333
Flaherty, Ellen, 145
Fletcher, Jane, 317
Flood, Mary, 362
Flyn, Alice, 238, 358
Flynn, Eleanor, 72
Flynn, Honora, 284, 365
Flynn, Mary, 23
Fogarty, Elizabeth, 364
Folks/Fowkes, Mary/Margaret, 121, 153, 337, 342
Forbes, Ann, 256
Ford, Elizabeth, 76
Ford, Mary, 358
Fowkes/Folks, Mary/Margaret, 121, 153, 337, 342
Fowles, Ann, 56-7
Frall, Ann, 244
Francis, Rose, 350
Frankland, Mrs, 244, 359
Franklin, Ann, 327
Fraser, Ellen, 19, 309
Freeman, Elizabeth, 366
French, Elizabeth, 153, 342
French, Mary, 68
Fristan, Elizabeth, 307
Fry, Elizabeth, 43, 51, 53, 86-8, 89, 98, 99, 189, 316, 328, 331

Gafney, Susan, 341
Gahan, Elizabeth, 133
Gamble, Ann, 164, 344
Gamble, Esther, 71
Garland, Mrs, 161, 343
Garvey, Harriet, 83
Gascoyne, Olive, 220
Gatty, Ann, 214, 354
Geentry, Sarah, 141, 340
Geoghegan, Bridget, 44-5
George, Ann, 220
Gernon, Mary, 341
Gibbs, Elizabeth, 74
Gibson, Sarah Jane, 142
Gilbert, Ann, 255
Giles, Elizabeth, 236, 328, 357
Gilles, Mary, 78
Godber, Rebecker, 299, 347
Goff, Catherine, 140
Goodwin, Mary, 257, 354
Goodwin, Mrs, 206, 351
Goodwin, Sarah, 331

Gordon, Harriet, 142
Gordon, Phillis, 203, 350
Gotham, Mary, 235, 357
Grady, Mary, 199-200, 206, 349
Graham, Elizabeth, 44-5, 239, 358
Graham/Wood, Jane, 203, 350
Graham, Margaret, 84
Gray, Dorothy, 34
Gray/Carney, Mary, 34
Green, Sarah, 328
Greenwood, Mary, 360
Greggs, Sarah, 223
Grey, Elizabeth, 298
Griffin, Mary, 151, 152, 154, 342
Griffiths, Anne, 288, 366
Griffiths, Elinor, 114, 251
Grimes, Sarah, 95
Groom, Emma, 89, 329
Guest, Ann, 327
Guild, Helen, 310
Gulliver, Elizabeth, 65

Hackett, Mary, 337
Haddock, Mary, 357
Haggarty, Catherine, 333
Haigney, Mary, 322
Hall, Ann, 223
Hall/Hull, Catherine, 251
Hamilton, Sarah, 291, 366
Hand, Esther, 239
Handland, Dorothy, 34, 59, 172, 321
Hannah, Mary, 146
Hanning, Bridget, 123
Hardy, Mary, 92
Harebut, Maria, 288, 366
Harrington, Margaret, 93, 332
Harrington, Mrs, 240
Harris, Betty, 273-4, 363
Harris, Elizabeth, 310
Harris, Mary, 158, 343
Harrison, Ann, 323
Hart, Elinor, 328
Hartford, Mary, 285, 365
Hartigan, Mary, 120, 207, 351
Hartley, Mary, 194, 197, 348
Harvey, Catherine, 25
Harvey, Mary, 120
Haynes, Harriet, 331
Haynes, Maria, 342
Hayward, Elizabeth, 56, 57, 320
Healy, Ann, 362
Healy, Elizabeth, 149
Healy, Elizabeth Catherine, 339
Heatherall, Elizabeth, 98
Hennegan, Bridget, 49, 319

Hensley, Maria, 223
Heron, Mary, 337
Hewett, Isabella, 30
Hewison, Martha, 96-7
Hill, Mrs, 239
Hill, Rose, 341
Hill, Sarah, 283, 365
Hinchcliff, Elizabeth, 325
Hinnegan, Cecilia, 169, 345
Hite, Mary, 288, 366
Hodges, Mrs Peter, 360
Hodges, Rebecca, 225
Hodley, Mary, 354
Hogan, Margaret, 337
Hogan, Mary, 146, 337
Holford, Mary Ann, 274, 363
Holland, Mrs, 344
Hollis, Anne, 282
Holmes, Harriet, 355
Holmes, Susannah, 215, 220, 354
Homan, Elinor, 335
Hook, Mary, 354
Hope, Elizabeth, 309
Hopkins, Charlotte, 97
Horn, Ann, 220, 355
Horsley, Ann, 84
Howard, Ann, 338
Howard, Sarah, 341
Hughes, Margaret, 92
Hughes, Mary, 327
Hull/Hall, Catherine, 251
Humm, Mary, 354
Humphreys, Ann, 178, 346
Hunt, Maria, 214
Hurley, Catherine, 146
Hurley, Elizabeth, 21, 309
Hurst, Jane, 362
Hyland, Elizabeth, 333

Ingram/Draper, Sarah, 332
Innett/Robinson, Ann, 220, 235, 239, 357, 358

Jackson, Catherine, 333
Jackson, Elizabeth, 137, 241, 340
Jackson, Jane, 285, 365
Jackson, Katherine, 287, 365
Jackson, Mrs, 354
James, Mrs, 244, 359
Jamieson/Trotter, Ann, 112, 238, 358
Jeines, Mary Ann, 78
Jenkins, Elizabeth, 92
Jenkins, Mrs, 215, 354
Jennings, Ann, 120
Jennings, Charlotte, 92

Women Mentioned in the Text

Jennings, Maria, 287-8, 366
Johnson, Ann, 92
Johnson, Mary, 83, 265, 362
Johnson, Mary (chaplain's wife), 258, 307
Johnson, Sarah, 71
Johnston, Margaret, 285, 365
Johnston, Mary, 74
Johnston, Mrs, 238
Jones, Elizabeth, 91, 194, 198, 244, 245, 348, 349, 359
Jones, Jane, 69, 213, 330, 354
Jones/Davis, Judith/Ann, 200, 349
Jones, Martha, 86, 231-2, 357
Jones, Mary, 27, 227, 283, 312, 330-1, 364
Jones, Mary Ann, 90
Jones, Mrs, 239, 243, 359
Jones, Sarah, 90, 354
Jones, Susannah, 329-30
Joyce, Bridget, 77, 332
Joyce, Mary, 212, 353
Julian, Esther, 361

Kable, Susannah, 354
Kane, Elizabeth, 339
Kavanagh, Charlotte, 116, 336
Kearns, Mary, 351, 366
Keating, Elinor, 145
Keith, Anne, 287, 365
Kelly, Ann, 90, 220, 364
Kelly, Catherine, 86, 339
Kelly, Doreen, 319
Kelly, Judith, 360
Kelly, Mary Ann, 289, 366
Kelsh, Bridget, 225
Kennedy, Ann, 205, 231, 351, 357
Kennedy, Bridget, 140
Kennedy, Catherine, 359
Kennedy, Jane, 205
Kennedy, Margaret, 18, 308
Kennedy, Mary, 364
Kennington, Ann, 327
Kenny, Rose, 147-8
Keogh, Ann, 226, 356
Kerr, Ann, 279-80, 364
Kette/Kettle, Mary, 166, 344
Kibrea, Mary, 336
Kiernan, Katherine, 53
Killett, Elizabeth, 242-3, 359
King, Margaret, 324
King, Mary, 338
Kingsmill, Mrs, 244, 359-60
Kirk, Elizabeth, 357
Kirkby, Hannah, 347
Kirwan, Catherine, 130
Kit, Catherine, 50-1, 319

Kite, Mary, 95
Knowles, Mrs, 344

Lalor, Mary, 318
Lamb, Ann, 76
Lambert, Elizabeth, 245
Lang, Anne, 341
Larkham, Mary, 266, 362
Laron, Mary, 337
Lather, Harriet, 360
Laughlin, Catherine, 146
Lawton, Sarah, 184, 347
Laycock, Mrs, 359
Leadbeater, Mrs, 245, 360
Lear, Elizabeth, 241, 359
Leary, Honora, 341
Lee, Ann, 21
Lee, Elizabeth, 289-90, 366
Lee, Martha, 21
Leech, Eleanor, 123
Leeke, Judith, 133
Leisted, Ann, 73
Lester, Sarah, 84
Levitt, Ann, 99, 332
Levy, Mrs, 214
Lightly, Judith, 74
Lines, Catherine, 96
Linton, Mary, 330
Lloyd, Ann, 61, 327
Lloyd, Jane, 212
Lock, Ann, 93
Long, Mary, 213, 241, 297-8, 367
Longfield, Mary, 90
Longhurst, Jane, 357
Lovatt, Rosetta, 352
Lovell, Diana, 325
Luke, Martha, 90
Lurry, Sarah, 227, 356
Luscombe, Mary, 93
Lynch, Mary, 146, 182, 347

MacAdams, Ann, 204
McAdams, Ann, 351
Macarthur, Elizabeth, 220, 258, 307
Macarthy, Mary, 95
McBride, Ann, 288, 366
McCabe, Ann, 337
McCabe, Eleanor, 220
McCabe, Eliza, 204
McCabe, Mrs, 239
McCarroll, Mary, 121, 337
McCarty, Johanna, 121, 337
McCarty/McCarthy, Mary, 69, 95
McCluffon, Rose, 341
McConolly, Elizabeth, 284, 365

McCormick, Sarah, 19, 309
McDade, Mary Ann, 282, 364
McDermott, Sarah, 338
McDonagh, Mary, 357
McDonald, Catherine, 148
McDonald, Elinor, 113-15, 251, 336
McDonald, Margaret, 262-3, 362
McDonald, Mary, 228
McDonnell, Bridget, 112
McDuel, Elizabeth, 193, 348
McElroy/Alroy, Mary, 238, 358
McEntee, Mary, 146
McEvoy, Margaret, 341
McFae, Jane, 209, 352
McGouran/McGournan, Sarah, 358
McGrady, Sarah, 116, 226, 356
Mack, Elizabeth, 239, 358
McKay, Jane, 213, 354
Mackellar, Janet, 204, 350
Mackenzie, Penelope/Penwell, 48, 318
McKeon, Ann, 140
Maclean, Elizabeth, 23
McLean, Sarah, 333
McLeod, Beatrice, 262, 362
McLoghlin, Mary, 138
McMahon, Mary, 232, 255, 290, 357, 366
McPherson, Mary, 166, 344
Madden/Marsh, Rosetta, 229, 239, 356, 358
Maginness, Ann, 140
Maher, Jane, 338
Malcolm, Ann, 61
Maloney, Sarah, 354
Mandeville, Elizabeth, 67, 95
Manson, Isabella, 234, 357
Marborough, Mary, 236, 357
Marcus, Jane, 193-4, 348
Margerum, Mary, 362
Markwell, Maria, 354
Marr/Driver, Elizabeth, 239, 266, 362
Marsden, Elizabeth, 307
Marsh, Harriet, 225
Marsh/Madden, Rosetta, 229, 239, 356, 358
Marshall, Mary, 41, 133, 254, 314, 339, 361
Martin, Catherine, 360
Marum, Catherine, 119
Mason, Elizabeth, 274-5, 363
Masterton, Catherine, 53
Masterton, Mary, 146, 255, 361
May, Sarah, 274, 363
Mazzagora, Mary, 29, 291, 366
Meagher, Sarah, 277, 364
Mears, Mary, 351

Mellon/White, Catherine, 366
Mercer, Mary, 70
Metcalf, Ann, 328
Mills, Sarah, 95
Milton, Mrs E S, 245, 360
Mitchell, Elizabeth, 290, 366
Mitchell, Hannah, 290
Mitchell, Margaret, 149
Moen, Mary, 277, 364
Molloy, Catherine, 149-50
Monroe, Lydia, 256-7, 361
Montague, Mary, 287
Moon, Elizabeth, 341
Mooney, Elizabeth Catherine, 252
Moore, Elizabeth, 93, 327
Moore, Mary, 357
Moran/Morris, Mary, 231, 357
Moreton, Frances, 200, 349
Morey, Mary Ann, 329
Morgan, Rose, 341
Morley, Ann, 366
Morley, Hannah, 236, 358
Morris, Christina, 65
Morris, Martha, 216
Morris/Moran, Mary, 231, 357
Morrison, Ann, 339
Moss, Elizabeth, 339
Moss, Mrs Isaac, 238, 358, 366
Moulds, Ann, 310
Muckle, Jane, 239, 358
Mulhall, Elizabeth, 109-10, 334
Mulholland, Elizabeth, 349
Mullens, Hannah, 251
Mullens, Johanna, 223
Mulligan, Mary, 178, 346
Munroe, Eleanor, 99
Munroe, Leticia, 256-7
Murphy, Catherine, 146, 213, 341, 354
Murphy, Elizabeth, 133, 339
Murphy, Mary, 122, 327, 336, 337, 339
Murphy/Murray/Welsh, Mary, 328
Murray, Hannah, 296
Murray, Mary, 328
Murtagh, Rose, 145

Nash, Maria, 342
Neal, Catherine, 116
Neale, Lucy, 266, 362
New, Mrs, 205, 351
Newbury, Mary, 74
Newman, Charlotte, 78
Newman, Mary, 84
Newton, Sarah, 84
Nightingale, Mrs, 243, 359
Nixon/Bennet, Jane, 240, 359

Noble, Ann, 24
Nolan, Eleanor, 339
Norman, Elizabeth, 70
Nowlas/Nowland, Bridget, 112, 114, 336
Nunn, Jane, 84

Oakes, Mary, 66
O'Brian, Julia, 226, 356
O'Brien, Bridget, 354
O'Brien, Elizabeth, 351
O'Brien, Mary, 223
O'Donnell, Bridget, 339
Ogle, Matilda, 331
Ogleby, Mrs, 206
Oldfield, Isabella, 19, 309
Oliver, Barbara, 88
Oliver, Mary, 228, 356
O'Neel, Sarah, 173
Owen, Ann, 70
Owen, Elizabeth, 344
Owen, Mary, 70, 84, 337
Owen, Sophia Charlotte, 330
Ozely, Bet, 84

Packer, Eleanor, 93
Parish, Mary, 167, 345
Parker, Ann, 251, 325, 337, 360
Parker, Mary, 220, 223, 321
Parker, Mercy, 59
Parker, Sophia, 359
Parkinson, Jane, 19, 309
Parsons, Clara, 216, 354
Partridge, Mary, 18
Pate, Mary, 366
Paterson, Elizabeth (wife of Col. Paterson), 109, 334
Pawley, Hannah, 239
Payne, Elizabeth, 69
Pearce, Charlotte, 97
Pearce, Mary, 281, 364
Peat, Hannah, 251
Perry, Ann, 342
Perry, Margaret, 140
Phillips, Bridget, 354
Phillips, Mary, 223
Phillips, Sophia, 276-7, 364
Phippard, Eliza, 311
Pickup, Sarah, 344
Piggett, Elizabeth, 214, 354
Pile, Rebecca, 308
Pleasant, Eliza, 91, 327
Plowright, Mary, 238, 358
Polley, Hannah, 78
Powell, Ann, 220
Powell, Elizabeth, 327

Power, Mary, 146
Prendergast, Mary, 336
Pritch, Mary Ann, 317
Pritchard, Hannah, 310
Proctor, Elizabeth, 347
Prodican/Brodican/Boddican, Bridget, 122, 337
Puddiford, Ann, 329
Pulley, Elizabeth, 220

Quigley, Jane, 145, 206, 351
Quin, Mary, 146
Quinion, Mary, 322
Quinn, Margaret, 44

Ralph, Mrs, 205, 351
Randall, Mary, 70
Rawlins, Abigail, 330
Rawlins, Alice, 330
Raymond, Mrs Susannah, 216, 354
Read, Sophia, 357
Redchester, Ellen, 309
Redman, Mary, 239, 358
Redmond, Ann, 361
Redmond, Mrs, 242
Reed, Ann, 48
Reed, Ann/Mary, 318
Rees, Mrs Margaret, 202
Reeson, Rebecca, 34
Reibey, Mary, 239, 265, 298, 357, 358
Reid, Helen, 326
Rens, Josephina, 243, 359
Reynolds, Mary, 311-12
Reynolds, Mrs, 214, 243
Reynolds, Sarah, 366
Rhodes, Ann, 84
Rice, Eleanor, 71
Richey, Rose, 339
Riley, Ann, 329
Riley, Catherine, 123
Roanes, Elizabeth, 199, 349
Roberts, Charlotte, 95, 317
Roberts, Jane, 357
Roberts, Mary, 289, 366
Roberts, Sophia Charlotte, 257
Roberts, Susan, 23
Robertson, Ann, 282, 364
Robertson, Mrs, 244, 359
Robinson, Sarah, 123
Rochfort, Ann, 34
Roe, Isabella, 234, 357
Roe, Judith, 146
Rogers, Anne, 69, 330
Rogers, Mary, 21, 93
Rogers, Mrs, 245, 360

Rooney, Mary, 44, 317
Rourke, Catherine, 44, 317
Rowe, Mary, 349
Roy, Ann, 90
Ruby, Mary, 34
Rumbold, Catherine, 337
Russell, Mary, 93
Ryan, Jane, 160, 343
Ryan, Mary, 120, 146, 150, 151, 154, 341
Ryan, Rose, 350

Sage, Frances, 87
Sarjant/Sarjent, Mary, 229, 356
Saunders, Sarah, 41, 314
Schofield, Ann, 343
Scott, Harriet, 338
Scott, Jane, 342
Scott, Margaret, 340
Scott, Mary, 207, 351, 353
Scrobie, Ann, 342
Sellers, Mary, 282, 364
Sewell, Ellen, 281, 364
Shadwell, Mary, 72
Shannan, Frances, 323
Shannon, Mary, 134
Sharp, Jane, 333
Shaw, Jane, 118, 321, 336
Shaw, Juliet, 34
Sheen, Mary, 88, 91, 329
Shipley, Mary, 357
Short, Ann, 333
Shorter, Ann, 357
Sidebotham, Elizabeth, 359
Simpson, Catherine, 317
Simpson, Judith, 359
Sims, Mrs, 175
Sims, Sarah, 90
Sivier, Frances, 309
Skelton, Susan, 72
Slater, Ann, 112, 113
Slater, Catherine, 156, 284, 342, 365
Slater, Sarah, 41
Smith, Ann, 201, 209, 349
Smith, Catherine, 24
Smith, Elizabeth, 50, 65
Smith, Hannah, 220
Smith, Harriet, 204
Smith, Isabella, 357
Smith, Jane, 87
Smith, Louisa, 84
Smith, Margaret, 362
Smith, Maria, 323
Smith, Mary, 88, 202, 289, 329, 349, 366
Smith, Mrs, 243, 359
Smith, Sarah, 95, 223

Sophie (a Negress), 323
Southern, Margaret, 308
Sowden, Mary, 73
Sparrow, Rosamond, 208-9, 352
Squires, Mary, 93, 362
Stacey, Elizabeth, 71-2
Stacey, Mrs, 212
Stafford, Catherine, 118, 336, 342
Stafford, Mary, 354
Stambles, Mary, 60, 321
Stanfield/Stanford, Sarah, 180, 346
Stanley, Charlotte, 93
Stephens, Mary, 351
Stephenson, Margaret, 112
Stephenson, Sophia, 322
Steward, Sarah, 87
Stewart, Helen, 89
Street, Margaret, 161, 343
Stroud, Charlotte, 333
Stuart, Mrs, 243, 359
Stubbs, Jane, 360
Sullivan, Barbara, 362
Sullivan, Mary, 142, 151-2, 330
Sullivan, Peggy, 332
Sullivan, Sarah, 34, 354
Supple, Mary, 30
Surkins, Jane, 358
Surman, Elizabeth, 71, 324
Surrins, Jane, 354
Susannah (a Negress), 66, 323
Sutherland, Barbara, 362
Swatman, Ester, 72
Swatman, Sarah, 72
Swinney, Hannah, 68
Swinns, Alice, 73

Talbot, Mary, 332
Tate, Maria, 93, 326
Taylor, Ann, 65, 76, 84, 201, 349, 363
Taylor/Baylis, Ann (Nancy), 275-6, 363
Taylor, Hannah, 231, 357
Taylor, Mary, 352
Terrie, Elizabeth, 352
Thirkill, Isabella, 20
Thomas, Mary, 31, 358
Thomas, Sarah, 354
Thompson, Isabella, 329
Thompson, Mary Ann, 31
Tibbutt, Ann, 194-6, 348
Tierney, Ann, 362
Todd, Martha, 237, 358
Tounkes, Rachael, 230, 356
Townsend, Sarah, 75, 325
Tracey, Ann, 75-6, 94
Traynor, Judith, 168, 345

Women Mentioned in the Text 485

Trotter/Jamieson, Ann, 112, 238, 358
Trotter, Jane, 230, 356
Tuckey, Ann, 194, 197, 348
Tuckwell, Elizabeth, 359
Tull, Sophia, 233, 357
Tully, Margaret, 206
Turner, Catherine, 65
Tyler, Ann, 84
Tyrrell, Mary, 135-6, 193, 340, 348

Vallance, Agnes, 75, 325
Varlow, Margaret, 322
Vaughan, Lucy, 22, 310
Voller, Elizabeth, 20

Wakelin, Ann, 18, 308
Waldron, Phebe, 239, 358
Wales, Elizabeth, 204, 350
Walker, Mary, 322
Wall, Mrs, 366
Wallis, Ellis, 65
Walsh, Bridget, 149
Walsh, Elizabeth, 350
Walsh, Jane, 146
Walsh, Rose, 134
Walters/Waters, Susannah, 181-2, 347
Waples, Sarah, 358
Ward, Clara, 67, 323
Ward, Elizabeth, 202
Ward, Mary, 215, 354
Ward, Mrs, 325
Ward, Sarah, 99, 332
Waring, Elizabeth, 50, 330
Waters/Walters, Susannah, 181-2, 347
Watkins, Mary, 319
Watkins, Sarah, 360
Watson, Margaret, 92
Watt, Eleanor, 289, 366
Weavers, Mrs, 243, 359
Webb, Mary, 95
Webb, Sarah, 207, 351
Webber, Mary Ann, 31
Welsh, Mary, 354
Welsh/Murphy/Murray, Mary, 328
Weston, Mary, 91, 330
Wheatley, Jane, 123
Wheelan, Eliza, 142
Whelan, Elizabeth (Jessie), 251

Whelan, Mary, 112
White, Mary Ann, 94
White, Rose, 333
White/Mellon, Catherine, 366
Whiteby, Hannah, 204, 350
Whitfield, Mary, 239, 245, 359
Whitfield, Mary Ann, 245, 360
Whiting, Anne, 214
Whiting, Sarah, 359
Whittaker, Ann, 238, 358
Wicks, Ann, 45
Wiggins, Mrs, 166, 344
Wilby, Margaret/Mary, 96
Wilkinson, Hannah, 350
Wilkinson, Marianne, 194, 196, 348
Williams, Ann, 92
Williams, Elizabeth, 27, 312, 318
Williams, Eliza, 69
Williams, Jane, 138
Williams, Mary, 69, 89
Williams, Sarah, 124
Williams, Susannah, 328
Wills, Catherine, 140
Wilmot, Elizabeth, 69
Wilmott, Sarah, 164, 344
Wilson, Amelia, 124
Wilson, Anne, 349
Wilson, Elizabeth, 193, 348
Wilson, Frances, 20
Wilson, Maria, 352
Wilson, Mary, 90, 329
Wilson, Sarah, 142, 145
Wingfield, Elizabeth, 78
Winlock, Catherine, 337
Wise, Sarah, 256, 257, 361
Witts, Johanna, 91, 330
Wood, Frances, 359
Wood/Graham, Jane, 203, 350
Wood, Sarah, 239, 358
Woodford, Elizabeth, 236, 357
Worthington, Catherine, 340
Wray, Elizabeth, 123
Wright, Mrs, 243
Wyatt, Rachael, 350

Yardley/Yarley/Yearly, Catherine, 335
Yardley, Hannah, 161, 183, 343, 347
Yardsley, Ann, 327
Yarley, Mary, 335

General Index

Notes
1 References to districts and places are not exhaustive.
2 Trial places, trial years and ships of arrival are included in Lists A-1 and B-1.

Aborigines, 65
Admiral Barrington, 172
Age Monthly Review (Melbourne), 308
Albemarle, 172
alcohol, *see* brewing; drunkenness; liquor; spirits
Alders, Joseph, & Frances Bell, 141
Alexander, 215
Archenholtz, von, 67-8, 323
Archer, F, Inspector-General of Prisons (Dublin), 52, 58-9, 122, 139, 143-4, 320-1, 340, 368-9
Armstrong, Joshua, & Mary Holford, 274
Arndel, Surgeon Thomas, & Elizabeth Burleigh, 223
Arnold, Surgeon, *Northampton*, Report to, 24
assignment: complaints re assigned women, 220; & crime, 203-4; from Female Factory, 225-6; Hunter's report on, 222-3; husbands to be assigned, 240, 262, 277-89; labour of assigned women, 219-20; legal basis of, 224; opinions re: Castlereagh, 224, Hunter & King, 222-3, 356, Plummer, 249-52; refusal of women assigned, 282-3; servants requested by women, 265-6, 359; statistics, 225
Association for the Improvement of Females at Newgate, 88

Australian, 3, 214, 216, 245, 349, 351, 353-4, 358-9, 360

Bacon, Henry, & Mary Ann McDade, 282
Baker, Benjamin, & Elizabeth Lee, 289-90
Baker, Thomas & Ann, 72
Balmain, Surgeon William, & Margaret Dawson, 223
Barnes, Thomas, & Lydia Astell, 241
Barret, John & Mary, 283
barrow-women, 245
Bassingbourne Chronicle, 107, 334
Bathurst, Lord, Secretary of State, 174-8, 346
Baylis, Joseph, & Ann Taylor, 275-6
Bayly, Nicholas, 219, 355
Beattie, J M, 68, 324
beggars, mendicants, tinkers & gypsies, *see* native place; poverty; vagrants
Bellinger, John & Sarah, 288
Bentham, Jeremy, 46, 317-18
Best, George, & Martha Chamberlain, 223
Bidon, G, & Jane Walsh, 146
Bigge, Commissioner J T, 203, 259, 261, 263, 267, 275, 278, 300, 352, 355, 358, 361, 363, 364
Bills of Mortality (London), 312
Blackburn, David, letters of, 336, 352

General Index 487

Blackstone, Sir William, on slavery, 323
Blake, & wife Susannah, 25
Bland, Surgeon William, describes 'women of colour', 67
Bligh, Governor William, 224-5; to Windham, 356
Bloodsworth, James, & Sarah Bellamy, 251
Botany Bay: assumptions re characteristics, 3-4, 47, 162-3, 189-92, 267; debate on settlement, 12, 38-9, 306-7; defined, 3; limits of settlement, 15-16; preparation for settlement, 54-6
Bowes, Surgeon Arthur, 309, 360
Brannigan, Hugh & Catherine Donnelly, 136
Brazeley, Edward & Susannah, 24
brewing, 236, 357-8; *see also* liquor licences; public houses
bridewell, *see* gaols
Britannia, 172
Brothers, 123
Brown, Thomas, & Ellen Campbell, 120
Bruxton, F, MP, 44, 317
Bryan, Michael & Mary Ann, 120
Burn, Simon, & Mary Davidson, 114
bushwomen, 226-7, 229-30; *see also* farming & grazing by women; land grants to women
Butler, Phillip, schoolmaster, 185
Buxton, Thomas, & liquor licence, 241

Callaghan, John, & Mary Charlton, 148
came-free women, 13-14; *see also* colonial women; convict wives
capital punishment, *see* executions, punishment
carts, barrow-women, 245, 360
Cartwright, Revd Robert, 268
Carver, Robert & Elizabeth, 286
Castle Hill Rebellion, 110-12; *see also* Irish
Castlereagh, Viscount: to Bligh, 253, 360; from King, 252-3; to/from Macquarie, 224, 253, 356, 360
Catherine, 58
Cavanagh, Owen, & Margaret Darnell, 22-3
Census of NSW 1828, 313
Chalker, William, wife & 'Miss Sprightly', 291
chaplains, colonial, *see* Johnson, Chaplain Richard; Marsden, Revd Samuel

children: applications for free passages to Botany Bay: from convicted parent/s in Britain/Ireland, 26-7, 116-21, from parent/s in NSW, 27-8, 121, 311, 324, from parishes, 27-8, 161-3; boys over 14 years not to accompany parent/s, 162, 343; came free with parent/s, 97, 99; crimes against (in Britain), 40-2, 90-1, 329, (in NSW), 204-5, 350-1; crimes by, 34, 50; death of, 32-3; death sentence passed on, 50, 72-3, 75-6, 330; mortality of (in London), 312, (on First Fleet), 26; pleas for clemency or mitigation of sentence by women with children, 49, 94, 99-100, 340, 341-2; refused passage, 26-7, 116-21, 150-3; statistics (mortality), 33; stolen, 90-1, 329; taken from parent/s, 56-7; *see also* native born
Chitham, Joseph, & Mary Doolan, 141
civil condition of women at Botany Bay, 259; *see also* colonial women
Clark, Lieutenant Ralph, 267, 360, 362
Clarke, James, & Mary Hartford, 285
Clarke, William, & Mary Shannon, 134
'class', economic & social: in Britain, 5-6, 188-9; in NSW, 3-4, 191-2, 221-2; origins of convicts, 273-4
Clode, Samuel, murdered missionary, 198
cohabitation, *see* marriage
Colethread, John, & Ann Colpitts & Elizabeth Mooney, 252
Collins, David, Deputy Judge-Advocate, 237, 307, 321, 335-6, 348-9, 350, 351, 352, 353, 358, 360, 363
Collman, Edward & Anne, 167-8
colonial women: assumptions re characteristics/skills, 219; criminality of at Botany Bay, 192-4, 204-7; defined, 12-14; as defendants, 213-16; feminist interpretations of, 7, 9-10, 164, 259-60; pioneers, 6-7, 113-14; ratio of to men, 164-5, 259; roles of in Botany Bay society, 191-2, 263-4, 268-9; roles of in British society, 47; social origins, 272-4; structure of female society, 6, 12-13, 259; *see also* convict wives; convict & ex-convict women; Irish; marriage
Colquhoun, Patrick, 42, 68, 96, 316, 323, 324, 331

488 *Indexes*

comers & goers, 29; *see also* native place; poverty
Commissariat store, sales to by women, 244
Committees, *see* Reports
common law marriages, *see* marriages
concubines, *see* Female Register
Conspiracy of 1800, 111, 335; *see also* Irish
conspiracy on *Marquis Cornwallis*, 108, 334
convicts & ex-convict women: ages of, 32-4, 58-60, 341; arrival of, 25-6, 248-9; assumptions re, 5-6, 12-13, 248-50; attempted escape of, 335-6; descriptions of, 123-5, 130-1, 314, 322, 323, 327-9, 333, 336-7, 338-9; free husbands accompanying, 25; social origins of, 17, 33-5, 188-90; speech of, 31-2, 67, 130; stereotype of, 12-14; *see also* children; colonial women; crime; Irish; land grants to women; London; marriage; native place; occupations; prostitution; punishment; for trial places, trial years & ships of arrival *see* Lists A-1 & B-1
convict wives, 12-14, 69-71, 223-4, 226-31; applications/petitions: for passage to/with husbands, 156, 158-9, for husbands to be assigned, 277-81, from husbands, 158-9, 163-4; attitudes of (British government), 160, 168-72, 173-8, (colonial governors), 173-8, (local parishes, etc.), 160-1, 163, 168-9, 179-82; conditions of, in Britain/Ireland, 160ff, 183ff; numbers, 173-4; roles of at Botany Bay, 156-8, 229-30; Select Committee on Transportation re, 175; social origins of, 157-8; *see also* children; Governors of the Poor; marriage; settlement rights
Cooper, George & Margaret, 284
Cork Advertiser (Ireland), 328
Cosgreave, Surgeon Peter, 88-9
Cosgrove, David & wife, 173
county women, *see* native place
Court of Civil Jurisdiction (NSW), 354
Court of Criminal Jurisdiction (NSW), 347-8, 349, 350, 351, 352, 354
Cowper, Revd William, 267
Cox, William, & assigned servant, 226
Creighton, John, & Mary Coglan, 120
crime: in Britain, 5-6, 29-31, 34, 39-46,
44-6, 71-3, (statistics), 316; in Ireland, 130-7, 148-51; in London, 64-6, 73-7, 89-97; in NSW, 191-216; & poverty, 72-3; remedy for, 41-3, 54; victims of, 40-2, 65-8, 74-6, 83-4; of women at Botany Bay, 204-7; *see also* punishment
'criminal class': Britain, 47; NSW, 190-3, (defined), 204-7; callousness of, 40-1; motivation of, 68-9
criminality of women: in NSW, 190-3, 204-6; determining attitudes towards, at Botany Bay, 14-15; linked with immorality & depravity, 5, 12-16, 94-6; of convict women, 68-70, 190-3; of Irish women, 113-14, 128-37; & respectability, 191-2, 261-2
criminals, female, convicted at Botany Bay (named in text): Baker, Ann, 324, 353; Banks, Mary, 353; Campbell, Anne, 214; Campbell, Eliza, 204; Carney, Mary, 352; Chambers, Elizabeth, 353; Cole, Mary, 214; Connelly, Bridget, 193; Connor, Kitty, 207; Davis, Ann *(alias* Judith Jones), 349; Davis, Mary, 206; Davis, Sophia, 214; Dixon, Betty, 206; Dunlevey, Mary, 214; Elliott, Catherine, 214; Finlay, Elizabeth, 352; Gatty, Ann, 214; Goodwin, Mrs, 206; Grady, Mary, 199; Grady, Mary, 206; Hartigan, Mary, 207; Hunt, Maria, 214; Jones, Elizabeth, 198; Jones, Jane, 213; Jones, Judith, 200; Lovatt, Rosetta, 352; McDuel, Elizabeth, 193; McFae, Jane, 209; Marcus, Jane, 193; Piggett, Elizabeth, 214; Quigley, Jane, 206; Roanes, Elizabeth, 199; Scott, Mary, 206, 351; Sparrow, Rosamond, 208-9; Taylor, Mary, 352; Terrie, Elizabeth, 352; Tyrrell, Mary, 193; Ward, Mary, 215; Webb, Sarah, 207; Wilson, Elizabeth, 193; Wilson, Maria, 352
criminals, male, convicted at Botany Bay (named in text): Bennett, –, 201; Boggis, William, 257; Bryant, Michael, 194-5; Clives, John, 204; Cunninghame, William, 204; Daly, James, 207-8; Day, Thomas, 209; Deegan, James, 204; Eldberry, William, 198; Green, John, 195-6; Hennessey, J, 204; Jones, Thomas, 198; Kenny, John, 202; McCarty, Dennis, 213; McNamara, Lot, 204;

Mahoney, Cornelius, 241; Massie, John, 209; Parsons, Thomas, 242; Taylor, Simon, 201; Whitehouse, Abraham, 348; Wright, Henry, 350
Cunningham, Surgeon Peter, 148, 341

Daily/General Orders and Proclamations, 110, 210, 341, 352
Daily Register (London), 78, 326
dairywomen, 225, 244
Darling, Eliza, & Ladies Committee, 207
Darling, Governor Ralph, petitions to, 185, 362
Davis, James & Jane, 181
deaths: in hulks, 39-40; of women on First Fleet, 56; *see also* executions
Defoe, Daniel, 188
depravity at Botany Bay: assumptions re, 12-13, 248-9; & Irish, 128-9, 137-8, 145-7; & women convicts, 55-8, 82-3, 97-8, 162-3, 203-4
'desolate boys' (Dublin), 119, 311, 336
Devonport, James, & wife & James Smith, 289
Diaper, Richard, 300
diet: in Ireland, 115; in prison, 79
disease: on convict ships, 51-4; in gaols/hulks, 51-2
Dispensary Movement, 32-4, 312
dissection by surgeons, 79, 100, 326; *see also* punishment
distilling, *see* liquor
Dogherty, Hugh, & Mary Dunbar, 136
Donohue, James, & Elizabeth Lee, 289-90
Donovan, Martin & family, 185
Downes, Thomas & Rosetta, 173
Driscoll, Dennis, & Catherine Edwards, 113
drunkenness: plea of at trials, 87, 327, 353, 354; *see also* liquor
Dublin, crimes of women transported from, 131-2
Duffield, Ian, 66
Dunn, James, & Catherine Barry, 297-8
Dunn, Thomas, & Ann Tuckey, 197
Dwyer, Michael & wife, 173

economic roles of colonial women, 6-7, 218-19, 221-2, 245-6, 266; assumptions re skills, 218-20; attitudes of governors, 219-22; *see also* assignment; colonial women; convict wives; occupations
Edinburgh Review, 316, 344

Egan, Thomas & wife, 279
Evans, Evan, & Eleanor Crozier, 286
Evans, George, & Elizabeth Jackson, 137
Evatt, John, & Bridget Nowlas, 114
ex-convict women/emancipists, *see* convicts & ex-convict women; colonial women
executions: (described) in Britain, 77-8; at Botany Bay, 195-6, 198, 199-200, 206-7; fear of, 48-9; pregnancy &, 140-1, 200, 332, 349; reprieves from, 34, 46, 65-6, 73-5, 77-8, 99-101, 199; women executed: Botany Bay, 198, 199, 201, 204; Britain, 76-9; Ireland, 49-50, 141
expense: of establishing colony, 55; of convict wives, 175-6; of convict women, 222; of transportation, 105-6

families: concern for transported husbands, 165-6, 343-4, wives, 311; convicted together, 50, 72, 276-7, 310, 319, 330; disputes in, 288-91; family women, 34-5, 142, single on arrival, 26; partner left in Britain/Ireland, 22-3, 170; petitions for reuniting in NSW, 120-2; refused passage, 311; reunited, 24-6, 118, 157-62; role of convict husbands at Botany Bay, 164-6, 183-6; separation at Botany Bay, 276-7; *see also* children; colonial women; convict wives; marriage
farming & grazing, 226-35; *see also* landholders/farmers, female
Farraugher, Murty & Bridget, 285
Female Factory (Parramatta), 12, 17, 145, 148-9, 206-7, 214, 225, 260, 350
Female Register (1806), 250-3, 254-6, 259
Fernee, Joseph, & Mary Clare, 286
Field, Andrew, & Mary Bergen, 251
fines passed on free persons, 354
First Fleet, 19, 22, 26, 55-8, 320
Fletcher B H (Sydney), 307, 348, 351
Flynn, Patrick & Honora, 284
Folks, William & Mary, 121
Foster, Andrew, & Mary French, 68
Fraser, William & Ellen, 19
Freeman, William, & Elizabeth Mitchell, 290
Freeman's Journal (Dublin), 110-11, 133-7, 264, 318, 335, 339, 340, 341, 362
free passengers, 156-62, 168-85; *see also* children; convict wives

Fry, Elizabeth, & prison reform, 42, 86-8, 98-9, 316; Ladies Association, 98-9, 328; *see also* Index to Women
Fulbourn Chronicle, 334
Fulton, Revd Henry & wife, 173

gallows speeches, 194, 200, 207, 319
Gamble, John & Ann, 164
gaols: attitudes towards, 42-3, 79; conditions in, 23, 39-40, 51-2, 61, 310; bridewell (Winchester), 21, 310; named, 23-4, 49, 51-2, 53, 59-60, 86-7, 97-8, 309, 318, 319, 321, 322, 324, 339, 340, 352
General Orders, *see* Daily Orders
George, M Dorothy, 308, 310, 323, 330
Godber, Josiah & Rebecca/Rebecker, 183, 299
Goodwin, Andrew & Leticia, 256-7
Goulburn, Frederick, Under-Secretary of State to Macquarie, 310
Governors of the Poor/Guardians of/Corporation of/Overseers of/Parishes on behalf of, 161, 181, 312; Parish refusing assistance, 70; & Irish in England, 106-8; *see also* convict wives
Gray, John, & Elizabeth Killett, 242-3
Green, John, 195-6
Grenada, 30
Griffiths, Jonathon, & Elinor McDonald, 114, 251
Guy, James, & Judith Lightly, 74

Hacking, Henry, & Ann Bowen, 202
Hall, William, & Catherine Corrigan, 251
Halliday, John P, & Mary Oakes, 66, 323
Hamilton, Jonathon, & Mary McEntee, 146
Hamilton, Samuel & Sarah, 291
hanging, *see* executions, punishment
Harris, Robert, & Elizabeth Maclean, 23
Harris, Silas & Mary, 343
Harrold, Father James, 111, 335
Harvey, – & Catherine, 25
Hatton, Joseph, & Rosamond Sparrow, 208
health of women before transportation 33-5, 51-3, 58-60; in gaols, 117; Report of F Archer, 143-4; *see also* Dispensary Movement
Hembridge, W, 250
Hicks, Richard & family, 169

Higgins, Mick, & Isabella Roe, 234
highway robbery, 76-80, 83-4, 94, 327
Hill, Thomas, & Catherine Devereux, 114
Hinnegan, James & Cecilia, 169
Holland, William & family, 166
Holmes, William, & Rebecca Davison, 57
Holt, Joseph, & Ann Tuckey, 197-8
housekeepers, 145, 228, 356
House of Correction/House of Industry, 94, 138, 207
Howard, John, 52
Hue and Cry and Police Gazette (London), 67, 312, 319, 323
Hughes, Robert, 15
hulks, 24, 39, 55; petition from, 313; *see also* gaols
Hunter, Governor John, 108, 111, 221-3, 334, 335, 355

illegitimacy: bastards, Petitions for Maintenace of, 147-8
infant mortality in Britain, 33-4
infanticide, 317
informers, 173
innkeepers/publicans, 238-42; *see also* liquor licences; public houses
Ireland, female criminality in, 137-40
Irish: age of, 104; accompanied by children, 112; arrival at Botany Bay from England, 104-6, 108-9; assumptions re, 104, 128-9; Catholic women in NSW, 254-5; colonial women, 104-25; crimes in Ireland, 104, 113-14, 129ff; crimes, 'political', 106; descriptions of, 129-30, 145-7, 151-3; diet, 115-16; differences from British convicts, 2-3, 122-3; in England, 22-3, 29-30, 65-6, 106-12, 123-4, 322-3; family women, 145-8; fear of in NSW, 106, 109-10; Gaelic in NSW, 130; in Ireland, 115-17, 128-54; in NSW, 108-15, 128-9; marriage & morality of, 254-56; Northern Ireland, 29-31; numbers in Irish gaols, 116-17, 142-4; petitions re children in Ireland, 116-17, 120-1, 122-3; proportion of, at Botany Bay, 104; religion of, 31, 114, 317; Ribbonism, 50, defined, 319; riots against/by, 106-8; roles of, at Botany Bay, 128-9, 146-7; stereotype of female convict, 109-10, 146-8; transportation, 104-6, 111-13;

women on *Kitty* (named), 333; *see also* children; families; native place; for trial years, trial places & ships of arrival *see* Lists A-1 & B-1

Jamieson, Sgt & Ann, 112, 238, 358
Janus, 106
Jarrett, Derek, 308
Johnson, Chaplain Richard, 12, 19, 223; letter from, 348; & wife Mary, 57, 307
Jones, John & Mary, 283
Judd, William & Sarah May, 274

Kable, Henry, & Susannah Holmes, 215
Kangaroo, 174-5
Keith, John & Anne, 287
King, Governor P G, 111, 224, 252; & Ann Innett, 235, 357
Kirkby, Matthew & wife, 184
Kitty, 105

labour of women, 218-19; *see also* assignment; occupation
Lancet, 312
land grants to women, 229-35; *see also* landholders/farmers, female
landholders/farmers, female, 226-7, 232-36, 356-7; & respectability, 261-2; *see also* farming & grazing; land grants to women
Lang, John Dunmore, 240
leases, confirmed, 234-6
Lee, Joseph, & Elizabeth Bason, 290
legislation: Macquarie against cohabitation, 341; *see also* Daily/General Orders
Lennard, Patrick, & Elizabeth Coak, 135
letters from convict men at Botany Bay, 163, 177-8, 182-3, 299, 342; from women at Botany Bay, 228, 261-2, 358, 362
licences, bakers', butchers', etc, 359
life expectancy in Britain, 32-4; aged convict women, 60
Limerick Evening Post, 115
liquor: & crime, 210-13, 214-15, 237-8; problems of, 210-11, 237-8; trade & women, 238-46; *see also* public houses; spirits
Liquorish, John & Rachel, 230
liquor licences, 236-43, 358, 359; & husbands, 236
Littleport Chronicle, 334

lodging houses/lodgers, 16-18, 64-5, 91-2, 324, 329-30
London: beggars, 32, 323-4; blacks, 66-7; county women in, 64-5; crime in, 68-9, 75-7; descriptions of, 64-5; employment of Shropshire and Welsh girls, 322; health, 32-4; housing, 16-19; living conditions of lower orders, 16-19; migration to, 32, 64-5, 66-7; poverty, 20-1, 73-4; *see also* crime; families; Irish; native place
Longstaff, Mr, & Elizabeth Bason, 74
Lord Wellington, 74
Louisa, 31
Lowe, Joseph, & Elizabeth Hayward, 57
Lownes, James, & Mary Masterton, 255
Lynch, Thomas, & Mary Quin, 146

Macarthur, John, 219-20, 223, 268, 363; & wife Elizabeth, 258, 307
McBride, Patrick, & Anne Griffiths, 288
McDonald, Alexander, & Mary Oliver, 228, 356
McGuigan, Simon, & family, 179
McHale, Patrick, & Mary Charlton, 148
Mackintosh, Sir James, 45, 317
McMahon, Owen, & Ann Byrne, 255
Macquarie, Governor Lachlan, 58, 79, 175-9, 182, 210, 224, 225-6, 230-1, 254, 368; Diary, 308; legislation re marriage, 341; letters to/from Bathurst, 346, 353, Marsden, 344
Manchester: living conditions, 18-19; description, 308, 309; Samuel Owen from, 166; women from, 19, 24, 343
Marines, wives accompanied, 307, 342
marriage: absconded wives, 291-2; adultery/misconduct by wife, 291-2; applications for assignment of husbands, 240, 276-92; applications for marriage licences, 336-7; applications for permission to marry, 336-7, 341; attitudes of British government & governors to, 252-4; authority of governors re, 253-4, 272-3, 290-2; at Botany Bay, 272-3; in Britain, 272-4; & class, 272-4; of colonial women, 119-20, 223-4, 252-3; concern for transported husband, 166-7; to convict men, 223-4, 261; de facto/common-law, 249-56, 273-6; encouragement of, 171-3, 252-4; evidence to Bigge re, 259; Irish women &, 146; married convicts

from Britain/Ireland, 23-5, 68-9, 122-3, 250-4, 274-9; problems of, 165-70, 262, 273-4, 287-8, 291-2; remarriage, 119-20, 275-6, 363; & respectability, 256, 261, 265, 267, 268, 275; role of free wife in convict marriage, 232ff; role of convict husbands, 164-6, 183-6; of women of former bad character, 145; *see also* Female Register

Marsden, Revd Samuel, 12, 164-5, 224, 249-52, 260-1, 275; evidence to Bigge, 363; & Female Register, 249-54, 307; letter to Macquarie, 344; 'Observations of Female Convicts', 362

Marsh, Henry, & Rosetta Madden, 229

Marshall, George, & Mary McCarroll, 121

Masterton, J, & Mary Consadine, 255

Matilda, 172

Meagher, William & Sarah, 277

Mendicity Report 1814-15 (London), 20-1

Middlesex gaols, description of women, 22-4; *see also* Lists A-1 & B-1

Minerva, 106, 109

morality & assumptions re immorality of convicts/colonial women, 248-53, 254-7, 291-2; *see also* marriage

Morley, George, & Margaret Wilby, 96

Morning Advertiser (London), 78, 326

Morning Herald (London), 77, 107-8, 325, 328

Morning Star (Dublin), 111, 335

Mould, Simon, & Ann Davis, 227

Murray, Kennedy, & Ann Parker, 250

musters, land & stock & population (NSW), 312

native born/colonial born, 6-7, 16-17; *see also* children; families; marriage

native peoples: blacks in London & 'St Giles black birds', 65-6; & crime, London, 65-7; 'women of colour', 67, 323

native place, 67, 87, 123-4, 129-30

Newman, Thomas & wife, 180

Newgate Calendar, 315

Newgate Gaol (London), descriptions of, 328

Newgate women: ages of, 82; assumptions re, 82; crimes of, 64-6, 68-9, 71-3, 82-3, 89-90; descriptions of, 86-90, 101; native place of, 87;

pleas (of distress), 69-70, (of intoxication), 95; occupations of, 82-4, 100; opinions of, 328; reformation of, 87-8; reputation of, 87-8; second offenders, 93-4; *see also* Fry, Elizabeth

New South Wales Corps, wives of, 112

Nixon, John, & Jane Bennet, 240

Noah, William, & Catherine Lines, 96, 331

Noble, Benjamin, & Mary Brown, 72

Noble, Robert & Ann, 24

'noble convict' legend, 8

Norfolk Island, 4, 57, 114

North American Colonies, transportation to, 39, 170, 313

O'Brien, Terence & family, 159-60

OBSP, *see* Lists A & B, trial places

occupations, women: Botany Bay, 6, 218-23, 245-6; Britain, 19-20, 30-1, 56, 322, 329, 330; on First Fleet, 56; Ireland, *see* Irish; London, 17-18, 64-6; given at trials, 83-4; & good character, 85; of husbands, 24-5, 365-6; *see also* economic roles of colonial women

O'Neel, Daniel & Sarah, 173

Owen, John, & Ann East, 330

Owen, Samuel & wife, 166-7

Parish, - & Mary, 167

parish relief, *see* Governors of the Poor

Paterson, Lieut Gov William & land grants, 114

Patfield, George & Mary, 223

Peat, Charles, & Johanna Mullens, 223, 251

Peel, Sir Robert: & crime, 46; letters/petitions to, 27, 46, 162-4, 317, 343

penal settlements/secondary transportation, 4

penal theories/theorists: Becaria, 317-18; Bentham, 317-18; newspapers, 54; *see also* Fry, Elizabeth; Reports

penitentiaries: proposal to build in Ireland, 40, 314; Quarterly Reports of Female (Dublin), 340; Richmond Central, 339

Phillip, Governor Arthur, 55-6, 171-2, 211-12, 219-20, 228, 320, 321, 353

Phillips, William & Sophia, 276

Phillips, Zachariah & family, 159

Phippard, Mr & wife Eliza, 311

General Index

pioneer women, 5-7; *see also* colonial women
Plummer, T W, 249
Plymouth, 364
Poor Laws, laws of settlement, *see* vagrants
poor, casual, 69-71; deserving, 50-1, 73-4
Porter, Roy, 85
poverty: in Britain, 19-20, 29-30; & childbirth, 18; & criminality, 20-1, 39-40, 72-4; in Ireland, 157-8; in London, 68-70; & parish charity, 20-1, 163, 178, 180-1; *see also* Governors of the Poor; London
Power, James, & Harriet Gordon, 142
prisons, *see* gaols
Proclamations, *see* Daily Orders
Proctor, John & wife, 184
prostitutes/whores/harlots/streetwomen/ 'unfortunate girls': at Botany Bay, 96, 164, 171-2, 260-1, 264-5, 288-9, 350; in Britain, 33-5; in Ireland, 134-5, 264-5, 339; in London, 94-8, 264-5; *see also* Marsden, Revd Samuel; Female Register
prostitution: inquiry into on *Janus*, 359; reluctance of men to prosecute prostitute-thieves, 84, 331
Public Advertiser, 41, 66, 73, 314, 315, 319, 323, 325
publicans, 92-3, 240-2, 360
public houses/inns/taverns, 75, 93-4, 235-8; crimes in, 91-4; named (Sydney), 238-43, 358-9
public labour (women convicts), 218-19, 263
Pugh's Hereford Chronicle, 319
punishment, legal: at Botany Bay, 193, 195-6, 206-10; aims/theories re, 41-4, 46-7, 79; capital, 45-7, 48, 77-8, 348-9 (*see also* executions); corporal, 22, 48, 56-7, 66; compassion for sufferers, 50-1; as deterrent, 78-9; fear of, 141, 199-200; gibbetting, 42, 79; mutilation, 42; physical & symbolic, 315-16; pillory/stocks, 206-7, 352, 353; restrictions, diet, 43; & toil, 43; transportation as, 39; of the body, 43-4; of family women, 49; of rogues, vagrants & vagabonds, 21-3; of women compared with men (NSW), 209-11; *see also* Delaney, John; penal theories
Purtell, Michael, & Bridget Carroll, 120
Pye, John, & Mary Phillips, 223

Queen, 112-15

Rebellion, Irish 1798, 335
Refuge for the destitute (London), 98
Reports: Quarterly Report of Adult Female Penitentiary (Dublin), 340; on the Agriculture of Middlesex (1793), 322; on the Laws relating to Vagrants 1821 (H of C), 310; on Problems of Transportation, 313; on State of Mendicity in the Metropolis (London) 1814-18, 308, 324; on State of Prisons & Prison Discipline, 189-90, 347; of Committee of Society for the Improvement of Prison Discipline (Third Report), 42-3, 98; of Royal Commission on Labour of Women & Children in Mines & Factories, 273, 363; of Select Committee on Transportation (1812), 175; to Surgeon Arnold (*Northampton*), 24
Ribbonism, 50, defined 319
Richards, William, 105
Roberts, John, & Sarah Wise, 257
Roberts, Michael, 210
Robinson, Richard John, & Ann Innett, 235
Robson, L L, 46
Rochester, John, & Ellen Flaherty, 145
rogues, *see* vagrants
Ryan, James, & Jane Trotter, 230
Ryan, John & Jane, 160

Scarr, Thomas, & Mary Sellers, 282
schoolmistresses/seminaries, 244-5, 357, 360
Scofield, Edward & daughter, 162
Scotland: native place, 65, 214, 287, 342; married in, 24; women tried in, 30, 48, 318, 326
seamstresses, dressmakers, needlewomen, mantua-makers, 245
secondary transportation, *see* punishment
Select Committees, *see* Reports
settlement, rights of, 20-3; statistics, 20; *see also* Mendicity Report; poverty
Sewell, George & Ellen, 281
Shaw, J & B, *see* Lists A & B, ships of arrival
shoplifters, 27, 34, 99, 135, 213-14
Sidaway, Robert, & Mary Marshall, 254
Simple, John, & Margaret Johnston, 285

494 Indexes

Sinclair, Duncan, 215
Small, John, & Mary Parker, 223
Smith, Edward, & Ann Horn, 220
Smith, Francis & wife, 159
Smith, Martin, & Bridget Burke, 130-1
Smith, Neal & Mary, 289
Smith, Sydney, 79, 163, 344, 347; see also *Edinburgh Review*; penal theories/theorists
Smith, Thomas, & Ann Colpitts, 252
Society for the Improvement of Prison Discipline (Third Report), 42-3
Society for the Suppression of Vice (London), 210; see also Roberts, Michael
Sommervail, James, & Mary Linton, 330
spirits, 237-9; see also liquor; liquor licences
Squires, James, & Betty Mason, 275
statistics, 20, 28, 33, 132, 143-4, 225, 258, 259
Stone, Thomas, & Hannah Murray, 296
Sunday Tribune (Dublin), 308
Surgeons' Journals/Reports: *Almorah*, 150; *Brothers*, 337; *Friendship*, 88, 277; *Lord Melville*, 350; *Tellicherry*, 53, 320; *Woodman*, 142
Surrey, 177
'suspicious characters', 54, 330
Sydney Gazette, 194, 197, 200, 242, 245, 317, 326, 348, 353, 358, 359, 360, 366
Sydney, Lord, from Phillip, 55
Sydney Morning Herald, 307, 318, 334

Tallentyre, George, & Ann Robertson, 282
Tatt, Thomas & wife, 163
Taylor, Simon, & Ann Smith, 201
Tellicherry, 53, 173
Tench, Watkin, 248
Thurgate, William, & Margaret Boyle, 123
Tibbutt, John & Ann, 195
tickets-of-leave applications, 344; see also assignment; marriage; convict wives

The Times (London), 77, 308, 324, 325
Three Bees, 58
Todhunter, William & Elizabeth, 120
trade/commerce: women in, 242-4
transportation: Act, 316; alternatives to, 43; & Botany Bay, 38-9; & North American Colonies, 38; fear of, 47; petition for, 53; selection for, 57-9, 137-40; self-transportation, 334; system, 4
Traynor, Barnabas & wife, 168
trial places, see Lists A-1 & B-1; statistics, 28
True Briton, 362

vagrants, vagabonds, vagrancy, beggars, tinkers, mendicants, gypsies, 17-23, 34; in London, 64
vice, 210-12

Wales, 32; Welsh girls, 129, 322; Welsh on the *Kitty*, 105
Ward, James, & Mary Long, 297
Ward, Russel, 15
Wentworth, D'Arcy, 236, 238, 244, 358
Wentworth, William Charles, 308
West, William, & Martha Hewison, 97
Whelan, Charles, & Elizabeth Berry, 251
Whitely, Fred, & Jane Quigley, 145
Whiteman, William, & Mary Tyrrell, 135-6
widows, 99, 120, 265-6; tried in London, 322-3
Wiggins, James & wife, 166
Williams, Thomas, & Ann Coleman, 289
Willmott, John & Sarah, 344
Wood, G A, 8, 10
Woodman, 130, 173
Worgan, G B, letter of, 211, 320
working women/ 'business' women, 242-3; see also economic roles of colonial women

Yarrow, Thomas, & Elizabeth Gibbs, 74
Yearly, Wickham, & Catherine Edwards, 113